THE ARCHAEOLOGY OF LOU

The archaeology of Lough Gur

Rose M. Cleary

Graphics: James O'Driscoll

Wordwell

This book is dedicated to the people of Lough Gur and to all the archaeologists who worked in the area.

First published in 2018
Wordwell Ltd
In association with UCC and Limerick County Council
Unit 9, 78 Furze Road, Sandyford Industrial Estate, Dublin 18
www.wordwellbooks.com

Front cover image—The Great Stone Circle with Knockfennell and Lough Gur in the background.
Back cover (top left): Socketed bronze axehead (National Museum of Ireland).
(middle right): Megalithic tomb known as the Giant's Grave, Killalough Hill (National Monuments Service).
(middle left): Aerial photograph of Lough Gur.
(bottom right): Class Ia Neolithic pottery from Lough Gur (National Museum of Ireland).

ISBN 978-1-9997909-7-4

British Library Cataloguing-in-Publication Data.
A catalogue record for this book is available from the British Library.

This publication has been funded by Limerick City and County Council, the Thomond Archaeological Society and Creative Ireland.

Typeset in Ireland by Wordwell Ltd
Copy-editor: Emer Condit
Cover design and artwork: James O'Driscoll
Printed by Gráficas Castuera, Pamplona

Contents

List of figures   viii
Acknowledgements   xviii
Preface   xix

1. The landscape   1
    Introduction   1
    The physical landscape   4
    Geology, glaciation and soils   4
    Raw materials   9
    Food sources   9
    Lake drainage   10
    Archaeological time   13

2. Antiquarian and archaeological research   17
    Antiquarian accounts   17
    Survey   27
    Excavations   37

3. The Stone Age   43
    3.1: Mesolithic   43
        Mesolithic activity around Lough Gur
    3.2: Neolithic settlement   47
        Early Neolithic (3800–3500 BC) rectangular houses and
        settlement evidence
        Middle Neolithic round houses (3500–3000 BC)
        Residual Neolithic material on later sites
    3.3: Neolithic burial   93
        Unprotected burials on Knockadoon Hill
        Caherguillamore

4. Late Neolithic Grooved Ware, Chalcolithic and early Bronze Age   102
    4.1: Grooved Ware culture   102
        Grange monument complex
        Great Stone Circle (B)
        Geroid Island
        Maceheads
        Circles O and P
    4.2: Beaker cultures   123
        Knockadoon Hill
        Rockbarton Bog
        Rathjordan
        Ballingoola

Caherguillamore
Stone wrist-bracers
Bronze axeheads
Bronze awls and bracelets
Halberd
4.3: Megalithic tombs   134
The 'Giant's Grave', Killalough Hill
Other megalithic tombs around Lough Gur
Destroyed megalithic tombs
4.4: Food Vessels   145

5. The Bronze Age   149
5.1: Settlement   150
Enclosures
Unenclosed settlement
5.2: Burial   189
Megalithic tomb
Knockadoon Hill
Ballynagallagh
Newchurch
Circle J
Ring-barrows and ring-ditches
Rathjordan
Ballingoola
Cahercorney
Knockfennel Hill
Grange Stone Circle B
Other burials?
5.3: Metalwork   203
5.4: Monumental remains   210

6. The Iron Age   215

7. The Roman period   220

8. The early medieval period   224
Political history   224
8.1: Settlement   227
Carraig Aille
The Spectacles
Grange ringfort and hut sites in Ballingoola
Ballynagallagh
Knockadoon
Overview

8.2: Crannogs   277
8.3: The Church   280
8.4: Burials   281

9. The Vikings   283

10. The Anglo-Normans, 1170–1300   289
    Political history   289
    Settlement   290
        Caherguillamore
        North-east shore of Lough Gur
    The Church   315

11. Tower-houses and settlement, 1400–1700   319
    The emergence of the Fitzgerald dynasty and the earls of Desmond   319
    Fortifications on Knockadoon   322
    Bourchier's Castle   322
        Historical references to Bourchier's Castle
        The Great Earl
        Elizabethan plantation
        George Bourchier
        The Sugán Earl rebellion
        Surrender of Bourchier's Castle, 1600
        The 1641 rebellion and the siege of Bourchier's Castle
        Cromwellian plantation
        Bourchier's Castle 1655–1800
    Black Castle (Killalough Castle)   340
    Geroid Island   344
        Gearóid Iarla
    Grange Castle   346
    Caherguillamore   347
    Rawleystown Castle   347
    Caherelly Castles   349
    Archaeological excavations   351
        Car-park excavations
        Site J, Knockadoon
    Newchurch   356
    Caherelly church   357
    Appendix 1: Account of the capture of Bourchier's Castle in May 1600   363
    Appendix 2: Account of the 1641 siege of Bourchier's Castle   364

12. Summary   367

Bibliography   371

List of figures

Chapter 1. The landscape
Fig. 1.1—Lough Gur: location and river network.
Fig. 1.2—Lough Gur: general photo.
Fig. 1.3—Low-lying land (under 76m OD)—locations of former lakes?
Fig. 1.4—The Red Bog.
Fig. 1.5—Local geology.
Fig. 1.6—Knockfennell Hill.
Fig. 1.7—Extinct volcanic plugs, Knockderc.
Fig. 1.8—Giant Irish deer (*Megaloceros giganteus*).
Fig. 1.9—Dineley's 1681 sketch of Lough Gur.
Fig. 1.10—Extent of lake mapped by Ordnance Survey in 1840.
Fig. 1.11—Area drained in 1847–8.
Fig. 1.12—Spearhead.

Chapter 2. Antiquarian and archaeological research
Fig. 2.1—John Ware plaque.
Fig. 2.2—Du Noyer's sketch of Bourchier's Castle.
Fig. 2.3—Du Noyer's sketch of scenery at Lough Gur.
Fig. 2.4—Crofton Croker's survey (1833).
Fig. 2.5—Crofton Croker's sketches of megaliths at Lough Gur.
Fig. 2.6—Sketch of megalithic tomb by Margaret Stokes.
Fig. 2.7—Ordnance Survey first-edition map (1844) of Grange.
Fig. 2.8—Windle's map, 1912.
Fig. 2.9—Windle's 1912 survey at Grange.
Fig. 2.10—Windle's 1912 survey of Stone Circles C and D and possible megalithic tomb at Site E.
Fig. 2.11—Sketches of *Leaba na Muice* and the Giant's Grave (Windle 1912).
Fig. 2.12—Bruff Aerial Photographic Survey (extract around Lough Gur).
Fig. 2.13—Geophysical survey, Grange, 'Site of Stone Circle'.
Fig. 2.14—Geophysical survey, Grange.
Fig. 2.15—Geophysical survey, Circle D.
Fig. 2.16—LiDAR image of trackway at Grange.
Fig. 2.17—Harkness's drawings of a child's bone from his excavation at Circle J.
Fig. 2.18—Seán P. Ó Ríordáin and his team on Knockadoon.
Fig. 2.19—Seán P. Ó Ríordáin on Knockadoon.
Fig. 2.20—Survey work in progress on Knockadoon.
Fig. 2.21—Beechwood Cottage, Lough Gur.

Chapter 3. The Stone Age
Fig. 3.1.1—Mesolithic sites in the environs of Lough Gur.
Fig. 3.1.2—Location of Mesolithic finds at Knockadoon.

Fig. 3.1.3—Microliths from Rathjordan; Bann flake (?) from Grange ringfort; blade from Site A, Knockadoon; points from Site A, Knockadoon; blades from Site C, Knockadoon; Bann flakes (?) from Site C, Knockadoon; Bann flakes (?) from Site F, Knockadoon; and microlith (?) from Site J, Knockadoon.

Fig. 3.2.1—Location of Neolithic sites on Knockadoon: Sites A–D, Circles J–L, Site J and Site 10.

Fig. 3.2.2—Site A, Knockadoon: house foundations.

Fig. 3.2.3—Reconstruction of Site A house.

Fig. 3.2.4—Site A, Knockadoon: reconstruction of house cross-section showing roof detail.

Fig. 3.2.5—Site A, Knockadoon: roof detail in reconstruction of house during excavation.

Fig. 3.2.6—Neolithic pottery from Lough Gur.

Fig. 3.2.7—Bronze Age Class II pottery.

Fig. 3.2.8—Polished stone axeheads from Lough Gur.

Fig. 3.2.9—General landscape view showing location of Sites A, C and D and Circle K.

Fig. 3.2.10— Plan of house at Site A, Knockadoon.

Fig. 3.2.11—House at Site A during excavation.

Fig. 3.2.12—Finds from Site A: stone axehead, slate spearhead, leaf-shaped arrowheads, scrapers and blade tool.

Fig. 3.2.13—Site B, Knockadoon: plan of house.

Fig. 3.2.14—Site B, Knockadoon: Class Ia pottery.

Fig. 3.2.15—Finds from Site B, Knockadoon: stone beads, leaf-shaped arrowheads, chert blade and thumbnail scraper.

Fig. 3.2.16—Circle K, Knockadoon: Neolithic house foundations within Bronze Age enclosure.

Fig. 3.2.17—Circle K, Knockadoon: overall plan.

Fig. 3.2.18—Circle K: plan of House 1.

Fig. 3.2.19—Finds from House 1, Circle K: laurel-shaped arrowhead, leaf-shaped arrowheads, flint knife, stone beads and bone points.

Fig. 3.2.20—Circle K: plan of House 2.

Fig. 3.2.21—Neolithic finds from the enclosure, Circle K: leaf-shaped arrowheads, lozenge-shaped arrowhead, flint knife, polished stone axeheads, bone pin and bone bead.

Fig. 3.2.22—Circle L, Knockadoon: overall plan.

Fig. 3.2.23—Circle L: location of Houses A and B and the Central House (Phase 1).

Fig. 3.2.24—Finds from Circle L: leaf- and lozenge-shaped arrowheads, scrapers, knives and blade.

Fig. 3.2.25—Bone points from Circle L.

Fig. 3.2.26—Finds from Circle L: stone beads and bone beads.

Fig. 3.2.27—Plan of Site 10, Knockadoon.

Fig. 3.2.28—Finds from Site 10: leaf- and lozenge-shaped arrowheads, scrapers, knife, blades and fragment of mudstone spearhead.

Fig. 3.2.29—Finds from Site 10: stone beads, bone beads and bone points.

Fig. 3.2.30—Plan of Circle J, Knockadoon.

Fig. 3.2.31—Finds from Circle J: leaf-shaped arrowheads, stone spearhead (?), string-winder (?) and bone points.

Fig. 3.2.32—Site C, Knockadoon: reconstruction of round house.

Fig. 3.2.33—Plan of Site C, Knockadoon.

Fig. 3.2.34—Site C (1940): House I (from north-east) during excavation.

Fig. 3.2.35—Site C (1940): House II (from south) during excavation.

Fig. 3.2.36—Site C (1949): House III (from north) during excavation.

Fig. 3.2.37—Finds from Site C: leaf-shaped arrowheads, scrapers and perforators.

Fig. 3.2.38—Bone points from Site C.

Fig. 3.2.39—Plan of Site D, Knockadoon.

Fig. 3.2.40—Site D: House II (from south-west) during excavation.

Fig. 3.2.41—Site D: House III (from south) during excavation.

Fig. 3.2.42—Finds from Site D: Class I and Class Ia pottery.

Fig. 3.2.43—Finds from Site D: leaf- and lozenge-shaped arrowheads and scrapers.

Fig. 3.2.44—Finds from Site D: bone bead, notched bone and antler pick (?).

Fig. 3.3.1—Site E, Grange.

Fig. 3.3.2—Site E, Grange (after Windle 1912).

Fig. 3.3.3—Finds from Circle K: pendant and bone beads.

Fig. 3.3.4—Site C (1949): burial with Neolithic pot adjacent to head.

Fig. 3.3.5—Caherguillamore: plan and section of burial.

Fig. 3.3.6—Finds from Caherguillamore: Carrowkeel Ware from crouched burial and Linkardstown-type pottery from burial chamber.

Fig. 3.3.7—Finds from Caherguillamore: bone pins, mushroom-headed pins, stone beads and shell beads.

Chapter 4. Late Neolithic Grooved Ware, Chalcolithic and early Bronze Age

Fig. 4.1.1—Location map, showing Grange Stone Circle complex, megalithic tomb (Giant's Grave, Killalough), *Leaba na Muice* and Garret Island.

Fig. 4.1.2—The Grange Stone Circle complex.

Fig. 4.1.3—Geophysical survey, Circles C and D.

Fig. 4.1.4—Circle C, Grange.

Fig. 4.1.5—Plan of Grange Stone Circle B.

Fig. 4.1.6—Grange Stone Circle B, looking west.

Fig. 4.1.7—Grange Stone Circle B, looking east.

Fig. 4.1.8—Grange Stone Circle B: entrance.

Fig. 4.1.9—Grange Stone Circle B: V-notched stones.

Fig. 4.1.10—Grange Stone Circle B: sunset, 9 November 2016.

Fig. 4.1.11—Grange Stone Circle B: elevation of stones of circle.

Fig. 4.1.12—Grange Stone Circle B: sectional profiles across bank.

Fig. 4.1.13—Grange Stone Circle B: sectional profiles across bank.

Fig. 4.1.14—Grange Stone Circle B: Grooved Ware pottery from under the bank and from the circle interior.

Fig. 4.1.15—Grange Stone Circle B: reconstructed Beaker pottery from old ground surface near and within the socket of Stone 12.

Fig. 4.1.16—Grange Stone Circle B: Beaker pottery from interior of circle.

Fig. 4.1.17—Finds from Grange Stone Circle B: hollow-based arrowheads, lozenge-shaped arrowhead, Petit Tranchet Derivatives (lop-sided arrowheads), barbed and tanged arrowhead, round scrapers and blades.

Fig. 4.1.18—Finds from Grange Stone Circle B: copper (?) bracelet fragment, copper (?) awl, bronze (?) end mount for dagger sheath (?), clay bead, bone point from under bank and bone points from old ground surface within the circle.

Fig. 4.1.19—Grange Stone Circle B: excavation in progress in 2012.

Fig. 4.1.20—Grange Stone Circle B: sectional profiles.

Fig. 4.1.21—Grange Stone Circle B: stone revetments exposed during 2012 excavation.

Fig. 4.1.22—Finds from Geroid Island: Grooved Ware pottery, scrapers and Petit Tranchet Derivative.

Fig. 4.1.23—Stone maceheads from Site C and Lough Gur.

Fig. 4.1.24—Circle O.

Fig. 4.1.25—Circle O: plan of excavation.

Fig. 4.1.26—Circle P.

Fig. 4.1.27—Circle P: plan of excavation.

Fig. 4.1.28—Circle P: geophysical survey.

Fig. 4.2.1—Site D: Beaker pottery.

Fig. 4.2.2—Barbed and tanged arrowheads from Site C (1940), Site D, Circle K and Site 10.

Fig. 4.2.3—Rathjordan: plan of excavation.

Fig. 4.2.4—Finds from Rathjordan: stone axehead, rubbing stone, yew pole, notched end of yew pole and Beaker (?) pottery.

Fig. 4.2.5—Finds from Barrow 3, Rathjordan: Beaker pottery and Food Vessel pottery.

Fig. 4.2.6—Finds from Ballingoola: Beaker pottery and barbed and tanged arrowheads.

Fig. 4.2.7—Caherguillamore Beaker.

Fig. 4.2.8—Stone bracers from Lough Gur and from Site C.

Fig. 4.2.9—Bronze axeheads from Ballynagallagh townland, from Lough Gur and from the Hunt Collection.

Fig. 4.2.10—Bronze axeheads from Knockadoon.

Fig. 4.2.11—Copper awls from Circle K, Site C and Site D, and bronze bracelet from Site D.

Fig. 4.2.12—Halberd from Lough Gur.

Fig. 4.3.1—Distribution map of megalithic tombs and sites of megalithic tombs.

Fig. 4.3.2—Megalithic tomb, looking north.

Fig. 4.3.3—Megalithic tomb, looking west.

Fig. 4.3.4—Plan and sectional profiles of megalithic tomb.

Fig. 4.3.5—Beaker pottery from megalithic tomb.

Fig. 4.3.6—Finds from megalithic tomb: thumbnail scrapers, hollow scraper, perforator and blades.

Fig. 4.3.7—*Leaba na Muice.*

Fig. 4.3.8—*Leaba na Muice.*

Fig. 4.3.9—Plan of *Leaba na Muice.*

Fig. 4.4.1— Food Vessel sherds from Grange Stone Circle B.

Fig. 4.4.2—Food Vessel sherds from megalithic tomb.

Chapter 5. The Bronze Age

Fig. 5.1.1—Location map, showing Circles K and L, Site 10, Site 12, Sites D, E, F, G, H and I, Knockadoon; 1985–8 excavations; 1991–2 excavations; car park and interpretative centre.

Fig. 5.1.2—Site C, Knockadoon: Lough Gur Class II pottery.

Fig. 5.1.3—Site C, Knockadoon: decorated Lough Gur Class II pottery and Lough Gur Class II pottery with perforations below rim.

Fig. 5.1.4—Plan of middle Bronze Age C-shaped enclosed habitation site, Knockadoon.

Fig. 5.1.5—Knockadoon: C-shaped enclosed habitation site.

Fig. 5.1.6—Knockadoon: C-shaped enclosed habitation site.

Fig. 5.1.7—Knockadoon: C-shaped enclosure wall.

Fig. 5.1.8—Knockadoon: reconstruction of house within C-shaped enclosed habitation site.

Fig. 5.1.9—Knockadoon: plan of earlier house within C-shaped enclosure.

Fig. 5.1.10—Knockadoon: plan of later house within C-shaped enclosure.

Fig. 5.1.11—Finds from Knockadoon: lignite pendants, bone bead and polished animal tooth fragment.

Fig. 5.1.12—Finds from Knockadoon: gold bar and gold foil.

Fig. 5.1.13—Finds from Knockadoon: hammer-stone, rubbing stone and perforated disc (spindle-whorl).

Fig. 5.1.14—Knockadoon: field fence west of C-shaped enclosed habitation site.

Fig. 5.1.15—Field walls on Knockadoon.

Fig. 5.1.16—Aerial photograph of enclosures Circle J and K, Knockadoon.

Fig. 5.1.17—Knockadoon: plan of Circle J.

Fig. 5.1.18—Knockadoon: pottery from Circle J.

Fig. 5.1.19—Knockadoon: Circle K.

Fig. 5.1.20—Knockadoon: plan of Circle K.

Fig. 5.1.21—Bronze artefacts from Circle K, Knockadoon: awl, decorated disc, toggle, pin fragment, button and casting waste.

Fig. 5.1.22—Knockadoon: overall plan of Circle L (Neolithic houses and Bronze Age enclosing wall).

Fig. 5.1.23—Knockadoon: plan of Bronze Age house within Circle L.

Fig. 5.1.24—Knockadoon: pottery from Circle L.

Fig. 5.1.25—Knockadoon: Site 10 enclosure.

Fig. 5.1.26—Knockadoon: Site 10 enclosure and possible house.

Fig. 5.1.27—Knockadoon: excavation in progress at unenclosed Bronze Age houses.

Fig. 5.1.28—Knockadoon: plan of Bronze Age round house.

Fig. 5.1.29—Knockadoon: reconstruction of Bronze Age round house.

Fig. 5.1.30—Knockadoon: plan of Bronze Age rectangular house.

Fig. 5.1.31—Knockadoon: plan of Bronze Age oval house.

Fig. 5.1.32—Finds from Knockadoon: scrapers, blade, arrowheads and bronze earring.

Fig. 5.1.33—Car-park excavations: hut sites.

Fig. 5.1.34—Excavations 1977: plan of Bronze Age hut.

Fig. 5.1.35—Bronze artefacts from Site C, Knockadoon: 'nail-headed' pin, pin, rapier blade, razor and socketed and looped axehead.

Fig. 5.1.36—Site D, Knockadoon: plan of Bronze Age house and enclosing walls.

Fig. 5.1.37—Site D, Knockadoon: Bronze Age house during excavation.

Fig. 5.1.38—Finds from Site D, Knockadoon: fragment of clay mould for bronze spearhead and fragment of stone mould for palstave axehead.

Fig. 5.1.39—Gold disc from Site D, Knockadoon.

Fig. 5.1.40—Site E, Knockadoon: plan of hut.

Fig. 5.1.41—Knockadoon: Site E during excavation (from north).

Fig. 5.1.42—Site G, Knockadoon: plan of hut.

Fig. 5.1.43—Knockadoon: Site G during excavation.

Fig. 5.1.44—Site H, Knockadoon: plan of hut.

Fig. 5.1.45—Site I, Knockadoon: plan of hut.

Fig. 5.1.46—Knockadoon: Site I during excavation.

Fig. 5.2.1—Plan of burials on Knockadoon Hill.

Fig. 5.2.2—Grave 1, Knockadoon hill.

Fig. 5.2.3—Grave 3, Knockadoon Hill.

Fig. 5.2.4—Knockadoon: child's skull in pit within house floor.

Fig. 5.2.5—Ballynagallagh: plan of graves.

Fig. 5.2.6—Rathjordan: location of barrows.

Fig. 5.2.7—Rathjordan: plan and sectional profile of Barrow 1.

Fig. 5.2.8—Rathjordan: sectional profiles of Barrows 2 and 4.

Fig. 5.2.9—Rathjordan: plan and sectional profile of Barrow 3.

Fig. 5.2.10—Ballingoola: location of Barrows 1 and 2.

Fig. 5.2.11—Plan of Ballingoola 1 and 2.

Fig. 5.2.12—Sectional profiles of Ballingoola 2.

Fig. 5.2.13—Grange Stone Circle B: location of excavated ring-ditches and ring-ditches detected by geophysical survey.

Fig. 5.3.1—Gold-mounted spearhead.

Fig. 5.3.2—The Lough Gur bronze shield.

Fig. 5.3.3—Bronze axeheads of Ballyvalley type and of Derryniggan type.

Fig. 5.3.4—Decorated axehead.

Fig. 5.3.5—Palstave axehead.

Fig. 5.3.6—Socketed axehead.

Fig. 5.3.7—Swords and scabbard chape.

Fig. 5.3.8—Stone mould fragment from Lough Gur wedge tomb and suggested reconstruction of socketed spearhead from mould.

Fig. 5.3.9—Mould for kite-shaped spearheads found in Lough Gur and now in the British Museum.

Fig. 5.4.1—The 'Pillar Stone' on Ardaghlooda Hill.

Fig. 5.4.2—*Cloghavilla* standing stone.

Fig. 5.4.3—Linear group of standing stones to east and north-east of Lough Gur, and standing stones around Lough Gur.

Fig. 5.4.4—Standing stone incorporated into modern field boundary.

Chapter 6. The Iron Age

Fig. 6.1—Reconstruction of Irish Iron Age chariot.

Fig. 6.2—Chariot-yoke mounts from Lough Gur.

Fig. 6.3—Iron sword with bone handle from Lough Gur townland.

Fig. 6.4—Safety-pin brooch (fibula) from Site C, Knockadoon.

Fig. 6.5—Slab-lined grave on Knockadoon.

Chapter 7. The Roman period

Fig. 7.1—Coin of Constantius II from Carraig Aille II.

Fig. 7.2—Bronze toilet implement and bronze stylus from Carraig Aille II, and bronze ring from Ballinard townland.

Fig. 7.3—The Balline silver hoard: ingots, dish with hunting scene and dish with foliage and acanthus pattern.

Chapter 8. The early medieval period

Fig. 8.1.1—Location map showing Carraig Aille I and II, the Spectacles, Grange ringfort, Ballynagallagh, Ballingoola and Site F, Knockadoon.

Fig. 8.1.2—Carraig Aille forts, looking west.

Fig. 8.1.3—Carraig Aille forts, looking east.

Fig. 8.1.4—Carraig Aille II: steps.

Fig. 8.1.5—Carraig Aille II: entrance.

Fig. 8.1.6—Carraig Aille II: plan of Phase I occupation.

Fig. 8.1.7—Carraig Aille II: plan of Phase II occupation.

Fig. 8.1.8—Carraig Aille II: House 1, Phase II. Plan of rectangular stone-built house south of rampart.

Fig. 8.1.9—Carraig Aille II: extramural houses north of rampart.

Fig. 8.1.10—Carraig Aille II: extramural Houses VI (a)–(c).

Fig. 8.1.11—Finds from Carraig Aille II: bronze ring-pin/brooch, bronze ring-pin, bronze enamelled hand-pin, bronze ring-pins, iron ring-pins, iron pin with spiral head, flat-headed iron pin, decorated bronze strip and bronze button.

Fig. 8.1.12—Finds from Carraig Aille II: iron knives, iron shears, axehead and plough-sock.

Fig. 8.1.13—Finds from Carraig Aille II: bone combs, bone pins, bone needle, bone spindle-whorls, bone scoops or gouges and bone gaming pieces (?) or beads (?).

Fig. 8.1.14—Finds from Carraig Aille II: quernstones, whetstones, rotary grindstone and single-cresset stone lamp.

Fig. 8.1.15—Finds from Carraig Aille II: stone spindle-whorls, stone disc, stone handle, stone bracelet, jet bracelets and stone bead.

Fig. 8.1.16—Finds from Carraig Aille II: glass beads and glass bracelet fragment.

Fig. 8.1.17—Clay crucibles from Carraig Aille II.

Fig. 8.1.18—Plan of Carraig Aille I.

Fig. 8.1.19—Iron artefacts from Carraig Aille I: hand-pin, ringed pins, ring, strap end, horse-bit, scribing tools (?) and punch.

Fig. 8.1.20—Finds from Carraig Aille I: bone combs, decorated bone strip, bone gaming piece or bead, antler handle, bone spindle-whorls and bone scoop or gouge.

Fig. 8.1.21—Glass beads from Carraig Aille I.

Fig. 8.1.22—Enclosed cattle corral west of Carraig Aille I.

Fig. 8.1.23—Plan of Structures A–C north-west of Carraig Aille I.

Fig. 8.1.24—The Spectacles.

Fig. 8.1.25—The Spectacles: Houses A and B.

Fig. 8.1.26—The Spectacles: House D.

Fig. 8.1.27—Grange ringfort before excavation.

Fig. 8.1.28—Grange ringfort: plan of excavation.

Fig. 8.1.29—Grange ringfort: plan of house.

Fig. 8.1.30—Grange ringfort: house site during excavation.

Fig. 8.1.31—Ballingoola III: plan of house site.

Fig. 8.1.32—Ballingoola IV: plan of house site.

Fig. 8.1.33—Ballynagallagh: site location.

Fig. 8.1.34—Aerial photograph of Ballynagallagh.

Fig. 8.1.35—Plan of circular house at Ballynagallagh.

Fig. 8.1.36—Palisade trench, Ballynagallagh.

Fig. 8.1.37—Stone-lined pit within the enclosure at Ballynagallagh.

Fig. 8.1.38—Site F, Knockadoon: general plan.

Fig. 8.1.39—Site F, Knockadoon: plan of stone house.

Fig. 8.1.40—Silver penny of Plegmund, archbishop of Canterbury, and silver penny of Edward the Elder.

Fig. 8.2.1—Location of crannogs (Bolin Island, Crock Island, Balic Islands and Ballynagallagh).

Fig. 8.2.2—Bolin Island.

Fig. 8.2.3—Bolin Island.

Chapter 9. The Vikings

Fig. 9.1—Viking period child's sword from Lough Gur.

Fig. 9.2—Carraig Aille Viking hoard: ring, bracelet, arm-rings and ring.

Fig. 9.3—Silver ingots from Carraig Aille.

Fig. 9.4—Finds from Carraig Aille: drinking-horn and chain link.

Chapter 10. The Anglo-Normans, 1170–1300

Fig. 10.1—Location map.

Fig. 10.2—Caherguillamore: site location; X marks the excavation site.

Fig. 10.3—Field systems at Caherguillamore.

Fig. 10.4—Plan of medieval houses at Caherguillamore.

Fig. 10.5—Caherguillamore: the houses during excavation.

Fig. 10.6—Caherguillamore: quernstone *in situ* in yard between Houses I and II.

Fig. 10.7—Finds from Caherguillamore: cheek-pieces, strip of bronze and loop.

Fig. 10.8—Finds from Caherguillamore: iron knives, door keys, latch-lifter, hasp, spur rowel, buckle, shears and chisel.

Fig. 10.9—Finds from Caherguillamore: bone box, spindle-whorls, stone lamp, whetstone, rotary grinding stone and quernstones.

Fig. 10.10—Car park: site location.

Fig. 10.11—Car park: plan and reconstruction of House 1.

Fig. 10.12—Finds from House I: iron hook, horseshoe fragment, iron buckle and bone die.

Fig. 10.13—Car park: plan of House II and yard enclosure foundation trenches.

Fig. 10.14—Car park: foundations of House II.

Fig. 10.15—Car park: reconstruction of House II.

Fig. 10.16—Car park: foundation of east wall of House II.

Fig. 10.17—Car park: threshold of House II.

Fig. 10.18—Car park: House II stone annexe.

Fig. 10.19—Iron artefacts from House II, car park: door keys, barrel padlock keys, stirrups, horse-bits, knives, arrowhead, stick-pin and needle.

Fig. 10.20—Finds from House II, car park: bronze stick-pins, bronze ring, bone pin, bone comb, amber bead and bone bead.

Fig. 10.21—Finds from House II, car park: whetstones, reused stone axehead, quernstone and plough pebble.

Fig. 10.22—Ploughing scene from the Luttrell Psalter.

Fig. 10.23—Ballynagallagh nunnery.

Chapter 11. Tower-houses and settlement, 1400–1700

Fig. 11.1—Location map.

Fig. 11.2—Bourchier's Castle.

Fig. 11.3—Bourchier's Castle.

Fig. 11.4—Bourchier's Castle.

Fig. 11.5—Bourchier's Castle: elevation.

Fig. 11.6—Bourchier's Castle: elevation.

Fig. 11.7—Bourchier's Castle: door.

Fig. 11.8—Bourchier's Castle: door.

Fig. 11.9—Bourchier's Castle: cross-section.

Fig. 11.10—Bourchier's Castle: cross-section.

Fig. 11.11—Bourchier's Castle: ground-floor plan.

Fig. 11.12—Bourchier's Castle: first-floor plan.

Fig. 11.13—Bourchier's Castle: second-floor plan.

Fig. 11.14—Bourchier's Castle: third-floor plan.

Fig. 11.15—Bourchier's Castle: fourth-floor plan.

Fig. 11.16—Bourchier's Castle: second-floor fireplace.

Fig. 11.17—Bourchier's Castle: third-floor fireplace.

Fig. 11.18—Dineley's sketch of Bourchier's Castle.

Fig. 11.19—Black Castle: Ordnance Survey map showing castle and causeway.

Fig. 11.20—Black Castle: Du Noyer's sketch (1860s).

Fig. 11.21—Black Castle c. 1870.

Fig. 11.22—Black Castle: bawn wall and entrance.

Fig. 11.23—Geroid Island in the centre of the lake, with Knockfennell and Knockadoon.

Fig. 11.24—Down Survey sketch of Rawleystown Castle.

Fig. 11.25—Rawleystown Castle: bawn wall.

Fig. 11.26—Rawleystown Castle: bawn wall.

Fig. 11.27—Rawleystown Castle: three-storey building within bawn wall c. 1940.

Fig. 11.28—Caherelly Castle.

Fig. 11.29—Down Survey sketch of Caherelly Castle.

Fig. 11.30—Confederate coin.

Fig. 11.31—Plan of Site J.

Fig. 11.32—Finds from Site J: spoon, ornamental piece, jew's harp, bone handle and whetstones.

Fig. 11.33—Newchurch.

Fig. 11.34—Newchurch: west gable.

Fig. 11.35—Newchurch: door with modern coloured glazed plaque of the Madonna and Child.

Fig. 11.36—Newchurch: window in south wall.

Fig. 11.37—Caherelly church.

Fig. 11.38—Caherelly church: window in south wall.

Chapter 12. Summary

Fig. 12.1—The Lough Gur shield.

Acknowledgements

The preparation of this book was facilitated by a number of individuals, and the author wishes to credit the following: James O'Driscoll, formerly of the Department of Archaeology, UCC, and currently in the University of Aberdeen, Scotland, for designing and producing the graphics; Mary Cahill, Keeper of Antiquities, National Museum of Ireland, for Figs 3.2.6a, 5.1.2, 5.1.39, 5.3.5–6, 6.3 and 7.3.1–4; Colin Rynne for Figs 10.11b and 10.15; Michelle O'Dea, Office of Public Works, for providing Figs 11.5–6 and 11.9–15; Joseph Lennon for Figs 11.7–8, 11.16–17, 11.22 and 11.29; Tony Roche, Photographic Unit, National Monuments Service, for providing Figs 4.1.4, 4.1.6–9, 4.1.24, 4.3.2–3, 5.1.16, 8.1.2–3 and 11.2–4; Nick Hogan for Fig. 8.1.24; Carleton Jones, Archaeology Department, NUI Galway, for Figs 3.1.16 and 5.1.19; Dan Breen, Cork Public Museum, for Fig. 5.3.4; Conor McDermott, Archaeology Department, UCD, for providing the available record of Ó Ríordáin's excavations at Lough Gur; Professor William O'Brien, Department of Archaeology, UCC, for various facilities; Maurice Hurley for reading and advising on Chapters 10 and 11; Kevin Kearney, Department of Archaeology, UCC, for useful discussion on the pollen record at Lough Gur; Clare McCutcheon for information on the Caherguillamore medieval pottery; Joanne O'Sullivan for help with the glass beads from various sites; Paul Rondelez for reviewing iron-working waste from the car-park site; Anna Brindley, Rijksuniversiteit, Groningen, for reviewing the radiocarbon dates from the 2012 excavation at Grange Stone Circle; Katharina Becker, Archaeology Department, UCC, for information on the radiocarbon evidence from Rathgall hillfort; Ed O'Riordan for information on the Famine period drainage at Lough Gur; Michael Quinlan for encouraging me to write this book and for various contributions; Limerick City and County Council and the Thomond Archaeological Society for financing publication; Sarah McCutcheon, Archaeologist, Limerick City and County Council, for arranging finance; and Wordwell Ltd.

DISCLAIMER

Many of the archaeological sites around Lough Gur are on private property and the owner's permission should be sought before visiting these. No responsibility is accepted by the author or publisher for any loss, injury or inconvenience sustained by anyone as a result of using this book.

Preface

The landscape around Lough Gur is one of the richest in Ireland as regards field monuments. The lake and its hinterland have been the focus of archaeological research, including excavation and survey, over the past 150 years. Many portable antiquities have also been recovered from the lake and the surrounding countryside. Archaeological research at Lough Gur has provided a vast amount of knowledge, published in various academic journals. This information is gathered together here to present a synthesis of the archaeology of Lough Gur. The archaeological evidence is set within the context of research in Ireland over the past 70 years and, where possible, a chronology and interpretation of sites is offered. Radiocarbon dating was unavailable for the early excavations, but by analogy with the results of more modern excavations it has been possible to provide good chronological perspectives on the results from older explorations.

All that is left of our distant ancestors are fragments of where they once lived and the materials they shaped into use. These remains constitute the archaeological evidence of communities remote from us in time. This evidence enables a reconstruction of the story of long-forgotten lives, which are pieced together and put into a sequence. The story, however, remains incomplete—more so for prehistoric times than for the historic period, in which the narrative of past lives is augmented by the written word. Even then the written word can be selective, and archaeological evidence presents a fuller picture of society.

Excavations began in Lough Gur almost 150 years ago, and the great campaigns of investigation by Seán P. Ó Ríordáin between 1936 and 1954 opened up a previously unknown world of past inhabitants. These excavations were one of the first of their kind in Ireland, where archaeology had hitherto been focused on upstanding monuments. In contrast, Ó Ríordáin's excavations explored places and landscapes inhabited by our ancestors. The archaeological fieldwork at Lough Gur established a basic chronology of settlement and helped fill in the gaps in our knowledge of how people lived, their beliefs and their connections with early communities elsewhere in Ireland and abroad. While the techniques of field excavation have improved and radiocarbon dating is standard, the pioneering work contributed greatly to our understanding of both the prehistoric and the historic populations that inhabited the Lough Gur area, and of the inhabitants of Ireland as a whole. Modern excavations at Lough Gur and large-scale archaeological projects undertaken as part of infrastructural works within Ireland have provided information, including close dating of material culture, that can be used to set the chronology of settlement at Lough Gur on a sounder footing.

Ó Ríordáin's excavations confirmed that Mesolithic hunter-gatherer communities probably roamed the landscape around Lough Gur 10,000 years ago, leaving little trace except for a few stone implements. At the time of Ó Ríordáin's excavations, the Irish Neolithic was understood to be 500 years long, and now the archaeological record confirms that the first agriculturists were settled in Ireland just after 4000 BC. Archaeological excavation of Neolithic settlements on Knockadoon Hill formed the basis of the study of Neolithic communities in Ireland for many years. A period in the late Neolithic known as Grooved Ware cultures (3000–2500 BC) was first discovered in Ireland at the Great Stone Circle at Grange. Similarly, excavations at the stone circle and elsewhere on Knockadoon Hill demonstrated the presence of the first metallurgists, known in Ireland as Beaker cultures (2500–2000 BC). The Bronze Age (2000–800/700 BC) in Ireland was previously marked by a proliferation of metal artefacts. Work at Lough Gur also explored Bronze Age settlement and burial evidence. The Iron Age (800/700 BC–AD 400) remains obscure in the Irish archaeological record but artefacts from that time have been recovered from excavations at Lough Gur. Evidence of connections with the Roman Empire was recorded at Lough Gur and its hinterland and affirmed by the historic connection between the Déisi and Roman Britain. The archaeology of the early medieval period (400–900) is augmented to some extent by written records, but the everyday lives of the people can only be revealed and examined through archaeological field exploration, and excavation of these sites at Lough Gur has contributed to such knowledge. Similar to the Iron Age, a Viking (870–1000) presence at Lough Gur is shown by some artefacts recovered from excavations and as stray finds. The arrival of the Anglo-Normans changed the political, social and economic landscape of Ireland. Much of the archaeological research on this period (1166–1400) in Ireland has focused on castles and, in more recent years, on the urban archaeology of Anglo-Norman towns and cities. Lough Gur has, however, provided evidence of the rural settlements which to date in Irish archaeology have been little researched. The emergence of the Desmond dynasty and their ultimate demise (1400–1650) is documented in political history. Their castles at Lough Gur were important strategic and economic centres and remain in the landscape as a reminder of past glory.

Allied to excavations was a tremendous amount of survey, beginning with Windle in 1912, followed by O'Kelly in the early 1940s and latterly using modern survey methods, including aerial photography, geophysical survey and LIDAR. The research at Lough Gur has also been augmented by various antiquarian accounts of monuments which are no longer visible on the landscape. These accounts enable the archaeologist to track landscape changes and the provenance of finds recovered in the past.

1. The landscape

INTRODUCTION

Lough Gur is an antique and storied land, inhabited continuously for over 8,000 years. The lake was and still is a focus both within the community of Lough Gur and for the greater hinterland of east Limerick. Dowd (1896, 65) wrote that

> 'Very few places which will be found more interesting by the visitor than Lough Gur and its neighbourhood. From long distant ages man has found a home here, and the shores of the lake still bear witness to the ancient race whose monuments have survived all changes that have passed over the county.'

Limited tillage has helped to preserve the archaeological landscape and monuments tend to survive above ground, in contrast to many areas where the remains of past societies have been almost obliterated by the plough. Today the area surrounding Lough Gur has a variety of visible field monuments, ranging in date from the Stone Age or Neolithic up to the late medieval period. These sites reflect how past societies shaped the landscape, and conversely how the landscape shaped daily lives. Human activity is seen in the ordinary lives of people whereby land was cultivated, houses were built, families were reared and beliefs were expressed in things outside daily life. These acts have moulded and formed the landscape. The impact of past societies is visible in such monuments at Lough Gur as the Great Stone Circle at Grange or the imposing tower-house of Bourchier's Castle, but also in less monumental sites such as the low earthworks that may mark the places of ancient burial sites or houses and the field fences, some of which are of great antiquity.

Lough Gur is a place renowned in archaeology not only in Ireland but also in western Europe. It was a place where Neolithic and Bronze Age settlements were discovered from 1940–51, when these prehistoric sites were practically unknown elsewhere in Ireland. Much archaeological research and fieldwork in Ireland has altered this picture, but Lough Gur remains one of the few places where the monuments are both abundant and varied within a relatively small area and where some date back several millennia. Excavations on both prehistoric and historic sites formed the basis of archaeological studies in Ireland for several generations. Excavations by Seán P. Ó Ríordáin, and to a lesser extent by Máire MacDermott and David Liversage, were at the time exemplary but by modern standards were less methodical. Archaeological excavations in the 1930s and 1940s were carried out without the benefit of radiocarbon dating, which now provides a reliable chronology. Dating relied on the artefactual finds, particularly on pottery from prehistoric sites and on art history and artefact form for historic sites. Other studies, for example of animal bone and charred plant

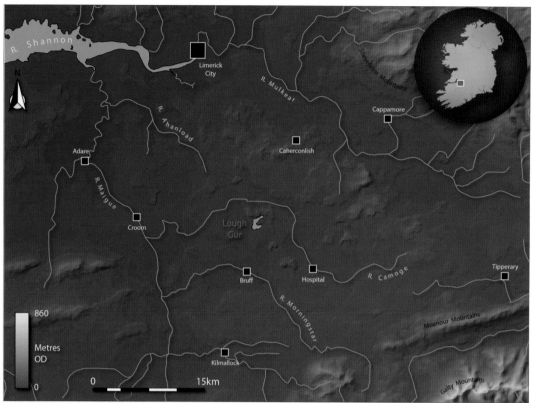

Fig. 1.1—Lough Gur: location and river network.

Fig. 1.2—Lough Gur: general photo.

Fig. 1.3—Low-lying land (under 76m OD)—locations of former lakes?

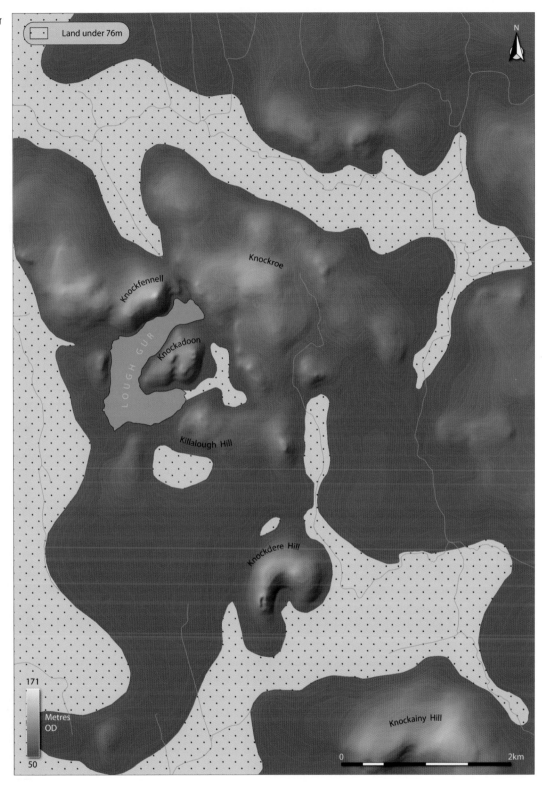

Land under 76m

Knockroe

Knockfennell

LOUGH GUR

Knockadoon

Killalough Hill

Knockdere Hill

Knockainy Hill

171

Metres
OD

50

0   2km

remains, which enable the archaeologist to reconstruct past economies had not developed, and much of this type of information can now only be inferred from more modern excavations. It is only in the recent past, with large-scale developmental works such as road and gas pipeline schemes, that similar prehistoric sites to those at Lough Gur have been uncovered. Information from modern excavations has helped to confirm the chronological sequence and to reconstruct past societies at Lough Gur.

THE PHYSICAL LANDSCAPE

Lough Gur is located south of the Shannon estuary (Fig. 1.1) and was accessible in prehistoric and early historic times via the Maigue River, which flows south from the estuary, or through the Mulkear River, which enters the River Shannon to the east of Limerick City. The west-flowing Morningstar River to the south of Lough Gur and the Camoge River to the north are tributaries of the Maigue River, and they also have a network of streams that generally flow north–south. These rivers were pivotal for the accessibility of the Lough Gur area.

Lough Gur is, at present, the largest inland water body in the east Limerick area and was attractive to early settlers (Fig. 1.2). Some low-lying tracts of boggy land in the environs of broad, flat river valleys to the south of Lough Gur (Fig. 1.3) previously included lakes, some of which survived into historic times (Synge 1966, 19). Low-lying boggy areas such as Rockbarton Bog were former lakes. Caherelly West Castle was also built near a lake (Grene Barry 1905–8, 138), and a lake known as 'Loch Ceann' was recorded between Knockainy and Lough Gur (Lynch 1895, 247). These lakes must have facilitated travel by boat across the landscape surrounding Lough Gur. This ease of travel in and out of Lough Gur in antiquity is confirmed by the identification of imported objects such as Neolithic stone axeheads from Cumbria in north Wales, Cornwall and the north Antrim coast (Dempsey 2013). In historic times, Vikings from Waterford launched their ships on Lough Gur in AD 926 (Ó Corráin 1972, 103), possibly having traversed the countryside via a network of lakes and rivers.

The 'Red Bog', close to the southern shore of Lough Gur, was investigated by Mitchell (1951, 171–2) as part of his work on reconstructing past landscapes based on pollen records, and he suggested that the Red Bog was a raised bog in antiquity. It was extensively drained and turf was cut there in the past century (Fig. 1.4).

GEOLOGY, GLACIATION AND SOILS

Geology

The geology of the Lough Gur area of County Limerick includes a mix of rock types within a syncline known as the 'Limerick Basin' (Fig. 1.5). The Carboniferous series in the region comprises shales and limestones that surround the lake. The limestone hills in the immediate environs of Lough Gur are Knockadoon, which is surrounded by the lake, Knockfennell to the north (Fig. 1.6), Ardaghlooda to the west and Grange Hill to the north-west. The ground also rises to the north and east and the contours enclose the lake in a bowl-shaped landscape. A volcanic ring-dyke complex is located to the north and east of the lake; these volcanic rocks are igneous, ranging from alkaline

Fig. 1.4—The Red Bog.

Fig. 1.5—Local geology.

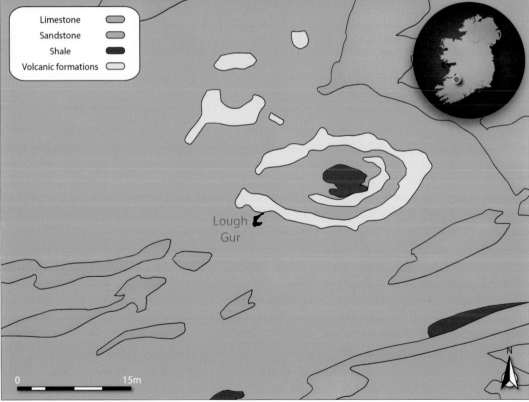

5

Fig. 1.6—Knockfennell Hill.

syenites to basic basalts, and are known as the 'Limerick Volcanics'. They are interbedded with layers of volcanic ash (tuffs) as well as Carboniferous limestone and shale. The ring-dyke complex is visible as conical volcanic plugs (Fig. 1.7) such as the hills of Knockderc to the south and Knockroe to the north of Lough Gur, and these interrupt an otherwise flat plain surrounding the Lough Gur area.

Glaciation

The Pleistocene Ice Age was a series of glacial advances and retreats and interglacial or interstadial warm periods. The last glaciation in Ireland, known as the 'Late Midlandian', was over 25,000 years ago, and the maximum extent of ice sheets is marked by a terminal moraine in the Ballylanders area. A subsequent re-advance of ice is also recorded at Fedamore. Much of the information on the glacial history of north Munster was derived from deposits exposed in a well-shaft dug in Baggotstown, to the south of Lough Gur, where sequential deposits helped reconstruct the development of the landscape (Mitchell 1976, 54). Climatic improvement provided an environment that allowed animals to occupy the island of Ireland during warm periods, and they may have crossed via land-bridges which existed between Ireland and Britain. Cave excavations at Castlepook, near Doneraile in north Cork, have produced animal bones which show that woolly mammoth (*Elephas primigenius*), reindeer (*Ranifer tarandus*), brown bear (*Ursus arctos*), hare (*Lepus lemmus*), hyena (*Crocuta crocuta*), lemming (*Lemmus lemmus*) and Arctic fox (*Alopex lagopus*) were among the animals that roamed the countryside (*ibid.*, 59). These remains may date from at least 30,000 years ago (Woodman 2015, fig. 2.2). Some evidence of interstadial animal remains was recovered during an excavation in 1938 by Seán P. Ó Ríordáin of the Red Cellar Cave on Knockfennell Hill.[1] The cave itself was a narrow solution crevice on the south-facing slope of the hill. Bones of elk, Arctic lemming, brown bear and other unspecified

Fig. 1.7—Extinct volcanic plugs, Knockderc.

species were recovered from the cave (O'Kelly 1941). The bones of larger animals may have been brought into the cave by scavengers such as hyenas or foxes. The bear bones were dated to the period between 12,747 and 12,247 years ago (Woodman 2015, table 2.1) and may have been the last in the sequence of animal bones from the Red Cellar Cave.

Interglacial and postglacial
When the Midlandian phase of the last Ice Age ended about 15,000 years ago (Woodman 2015, 20), soil began to develop over the exposed bedrock; as temperatures rose, the landscape was one of open grassland with scattered copses of willow and birch. The Giant Irish Deer (*Megaloceros giganteus*) lived in Ireland at various times during interglacial and interstadial warm periods; it is recorded 30,000 years ago and continued to exist up to 14,000–13,000 years ago (*ibid.*, 22). As colder episodes occurred, the deer moved south to open grassland (Mitchell 1976, 75). These giant deer stood up to 2m high and had an antler span of up to 4m (Fig. 1.8). The antlers, though massive, were frail and were for show rather than combat. A return of Arctic conditions about 12,600 years ago, known as the 'Younger Dryas', saw the environment revert to tundra-like conditions, and this phase may have seen the extinction of most of the mammals in Ireland. The grasslands essential for the Giant Irish Deer disappeared, resulting in their demise.

Bones and antlers of the Giant Irish Deer have been found frequently in east Limerick along the banks of the rivers and the edges of former lakes at Cahercorney and in the Red Bog (Mitchell 1951, 169, 172). Bones were recovered during arterial drainage works along the valley of the Camoge River in the 1940s (*ibid.*, 169–70), and in more recent times during the Maigue Drainage Scheme from 1973 to 1986. Carte (1866) details the finding of bones of Giant Irish Deer by a Mr Hinchy

Fig. 1.8—Giant Irish deer (*Megaloceros giganteus*) (after Mitchell 1976).

in 1864 on the bank of the Camoge River near Kilcullane House, to the south-east of Lough Gur. The bones included twenty skulls, and the account refers to the finding of 40 more skulls by John Abel of Limerick around 1839 (Carte 1866, 152). The skulls that Hinchy found were *c.* 4–5ft (1.2–1.5m) below the surface in blue marl. Some bones were sent to Carte and included leg bones and antlers. The discovery of so many skulls confirmed that the Giant Irish Deer roamed in herds, and the blue marl indicated a former lake or waterlogged river valley. Mitchell (1976, 76) suggested that the lake edges were areas of soft mud and that when the deer came to drink or to eat the water-plants it became stuck in the mud, and in a struggle to free itself it caused itself and other deer in the herd to sink into the mire; its huge antlers made it impossible to regain its feet and death followed.

After the cold period of the Younger Dryas, which lasted around 1,000 years, the climatic phase known as the Holocene began around 11,600 years ago, with a drier, more continental climate followed by a warmer and wetter climate similar to today, which was fully established by about 8,000 years ago (Woodman 2015, 22).

Soils

The last glacial advance shaped the east Limerick landscape. As the ice retreated, a limestone-derived boulder-clay plain was laid down. Lough Gur is part of the wider 'Golden Vale', where good agricultural land is best suited to pasture for dairying and cattle. The soils to the west of Lough Gur are grey-brown podzolic soils of the Elton Series, which were developed mainly from glacial drift of limestone derivation (Finch and Ryan 1966). To the east, in the vicinity of Circles O and P and approximately 500m to the east of the lake, the Elton Series podzolic soils merge with brown earths of the Derk Series, the latter being developed from glacial drift of predominantly volcanic origin and containing an abundance of pebbles derived from the volcanic outcrops. The soils around Lough Gur are in general suitable for pasture, and the Derk and Elton Series are excellent for grazing (*ibid.*, 94, 99). The light soil cover in Lough Gur was easy to bring into farmland in prehistoric times and must have facilitated early farming methods.

The areas where the former lakes existed are now seasonally waterlogged, although they produce good grassland, but were not in use in prehistoric or early historic times. The Camoge River valley to the north of Lough Gur is liable to periodic flooding, although the grassland is good. The land around the Camoge was recorded in the Civil Survey (Simington 1938), where in 1655 the rivers Camoge and 'Cavoyer' were described as 'meares' (pools; wet land) (Westropp 1906–7, 174). Fitzgerald and McGregor (1826, 304) recorded that in Ballingoola townland the level land on either side of the Camoge comprised corcass lands 'covered with water for nearly six months in the year' as a result of the overflowing river. They also noted that, as a consequence of flooding, 'the air is cold, and the houses and furniture very damp; and in Spring, when the extent of the stagnant water thus collected, is exhaling by the sun's heat, the inhabitants are subject to colds, coughs and sore throats'.

RAW MATERIALS

The availability of flint and chert for stone tools made Lough Gur attractive to early settlers. The stone tool assemblages from many excavated sites included artefacts manufactured from flint derived from the glacial tills and chert from the Carboniferous limestone. Woodman and Scannell (1993, table 6.2) have shown that, although chert is readily available in Lough Gur, there was a marked preference for glacially derived nodular flint. A study of the Neolithic stone axeheads from Lough Gur confirmed that 64% were imported and that local raw materials were used in only about a third of the examples (Dempsey 2013). The extinct volcanic plugs provided glacial erratics used in monument construction, principally at the Great Stone Circle in Grange townland. Wood was also a raw material necessary for daily life and was used to build houses, as firewood, for furniture, for artefacts such as handles and in parts of machinery such as ploughs and looms. The soils around Lough Gur are light and may never have supported oak forests but oak has flourished in the clay soils of the hinterland. Ash and birch still grow around Lough Gur and hazel is common. These species are the most frequently recorded from analyses carried out on charred wood from excavated sites at Lough Gur.

FOOD SOURCES

The earliest inhabitants of Lough Gur were Mesolithic hunter-gatherers who foraged for food and consequently had a transient presence in the landscape. Food sources included fish, wild birds and animals, and seasonal berries and nuts. The native fish stock in Lough Gur itself is limited, as the lake is a solution lake with no surface inlet or drainage, preventing spawning fish from reaching it. Eels, which can travel overland, are present today and were likely there in the past. Mary Carbery (1973, 39) recorded an eel weir on the lake in the late nineteenth century. There were undoubtedly salmon and trout in the Camoge and Morningstar rivers surrounding Lough Gur, and these rivers may also have contained freshwater oysters (Van Wijngaarden-Bakker 1995). The abundance of water at Lough Gur attracted resident and migratory birds, and a variety of bird bones from excavated sites include greylag and white-fronted geese, sea eagles, ducks, cranes, coots, gulls, corncrakes, ravens, owls and marsh harriers around the lake (*ibid.*, table 10). Fowl probably provided a significant food source. Charred hazelnuts have been found on many of the excavations, and hazel grows well on the shallow limestone-derived soils surrounding Lough Gur. Charred hazelnuts have been found on many Mesolithic and Neolithic sites and represent a frequently foraged food. Other food sources probably included crab-apples, blackberries, wild raspberries and strawberries, as well as herbs and edible weeds.

The advent of farming and a sedentary lifestyle in Lough Gur about 4000 BC saw the management of food sources rather than opportunistic hunting and foraging. The soils around Lough Gur were, as now, suitable for pasture. The light soils probably never supported a dense tree cover and it may have been relatively easy to create farmland. Despite the shallow soils on the hills of Knockadoon and Knockfennell, crop cultivation is indicated by ancient field enclosures, some of which date from at least the Bronze Age. Fences may have been erected to protect crops. There is ample evidence in historic times for cereal cultivation.

LAKE DRAINAGE

The lake is now 'C'-shaped, fed by a spring, and drains through a rock cave or crevice at Pollavaddra[2] on the south-east side of Knockfennell Hill. Lake levels fluctuated in antiquity, possibly owing to climatic changes or because the underground outlet at Pollavaddra was periodically blocked (Ahlberg *et al.* 2001, 370). Mitchell (1954, 484) also recorded that Garret Island was only slightly elevated above the modern lake level and suggested that the lake was lower than today when the island was occupied in Neolithic and medieval times.

Prior to a Famine Poor Law Relief drainage scheme in 1847–8,[3] the lake almost completely surrounded Knockadoon Hill. A Commission for Drainage was established in 1842, and schemes for arterial drainage were planned by the then Board of Works; part of the scheme included the Camoge River, where drainage works were in place in 1849.[4] Robert Peel introduced legislation for Famine Relief through drainage works in 1846, and the Lough Gur drainage came under that initiative. Drainage at the lake was achieved by cutting a channel from the north-west shore at the foot of Knockfennell Hill to Grange, where water disgorged into a tributary of the Morningstar River. An antiquarian visitor identified as 'B.R.R.'[5] (1865, 243), from Sunday's Well in Cork City, described the Lough Gur drainage as being achieved 'by making a cut through the townland of Grange, which was successfully deepened until the lake has been lowered nearly 16 feet [4.8m] below its original level'. This channel was dug sometime around 1847–8. The old shore line is traceable along the edge of Lough Gur and the water is now *c.* 2m below the original lake level. The extent of the lake in the late seventeenth century was shown in Dineley's sketches (Fig. 1.9) of 1681 (Hayman 1868–9, 414–15), and its early nineteenth-century extent was recorded on the first-edition Ordnance Survey map published in 1844 (Fig. 1.10). Part of the original lake is now visible as a large tract of bog which extends between the east side of Knockadoon Hill and the ridge to the east, where the stone forts at Carraig Aille are located (Fig. 1.11). This bog is reputed to be the find-spot of the Lough Gur shield.

Fig. 1.9—Dineley's 1681 sketch of Lough Gur.

Fig. 1.10—Extent of lake mapped by Ordnance Survey in 1840 (published 1844).

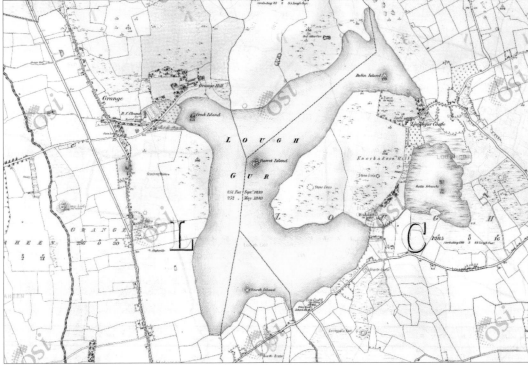

The 1847–8 drainage reduced the lake in size to about 80% of its original extent, and several artefacts, including the late Bronze Age Lough Gur shield, were recovered from the lake shore immediately after the lake was lowered. The antiquarian Day (1895, 303) recorded that the partial drainage at Lough Gur resulted in the recovery of many artefacts, and that Lough Gur 'has been a rich and fruitful storehouse, from whence antiquities of stone, bone, copper, bronze, silver and gold have been sought after and gathered by the country-folk'. He listed the antiquities in his collection acquired from friends at Lough Gur, found by himself or 'bought from rag and bone men in Bruff' (Day 1895, 304): 23 stone axeheads, five bronze axeheads, two socketed bronze spearheads, three bronze

Fig. 1.11—Area drained in 1847–8.

pins/brooches and an unspecified number of bone pins. He also referred (*ibid.*, 305) to the partial drainage of Lough Gur in the 'fifties' (the 1850s) and mentioned that antiquities from Lough Gur had been dispersed to museums and private collections in Britain. Amongst the items found was a gold-mounted spearhead (Fig. 1.12) which was brought to Lord Guillamore, who 'bought it for a trifle' and put a handle on it, after which 'the spearhead was then added to a trophy of arms in the hall of Rockbarton' (*ibid.*, 303). The spearhead was subsequently sold at auction to the Revd W.C. Neligan, DD, who in turn sold it with some other antiquities at a Sotheby's auction to Colonel Lane Fox (later known as General Pitt-Rivers). The spearhead was exhibited at a meeting of the Ethnographical Society in London in 1869 by Colonel Lane Fox, who stated that it was found in a peat bog adjoining Lough Gur in 1857 or 1858 and gave details of measurements and of the gold inlay on the socket, which at the time was the only known example from either England or Ireland. Lane Fox also had the oak shaft examined by J.D. Hooker of Kew Gardens, who confirmed that the shaft was shaped from a solid block of oak, tapered at both ends. Hooker considered the shaft to be original.

Dowd (1896, 65) recorded that the drainage exposed 'bones and skeletons of extinct animals' and 'implements of stone and bronze, ornaments of bone and silver, weapons of various kinds … [that] bear witness to the number and variety of the antiquities which were discovered when the surface of the lake was lowered by drainage some half a century ago'.

There appear to have been a few previous attempts to drain the lake prior to the 1847–8 drainage. Fitzgerald and McGregor (1826, 312) referred to a landlord, Stackpoole Baylee, who cut a drain near the Black Castle which drew off a considerable amount of water from the lake; he was 'killed by a fall from his horse, on his return at night from a neighbouring gentleman's house where he had dined'. Baylee's drainage scheme appears to have taken place around 1795 (Lynch 1895, 242–3). The antiquarian 'B.R.R.' (1865, 243) also recorded Stackpoole Baylee's death and that

'Three other persons, who successfully continued the operations, met either with serious accidents or misfortunes; all of which the country people believe to be the result of the

Fig. 1.12—Spearhead (after Evans 1881).

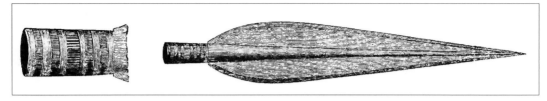

vengeance of the good people [the fairies], for so outrageous a violation of their territorial rights'.

Lenihan (1866, 726) noted that 'the peasantry attribute his [Baylee's] death to the indignation of the Earl of Desmond on account of the attempt [at drainage]'. Lynch also recorded that since the publication of Fitzgerald and McGregor's history of Limerick (1826) other attempts to drain the lake had been only partially successful, adding that

> 'The country people firmly believe that whoever attempts to drain the lake will incur the vengeance of Garrett Fitzgerald, Earl of Desmond. They say that the great earl rides over the lake once every seven years on a horse whose shoes are made of molten silver, and that, when the shoes are worn out, the spell of the enchantment which now holds him will be broken, and the earl will return to life again' (Lynch 1895, 242).

Local tradition holds that Gerald, the Great Earl of Desmond, is alive and detained by enchantment in a fairy place beneath the lake. The belief is that once very seven years he is to be seen at night careering over the lake, accompanied by a cavalcade of knights and ladies, and that when his silver horseshoes are worn out he will again return to life and recover his territory.

An account of the lake drainage appeared in the *Cork Examiner* on 8 September 1843 by way of a letter entitled 'A Way-Faring about Kilmallock' written by 'Comes', whose identity is unknown. Comes recorded that the property around Lough Gur belonged to Count de Salis and continued: 'The Count is, unfortunately for the beauty of Lough Gur, an Utilitarian, one of a race not well to do in my estimation … The foreigner intends to deprive the country of its only picturesque attraction by draining the lake'. Comes recounted that de Salis had already drained the eastern part and 'obtained as a result an extent of bog, which formed its bottom, the turf in which … is … 18 spades in depth'. Glennon (1847) also recorded the count's attempts to drain the lake by sinking a canal which lowered the lake and reduced the lake size, and noted that the exposed turf in the drained area was used as fuel.

The retrieval of part of a cart and a leather shoe from the bog exposed by drainage was recounted by Carbery (1973, 125–6, 132), who also mentioned a nearby causeway and made reference to previous finds of 'big deer' bones, presumably Giant Irish Deer.

ARCHAEOLOGICAL TIME

All archaeological sites, be they prehistoric or historic in date, are assigned specific archaeological phases; some are of single-phase and others of multi-phase use. At Lough Gur, the main phase of activity on sites was frequently preceded by some earlier occupation or succeeded by later cultural phases. The chronology of sites at Lough Gur is set out in Table 1.1 (overleaf).

Table 1.1—Archaeological time.

Archaeological phase	Major cultural developments	Sites at Lough Gur	Main features
MESOLITHIC			
Early Mesolithic, 8000–6500 BC	First settlers in Ireland; hunter-gatherer communities.	Rathjordan; Sites A and J, Knockadoon.	Microlithic artefacts; polished stone axeheads.
Late Mesolithic, 6500–4000 BC	Continued hunter-gatherer communities.	Sites C and F, Knockadoon; Grange ringfort.	Large flake tools, including 'Bann Flakes'.
NEOLITHIC			
Early Neolithic, 4000–3600 BC	First farmers; introduction of cereal cultivation and domestic animals (cattle, sheep and pig).	Rectangular houses at Sites A and B, Knockadoon; pre-enclosure houses at Circle K, Knockadoon; Houses A, B and Central House (phase 1), Circle L; pre-enclosure activity at Sites 10, 12 and Circle J; unprotected burials at Circle K.	Houses of rectangular or square plan; Class I pottery; polished stone axeheads; flint and chert leaf-shaped arrowheads.
Middle Neolithic, 3600–3000 BC	Farming economy.	Houses I–IV, Site C; Houses II and III, Site D, Knockadoon; possible court tomb at Site E; burials at Caherguillamore.	Houses of circular plan; Class I pottery.
Late Neolithic, 3000–2500 BC	Henge monuments; timber circles.	Great Stone Circle (B) and Circle D, Grange.	Grooved Ware pottery.
CHALCOLITHIC			
2500–2000 BC	First metallurgists producing copper artefacts; wedge tomb construction and use.	Megalithic tomb at Killalough; Circle C, Grange; Circles O and P.	Copper axes; Beaker pottery.
BRONZE AGE			
Early Bronze Age, 2000–1600 BC	Bronze-working.	Food Vessel burial at site of interpretative centre.	Bronze axeheads; Class II pottery; gold disc, Site D.
Middle Bronze Age, 1600–1100 BC	Increased production of bronze tools and weapons.	Enclosures on Knockadoon at Circles J, K and L, Sites 10 and 12; C-shaped enclosure; unenclosed settlements at Sites C and D and north slope of Knockadoon; huts in car park; hut sites E–I; field fences; ring-barrows and ring-ditches at Rathjordan, Ballingoola, Cahercorney and Knockfennell Hill; standing stones.	Class II pottery; Bronze Age burial inserted into wedge tomb; slab-lined graves and unprotected burials on Knockadoon; bronze axeheads and spearheads.
Late Bronze Age, 1100–800/700 BC	Increased production of bronze tools and weapons.	Socketed axehead, Site C; stone mould from megalithic tomb; bronze metalwork, including axeheads, swords and rapiers; the Lough Gur Shield; gold-mounted spearhead recovered after lake drainage.	Stone and clay moulds and clay crucibles for the production of weapons.

Table 1.1 (cont.)—
Archaeological time.

Archaeological phase	Major cultural developments	Sites at Lough Gur	Main features
IRON AGE			
Early Iron Age, 800/700 BC–AD 100	Iron-working.		Development of iron-working technology and continued use of bronze-casting.
Late Iron Age, AD 100–400	Déisi tribe in east Limerick.	Burials on Knockadoon Hill; yoke mounts and sword from lake; safety-pin brooch or fibula from Site C (1940).	Increased iron-working.
Sub-Roman, AD 100–400	Contact with Gaul and Roman Britain.	Balline hoard; Ballinard finger-ring; coin from Carraig Aille.	
EARLY MEDIEVAL			
AD 400–900	Introduction of Christianity; beginning of written history; Lough Gur area under rule of Eóganacht Áine; farming economy dominated by cattle; some evidence for cereals.	Carraig Aille stone forts; the Spectacles; Grange ringfort and hut sites in Ballingoola; large enclosure in Ballynagallagh; crannogs; church at Killalough; burials at Circle J.	Houses of circular plan later replaced by houses of rectangular or square plan; evidence of domestic crafts (spinning, leather-, bone-, bronze- and iron-working, etc.); personal ornaments.
VIKING			
870–1000	Historical references to Vikings in Lough Gur; Knockadoon Hill fortified by Brian Boru in 1002.	Carraig Aille II.	Child's sword; Viking silver hoard and bronze mount for drinking horn from Carraig Aille II.
ANGLO-NORMAN			
1166–1400	Anglo-Norman settlement in Lough Gur; emergence of Fitzgerald dynasty, who were created earls of Desmond in 1329; castle construction and development of manorial system.	Caherguillamore houses; 13th/14th-century houses in car-park area; Augustinian nunnery at Ballynagallagh.	Medieval artefacts, including pottery.
TUDOR			
1400–1650	Consolidation of Desmond lordship; increasing Gaelicisation of earls of Desmond; 1641 rebellion; Plantation of Munster, 1622; Cromwell, 1649.	Tower-houses at Bourchier's Castle, Black Castle; Geroid Island Castle; Grange Castle; Caherguillamore Castle; Rawleystown Castle; Site J, Knockadoon.	

NOTES

[1] The excavation results are unpublished and the site archive appears to be lost.

[2] *Pollavaddra* can be translated as 'hole of the dog'.

[3] The Poor Law Relief Scheme was implemented to relieve starvation during the Great Famine. Works may have begun at Lough Gur at the height of the Famine in 'Black '47' and continued until the 1850s.

[4] House of Commons Sessional Papers, 1849; Vol. 23, 212. The report recorded that 4¾ miles were being drained.

[5] Michael Quinlan, Lough Gur, identified 'B.R.R.' as Richard Rolt Brash (1813–76), a Cork-based architect who was a member of various antiquarian societies and whose work on ogham stones (*The ogham inscribed monuments of the Gaedhil in the British Isles*) was published posthumously in 1879.

[6] The designation of monuments by letters was the format used by Windle (1912) and is used throughout this book.

2. *Antiquarian and archaeological research*

ANTIQUARIAN ACCOUNTS

Antiquarian interest in the Lough Gur region has been recorded since at least the seventeenth century, when the area was visited by tourists and travellers whose early topographical and descriptive works reflect their interests. Some early visitors to Lough Gur did not publish accounts, of course, but there are hints of their presence there. A bronze plaque (Fig. 2.1) found during excavations at the car park in 1978 bears the inscription 'John Ware' on one side. The identity of John Ware is unknown, although he may have been related to Sir James Ware (1594–1656), the historian and antiquarian,[1] who possibly visited Lough Gur in the seventeenth century. The plaque includes an inscription—*Walls of Troy*—and a representation of the walls. Other motifs are biblical in inspiration and include a tonsured head on a platter (John the Baptist), a swan and cygnet, a phoenix or dove, a cockerel and a hound. The plaque's owner obviously had an interest in antiquities and must have lost it when he visited Lough Gur.

Fig. 2.1—John Ware plaque.

One of the earliest accounts of Lough Gur can be found in the text of *Pacata Hibernia*, which was compiled in 1633 by Thomas Stafford, secretary to Sir George Carew and a captain in Carew's army. Stafford based the text on detailed war reports and gave an account of the military campaigns during the Elizabethan wars at the beginning of the seventeenth century (Stafford 1633). These chronicles describe the taking of Bourchier's Castle in May 1600 (*ibid.*, 80–4) (see Chapter 11).

A survey known as the 'Down Survey', as the information was written down and recorded in maps, was undertaken in 1655–8 by Sir William Petty, a physician in Cromwell's army. He hired over 1,000 assistants to carry out the surveys of escheated or forfeited lands in advance of the Cromwellian plantation of Munster (Grene Barry 1900, 28). After the Cromwellian wars in 1652, forfeited lands were given to settlers, many of whom had invested in the Cromwellian campaign in Ireland. Mr Thomas Jackson surveyed a great part of County Limerick. The Books of Survey and Distribution give the names of the old proprietors and the grantees, the townlands within the area and lists of baronies and parishes (*ibid.*). The lands around Lough Gur remained in the hands of the Bourchier family and the proprietor is listed as the earl of Bath (Bourchier). Sketches in the Down Survey include Caherelly and Rawleystown castles in the Lough Gur area; the castle at Rawleystown does not survive and the sketch is a useful survey of the building (see Figs 11.23 and 11.27).

The difficulty with some of the early antiquarian accounts lies in assessing their value and accuracy. The descriptions are useful where the surface remains have been altered or removed, and the accounts provide clues to the original form of monuments, as in the case of the Great Stone Circle (B) at Grange. There are varying accounts of the number of original stones at the Great Stone Circle—up to 1840 the numbers given varied from 40 to 65 stones. Five[2] antiquarian accounts indicate the number of stones as 60–65, which is possibly the correct figure. As the Great Stone Circle was 'restored' possibly around the 1870s (see Chapter 4), subsequent accounts described a monument that had been substantially added to and altered. Windle (1912) and Westropp *et al.* (1916) recorded 113 stones in the circle. Harkness (1869, 389) wrote that on the 'E.N.E. side of the circle a passage has recently been discovered by Mr Fitzgerald [of Holycross Cottage], leading to the enclosed portion'. A certain amount of investigative digging around the Great Stone Circle no doubt damaged the archaeological layers prior to the excavation carried out by Seán P. Ó Ríordáin in 1939 (Ó Ríordáin 1951). Harkness (1869, 389) also recorded the enclosing bank as 9ft (2.7m) high and 34ft (10.3m) wide, dimensions which are much the same as today. Excavation has, however, confirmed substantial alteration to the bank height (Cleary 2015).

Antiquarian accounts frequently link archaeological sites to druidism, and focus on celestial alignments and astronomical readings. Crofton Croker (1833, 105) remarked on this tendency when he observed that 'on no subject has Fancy [imagination] roamed with more licentious indulgence than that of the Druids and their works'. In some ways, the attribution of druidical origins to ancient remains probably reflects the idea that the sites were constructed in pagan times, when religion and beliefs were guided by the natural world. Antiquarian interpretations of monuments were also influenced by medievalism, and to some extent by the nineteenth-century revival of Celticism and interest in Celtic culture, including druidical mysticism. Indeed, the entire landscape at Lough Gur was considered magical by some visitors. The antiquarian Richard Rolt Brash (B.R.R. 1865, 242) wrote of 'Lough Gur, lying lone and solitary, embosomed in high rocky hills; it is indeed a wild and weird-looking spot, it is still a place that a college of Druids might select for their mysterious rites'. As part of his survey of megalithic remains around Lough Gur, Windle (1912, 287) commissioned his cousin, Captain Boyle Somerville, to review the astronomical alignment at Grange Stone Circle

B to determine whether the circle was aligned on a significant event; the survey concluded that the site was aligned[3] on the *Samhain* sunset (8 November). Boyle Somerville was correct in his assessment; recent observation has confirmed that the sun sets between the V-notched stones on the west side of the circle in early November (Chapter 4).

The accounts of travellers and antiquarians contribute to the reconstruction of effaced landscapes. Thomas Dineley (or Dingley) was described as 'a learned and industrious topographer', 'a man of very considerable learning, and very ingenious in drawing with his pen' (Shirley 1856, 143, 144). Westropp (1907, 27) was less effusive, describing Dineley as 'no very sound historian'. Dineley compiled *A voyage through the kingdom of Ireland* in 1681, in which he described and sketched Bourchier's Castle (Shirley 1867). His sketch showed the lake as completely surrounding Knockadoon, a drawbridge across the now-infilled moat to what was then the mainland, and buildings—including a gatehouse and outer defences adjacent to the castle which do not survive, with the exception of the pigeon-house—to the north of the castle (Fig. 1.10). Dineley also described the lake:

> 'The lough or large mote which encompasseth this Island and Castle aboundeth in Fishes, Pike, Eeles, and Roches in vast quantity. Mr Henry Bayly [agent of the Fane family, who owned Bourchier's Castle and land around Lough Gur], son to the sd. Jno. Bayly told me of a prodigious Pike there lately taken 4 feet and a half [1.37m] in length with one in its belly of above two feet [0.6m] long' (*ibid.*, 196).

The late seventeenth/early eighteenth century introduced a new type of visitor to Ireland—tourists who came to observe the landscape and reported on this and on the manners of the people (Kelly 2004). The fashionable Grand Tour of Europe was rendered unsafe in the late eighteenth century by the French Revolution (1789) and its aftermath, as well as by the Napoleonic Wars, which culminated in the Battle of Waterloo (1815). Indeed, there is a Lough Gur connection to the Battle of Waterloo, as Colonel O'Grady's horse, which survived an engagement at Genappe, is buried in Caherguillamore (Dowd 1896). Those who came to Lough Gur included the travel writer Richard Twiss, who toured Ireland in 1775. His unflattering observations of the Irish made him unpopular—so much so that a chamber-pot was created in his honour, with the following rhyme on the bottom: 'Let everyone piss / on lying Dick Twiss' (Finnegan 2008, ix). His observations at Lough Gur presented only an account of the Great Stone Circle at Grange:

> 'I made an excursion of nine miles, on the road to Cork, to see three circles of stones, supposed to have been placed there by the druids; they are near a small lake, called Gur; the principal, which is about a hundred and fifty feet [45m] in diameter, consists of forty stones, of which the largest is thirteen feet [3.9m] long, six [1.8m] broad, and four [1.2m] thick. These kinds of circles are to be met with in many parts of Ireland. Several of these are described and engraved in this Louthiana [book], to which I refer. Near these on a hill is a small cromlech' (*ibid.*, 58–9).

The development of what can be called 'public transport' in the early 1800s in County Limerick facilitated travellers and visitors. The Grange stone circle complex was beside the mail-coach route (from Limerick to Cork) and, as Crofton Croker (1833, 107) noted, the monuments were 'thus

Fig. 2.2—Du Noyer's sketch of Bourchier's Castle.

slightly noticed by the tourists and topographers'. The development of the postal service and post towns, of which Bruff was a major link between Limerick, Kilmallock and Cork, also contributed to 'a quickening in the pulse of communication, and a keen appraisal of improving arterial lines' (O'Connor 1988, 166, fig. 8.8).

The artist Austin Cooper (1759–1830) produced an illustrative survey, possibly around 1780–5, entitled 'Plan and sections of three circles of stone near Loch Gower', and this is now housed in the Cooper collection in the National Library (Ó Nualláin and Cody 1996, illus. 6). The survey showed Circles B (the Great Stone Circle), C and D; Circle B was shown as embanked, *c.* 90ft (27.4m) in diameter, when the correct measurement should be *c.* 46m. Circle D was depicted as a circle of free-standing stones. Circle C was recorded as a circle of seventeen stones whereas fifteen remain *in situ*, although it is possible that two were removed and that the Cooper illustration recorded Circle C in a more intact state than it is in today. George Du Noyer (1817–69) was an antiquary and geologist who worked initially from 1834 with the Ordnance Survey and then from 1848 with the Geological Survey of Ireland. His sketches at Lough Gur show Bourchier's Castle (Fig. 2.2) and Black Castle (Chapter 11; Fig. 11.20) on the south-east side of the lake, with the causeway extending to the south from Black Castle. Du Noyer also sketched the scenery at Lough Gur and produced a landscape drawing showing the lake with the Galty Mountains in the distance (Fig. 2.3).

Some observations by travellers and tourists provide little information on the monuments—for example, Trotter's walks through Ireland in the years 1812, 1814 and 1817, which were described in 'a series of letters to an English gentleman'. Trotter (1819, 319) lamented the lack of care for monumental remains throughout Ireland at the time and wrote that 'it is truly melancholy that in Ireland there is not more general respect for her ruins. Are they not a guide to history, and affecting memorial of the past?' He did, however, provide a short description of the Grange stone circles, and also recorded social conditions in the early nineteenth century:

Fig. 2.3—Du Noyer's sketch of scenery at Lough Gur.

'The road from Bruff to Limerick leads through a very fine country, but we heard with fresh sorrow, of fever in every part, and the language of despair from some of those poor people who had relatives ill or had themselves recovered recently' (Trotter 1819, 330–1).

In 1826 Revd Patrick Fitzgerald and John James McGregor published a two-volume work entitled *The history and topography of the county and city of Limerick with a preliminary view of the history and antiquities of Ireland*. Revd Fitzgerald was the vicar of Cahercorney and did most of the research, while McGregor, who was a journalist and topographer, put the work in chronological order (Kemmy 1996, 11). McGregor, a Methodist, was born in Limerick in 1775 and became editor of the *Munster Telegraph* in Waterford before moving to Dublin to edit the *Primitive Wesleyan Methodist Church Magazine*. Fitzgerald was originally from Bruff and worked in Mr Buckley's Academy and as a tutor for the local landlord's children. He secured a scholarship to Trinity College, where he became a Protestant and ultimately a Church of Ireland clergyman (*ibid.*). He was appointed to Cahercorney and lived near Grange. Fitzgerald and McGregor's history provided descriptions of some of the monuments around Lough Gur; these were referred to in subsequent histories, such as those by Crofton Croker (1833) and Grene Barry (1903a), and were cited as a frequent source in O'Donovan's Ordnance Survey letters of 1840. It is possible that in the case of certain monument descriptions some writers such as Lynch (1895) and Richard Rolt Brash (B.R.R. 1865) relied heavily on published works such as Fitzgerald and McGregor's and may not have actually measured the sites. Fitzgerald and McGregor (1826, 295) described Grange stone circles, Bourchier's Castle and Black Castle on Knockadoon, Rawleystown Castle and Newchurch.

Fitzgerald and McGregor (1826, 313) referred to a 'Danish Fort'[4] 'on the [west] pinnacle of Knockfennell', describing it as 'circular, and about 360 feet [110m] in circumference; the wall that surrounds it is ten feet [3m] in thickness'. Almost 70 years later Lynch (1895, 249) stated that 'very few stones are now left' and surmised that the surrounding 3m-wide wall

'must have been proportionally high from the quantity of stone that has fallen outside. That part of the wall that still remains is built of large stones nearly three feet [0.9m] every way, regularly fitted to each other, and the interstices filled up with small ones, but there is no sign of mortar.'

Thomas Crofton Croker (1798–1854), a Cork-born antiquarian, compiled an illustrated survey

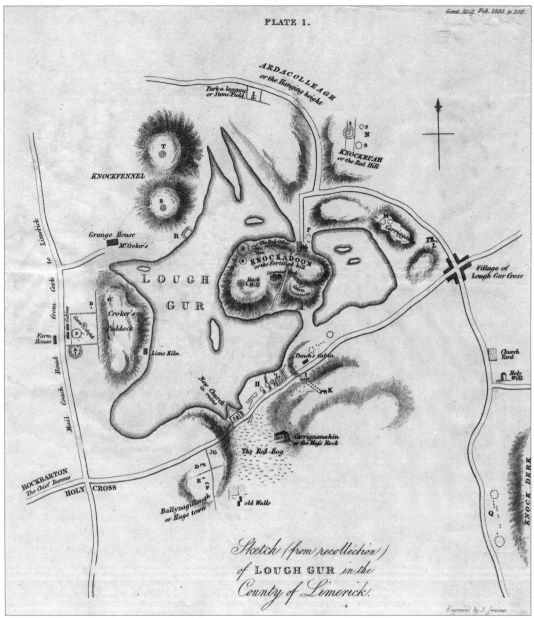

Fig. 2.4—Crofton Croker's survey (1833).

of some of the monuments at Lough Gur, published in 1833 in the *Gentleman's Magazine* (Fig. 2.4). His account details the circumstances of the survey, including

> 'unfavourable weather, an inability at the time to walk any considerable distance, and the nature and extent of the ground which it is necessary to traverse, rendering my investigation in many parts extremely hurried and imperfect, although the greater portion of three days were devoted to it' (Crofton Croker 1833, 105).

The survey was also fraught with danger and Crofton Croker had to shelter in the home of Mr Baylee, who occupied the house beside Bourchier's Castle, as 'an assembly of the peasantry, who collected upon observing me measuring some distances, … warned me off, declaring that "as the ground never had been measured; and that all tythe proctors[5] and their surveyors were marked men"' (*ibid*.). The peasantry may have mistaken Crofton Croker for a government official, or at least his bearing was that of a Protestant gentleman. The countryside around Bruff, like much of Limerick and Ireland in the early part of the nineteenth century, was an area where social unrest and sectarianism were rife and dominated by the secret agrarian societies, including the Rockite movement (O'Connor 1988, 153–5).

Crofton Croker's visit to Lough Gur took place before the drainage in 1847–8 and thus the lake was more expansive. He wrote that it 'contains six islands; four of which, however, scarcely deserve the name, as their appearance is merely that of tufts of trees rising out of the water … the sixth or principal island, called Knockadoon, or fortified hill' (Crofton Croker 1833, 105). His account (*ibid*., 107) provided measured descriptions of the stone circles at Grange, three of which were still extant in 1833, and he recorded stones to the east of Circle 2 (Circle D[6]) that were not noted in any other account of the Grange complex and may have been outliers or surface boulders subsequently removed. Fitzgerald and McGregor (1826, 295) also recorded a large stone lying flat a few yards to the east of the stone circles; they described it as 'seven feet and a half [2.2m] in length, six [1.8m] in height, and four and a half [1.3m] in breadth, which is generally supposed to be an altar for sacrifice'. This stone is no longer to be found.

Crofton Croker (1833, 108) recorded a megalithic tomb to the south of the Holycross–Lough Gur road and marked it 'D' on his plan, as 'this altar is called by country people Labigdiarmud, or Edward's Bed' (Fig. 2.5: D). This site is the same as that recorded by Windle (1912, Site F) as '*Leaba na Muice*'. Crofton Croker (1833, 109) also recorded three stone circles (Fig. 2.4: H) on the west side of the road near the megalithic tomb, and he gave their dimensions as follows: 'Circle 1 twenty yards [18m] diameter and comprising fifteen stones; Circle 2 thirteen yards [12m] diameter and eight stones with parallel lines of stones extending to the lakeshore; Circle 3 eight yards [7m] in diameter and seven stones'. Windle (1912, 296; Site G) considered these sites to be natural boulders, as the land was under water before the 1847–8 lake drainage,[7] although the sites were on dry land at the time of Crofton Croker's visit in 1833. They were not marked on the first-edition Ordnance Survey map (1844) but were subsequently recorded on the 1924 edition as 'Stone Circles'. Crofton Croker also recorded a track from the stone circles to the Red Bog (Fig. 2.4). Nothing survives above ground of two stone circles recorded by Crofton Croker to the north-east (east of Punch's Cabin) (Fig. 2.4).

Of interest in Crofton Croker's (1833, 109) account is his description and drawing of the Mass rock named as 'Carrignanahin' (Figs 2.4–5). He was accompanied to the Mass rock by a 'countryman' who

> 'blessed himself more than once, spoke in an under-tone, and at length cautiously pointed out to me what he called the holy chamber, a hollow in the rock, with evident marks of fire, and from which he affirmed there was a passage into the centre, although I could perceive no opening whatever. He [the countryman], however, insisted that such existed, as he knew a man who had been taken into the grand room within, which resembled a chapel. This superstitious veneration may be attributed to the remarkable and artificial appearance of the rock itself, as well as the tradition connected with its name, which is

Fig. 2.5—Crofton Croker's sketches of megaliths at Lough Gur: D = *Leaba na Muice*; G and L = destroyed megalithic tombs?; I = megalithic tomb at Killalough (excavated by Ó Ríordáin in 1938) and natural outcrop known as a Mass rock and recorded by Croker as Carrignanahin.

said to be derived from a priest having regularly celebrated mass in the holy chamber at a period when the Roman Catholic religion was under proscription.'

Crofton Croker's surveys at Lough Gur were referred to by a correspondent known as 'Comes', who wrote in the *Cork Examiner* in 1843 that 'Crofton Croker was lately in the neighbourhood exploring and brought to light a vast amount of antiquities hitherto unnoticed'.

William Wakeman published *Archaeologia Hibernica: a hand-book of Irish antiquities, pagan and Christian: especially of such as are easy access from the Irish metropolis* in 1848 while working as a drawing master at St Columba's College, Stackallan, Slane, Co. Meath. Wakeman was a student of the antiquarian George Petrie and secured employment as a draughtsman and assistant in the topographical department of the Ordnance Survey. He accompanied O'Donovan and, under the direction of Larcom, drew, measured and described the monuments of various survey areas, including County Limerick. Wakeman (1891, 130) wrote of Lough Gur: 'Some of the finest monuments of the class under notice I have seen in Ireland occur near the shore of Lough Gur, at a short distance north of the little town of Bruff, in the county of Limerick'.

Maurice Lenihan was born in Waterford in 1811 and as his mother was from Limerick he went back to his roots. He trained as a journalist and in 1849 founded a paper known as the *Reporter* in Limerick and the *Vindicator* in Tipperary. Lenihan published *Limerick; its history and antiquities, ecclesiastical, civil and military from the earliest ages* in 1866. He prefaced his gazetteer of sites in Lough Gur by writing that 'The "enchanted lake"; Its druidical remains, castles, a cromleach, natural curiosities, and beauty, have won admiration of every tourist and antiquary' (Lenihan 1866, 723). The gazetteer included a survey of the stone circles at Grange, where the measurements were paced. Lenihan recorded 55 stones at the Great Stone Circle (B) (*ibid.*, 723–4). Circle D was still extant at that time; Lenihan noted 58 stones and that the ground within the circle had been tilled. He described and provided some of the history of Bourchier's Castle; at that time the agent for Count de Salis was a Mr Harte, who lived beside Bourchier's Castle. Lenihan also referred to a wall that skirted the lower south-eastern slope of Knockadoon Hill and linked Bourchier's Castle with Black Castle (*ibid.*,

725). He noted the destruction of monuments in writing about the megalithic tomb located on 'Bailinallycailleach [Ballynagallagh] Hill':

'*Leaba-na-Mucka*, or Pig's Bed, near which a stone coffin was found some years since, with a human skeleton . . . at less than half a mile [800m] south of this are two others, one of which has been lately broken down by a farmer, who had the stones taken to make pillars for his gateway' (*ibid.*, 726).

Two megalithic tombs[8] recorded by the Ordnance Survey (1844) as 'Giant's Grave' in the townland of Ballynagallagh are no longer extant but seem to have survived into the early 1900s. Lynch (1913, 19) described the sites as

'Three different cromleacs immediately beside it [the linear trackway *Claidhe na leac*], and all south of the cairn of Baile na gCailleach. The first of these cromleacs is about 200 yards [180m] away, and quite close to the house of Mrs Bennett. It resembles the one (*Leaba Dhiarmada agus Ghrainne*) near John Punch's house, but is more dilapidated … some of the stones were taken away by the late Mr John Fitzgerald to adorn the circle of *Rannach Chruim Dhuibh* [the Great Stone Circle (B)] near his own residence.'

The Revd J. Dowd, who published *Round about the county of Limerick* in 1896, was a Church of Ireland minister who, after graduation from Trinity College in 1874, was ordained in 1876 for the combined Church of Ireland dioceses of Limerick and Ardfert. He also edited the *Chronicle* newspaper and promoted education and the Free Library in Limerick. Of the monuments of Lough Gur he wrote (Dowd 1896, 65):

'The Pillar stone, the lonely Cromlech, the mysterious Stone Circle, tell of a people who existed here before the dawn of history, and of whom little is known unless what can be learned from their very graves. The long deserted military works that still bid defiance to time, have each their story to tell. The bed of the lake itself reveals the secrets that have long been buried beneath its waters. Bones and skeletons of extinct animals have been brought to light. Implements of stone and bronze, ornaments of bone and silver, weapons of various kinds, from those of the rudest construction to the gold-mounted spear head and round shield, bear witness to the number and variety of the antiquities which were discovered when the surface of the lake was lowered by drainage some half a century ago.'

Dowd provided descriptions of many of the monuments, including Black Castle, Bourchier's Castle, Grange Castle, the Grange stone circle complex, the megalithic tomb and church at Newchurch, Carraig Aille, the medieval nunnery at Ballynagallagh, a stone circle and a deserted medieval village in Caherguillamore. Like many writers in more recent centuries, he also remarked on the beauty of the landscape around Lough Gur.

William Borlase (1848–99) published *The dolmens of Ireland, their distribution, structural characteristics, and affinities in other countries; together with the folk-lore attaching to them and traditions of the Irish people* in 1897. This was the first comprehensive survey of Irish megalithic tombs. The megalithic tomb at Killalough, near Newchurch, was described and sketched by Margaret Stokes (Fig. 2.6).

Fig. 2.6—Sketch of megalithic tomb by Margaret Stokes, published in Borlase 1897.

Borlase (1897, 48) referred to five megalithic tombs near Lough Gur; at the time of his writing two of these near the Grange stone circles were destroyed. He also described the 'Leaba na Muice' megalithic tomb as

'half a furlong [200m] to the N. of this old graveyard [Mainister na gCalliagh], and on the northern summit of the same hill, there is a Giant's Grave or cromlech which has often attracted the attention of the curious. It is now thrown down, but the stones are on the ground, and one may easily perceive how they were originally fixed' (Borlase 1897, 48).[9]

P.J. Lynch (1906–7, 129) was of the opinion that Borlase never visited Lough Gur and that his descriptions were taken from the Ordnance Survey letters.

One of the most prolific antiquarian writers on Lough Gur was the Revd J.F. Lynch, who wrote lengthy articles on the monuments at Lough Gur as well as on the folklore in the *Journal of the Cork Historical and Archaeological Society* in 1895 and 1913, and also contributed articles to the *Journal of the Limerick Field Club*. Lynch (1895, 246) deplored the vandalism that had taken its toll on the monuments around Lough Gur, including the destruction of megalithic tombs and the despoiling of castles to provide stone for mansions. He drew on ancient historical sources such as the *Chronicon Scotorum* and *The Book of Rights* (Lynch 1895; 1913). His work cited published material relating to Lough Gur, including Dineley (1870 [1681]; Shirley 1856; 1867), Ferrar (1767), Fitzgerald and McGregor (1826) and others. He also drew on local folklore and conversations with local people.

Thomas Johnson Westropp published widely on archaeological sites in County Limerick, including those around Lough Gur, as well as a history of Monasteranenagh in 1889. He produced detailed surveys and sketched important features. His publications on castles and churches from 1904 to 1907 in the *Journal of the Royal Society of Antiquaries of Ireland* and the *Proceedings of the Royal Irish Academy* are particularly valuable, and include sources such as the *Calendar of State Papers* (published in 1870) and the *Irish Chancery Rolls* (1828). Westropp was born in 1860 at Attyflin near Patrickswell, Co. Limerick; initially educated at home, he went to Trinity College in 1879 and qualified as a civil engineer (Irwin 2009, 484). He had a private income that enabled him to devote his life to recording and studying archaeological monuments. His basic tool kit consisted of a sketch-book, field-glasses and camera (Ashe-Fitzgerald 2000, 43). Westropp's main aim was to record and classify and to 'put on record what survived so that future generations would be able to study the historical and archaeological heritage that he felt was under threat and might not survive' (Irwin 2009, 483).

SURVEY

The Ordnance Survey was established in 1823 to provide mapping for a new valuation of land to enable the collection of rates. The survey corps was a branch of the army under the command of Colonel Thomas Colby (Herity and Eogan 1977, 7), assisted by Lieutenant Thomas Larcom from 1828. As Larcom saw the importance of marking names on maps, he studied Irish under the guidance of John O'Donovan. O'Donovan joined the survey in 1830; his job was to follow the surveyors into the field, to collect place-names and to establish the pronunciation and derivation of the names (*ibid.*, 8). The Lough Gur area was mapped *c.* 1840 (and published in 1844) by Captain Stotterd and Lieutenants Burnford and Boteler under Larcom's direction. The 6in.-scale maps were engraved in 1843. O'Donovan's accompanying 'Letters containing information relative to the antiquities of the county of Limerick collected during the progress of the Ordnance Survey in 1840' provided detailed descriptions of the monuments. Some of the Ordnance Survey representations of the antiquities were probably schematic, as is illustrated at the three stone circles in Grange townland, where the Great Stone Circle (B) is depicted as fifteen separate stones, Circle C is shown as nine separate stones

Fig. 2.7—Ordnance Survey first-edition map (1844) of Grange.

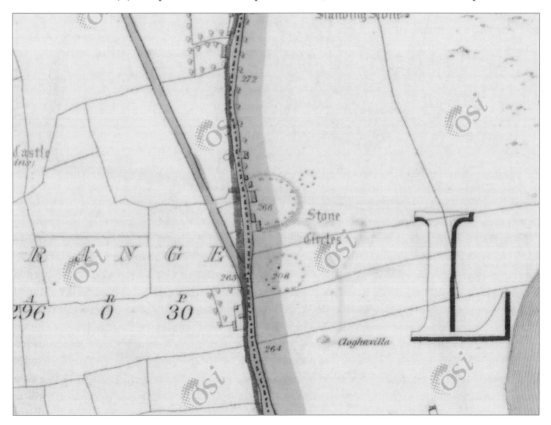

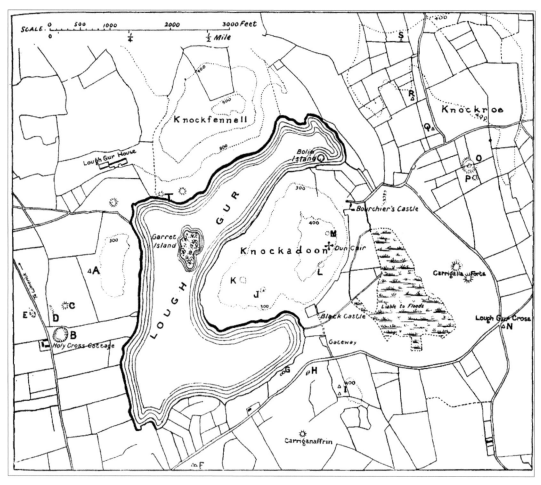

Fig. 2.8—Windle's map, 1912.

and Circle D as an embanked stone circle (Fig. 2.7). O'Donovan (1840, 249–52) recorded 45 stones at the Great Stone Circle. While the Ordnance Survey was not an archaeological survey, the mapping provided the building blocks for future work. The locations of antiquities were recorded and were mostly correct. There were some omissions, and these were later rectified by O'Kelly (1941; 1942–3; 1944) in his survey of the barony of Small County.

Sir Bertram Windle, a former president and professor of Archaeology in University College Cork, was the first archaeologist to undertake specific monument surveys at Lough Gur, with detailed surveys of the megalithic remains (Fig. 2.8). On his first visit to Lough Gur he was so 'much impressed by them [the antiquities] that I made up my mind to make a prolonged visit in order to obtain a complete and accurate survey' (Windle 1912, 283). Windle measured 111 stones in the Great Stone Circle (B), provided detailed plans of the Grange stone circle complex and a possible megalithic tomb (Site E) to the south (Figs 2.9–10), and gave descriptions of sixteen other monuments. As he could not use 'a theodolite and other instruments', he enlisted the help of Professor Alexander and his student Mr J.F.X. Hartigan; Windle's wife drew up some of the illustrations (Fig. 2.11). Windle's monument designation was by letters of the alphabet and this nomenclature was retained in subsequent surveys (O'Kelly 1942–3; 1944; Cleary and Hogan 2013; O'Driscoll and Cleary 2016) and excavations (Ó Ríordáin 1951; Cleary 2015). The monuments surveyed by Windle were as follows (Fig. 2.8).

A—The standing stone or pillar stone on the lower slope of Ardaghlooda Hill.

B—The Great Stone Circle at Grange.

C—The smaller extant stone circle to the north of the Great Stone Circle.

D—Stone circle to the west of Circle C, of which twelve stones remained at the time of Windle's survey (Windle 1912, fig. 4).

E—Described as an 'avenue' and comprising a double row of stones converging slightly at the north-west end.

F—Small megalithic tomb known locally as *Leaba na Muice*.

G—A formation of what Windle considered to be natural boulders, recorded by the Ordnance Survey as 'Stone Circles'. Windle considered that they were under water before Lough Gur was drained. There remains the possibility that these are in fact of archaeological significance; they were recorded by Crofton Croker (1833), who was certain that they were prehistoric monuments (see above).

H—The 'Giant's Grave', the wedge tomb near Newchurch.

I—Two standing stones ('gallauns') to the south-east of the Giant's Grave.

J, K and L—These were designated 'stone circles' by Windle.

M—A small stone circle on Knockadoon.

N—A large boulder at Lough Gur Cross.

O and P—Stone circles.

Q, R and S—Standing stones north of Circles O and P.

T—Stone circle at the base of the south-western slope of Knockfennell Hill.

Windle (1912, 304) also noted that standing stones N, Q, R and S may have been an alignment of stones along a ridge to the east of Lough Gur and this was confirmed by O'Kelly's survey (1944, 29), which included a further five standing stones; the alignment extended from Lough Gur Cross to Ballingoola (see Chapter 5). Circles J, K and L were subsequently excavated by Seán P. Ó Ríordáin and were identified as enclosed prehistoric settlements rather than stone circles. Windle (1912, 302) identified Site M on Knockadoon as a stone circle but it may be a natural rock outcrop (O'Kelly 1944, 26). Site M was marked by the Ordnance Survey as 'Dun Gair (site of)', which was one of the fortifications attributed to Brian Boru (Chapter 9), although it is probable that Brian Boru's fortification was at the entrance to Knockadoon and in the vicinity of Bourchier's Castle. Windle (1912, 286) referred to the 'restoration' of the Great Stone Circle (B) and noted that 'it is, therefore, difficult to feel quite certain which of the stones are in their ancient position and which have been placed there by the restorers'. Windle considered that the larger stones projecting above the bank were ancient.

In 1916 Westropp, Macalister and MacNamara published *The antiquities of Limerick and its neighbourhood*, including a historical introduction, an account of previous surveys, descriptions of the Grange stone circle complex and the megalithic tombs. The derivation of the names for the megalithic tombs was scathingly reviewed; the origin of the name *Leaba na Muice* ('the Pig's Bed') was supposed to relate to the use of the site at some time as a pigsty, or was 'a mere corruption of the common place-name Leaba Dhiarmada, picked up by someone with an imperfect ear, a vivid

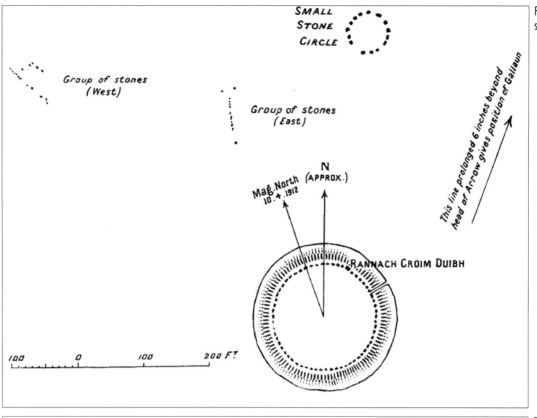

Fig. 2.9—Windle's 1912 survey at Grange.

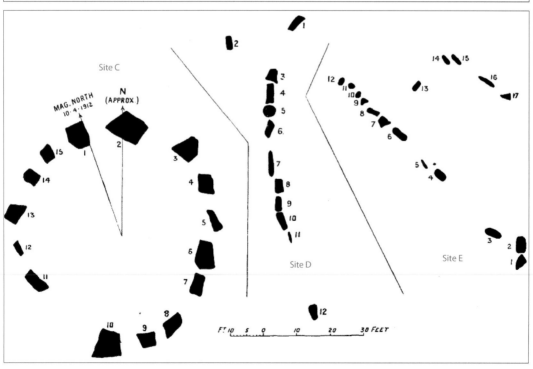

Fig. 2.10—Windle's 1912 survey of Stone Circles C and D and possible megalithic tomb at Site E.

Fig. 2.11—Sketches of *Leaba na Muice* and the Giant's Grave (Windle 1912).

imagination, and (worst of all!) good intentions' (Westropp *et al.* 1916, 124). The name of the megalithic tomb at Killalough (near Newchurch) 'called by Croker "Labig yermiddagh a Grana" [is] a hideous corruption, but still more hideously translated "Ned and Grace's bed"' (*ibid.*, 124). The writers also recorded that Garrett Punch, who lived near the megalithic tomb, told Crofton Croker that an old woman lived in the tomb and that on her death the capstones were removed by 'money diggers', who 'found some burned bones in an old jug that surely was not worth one brass farthing' (*ibid.*). It is possible that the diggers found some type of cinerary urn containing cremated human bones.

M.J. O'Kelly began his archaeological career as a surveyor during the excavation of the Great Stone Circle (B) at Grange, and by the end of the excavation he had changed his course of study from Civil Engineering to Archaeology at University College Cork. O'Kelly carried out extensive fieldwork in 1941, surveying almost 400 monuments in the barony of Small County and providing measured drawings of some of the upstanding monuments (O'Kelly 1942–3; 1944). His survey included information on archaeological artefacts recovered in the survey area and these were particularly numerous from the Lough Gur area, although specific locations were not always available.

Fig. 2.12—Bruff Aerial Photographic Survey (extract around Lough Gur).

The survey (O'Kelly 1942–3, 83–4) also confirmed that Lough Gur was a centre for prehistoric activity, and most of the megalithic tombs, stone circles, standing stones and barrows were in the hinterland of the lake. This survey of antiquities earned O'Kelly an MA degree and the National University of Ireland Travelling Studentship in 1941.

The Archaeological Survey of Ireland began in 1981 and the Limerick Archaeological Survey was undertaken under its auspices. This built largely on the Ordnance Survey of Ireland maps. The Limerick Archaeological Survey was issued in 1989 as a series of maps known as the Record of Monuments and Places (RMP), within which all the archaeological sites in the area around Lough Gur were given specific monument designations, with limited information on each site. The survey has yet to be published.

A medium-altitude aerial survey of an area centring on Lough Gur, extending north–south between Caherconlish and Knocklong and east–west between Bruff and Emly, was undertaken in 1986 as a joint project between the Department of Archaeology, University College Cork, and *Dúchas* the Heritage Service. The aerial photographs were at a scale of 1:10,000 and allowed for the recognition and mapping of sites that are barely visible on the surface but can be observed from the air (Fig. 2.12). Many of these newly mapped sites are earthworks whose surface features had become denuded over time and are not easily seen in field-walking. Overall, 1,074 new sites were recorded within the survey area, including previously unknown sites in the Lough Gur area (Doody 2008, 67). The absence of tillage contributed to the survival of a huge number of earthworks and this was confirmed by the Bruff aerial survey, where the number of known monuments was increased by

Fig. 2.13—Geophysical survey, Grange, 'Site of Stone Circle'.

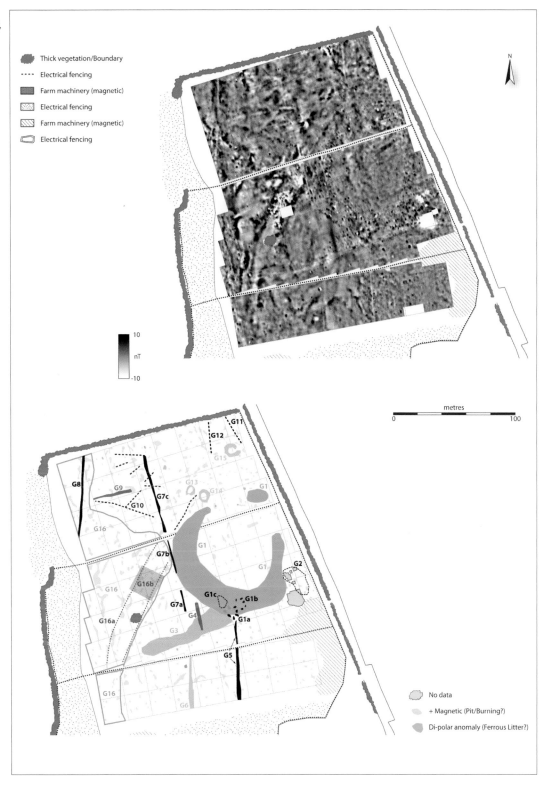

Thick vegetation/Boundary

Electrical fencing

Farm machinery (magnetic)

Electrical fencing

Farm machinery (magnetic)

Electrical fencing

10

nT

-10

metres

0   100

G11

G12

G15

G8   G9   G13   G1

G7c

G10   G14

G7b   G1

G16   G1

G2

G16b   G1c   G1b

G16   G7a   G4

G16a   G1a

G3

G5

G16

G6

No data

+ Magnetic (Pit/Burning?)

Di-polar anomaly (Ferrous Litter?)

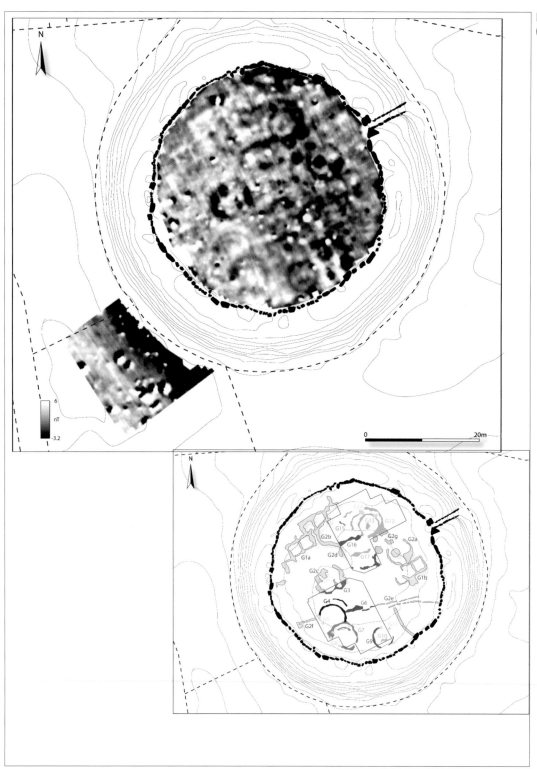

Fig. 2.14—Geophysical survey, Grange.

Fig. 2.15—Geophysical survey, Circle D.

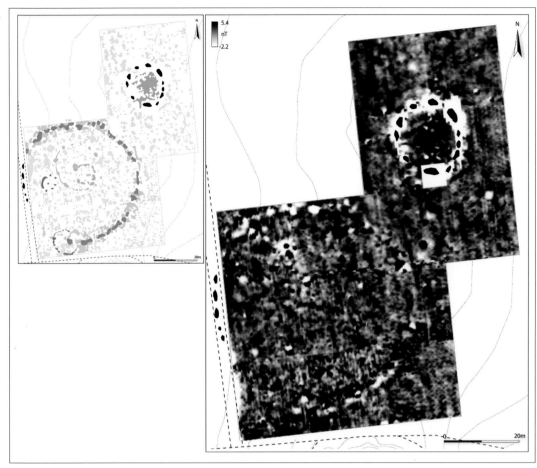

almost 70% (Doody 1993; 2008). Dating of these sites is problematic, as there was no excavation to confirm what they were used for or when they were constructed. An exception to this is a site in Ballynagallagh townland, where excavation established that the enclosure was early medieval in date (Cleary 2006). The aerial survey also confirmed the extent of a large enclosure just west of the Grange stone circle complex, and this was subsequently surveyed using geophysical prospection techniques (Cleary and Hogan 2013).

A survey project aimed at examining and chronicling monuments in their landscape setting using modern survey technology was undertaken at Lough Gur in 2008–9 (Cleary and Hogan 2013) and 2012–13 (Cleary and O'Driscoll 2014; O'Driscoll and Cleary 2016). The results of these geophysical surveys show a hidden archaeological landscape, and visible monuments in the survey areas are part of a greater monument complex of low-visibility and subsurface archaeological sites (Fig. 2.13). The study areas were around the Grange stone circle complex (Fig. 2.14) on the western shore of Lough Gur and around Circles O and P to the north-east of Lough Gur.

Geophysical survey at Grange (Fig. 2.14) was concentrated within the Great Stone Circle (B), immediately to the south of the circle and in fields to the west of the stone circles (Cleary and Hogan 2013; Cleary and O'Driscoll 2014; O'Driscoll and Cleary 2016). The survey identified seven possible prehistoric ring-ditches within the Great Stone Circle (Chapter 5). While the dating of ring-ditches has a broad spectrum, there is a tendency towards a middle/late Bronze Age date. There is therefore a strong probability that the Great Stone Circle continued in use for over 1,500 years after it was built and was used as a place of assembly for rituals linked to life and death. A possible site of a stone circle which was removed from the landscape was detected *c*. 90m east of the Great Stone Circle; all that now remains are the sockets of the stones.

Geophysical survey around the almost ruinous Circle D (Fig. 2.15) confirmed that it was once surrounded by a bank similar to that of the Great Stone Circle (B). Circle D originally had an overall maximum diameter of 78m and was larger than Circle B (O'Driscoll and Cleary 2016). The survey at Circle D also recorded an internal circular feature with a diameter of 20m which may have been a timber circle or some other type of timber-built structure (Chapter 4).

Survey work in the fields west of the Grange stone circles was undertaken around the site of a stone circle and stone avenue recorded by the Ordnance Survey in 1924 (Cleary and Hogan 2013). The stone circle site was also recorded on the Bruff aerial survey as a large enclosure (Doody 2008). The geophysical survey showed that the enclosure was a C-shaped earthwork with an opening on

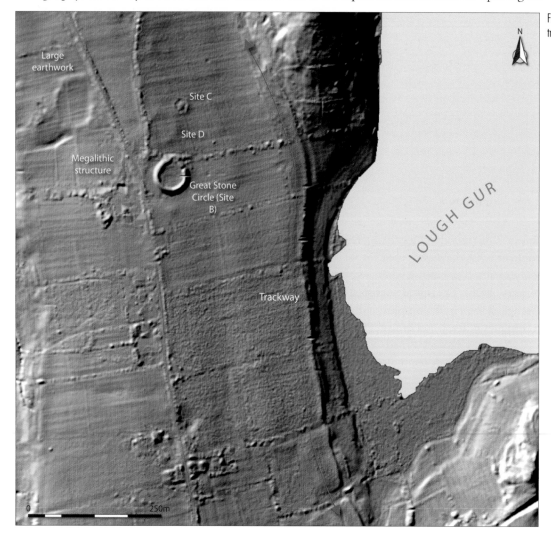

Fig. 2.16—LiDAR image of trackway at Grange.

the north-east and a maximum diameter (east/west) of almost 100m. There were also indications of internal features but without excavation it is not possible to establish what these are. The survey around the stone avenue showed that the monument is more complex than indicated by the surviving stones (see Fig. 3.3.1).

The geophysical survey at Circle P uncovered an outer enclosure that now has no visible surface remains and was unrecorded during the excavation (Cleary and Hogan 2013). This allows reinterpretation of the site and shows that it was similar to the adjacent Circle O. Two subsurface sites to the north of Circle P are interpreted as a levelled mound with a diameter of *c.* 13m, similar in size to the upstanding remains at Circle P, and a small possible stone enclosure. A small structure, *c.* 11m in diameter and possibly made from timber uprights, was also recorded north of Circle O.

Airborne LiDAR is a survey method which uses a laser light detection and ranging system to record the topography of an area in great detail. The technique can rapidly map large areas of ground and also has the potential to penetrate vegetation cover. As an archaeological tool, LiDAR has the ability to record low-relief sites and landscapes, even those masked by trees and overgrowth. An analysis of LiDAR coverage of the Lough Gur area included a study of Grange, around Circles O and P, Carraig Aille and Rawleystown (Motherwell 2012). LiDAR survey detected the circular enclosure to the south-west of the Great Stone Circle (B) which had also been recorded by the geophysical survey. The outline of the former bank of Circle D was clearly visible, and LiDAR confirmed that the levelled bank was spread over a width of 15m outside the perimeter of the stone circle (*ibid.*, 238). An ancient trackway (Fig. 2.16) near Grange church and a previously unknown ring-barrow were also detected using LiDAR (*ibid.*, 248, 250). The LiDAR survey recorded a network of ancient field enclosures near Carraig Aille and a possible ancient trackway and field systems near Rawleystown.

EXCAVATIONS

Various surveys, from antiquarian to modern scientific methods and archaeological excavations, have established a broad chronological framework for the sequence of settlement and monuments at Lough Gur. Antiquarians were primarily concerned with collection, but some, such as J.F. Lynch, also added discourse. Archaeologists concern themselves with the recovery of information, but behind this is a reconstruction of the lives of the past inhabitants, their connections and patterns of behaviour.

The first excavation was carried out in the 1860s at Circle J on Knockadoon by J. Harkness, professor of Anatomy at University College Cork (Harkness 1869; Grogan and Eogan 1987, 332–4). The excavation team consisted of Harkness, Mr Day (presumably Robert Day) and Mr Fitzgerald of Holycross Cottage (Harkness 1869, 390). Harkness's excavation was west of the standing stone within Circle J, where he discovered the bones of a child aged 6–8 years in an unlined grave at a depth of *c.* 0.3m (Fig. 2.17). He referred to a small, circular stone setting with a diameter of *c.* 2.45m that surrounded the standing stone, but this had disappeared by the time the site was surveyed by Windle (1912, 298). A second area excavated by Harkness was in the south-west quadrant of the Circle J enclosure and comprised a cist grave which was partly covered by a flagstone and paved at the base (Harkness 1869, 391; Windle 1912, 299). The cist grave was 0.45m below the surface, 1.3m long and 0.45m deep, and contained an adult burial, which may have been female, and a child aged 6–8 years; some pig bones and an antler fragment were also placed in the grave with the burials

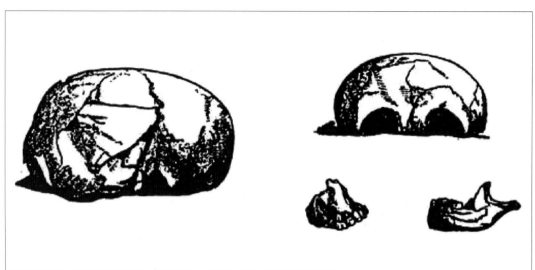

Fig. 2.17—Harkness's drawings of a child's bone from his excavation at Circle J.

(Harkness 1869, 392; Grogan and Eogan 1987, 333). The skeletal remains were aligned north/south, with the heads to the south. Harkness noted that the child's jaw was particularly thick and concluded that the bones were from 'broad-headed people, with small eyes and of short stature' (Harkness 1869, 392). His comments on the shape of the skull were in keeping with the pseudo-science of the late nineteenth century, whereby head shape was taken as an indicator of race and personality.

A campaign of excavations at Lough Gur began in 1936, when Seán P. Ó Ríordáin, the then professor of Archaeology in University College Cork, started work at Circles O and P. Apart from 1952–3, this work continued until his death in 1954 (Figs 2.18–20). These large-scale excavations were financed by a Free State government initiative to alleviate unemployment (Ó Ríordáin 1946, 142). The funding continued during the early years (1939–40) of World War II but was then discontinued, as labour was diverted towards increased food and turf production. Ó Ríordáin's investigations were the first scientific excavations at Lough Gur and covered a broad range of sites, including fifteen Neolithic and Bronze Age sites on Knockadoon, nine of which were published in the *Proceedings of the Royal Irish Academy* (1954), while a further six were published posthumously by Grogan and Eogan in that journal in 1987.

Ó Ríordáin was appointed as a museum assistant in the National Museum of Ireland in 1931 and, under the tutelage of Adolf Mahr, the Keeper of Antiquities and Director of the National Museum, was granted study leave that enabled him to travel widely in Europe (Wallace 2004, 255). Ó Ríordáin visited museums in England, Scotland and Wales in 1932, cataloguing Irish material and familiarising himself with museum practice. Mahr's connections also made it possible for Ó Ríordáin to visit and work on various excavations, including those being directed by notable British archaeologists such as Vere Gordon Childe, Mortimer Wheeler and W.H. Hemp (*ibid.*, 256). This allowed Ó Ríordáin to experience excavation techniques and methods which at the time were not available in Ireland. In 1932 he travelled to Groningen in the Netherlands, where he examined museum collections and worked on an excavation with E. Van Giffen. The following year he moved on to Germany, where similar access to museums and excavations was facilitated by Mahr's connections (*ibid.*, 256–7) and where he also attended various lectures. From Germany he went to Switzerland, where he attended a course on prehistory as well as visiting museums (*ibid.*, 258–9). In

Fig. 2.18 (top)—Seán P. Ó Ríordáin (centre) and his team on Knockadoon (O'Donovan Collection, UCC).
Fig. 2.19 (left)—Seán P. Ó Ríordáin on Knockadoon (O'Donovan Collection, UCC).
Fig. 2.20 (above)—Survey work in progress on Knockadoon (O'Donovan Collection, UCC).

late 1933 Ó Ríordáin was back in Britain and worked with Mortimer Wheeler on his excavations. He also travelled to museums in Sweden and Denmark and returned to Ireland via Paris and London (*ibid.*, 260–1). These years abroad and the garnered experience of excavation and artefact study enabled Ó Ríordáin to bring (then) modern archaeological methods back to Ireland (Daniel 1960, 60). Ó Ríordáin left the National Museum in 1936 to succeed Canon Patrick C. Power as professor of Archaeology in University College Cork, and continued in this post until his appointment to the chair of Archaeology in University College Dublin in 1943. He married the artist Gabrielle Hayes in 1936 and they spent their years at Lough Gur in Beechwood Cottage (Fig. 2.21), which was owned by Count de Salis and conveniently located at the cross where the road leads into Lough

Fig. 2.21—Beechwood Cottage, Lough Gur (O'Donovan Collection, UCC).

Gur. Gabrielle Hayes lived until 1978 and continued sculpting; she also designed the halfpenny, penny and twopenny coins introduced with decimalisation in Ireland in 1971.

Ó Ríordáin collaborated with Gearóid Ó h-Iceadha on the excavation in 1938 of the megalithic tomb at Killalough near Newchurch, on the southern shore of Lough Gur (Ó Ríordáin and Ó h-Iceadha 1955). Frank Mitchell and Ó Ríordáin excavated temporary settlement sites of Neolithic and Beaker period date at Rockbarton Bog in 1941, and Mitchell also studied the pollen sequence of the bog (Ó Ríordáin and Mitchell 1942). John Hunt and Ó Ríordáin excavated two thirteenth/fourteenth-century stone houses in Caherguillamore in 1940; this excavation was one of the first undertaken in Ireland of an Anglo-Norman peasant rural settlement, as well as one of the first times that aerial photography was used to map earthworks and extensive field enclosures (Ó Ríordáin and Hunt 1942). Caoimhín Ó Danachair and Ó Ríordáin excavated a seventeenth-century house at Site J, Knockadoon, in 1945 (Ó Ríordáin and Ó Danachair 1947); research on this site was innovative, as at that time Irish archaeology was focused on prehistoric sites or upstanding monuments. Ó Ríordáin's interest in the more recent phases of Irish archaeology is also seen in his survey with Michael J. O'Kelly of the vernacular architecture of Lough Gur, where they completed a survey of traditional mud-walled houses (Ó Ríordáin and O'Kelly 1940). Máire MacDermott, a pupil of Ó Ríordáin's in UCD, excavated ring-barrows at Ballingoola and Cahercorney and published summary accounts of these in 1949. She also excavated a platform-type ringfort at the western foot of Knockfennell Hill, which remains unpublished.

More recent work was carried out by the author from 1977 to 2012 (Cleary 1982a; 1982b;

1983; 1995; 2003; 2006; 2015; Cleary and Jones 1980; Cleary and Hogan 2013; Cleary and O'Driscoll 2014; O'Driscoll and Cleary 2016). The initial excavations in 1977–8 at Lough Gur were financed jointly by Shannon Development and Limerick County Council. The excavation was carried out prior to the development of an interpretative centre and car park on the north-eastern shore of Lough Gur. The interpretative centre was designed to tell the story of Lough Gur and the car park facilitated the ever-increasing number of visitors. The excavations were initially exploratory, to determine whether any archaeological remains existed within the footprint of the development, and a series of test trenches were cut. It became clear that the area included archaeological remains, the foundations of a Bronze Age house and an early Bronze Age burial with associated pottery on the site of the proposed interpretative centre. The car park included the foundations of two medieval houses of thirteenth–fourteenth-century date, a yard enclosure around the fourteenth-century house, a corn-drying kiln and the foundations of four hut sites of probable Bronze Age date (Cleary 1982a; 1982b; 1983). The medieval houses, similar to those excavated at Caherguillamore, were for many years exceptional in the Irish archaeological record, as little research was carried out on rural medieval settlement in Ireland. An excavation undertaken at Ballynagallagh in 1979 at the site of a destroyed megalithic tomb uncovered the remains of two burials (Cleary and Jones 1980).

As most of Ó Ríordáin's excavations on Knockadoon were undertaken prior to the development of radiocarbon analysis, a programme of excavation began in 1986 to address the issue of dating prehistoric settlement at Lough Gur. Ó Ríordáin based much of his dating of sites on artefacts, particularly pottery, and the sequence produced a chronology for settlement which was not fixed in real time. The aim of the excavations in the 1980s and 1990s was to place Ó Ríordáin's excavations within a firm chronological framework and, allied to this, to redress the lack of information on other aspects of prehistoric settlement, such as the economy, sources of raw materials and a reconstruction of the environment. This was done by modern methods of recovery of charred seed remains and detailed studies of animal bones. A site detected in Ballynagallagh during the Bruff aerial survey was also investigated to determine its date (Cleary 2006). Excavation work at Grange Stone Circle B was carried out to establish its construction date and sequence of use. These recent excavations have established a broad chronological framework for the various monuments at Lough Gur. In addition, the results of other excavations outside the Lough Gur area where similar artefacts— and pottery in particular—have been recovered have enabled a better understanding of the dating and sequence of archaeological sites at Lough Gur. The archaeological remains are fragmentary and provide the merest glimpse of the past inhabitants of Lough Gur, the nature of whose lives, beliefs and customs can to a large extent only be surmised. Many of the inhabitants of Lough Gur over the past six millennia have left little trace on the landscape.

NOTES

[1]   Ware's *The antiquities and history of Ireland* was published posthumously in 1705.

[2]   Crofton Croker (1833) specified 63; Lewis (1837) and Fitzgerald and McGregor (1826) recorded 65; Harkness (1869) and Camden (1607, vol. 3) gave 60 as the number. Other antiquarians record lower numbers: Twiss in 1775 said 40 (Finnegan 2008), while Beaufort (1828) indicated 43; O'Donovan (1840) recorded 45 but largely followed Beaufort's description.

[3]   February 4th was suggested as an alternative alignment; this was around the time of the Celtic

festival of *Imbolc* or St Bridget's Day, which marked the beginning of spring.

4 Recorded in the Archaeological Inventory of County Limerick as RMP 032-014-006; the maximum diameter of the cashel is *c.* 41m.

5 Tythes (tithes) were taxes of 10% levied mainly on tenant farmers but also on some tradesmen and used to support Protestant clergy. The tythe proctor collected the tax.

6 Designation after Windle 1912.

7 Windle (1912, 296) also recorded that the area was prone to flooding and that water levels could rise to the road boundary wall, and thus the 'stone circles' were periodically flooded.

8 These are recorded in the Limerick Archaeological Survey as LI 032-120 and 158.

9 Borlase (1897, 48) gave detailed measurements of *Leaba na Muice* as follows: 'The flag, supported by the galláns, or uprights, is nearly the shape of an equilateral triangle measuring 7 feet [2.1m] in height, 6 feet 6 ins. [2m] at the base, and 1 foot 6 ins. [0.46m] in thickness. The upright stones measure, one 4 feet [1.2m] in length, 2½ feet [0.76m] in height, and 10 inches [0.25m] in thickness; the other 6 feet [1.8m] in length, 3 feet [0.9m], and 1 foot [0.3m] in thickness.'

3. The Stone Age

3.1: MESOLITHIC

Hunter-gatherer communities or Mesolithic people reached Ireland around 8000 BC (Woodman 2015, 119). Similar stone tools to those found on British Mesolithic sites suggest that these colonists probably travelled by boat to the island of Ireland from Britain (*ibid.*, 185). Early Mesolithic sites in Ireland are frequently found in coastal areas or further inland along river valleys. The initial colonisation of the north Munster area was presumably via the River Shannon, and access to the inland area of Lough Gur must have been via the Maigue and Mulkear rivers and their tributaries, the Camoge and Morningstar rivers, and perhaps across other lakes in the hinterland of Lough Gur (Fig. 3.1.1). These hunter-gatherer people were nomadic and have left little trace on the landscape.

Fig. 3.1.1—Mesolithic sites in the environs of Lough Gur.

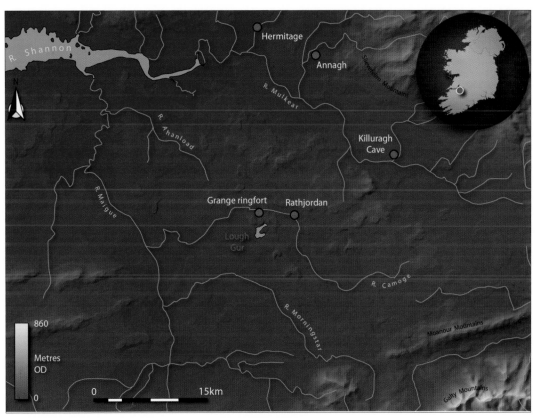

Most Mesolithic sites are found accidentally, often by field archaeologists who recover Mesolithic stone tools from ploughed fields. Tillage is not common around the Lough Gur area, which hinders the recovery of artefacts and the identification of sites, and the known Mesolithic material has been found on archaeological excavations.

After the last Ice Age or the early Holocene,[1] Ireland was an island cut off from Britain and Europe. Animals that were present and could be hunted by the Mesolithic population were wild boar, brown bear, otter, lynx, stoat and perhaps wild cat (*ibid.*, 26). The landscape around Lough Gur was probably one of small and large lakes and rivers and fish may have provided a food source, although Woodman suggests that fish stocks were limited in Irish rivers (*ibid.*, 194). Eels were also part of the diet (*ibid.*, 285). Lampreys or jawless fish which grow to 30–40cm in adulthood are still common in the Mulkear River, and were presumably eaten by hunter-gatherer communities in the Lough Gur area. Birds and foraged foods must have provided some sustenance. Hazelnuts are frequent on Mesolithic sites, and wild fruits and edible wild plants presumably supplemented the diet.

The Mesolithic cultural phase of archaeology is divided into two periods, early (*c.* 8000–6500 BC) and late (6500–4000 BC), based on the type of tools and the technology of production. Diagnostic early Mesolithic tools are small struck stones, known as 'microliths', which were composite implements used as projectiles for hunting and as cutting tools for butchering, preparing hides and woodworking. From about 6500 BC tools were made from larger flakes, and in the final stages of the later Mesolithic tools known as 'Bann flakes' or butt-trimmed, leaf-shaped points were characteristic (*ibid.*, 141, 231–2; Woodman *et al.* 2006, 61). Ground stone axeheads were also part of the Mesolithic tool kit, and the raw material was mostly opportunistically sourced and manufactured from suitable pebbles. The axeheads were probably used as weapons and for woodworking.

The raw material for stone tools in the Mesolithic was flint and chert for small tools and rocks of volcanic origin for stone axeheads. In the initial stages of colonisation Mesolithic populations appear to have preferred to use flint as the main raw material for tool production and, as flint has a limited distribution in the southern part of Ireland, the main source was on the coast (Woodman 2015, 33). In the case of early Mesolithic sites in east Limerick, the nearest coastal sources were 60–80km away (*ibid.*, 255). The flint source at Lough Gur may have been small *remanié* pebbles, while chert is found as nodules in the local Carboniferous limestone. Other raw material used for stone tool production at Lough Gur included quartz (Woodman and Scannell 1993).

In the wider Limerick area fifteen sites have produced evidence for Mesolithic activity. Mesolithic artefacts were found in a cave site at Annagh, and early Mesolithic human remains dated to around 7500–7000 BC and artefacts were recovered from Killuragh Cave near Cappamore (Fig. 3.1.1) (Woodman 2015, 210, 212). Two cremated Mesolithic burials were recovered from the bank of the Shannon at Hermitage, near Castletroy in Limerick City (Collins and Coyne 2006). Mesolithic stone tools were found at Grange and Rathjordan (Fig. 3.1.1) and at four sites on Knockadoon Hill, Lough Gur (Fig. 3.1.2).

Mesolithic activity around Lough Gur

All finds of Mesolithic date were recovered from excavations and provided some evidence of earlier activity around sites which were in the main occupied in the Neolithic and the Bronze Age. The finds were early Mesolithic microliths and possible Bann flakes from late Mesolithic cultural phases.

Fig. 3.1.2—Location of Mesolithic finds at Knockadoon.

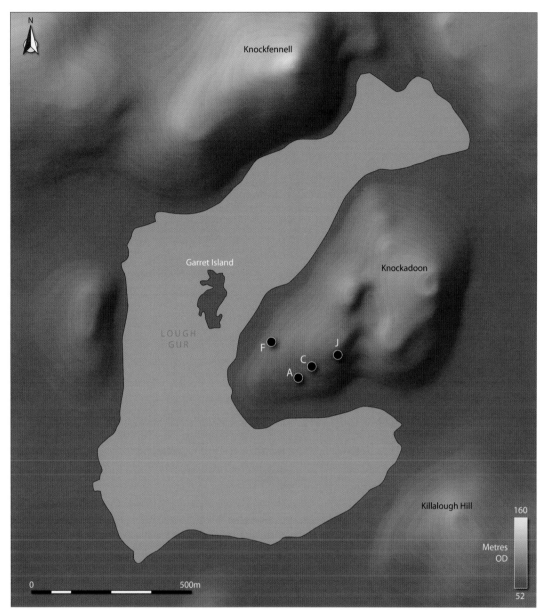

Rathjordan

The barrows at Rathjordan were small enclosures linked to Bronze Age ritual (Chapter 5) and included some finds, such as Neolithic pottery, from earlier activity at these locations. The barrows were on the banks of the Camoge River, and Mesolithic hunter-gatherer communities along the river would not be unexpected. The artefacts date from both the early and the late Mesolithic, spanning 4,000 years, and were residual on the barrow sites. The excavation of Barrow No. 1 at Rathjordan (Ó Ríordáin 1947a) exposed an off-centre pit in the south-east quadrant. The pit fill yielded a small quantity of cremated pig bone, Neolithic pottery and two quartz microlithic points (Fig. 3.1.3: 1–2). The microliths are early Mesolithic in date and were accidentally incorporated into

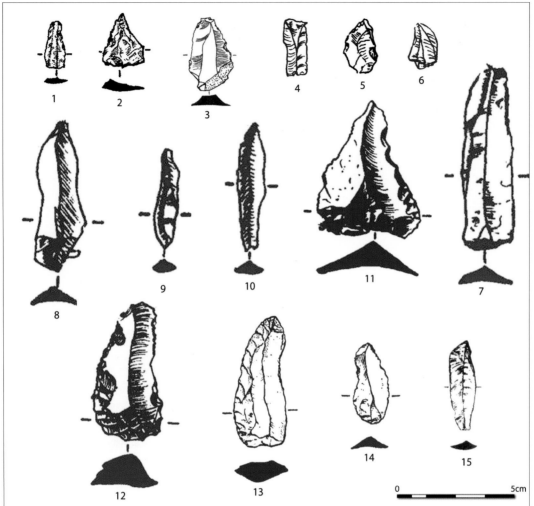

Fig. 3.1.3—1–2 Microliths from Rathjordan; 3 Bann flake (?) from Grange ringfort; 4 blade from Site A, Knockadoon; 5–6 points from Site A, Knockadoon; 7–10 blades from Site C, Knockadoon; 11–12 Bann flakes (?) from Site C, Knockadoon; 13–14 Bann flakes (?) from Site F, Knockadoon; 15 microlith (?) from Site J, Knockadoon.

the pit fill. The fill of a central pit at Barrow No. 2, Rathjordan, included a leaf-shaped flint point, identified as a possible Bann flake, three quartz microlithic points and a small chert blade (Ó Ríordáin 1948, pl. III). A second possible chert 'miniature Bann flake' was also recovered from Barrow No. 2 (*ibid.*, 22). If the identification of the Bann flakes is correct, they indicate late Mesolithic communities on the banks of the Camoge River.

Grange ringfort

A flint flake (Fig. 3.1.3: 3), 'the form of which shows something of Bann flake tradition' according to Ó Ríordáin (1949a, 133), was found on the clay floor just outside the hut in Grange ringfort.

Knockadoon

Woodman and Scannell (1993, 58) noted that the lithic assemblages from excavations on Knockadoon represented an accumulation of material over time and that it was not possible to separate the assemblages into discrete Neolithic and Bronze Age components. Some of the flint and chert assemblages included Mesolithic artefacts left behind by transient hunter-gatherer communities. At Site A, a small blade (Fig. 3.1.3: 4) and two very small points (Fig. 3.1.3: 5–6), possibly intended as tips for darts, may have been microliths. Some small quartz points from Site A were also described by Ó Ríordáin (1954, 308) as 'microlithic'. Small, narrow blades from Site C, Knockadoon (Fig. 3.1.3: 7–10), were considered by Ó Ríordáin (1954, 351) to be Mesolithic in date. Two curved points (Fig. 3.1.3: 11–12), also from Site C, were described as of the Bann flake tradition and similar to those from Rathjordan, late Mesolithic in date. Ó Ríordáin (1954, 423) also recorded flint blades (Fig. 3.1.5: 13–14) from Site F as having 'something of the Bann flake tradition in their form'.

Site J, Knockadoon, was a seventeenth-century house where settlement from the Neolithic period was also recorded around a hearth site (Ó Ríordáin and Ó Danachair 1947). The fill of a pit below the hearth contained Neolithic pottery, a stone axehead chip and a quartz microlith. The microlith (Fig. 3.1.5: 15) was 22mm long and was described as exceptionally well made (*ibid.*, 45–6). Some débitage (waste flakes) from the production of quartz artefacts was also recovered from the later walls at Site J and suggests on-site production of quartz tools.

3.2: NEOLITHIC SETTLEMENT

The onset of arable and pastoral farming in Ireland was marked by landscape changes, including a decline in tree cover. Woodland and scrub vegetation clearance was essential for the creation of fields for crop cultivation and pastureland. These environmental changes were marked by a decline in tree pollen and a rise in grass and weed pollen. Pollen is preserved in bogs and lake sediments. Two studies of the Lough Gur pollen record have been undertaken, one in 1948 by G.F. Mitchell (1954) and one in the mid-1980s by Elizabeth Almgren (1989; 2001). Mitchell's study was undertaken before the development of radiocarbon dating and consequently his sequence of changes over time in pollen was not linked to an absolute chronology with specific dates. After lake drainage from the late 1840s, pollen in lakeshore sediments began to decay once exposed to the air or was washed into the lake bed, where the upper 0.3m of sediments were redeposited (Mitchell 1954, 484–5). Other factors that contributed to the disturbance of the sediments were the rate of water flow, water-level fluctuations and cattle trampling in the lake mud, both in modern times and in antiquity. Mitchell's pollen core (1954, pl. XL) provided information on broad landscape changes, including an elm decline and a rise in herbaceous pollen such as *Plantago lanceolata* (ribwort plantain), which reflect an open landscape linked to the onset of agriculture. At the time of Mitchell's writing, the beginning of the Neolithic in Ireland was dated by analogy with the British Neolithic to about 2000 BC. The now-standard use of radiocarbon dating has shown, however, that the Irish Neolithic began just after 4000 BC and continued until the advent of the knowledge of copper-working around 2500 BC.

A pollen core from the Bog of Cullen, *c.* 15km east of Lough Gur, showed the broad landscape changes around Lough Gur (Molloy 2008, 23). Tall oak and elm trees with an understorey of hazel were established by 4585–3900 BC in the east Limerick/west Tipperary area. The light soil cover in the immediate environs of Lough Gur, particularly Knockadoon and Knockfennell hills, probably had more scrub-like vegetation such as willow (*Salix* sp.), birch (*Betula* sp.), hazel (*Corylus avellana*) and alder (*Alnus glutinosa*). Woodland clearance (*Landnam*) and a decline in tree pollen, including elm (*Ulmus*), marked the beginning of the introduction of farming around 3850 BC (*ibid.*, 29; McSparron 2008). Vegetational changes in the pollen record for Lough Gur suggest early farming close to the lake shore (Almgren 1989, 66).

Woodland clearance may have been carried out by ringing the bark of large trees to kill them, cutting down smaller trees with stone axes and burning off scrub. The amount of charcoal or charred wood in the pollen core from the Bog of Cullen suggested that woodland was burnt off (Molloy 2008, 26). An increase in grass pollen included pollen from what are known as 'the weeds of light', such as ribwort plantain, dandelions, daisies, clover and buttercups, indicating open pastureland in east Limerick (*ibid.*, 26).

The Neolithic period can be divided into an early phase, *c.* 4000–3600 BC, a middle phase, 3600–3000 BC, and a late phase, 3000–2500 BC. The earliest Neolithic settlements at Lough Gur are likely to date from around 3750–3600 BC. The earlier phase (4000–3750 BC) may have seen some initial colonists whose first settlements are difficult to detect in the archaeological record. It is also possible that the livelihood of these first farmers was based on stock husbandry rather than crop cultivation, and the changes brought about may not be very visible in the pollen sequence. As Ireland had a very limited native fauna, large animals such as cattle, sheep/goat and pigs were introduced onto the island. Seed corn for wheat and barley was also brought in, as well as new technology for the production of pottery in which to cook the cereals and for the production of new flint and chert tools and weapons. Cereal cultivation in the period 3750–3600 BC was primarily of wheat, and to a lesser extent of barley (McClatchie *et al.* 2015). There was also opportunistic foraging, and hazelnut shells and the remains of crab-apples are found on early Neolithic sites. There was probably consumption of wild plants, including berries, herbs and fungi, which have left no trace on excavated Neolithic sites.

As the Neolithic advanced, there was a drop-off in cereal cultivation, with fewer records of cereal remains from excavated sites; wheat continued to be the preferred crop (*ibid.*, 306, 310). As all of the Neolithic houses in Lough Gur were excavated at a time when charred plant remains were not retained, early farming practices can only be deduced from evidence from more recently excavated sites. The light soil cover around Lough Gur and in the immediate hinterland was suitable for arable farming. While much of Knockadoon Hill has rock close to the surface and little soil cover, the valley between Knockmore on the north and Back Hill on the south has a relatively good soil cover. There are field enclosures on Knockadoon, suggesting crop cultivation within plots. Only one of these field fences has been scientifically dated and was middle Bronze Age in date (see Chapter 5), although it is likely that other fences were earlier and perhaps Neolithic, while some date from early medieval times (Chapter 8).

The field monuments at Lough Gur, in contrast to elsewhere in Ireland, reveal a visible presence of prehistoric communities. The excavated Neolithic houses on Knockadoon were on the south and south-west side of the hill (Fig. 3.2.1). The excavations on Knockadoon began in 1939, following those at Carraig Aille, and the discovery of Neolithic and Bronze Age sites was completely unexpected (Ó Ríordáin 1954, 299). At that time little was known about Neolithic settlements, and excavations of megalithic tombs were the standard field of prehistoric archaeological research. Indeed, the Irish Neolithic as understood in the 1930s and 1940s was considered to be no more than 500 years long.

The number of Neolithic houses excavated in Ireland is estimated at about 90 buildings from 54 sites; most of these had no surface remains and were detected only when topsoil was stripped (Smyth 2014, 21). At Lough Gur, in contrast, the footings of Neolithic houses at Site A (Fig. 3.2.2), part of Site B and House 2 at Circle K were visible prior to excavation. Sites A and B and Houses 1

Fig. 3.2.1—Location of Neolithic sites on Knockadoon: Sites A–D; Circles J–L; Site J and Site 10.

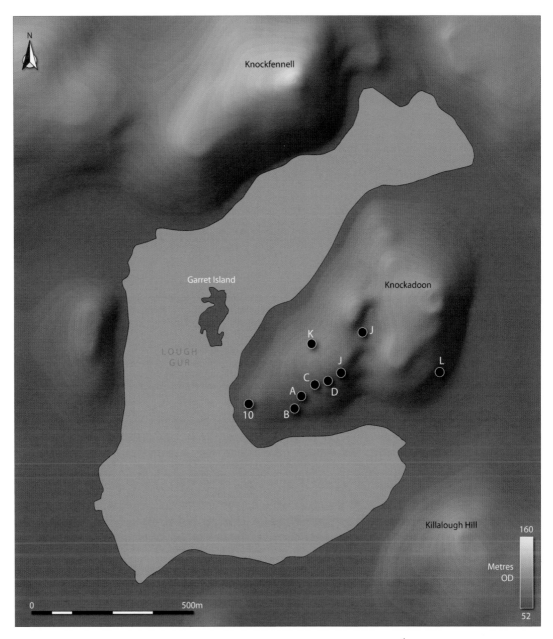

and 2 at Circle K on Knockadoon were rectangular or square in plan (Ó Ríordáin 1954), a shape characteristic of the Irish early Neolithic house (Smyth 2014, 1, 27). A radiocarbon-dating programme on Irish early Neolithic houses indicated that construction began about 3715–3650 BC and ended around 3690–3625 BC (McSparron 2008; Smyth 2014, 48). The houses excavated by Ó Ríordáin at Lough Gur, although not dated by radiocarbon, were architecturally similar to early Neolithic houses in Ireland and were also associated with early Neolithic pottery and Neolithic flint/chert artefacts.

The early Neolithic houses at Lough Gur were rectangular or (less frequently) square in plan.

Fig. 3.2.2—Site A, Knockadoon: house foundations.

Fig. 3.2.3—Reconstruction of Site A house (after Ó Ríordáin 1954).

The long axes of the Knockadoon examples were also typical of Irish Neolithic houses, of which *c.* 70% lay on north-east/south-west and north-west/south-east or north/south alignments (Smyth 2006, 237). The best surviving evidence for the ground-plan was from Site A, which was a rectangular, three-aisled building with a central hearth (Fig. 3.2.3). The internal division into compartments may suggest that the side aisles were used as sleeping/storage areas, set apart from communal space. The floor plan of Site B was less clear and the original house may have been replaced or repaired after a fire. The ground-plan of the primary house may have been square, and internal divisions were

Fig. 3.2.4—Site A: reconstruction of house cross-section showing roof detail.

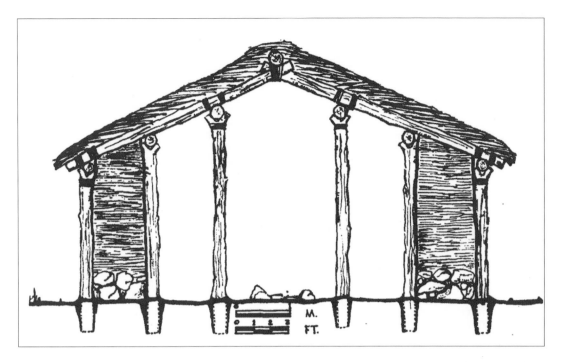

indicated by post-holes. The second phase of house construction/repair was in the footprint of the earlier house but used different construction techniques. A large central hearth was also recorded at Site B. Houses 1 and 2 at Circle K were roughly square in plan and did not appear to have internal divisions. An internal hearth was only recorded at House 1.

The majority of the Neolithic houses on Knockadoon were constructed using paired upright posts that formed the wall frame, while internal structural posts supported the roofs. A foundation trench perhaps for oak plank-built walls was used at Site B (phase 2). A stone wall base was recorded at Site A, on the south side of Site B (phase 2), at House 2, Circle K, and along the north wall of House 1, Circle K. This stone base was not a structural feature and merely formed a foundation course on which the upper walls were laid. The nature of the walls is a matter of conjecture and Ó Ríordáin (1954, 302) was of the opinion that they were made of organic material such as brushwood, grass or rushes. Walls may also have been built from dried mud, a tradition of house-building which survived in the Lough Gur area until the late nineteenth century (Ó Ríordáin and O'Kelly 1940). More recent excavations indicate that Neolithic houses were constructed using a combination of posts, planks and wattle walling (Smyth 2014, 34). The double rows of upright posts that formed the wall frame on some of the Knockadoon Neolithic houses may have had intermediary wattle walling that was plastered over with mud; the space between the double walling was probably filled with some type of organic material such as moss, brushwood or reeds. Neolithic houses in Ireland were generally 6–8m long and 4–7m wide (Smyth 2014, 27), and those at Lough Gur were of similar size. The best-preserved and largest building was Site A, where the estimated internal floor area was in the region of 60m², while that of Site B was c. 52m². The floor areas of Houses 1 and 2 at Circle K were smaller, c. 42m² and 49m² respectively.

The precise structure of the roofs is unknown and subject only to speculation. If the walls were of solid dried mud they may have been load-bearing and supported the roof. Ó Ríordáin's (1954)

Fig. 3.2.5—Site A: roof detail in reconstruction of house during excavation.

illustration of the roof of Site A (Fig. 3.2.4) shows horizontal beams along the top of the external and internal wall posts, with rafters tied into these. Rafters resting on the top of a mud wall or on the horizontal beams would have extended upwards to a central ridge. Additional roof support was provided by internal posts, and the best evidence of these was recorded at Site A. Ó Ríordáin reconstructed a full-scale model of the Site A house during his excavations on Knockadoon; it had low walls with an overhanging roof, which was constructed of woven withies to which thatch was pegged (Fig. 3.2.5). Reeds growing along the adjacent shore of Lough Gur could have been used as thatch.

Ó Ríordáin (1954, 302) recorded that at Site A 'a considerable amount of charcoal in the soil, especially in the neighbourhood of the walls, indicates that the existence of the house ended by its having been burnt'. Burning was also recorded at Circle L, although these burnt areas were also interpreted as 'fireplaces' or hearths (Grogan and Eogan 1987). Smyth (2006, 246) concluded that 'at over half the [Irish Neolithic house] sites, there has been substantial burning of structures, with additional sites producing evidence for partial burning of structures'. The causes of house-burning are explained in a number of ways, including accidental fires and attack, but the most likely reason is deliberate destruction by the householders when a resident died (Smyth 2006, 245–6; 2014, 62–70). This practice is also part of the tradition of the Irish traveller community, whereby the caravan and possessions are burned when an individual dies; burning was also used by Native Americans to purify a house after the death of a resident. House-burning was probably linked with the idea that fire was the source of rebirth and renewal, and as a means of purification and healing. Oddly enough, Houses 1 and 2 at Circle K had burials within the floor areas but neither of these houses showed evidence of deliberate burning.

After the initial early Neolithic rectangular and square houses architectural forms appear to have become less rigid. In the absence of a sequence of radiocarbon dates the chronology of circular houses on Knockadoon is imprecise, and dating is based primarily on the pottery assemblages and diagnostic stone tools. Grogan (1996; 2002) has argued that houses of circular plan may date from the middle Neolithic (3600–3000 BC), and the houses of circular plan at Sites C and D probably date from this time.

The excavated Neolithic houses at Lough Gur were constructed in relatively exposed areas on Knockadoon Hill without regard to shelter. Houses at Sites A, B, C and D were on the south-west side of Knockadoon Hill, where they were exposed to the prevailing south-westerly winds, particularly in winter. Houses 1 and 2 at Circle K, although located in the lee of the hill, and settlement at Circle J were also in a fairly exposed landscape, whereas Circle L was more sheltered.

The difficulty with sites excavated over 75 years ago is the absence of secure dating based on a radiocarbon sequence. Dating of sites from older excavations was primarily based on ceramic finds, which were a key indicator of cultural phases, and to a lesser extent on lithics and metal artefacts for later prehistoric sites. Find locations were not always precisely recorded and thus the determination of a distinct sequence or phasing based on finds is not always possible. The second problem at Lough Gur is the relatively thin soils on Knockadoon and the lack of clear stratigraphic sequences; part of this is due to the continued use of sites, where there was clearly a mixing and churning up of artefacts, including pottery. Some sites of later date had residual artefacts from an earlier period of use. A further contributing factor to the disturbance of occupation layers on sites was animal and, to a lesser extent, root disturbance. Ó Ríordáin (1954, 341–2) noted these problems in relation to dating at Knockadoon and elsewhere at Lough Gur, where continuous activity, disturbance and mixing of material were a feature of the excavated sites. The difficulty of dating Neolithic settlement at the Lough Gur sites is somewhat ameliorated by series of radiocarbon dates from a settlement site at Tullahedy, Co. Tipperary, on the western side of Lough Derg on the River Shannon and easily accessible from Lough Gur (Cleary and Kelleher 2011). There are many similarities between the pottery and stone tools from Tullahedy and Lough Gur, and the radiocarbon evidence from the Tullahedy site allows the creation of a time-frame for the onset of and evolution of Neolithic communities at Lough Gur.

At the post-excavation phase of the study of Site C, the pottery was the only mechanism for dating; the ceramic sequence from Site C was applied to all of Ó Ríordáin's excavations on Knockadoon (Ó Ríordáin 1954) and other sites, including the Great Stone Circle at Grange (Ó Ríordáin 1951). The pottery sequence at Site C was studied by Ó Ríordáin and M.J. O'Kelly (Ó Ríordáin 1954, 342) and examined relative to the depth at which it was found. The pottery was divided into three types: Class I, Class Ia and Class II. Ó Ríordáin concluded that Classes I and Ia were in use at the beginning of the occupation of Site C and were gradually replaced by Class II (*ibid.*, 326–33). Modern excavation and radiocarbon dating have confirmed that Classes I and Ia can be dated to the early/middle Neolithic (3800/3700–3300 BC). They were large, round-bottomed bowls with rim diameters of up to 28cm and estimated heights of 20–22cm, and were used for cooking and storage. They had angled profiles or shoulders, which varied from being acute or sharp (Fig. 3.2.6a, b) to instances where the shoulder angle was just a slight thickening of the vessel wall and the vessels were almost straight-sided (Fig. 3.2.6c). The Class Ia pottery had expanded rims decorated with incised lines (Fig. 3.2.6b), but apart from decorated rims and occasional decoration on the shoulder it was not possible to separate Classes I and Ia; the probability is that both were in

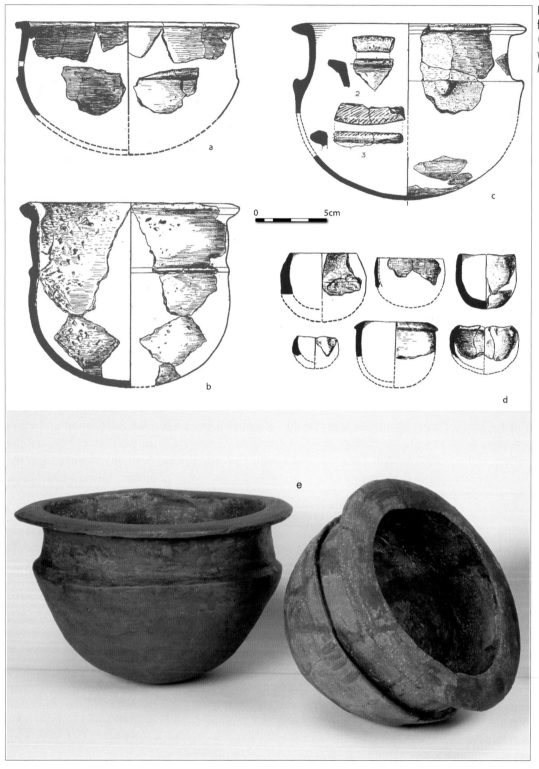

Fig. 3.2.6—Neolithic pottery from Lough Gur: (a, b) Class I; (c) Class Ia; (d) small cup-like vessels; (e) Class 1a (National Museum of Ireland).

Fig. 3.2.7—Bronze Age Class II pottery.

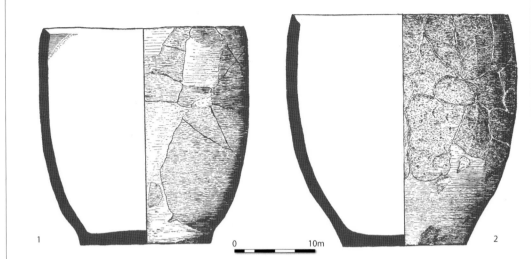

concurrent use, the decorated pottery being a variation rather than a discrete type. Even at an early stage the Neolithic potters began to produce local styles (Cleary 2011, 336). Pottery from Tullahedy that was similar to Classes I and Ia from Lough Gur was dated to *c.* 3700–3300 BC (*ibid.*, 337). Small, cup-like, round-based vessels (Fig. 3.2.6d: 1–6) were also in use on the Neolithic occupation sites on Knockadoon and were contemporary with Class I and Class Ia wares. These cups had rim diameters of 8–9cm and an estimated height of *c.* 7cm and were probably used as drinking vessels. Ó Ríordáin (1954) described the pottery fabrics in detail and recent study of the pottery has confirmed that most was made locally (Cleary 2000, 125–8).

Class II pottery was bucket-shaped and flat-based, with estimated rim diameters of *c.* 20–26cm and heights of *c.* 26–29cm (Fig. 3.2.7). Some of the Class II pottery was decorated with incised lines, either as haphazard scorings or in lattice patterns. Flat-based decorated pottery from the Great Stone Circle at Grange (see Chapter 4) has been identified as Grooved Ware and late Neolithic in date (3000–2500 BC; Chapter 4). Radiocarbon dating from excavations on Knockadoon Hill (Cleary 1995; 2003) confirmed that flat-based, bucket-shaped pottery (albeit undecorated) was in use in the middle–late Bronze Age (1500–700 BC; Chapter 5). Excavations at Chancellorsland, near Emly, Co. Tipperary, and close to Lough Gur, provided middle Bronze Age dates for decorated pottery similar to the Class II type from Knockadoon (Cleary 2008). The occurrence of Class II pottery on early Neolithic sites was due to disturbance from later occupation. While the excavated Neolithic houses on Knockadoon represent permanent settlement, artefacts such as pottery and stone axeheads that belong to later cultural phases probably represent short-term settlement, accidental loss or casual deposition.

The dating of struck stone tools (lithics) is imprecise. Woodman and Scannell (1993, 55, 60) noted the difficulties in separating the different chronological components of the Lough Gur lithic assemblages. While leaf- and lozenge-shaped arrowheads are Neolithic and barbed and tanged arrowheads belong to the Beaker period, many lithics cannot be ascribed to a particular period. Scrapers are ubiquitous in Neolithic and Bronze Age levels at Lough Gur and are not closely datable, although Woodman and Scannell (1993, 55, fig. 6.1) identified the small, invasively retouched scrapers as Bronze Age.

0   8cm

Fig. 3.2.8—Polished stone axeheads from Lough Gur.

Polished stone axeheads were frequent finds on the Lough Gur excavations and many were also recovered as chance finds in the fields around the lake. At least 400 stone axeheads are known from Lough Gur, many of which are to be found in museums in Ireland, in Britain and across Europe. While some may have been Mesolithic in date, most were probably Neolithic. An account by Ó Ríordáin and Lucas (1946–7, 68) detailed the discovery of a 'full box-cart' of stone axeheads in a field in Rathjordan when the field was ploughed during World War I. Many of these are presumably lost, in private hands or acquired by various museums. Apart from use in the construction of solid timber-framed houses, stone axes were an integral part of the tool kit of early farmers for forest clearance and were most likely also used to prepare the ground for growing domesticated plants such as cereals. The stone axeheads invariably have a narrow butt end and a sharp cutting edge (Fig. 3.2.8). They vary in size, and some very small and very large examples are known. The smaller examples may have been used for tasks within a domestic setting, such as cutting food, hair, leather etc., while the larger examples may have been prestige items. Many chips from axeheads were found on the excavations and the stone had been recycled to produce scrapers.

Dempsey's (2013) study of a sample of 50 stone axeheads from Lough Gur established that they were made from a variety of raw materials. Axeheads of fine-grained shale, mudstone, siltstone and sandstone constituted *c.* 40% of Dempsey's study and the raw materials were most likely locally sourced. Axeheads made of tuffs, frequently referred to as 'greenstone' in the published record, comprised *c.* 22% and were imported from the Great Langdale axe factory in Cumbria, probably as finished products rather than as rough-outs. Axeheads of gabbro/dolerite comprised about 15% of the sample and the source of these rock types may have been in Cornwall or Wales. Porcellanite axeheads from Lough Gur, which comprised *c.* 10% of Dempsey's sample, were sourced from the axe factories at Tievebulliagh, Co. Antrim, or Rathlin Island, off the Antrim coast. Other raw materials

Fig. 3.2.9—General landscape view showing location of Sites A, C, D and Circle K.

included andesite, basalt, rhyolite, schist and limestone, which were used in minor quantities. The axeheads from Ó Ríordáin's excavations were also examined by J.C. Brindley, who identified the rock types of some from Site D as shale and sandstone, while G.F. Mitchell identified others as porcellanite. One can only speculate about how stone axeheads from these distant regions arrived in Lough Gur. They may have been traded for other goods or been part of a gift-exchange system.

Early Neolithic (3800–3500 BC) rectangular houses and settlement evidence

Site A, Knockadoon

This site was at the foot of the lower south-western slope of Back Hill on Knockadoon (Figs 3.2.1 and 3.2.9) and a stone footing was visible on the ground prior to excavation (Fig. 3.2.2). The house was rectangular in plan with a north–south long axis; the site slope resulted in the southern end being *c.* 2ft (0.6m) lower than the northern end. The overall internal dimensions were 6.1m (east/west) by 9.75m (north/south). The stone footing was continuous along the perimeter except on the south-west corner, where the entrance was located (Figs 3.2.10–11). The stone foundation was randomly set without a formal wall face. The stones were irregular and in places comprised large stones set directly on boulder clay, while other stones sat on the old ground surface or pre-wall sod level. Some of the footing stones were supported and steadied with smaller stones or sods, and clusters of smaller stones also occurred along the line of the footing. The stone foundation stood to a height of one or two courses and possibly formed a type of damp-proof course at the base of a wall made from organic material.

Paired post-holes were set along the external and internal perimeters of the stone footing (Fig. 3.2.10). The post-hole diameters were recorded as *c.* 7in. (0.18m), with depths of 5–10in. (0.12–0.25m). These dimensions most likely represented the tips of posts where they were driven into boulder clay levels rather than the actual sizes of the posts. Post-holes on Knockadoon Hill are only

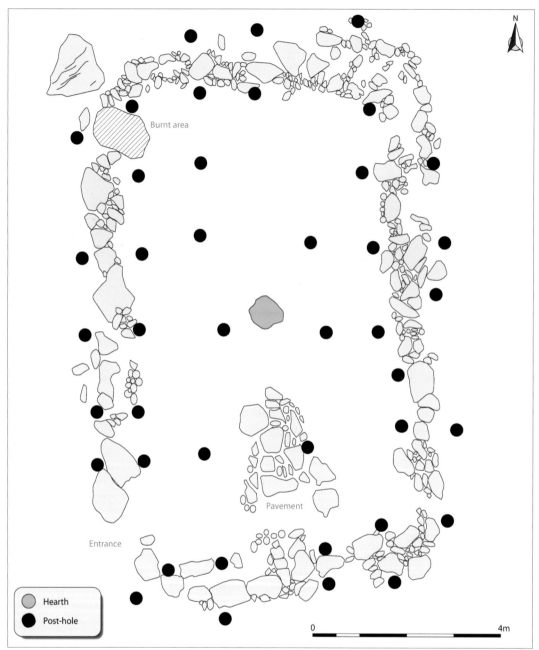

Fig. 3.2.10—Plan of house at Site A, Knockadoon.

Burnt area

Hearth

Post-hole

Entrance

Pavement

0   4m

easily recognisable at boulder clay level and are not usually detectable in the upper humic soil. These perimeter post-holes at Site A marked the line of upright posts, and intermediary wattle walls between the posts may have formed the shell of the house wall. The cavity between the wattle walls may have been filled with moss, brushwood or rushes (Ó Ríordáin 1954, 302). Ó Ríordáin considered that the absence of clay around the stone foundation precluded an interpretation of clay/mud or sod walls. This may not have been the case, however, as once the roof collapsed and the

Fig. 3.2.11—House at Site A
during excavation.

mud walls were exposed to the elements they would disintegrate or wash away and leave little trace. The perimeter posts along the walls also supported the roof. A reconstruction drawing of Site A (Fig. 3.2.3) shows a long house with gabled ends and a thatched roof. Post-holes within the house were 1.5–1.8m distant from the external walls, *c*. 2m apart and formed aisle divisions within the house, and were also considered by Ó Ríordáin to be structural and part of the roof supports (Fig. 3.2.4).

The occupation level within the Site A house was recorded under an 8–12in.-thick (0.2–0.3m) humic soil layer or the modern soil accumulation. The basal layer described as a 'clay floor' was not deliberately laid but was likely to have been the exposed boulder clay. It may have been that the builders stripped the site of sod and soil prior to construction in order to expose the boulder clay, which then provided a hard, firm floor surface. Over time, debris from occupation accumulated on this surface and was recorded particularly south of the central hearth towards the southern wall (Fig. 3.2.10). This section of the floor was subsequently paved to level up the southern floor area (Fig. 3.2.11). Ó Ríordáin (1954, 300) considered that the paving was originally more extensive than the section that survived. A *c*. 1m-wide break in the wall stones in the south-west corner marked the doorway. A central hearth over the 'clay floor' was *c*. 0.7m in diameter.

The architectural style and pottery from House Site A suggest a date range of 3750–3600 BC. The pottery was identified as Neolithic Class I ware and flat-based Bronze Age Class II pottery. Class I wares were round-based with angled profiles and undecorated, typical of Neolithic pottery. One sherd described as 'decorated' (Ó Ríordáin 1954, 308, fig. 3:12) was probably later than the primary occupation and may have been from the Beaker period. The Class II wares were thicker 'coarse wares'

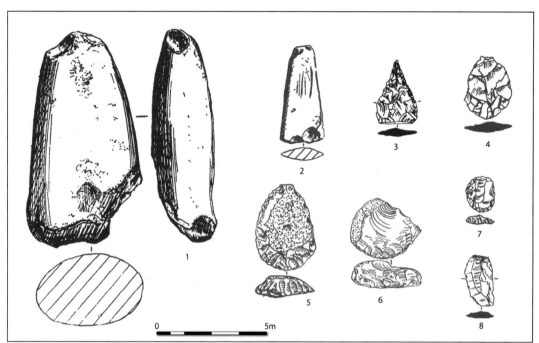

Fig. 3.2.12—Finds from Site A: 1 stone axehead; 2 slate spearhead; 3–4 leaf-shaped arrowheads; 5–7 scrapers; 8 blade tool.

and date from the late Bronze Age (Cleary 1993, 118–19). The Bronze Age pottery was found on the clay floor as well as at higher levels, suggesting some disturbance of the primary Neolithic occupation layers. Most of the pottery came from the north-eastern area of the house around the hearth.

The stone artefacts from Site A comprised an almost complete greenstone axehead (Fig. 3.2.12: 1), four axehead chips which were reused as scrapers and a slate spearhead (Fig. 3.2.12: 2). The axehead was found under the inner side of the northern stone foundation and may have been deliberately placed there or perhaps casually used as a convenient stone. Eighty-six mainly flint artefacts were also recovered, including two leaf-shaped arrowheads (Fig. 3.2.12: 3–4), scrapers (Fig. 3.2.12: 5–7) and blade tools (Fig. 3.2.12: 8). Quartz was also worked at Site A.

Site B, Knockadoon

Site B was south-west of Site A, nearer to the lake shore and on the same ridge as Sites A, C and D (Fig. 3.2.1). Ó Ríordáin (1954, 312) interpreted the site as one where successive building occurred and consequently the ground-plan was not as clear as that of the house at Site A. Sequential building on the same location is uncommon on early Neolithic house sites in Ireland and the house may have been repaired, perhaps after a fire or when some of the structural posts rotted. Post-holes under a stone foundation course on the south side and on the west and north sides and a single post-hole on the east side mark the ground-plan of the primary building (Fig. 3.2.13). The east/west long axis of the primary house was approximately 7m in length and the house was 6m wide (north/south). An area of burning recorded on the floor level at a depth of 2ft 6in. (0.76m) indicated that the primary house was partly destroyed by fire.

Phase 2 of the building may have been a partial reconstruction of the earlier house; it comprised a *c.* 20ft-long (6.1m) stone foundation course along the southern side and a foundation trench for

Fig. 3.2.13—Site B,
Knockadoon: plan of house.

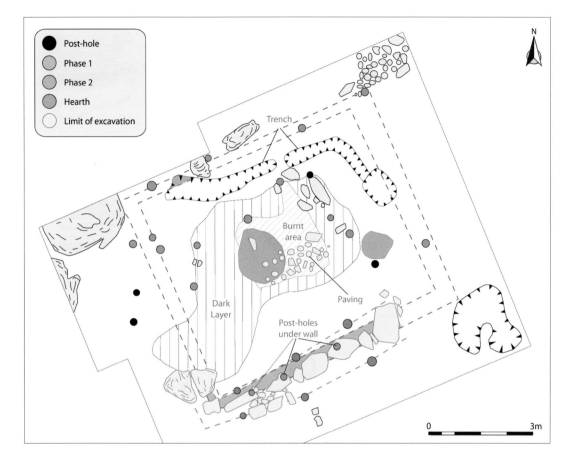

a plank-built wall on the northern side. Outcropping bedrock may also have been used as part of the foundation like the stone at the base of the southern wall. Ó Ríordáin (1954, 314) considered that the accumulation of an intermediary layer of humic soil between the base of the wall stones and the old ground level suggested an interval between the construction of the original southern wall and the later addition of a stone wall course. Paired post-holes were recorded on either side of the stone foundation and, as at Site A, these must have held structural posts for the second phase of wall construction, as well as providing roof supports. A trench 5–7in. (0.13–0.18m) deep along part of the northern side, which turned and also marked the north-east corner, was probably a foundation for a plank-built wall. This trench terminated on the eastern side at a large post-hole, 16in. (0.4m) deep. No real evidence survived to confirm whether the western wall, which was built of posts, had remained in place after the first house was damaged or whether it was also rebuilt in a second phase of construction.

Internal post-holes, suggesting an aisled building similar to Site A, may indicate an internal division and structural posts used as roof supports; these may have been part of Phase 1 or Phase 2 house construction. A 'black stratum' (Ó Ríordáin 1954, 314) in the north-east quadrant of the house floor was 0.3m above the primary burnt layer and suggested an occupation layer associated with rebuilding/repair of the house. A paved area was recorded immediately over this occupation layer. A central hearth was evident as a *c.* 1.5m-diameter area of burning; it was recorded at a high level and

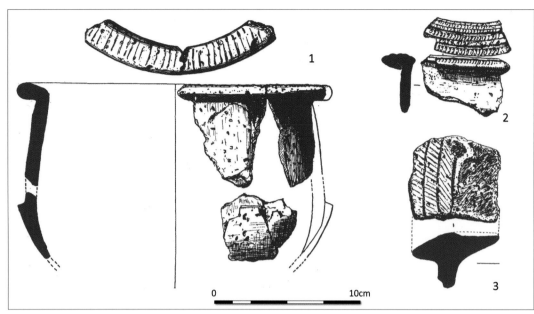

Fig. 3.2.14—Site B, Knockadoon. Class Ia pottery.

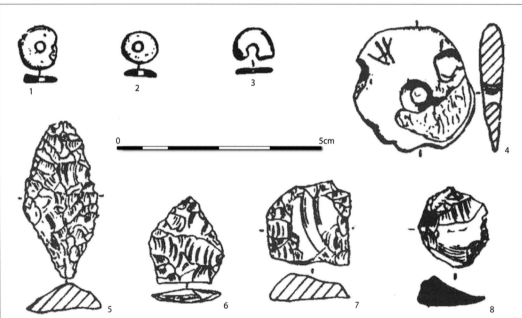

Fig. 3.2.15—Finds from Site B, Knockadoon: 1–4 stone beads; 5–6 leaf-shaped arrowheads; 7 chert blade; 8 thumbnail scraper.

was probably associated with a second phase of house use. A *c.* 1m-diameter hearth located *c.* 0.8m from the eastern wall and a 'C'-shaped pit outside the south-east corner were shown on the published plan but there were no other details.

The pottery from Site B was almost exclusively Neolithic and comprised plain (Class I) and decorated (Class Ia) wares. The rectangular plans of both phases of the house and the pottery from Site B suggest a date range of 3750–3600 BC. Most of the 650 sherds of pottery came from the north-east quadrant of the house floor. The pottery (Fig. 3.2.14: 1) was round-based with sharp shoulders and either plain or decorated rims; some vessels had lugs or short handles at the shoulders. Ó Ríordáin (1954, 317–18) recorded that Classes I and Ia were found together, and Class Ia or decorated pottery predominated at the earliest level. Some Class Ia pottery found at the lowest levels at Site B (Fig. 3.2.14: 2–3) had very exaggerated expanded rims, which probably shows a preferred local style. Ó Ríordáin (1954, 317) referred to the pottery as 'corky'-textured, particularly in the Class Ia, as a result of the use of crushed bone, which was mixed with the clay to improve the strength of the clay for pottery production and which dissolved over time, leaving the surfaced pitted (Cleary 1984).

One complete stone axehead, two butt ends of stone axeheads and eight fragments were recovered at Site B. Three (Fig. 3.2.15: 1–3) of the four stone beads from Site B were small, with diameters of 7–11mm; one (Fig. 3.2.15: 2) was identified as serpentine, which is not found at Lough Gur and may have come from the Connemara area of County Galway. One large bead (Fig. 3.2.15: 4) was 30mm in diameter and, like two of the smaller beads, was made from local rock. Fifty-six pieces of struck flint, chert and quartz were found at Site B but the assemblage did not include many finished artefacts. Two leaf-shaped arrowheads (Fig. 3.2.15: 5–6), one blade (Fig. 3.2.15: 7) and one scraper (Fig. 3.2.15: 8) were recovered.

The animal bones from Site B were fragmentary and were identified as of cattle, sheep or goat and pig. Red deer bones were also recovered. Bones of a dog or wolf may represent a pet. Bird bones were from barnacle geese and mallard, presumably caught when the opportunity arose and consumed on site.

Circle K

Circle K, situated on a level plateau on the west side of Knockadoon Hill (Figs 3.2.1 and 3.2.9), was excavated by Seán P. Ó Ríordáin in 1940 (Grogan and Eogan 1987). The enclosure wall and stone

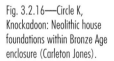

Fig. 3.2.16—Circle K, Knockadoon: Neolithic house foundations within Bronze Age enclosure (Carleton Jones).

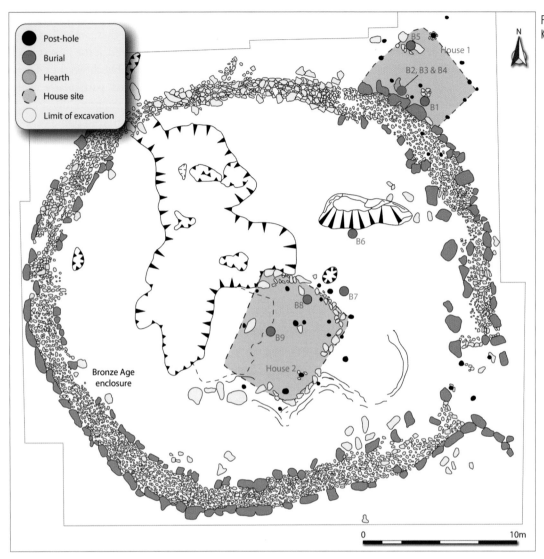

Fig. 3.2.17—Circle K, Knockadoon: overall plan.

footings of a central house were visible before excavation (Fig. 3.2.16). The site had two houses, one under the enclosure wall and another off-centre within the enclosure (Fig. 3.2.17). There was also evidence of burial on the site. The bulk of the ceramic finds within the infill of the enclosure wall was Class II pottery, confirming that it was constructed in the Bronze Age (Cleary 2003, 145–6). The enclosing wall was most likely fortuitously built on the early Neolithic site. The finds from Circle K had accumulated over perhaps three millennia of occupation, extending from the Neolithic to the late Bronze Age. The soil cover was very thin and less than 0.1m over most of the area, except in a natural hollow that extended across the western side of the site (Fig. 3.2.17) and where the average depth of soil was 0.75m. The absence of clear stratigraphy and details of the locations of finds from Circle K makes precise dating difficult. The plans of Houses 1 and 2, the frequency of Class I pottery and the stone artefacts suggest an early Neolithic date range of 3750–3600 BC for the houses.

Fig. 3.2.18—Circle K: plan of House 1.

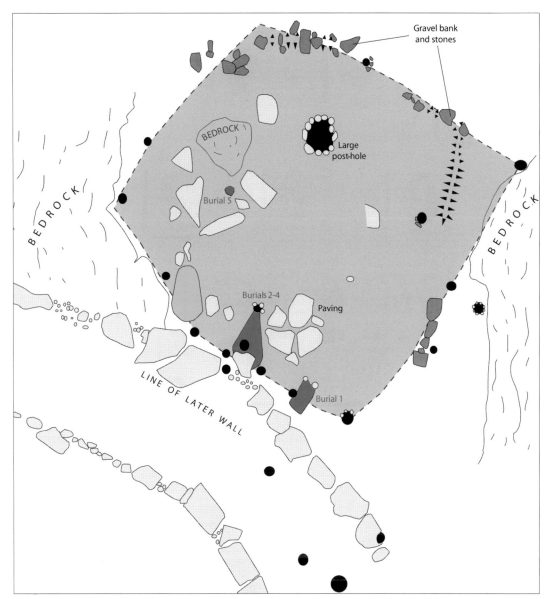

House 1. House 1 (Fig. 3.2.18) lay under the north-east quadrant of the Bronze Age stone enclosure and in a saucer-shaped natural hollow. It was roughly square in plan, measuring 7.25m (east/west) by 6.65m (north/south). A 0.3m-thick layer of Neolithic occupation soil within the house extended under the later enclosure wall, suggesting that the house was larger than the ground-plan recorded in the excavation. A 0.1m-high gravel bank topped with stones formed the base of the northern and eastern walls; the stones were irregular on the northern wall and a stone row remained midway along the eastern wall. A line of post-holes along the southern side may have marked the southern wall, or an internal division if the house floor continued under the later enclosure wall. Two extant post-holes were recorded along the western wall. A gap in the northern wall with a post-hole on

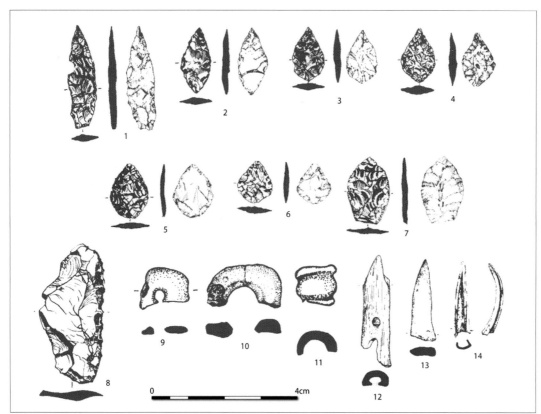

Fig. 3.2.19—Finds from House 1, Circle K: 1 laurel-shaped arrowhead; 2–7 leaf-shaped arrowheads; 8 flint knife; 9–11 stone beads; 12–14 bone points.

the west side may have marked the entrance. A large internal post-hole towards the northern end and a smaller post-hole at the southern end may have contained posts for internal roof supports. A layer of burnt clay and charcoal, 0.9m by 0.6m and 0.15m thick, marked a hearth on the south-west side, with a paved surface to the east. The positioning of the hearth near the southern side also suggested that the house may have been longer than the ground-plan indicated.

The pottery from the house was identified as Class I, and fragments of at least six vessels were recovered. The worked stone from House 1 included one laurel-shaped arrowhead (Fig. 3.2.19: 1), six leaf-shaped arrowheads (Fig. 3.2.19: 2–7) and a rough-out for a lozenge-shaped arrowhead. Seventeen scrapers, two knives (Fig. 3.2.19: 8) and five blades were also recovered. Two greenstone axehead fragments and one granite axehead fragment were found, as well as some axehead chips. Three beads were found within the house; one (Fig. 3.2.19: 9) was of serpentine, one was of local siltstone (Fig. 3.2.19: 10) and the third was of bone (Fig. 3.2.19: 11). Three polished bone points (Fig. 3.2.19: 12–14), possibly used as perforators or spearheads (Mullins 2007), were also recovered.

Five burials were recorded in the environs of House 1, although there was no evidence that they were associated with the construction or use of the house. There is no absolute dating of the burials but it is clear from the published information that they were not all contemporary interments and that some were later than others. Burial 1 was inserted into the habitation layer overlying the house floor, perhaps after the house was abandoned. Burial 2 underlay a structural post in the southern wall of House 1. Burials 3 and 4 pre-dated the enclosure wall, and no information was recorded on the stratigraphic position of Burial 5. The burials are detailed below (Section 3.3).

Fig. 3.2.20—Circle K: plan of House 2.

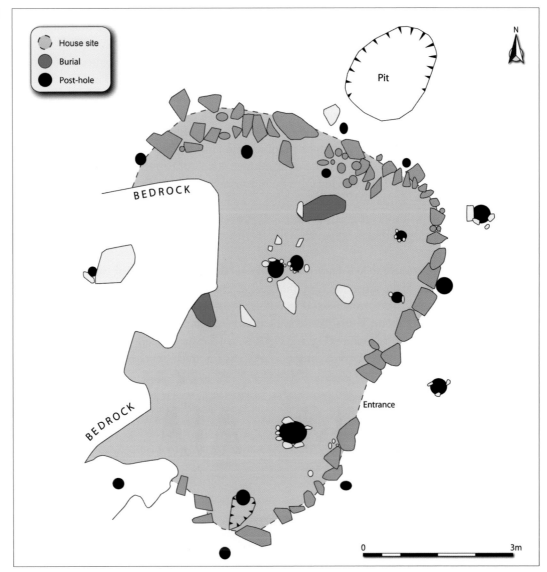

House site
Burial
Post-hole

Pit

N

BEDROCK

BEDROCK

Entrance

0   3m

House 2. The house was within the enclosure, off-centre and mainly in the south-east quadrant (Fig. 3.2.17). It was rectangular in plan, measuring 8.2m (north-east/south-west) by 6.4m (north-west/south-east), and was built on a level limestone outcrop that formed the floor (Fig. 3.2.20). A 0.25m-high earthen bank on which stones were placed was recorded at foundation level. The stones varied in size (0.3–0.5m), forming a double row on the north-west side and a single row elsewhere (Grogan and Eogan 1987, 367). This stone foundation was similar to foundation courses at Sites A and B. Post-holes, some of which were paired, were recorded on either side of the foundation and presumably held structural posts which formed the wall and supported the roof, similar to Site A. Two large post-holes that were slightly off-centre may have held additional internal roof supports. The entrance was marked by a 0.8m-wide gap in the eastern wall. The published report confirmed that there was no stratigraphic evidence to link the house with the later enclosure wall (*ibid.*, 368) and its position within the enclosure was fortuitous. There are no details on a large oval pit, almost 2m in diameter, which was shown on plan immediately north of House 2.

Disturbance was recorded within the floor area of the house, and some fragments of pottery from outside its perimeter belonged to vessels found within the floor area (*ibid.*). Finds from House 2 came mainly from the south-east corner of the floor area and included sherds from at least nine vessels of Class I pottery. The struck stone tools were six scrapers, a blade, two knives, one leaf-shaped arrowhead and one lozenge-shaped arrowhead. One almost complete greenstone polished axehead and small chips of a sandstone axehead, similar to those from House 1, were also found within House 2. Nine fragments of Beaker pottery and sherds from three vessels of Bronze Age Class II ware were recovered around the house, reflecting intrusive finds from a later phase of site use. Two infants were buried in shallow graves in the floor of House 2 (Section 3.3), and a child burial in a shallow grave was found immediately outside its north-eastern wall. Two child burials were also recorded between Houses 1 and 2.

Finds. Excavation within the Circle K enclosure recovered Neolithic artefacts that were detritus from the primary occupation of the site in the Neolithic period. These included 56 flint and chert artefacts, eight leaf- and lozenge-shaped arrowheads (Fig. 3.2.21: 1–3), eleven scrapers, fragments of flint and chert knives (Fig. 3.2.21: 4) and blades. Two complete stone axeheads, one made from volcanic ash (Fig. 3.2.21: 5) and the other of granite (Fig. 3.2.21: 6), were recovered. There was also débitage from on-site flint- and chert-working. Fifty-eight sherds of Class I pottery (representing four vessels), six

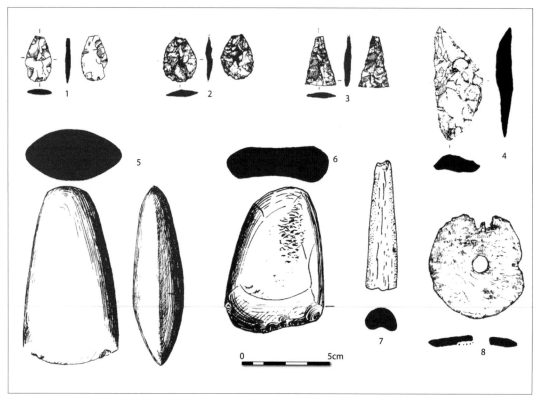

Fig. 3.2.21—Neolithic finds from the enclosure, Circle K: 1–2 leaf-shaped arrowheads; 3 lozenge-shaped arrowhead; 4 flint knife; 5–6 polished stone axeheads; 7 bone pin; 8 bone bead.

Fig. 3.2.22—Circle L,
Knockadoon: overall plan.

siltstone beads, and a bone pin (Fig. 3.2.21: 7) and a bone bead (Fig. 3.2.21: 8) were found. A granite axehead and axehead chips and 167 fragments of Class I pottery from at least six vessels were recovered from the vicinity of House 1.

Circle L

The site, on the south-east side of Knockadoon Hill (Fig. 3.2.1), was excavated in 1951 by Seán P. Ó Ríordáin (Grogan and Eogan 1987). Cuttings were opened in the central area and across the enclosing rampart on the cardinal points (Fig. 3.2.22). The enclosure wall at Circle L, as at Circle K, probably post-dated Neolithic activity on the site. The excavation uncovered a large number of post-holes and pits in the central area, indicative of rebuilding or remodelling of the houses (*ibid.*, 387). Truncation and disturbance in antiquity of pre-existing structural features made it difficult to separate out elements of the houses, but it was possible to discern at least three Neolithic houses—House A,

Fig. 3.2.23—Circle L: location of Houses A and B and the Central House (Phase 1).

House A

Central House (Phase 1)

House B

#	Fireplace
	Hearth
	House
	Limit of excavation

0   5m

House B and Phase 1 of the Central House (Fig. 3.2.23). Phase 2 of the Central House, which had a stone foundation, was probably Bronze Age in date (see Chapter 5) and contemporary with the construction of the enclosing wall of Circle L.

There are few details[2] on finds directly associated with the houses. Most of the finds came from north of House A or in the vicinity of the Central House (see below). The ceramic assemblage comprised fragments of at least 40 vessels, of which 25 were from the primary occupation or pre-enclosure phase. All were undecorated and the profiles suggest early Neolithic pottery of Ó Ríordáin's Class I wares, with a date range of 3750–3600 BC, providing a broad chronological framework for pre-enclosure Neolithic occupation at Circle L.

House A. This was on the northern side of the enclosure and best preserved on the north-east corner. Its southern side lay under Phase 1 of the Central House, the construction of which had disturbed some of its structural features. The floor plan of House A suggests a square or rectangular[3] building on a north-east/south-west axis (Fig. 3.2.23), with an estimated width (north-east/south-west) of *c.* 5.5m. The structural elements consisted of a double row of paired posts forming the external walls, probably with intermediary double wattle walls with an organic layer between them. A pit in the north-east corner was of sufficient size to hold a substantial corner post for the building. Three pits parallel to the northern wall (Fig. 3.2.23), 0.3–0.5m in diameter and aligned north-west/south-east, suggest the locations of internal roof-support posts. The intermediary distance between the pits and the northern wall was *c.* 1m, and these internal posts may have formed an aisle along the northern side of the house. One pit to the north and one to the south of this line of pits may also have held structural roof-support posts. Grogan and Eogan (1987, 388) described an area of burning within the building as 'fireplace 1' or the vestiges of a central hearth. The spread of burnt material measured a maximum of 0.9m and may have comprised rake-out as well as the hearth itself. If the hearth was centrally located, the estimated length of the building was in the region of 6m, making the ground-plan roughly square. A number of small post-holes/stake-holes around the hearth probably represented the remains of a spit adjacent to the fire. Other post-holes/stake-holes within the building suggest uprights which were part of fittings such as drying-racks or screens.

The elements of House A, including the paired posts used for walls, the large internal (post-?) pits, the central hearth and the general north/south alignment, are paralleled at Site A, Knockadoon, and at Circle K. Houses excavated at Tullahedy, Co. Tipperary, which had similar Neolithic pottery and large internal pits interpreted as internal post-pits were dated to 3795–3385 BC (Cleary and Kelleher 2011, 417).

House B. This was on the southern side of the enclosure and was best preserved on the southern and western sides. The floor plan suggests a rectangular[4] building on a north-west/south-east axis (Fig. 3.2.23). It sat on the old ground surface (Grogan and Eogan 1987, 391) and may have been contemporary with House A (above). The structural features included the vestiges of a west wall and part of the south-west wall, constructed from a double row of posts, and a slot-trench along the southern side, perhaps used to house a plank-built wall. The estimated length of the building was *c.* 7.5m and its internal width may have been in the region of 5m. Four central post-holes *c.* 2.2m from the southern wall may have held roof-support posts and also created two compartments within the building. A large post-hole adjacent to the inner edge of the slot-trench may also have held a roof-support post. Areas of burning within the house around the line of internal posts and on the eastern side suggest that the house burnt down. While there are no precise details of directly associated finds, fragments of at least four early Neolithic pottery vessels (Class I) came from the area of the house (*ibid.*, 391). Later pottery from around House B comprised Beaker pottery and Bronze Age Class II Ware, indicating post-Neolithic activity.

Central House (Phase 1). This was built later than House A, as an occupation layer of the Phase 1 Central House overlay the post-holes of House A. The structural remains of the Central House were poorly preserved and the main evidence for it was a thin[5] layer of habitation soil, post-holes on the eastern side and a line of large post-pits up to 0.58m deep on the western side (Fig. 3.2.23). The eastern post-holes may have been the vestiges of the eastern perimeter wall. The post-pits on the western side were on a north-east/south-west axis and, as a habitation layer extended to this line of posts, they were interpreted as marking a western perimeter wall (*ibid.*, 413). As these large pits were at a distance of *c.* 2.5m from the eastern wall, it is probable that they were internal features similar to those at House A, Circle L. A cluster of post-/stake-holes occurred near the large pits and there was a single post-hole *c.* 1.9m to the east of the pits. An area of extensive burning was recorded within the Central House, suggesting that the structure burnt down. Neolithic pottery (Class I) was recovered from the burnt area and later Beaker pottery came from a higher level (*ibid.*, 391).

A hearth (Fig. 3.2.23) on the old ground surface to the east of the eastern wall may have been external to the house. The hearth was a circular spread of charcoal and ash that lay between and over large stones. It was interpreted as having been used throughout the early phase of occupation (*ibid.*, 388) and was overlain by a layer of blackish gravelly earth that separated it from the later Bronze Age Phase 2 Central House (Chapter 5).

Finds. The main finds from the pre-enclosure phase at Circle L were pottery, stone tools, stone axeheads, bone points, a collection of stone and bone beads and animal bones. Two radiocarbon

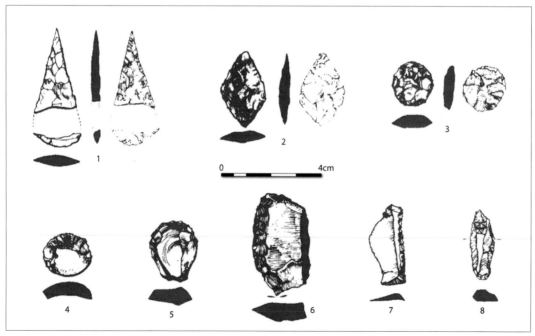

Fig. 3.2.24—Finds from Circle L: 1–2 leaf- and lozenge-shaped arrowheads; 3–5 scrapers; 6–7 knives; 8 blade.

dates[6] were obtained from the first phase of the Central House. Both dates had large standard deviations and, coming from a site where there was intensive later activity, they have limited value for dating the site. As the site archive did not survive well, it is not possible to draw definitive dating evidence from the pottery. The remains of 47 vessels of Class I pottery were recovered, and the forms suggest an early Neolithic date (3800/3700–3500 BC). Fragments of at least seven decorated Neolithic vessels (Class Ia) were also recovered from the primary pre-enclosure phase. These vessels had broad, out-turned rims with broken incised lines along the top of the rim and may also date from *c.* 3800/3700–3500 BC. One large vessel with a rim diameter of 30cm was highly decorated, with scorings within panels, applied vertical lugs and concentric grooving around the vessel. The vessel size and motifs are reminiscent of decoration on pottery usually associated with burials in megalithic cists and known as Linkardstown-type pottery, dated to 3600–3300 BC. These decorated pottery vessels were recovered from the centre of the site (*ibid.*, 400) and, while there was no direct association with the Phase 1 Central House, it may confirm the relative structural sequence and that the Central House post-dated Houses A and B by some years. Some Class II Ware from Circle L was considered to be contemporary with Class I and Ia (*ibid.*, 437). This is unlikely, and most of this later pottery was probably associated with the construction of the enclosure and the Phase 2 Central House. The later pottery may have intruded on earlier levels through various activities on the site, including house construction and pit-digging.

Chert and flint struck stone artefacts from Circle L consisted of three leaf- and lozenge-shaped arrowheads (Fig. 3.2.24: 1–2). There was some evidence of on-site stone tool manufacture, as 28 pieces of waste flint and chert were recovered. Eight complete stone axeheads were also found. There is no surviving information on the original provenance of the stone finds, but leaf- and lozenge-shaped arrowheads are clearly of early Neolithic date (Woodman and Scannell 1993, 60) and are probably associated with the occupation of Houses A and B and the Central House (Phase 1). Twenty-four scrapers were found, including thumbnail (Fig. 3.2.24: 3), round (Fig. 3.2.24: 4) and end scrapers (Fig. 3.2.24: 5). Knives (Fig. 3.2.24: 6–7) and blades (Fig. 3.2.24: 8) were also recovered. Eight complete and five large fragments of stone axeheads were found at Circle L. These were ground and polished and were manufactured from a variety of rock types, including granite, greenstone, tuff, sandstone, andesite and mudstone. There were 24 pieces of bone worked into single-sided points (Fig. 3.2.25: 1–4) and one example in which both ends were pointed (Fig. 3.2.25: 5).

A mixed collection of 26 stone and 21 bone beads from a necklace were found on the old

Fig. 3.2.25—Circle L: 1–5 bone points.

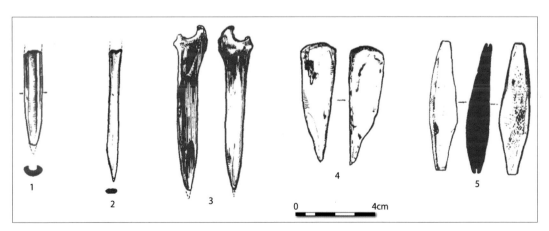

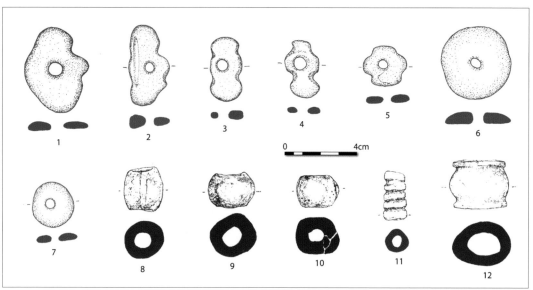

Fig. 3.2.26—Finds from Circle L: 1–7 stone beads; 8–12 bone beads.

ground surface on the east side of Circle L. The stone beads were of siltstone and either had a notched outline (Fig. 3.2.26: 1–5) or were roughly circular (Fig. 3.2.26: 6–7). The bone beads were barrel-shaped (Fig. 3.2.26: 8–10) and highly polished and had been burnt, perhaps to blacken them and make them similar in colour to the stone beads. One other bone bead from Circle L had a long, segmented profile (Fig. 3.2.26: 11), while a second bead had a collar at either end (Fig. 3.2.26: 12). A grey siltstone bead of Neolithic date from Tullahedy (K. Cleary 2011) may provide a broad date range of 3795–3385 BC for the beads from Circle L.

Most of the animal bone assemblage from Circle L had been lost by the time the site report was being prepared for publication (Grogan and Eogan 1987, 436). Fragments of red deer antler tines and some pig and cattle bones remained in the collection from the site.

Site 10

Site 10 was on a level platform on the south-west of Knockadoon Hill (Fig. 3.2.1). The north-eastern area, including part of the enclosing wall and a section of the interior (Fig. 3.2.27), was excavated by Seán P. Ó Ríordáin in 1954 (Grogan and Eogan 1987). The primary occupation phase of Site 10 was a charcoal-rich layer of habitation material that extended under the later enclosing wall and included Neolithic pottery, stone tools and axeheads, and bone points and beads. The excavation recorded seventeen post- and stake-holes on the southern side of the excavated area, and these may be the vestiges of a lean-to building against a rock outcrop (Chapter 5). The relationship of this building to the Neolithic layer is unknown. A similar structure, dated to the Bronze Age, was recorded further to the north on Knockadoon Hill within a Bronze Age enclosure (Cleary 2003). Given the number of finds from the habitation layer, it is possible that an early Neolithic house stood within or close to the Site 10 enclosure in an unexcavated area.

The pottery from Site 10 was primarily Class I ware and fragments of at least 35 vessels were recovered. The pottery form, with simple out-turned or some bulbous rims and angled shouldered profiles, suggests a date for the accumulation of the Neolithic habitation layer in the period 3800/3700–3500 BC. Only three sherds of decorated Neolithic pottery (Class Ia) were recovered.

Fig. 3.2.27—Plan of Site 10, Knockadoon.

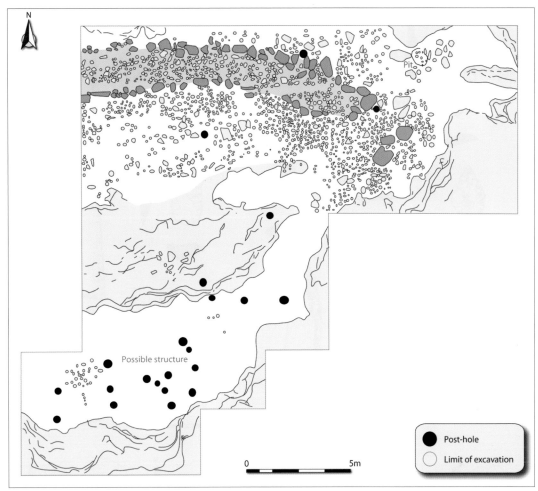

The stone tool assemblage comprised flint and chert artefacts and some waste from on-site knapping. Site 10 had the highest incidence of retouched tools and also the most frequent use of chert in the manufacture of stone tools (Woodman and Scannell 1993, 55). Seventeen flint and chert leaf- and lozenge-shaped arrowheads (Fig. 3.2.28: 1–4) were found in the Neolithic habitation layer, and ten of these were made from good-quality chert (*ibid.*, table 6.2). The layer also produced 40 scrapers, including round (Fig. 3.2.28: 5–6), end (Fig. 3.2.28: 7–8) and side scrapers (Fig. 3.2.28: 9). Knives (Fig. 3.2.28: 10) and blades (Fig. 3.2.28: 11–12) were also recovered. Three complete and five large fragments of polished stone axeheads made from tuffs and greenstone were found in the Neolithic layer. A broken mudstone spearhead (Fig. 3.2.28: 13) had a sharp pointed end. Nineteen stone and thirteen bone beads were also recovered from the layer. The stone beads were made from pebbles (Fig. 3.2.29: 1–5) and were irregularly shaped, with central and off-centre perforations. Eight bone beads were found under the enclosure wall and were all probably part of the same necklace (Fig. 3.2.29: 6–12). Most of the bone beads were segmented (with from two to four segments) or simple oval beads. Bone cylinders from the site show that the bone beads were manufactured at Site 10. Two polished bone points (Fig. 3.2.29: 13–14) from Site 10 may have been used for leather-working.

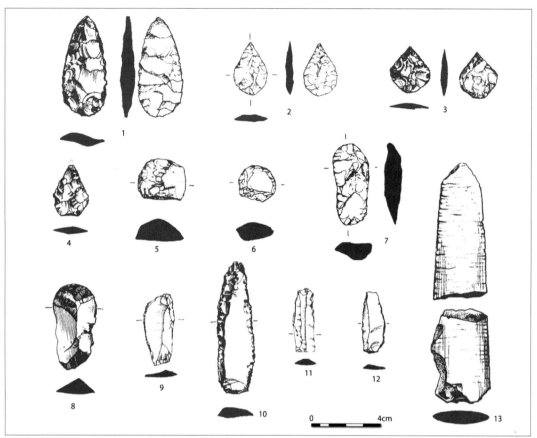

Fig. 3.2.28—Finds from Site 10: 1–4 leaf- and lozenge-shaped arrowheads; 5–9 scrapers; 10 knife; 11–12 blades; 13 fragment of mudstone spearhead.

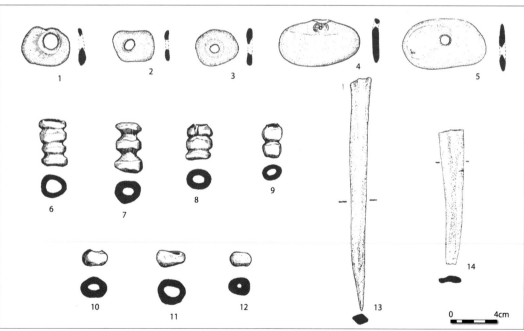

Fig. 3.2.29—Finds from Site 10: 1–5 stone beads; 6–12 bone beads; 13–14 bone points.

Site 12
This was located on the western side of Knockadoon Hill (Fig. 3.2.1) and was excavated by Seán P. Ó Ríordáin in 1954 (Grogan and Eogan 1987). The site was enclosed on the eastern side by a curved wall, which formed a D-shaped enclosure, while the western side was at the top of a cliff. The site was relatively level on the west but sloped upwards towards the east. The excavation was on the western side, with two cuttings extending across the enclosing wall; no plans or site drawings of the excavation survive (*ibid.*, 462). Fragments of six Class I vessels with out-turned rims and angled shoulders were recovered, probably dating from 3800/3700–3500 BC. The stone tools found consisted of one lozenge-shaped and four leaf-shaped arrowheads, scrapers, fragments of six polished stone axeheads and evidence of on-site production of flint and chert tools. Half of a large stone bead with an estimated diameter of *c.* 44mm was also recovered.

Circle J
This site was on a level platform in the centre of Knockadoon Hill (Fig. 3.2.1), with steeply sloping ground to the south, east and west. It was enclosed by a stone wall, similar to Circles K and L, and included a standing stone in the south-east quadrant (Fig. 3.2.30). A second recumbent stone recorded

Fig. 3.2.30—Plan of Circle J, Knockadoon.

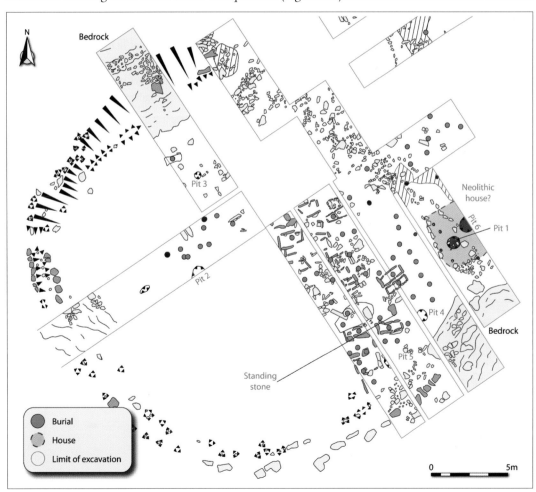

77

on the excavation may have been a fallen standing stone (Grogan and Eogan 1987, 312). The area immediately west of the standing stone and a cist grave possibly also in the south-east quadrant were excavated by Harkness in the 1860s (Harkness 1869, 390). The south-east quadrant, part of the western and northern sides, through the enclosing wall and sections on the north-east side outside the enclosure were excavated by Seán P. Ó Ríordáin in 1946 and 1947. Like Circles K and L, Circle J had a pre-enclosure Neolithic occupation layer and the enclosure wall was subsequently built in the Bronze Age. The site was used as a burial ground, possibly beginning in the late Iron Age and continuing into the early medieval period, when burial orientation was generally east/west (Chapter 8). This later use as a cemetery disturbed most of the earlier activity, but evidence for a Neolithic phase survived under the eastern enclosure wall and as spreads of occupation material inside and outside the enclosing wall.

The Neolithic phase at Circle J comprised two pits (Pits 1 and 6), 0.85–1m in diameter, with adjacent clusters of post-holes and two post-holes to the north of the main group (Fig. 3.2.30) and a 0.1m-thick layer of Neolithic occupation material under the enclosure wall. The post-holes were possibly the remains of a Neolithic house of square or rectangular plan with an estimated width (north-west/south-east) of *c.* 4m. The internal pits may have held roof supports. Two other spreads of Neolithic habitation material were on the north-east outside the enclosure wall. Four pits (Pits 2–5) within the enclosure were recorded on the site plan (Fig. 3.2.30) but few details survive.

The pottery from the Neolithic level at Circle J included fragments of at least five Class I vessels, and the Neolithic stone tools included leaf-shaped arrowheads (Fig. 3.2.31: 1–4), fifteen scrapers, knifes, blades and points, as well as débitage from on-site flint- and chert-working. Five stone axehead fragments were recovered from the Neolithic layer, while four stone axeheads, axehead fragments

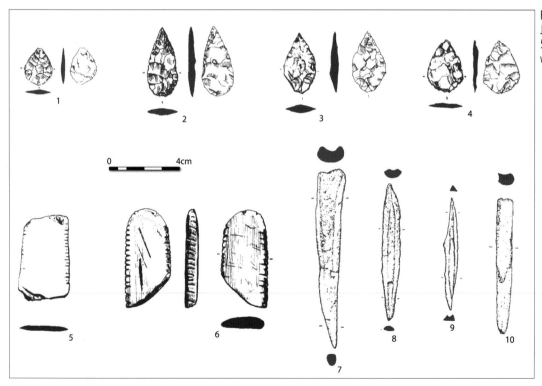

Fig. 3.2.31—Finds from Circle J: 1–4 leaf-shaped arrowheads; 5 stone spearhead (?); 6 string-winder (?); 7–10 bone points.

and several axehead chips were found both inside the enclosure and in the excavated area to the north-east. A sandstone spearhead (Fig. 3.2.31: 5) from within the enclosure had been ground smooth; the edges were sharpened and a series of grooves were cut across them. A similar but thicker stone (Fig. 3.2.31: 6), of siltstone, had a rounded end and deep lateral grooving and may have been used for winding string. Two rounded stones from within the enclosure were interpreted as rubbing stones for use on a saddle quern (Grogan and Eogan 1987, 316). Six mudstone circular beads of *c.* 12mm diameter were found randomly within the enclosure and were probably from the primary Neolithic occupation. Two larger stone beads were *c.* 21mm in length and may have been the centre-piece of a necklace or a pendant. Four bone points (Fig. 3.2.31: 7–10) from within the enclosure were made from split bone and were pointed at one or both ends for use as perforators or some other type of implement.

Middle Neolithic round houses (3500–3000 BC)

Although the dating of Irish Neolithic houses of circular or oval plan is imprecise, the architectural style suggests a middle Neolithic date (Grogan 1996; 2002). Dating of the circular/oval houses excavated at Lough Gur was based on the pottery assemblages and diagnostic stone tools. Construction techniques varied; Houses I and II at Site C were built using double walling similar to Site A, while House III at Site C had a single wall. The house walls were probably of woven wattle around upright posts and may have been plastered with mud or covered with skins. Up to four[7] phases of Neolithic house construction were apparent on Site D, and each house was erected over the footprint of the preceding house. Houses IIa, IIb and IIIa at Site D were built using a combination of structural techniques of plank-built walls set in foundation trenches and post-and-wattle walling. House IIb was built of free-standing posts, presumably with intermediary wattle walling. The walls of Houses IIIb and IIIc were probably made from split oak planks. The reconstruction of a house at Site C envisaged a conical roof (Fig. 3.2.32), possibly supported by upright posts both around the

Fig. 3.2.32—Site C, Knockadoon: reconstruction of round house.

perimeter walls and within the buildings. Similar types of roofs were probably in use at Site D. With the exception of House III, Site C, the houses had internal hearths. Internal hearths were also a feature of the Site D houses.

Site C

Site C lay to the east of Site A, at the southern end of Knockadoon Hill on slightly elevated ground near the old shore line (Fig. 3.2.1). An extensive area of *c.* 604m² (6,500 square feet) was excavated by Seán P. Ó Ríordáin. The initial excavation on the southern side was undertaken in 1940, and the excavated area was extended to the north in 1949. Lines of stones on the surface drew Ó Ríordáin's (1954, 321) attention to the site, but on excavation these were interpreted as later enclosure walls. The depth of soil varied and was deepest at 3½ft (*c.* 1m) on the northern side. A gravel surface in the area excavated in 1940 and on the southern side of the 1949 excavation originated from hill-wash and was a natural accumulation under the modern sod level. A layer of larger stones at the northern end (1949 excavation) had the appearance of deliberately laid cobbling but was also a natural occurrence. These layers (gravel and larger stones) were important in the interpretation of the occupation sequence of Site C, as Ó Ríordáin (1954, 323) considered material below the gravel/stone layer to be no later than the Beaker phase. Food Vessels were found in and under the gravel/stone layer (Ó Ríordáin 1954, 341), which may indicate a date of *c.* 2000 BC for the occurrence of hill-wash across Site C. Artefacts in and above the gravel/stone layer were late Bronze Age, early medieval and later, and derived from both occupation on and intermittent use of Site C. As a consequence, there was inevitably some disturbance of material in earlier occupation strata owing to the digging of pits, trenches and post-holes. Ó Ríordáin argued for continuity of settlement, stating that 'there was no sterile layer, and finds, especially pottery, were forthcoming at all levels' (*ibid.*, 322). The archaeological evidence, however, suggests a main phase of occupation in the middle Neolithic, followed by some late Neolithic (Grooved Ware), Beaker period and Bronze Age site use.

The initial phase of occupation at Site C was middle Neolithic (3600–3000 BC), represented by three houses of circular or oval plan. Apart from structural features related to house construction, prehistoric levels at Site C included numerous pits, randomly scattered post-holes and some trenches (Fig. 3.2.33). The dates of these pits and trenches are unknown and the activity may have extended from Neolithic to Bronze Age times. Pit-digging can be interpreted as intermittent landscape use, whereby temporary settlement was reflected in a number of pits where Neolithic or Bronze Age material, including artefacts and food waste, was buried. Almost 60%[8] of the pottery from the northern end of the Site C excavation (1949) was Class II ware and suggests a Bronze Age date for much of the pit-digging in that area. Pits were more frequent at the northern end of Site C (1949 excavation) and were larger and deeper than those on the south (*ibid.*, 370). Ó Ríordáin described the pits as 10–24in. (0.25–0.61m) deep with sloping sides, and the largest and deepest usually had associated post-holes (*ibid.*, 324). The pits to the east of House III varied from 0.16m to 0.37m in depth. One pit[9] to the east of House III was 0.5m deep and contained burnt soil and ash in the fill. Two pits on the northern side[10] of the excavation were 1.1m deep and one of these contained a child burial (see below). Apart from disposal, some pits may have been used in food preparation, such as the roasting or drying of plant foods, and the evidence for this usually survives as charring of the pit sides. Shallow pits may have been used as pot-stands for the round-based Neolithic pottery. Pits may also have been dug for other reasons that are now unclear.

Fig. 3.2.33—Plan of Site C,
Knockadoon.

Fig. 3.2.34—Site C (1940): House I (from north-east) during excavation.

House I. This was in the centre of the 1940 excavation area (Figs 3.2.33–34). The footprint of the house suggests an internal diameter of *c.* 5.5m and an external diameter of *c.* 7.7m (east/west) by 6.3m (north/south). The walls were constructed using double posts along most of the perimeter, presumably with intermediary wattle walls between the upright posts, and a slot-trench 14ft (4.2m) long on the northern side as a footing for vertical planks. Ó Ríordáin suggested that the wall cavity between the outer and inner wattle walls was filled with some type of organic material, such as rushes or brushwood (*ibid.*, 325). These types of walls were postulated for earlier houses at Site A, Houses 1–2 at Circle K and House B, Circle L. House B at Circle L had a combination of double post-built and vertical planked walls. An inner setting of post-holes at House I, Site C, with a projected diameter of 8ft (2.4m), suggested upright posts that supported the roof. The intermediary space between the wall and the inner post setting varied from *c.* 0.6m to 1.1m, and this may have formed a compartment separated from the central 'living area'. Similar internal divisions of space were recorded at Sites A and B and at Houses A and B, Circle L.

There was no clear evidence for a door in House I, Site C, although stones marked on the site plan (Fig. 3.2.33) suggested a threshold on the southern side. Ó Ríordáin considered that the wider post spacing on the west and south-west may have indicated a south-facing door (*ibid.*, 325). A 0.6m-diameter spread of burned material marked an off-centre hearth within House I. The hearth site had seven small (*c.* 0.1m in diameter and 0.15m deep) stake-holes on the southern side, suggesting a spit or pot-hanger over the fire. Ó Ríordáin interpreted a large kidney-shaped pit, *c.* 2.2m long (north/south) by 1.6m wide (east/west) and 0.6m deep, on the eastern side of the floor area as an internal rubbish pit (*ibid.*).

Fig. 3.2.35—Site C (1940): House II (from south) during excavation.

House II. This was *c*. 7m to the north-west of House I. Paired posts formed most of the wall circumference, and there was a slot-trench for a plank-built wall on the northern and eastern walls (Figs 3.2.33 and 3.2.35). Similar to House I, the upright wall posts probably had intermediary wattle walling and partly plank-built walling. The footprint of the house was oval in plan, with estimated diameters of *c*. 7.6m (north-west/south-east) by 6.5m (north-east/south-west) externally and 5.2m (north-east/south-west) by 6.3m (north-west/south-east) internally. Four large post-holes (Fig. 3.2.33) that were slightly off-centre may have held roof-support posts. Nineteen other post-holes within the floor area of House II did not form any clear pattern. A hearth on the north-west side was off-centre and described as sunken and 6in. (0.15m) deep (*ibid.*, 325).

The entrance may have been on the southern side but the evidence for this was not conclusive, as a 0.3m-deep pit was cut across the possible entrance area. This pit may have been contemporary with or pre- or post-dated the house and was one of a series of three sequential pits on the southern side of the house. Three other pits were recorded (Fig. 3.2.33) within House II: an irregularly shaped pit, *c*. 1.8m long (east/west), on the eastern side, and two pits with maximum diameters of *c*. 1m on the western side. Their function and their relationship to House II is unknown, although Ó Ríordáin considered that they were contemporary with the occupation of the house (*ibid.*, 325).

House III. This house, located immediately north-east of House II, was excavated in 1949. House III was structurally different to Houses I and II in that the perimeter wall was a single line of posts set at irregularly spaced intervals, from 0.2m to 1.5m apart (Figs 3.2.33 and 3.2.36). The posts were described as light, with depths of 0.1–0.2m, but these depths only represent the tips of the posts

Fig. 3.2.36—Site C (1949): House III (from north) during excavation.

where they had been driven into the boulder clay (*ibid.*, 370). House III was roughly circular in plan, with a diameter of 5m. A slightly off-centre large (diameter 0.3m) internal post-hole may have held a roof-support post. Two burnt patches within the house were possible hearth sites.

A yellow clay bank *c.* 4.2m to the north-west of House III was composed of a mixture of redeposited boulder clay, charcoal, organic matter and some unspecified finds (*ibid.*, 369). It sat on a layer of occupation soil and a possible hearth. Ó Ríordáin suggested that the bank was backed by posts and postulated some type of enclosure on the north-west side of House III (*ibid.*), but the evidence for this is not convincing. Concentrations of post-holes were recorded to the north-east of House III but there was no clear pattern, although these may have been the vestiges of a house. Stone 'walls' traversed the area excavated in 1949; these were in the south-west corner, across the yellow clay bank, to the west of House III and on the northern periphery of the excavated area. The walls appeared to have been single courses of stones and it is unlikely that they ever stood to any great height. Some walls were high up in the stratigraphy and unrelated to the Neolithic occupation of the site.

Finds. The 1940 excavation produced a large number of finds, including over 11,000 pottery sherds, and a further 3,500 were recovered in 1949. Ó Ríordáin described the pottery from Site C in detail (*ibid.*, 326–41) but with little reference to where it was found. His summation of the sequence of pottery from the site concluded that Neolithic Classes I and Ia were in contemporary use and found at the earliest levels (*ibid.*, 450). He suggested that where the stratigraphy was best preserved at the northern end (Site C, 1949) Classes I and Ia were sealed by a yellow clay layer (*ibid.*, 372). This yellow

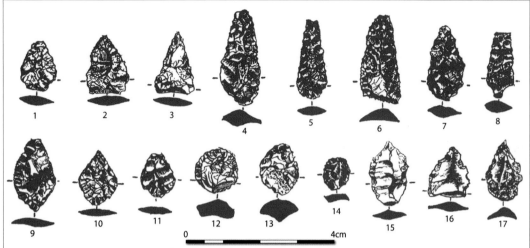

clay layer was intermittent and localised (*ibid.*, pl. XXIV) and may have been upcast from pit-digging. Class I and Class Ia pottery from earlier levels was probably disturbed by later activity and became mixed with Bronze Age Class II pottery.

Apart from Class I and Class Ia pottery, the finds included struck stone tools and polished axeheads. One complete and seven fragments of polished stone axeheads were recovered from Site C in 1940, and a further four complete and eight large fragments of axeheads were found in 1949. The latter were identified as of shale, sandstone and felsite. There was evidence of on-site production of stone artefacts, including flint and chert cores and split pebbles (Woodman and Scannell 1993, table 6.3). Some polished stone axeheads were reused when broken, and chips were removed to make scrapers. Given the size of the area excavated in 1940 and 1949, the number of struck stone tools was not large. Almost 55% were made from flint; there was a high proportion (27%) made from quartz, and the remainder were of chert. Twelve leaf-shaped arrowheads were recovered from Site C (Fig. 3.2.37: 1–11) and these tended to be broad in proportion to their length. There were also *c.* 28 scrapers (Fig. 3.2.37: 12–14), blades and pointed tools (Fig. 3.2.37: 15–17) that may have been perforators. Thirty stone beads from Site C were mostly circular with central perforations. They were identified as being made from chlorite, shale and slate, while one was made from serpentine; chlorite and serpentine are not found in the Lough Gur area and must have been imported, perhaps from the Connemara region, while the slate may have come from County Tipperary. Other stone objects of possible Neolithic date from Site C were two rubbing stones (1940) and seventeen 'hammer-stones' (1949). Some of these spherical stones may have been used with saddle querns to grind corn, while others could have been used to grind and polish axeheads. All of the stones had facets from use.

About 370 bone points, made primarily from the long bones of cattle and sheep and some from pig bones, were found on Site C. The number of bone points is high compared to other sites and indicated on-site specialist craft bone-working. Some bone points were pointed at one end and others at both ends (Fig. 3.2.38: 1–4). Some had been cut diagonally (Fig. 3.2.38: 5–6), some were perforated (Fig. 3.2.38: 7) and some were small (Fig. 3.2.38: 8–9). Mullins (2007) interpreted these artefacts as bone spearheads which were perforated to secure a haft; they may have been used for hunting and fishing. The dating of bone spearheads in Britain and on the Continent indicates a late

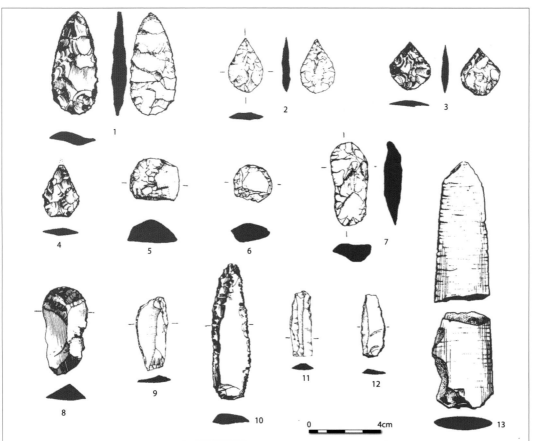

Fig. 3.2.38—Bone points from Site C.

Bronze Age or Iron Age period of use (Mullins 2007, 44). The bone spearheads, like the Class II pottery, suggest a continuity of occupation into the Bronze Age.[11] Five bone beads from Site C (1940) and a further three found in 1949 came from the lower levels on the site and were probably Neolithic in date. They were annular with central perforations. A piece of notched bone from the 1949 excavation may have been raw material used for bead manufacture. A perforated bear claw found in 1940 was possibly used as an amulet or charm. Bear bones may have been found by Neolithic people in a local cave.

Animal bones from Site C (1940) were primarily of cattle (95%), with some pig (4%) and minor quantities of sheep or goat. Dog (or wolf) bones were also recovered, and coprolites (fossilised faeces) found on the site suggested that domestic dogs were kept (Ó Ríordáin 1954, 366). Other bones from Site C were identified as two fragments of red deer antler and bird bones, including wild geese, duck, crane, gulls and barn owl; there are, however, no details on where these were found and they may not be contemporary with the Neolithic settlement. Arrowheads from the site indicated opportunistic hunting, and it is probable that some of these birds were caught and eaten by the inhabitants.

Human bones from Site C consisted of fragments of children's limb bones, some skull fragments and the clavicle or collar-bone of a newborn or unborn child, and adult teeth which may have fallen out. There is no information on where the bones came from, although it is possible that they were from burials that were disturbed by later activity and scattered throughout the site. The Neolithic burial (see below) from the northern end of Site C (1949) and those from around Circle K confirmed that unmarked Neolithic interments took place on Knockadoon Hill.

Site D

This site was in a small, narrow valley east of Site C (Fig. 3.2.1). The architectural style of circular and oval houses suggests a middle Neolithic date (3600–3000 BC), although there are few details on the provenance of the finds. Two post-built houses (Houses II and III) were recognised on the excavation, although Ó Ríordáin (1954, 386–7) suggested that more than one construction phase was evident at both houses and that each may have been rebuilt (Fig. 3.2.39). Bedrock in the area of Site D was close to the surface, and some of the structural posts may have been wedged into bedrock crevices. House I at Site D was rectangular in plan with a stone foundation and was built in the Bronze Age (Chapter 5).

Houses IIa and IIb. House IIa was circular; a later, larger house (House IIb) of oval plan was rebuilt on the same site (Figs 3.2.39–40). The evidence for this two-phase construction was a clay floor on the southern and western sides of the later house that covered some of the post-holes and a foundation trench of House IIa. The foundation of House IIa was a curved slot-trench for a plank-built wall on the western side; the south-west side of this trench was cut into by later pits. The projected arc of House IIa continued across exposed bedrock; structural posts were probably fixed in place into rock crevices and would have been difficult to detect on an excavation. The estimated diameter of House IIa was *c.* 6m.

House IIb (Fig. 3.2.39) was constructed over the footprint of House IIa and built from free-standing posts which formed a roughly oval plan. The estimated dimensions were *c.* 7.5m (north/south) by 5m (east/west). An off-centre internal hearth recorded on the north-east side of the house may have belonged to either House IIa or House IIb. Three large (up to 0.5m) stones or flagstones were on three sides, while a post-hole on the southern side may have held a pot-hanger over the fire. Three post-holes within the footprint of the houses may have held structural roof supports for either House IIa or House IIb. There was no evidence for a door in either house, but this was likely to have been on the southern or western side rather than on the northern or eastern side, where the ground level rose and the bedrock was high.

Houses IIIa–c. Houses IIIa–c were to the south side of House II at a distance of *c.* 2m. At least two houses and possibly a third appear to have been built. It is not possible to determine the stratigraphic sequence based on the published record, but it may be that the smaller circular house (House IIIa) was contemporary with House IIa and was replaced by a larger oval-shaped house (House IIIb) similar to House IIb. House IIIa was circular in plan with an estimated diameter of *c.* 6m (Figs 3.2.39 and 3.2.41). The evidence for a foundation on the northern side was a 1.5m-long slot-trench for a plank-built wall, a line of stones and a feature that Ó Ríordáin (1954, 387) described as a 'step'. This 'step' extended along the northern and western sides of the projected outline of House IIIa and probably marked the line of a more extensive slot-trench. Post-holes on the southern and eastern sides marked upright posts, which probably had intermediary wattle walling plastered with mud.

House IIIb was larger and oval in plan, with estimated diameters of 7.5m (north/south) and 5m (east/west). Its foundation outline was a slot-trench along the eastern and part of the southern

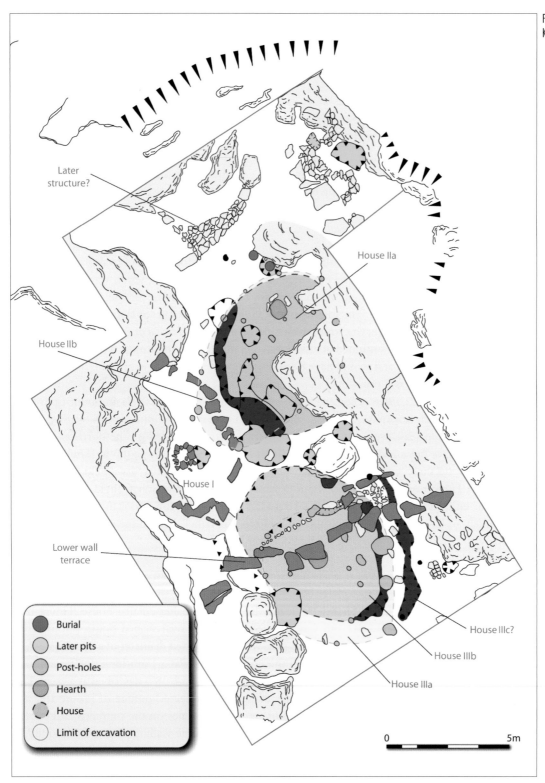

Fig. 3.2.39—Plan of Site D, Knockadoon.

Later structure?

House IIa

House IIb

House I

Lower wall terrace

House IIIc?

House IIIb

House IIIa

Burial
Later pits
Post-holes
Hearth
House
Limit of excavation

0   5m

Fig. 3.2.40—Site D: House II
(from south-west) during
excavation.

Fig. 3.2.41—Site D: House III
(from south) during excavation.

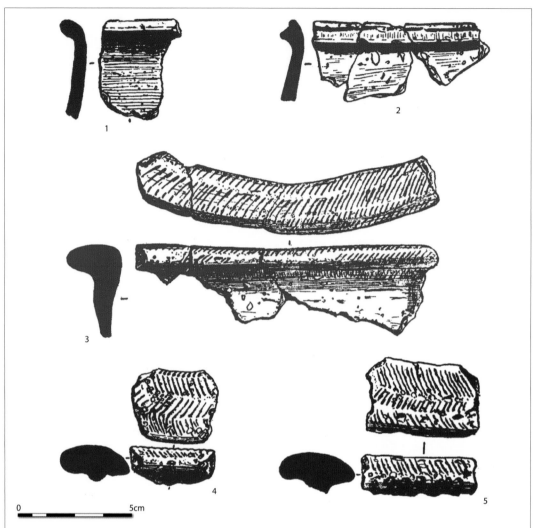

Fig. 3.2.42—Finds from Site D: 1–2 Class I pottery; 3–5 Class Ia pottery.

0   5cm

sides; a 'step' in the ground level on the northern side was also likely to have been part of the slot-trench (Fig. 3.2.39). Large post-holes within the slot-trench on the eastern side marked upright posts. On the southern side the trench terminated at a post-hole, possibly indicating a door-jamb for a south-facing entrance. A third slot-trench (Fig. 3.2.39) was cut *c.* 0.5–0.7m from the eastern perimeter of House IIIb and may represent the remains of a third house (House IIIc) or a rebuilding of the eastern side of House IIIb. It varied in width, with a maximum of 0.5m; no depths are recorded. A post-hole at the terminus on the southern side may have held a door-jamb for a south-facing door. A centrally placed hearth was recorded within the footprint of Houses IIIa and IIIb. Ó Ríordáin (1954, 387) described the hearth as a heavily burnt area, suggesting longevity of use whereby the hearth was in continuous use in two sequential houses. Five post-holes (Fig. 3.2.39) within the floor area of Houses IIIa and IIIb may have marked the locations of structural roof-support uprights in either house.

Over 4,000 pottery fragments, including a large quantity of Beaker ware, were recovered from

Site D. Class I and Class Ia pottery was recorded at the lowest levels and was associated with Houses II and III. Class I pottery was similar to the Site C pottery and had mostly out-turned rims (Fig. 3.2.42: 1–2); some vessels had lugs or handles at the shoulders. The Class Ia pottery had wide, out-turned rims with incised short lines or lines in a herringbone pattern across the rims (Fig. 3.2.42: 3–5). Parts of small, cup-like vessels comparable to pottery from Site C were also found and these were probably Neolithic in date.

Two complete polished stone axeheads and fragments of another three as well as over 70 small fragments and chips of axeheads were recovered from the lowest levels at Site D and were probably used by the inhabitants of Houses IIa–b and IIIa–c. At least two axeheads were of porcellanite from the axe factories at Tievebulliagh, Co. Antrim, or Rathlin Island, off the Antrim coast. The rock types used in other axeheads from Site D were close- and medium-grained volcanic rocks and a rock type referred to as 'greenstone', which was sourced from the axe factory at Great Langdale in Cumbria.

Fig. 3.2.43—Finds from Site D: 1–5 leaf- and lozenge-shaped arrowheads; 6–7 scrapers.

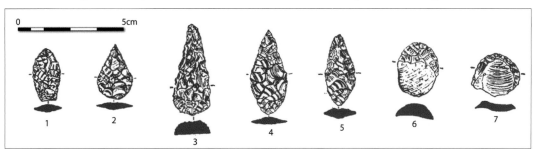

Two flint and six chert finely finished leaf- and lozenge-shaped arrowheads (Fig. 3.2.43: 1–5) were found at Site D, as well as scrapers (Fig. 3.2.43: 6–7), blades and points. There was also evidence of on-site flint, chert and quartz stone tool manufacture, as flakes, cores and split pebbles were recovered. Two rubbing stones that may have been used to grind corn on a saddle quern or to polish stone axeheads were found at Site D, but the association with middle Neolithic settlement was not confirmed. Thirty stone beads were also recovered and found at all levels, although the majority occurred in the lower strata. Some beads were circular or irregularly shaped with central perforations, while others had notches similar to those from Circle L. The beads from Site D were made of serpentine and chlorite schist, rock types that were probably sourced in Connemara, as well as of grey-blue slate from County Tipperary. One bead was made from fluorspar, which is found in the limestone around Lough Gur.

Twenty-one bone points from Site D were similar to those from Site C. Eleven bone beads were also found and were mostly circular (Fig. 3.2.44: 1). A notched bone (Fig. 3.2.44: 2) showed how bone was cut through to make beads, and an unfinished bead indicated on-site bone-working. Grooves were cut around the bone and it was then easy to break off segments for beads, which were subsequently polished. There was also evidence of antler-working; one antler from the site had a circular hole cut through it, and Ó Ríordáin (1954, 409) considered that this could have been used as some type of pick (Fig. 3.2.44: 3).

Residual Neolithic material on later sites

Evidence of some Neolithic activity was found on sites where the main phase of occupation was of a later date. Neolithic pottery and stone tools confirm some occupation, although there was little tangible evidence of any prolonged settlement. Eighteen sherds of Class I pottery and a Neolithic

Fig. 3.2.44—Finds from Site D: 1 bone bead; 2 notched bone; 3 antler pick (?).

leaf-shaped arrowhead were found in a Bronze Age enclosure on Knockadoon Hill (Cleary 2003). A Neolithic habitation layer, pit and hearth underlay the floor of a seventeenth-century house at Site J, Knockadoon (Ó Ríordáin and Ó Danachair 1947, 43); 150 sherds of Neolithic pottery (Classes I and Ia and a small cup-like vessel), four stone axeheads, a scraper made from a stone axehead chip and quartz microliths were recovered from the pit fill and the habitation layer. Neolithic finds were also recovered *ex situ* from the walls of and within the seventeenth-century house.

Excavations of small hut-like structures on plateaux above the shore line (Sites E–H) and in the north/south valley (Site I) on Knockadoon produced evidence of Neolithic activity pre-dating the huts. A chert leaf-shaped arrowhead and a fragment of a small, cup-like Neolithic vessel were recovered from a 'floor' which extended outside the stone foundations of the hut at Site E (Ó Ríordáin 1954, 414). The hut at Site F was built in the early medieval period (Chapter 8) and the site also had evidence of Bronze Age metal-working (Chapter 5). A layer near the stone hut contained fragments of Class I pottery, two stone axehead fragments, a leaf-shaped arrowhead, flint blades and waste from flint- and chert-working. A small (63mm long) perforated stone axehead pendant was an unusual find, and Ó Ríordáin compared it to similar pendants used as charms in Europe and the Mediterranean regions in the late Neolithic (*ibid.*, 423). A leaf-shaped arrowhead, an axehead chip, a bone bead and 120 sherds of Class I pottery were found in a clay layer which pre-dated a Bronze Age hut at Site H. Class I pottery was recovered from a hearth and an adjacent pit at Site I, and other fragments of Class I pottery were found scattered around later stone walls. Other Neolithic artefacts from Site I included two axehead fragments, two leaf-shaped arrowheads, waste from flint- and chert-working and two chlorite stone beads, similar to those found on other Neolithic sites on Knockadoon.

Class I pottery was found during excavation at the wedge tomb and was residual from earlier use of the site (Ó Ríordáin and Ó h-Iceadha 1955). Excavations at Carraig Aille and the Spectacles also uncovered some Neolithic finds, which were evidence of site occupation prior to the main early medieval settlement phase. These finds consisted of 25 sherds of Neolithic pottery and one stone axehead fragment from the Spectacles, eight stone axeheads from Carraig Aille II and six stone axeheads from Carraig Aille I (Ó Ríordáin 1949b, 86, 100, 106). Some axeheads from these sites had been reused as whetstones in the early medieval period, and some may have been collected from elsewhere around Lough Gur for sharpening metal tools (Chapter 8). A chert arrowhead was found in a clay layer around the hut excavated at Grange ringfort (Ó Ríordáin 1949a, 133). A polished greenstone axehead was recovered at a depth of 1m in the bottom of a pit outside the north-west corner of the medieval House I at Caherguillamore (Ó Ríordáin and Hunt 1942, fig. 6: I.3). A chert scraper and a piece of worked flint were found around House II at Caherguillamore.

Barrows of probable Bronze Age date were excavated at Rathjordan, Cahercorney and Ballingoola, and Neolithic, Beaker and Bronze Age phases were recorded on some sites. A broken undecorated Neolithic pottery vessel dating from *c.* 3800–3500 BC was recovered from the base of a slightly off-centre pit at Barrow 1, Rathjordan (Ó Ríordáin 1947a). The pottery had a rim diameter of *c.* 20cm and a height of *c.* 17cm; it had perforations below the rim and was comparable to pottery from Neolithic house sites on Knockadoon Hill. One sherd of undecorated Neolithic pottery was found in the central pit at Barrow 2, Rathjordan (Ó Ríordáin 1948, 21). Twenty-two sherds of Neolithic pottery were also recovered from Barrow 2, but the published account contains no details of their provenance. The form of the rim sherds and one decorated example confirm an early–middle Neolithic date (*c.* 3800–3500 BC). A chert scraper, one large axehead and two fragments of deliberately broken axeheads of greenstone were also found at Barrow 2, and flint and chert débitage showed on-site manufacture of stone tools. Neolithic pottery was also found at Barrow 3, Rathjordan. Neolithic pottery and stone axehead chips were found on an extensive stony surface near Barrow 2 at Ballingoola (MacDermott 1949a). Finds from the excavation of a barrow at Cahercorney comprised a polished greenstone axehead fragment, an unfinished chert arrowhead and one sherd of undecorated Neolithic pottery in the barrow mound (MacDermott 1949b).

3.3: NEOLITHIC BURIAL

County Limerick has seven extant megalithic tombs (de Valera and Ó Nualláin 1982, xvii) and of these only the wedge tomb (Giant's Grave) at Lough Gur has been excavated (Ó Ríordáin and Ó h-Iceadha 1955). The remaining tombs are dated on morphological grounds and, with the exception of a passage tomb at Duntryleague near Galbally, most appear to be of the wedge tomb type and belong to the period 2500–2000 BC (Chapter 4).

A monument[12] west of the Grange stone circle complex, marked as a 'Stone Avenue' on the 1902 and 1924 revisions of the Ordnance Survey mapping, may be the vestiges of the kerb of a court tomb (Figs 3.3.1–2). The orientation (north-west/south-east), siting and altitude of the monument show similarities with court tombs that date from *c.* 3800–3500 BC (Cooney and Grogan 1994; Schulting *et al.* 2011). Dowd (1896) and Harkness (1869) suggested that the stones were part of Stone Circle D but this is not the case, as indicated by recent geophysical survey at the Grange stone circle complex (Cleary and Hogan 2013; O'Driscoll and Cleary 2016). The site was designated 'Site E' by Windle (1912), and he and Lynch (1895) described the stone setting as 'an avenue'. Lynch believed that the 'avenue' led to a stone circle in the same field.[13] Ó Ríordáin (1951, 39) described Site E as two lines of stones converging towards the north-west and suggested that these were the

Fig. 3.3.1—Site E, Grange.

Fig. 3.3.2—Site E, Grange
(after Windle 1912).

'kerb of a megalithic tomb of long barrow or long cairn type. A single stone between the lines may be a portion of a chamber, while the position of two stones at the south-eastern end of one of the lines suggests the curved façade of a forecourt.'

The northern row of three stones is 6.5m long, and the southern row of twelve stones is 23m long (Ó Nualláin and Cody 1996). The distances between the stones are 7.3–8.3m and there is one extant intermediary stone on the north-west end. The stones vary from 0.35m to 1.16m in height, the largest being Stone 4 on the western side (Fig. 3.3.2).

Unprotected burials on Knockadoon Hill

One Neolithic burial was found on the northern slope (Cleary 1995) and fifteen were recorded from the excavations of Neolithic houses (Ó Ríordáin 1954; Grogan and Eogan 1987). The burials were unprotected, in shallow graves, and contrast with burials in megalithic tombs. Ó Ríordáin (1954, 371) was of the view that the pit in which an adolescent was buried north of House III on Site C (1949) was originally dug for some other purpose but this may not have been the case. All the other graves were pits that were backfilled once the interment had taken place. Two burials outside House 1 at Circle K were covered by stones, but otherwise the graves were just filled with soil. Dating evidence for these unprotected burials centres on c. 3600 BC (Brindley and Lanting 1989–90, 3). A radiocarbon date of 3641–3372 BC from one child burial (Cleary 1995, 40) and an associated Class Ia pottery vessel from an adolescent burial at Site C confirmed early/middle Neolithic dates for the burials. The remaining burials are dated by association with early Neolithic houses on Knockadoon; Burial 2 at Circle K pre-dated the erection of House 1 but the time interval may not have been significant. At Circle K, six burials were recorded within House 1 and a further two within House 2.

The reason for burying the dead within the house may have stemmed from a socio-religious belief. Children and females are linked to the home, and interment within the house may have provided a connection or continuity between the dead and the house. Three burials were associated with pottery vessels; the adolescent in the pit at Site C was buried with a complete pot, while fragments of pottery were recovered from Burial 1 at Site D (Ó Ríordáin 1954) and from the child's grave on the northern slope (Cleary 1995). Pottery is linked to food and nourishment and perhaps provided a further tie to the home. Burials 1 and 6 from House 2 at Circle K had necklaces placed with the children's remains, suggesting affection and perhaps privilege.

The burials on Knockadoon were in the main those of infants or children, and the age at death of the majority ranged from newborn to fourteen years. One burial from House 1, Circle K, was that of a woman who was pregnant with a full-term foetus and she may have died in childbirth. Three children were buried close to the woman, and the proximity suggests a familial group. Except for two burials outside House 2 at Circle K, which were laid north/south, the bodies were mostly aligned east/west; this raises the possibility that the alignment of the bodies in the graves was significant and possibly dictated by the rising and setting sun.

Knockadoon Hill (northern slope)

A burial excavated on a narrow plateau on the northern slope of Knockadoon Hill was in a shallow pit measuring 1.05m by 0.77m and 0.13m deep (Cleary 1995). The soil at the base of the pit showed evidence of burning, and the grave may have been purified by fire before the body was placed in it. The body was that of a child aged 6–8 years, in a flexed position with the legs drawn up to the chest and the arms across the chest. Defects in the teeth showed that the child had been ill in the two years prior to death (Ó Donnabháin 1995). Finds from the grave included a greenstone axehead chip near the child's skull, fragments of Class I pottery and flint flakes. A radiocarbon date of 3641–3372 BC was obtained from charcoal in the fill of the grave.

Circle K

Six burials were recorded in the environs of House 1, Circle K. Burial 1 was found in the upper level of the habitation soil within House 1 and at the base of an upright stone forming the later enclosure around Circle K. The burial may have been in a pit, but this was not detected on the excavation and the construction of the later enclosure probably disturbed the grave. Only parts of the skeleton were recovered and were those of a child aged 1–2 years at the time of death. The child had a necklace comprised of a slate pendant (Fig. 3.3.3: 1) and six bone beads (Fig. 3.3.3: 2–7). Burial 2 was below a gravel patch that formed part of the floor of House 1. A structural post of House 1 was driven into the burial pit, indicating that the burial pre-dated the house. Burial 2 was of a young woman who may have died during childbirth. She had been placed in the grave in a flexed position, with her head on the north-east side, the knees drawn up near the chin and her right hand under her body. The unborn child, nearing full term, was in her pelvis. Bones of a child aged about two years were also found in the grave. Burial 3 was of a child aged 3–6 years but probably closer to three years. It lay on a flat limestone slab, against which the feet of the woman (Burial 2) were also laid. Burial 3 was adjacent to the outer ring of the enclosure wall of Circle K and may have been disturbed when the wall was erected. Burial 4 was on a flat slab and at a right angle to Burial 3. The skeleton was of a child aged about three years. Children's teeth from within the enclosure wall of Circle K were from a 3–6-year-old and may have been from Burial 4. Some teeth from a child aged 11–13 were also recovered, and these may have come from a burial that was destroyed during the construction of the Circle K enclosure wall. Burial 5 was within the floor area of House 1, but there was no evidence to establish whether the burial pre-dated, was contemporary with or was later than the house. The burial was in a natural hollow and was of a newborn or child in its first year of life.

Burials 6 and 7 were within the Circle K enclosure between House 2 and a cave. Burial 6 was near the southern edge of a hollow, and the anatomical and dental reports show that the grave contained at least two bodies. The skeletons were aligned north/south and were covered by closely spaced angular stones, sealed by a 0.5m-thick layer of dark habitation material. The skull and jaw of one individual had been crushed by the overlying stones, and some of the teeth lay amongst the stones. The remains consisted of a large number of skull fragments, ribs and fragments of the backbone of a young person. Twelve green-black siltstone stone beads came from immediately above and to the south of the burials. Burial 7 was found in a shallow pit immediately outside the north-east wall of House 2. The skeleton, of a newborn or almost full-term unborn child, was aligned north-

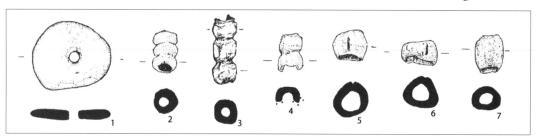

Fig. 3.3.3—Finds from Circle K: 1 pendant; 2–7 bone beads.

east/south-west, extended on its back with the head turned slightly to the left.

Burials 8 and 9 came from the floor of House 2. Burial 8 was of a young child, possibly newborn or in the early part of the first year of life, and was in a shallow pit near the north-eastern wall. The body was aligned east/west with the head towards the west, turned slightly to the left, and was lying on its back, with the arms by the sides and legs extended close together. The crushed skull rested against a rectangular limestone block but the burial was otherwise undisturbed. Burial 9 was of a child aged between newborn and about four months old and was in a shallow pit; the grave was disturbed, and the lower limbs and pelvis were separated from the upper part of the body. The burial was aligned north-west/south-east, with the head to the north-west and turned to the right; the body lay on its back, with the skull against a rock outcrop on the western side of the house. Small fragments of burnt animal bone and charcoal were found over the body.

Site C

The pit burial at Site C was uncovered at the northern end of the area excavated in 1949 (Ó Ríordáin 1954, 371–2). Ó Ríordáin considered that the burial of human remains was a secondary reuse of the pit, although there was no clear evidence presented for this interpretation and it may be that the pit was intended for burial. The sequence as proposed by Ó Ríordáin was that a 1m-deep pit was dug and while it was still open a hollow was made in the bottom (*ibid.*, 371). The burial was placed within the hollow and an intact Class Ia vessel with a decorated rim was placed on the west side near the head (Fig. 3.3.4). The pit was then partly filled with large stones and clay near the base and over the

Fig. 3.3.4—Site C (1949): burial with Neolithic pot adjacent to head.

burial, and subsequently with soil that included occupation material from the nearby settlement.

The burial was of a youth aged about fourteen years; the body was placed into the pit on its left side and the legs were drawn up close to the body in a tightly flexed crouched position. The right upper arm lay along the body, while the forearm was near the legs. The left arm was across the body with the hand in front of the face. Dating of the interment is based on the associated Class Ia pot, which may be early Neolithic (3750–3600 BC) or slightly later but probably before *c*. 3500 BC.

Site D

Two burials were found to the north-east of House II. Burial 1 was at the base of a pit, 23in. (0.58m) deep and partly in a cavity of the overhanging rock. The body of a child of 4–5 years of age lay on its right side, with the face turned towards the rock, the legs flexed, the arms close to the chest and the hands by the chin. The bones of the lower limbs were poorly preserved. The grave was subsequently infilled with dark soil, animal bones, fragments of Class I pottery, greenstone axehead chips and flints; this infill may have come from occupation debris from the nearby houses.

The head of Burial 2 lay directly on bedrock, while the torso and lower limbs were on the ground and covered by rubble. The bones were those of a child aged 5–5½ years. The body was aligned east/west and lay on its right side in a flexed position; the lower part was in poor condition. Other fragments of human bone collected during the excavation of Site D were identified as nineteen skull fragments and a clavicle (collar-bone) fragment. Details of the find-spots of the bones are unknown, but they were probably from disturbed burials as there was no evidence of the burial pits in the excavated area.

Caherguillamore

A Neolithic burial site on the eastern side of the old avenue to Caherguillamore House was discovered in 1948 during preparatory works for blasting for road-metal and was reported to John Hunt and Seán P. Ó Ríordáin (Hunt 1967). The site comprised a crouched burial adjacent to the rock face, a burial chamber sealed by a large rock against the rock face and a pottery vessel on a rock ledge above the burial chamber (Fig. 3.3.5). The crouched burial[14] was near the top of an earthen bank, and a round-bottomed bowl (Fig. 3.3.6) had been placed in the grave near the head of the body. The pottery type finds parallels among vessels found in megalithic cist graves known as 'Linkardstown-type' and dated to *c*. 3525–3350 BC (Brindley and Lanting 1989–90, 4). A stone axehead fragment was also found in the grave.

The burial chamber to the north of the crouched burial was formed by a large, naturally occurring boulder which rested against the rock face (Fig. 3.3.6), closing off a space in front of it. This space was opportunistically used to create a tomb in which at least fourteen individuals were interred. Hunt (1967, 20) argued that the earthen bank in which the crouched burial lay sealed the entrance to the burial chamber and that the crouched burial was therefore later than the burials within the chamber. The burial chamber was irregular in shape, 1.37–1.83m wide at the base (ground surface), and the entrance on the south side sloped into the chamber. The chamber had been deepened in antiquity to house the burials. There appeared to have been no stratification within the chamber and it 'was filled to within a foot [0.3m] of the apex with a dry and porous mixture of bones and pieces of broken limestone' (Hunt 1967, 22). The human bones were identified as being from at least eleven adults, one child and two infants. The anatomical study identified four females, four males and three adults whose sex was not determinable within the assemblage. The age at death

Fig. 3.3.5—Caherguillamore: plan and section of burial.

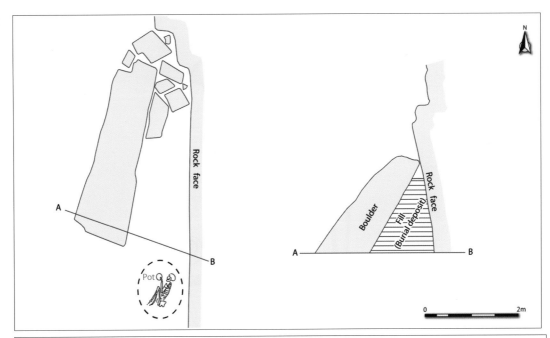

Fig. 3.3.6—Finds from Caherguillamore: Carrowkeel Ware (left) from crouched burial; Linkardstown-type pottery (right) from burial chamber.

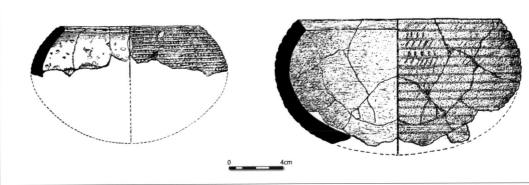

for adults ranged from 25 to 50 years and adolescents were aged at 12–18 years, with one child aged one year and one aged 8–9 years. Measurements of one adult femur gave an estimated height for that individual of 5ft 4in. (1.73m). There was marked wear on the teeth, probably from eating cereals ground with quernstones, whereby grit became incorporated in the food.

Most of the small finds came from the base of the chamber fill and comprised pottery fragments, seven bone pin fragments, four stone beads and some animal bones. The pottery from the burial chamber consisted of a sherd of Class I ware, sherds of Linkardstown-type pottery and a round-bottomed bowl identified as Carrowkeel Ware (Fig. 3.3.6). Carrowkeel Ware is frequently found in passage tombs and is dated to *c.* 3200–2900 BC. Other finds from the chamber were polished bone points (Fig. 3.3.7: 1–2), mushroom-headed bone pins (Fig. 3.3.7: 3–4) and beads of stone (Fig. 3.3.7: 5–6) and shell (Fig. 3.3.7: 7–8). Mushroom-headed pins are a recurrent find from passage tombs and are often found with Carrowkeel pottery. The stone beads were similar to those found on Knockadoon (see above). The shell beads were made from saltwater clam[15] shells, which must have been sourced on the coast.

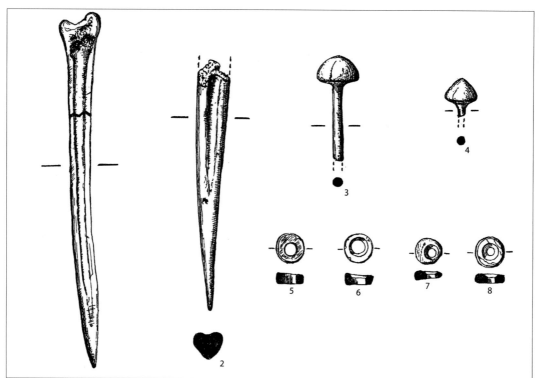

Fig. 3.3.7—Finds from Caherguillamore: 1–2 bone pins; 3–4 mushroom-headed pins; 5–6 stone beads; 7–8 shell beads.

Beaker pottery dated to *c.* 2500–2200 BC was found on the rock ledge above the burial chamber. The pottery was exposed rather than buried below the surface, and Hunt (1967, 22) considered that it had lain undisturbed on the rock for several thousand years. The pottery appears to be unweathered and was unlikely to have survived in good condition over time; it was probably *ex situ*, perhaps unearthed when the area was being prepared for rock-blasting. A second Beaker vessel was recorded from the burial chamber but its provenance is unknown and it may have been an intrusive find from later activity at the site.

NOTES

[1] After the last glacial period, the early Holocene began around 10,000 BC; initially the climate was drier but by about 6000 BC it had become wetter and similar to that of today (Woodman 2015, 22).

[2] The site archive (card index) for finds from Site L has been lost (Grogan and Eogan 1987, 391).

[3] This house was interpreted as being oval or circular in plan (Grogan and Eogan 1987, 388), but the published plan suggests a rectangular structure.

[4] This house was interpreted as subrectangular or circular in plan (Grogan and Eogan 1987, 391), but the published plan suggests a rectangular structure.

[5] This was described as 40cm thick in the published report (Grogan and Eogan 1987, 413) but this is unlikely, given the light soil cover on Knockadoon Hill.

[6] These dates were 4690 ± 240 BP and 4410 ± 240 BP (Grogan and Eogan 1987, 437), which

calibrate (at 95% probability) to 4037–2875 BC and 3662–2468 BC respectively.

7   A Bronze Age house was also recorded at Site D (Chapter 5).

8   Two thousand sherds out of an assemblage of 3,600 sherds were identified as Class II ware (Ó Ríordáin 1954, 375).

9   In Square 16.

10   Squares 23 and 24.

11   Bone spearheads were also recovered at the early medieval sites at Carraig Aille (Chapter 8) but they may have been residual from early occupation on the site.

12   RMP LI 032-003.

13   This site was marked on the 1925 edition of the map as 'Stone Circle (*Site of*)'.

14   A detailed anatomical report on the skeletal remains was published (Hunt 1967, 36–42) but this did not separate the crouched burial from the burials within the adjacent chamber.

15   Possibly *Venus striatula* and *Venus verrucosa* L. The marine habitat of these clams is at depths of 5–20m, although the shells were probably washed up on the shore and collected as a curiosity.

4. Late Neolithic Grooved Ware, Chalcolithic and early Bronze Age

The period 3000–2000 BC saw significant cultural changes, beginning with the introduction of new pottery styles known as 'Grooved Ware', along with new types of ceremonial sites and presumably new beliefs, spanning about 500 years. The Grooved Ware period was followed by the Beaker Culture (2500–2100 BC), which marked the introduction of the knowledge of copper-working and changes in pottery types, and perhaps changes in society and spiritual practices. A new type of megalithic tomb, known as the 'wedge tomb', was constructed towards the end of the millennium. The technology of metal-working changed about 2100 BC and bronze production became the norm. Excavations at Lough Gur have recorded evidence of Grooved Ware period cultures at Grange, Knockadoon Hill and Geroid Island (Fig. 4.1.1). Beaker remains were found on Knockadoon Hill, at the wedge tomb known as the 'Giant's Grave', at barrow sites at Rathjordan, Cahercorney and Ballingoola, and at a burial site in Caherguillamore.

Evidence from the pollen record suggests that farming activity in the later Neolithic (3000–2500 BC) was well established at Lough Gur (Molloy 2008, 29). Elsewhere in east Limerick/west Tipperary some woodland regeneration has been recorded, with a decline in grassland weeds during the period *c.* 3530–2580 BC. These changes may mark a time when pastoralism expanded and agriculture decreased (*ibid.*).

4.1: GROOVED WARE CULTURE

The Grooved Ware culture (3000–2500 BC) appears to have developed in the Orkney Islands off the north-west coast of Scotland, from where it spread to southern Britain and Ireland. Links between Ireland, Scotland and southern Britain were probably maintained by long-distance travel and by the transfer of ideas as well as goods across the Irish Sea. The impetus for the development of a new culture is unknown. New large, open-air enclosures were constructed, interpreted as places of assembly connected to prehistoric rituals. There is some evidence of feasting, and new types of pottery vessels may have been linked to the consumption of special foods. The culture is recognised by the presence of flat-based bucket- or bowl-shaped vessels, which in the early stages (*c.* 3000 BC) were decorated with incised motifs but became plainer towards the end of the period (*c.* 2500 BC). Grooved Ware pottery was recovered from under and within the bank and in the interior of the Great Stone Circle (B) and on Site H, Knockadoon (Ó Ríordáin 1954), and Geroid Island (Liversage 1958).

Other artefacts from the culture include oblique flint arrowheads (*petit tranchet* derivatives [PTD]) and discoidal polished knives. Stone maceheads with a perforation for a handle are found on Grooved Ware sites in both Ireland and Scotland. An ornate example from the Knowth passage

Fig. 4.1.1—Location map, showing Grange Stone Circle complex, megalithic tomb (Giant's Grave, Killalough), *Leaba na Muice* and Garret Island.

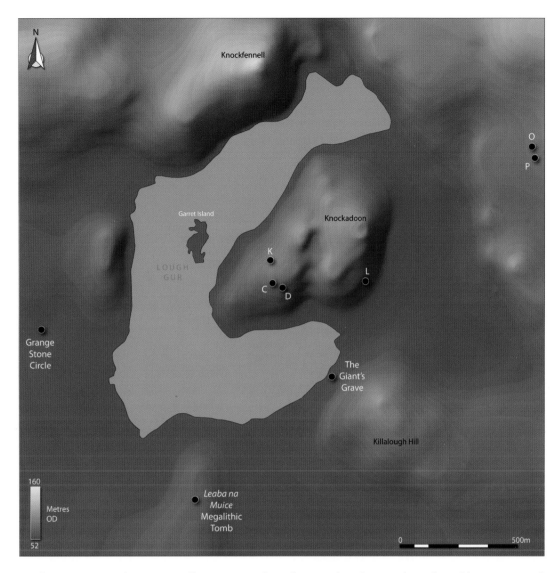

tomb cemetery in the Boyne Valley, Co. Meath, is decorated with carved spirals and lozenge motifs similar to maceheads and Grooved Ware pottery from the Orkney Islands. Two undecorated maceheads were found at Lough Gur; one was a stray find and the other was from the excavation of Site C, Knockadoon (Ó Ríordáin 1954, 343–5; Simpson 1988, 28).

By 3000 BC megalithic tombs, including portal tombs and court tombs, were no longer being constructed; the building of passage tombs was on the wane but probably overlapped with the introduction of Grooved Ware cultures. New monument types, including timber circles and earthen enclosures known as 'henges', replaced megalithic tombs as centres of assembly and ritual. The timber circles leave no surface trace on the landscape and are only discovered through archaeological investigation. Henge monuments are traceable on the landscape as circular or oval earthen banks and in some areas, such as the Boyne Valley, Co. Meath, can be up to 275m in diameter (Stout 1991, 247). The henges in County Limerick are smaller, although some are up to 100m in diameter.

Grange monument complex

The Grange area of Lough Gur was a microcosm of activity in the late Neolithic. The monuments are mainly located in a prominent position on the crest of a low ridge that rises from Lough Gur on the east and slopes downwards to a stream valley on the west (Fig. 4.1.2). This cluster of henges, embanked stone circles, stone circles and megalithic tombs suggests an extraordinary prehistoric landscape linked to congregation and ritual. Geophysical survey work in the environs of the upstanding monuments also recorded a number of low-visibility and subsurface archaeological sites, confirming a hitherto-unknown monument density at Grange (Cleary and Hogan 2013; O'Driscoll and Cleary 2016).

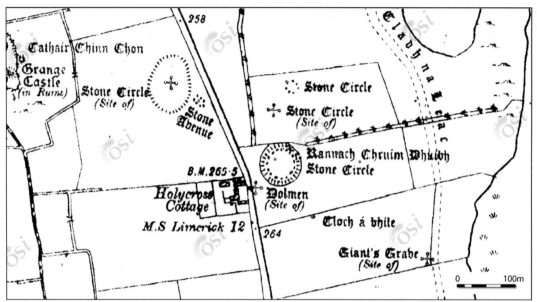

Fig. 4.1.2—The Grange Stone Circle complex.

The 'Great Stone Circle' (B[1]) is now the most prominent archaeological site at Grange. Adjacent monuments include Circles C and D and a large earthen embanked enclosure[2] to the north-west (Fig. 4.1.2). Circle C (Figs 4.1.3–4), comprised of fifteen stones, has a maximum internal diameter of 17m. The stones are set into a low external earthen bank and there is a low internal mound. Circle D, 10m north of the Great Stone Circle (B), is a largely levelled stone circle with nine extant orthostats on its north-western arc (Fig. 4.1.3). Windle (1912) recorded twelve stones at Circle D in the early part of the twentieth century. The Ordnance Survey letters (O'Donovan 1840) indicate that the majority of the orthostats were approximately 0.9m in height and that a number of outlying stones were originally present. Geophysical survey at Circle D showed a levelled embankment around it and a stone circle diameter of 78m, which was larger than that of Circle B (Fig. 4.1.3). A circle of pits within Circle D, reminiscent of a Grooved Ware timber circle, was detected by geophysical survey but this interpretation needs to be verified by archaeological investigation (O'Driscoll and Cleary 2016).

The earthen embanked enclosure to the north-west of Circles B and D was represented on the 1927 Ordnance Survey map by hachuring and marked as 'Stone Circle (site of)'. The site was also clearly visible as a large bowl-shaped or concave earthwork on the Bruff aerial survey (Doody 2008). A geophysical survey of the enclosure mapped a C-shaped earthwork measuring 102m by 85m, and the bank was 0.4–1.5m higher than the centre of the earthwork (Cleary and Hogan 2013). The absence of a ditch appears to corroborate Ó Nualláin and Cody's (1996) interpretation of the site as a henge

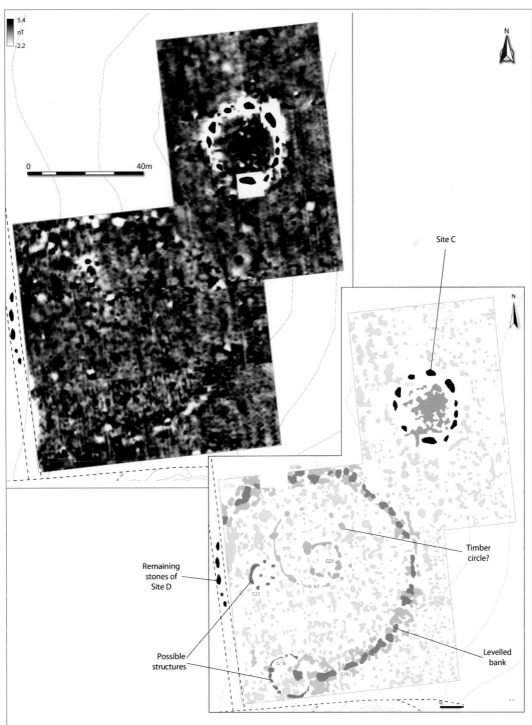

Fig. 4.1.3—Geophysical survey, Circles C and D.

Fig. 4.1.4—Circle C, Grange (Photographic Unit, National Monuments Service).

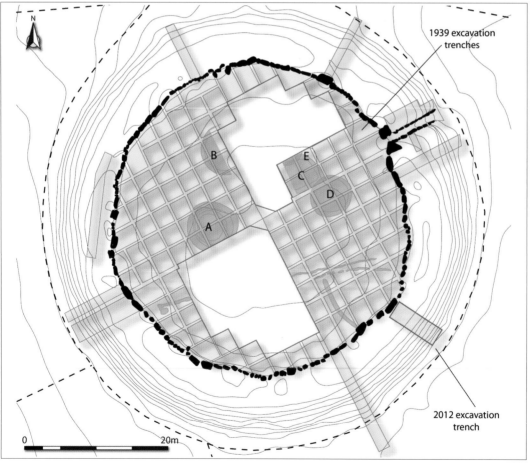

Fig. 4.1.5—Grange Stone Circle B.

1939 excavation trenches

2012 excavation trench

0   20m

Fig. 4.1.6—Grange Stone Circle B, looking west (Photographic Unit, National Monuments Service).

Fig. 4.1.7—Grange Stone Circle B, looking east (Photographic Unit, National Monuments Service).

Fig. 4.1.8—Grange Stone Circle B: entrance (Photographic Unit, National Monuments Service).

Fig. 4.1.9—Grange Stone Circle B: V-notched stones (Photographic Unit, National Monuments Service).

monument. Other monuments at Grange include a 3m-high standing stone, known as the 'Pillar Stone', on the west-facing slope of Ardaghlooda Hill, a trackway (*Cliadh na Leac*), a possible megalithic tomb (Site E; see Chapter 3) and the sites of two now-destroyed megalithic tombs.

Grooved Ware sites in the environs of Lough Gur include an earthwork at Longstone, Co. Tipperary, some 20km east of Lough Gur, and Duntryleague, near Galbally. The Longstone site was an embanked enclosure with an internal ditch and an overall diameter of 65m, a central mound and a standing stone on the mound (Danagher 1973, 24). A large assemblage of Grooved Ware pottery was found. The Duntryleague site was close to the passage tomb at Deerpark (Duntryleague) on a hilltop to the north of Galbally village. It was detected after topsoil-stripping during gas pipeline construction in 1986 and was dated to 2878–2299 BC (Gowen 1988). The vessels from Duntryleague were undecorated flat-based, bucket-shaped pots *c.* 20cm in height.

Great Stone Circle (B)

The Great Stone Circle (B) at Grange has an inner ring of contiguous orthostats, with an internal diameter of 45.7m, backed by an earthen bank 9m wide by 1.2m high (Figs 4.1.5–9). The circle

Fig. 4.1.10—Grange Stone Circle B: sunset, 9 November 2016.

stones are predominantly limestone, with some breccia, basalt and sandstone; all of these rock types are found relatively locally. The entrance to Circle B, on its eastern side, is stone-lined, with the stones set against the bank terminals (Fig. 4.1.8). Two stones almost opposite the entrance are placed so as to form an intermediary 'V'-notch[3] setting (Fig. 4.1.9) that frames the setting sun in early November (Fig. 4.1.10).

The number of original stones (Fig. 4.1.11) in the inner ring is recorded as 113 (Windle 1912, 288–91; Westropp *et al.* 1916; Ó Ríordáin 1951) and these vary in height; the tallest, at 4m, is in the north-east quadrant and is recorded on the 1927 OS map as '*Rannach Croim Dubh*'.[4] Ó Ríordáin (1951, 41–2) was of the opinion that most of the stones were original and that only six[5] were modern insertions, giving a number of 107 as original in the circle[6] (Fig. 4.1.11). Windle (1912, 287) recorded that the entrance passage was discovered by 'some men digging for treasure'. Ó Ríordáin (1951, 48) suggested that the entrance was only cleared of overgrowth and collapsed material and that there was 'no indication of the fill having been disturbed'. He also noted a tradition concerning the replacement of four stones in the entrance passage, and these inserted stones were confirmed by his excavation in 1939.

Up to 1840 the numbers given for the stones of Circle B varied from 40–45[7] to 60–65.[8] Beaufort (1828, 139) described the condition of the stone circle: 'Many of the intermediate stones have been removed, and a part of the north side of the circumference has been much disturbed by a ditch lately made close to it'. The addition of stones to Circle B has implications for the interpretation of the site, given that the stone circle was restored possibly around the 1870s.[9] Windle (1912, 286) recorded that Count de Salis and his tenants John and Edward Fitzgerald re-erected, or at least straightened, some of the circle stones and that drystone walling was constructed between

Fig. 4.1.11—Grange Stone Circle B: elevation of stones of circle (after Ó Ríordáin 1951).

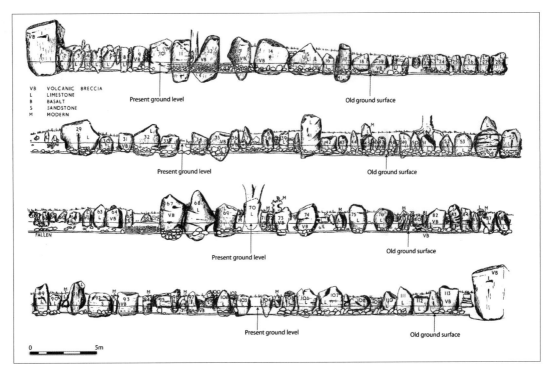

the stones. Straightening of the stones within the circle must have required some digging back into the bank as well as at the bases, and this undoubtedly disturbed stratigraphy along the internal perimeter of the stone circle and that of the bank. Lynch (1895, 294) initially described the work by the Fitzgeralds as minimal and wrote that only a few stones were added, although he later confirmed more interference with the site than hitherto suggested:

> 'I have been told since the publication [1895] of my article, by old men at Lough Gur that the late Mr John Fitzgerald introduced very many stones into this circle, which he obtained from the lake, and from other stone monuments in the district and that the mound was deformed by him' (Lynch 1913, 14).

There is a strong possibility that there were originally fewer circle stones and that many were added in the 1870s, creating the circle as it is today. The circle stones are now adjoining whereas originally they may have been separated. Accounts after 1870 probably described a monument that had been substantially added to and altered; although Dowd (1896) indicated 60 stones, he may have been citing earlier statements.

The 1939 excavation
The north-west and south-east quadrants were investigated, as well as the bases of all the circle stones and nine cuttings across the bank, including the northern and southern sides of the entrance (Fig. 4.1.5). The excavation recorded that the circle stones were set in sockets or rested on the old ground surface or old turf line, where they were held in position and supported by packing stones and gravel around their bases (Ó Ríordáin 1951, 45–6). Packing stones also raised some smaller circle stones

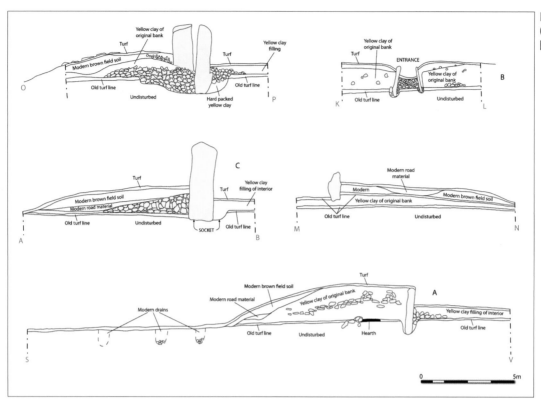

Fig. 4.1.12—Grange Stone Circle B: sectional profiles across bank (after Ó Ríordáin 1951).

above the old ground surface. Ó Ríordáin (1951, 45) suggested that, if left uncovered, the packing stones and gravel 'would have formed a low, irregular and unsightly bank inside the uprights', and that consequently the stone bases were covered by a layer, *c.* 0.46m (*c.* 18in.) thick, of introduced yellow clay (Figs 4.1.12–13). This yellow clay compacted the original ground surface of sod and humus (Fig. 4.1.12: Section AB; Fig. 4.1.13: Sections YW, ER and DF). Excavation in 2012 (Cleary 2015, 55–7) revealed considerable disturbance around the circle stones; this was likely to have occurred in the 1870s, when additional stones were inserted into the circle and existing stones were straightened up. The packing stones and gravel at the bases of some stones within the circle were likely to have been put in place when new stones were added, and all the stones whose bases were on or above the old ground level are probably modern additions (*ibid.*, 55). The number of original stones was probably 40–60. The infill layer was also a modern introduction, brought onto the site as part of the work undertaken in the 1870s.

The bank material was sourced locally from gravelly clay on the western side of Lough Gur and transported to the site. During construction the bank material was piled up and stone revetments were used in places to retain it; these were subsequently covered by the addition of further layers of bank clay. The bank was highest towards the inner side and tailed off at the outer edges. It was best preserved on the southern side (Fig. 4.1.12: Section SV), where it stood to a height of *c.* 1.8m, and was *c.* 1.4m high at the entrance (Fig. 4.1.12: Section KL); little of the original bank survived along the north-east quadrant (Fig. 4.1.12: Section AB). The regularity of the bank before the 1939 excavation suggested that modern layers had been added to the original bank to even up the surface. Excavation confirmed that a 0.8m-thick layer of limestone road-metal had been added on the northern (Fig. 4.1.12: Section

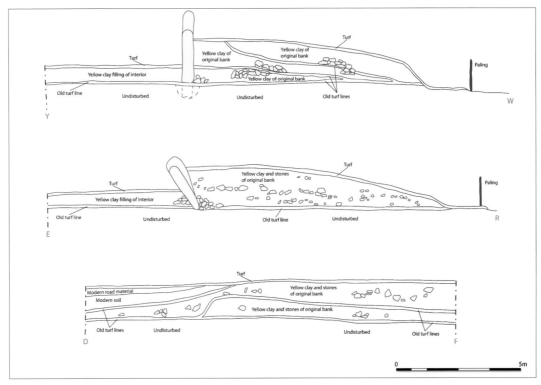

Fig. 4.1.13—Grange Stone
Circle B: sectional profiles across
bank (after Ó Ríordáin 1951).

SV) and south-western (Fig. 4.1.13: Section DF) sides of the bank. The main addition to the bank was 'brown soil such as could have been obtained by shallow digging in the neighbouring field' (Ó Ríordáin 1951, 47). This brown soil was up to 0.5m thick and in places overlay the limestone road-metal (Fig. 4.1.12: Sections AB, SV and OP). One section (Fig. 4.1.12: Section AB) indicated that the bank in the south-east quadrant was raised considerably in modern times and that the rubble packing behind the circle stones was originally not covered by bank material.

Ó Ríordáin (1951, 47) also recorded turf lines within the bank in his excavation cuttings across the bank behind Stones 67 and 68 (the 'V'-notched stones) and in the tangential section cut across the bank in the north-west quadrant (Fig. 4.1.13: Sections DF and WY). These were interpreted as deriving from workers' camps where organic material accumulated while the bank was being constructed. The probability is that these 'turf lines' were sods and topsoil that were transported onto the site when the bank was being constructed. The entrance on the eastern side had a paved surface and was lined with stones.

The archaeological evidence from the 1939 excavation led Ó Ríordáin (1951, 45–6) to suggest that the circle stones were supported by the surrounding bank as well as by packing stones and gravel around the internal bases, and he concluded that 'the monument was constructed as a unit—bank, uprights and packing'. This assumption did not consider significant remodelling of the stone circle and was based on the supposition that all the circle stones were original and in their original places; it also underestimated of the scale of 'restoration' in the 1870s.

Ó Ríordáin's excavation also uncovered 'five trenched enclosures' within Circle B (Ó Ríordáin 1951, 72). These were likely to have been ring-ditches that were part of Bronze Age funerary rites (Fig. 4.1.5; see Chapter 5). They confirm use of the site into the Bronze Age, and the Great Stone

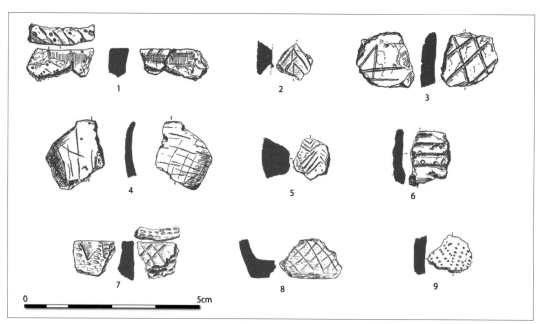

Fig. 4.1.14—Grange Stone Circle B: 1–4 Grooved Ware pottery from under the bank; 5–9 Grooved Ware pottery from the circle interior.

Circle must have been a magnet for communities who continued to practise rituals at the site for a considerable length of time.

At the time of Ó Ríordáin's excavation, dating was primarily based on the ceramic evidence and other finds. Neolithic round-based pottery (Lough Gur Class I) and flat-based pottery (Class II—Grooved Ware[10]), Beakers and Food Vessels were recovered from the site. Ó Ríordáin's description of the finds recorded that:

> 'Only Class I [Neolithic pottery] and Class II [Grooved Ware] are represented among the wares from under the bank. Class II [Grooved Ware] accounts for the main bulk of the pottery, the Class I sherds being exceptional. Sherds with ornament are very rare and are usually Class II' (*ibid.*, 64).

Ó Ríordáin compared the Class II pottery from Grange (Fig. 4.1.14: 1–9) to British Grooved Ware (*ibid.*, 69), and noted the absence at Grange of the elaborate decorative encrustations found on the Skara Brae Grooved Ware site on the Orkney Islands.

Beaker and Food Vessel pottery was only found in the interior of the circle and came from the old ground surface below the introduced layer (the yellow clay). The absence of Beaker pottery from under or in the bank strongly suggests that the bank was in place prior to the Beaker period. The types of Beaker pottery present at Grange included what can be described as early Beaker types, probably dating from 2500–2300 BC (Figs 4.1.15–16). It is possible that the Beaker-using people erected the stone circle adjacent to the pre-existing bank and that the monument was constructed in at least two phases. Indeed, as Ó Ríordáin pondered, 'we are left to wonder if the Beaker Folk were in fact responsible for inspiring the building of the stone circle or were only a contributing group in erecting the monument' (*ibid.*, 72). Food Vessel pottery on the site suggested activity at Grange into the early Bronze Age, beginning *c.* 2200 BC.

Fig. 4.1.15—Grange Stone Circle B: reconstructed Beaker pottery from old ground surface near and within the socket of Stone 12.

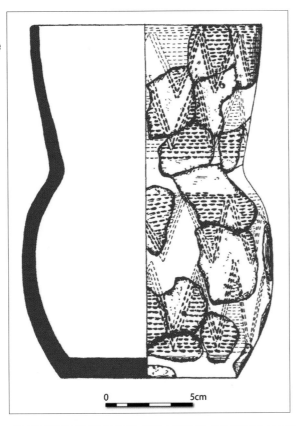

Other finds from Ó Ríordáin's 1939 excavation included about 400 struck stone artefacts; the majority were of flint and there were about twenty chert fragments. Twelve flint cores showed on-site flint-working (Woodman and Scannell 1993, table 6.1). The flints were in the main recovered from the interior of the circle on the old ground level, near the circle stones and from within and below the bank. The assemblage included hollow-based arrowheads (Fig. 4.1.17: 1–2), one of which was made of felsite, and one lozenge-shaped arrowhead (Fig. 4.1.17: 3). A review by Woodman and Scannell (1993, 55) of the lithic assemblage from Grange identified Ó Ríordáin's (1951, 50) 'lop-sided' arrowheads as 'Petit Tranchet Derivative' (Fig. 4.1.17: 4–6) and noted the similarities between the assemblage from Grange and the Grooved Ware and Beaker cultural phases at Newgrange, Co. Meath. One barbed and tanged (Fig. 4.1.17: 7) arrowhead can be dated to the Beaker period of site use. The site also produced round scrapers (Fig. 4.1.17: 8–9)

Fig. 4.1.16—Grange Stone Circle B: Beaker pottery from interior of circle.

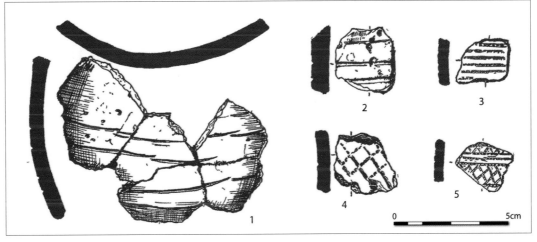

and blades (Fig. 4.1.17: 10–11). A felsite stone axehead was recovered from the old ground surface, an axehead fragment was found at a hearth site under the bank and a second axehead fragment was found in the gravel packing of one of the circle stones.

A bronze bracelet, an awl fragment and a mount for a dagger sheath were found on the old surface below the infill layer inside the circle and may date from the Beaker period or later. The bracelet fragment came from just south of the entrance and the awl was close to the circle stones in

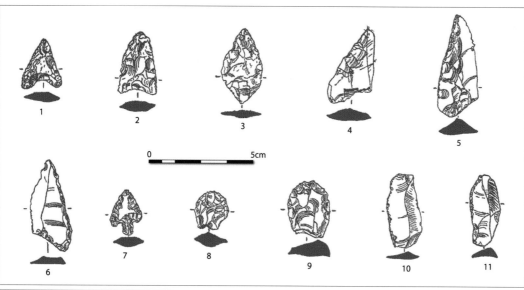

Fig. 4.1.17—Finds from Grange Stone Circle B: 1–2 hollow-based arrowheads; 3 lozenge-shaped arrowhead; 4–6 Petit Tranchet Derivatives (lop-sided arrowheads); 7 barbed and tanged arrowhead; 8–9 round scrapers; 10–11 blades.

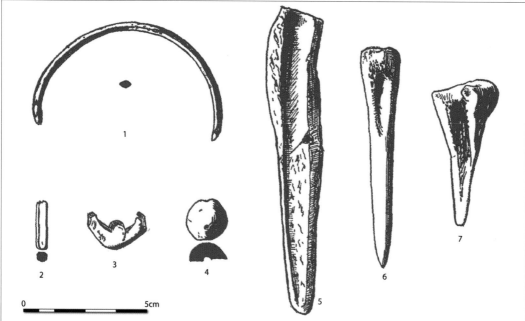

Fig. 4.1.18—Finds from Grange Stone Circle B: 1 copper (?) bracelet fragment; 2 copper (?) awl; 3 bronze (?) end mount for dagger sheath (?); 4 clay bead; 5 bone point from under bank; 6–7 bone points from old ground surface within the circle.

the south-west quadrant. The bracelet diameter was estimated at 80mm and it had an oval cross-section (Fig. 4.1.18: 1). The awl, 21mm in length, was broken in antiquity, showed traces of hammering and had edges that were rounded from filing (Fig. 4.1.18: 2). An object made from sheet bronze was identified as a possible end mounting for a leather sheath used to house a dagger (Fig. 4.1.18: 3). It was bent into a U-shape, with projecting tongues in the middle and at each end; these were used to attach the mount to leather. Half of a circular clay bead (Fig. 4.1.18: 4) with a diameter of 18mm and a central perforation was recovered near the circle stones in the north-west quadrant. Three bone points made from cattle bones were found; one large example (Fig. 4.1.18: 5) was under the bank and the other two (Fig. 4.1.18: 6–7) came from the interior near the circle stones in the north-west quadrant. An ox tooth and two boar tusks were also cut to provide sharp-edged tools.

Human bones from Ó Ríordáin's excavation came from the north-west quadrant and from within the bank. No complete skeleton was recovered; one collection of bones in the north-west quadrant consisted only of adult skull fragments, while parts of the femur, hip and pelvis were from a second adult. An arm bone fragment of a newborn child or a child within the first year of life was found within the bank. The bones were not from formal burials and the fragments may have been accidentally incorporated in layers from an original burial place.

The 2012 excavation
This excavation aimed to establish the date of bank construction using radiocarbon dating (Cleary 2015).[11] A trench was cut through the bank at the back of Stone 29[12] (Figs 4.1.5 and 4.1.19). Animal bone and charcoal samples[13] suitable for radiocarbon dating were recovered and returned dates ranging from 3020 to 2574 BC for layers within the bank. Three samples from residues preserved on Grooved Ware pottery recovered during the 1939 excavation returned determinations extending from 3020 to 2680 BC. A review[14] of the radiocarbon evidence provided a construction phase for the bank in the period 2950–2850 BC.

The bank was a mixture of redeposited boulder clay and thin lenses of humic soil (Fig. 4.1.20), and the height recorded in 2012 varied from 0.4–0.5m at the eastern end to 2–2.2m in the middle. The humic lenses probably derived from topsoil or sod in the environs of the areas where the boulder clay was sourced and were incorporated into the bank during construction. The 2012 excavation also exposed two stone revetments concentric with the stone circle that extended north/south across the cutting and comprised drystone walling; that closest to the stone circle was 0.8m high and the

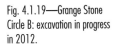
Fig. 4.1.19—Grange Stone Circle B: excavation in progress in 2012.

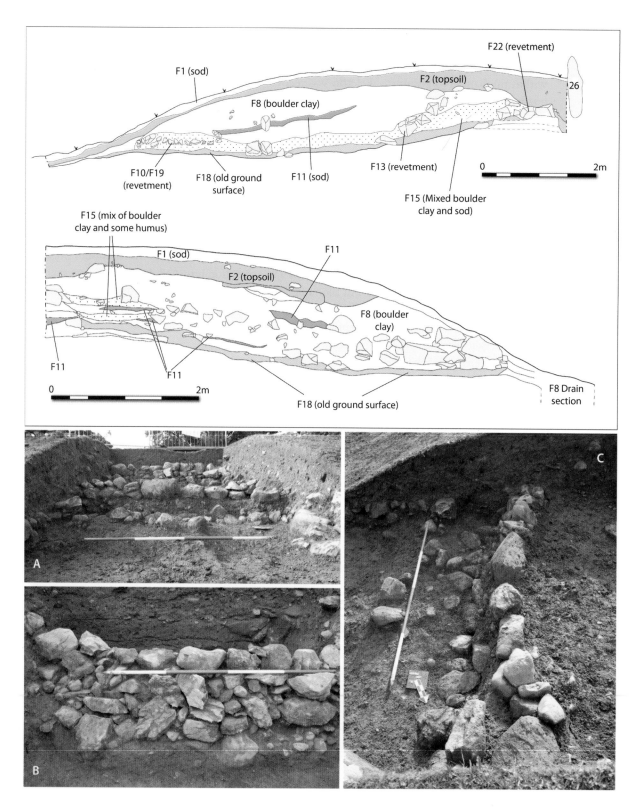

4.1.20 (opposite)—
ge Stone Circle B: sectional
les.

second was 0.2m high (Fig. 4.1.21). These revetments were similar to those recorded on Ó Ríordáin's 1939 excavation; they were put in place to contain the boulder clay during bank construction and also to strengthen the bank.

The 2012 excavation showed that the western end of the bank at the back of Stone 29 was severely disturbed and that the infill behind the stone was modern (Fig. 4.1.20). This disturbance was likely due to the 'restoration' of the stone circle in the 1870s and confirmed Lynch's (1895; 1913) account of considerable restoration work and damage to the monument when stones were straightened and new stones were added.

The dating of pottery from the Great Stone Circle suggests a long currency of use of the site. The earliest pottery is Neolithic (Class I), dating from *c.* 3800–3500 BC, and confirms activity (albeit probably intermittent and transitory) at Grange in the mid-fourth millennium BC. The enclosing bank was constructed 400–500 years later by people who were familiar with rituals that included the use of Grooved Ware pottery. The site continued to be used, and it is possible that the inner stone circle was added by people who were Beaker-using and had a different set of cultural rituals. The presence of Food Vessel pottery within the circle indicated use in the early Bronze Age. Later ring-ditches cut into the old ground surface suggest a continuity of use in ritual and assembly. The landscape around Grange is testament to prehistoric rituals. The construction of earthen enclosures and stone circles on prominent locations close to the lake must have provided a lure for communities within the Lough Gur area and perhaps from further away.

Geroid Island

4.1.21 (opposite)—
ge Stone Circle B: stone
tments exposed during
2 excavation.

Archaeological investigation on Geroid Island was undertaken by David Liversage in 1956 (Liversage 1958). The excavation was prompted by an earlier exploration on the island in 1947 by Frank Mitchell, who documented pollen associated with the beginning of his Atlantic phase (*c.* 5800–3800 BC) and recovered flints from peat layers (Mitchell 1954, 486). As lake levels rose, stones were brought to the island and a circular platform resembling the foundations for a crannog was laid down; the time at which this happened is unknown, as no dating evidence was recovered, but it preceded the construction of a castle. The island was fortified in the early fifteenth century when a Desmond castle was built, and the foundations of this were recorded on the excavation (Chapter 11).

Liversage's excavation was relatively limited but established that the island was a mud-bank and originally larger than it is today (Liversage 1958, 69). Layers derived from habitation on the island were recorded on the shore line and adjacent to the later stone platform on which the castle was built. A peat and sand layer outside the platform showed traces of occupation, including evidence of burning/fires, burnt animal bones, flint flakes from the production of flint tools and split stones (*ibid.*). A trench cut on the southern side of the stone platform found evidence of Neolithic occupation that was under and pre-dated the stone platform. The stratigraphy was disturbed and modern finds were found in layers that also contained prehistoric pottery and flints. The Neolithic layers below the stone platform were 'churned up peaty material with charcoal, heat-shattered stones, considerable quantities of bone (some burnt), flints and sherds' (*ibid.*, 71). Other features included a clay layer in the north-west corner of the excavation trench and an adjacent cobbled surface of water-worn stones. Habitation material was recorded in two natural hollows that were formed where trees had fallen. Two radiocarbon dates that were probably[15] late Neolithic were returned from charcoal in the habitation layer. Sherds from about ten pottery vessels (Fig. 4.1.22: 1–5) were recovered from the layer and from *ex situ* locations incorporated in the stone platform. The decoration and shape confirm

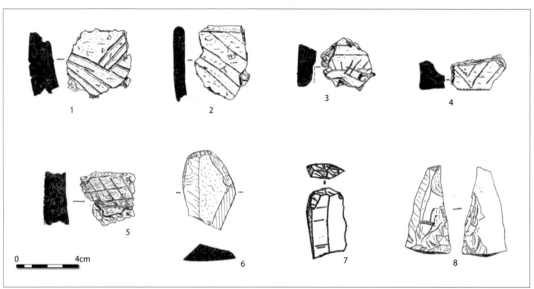

Fig. 4.1.22—Finds from Geroid Island: 1–5 Grooved Ware pottery; 6–7 scrapers; 8 Petit Tranchet Derivative.

that these pots were Grooved Ware, similar to those recovered below and in the bank at Grange Stone Circle (B), and date from *c.* 2900–2800 BC. The other artefacts included flint scrapers (Fig. 4.1.22: 6–7), a Petit Tranchet Derivative (Fig. 4.1.22: 8) and waste flakes and a core from flint-working on the island. A large quantity of animal bone included cattle, pig and, to a lesser extent, sheep and deer. The bones were fragmentary and some had been gnawed.

Maceheads

Two maceheads were found at Lough Gur. Half of a stone macehead from Site C, Knockadoon, was found in a gravel layer on the same level as Class II (Grooved Ware?) pottery and one Beaker sherd (Ó Ríordáin 1954, 345). It was made of a close-grained dioritic stone, *c.* 118mm in length, 60mm across the widest section and 37mm thick, with a central hourglass perforation (Fig. 4.1.23: 1). The

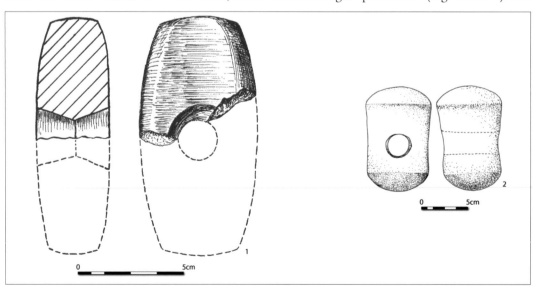

Fig. 4.1.23—1 Stone macehead, Site C; 2 stone macehead, Lough Gur.

profile was symmetrical and the surface well polished. This type of macehead is dated to the late Neolithic and belongs to the 'Cushion Macehead' type frequently found in Orkney, with examples from the Grooved Ware site at Skara Brae and from southern Britain at Stonehenge and Dorchester henge (Simpson 1988, 28–29, 34). The macehead is now broken and this may have been done in antiquity as a deliberate act (Simpson 1996, 69).

A second macehead, found when the lake waters were lowered, is now in the British Museum and is of the 'Pestle Macehead' type (Simpson 1988, 37). It is made from hornblende and is complete, *c.* 98mm in length, 58mm across the widest section and 58mm thick, with a central perforation (Fig. 4.1.23: 2). This macehead is described as an 'Orcadian pestle' macehead and has direct links with the Orkney Islands (*ibid.*, 33). The presence of these maceheads in Lough Gur confirms contact with the Orkney Islands, either directly or by exchange of gifts.

Circles O and P

Circles O and P on the east side of Lough Gur are set in a broad valley where the terrain rises steeply to the east and less so to the west. These sites are described here for convenience, as their construction date is unknown. The embankment around Circle O has parallels with the embanked Great Stone Circle (B) and Circle D at Grange. An internal ditch at Circle O is analogous to internal ditches recorded on henge monuments. Circles O and P were the first excavations carried out in Lough Gur by Seán P. Ó Ríordáin and were undertaken in 1936, beginning with a four-week period and a team of 22 men[16] at Circle P, and excavation at Circle O in 1936 and 1937 (J. Raftery 1936–9; Grogan and Eogan 1987, 496–501). The site archive was incomplete when these sites were published by Grogan and Eogan in 1987.

Circle O is a circular enclosure with a maximum diameter of 54.4m and surrounds an inner

Fig. 4.1.24—Circle O (Photographic Unit, National Monuments Service).

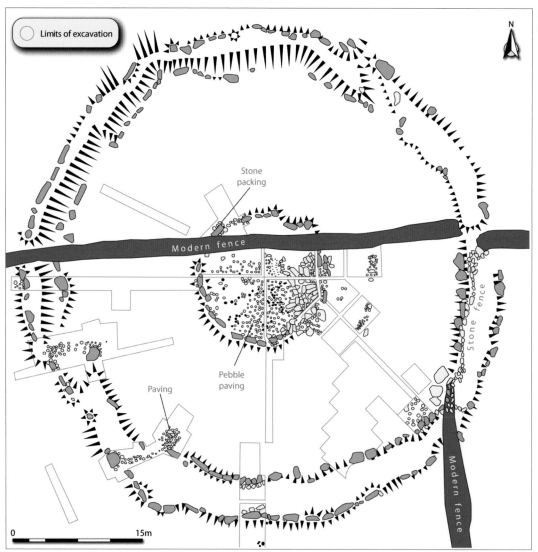

Fig. 4.1.25—Circle O: plan of excavation.

stone setting (Fig. 4.1.24). The surrounding earthen bank is *c.* 4.2m wide and faced internally and externally with contiguously set orthostats (Fig. 4.1.25). An internal ditch, concentric with the outer bank and inner stone circle, was exposed and partially excavated. It had completely silted up and had not been visible on the surface. The excavation did not locate an entrance to the circle; Ó Ríordáin suggested that there might have been a wooden gangway on the western side, although this feature was not fully excavated (Grogan and Eogan 1987, 496). A stone setting was also recorded on the eastern side between the inner circle and the outer bank (Fig. 4.1.25).

The central inner circle of orthostats has an overall diameter of 15m and was fully excavated in 1936. The inner stone circle was paved and infilled on the east side with large stones (J. Raftery 1936–9, 82). The stone infill was tentatively interpreted as a 'platform' by Ó Ríordáin (Grogan and Eogan 1987, 496). The inner stone circle may have been an unfinished feature and, like Circle P, the plan may have been to fill in the stone circle to form a flat-topped cairn. Randomly dispersed plank-

Fig. 4.1.26—Circle P.

Fig. 4.1.27—Circle P: plan of excavation.

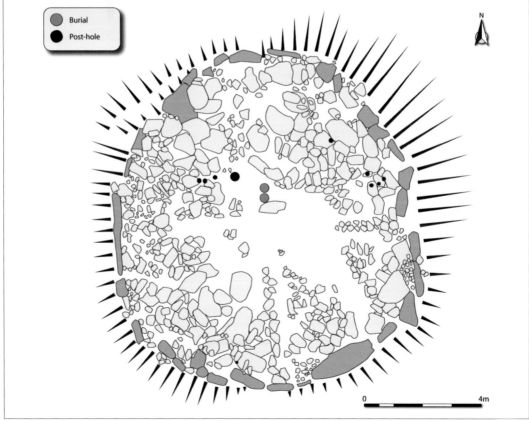

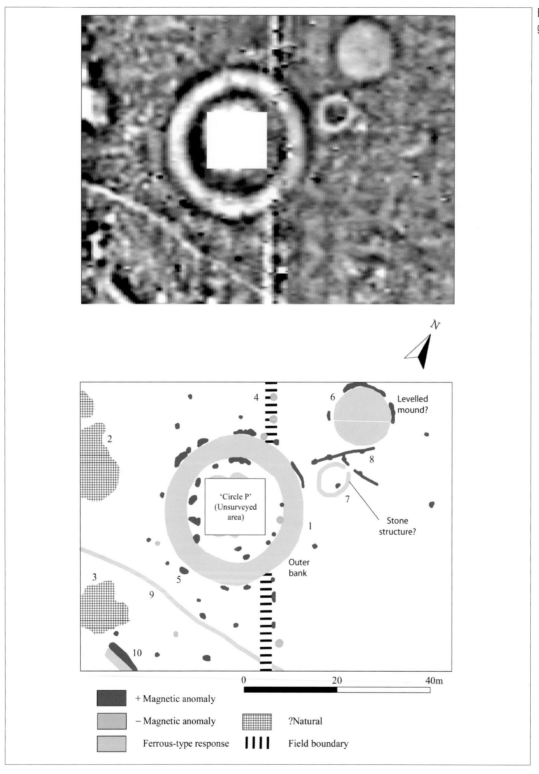

Fig. 4.1.28—Circle P:
geophysical survey.

and post-holes were recorded within the inner circle (*ibid.*). There were no finds from Circle O that could have indicated a construction date. Cremated bone was found under the outer bank.

Circle P, 30m south-east of Circle O, has an outer ring of 29 contiguous orthostats with a diameter of 10.3m (Fig. 4.1.26). 'None of the stones, even the largest, was well bedded in the underlying clay, their upright position being maintained by their being well balanced and when necessary banked with clay on the outside' (J. Raftery 1936–9, 82). The orthostats contained an infill of stones mainly adjacent to the inner side of the stone circle, and above this a mixture of clay and stones (Fig. 4.1.27). This infill included animal bone and a single human bone, of a child. Post-holes were recorded under the infill and included a centrally set post-hole interpreted as having held a post to set out the circumference. Two cremation burials within ceramic urns were found under the old ground surface and one burial disturbed an earlier insertion. The urns were undecorated and in an upright position. The two-phase urn burials under the infill may suggest that Circle P was a multi-period site, albeit in use perhaps over a short span of time.

The ground slopes away from Circle P and there are no visible surface features surrounding it. Geophysical survey uncovered evidence of an outer enclosing earthen bank with an overall diameter of 30m that now has no surface expression and was not recorded during the excavation (Fig. 4.1.28). The outer levelled bank has clear parallels with the enclosure at Circle O, and Circle P was undoubtedly a more complex monument than indicated by the visible remains.

4.2: BEAKER CULTURES

Beaker remains (2500–2100 BC) in Ireland are similar in some respects to British and Continental Beaker cultures in the use of a distinctive type of pottery. The pottery from which it takes its name is the strongest evidence for the culture in Ireland. The vessels were well made, small, flat-based and thin-walled. Decoration was usually all over the vessel or in zones, and executed by incised lines and comb or twisted cord impressions (Fig. 4.2.1). The mechanisms by which Beaker culture was introduced into Ireland are a matter of speculation. This was a time of movement within what is now known as Western Europe, including Britain and Ireland. There was undoubtedly contact between Ireland and Britain and the Iberian regions. Social exchange, including trade, may have led to the adoption of new ideas by Neolithic people, or small-scale migration may have resulted in changes in society. The technical knowledge of metal production and the control of copper and gold resources may have led to the emergence of an élite group and a more stratified society.

The Beaker period in Ireland is linked with the introduction of copper metallurgy and copper ore extraction from mines at Ross Island, Co. Kerry (O'Brien 2004a). Copper is a relatively soft metal but sources with trace elements of arsenic can better withstand cold-hammering and produce a hard cutting edge. The Ross Island copper ore sources or grey copper (*fahlerz*) ores contain arsenic and trace elements of silver and antimony and were deliberately chosen by Beaker metallurgists. Copper was alloyed with tin to produce bronze, and this technology was probably in use in the later period of Beaker cultures. Axeheads, halberds (large dagger-like blades with the handle at a right angle to the blade) and some daggers were produced by these early metallurgists. Sheet gold was also worked into ornate crescent-shaped collars known as 'lunulae', earrings and enigmatic discs known as 'sun-discs', which may have been attached to cloth or leather. Items made of stone included bracers or wrist-guards possibly used by archers to protect the wrist, V-perforated buttons,[17] barbed

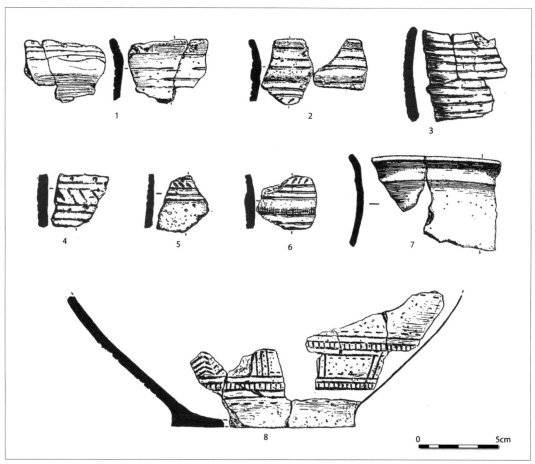

Fig. 4.2.1—Site D: Beaker pottery.

and tanged arrowheads, and small flint and chert scrapers.

As yet there are no recorded Beaker burials in Ireland similar to the evidence from Britain, where the burials were inhumations and had accompanying grave-goods, including a Beaker pot and sometimes a dagger. In the later part of the Beaker period, the emergence of Food Vessel burials about 2200 BC marked the development of a single-burial tradition reminiscent of Beaker graves in Britain and continental Europe.

Some insight into agricultural practices around Lough Gur in the Beaker period is provided by pollen records from the Bog of Cullen, Co. Tipperary. Increased land clearance by the burning off of scrub vegetation and pastoral farming are recorded from 2580–1730 BC (Molloy 2008, 27–8). The 'weeds of light' associated with pastureland, including ribwort plantain, daisy, docks, buttercup, clover and nettles, also occur in the pollen record. Weeds found on tilled ground, such as members of the cabbage family and goosefoot, indicate some cereal cultivation.

Beaker pottery has been recovered from many excavations at Lough Gur, in some cases representing a late phase of site use. It was the most frequent type found at the Great Stone Circle (B) at Grange, and was possibly linked to the stone circle construction adjacent to a pre-existing embanked enclosure. Beaker pottery was also recovered from the excavation at the megalithic tomb (Giant's Grave) at Killalough (Ó Ríordáin and Ó h-Iceadha 1955) and on Sites C and D and Circles

J and K on Knockadoon Hill. A single pottery vessel from the cave burials at Caherguillamore was influenced in shape and design by Beaker vessels. Beaker pottery was also recovered from Barrow III at Rathjordan (Ó Ríordáin 1948).

Knockadoon Hill

Beaker pottery on many sites excavated on Knockadoon is testament to Beaker settlement on the hill. There is no structural evidence of Beaker houses but this may be related to the type of shelter used or to the visibility of structures in the archaeological record. Those who used Beaker pottery undoubtedly had some type of houses; these may have been structures of an ephemeral nature and of a different form from earlier Neolithic houses or subsequent Bronze Age buildings. Structures of the Beaker period may have been built on sill-beams, whereby the structural posts were not driven into the ground, or tent-like buildings that enabled the occupants to move the shelters as required.

The contextual information about Beaker material from Knockadoon was not recorded in detail in the published record (Ó Ríordáin 1954; Grogan and Eogan 1987). The pottery is fragmentary, and the unweathered surfaces of most of the fragments suggest that it may have been incorporated in pits or in layers of habitation material as part of household waste. A small percentage of the Beaker pottery from Circle J and Site 10 was worn and abraded (Grogan and Eogan 1987, 319, 461) from exposure to the elements and was probably thrown on middens or surfaces outside shelters or houses. Beaker pottery was recovered from the northern area of the Site C (1949) excavation, where there was a concentration of post-holes but it was not possible to discern a house plan (Ó Ríordáin 1954, 370). A step or scarp was also formed in this area by cutting into the boulder clay, and Beaker pottery at the base indicated a date in the Beaker period.

Almost 80% of the 4,800 pottery sherds from Site D were Beaker (Ó Ríordáin 1954). The Beaker pottery was found beneath a lower terrace wall and appears to have come from a layer of occupation material. The forms from Site D are early in the Beaker pottery sequence and included All-Over-Ornamented and Bell Beakers dating from *c.* 2500–2300 BC (Fig. 4.2.1). Some Beaker pottery from Site D was also undecorated (Fig. 4.2.1: 7). Enough fragments were recovered to partially reconstruct one vessel, which had panels of decoration, a base diameter of *c.* 11.5cm and outward-sloping walls (Fig. 4.2.1: 8).

Beaker pottery was less frequent on the other excavated Neolithic and Bronze Age sites on Knockadoon Hill (Ó Ríordáin 1954; Grogan and Eogan 1987). About 250 sherds of Beaker pottery were found at the northern end of Site C (1949), and one vessel was a large All-Over-Ornamented pot with a rim diameter of 22cm (Ó Ríordáin 1954, pl. XXXVI). At Circle L, *c.* 600 sherds of Beaker pottery were found mainly within the enclosed area (Grogan and Eogan 1987, 407) and, as at other sites on Knockadoon, no evidence remained to indicate the type of Beaker period buildings. The pre-enclosure layer of occupation material at Site 10 included over 400 sherds of Beaker pottery (*ibid.*, 451) and represented occupation on the site prior to the construction of a Bronze Age enclosure. About 175 sherds of Beaker pottery were found at Circle K (*ibid.*, 377), including two fragments which were incorporated into the fill of the Bronze Age enclosure wall. The remaining sites (Sites A, B, C (1940), F, H and I) had little evidence of Beaker activity, and Beaker sherds from these sites numbered 1–18 fragments.

Six barbed and tanged Beaker arrowheads were also recovered on the Knockadoon excavations: one (Fig. 4.2.2: 1) from Site C, two from Site C (1949) (Ó Ríordáin 1954, pl. XXXIX), one from Site D (Fig. 4.2.2: 2), one from within the enclosure at Circle K (Fig. 4.2.2: 3) and one from pre-

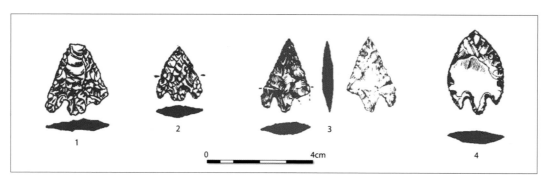

Fig. 4.2.2—Barbed and tanged arrowheads: 1 from Site C (1940); 2 from Site D; 3 from Circle K; 4 from Site 10.

enclosure activity at Site 10 (Fig. 4.2.2: 4). The limited numbers of these types of arrowheads may indicate that hunting was not an economic priority at Lough Gur during the Beaker period, or that other types of hunting equipment were used.

Rockbarton Bog

Turf-cutting on Rockbarton Bog in 1941 led to the discovery of three spreads of ash and burnt stone on fen that had developed on a former postglacial lake (Mitchell and Ó Ríordáin 1942). The site was once a reedy swamp with patches of open water where people came to fish and fowl (*ibid.*, 259). Fragments of Beaker pottery were recognised and collected from an ash spread (Site 1) by John O'Donovan, who had worked on the Knockadoon excavations with Ó Ríordáin. This ash spread (Site 1) was destroyed before excavation.

Site 2 was originally about 24m² but had been reduced by turf-cutting to 12m² at the time of the excavation. Mitchell and Ó Ríordáin (1942, 256) described the site as a 'pillow-shaped mass of burnt stones'. All the stones had been carried to the fen or marsh; they were used to build a hearth and as pot-boilers to heat water or cook food, and were heaped together after use. Although not mentioned in the report, this site has similarities to *fulachtaí fia*,[18] where water was heated to cook meat. Water held in open-air sunken pits or troughs was brought to the boil by the addition of heated stones, and meat joints were placed in the pits and boiled (Cleary and Hawkes 2014). Repeated reheating followed by immersion in cold water caused the stones to fracture until they shattered. The burnt stone detritus and remnants of fires were spread around the pits or troughs and ultimately formed a mound. Site 3 at Rockbarton was comparable to Site 2 except that the stones were not heaped and the stone spread was *c.* 20m².

The pottery from Sites 1–3 was predominantly Beaker. Few fragments can be identified as possibly Lough Gur Class II wares, which were Bronze Age although the pottery type may have overlapped with the end of Beaker cultures. Cordons on some sherds of Lough Gur Class II wares from Rockbarton can be paralleled with middle Bronze Age pottery from Chancellorsland, near Emly, Co. Tipperary (Cleary 2008, 269). The Rockbarton sites were probably used seasonally for hunting and fishing, beginning in the Beaker period and continuing into the Bronze Age. Charred hazelnuts, elderberry and raspberry/blackberry seeds were recovered during the excavation and interpreted as 'the relics of picnic meals' (Mitchell and Ó Ríordáin 1942, 259). Autumnal wild foods such as blackberries suggest that the site was inhabited in the autumn, when perhaps winter migratory birds were hunted on the bog.

Rathjordan

Rathjordan is about 3km north-east of Lough Gur, and an excavation undertaken in 1946 uncovered a low circular mound in low-lying ground on the east side of the Camoge River valley (Ó Ríordáin and Lucas 1946–7). The site was drawn to the attention of Ó Ríordáin and Lucas because of the number of stone axeheads recovered from the field when it was ploughed over a four-year period during World War I. The excavators had hoped to investigate the reasons for the proliferation of the stone axeheads but instead discovered a stone platform, which was dated from a single fragment of pottery to the Beaker period. The published report described the site as a 'crannog', but the excavation details suggest a platform with a basal layer of brushwood and an upper layer of stones. The site was

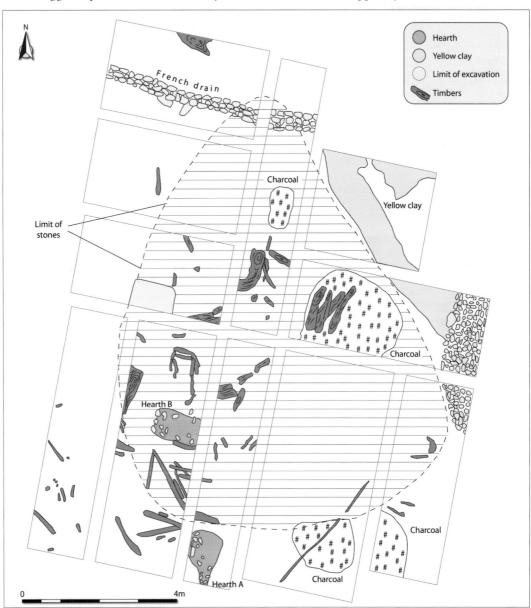

Fig. 4.2.3—Rathjordan: plan of excavation.

in the floodplain of the Camoge River, which was subject to flooding until recent times. Fitzgerald and McGregor (1826, 304) described the landscape in the early nineteenth century as 'a level plain consisting of corcass [marsh] lands, covered with water for nearly six months in the year, which is caused by overflowing of the Commogue'. The platform was probably built as a seasonally occupied site for fishing and fowling, like the Rockbarton site (above).

The lowest layer of the platform was laid on mud deposited during flooding and comprised bundles of brushwood which were pegged to the ground with pointed light stakes (Fig. 4.2.3). Overall, an area about 11m in diameter was covered with brushwood. The brushwood included hazel withies that retained hazelnuts, and this suggested to the excavators that the brushwood was laid in the autumn, when the hazelnuts were still attached to the branches. Large timbers of varying lengths (0.3–1.7m) were laid randomly across the brushwood base; most of these were in the round but some were split planks that appear to have been reused from buildings. In the south-east quadrant the timbers had disintegrated into a pulpy mass but elsewhere they retained some of their original form. Three stakes were also driven into the underlying mud but otherwise there was no evidence that the timbers were in any way secured to the underlying brushwood. A 0.2m-thick spread of charcoal at the level of the timbers indicated that the platform was occupied and that frequent fires were lit. A layer of mostly limestone stones was subsequently spread over the brushwood and timber layer; this was about 8m in diameter, up to 0.4m thick in the centre and tapered off towards the edges. Fires were lit on the stone layer but with concentrations on the southern side.

Animal bones were found at the edge of the mound and were primarily of cattle, with lesser quantities of pig, sheep or goat and horse. The horse bones may indicate that the earliest date for the site was in the Beaker period, as horse is unknown in Ireland in pre-Beaker cultural levels and may have been introduced into Ireland with the Beaker cultural package. The right thigh bone of a woman or young male was also recovered from the mound edge. This was most likely an accidental inclusion with the animal bones and may have come from a disturbed burial near the site. Other finds from the stone mound included a stone axehead (Fig. 4.2.4: 1), a chip from a stone axehead, a pebble which was smoothed from use as a rubbing stone or polisher (Fig. 4.2.4: 2), three flint flakes and a wooden pole (Fig. 4.2.4: 3). The pole was of yew wood, 3m long, slender and notched (Fig. 4.2.4: 3a) at one end, and the suggestion was that it was part of a trap or snare, which is in keeping with the interpretation of the site as a seasonal hunting camp.

The site was subsequently abandoned, and peat encroached onto the perimeter of the stone layer. Two hearths were built on the peat: one with a paved base was south of and outside the stone layer (Hearth A, Fig. 4.2.3), while the second was on peat that had encroached onto the stone layer (Hearth B, Fig. 4.2.3). A fragment of pottery (Fig. 4.2.4 :4) was recovered from Hearth A, and its decoration and thinness suggest Beaker pottery. This may give a date range of about 2500–2300 BC for the occupation of the site after the peat had encroached on the periphery of the mound, although the peat may have started to grow around the mound during the time it was in use as a temporary occupation site.

Excavations on the west side of Geroid Island (see above) identified 'a large circular pile of stones resembling a crannog' (Liversage 1958, 80). The stone platform was over 2m in depth and 40m in diameter (*ibid.*, 67) and on a more massive scale than the platform at Rathjordan. It may also have been laid to raise the ground level above water and provide a place for temporary or seasonal occupation linked to fowling on the lake, allowing the hunter to get close to flocks of birds.

Four other sites excavated in Rathjordan by Seán P. Ó Ríordáin in 1946 and 1947 were identified as ring-barrows (Ó Ríordáin 1947a; 1948). Ring-barrows are interpreted as sites connected to death and burial or rites of passage to the spirit world (Chapter 5). Dating is imprecise, as there was a reliance on artefacts for dating the older excavated sites and more modern excavations frequently do not yield suitable material for radiocarbon dating. The excavation of Barrow 3 at

Fig. 4.2.5—Finds from Barrow 3, Rathjordan: 1–6 Beaker pottery; 7–9 Food Vessel pottery.

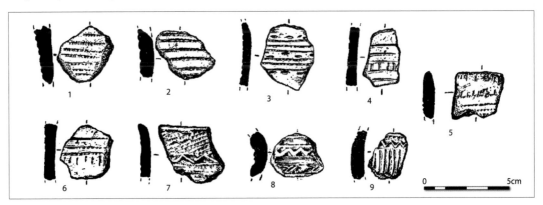

Rathjordan uncovered post-holes, spreads of dark soil and pits (Chapter 5). The pit fills included pottery fragments that ranged in date from the Neolithic to the Bronze Age and represented multi-cultural layers with material residual from previous, pre-barrow phases. Fifty Beaker pottery fragments (Fig. 4.2.5: 1–6) from the site had decorative elements that indicated early Beaker types dated to *c.* 2500–2300 BC. Sherds of Food Vessels (Fig. 4.2.5: 7–9) were also recovered.

Ballingoola

Barrow 2 at Ballingoola was partly built on a stony layer mixed with charcoal-enriched soil; the layer extended out from the barrow to the north-east and east (MacDermott 1949a). Over 200 sherds of pottery, 70 flint pieces and some chert were found on the excavation, and most of these came from the area around the stony spread. MacDermott (1949a, 142) considered that the finds from the area of the ring-barrow 'may have been introduced fortuitously' from the stony spread when the ring-barrow was constructed and were not contemporary with it. The pottery included sherds of Neolithic and Beaker pottery and suggests a lengthy period of use of the site. The Neolithic pottery included rim fragments that may date from as early as 3700–3400 BC. Beaker pottery formed the bulk of the ceramic finds. The motifs were impressed comb decoration, and some sherds have zoned decorative panels with fringe motifs (Fig. 4.2.6: 1–3). These decorative elements suggest All-Over-Ornamented and Bell Beakers dating from *c.* 2500–2300 BC. Most of the flint artefacts were waste fragments and flakes, indicating on-site production of flint and chert tools. The artefacts included scrapers, eight polished stone axehead chips, two barbed and tanged arrowheads (Fig. 4.3.6: 4–5) and several small blades. A small quantity of animal bone was identified as cattle, sheep, pig and dog. The charcoal was collected mainly from the stony area north and east of Barrow 2 and was mainly from birch, hazel and hawthorn, with minor amounts of willow/poplar, ash, cherry, alder and ivy.

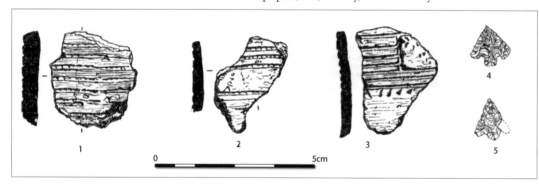

Fig. 4.2.6—Finds from Ballingoola: 1–3 Beaker pottery; 4–5 barbed and tanged arrowheads.

Caherguillamore

A Beaker-like vessel was found in the burial site at Caherguillamore (Hunt 1967). It had the shape of a Beaker but was thick-walled, with an incised chevron all over the external surface (Fig. 4.2.7). It was *c.* 27cm high with a rim diameter of *c.* 27cm and a base diameter of *c.* 19cm. The size and decorative motifs are not typical of Beaker pottery. The vessel was recovered from the Neolithic burial chamber but may have been from a secondary use of the site.

Stone wrist-bracers

Two Beaker period stone wrist-bracers were found at Lough Gur. These are interpreted as archer's wrist-guards, which prevented injury when the bowstring snapped forward after the arrow had been

Fig. 4.2.7—Beaker-like vessel from Caherguillamore.

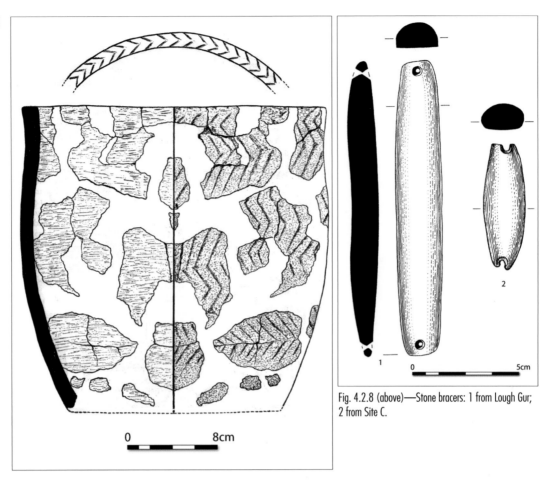

Fig. 4.2.7—Beaker-like vessel from Caherguillamore.

0   8cm

Fig. 4.2.8 (above)—Stone bracers: 1 from Lough Gur; 2 from Site C.

fired (Harbison 1976, 3). The bracers are rectangular in shape with perforations at the ends, where a leather thong or perhaps gut was passed through the holes and bound around the wrist. Bracers are found mainly in the north-east of Ireland, and Lough Gur is the only find location for these in the Munster and south Leinster regions (*ibid.*, fig. 2). The types of bracers found in Ireland are infrequent in Britain but more common in continental Europe, particularly Spain (*ibid.*, 13), indicating cultural links between Ireland and the Iberian Peninsula. One bracer described as being from Lough Gur is in the Hunt Collection in Limerick (Fig. 4.2.8: 1). It is straight-sided with a perforation at either end, *c.* 129mm long and 20mm wide with a D-shaped cross-section. The second bracer was recovered on the excavation of Site C, Knockadoon; the location was recorded as above the old ground surface but below the gravel layer, and it was associated with Class II pottery and stone beads (Ó Ríordáin 1954, 345–7). It is 54mm long and tapers towards the ends, with a maximum width of 19mm and a D-shaped cross-section (Fig. 4.2.8: 2).

Bronze axeheads

Early bronze axeheads have been found at Lough Gur but, except for a fragment of an axehead blade from Site D (Ó Ríordáin 1954, 411, fig. 43:8), all appear to have been stray finds. The early bronze axeheads from Lough Gur are slightly more developed than the first straight-sided types, and all have

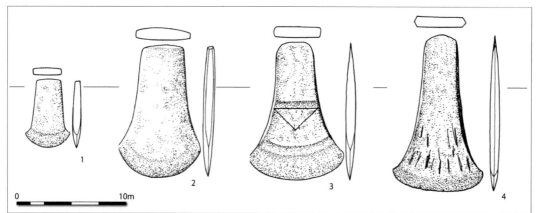

Fig. 4.2.9—Bronze axeheads: 1 from Ballynagallagh townland; 2 from Lough Gur (Ashmolean Museum); 3 from Lough Gur (Limerick City Museum); 4 in the Hunt Collection.

Fig. 4.2.10—Bronze axeheads from Knockadoon.

splayed cutting edges and thick butts. These are assigned to what Harbison (1969a, 10) calls his Lough Ravel Type and date from *c.* 2400–2200 BC. An axehead from Ballynagallagh townland (Fig. 4.2.9: 1) was recovered on the south shore of Lough Gur and is now in the National Museum of Ireland.[19] An axehead in the Ashmolean Museum, Oxford, is of a similar type and the provenance is listed as Lough Gur (Fig. 4.2.9: 2). The axehead fragment from Site D was found 2in. (0.05m) above the old ground level and near a small awl (Ó Ríordáin 1954, 411). Two bronze axeheads from Lough Gur belong to Harbison's (1969a, 24) Killaha Type; they have thin rounded butts, wide splayed sides and a large cutting edge, and date from *c.* 2200–2000 BC. One example (Fig. 4.2.9: 3) in the Limerick Museum has an incised triangular motif (possibly modern) across its face (Harbison 1969a, 25). The second example is in the Hunt Collection (Fig. 4.2.9: 4). Two bronze axeheads found on Knockadoon are on display in the visitors' centre (Fig. 4.2.10). These axeheads are straight from a mould[20] and do not show any traces of secondary hammering, which would have drawn out the cutting edge. They also belong to the Killaha Type.

Bronze awls and bracelets

Bronze awls may also date from the Beaker period. A bronze awl fragment (Fig. 4.1.18: 2) was found at Grange Stone Circle B below the infill layer (Ó Ríordáin 1951, 49). An awl (Fig. 4.2.11: 1) from Circle K was found 0.76m deep in the fill of a natural hollow on the north-western side of the enclosure (Grogan and Eogan 1987, 364). It was 42mm long with a square tang and round-sectioned body. A similar awl (Fig. 4.2.11: 2), 58mm long with a square-sectioned tang, was found under the gravel layer at Site C (Ó Ríordáin 1954, 360). Two awls (Fig. 4.2.11: 3–4) from Site C (1949) were recovered from 'a low level well beneath the sealing layer of stones' (*ibid.*, 411). They had square-sectioned tangs and pointed, rounded perforating ends, with extant lengths of 45mm and 53mm. Three awls and two bronze rods possibly intended as awls were found at Site D (Fig. 4.2.11: 5–7). One awl was *c.* 0.12m above the old ground surface and Ó Ríordáin (1954, 411) considered that it was associated with an early phase of site occupation, but the likelihood is that later on-site activity resulted in ground disturbance and the awl was probably in a pit dug from a higher level than the primary Neolithic phases. The other awls were from a high level to the south-east of House 1. They were 19–34mm long and double-ended, with square sections in the mid-points.

A bronze bracelet fragment (Fig. 4.1.18: 1) was recovered from the Beaker levels at Grange Stone Circle B (see above). A bronze bracelet from Site D was oval in outline with an internal diameter of 62mm (Fig. 4.2.11: 8) and was found in the material in the lower terrace wall (Ó Ríordáin 1954, 412). A curved bronze fragment from Circle K may suggest a bracelet with an estimated diameter of 80mm (Grogan and Eogan 1987, 364).

Fig. 4.2.11—Copper awls: 1 from Circle K; 2–4 from Site C; 5–7 from Site D; and 8 bronze bracelet from Site D.

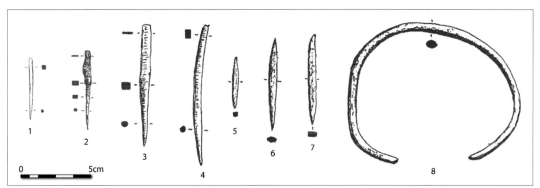

Halberd

A halberd had a metal blade with a midrib and was riveted at right angles to the shaft. The absence of wear on halberd blades suggests that they were used as ceremonial objects rather than as weapons. Halberds are difficult to date, as most are stray finds and frequently recovered from bogs (Harbison 1969b, 35–6). Similar objects are known in continental Europe, particularly Spain/Portugal, Italy and Germany, and less frequently in Britain, suggesting Continental cultural links to Ireland (*ibid.*, 37–8). Metallurgical analyses indicate arsenical copper sources, which suggest that the ore source was at Ross Island, Co. Kerry. A halberd blade recovered from Lough Gur is now in the National Museum of Ireland[21] (Fig. 4.2.12). It has an asymmetrical blade with a rounded hafting-plate where

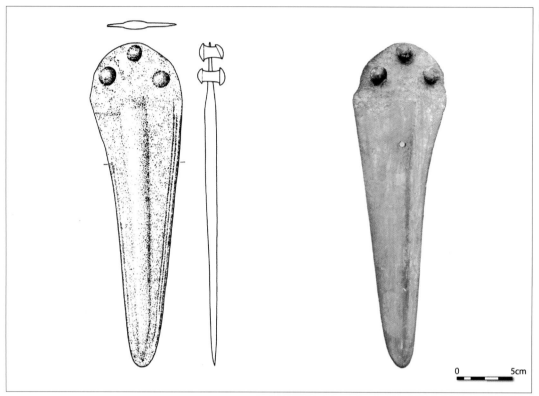

Fig. 4.2.12—Halberd from Lough Gur.

round-headed rivets are set along the upper edge. The central area of the blade has a raised midrib. The blade edges are bevelled and parallel to these are grooves known as 'blood-grooves'—so called because antiquarians considered halberds to be weapons and believed that the grooves allowed blood to flow from the blade after the halberd was plunged into a victim.

4.3: MEGALITHIC TOMBS

Megalithic tombs were frequently referred to as 'Giant's Grave', 'Diarmuid and Grainne's Bed', 'dolmen' and 'cromlech'. One site at Lough Gur is known as *Leaba na Muice* ('the Pig's Bed'). An antiquarian identified as B.R.R. (1865, 243) visited Lough Gur and wrote of the folklore of megalithic tombs:

> 'Among the most famous champions of the Fenian battalions, none excelled Diarmidh O'Duibhne for valour, beauty, and a taking way with the ladies; in particular he had a beauty spot which made him irresistible to the sex; this was neither less nor more than a very handsome mole on his right shoulder, the sight of which turned the heads of all the ladies who were favoured with a view'.

B.R.R. related that Fionn Mac Cumhal wanted to marry Grainne, daughter of Cormac, king of Tara. Grainne, however, thought Fionn 'too old and deficient in other qualifications requisite in the

Fig. 4.3.1—Distribution of
megalithic tombs and sites of
megalithic tombs.

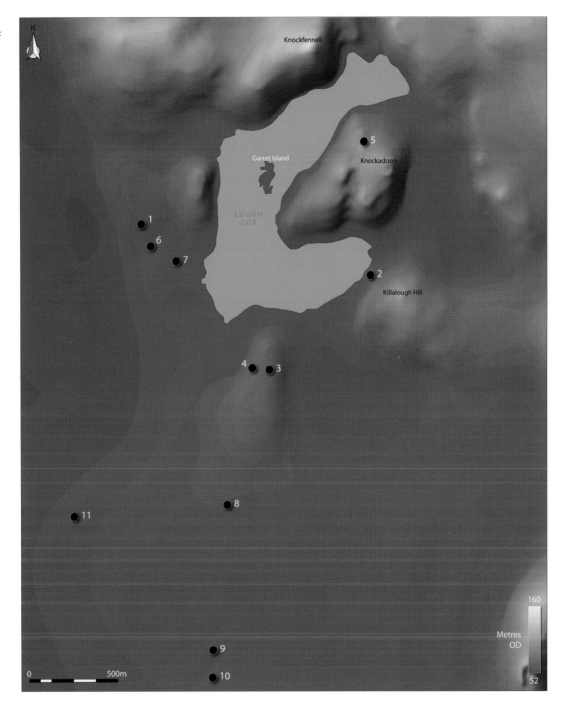

husband of so young and lively a damsel'. Grainne fell for Diarmidh, and they eloped and slept in a *leabha* (a bed or resting place) that they erected, and thereafter these became known as '*Leabha Diarmidh is Grainne*'.

Five megalithic tombs survive in the Lough Gur area. Site E, to the west of the stone circle complex at Grange (Fig. 4.3.1: 1), was described by Windle (1912, 294–5) as an 'avenue' leading to a destroyed stone circle. The remains may be the kerb of a court tomb and the site is discussed in Chapter 3. The other sites are the 'Giant's Grave' close to the east shore of Lough Gur (Fig. 4.3.1: 2), excavated in 1938 (Ó Ríordáin and Ó h-Iceadha 1955), *Leaba na Muice* (Fig. 4.3.1: 3), a site near *Leaba na Muice* which was recorded by Crofton Croker (1833) and as 'G' by O'Kelly (1941) (Fig. 4.3.1: 4) and one possible megalithic tomb on Knockadoon Hill (Fig. 4.3.1: 5). Seven other sites of megalithic tombs mapped by the Ordnance Survey (1844) have been destroyed. P.J. Lynch (1906–7, 129) wrote that, apart from the 'Giant's Grave' and *Leaba na Muice*, 'there were other cromleacs here but there is now no trace of them'. He also referred to his communication with Revd J.F. Lynch, rector of Caherconlish, who informed him that 'some of the Lough Gur cromleacs were destroyed "to improve" the stone circle of *Ronadh Crom Dubh*' and concluded that 'this was, certainly, a refined type of vandalism' (Lynch 1906–7, 130).

The 'Giant's Grave' is on the lower part of the western slope of Killalough Hill and about 70m from the lake shore (Fig. 4.3.1: 2). This is the only excavated megalithic tomb in County Limerick. J.F. Lynch (1920a, 29) recorded 'a dolmen marked and named by the Ordnance Survey map, *Leaba Dhiarmada agus Ghrainne*, and tales of Grainne are told in connection with this monument, but the name is late'. There were various accounts of the site, beginning with Crofton Croker's (1833) survey and sketch (Figs 2.4–5). Crofton Croker (1833, 109) recounted that:

> 'a countryman named Garrett Punch, nearly opposite whose cabin is situated, told me that an old woman had resided in it for many years, and on her death the covering stones were thrown off, and it was left in its present state by "money diggers", who, to use my informant's words, "only found some burned bones in an old jug, that surely not worth one brass farthing".'

Modern finds recovered during the excavation from the main chamber and between the chamber side stones and outer walling included corroded iron objects, a modern pottery fragment and a slate pencil, confirming recent disturbance (Ó Ríordáin and Ó h-Iceadha 1955, 46). Lynch (1913, 10) referred to the story of the finding of an urn and postulated that 'at Lough Gur carnal interment and burning of the bodies were practised at the same time, the latter mode of interment being much older'.

John O'Donovan (1840, 76) described the site as being two-chambered and gave measurements. Lynch (1895, 255) referred to the displaced capstones and that 'the grave lies east and west, and at its head there is part of a second grave, which was destroyed many years ago by a farmer, who took two stones to make pillars for his gateway'. Lynch's description of a partially destroyed tomb is inconsistent with the evidence from Ó Ríordáin and Ó h-Iceadha's excavation, and the removal of stones to make gateposts possibly related to one of the destroyed megalithic tombs in Ballynagallagh townland.

In his *The dolmens of Ireland* Borlase (1897, 47–8) confused the descriptions of the 'Giant's Grave' and *Leaba na Muice*. It is likely that he never visited Lough Gur; the published sketch was made by Miss Stokes (Fig. 2.6) and the text is from O'Donovan's Ordnance Survey letters of 1840 (Lynch

1906–7, 129). Dowd (1896, 78) recorded that one of the capstones was in place and two were dislodged. The megalith was also described and sketched (Fig. 2.11) by Windle (1912, 296), and at that stage the smaller chamber at the western end was filled with rubble and there was no capstone. Lynch (1906–7) provided a detailed description of the megalithic tomb; of particular interest is his reference to a clay mound which he suggested covered the tomb, and 'the filling still remains on the south side'. Lynch (1906–7, 132) recorded that

> 'The mound was oval in shape and is in part marked by a peristyle [kerbing] of small stones which can be traced on the S. side; others are disturbed around the cromleac. The peristyle or circle of stones at the base of the mound is a common form of construction.'

This clay mound and stone kerbing were not, however, noted in the excavation report (Ó Ríordáin and Ó h-Iceadha 1955).

Of the extant megalithic tombs at Lough Gur, only the excavated site (Giant's Grave) at the foot of Killalough Hill can be classified, and it was of the wedge tomb variety (*ibid.*). Wedge tombs are more numerous in the west of Ireland and are so called because they frequently decrease in height from west to east, narrowing towards the east (Fig. 4.3.2). The east end usually has a small chamber or 'portico', which is separated from the main chamber by a large stone or septal slab that blocks access to the main chamber. The entrance is usually considered to be on the wider western end, but a feature of the north Munster tombs is a septal slab which completely closed off the portico from the main chamber; Shee Twohig (1990, 53) suggested that the entrance was likely to have been from the lower eastern end at these sites (Fig. 4.3.3).

Fig. 4.3.2—Megalithic tomb, looking north (Photographic Unit, National Monuments Service).

Fig. 4.3.3—Megalithic tomb, looking west (Photographic Unit, National Monuments Service).

Where excavation has taken place at wedge tombs the burials have been both inhumations and cremations. As at Lough Gur, there appears to have been a long history of use of these tombs for interment and probable reuse in the Bronze Age, when secondary burials were inserted into existing monuments. Of the 470 recorded wedge tombs about 30 have been excavated, and the available radiocarbon dates suggest a period of construction and use spanning the years 2400–2000 BC. This time marks the end of the Neolithic period and saw cultural changes such as the introduction of copper-working and Beaker pottery.

The 'Giant's Grave', Killalough Hill

The 'Giant's Grave' was excavated in 1938 as part of the state-aided Archaeological Schemes financed by the Relief of Unemployment Scheme (Ó Ríordáin and Ó h-Iceadha 1955). The megalith has a main chamber and a smaller, subsidiary, open-ended chamber or portico at the western end (Fig. 4.3.4). Typical of wedge tombs, the megalith is higher (1.35m) at the western end and slopes downwards to the east, where the height is reduced to 0.7m. The tomb is almost straight-sided, however, with a 0.15m difference in width between the western and eastern ends, whereas many wedge tombs narrow towards the east. The two chambers are divided by a large slab or septal stone, which is keyed into the chamber walls and completely closed off the portico from the chamber. The megalith is aligned south-west/north-east or roughly east/west, with an overall length of 8.8m and width of 3.6m. Four capstones are now in place over the main chamber and two of these were replaced after the excavation in 1938; a stone lying flat in front of the entrance/portico may originally have been a capstone over the portico. At the end of the excavation this stone was set upright and blocked the entrance to the portico. The capstones rest on the chamber walls, which are formed by

Fig. 4.3.4—Plan and sectional profiles of megalithic tomb.

five large stones on the southern side and four large stones on the northern side. An outer or subsidiary wall built 0.25m beyond the chamber wall exists on both sides; the wall on the southern side is well preserved and ten stones survive, whereas on the northern side only two stones remain upright and four were recorded as collapsed (Fig. 4.3.4). The subsidiary wall stones are almost equal in height to the side stones of the chamber (Ó Ríordáin and Ó h-Iceadha 1955).

Excavation (Fig. 4.3.4) recorded that the western half of the main chamber had a 'loose filling about 9" [0.2m] deep, which was considerably disturbed, the place having been dug into for the erection of the notice post [a *fogra*]. Except for a few bone fragments and an extensive charcoal layer

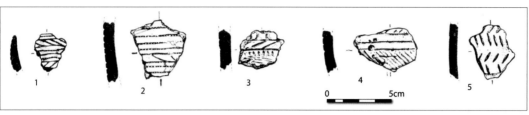

Fig. 4.3.5—Beaker pottery from megalithic tomb.

on the subsoil nothing was found' (Ó Ríordáin and Ó h-Iceadha 1955, 36). Human bones that were crushed by the stone fill and a considerable quantity of pottery were recovered under the extreme eastern capstones. A human skull fragment was also found under the recumbent slab at the east of the chamber. Finds from the chamber included a variety of pottery, including Neolithic (Class I), Beaker, Food Vessel and Bronze Age (Class II) wares. The western chamber (portico) was filled with stones mixed with human bones and pottery fragments. Ó Ríordáin and Ó h-Iceadha (1955, 36) recorded a small stone-lined grave beneath the western slab, which may have been a Bronze Age insertion into the tomb (Chapter 5). The filling between the chamber wall and the subsidiary outer wall was removed and was found to contain human bones and pottery at all levels. Other excavated features included the burial of a young ox south of the tomb, two hearths to the south and one hearth to the north of the tomb.

The anatomical report on the human remains confirmed at least eight adult inhumations within the main chamber, and other adult remains (unspecified) and at least four children from the wall fill and from outside the tomb. The child skeletons were of a newborn, an infant under one year of age, a child aged three–four years and a child aged about twelve years. Radiocarbon dating of the human remains confirmed a period of use in the years 2202–2162 BC, and one burial inserted in the Middle Bronze Age was dated to 1731–1409 BC (Brindley and Lanting 1991–2, 24). Radiocarbon evidence also indicated that the burials probably took place over several hundred years (*ibid.*, 24, fig. 2).

The pottery assemblage totalled over 400 sherds, the majority of which can be identified as early Beaker types (Fig. 4.3.5: 1–5) dating from the period *c.* 2500–2300 BC. The available dating for the human bones suggests an interval between these interments and the use of Beaker pottery, and it is possible that these burials were the last in a sequence; the primary burials in the main chamber were largely disturbed. The remains of two Neolithic Class I pottery vessels from the site can be dated to *c.* 3800/3700–3500 BC and were recovered at a depth of 0.45m within the western chamber on the old ground surface. These were obviously residual from earlier, pre-megalithic tomb activity on the site. Sherds from two Bowl Food Vessels dated to *c.* 2200–2000 BC were also recovered from the site. One Food Vessel was found with a modern pencil and was in a disturbed layer; the other was at the eastern end of the eastern chamber, but no depth or context was recorded and the association with the tomb is unknown. Class II wares of mid–late Bronze Age date were also found and were described as coming from both chambers, from outside the megalith and mainly associated with hearths to the south. This type of pottery dates at the earliest from 1800 BC and represents later use of the tomb; it may be linked to secondary use when the site was used for burial in the middle Bronze Age.

Other finds from the excavation were flint artefacts, including eight thumbnail scrapers (Fig. 4.3.6: 1–3), a hollow scraper (Fig. 4.3.6: 4), a perforator (Fig. 4.3.6: 5) and small blades (Fig. 4.3.6: 6–7). A stone bivalve mould (Fig. 5.3.8) used to cast a socketed spearhead was found just under the sod at a distance of 9ft (2.74m) from the western end of the southern wall (Ó Ríordáin and Ó h-Iceadha

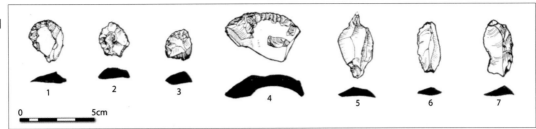

Fig. 4.3.6—Finds from megalithic tomb: 1–3 thumbnail scrapers; 4 hollow scraper; 5 perforator; 6–7 blades.

1955, 44). The type of spearhead produced in these moulds dates from the period *c.* 1400–700 BC and the mould was deposited long after the tomb had gone out of use as a burial place. Clay crucible fragments were also found in the western chamber. Three sandstone whetstones from the site were used for sharpening metal tools or weapons but the find-spots are unrecorded.

The excavation exposed the burial of a young ox to the south of the tomb. The location is not recorded on plan but it was described by Ó Ríordáin and Ó h-Iceadha (1955, 47) as 'presumably a complete burial, although the head was not in its natural position'. The condition of the bones and comparison with other animal bones from the tomb led the excavators to assume that the ox burial was ancient but this is not certain.[22] Other animal bones from the tomb were mainly ox from the main chamber, the wall fills between the chamber walls and the subsidiary walling, one fragment from the western chamber and a considerable quantity from outside the megalithic tomb, including around the hearth sites. To a lesser extent pig bones were also found, and these came from similar areas to the ox bones. Bones from sheep or goat, horse, dog or wolf and cat were recovered, but again it is unclear whether these were primary to the construction and use of the tomb or casual later deposition around the megalith. Remains of wild animals included hare, badger and bird bones. The most frequently recorded wood types represented by charcoal were holly, hazel and hawthorn, with lesser quantities of ash, willow and oak. It is again uncertain whether these were contemporary with the use of the tomb.

Other megalithic tombs around Lough Gur

A megalithic tomb known locally and recorded by the Ordnance Survey as *Leaba na Muice* is located on a low ridge overlooking Lough Gur (Fig. 4.3.1: 3). Lynch (1895, 247) related the name to the goddess Aine of Knockainy, as 'swine were sacred to Aine'. He got the name from, among others, Owen Bresnan and John Punch (who lived near the site) (Lynch 1920a, 29). He was scathing of Westropp *et al.* (1916) for their dismissal of the name *Leaba na Muice*, noting that 'The same writer, who has no knowledge of the traditions of Lough Gur, also mentions in his article that the local traditions at Lough Gur have been contaminated by the meddlesomeness of amateur dabblers in antiquarianism' (Lynch 1920a, 30). P.J. Lynch (1906–7, 130) recounted the folklore from which the name *Leaba na Muice* derived: Diarmuid was killed by a wild boar, which also died, and when Grania heard of the tragedy she died of grief and was buried in the same grave as Diarmuid.

Fitzgerald and McGregor (1826, 313) recorded that on Ballynagallagh Hill 'is a cromleach, near which a stone coffin was found a few years since with a human skeleton'. The 'stone coffin' was also referred to by O'Donovan (1840, 112) and Lynch (1895, 247), who noted that 'a stone coffin was found with a human skeleton close to Labanamuice, and there is a tradition in the neighbourhood that two gold swords are buried near the grave'. Lenihan (1866, 726) also referred to the stone coffin and to a local tradition that a giant and a golden sword were buried in the tomb. The 'stone coffin'

Fig. 4.3.7—*Leaba na Muice.*

Fig. 4.3.8—*Leaba na Muice.*

Fig. 4.3.9—Plan of *Leaba na Muice*.

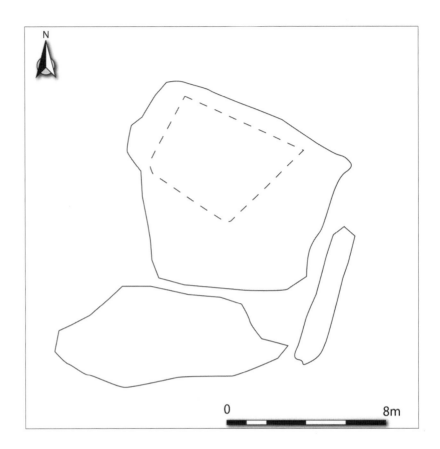

N

0   8m

may have been a Bronze Age cist grave and not contemporary with the megalith.

The remains of the megalithic tomb *Leaba na Muice* cannot be easily classified, as it is in a poor state of preservation and the stones are clearly displaced (Figs 4.3.7–8). The hilltop siting is atypical of wedge tombs in the east Limerick/west Tipperary region, where wedge tombs are generally located on slopes rather than hill summits. The axis is east/west, similar to wedge tombs, although the plan of the tomb is not wedge-shaped. Four stones remain at *Leaba na Muice* (Fig. 4.3.9). The southern stone leans towards the north and is 1.8m long and 0.25m thick; if erect it might be *c.* 1m high. A stone on the east, 1.2m long by 0.7m by 0.2m thick, also leans towards the east. Two stones between these lie on top of each other; the upper stone, presumably the fallen capstone, is *c.* 2m^2 by 0.4m thick, and the lower stone is 1.4m by 1m by 0.3m thick. The capstone rested on one upright when Windle (1912, 295) recorded the site. When the site was described by Westropp *et al.* (1916, 124) three stones were upright and the capstone was 'poised on one of the uprights', suggesting that it may have been ready to collapse. P.J. Lynch (1906–7, 131) described the site as typical of the Lough Gur megaliths, being 'covered by a single stone as this was, are of a distinct type, differing from the long, grave-like structures illustrated by the Lough Gur cromleac' (the 'Giant's Grave').

Crofton Croker (1833) marked a megalithic site as 'G' on his map and this was also recorded by O'Kelly (1941, Site 105). Crofton Croker (1833, 108) wrote that 'about 40 or 50 yards [36–45m] from the altar [*Leaba na Muice*] I found two large stones marked G on plan' (Figs 2.4–5), and gave measurements of 8ft (2.4m) by 3ft 5in. (1.05m) for one stone and of 5ft 6in. (1.4m) by 3ft 5in.

(1.05m) for the second. Lynch (1913, 19) noted that this site was on the farm of James Leahy and described three stones, of which 'two of these are perforated at the ends, were formerly taken away for the purpose of hanging gates on them when they holed, but they were afterwards brought back to the old site'. Local tradition also suggests that the site was a megalithic tomb (O'Kelly 1944, 19). The site has one upright stone (a possible side stone of a megalithic tomb) and one large stone resting on this. This large stone has a modern perforation on the top end and was presumably the stone removed for a gatepost and subsequently returned (*ibid*.). A third stone *c.* 1m to the east was embedded in the field fence (O'Kelly 1941). The megalithic structure may have been a wedge tomb but the remains are very disturbed.

A megalithic structure (Fig. 4.3.5) on the Knockmore peak on the eastern side of Knockadoon Hill may also be a megalithic tomb. This has a row of four stones aligned east/west and extending for a distance of *c.* 5m (*ibid*.). A further two stones *c.* 4.5m to the north may be part of the structure.

Destroyed megalithic tombs

Two now-destroyed megaliths recorded by the Ordnance Survey[23] as 'Dolmen (Site of)'[24] (Fig. 4.3.1: 6) and 'Giants Grave (Site of)'[25] (Fig. 4.3.1: 7) were located to the south-west and south-east of the Great Stone Circle (B). Lynch (1895, 296) located the dolmen 'at a distance of one hundred feet [30m] due south of the rath [Grange Stone Circle B] there formally stood a cromlech. This cromlech was destroyed many years ago; not a stone is left.' Lynch (1913, 15) later recorded that:

> 'The cromlech or dolmen attached to this circle [Great Stone Circle] was 105 feet [32m] from the outer edge of the mound, and SSW of the centre of the circle … From what he [Edward Fitzgerald] told me, there was, it appears, a passage from the circle to the dolmen, and that outside the mound was a fosse filled with water … the dolmen was destroyed by the father of Edward Fitzgerald, as it stood near the gate opening from the public road, and impeded his carts.'

The passage was described in the Ordnance Survey Name Books as a series of flagstones (de Valera and Ó Nualláin 1982, 77), which must have been visible on the ground and were probably a modern track rather than of any antiquity. Crofton Croker makes no mention of the dolmen (Fig. 4.3.1: 6) and it must have been destroyed before his visit to Lough Gur in 1830.

Lynch (1895, 299) noted of the 'Giant's Grave' (Fig. 4.3.1: 7) to the south-east of the Great Stone Circle (B) that:

> 'About one hundred and eighty yards [165m] south-east of Cloughavilla [a standing stone], in the corner of the field in which it stands, there was many years ago some kind of a stone structure. A very old man at Lough Gur said he took stones from this site which were very large, and which enclosed a space somewhat like a grave. The stones were broken up for building purposes. Some of the pieces may be seen in the stone wall near the site.'

O'Donovan (1940, 76) cited Camden (1607) as follows: 'Near Lough Gur … are remains of a druidical temple three circles of stones … near them on a hill is a small cromlech'. The same information on the cromlech was given by Twiss on his 1775 tour of Ireland (Finnegan 2008, 59). If the 'cromlech' was on a hill near the stone circles, it was most likely on Ardaghlooda Hill to the east. There is no other record of this site and it may have been destroyed before other topographers wrote on Lough Gur in the nineteenth century.

One site in Ballynagallagh townland recorded as 'Giant's Grave' by the Ordnance Survey (Fig. 4.3.1: 8) was excavated in 1979 (Cleary and Jones 1980). Prior to excavation the site comprised three boulders of megalithic proportions, but on excavation it was discovered that the boulders lay on modern soil and had probably been removed from the original site. A stone-lined cist grave (Chapter 5) was recorded immediately north of the boulders, and the boulders may have been fortuitously located adjacent to the burial.

Two other megalithic tombs in the townland of Ballynagallagh were recorded by the Ordnance Survey as 'Giant's Grave' (Fig. 4.3.1: 9–10). Fitzgerald and McGregor (1826, 313) noted that 'at less than half-a-mile south of this [*Leaba na Muice*] are two others, one of which has been lately broken down by a farmer, who had two of the stones taken to make pillars for his gateway'. Some of the sites may have been in existence when the area was first surveyed by the Ordnance Survey in 1840. Lynch (1913, 19) recorded

'Three different cromleacs immediately beside it [an ancient trackway known as *Cladh na leac*[26]], and all south of the cairn of *Baile na gCailleach*. The first of these cromleacs[27] is about 200 yards [183m] away, and quite close to the house of Mrs Bennett [Fig. 4.3.1: 9]. It resembles the one (*Leaba Dhiarmada agus Ghrainne*) near John Punch's house, but is more dilapidated ... some of the stones were taken away by the late Mr John Fitzgerald to adorn the circle of Rannach Chruim Dhuibh near his own residence.'

Lynch's comparison to the excavated 'Giant's Grave' on Killalough Hill suggests that the megalith was a wedge tomb.

A further site was recorded in Ardanreagh townland, immediately west of Ballynagallagh townland (Fig. 4.3.1: 11). Lynch (1913, 19) located the megalithic tomb:

'on one of two pinnacles of Ardanreagh, and near the house of Mr James Leo, is the second cromleac,[28] which consists of a large flagstone resembling the top one of Leaba na Muice; it is sloping eastwards and retains its position being concealed beneath the surface of the ground. The perpendiculars were taken away ... from beneath the elevated portion.'

At his site 'L', Crofton Croker (1833, 110) recorded 'a tabular stone supported by three stones. It measures in length 7' [2.1m], in breadth 6' [1.8m] at one end and 4' [1.2m] at the other and is about 1' [0.3m] in thickness.' This megalithic tomb is located at the Cross of Lough (Figs 2.4–5).

4.4: FOOD VESSELS

Food Vessels are usually associated with burial in slab-lined or unprotected graves, and fragments of these pottery vessels have been found on many excavated sites on Knockadoon, at the Great Stone Circle (B) and the megalithic tomb. Food Vessels were influenced by the decorative motifs on Beaker pottery and there was an overlap between Beaker cultures and the use of Food Vessels in the early

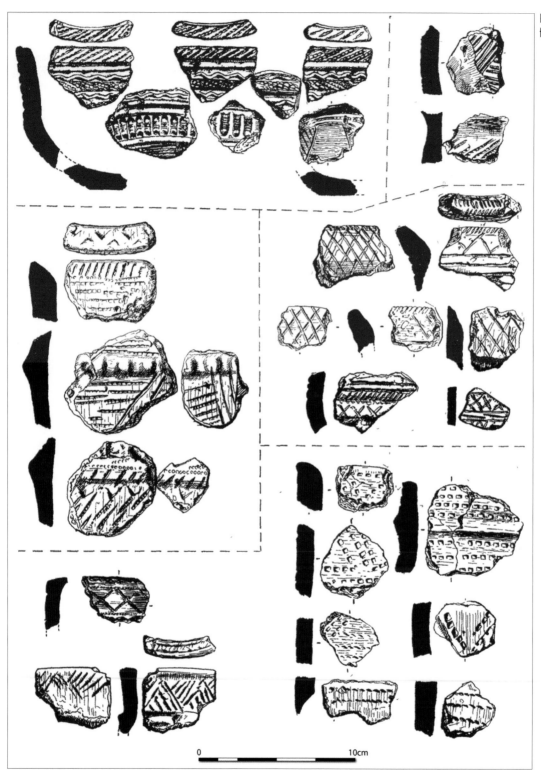

Fig. 4.4.1— Food Vessel sherds from Grange Stone Circle B.

0   10cm

Fig. 4.4.2—Food Vessel sherds from megalithic tomb.

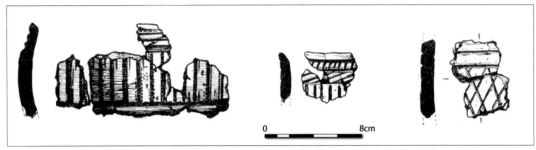

0   8cm

Bronze Age. Food Vessels are divided into Bowl and Vase forms; Bowls are slightly earlier, dating from *c.* 2200–1800 BC, while Vases date from 2100–1850 BC. Although fragmentary, most of the Food Vessels from the Lough Gur excavations appear to have been Bowls. A single sherd from Site B may be from a Vase (Ó Ríordáin 1954, fig. 9).

There are no graves in the Lough Gur area where Food Vessels have been found. A fragment of a Food Vessel, which may be of the Bowl tradition, was found in a small pit on the access road to the interpretative centre in 1977 (Cleary 1982a, 7–8). The pit also included minute fragments of unidentifiable bone. There was no evidence that the pit had been disturbed; the deposition of a fragment of Food Vessel pottery and bone fragments may represent a token burial.

Fragmentary remains of five Food Vessels were recovered from the interior of Grange Stone Circle B and these can be identified as Bowls on the basis of decoration and profile (Fig. 4.4.1), suggesting activity at Grange *c.* 2200 BC. Fragments of Food Vessels from the megalithic tomb are also of the Bowl form (Fig. 4.4.2: 1–3). Fragments of four Bowl Food Vessels were found on a paved surface at Site 10 (Grogan and Eogan 1987, 461, fig. 72); they pre-dated the Bronze Age enclosure. Two fragments of Food Vessels were found at Site B, thirteen at Site C, four at Site D and two at Site I (Ó Ríordáin 1954, 319, 343, 400, 440). Five small sherds of Food Vessel were recovered from Circle K (Grogan and Eogan 1987, 461). A single sherd of Food Vessel pottery was recovered from the C-shaped enclosure (Cleary 2003, 158) and, as at other sites on Knockadoon, was residual from earlier activity on the site. Fragments of at least three Food Vessel Bowls were recovered from Barrow 3 at Rathjordan, dating from 2160–1930/20 BC (Brindley 2007, 328).

NOTES

1   Windle's 1912 monument nomenclature is used as site designations. B = RMP LI032-00400; C = RMP LI032-006; D = RMP LI032-005; E = LI032-003; Standing Stone on Ardaghlooda Hill = LI032-010002.

2   RMP LI032-297.

3   Windle (1912, 287) suggested that the alignment for a solar event was the *Samhain* sunset (8 November).

4   *Rannach Croim Duibh* (1903 OS map); *Rannach Chruim Dhuibh* (1927 OS map); Windle (1912) recorded the nomenclature of Circle B as *Rannach Cruim Duibh*. Westropp *et al.* (1916, 121) suggested that the original form was *Rothanna Chruim Duibh* ('the wheels or circles of Crom Dubh') and that the derivation may be no earlier than the 'invention of some hedge school master of the 18th century'. Lynch (1895, 296) was also scathing about the derivation of the name,

ascribing it to 'some vagabond archaeologist, [who] may in recent times have imposed it on the stone'.

5   Stones 72, 77–9, 86 and 94.

6   Seven stones were also indicated as modern in the entrance passage.

7   Twiss (Finnegan 2008), Beaufort (1828) and O'Donovan (1840).

8   Crofton Croker (1833), Lewis (1837), Fitzgerald and McGregor (1826) and Camden (1607).

9   Lynch (1895, 294) recorded the restoration as 25 years before his paper on Lough Gur, giving a date of *c.* 1870 for the works.

10 'Lough Gur Class II pottery' was a term used to encompass all flat-based, bucket-shaped pottery from Lough Gur. Radiocarbon dating of organic residues on the flat-based pottery from Ó Ríordáin's excavation at the Great Stone Circle (B) has confirmed that it is Grooved Ware.

11 As Ó Ríordáin excavated all the stone circle bases, there were no intact archaeological layers from which to recover samples for radiocarbon dating or to determine the relative position of the stone circle to the bank.

12 The enumeration follows Ó Ríordáin's plan (1951, pl. l).

13 One sample was a carbonised barley grain and intrusive.

14 Anna Brindley, Rijksuniversiteit, Groningen.

15 The large standard deviations, the unknown age of samples (oak charcoal [?] and an oak stump above the habitation layer) and the early stage of radiocarbon dating reduced the value of the dates (Brindley 1999a, 31).

16 Typescript in the Department of Archaeology, UCC. The information differs in small details but is a fuller account than that published in the *North Munster Antiquarian Journal* (J. Raftery 1936–9).

17 There are no finds of V-shaped buttons from the Munster area.

18 Ancient cooking sites.

19 Ref. no. 191: 66.

20 These unfinished axeheads are also known as 'axe-ingots'.

21 Ref. no. 1891: 13.

22 A comparison of the ash and nitrogen content of the bones of the ox burial and bones from the tomb indicated similar ages (McCormick 1985–6, 43).

23 In 1844 and 1924.

24 RMP LI 032-004-002.

25 RMP LI 032-010-003.

26 'Ditch of the flagstones'.

27 RMP LI 032-158 (?).

28 RMP LI 032-010-118.

5. The Bronze Age

The Bronze Age began in Ireland about 2100 BC and continued until the introduction of iron sometime around 800–700 BC. The production of bronze, which is an alloy of tin with copper, became the norm in the manufacture of tools and weapons that were stronger than copper and easily cast in moulds. Bronze artefacts became the currency of wealth; they were used in exchange systems and undoubtedly as part of a display of social status. The production of weaponry also reflected a society that was becoming increasingly territorial and hierarchical, along with the evolution of a warrior class.

Metal use became more common as the Bronze Age progressed, and towards *c.* 1500 BC the use of bronze bivalve moulds that allowed for better hafting of tools and weapons represented a major technological change. This was also a time when metal objects were probably made by specialist craftsmen. Bronze axeheads known as 'palstaves' had high flanges and prominent stop ridges fused with the flanges, enabling more secure hafting and thus more useful implements. Socketed artefacts such as spearheads, daggers and sickles were also produced. By *c.* 1350 BC bronze rapiers, swords and spearheads with loops on the socket were being made. Metal output continued to increase and by *c.* 900 BC sheet bronze was used to make a range of items, such as buckets, cauldrons and musical instruments like horns and rattles. Swords, scabbard chapes and a variety of spearheads and shields were also manufactured, and the Lough Gur shield dates from this period.

Gold jewellery, including neck-rings or torcs, bracelets and earrings, was produced from *c.* 1350 BC. Beginning at about 900 BC, the variety of gold items for the display of wealth and status increased, and ornate dress-fasteners, lock-rings and gold collars known as gorgets were made. Much of the Bronze Age metalwork was recovered from wet places, including rivers, lakes and areas that are now boggy. The post-Famine drainage of Lough Gur, which began in the late 1840s, exposed many Bronze Age metal artefacts, and the recovery and subsequent dispersal of these was recorded by Day (1895) and Dowd (1896). The deposition of valuable bronze tools and weapons in the lake at Lough Gur must have been connected to some religious belief and ritual of giving precious items to the spirits of the lake.

Increased land clearance and a renewal of farming at the beginning of the Bronze Age were evident in the pollen record (Molloy 2008, 27). This picture changed towards the end of the Bronze Age and there is some indication of a regeneration of woodland around 1000 BC (*ibid.*, 28). Climatic deterioration may have been caused in part by volcanic eruptions in Europe, which are reflected in closely spaced tree-rings in Ireland, reflecting a worsening of climatic conditions. Dust from a volcanic eruption in 1159 BC in Iceland, known as Hekla 3, spread over northern Europe, including Ireland; this may have caused adverse weather, which led to reduced farming output (Baillie 1995a; 1995b). Ultimately the climatic deterioration may have led to food shortage or even famine and some social upheaval or unrest. The construction of ramparts encircling hilltops and linear earthworks to mark territorial boundaries and the proliferation of weaponry towards the end of the Bronze Age must reflect the consolidation of territories and the evolution of a hierarchical society and a warrior class.

The Bronze Age also heralded changes in society that were reflected in new burial practices and monument types. Most burials were unmarked at surface level; they were frequently in stone-lined cist graves or unprotected in pit graves. Pottery known as 'Food Vessels' (Chapter 4) was sometimes placed within the graves, and from about 1900 BC the dead were cremated and placed in cinerary urns. Existing megalithic tombs were sometimes used for Bronze Age burials, and this was the case at the wedge tomb at Lough Gur. These tombs must have continued as sacred places where the dead were buried. Simple ditched enclosures or ring-ditches and enclosures with a central mound, known as 'ring-barrows', were also part of funeral customs. Cremated human remains have been recovered from some ring-ditches and barrows, albeit rarely complete bodies. These sites may have been used as part of a rite of passage rather than as the final resting place for the dead.

Standing stones are a feature of the landscape around Lough Gur. Few of these sites have been excavated in Ireland, and token cremations have been recovered from the sockets of some. As many standing stones were located on prominent positions on the landscape, these sites have also been interpreted as prehistoric signposts, marking boundaries or territorial divisions or the sites of sacred places. It is possible that some stone circles in the Lough Gur area, such as the unexcavated Circle C at Grange, are Bronze Age in date. Similarly, Circles O and P, which were excavated but did not produce conclusive dating evidence, may have been constructed in the Bronze Age (see Chapter 4). The excavated embanked Great Stone Circle (B) at Grange was a multi-period site; construction of the embankment began around 2900–2800 BC, while the inner stone circle may have been built in the Beaker period or *c.* 2500–2200 BC (Chapter 4). Food Vessel pottery and ring-ditches at the Great Stone Circle show that the site continued to be a focus for ritual in the Bronze Age. Excavations at Lough Gur have recorded Bronze Age house sites and field systems on Knockadoon Hill and at Rockbarton.

5.1: SETTLEMENT

Bronze Age settlement sites were recorded from excavations on Knockadoon Hill (Fig. 5.1.1). The dating of sites found on older excavations (Ó Ríordáin 1954; Grogan and Eogan 1987) was based on the types of artefacts recovered, particularly pottery. Large bucket-shaped, flat-based vessels known as Lough Gur Class II were considered by Ó Ríordáin (1954, fig. 55) to date from the Neolithic and Bronze Age. They had rim diameters of up to 30cm and heights of 25–30cm and were probably used for cooking and storage (Fig. 5.1.2). The Class II pottery was better made in the earlier Bronze Age, the texture becoming increasingly coarse in the later Bronze Age (Cleary 2000). Some of the pottery was decorated with incised lines, sometimes haphazard but also in lattice patterns (Fig. 5.1.3: 1–4), and with impressed cord decoration (Fig. 5.1.3: 5). The flat-based Class II pottery[1] from Lough Gur has been dated from recent excavations on Knockadoon to *c.* 1600–800 BC (Cleary 1995; 2003). Excavation of a Bronze Age settlement at Site A, Chancellorsland, Emly, Co. Tipperary, which is *c.* 13km south-east of Lough Gur, produced similar pottery to the Lough Gur Class II wares found on Knockadoon, and the Chancellorsland pottery is dated to 1600–1400 BC (Doody 2008; Warner 2008). Elsewhere in Ireland, several radiocarbon dates from archaeological investigations on recent infrastructural development sites confirm the dating of flat-based, bucket-shaped pots to *c.* 1600–

Fig. 5.1.1—Location map, showing Circles K and L, Site 10, Site 12, Sites D, E, F, G, H and I, Knockadoon; 1985–8 excavations; 1991–2 excavations; car park and interpretative centre.

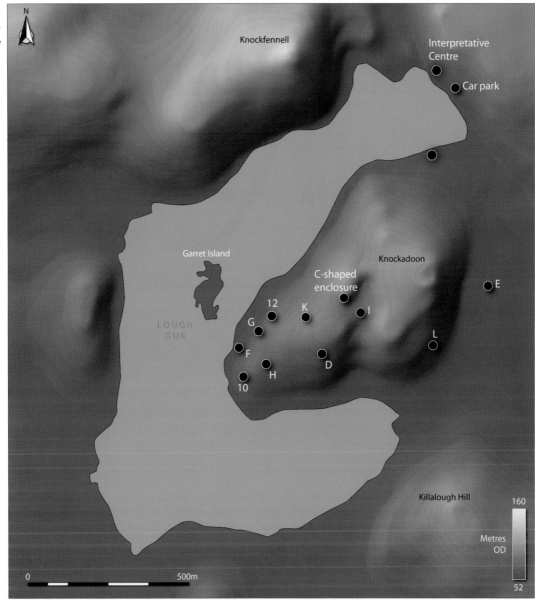

800 BC (Grogan and Roche 2010). The archaeological evidence from modern excavations therefore suggests that when Class II pottery is identified in the published excavation reports on Lough Gur (Ó Ríordáin 1954; Grogan and Eogan 1987) it can be dated to the Bronze Age. Some Class II vessels from Knockadoon have perforations below the rim (Fig. 5.1.3: 6) and have been dated to *c.* 1400–1150 BC (Cleary 2003). This type of pottery has been recovered from a hillfort at Tinoran, Co. Wicklow, where a radiocarbon date of 1214–1001 BC was returned from a residue on the pottery (O'Brien and O'Driscoll 2018, fig. 6.72). Perforations below the rim were also recorded on vessels from late Bronze Age layers on the hillforts at Rathgall and Freestone Hill, Co. Wicklow (Grogan and Roche 2010, 41), and from Navan Fort, Co. Armagh (McCorry 1997). The Rathgall pottery

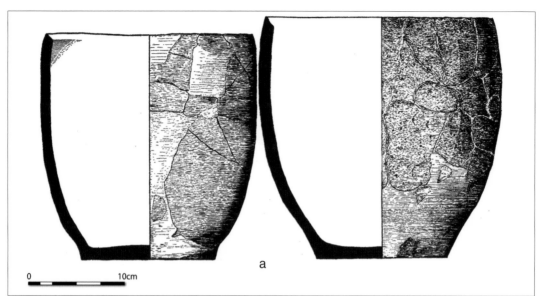

Fig. 5.1.2—(a) Lough Gur Class II pottery from Site C, Knockadoon; (b) Lough Gur Class II pottery (National Museum of Ireland).

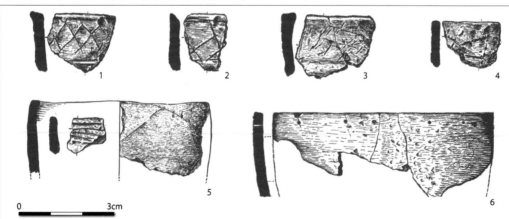

Fig. 5.1.3—Site C, Knockadoon: 1–5 decorated Lough Gur Class II pottery; 6 Lough Gur Class II pottery with perforations below rim.

has a date range of 1381–931 BC;[2] a radiocarbon date of 1260–1045 BC was returned from a residue on a vessel and provides a closer dating for this type of pottery.

Many of the settlement sites on Knockadoon had Neolithic, Bronze Age and medieval occupation phases. This resulted in the mixing of artefacts from later layers into earlier cultural phases when foundation trenches, pits and post-holes were dug into existing levels. Where Class II ware was found on Neolithic sites such as Circles J, K and L and Sites C and D, the pottery was intrusive in Neolithic layers and represented Bronze Age phases of site use when the enclosures and houses were constructed over earlier settlement.

Enclosures

Six settlement sites surrounded by enclosures have been excavated on Knockadoon Hill. One of these enclosures was excavated in 1990–1 and was dated by a series of radiocarbon determinations to *c.* 1400–1150 BC (Cleary 2003). The other sites (Circles J, K and L and Sites 10 and 12) were excavated in 1940 (Circle K), 1946–7 (Circle J), 1951 (Circle L) and 1954 (Sites 10 and 12). At the time, the understood sequence of pottery was that Lough Gur Class II ware was in contemporary use with Neolithic pottery (Ó Ríordáin 1954; Grogan and Eogan 1987), but recent radiocarbon dating of Class II pottery has confirmed that this supposition was incorrect.

The enclosures were in the main built around houses, and this seems to have been a trend in the Irish later Bronze Age. The reasons for enclosures may perhaps be linked to social unrest and consequent discord. The late Bronze Age appears to have been a time of territorial consolidation, and this was reflected on a more local scale in the construction of ramparts around houses, such as those that survive on Knockadoon Hill. Unenclosed settlements were also a feature on Knockadoon, albeit the surrounding lake provided an effective barrier. Bronze Age houses within enclosures were recorded on a C-shaped enclosure excavated in 1990–1, at Circle L and at Site 10. The use of Circle J as a later burial ground undoubtedly destroyed evidence for Bronze Age structures. There was no recorded evidence of a Bronze Age house within Circle K and this may have been due to the inability of the excavators to detect structures in the thin soil cover. There was some evidence of sword production at Circle K and a large number of blue glass beads were found. This may suggest a different purpose for the enclosure, possibly connected to metal production or the distribution of luxury items such as imported glass beads.

C-shaped enclosure

The enclosure was partially excavated in 1990–1 to recover material suitable for dating the Knockadoon enclosures and for reviewing the dating of Ó Ríordáin's excavations on Knockadoon Hill (Cleary 2003). The excavation showed that two sequential houses were constructed within the enclosure. Part of a field fence on the south-west side of the enclosure was also excavated and was in contemporary use with the occupation of the enclosure. Radiocarbon evidence gave a date range of *c.* 1500–800 BC for site use and for Class II pottery.

The enclosure was located on a small plateau on the west-facing slope of Back Hill, Knockadoon, from where the terrain descends in a stepped fashion towards the lake shore (Fig. 5.1.1). The enclosure wall was C-shaped in plan with internal dimensions of 18m (north/south) by 22m (east/west) and enclosed an area of 326m² (Fig. 5.1.4). The enclosed area comprised two plateaux, with a drop of *c.* 1m between the eastern and western sections (Figs 5.1.4–6). The enclosing wall was a double row of upright limestone slabs, set contiguously, with an intermediary fill of small

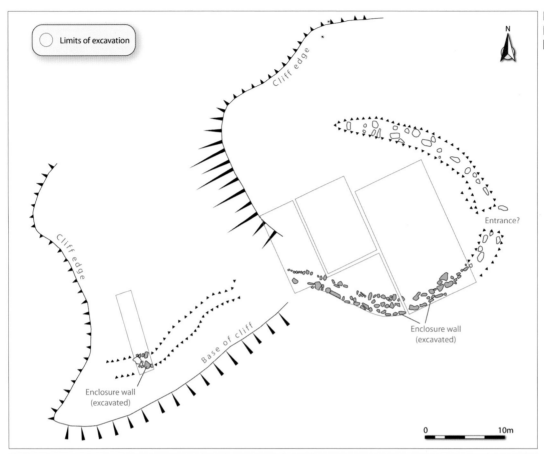

Fig. 5.1.4—Plan of middle Bronze Age C-shaped enclosed habitation site, Knockadoon.

Fig. 5.1.5—Knockadoon: C-shaped enclosed habitation site.

Fig. 5.1.6—Knockadoon: C-shaped enclosed habitation site.

Fig. 5.1.7—Knockadoon: C-shaped enclosure wall.

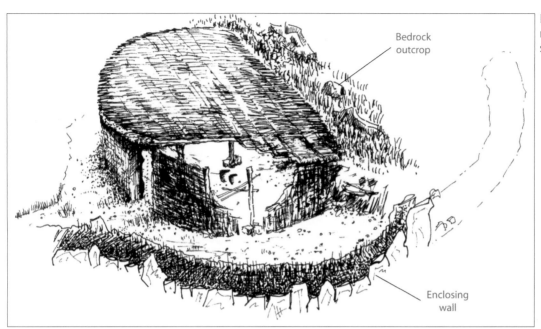

Fig. 5.1.8—Knockadoon: reconstruction of house within C-shaped enclosed habitation site.

stones mixed with earth (Figs 5.1.4 and 5.1.7). This infill may not have risen to the top of the kerbstones and it is probable that the upper level was completed with sod stripped from within the enclosure. The wall was up to 1–1.2m high in places and varied in thickness from 1.5m to 2.5m, the narrowest section being on the south-east side. The kerbstones were erected directly on the old ground surface or exposed bedrock and were propped up with packing stones; exposed bedrock was also incorporated into the wall. Where the wall was thickest along the south-east, an intermediary section of kerbing was constructed between the outer and inner wall faces, perhaps to counteract the steep ground slope in the area; alternatively, the wall may have been rebuilt. The inner line of the kerbstones had tilted inwards at the time of the excavation. The enclosure wall was not maintained during the occupation of the site and stones became displaced from their original positions. A layer of scree or slippage of small stones from the wall occurred on the southern perimeter and covered part of the occupation layer within the enclosure. Class II pottery was recovered from the upper level of the stone infill of the wall and from the slippage on the southern perimeter.

The area within the C-shaped enclosure had a very thin soil cover (Figs 5.1.5–6) and this may have been partly due to stripping of the sod from within the enclosure to provide material to build up the surrounding wall. Two Neolithic leaf-shaped arrowheads, one hollow-based arrowhead and some Neolithic, Grooved Ware, Beaker and Food Vessel pottery fragments were recovered from crevices in the bedrock and were residual from earlier site use. Bronze Age Class II pottery was also found in the crevices. The highest concentration of archaeological features was on the south-western side of the enclosure, where the finds comprised Class II pottery, a hammer-stone, two stone axehead fragments, flint blades and débitage from flint- and chert-working. Animal bone fragments and charcoal suggested that the area was a 'living floor' around two sequentially built houses. Radiocarbon dating from charcoal on the 'living floor' gave a range of 1496–1132 BC. Both houses within the enclosure were C-shaped in plan and the east sides may have incorporated a protruding ledge of bedrock as part of the eastern wall; the houses were envisaged as lean-to types of structures (Fig.

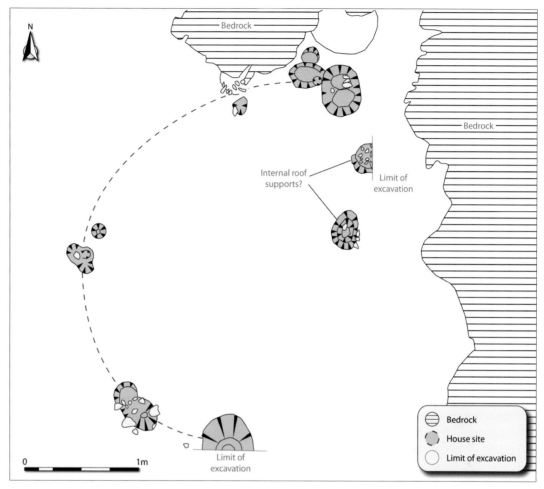

Fig. 5.1.9—Knockadoon: plan of earlier house within C-shaped enclosure.

5.1.8). There was no surviving evidence for an internal hearth in either building. The fill of one pit adjacent to outcropping bedrock on the east side of the houses suggested hearth rake-out but a radiocarbon date of 1029–814 BC confirmed that the pit was later than the houses.

The earlier house had an estimated diameter of 6.8m and structural posts marked the building perimeter (Fig. 5.1.9). If the building was a lean-to type of structure it is likely that the posts were high and that the roof sloped downwards to the east onto the bedrock shelf. Two large post-holes within the house may have held extra internal roof supports. The upright posts were of ash and the walls were probably of hazel withies woven into a wickerwork and plastered with mud. Paired posts suggested a door on the northern side. A radiocarbon date from charcoal in one of the post-holes gave a construction date of 1451–914 BC. Bronze Age Class II pottery was recovered from the fills of post-holes and from within the floor area.

The second house was larger, measuring 10.6m (north/south) by 7.2m (east/west). The structural features were two concentric rings of posts, the inner ring set 2m inside the outer ring (Fig. 5.1.10). Ash and oak charcoal from the inner ring indicated large structural posts, whereas charcoal from the outer ring was from willow, hazel, blackthorn and birch. These species could be woven into wickerwork and the outer line of posts may have been a frame for a light, outer, mud-

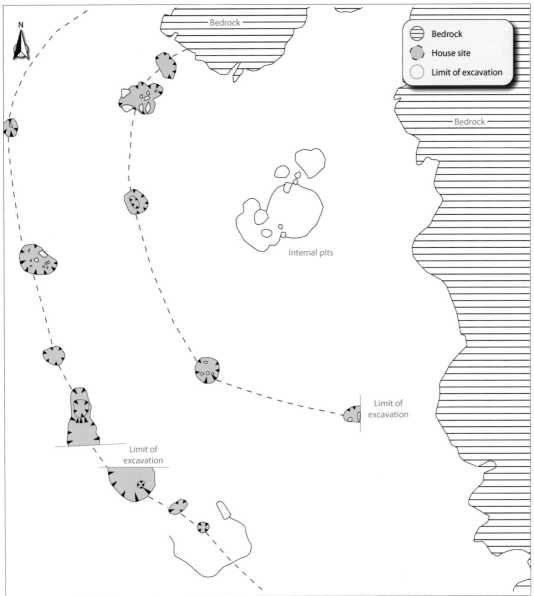

Fig. 5.1.10—Knockadoon: plan of later house within C-shaped enclosure.

plastered wattle wall similar to other Bronze Age buildings excavated on Knockadoon (see below; Fig. 5.1.29). Paired posts on the south-west side suggested a door at that location. A radiocarbon date of 1262–1115 BC was obtained from a structural post in the later house. A cluster of pits within the later house were central to the internal ring of posts, and a date of 1394–936 BC confirmed a chronological link to the second house. One large pit contained *c.* 300 fragments of Class II pottery, which were deliberately smashed and deposited. This may have been some symbolic act of destruction connected to the abandonment or destruction of the house.

There were five large pits at the base of the outcropping bedrock on the eastern side of the houses. Two radiocarbon dates of 1188–801 BC showed that they were later than the houses and

Fig. 5.1.11—Finds from
Knockadoon: 1–2 lignite
pendants; 3 bone bead; 4
polished animal tooth fragment.

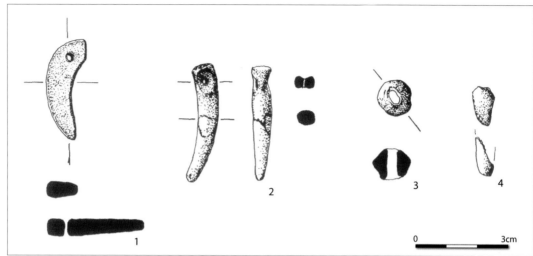

Fig. 5.1.11—Finds from
Knockadoon: 1–2 lignite
pendants; 3 bone bead; 4
polished animal tooth fragment.

Fig. 5.1.12—Finds from
Knockadoon: 1 gold bar; 2 gold
foil.

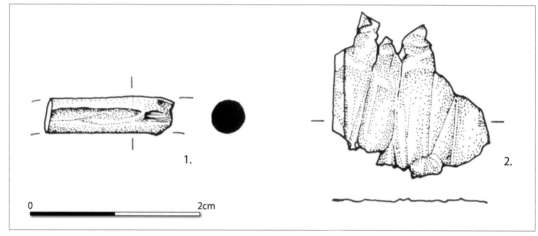

represented a secondary use of the enclosure. All contained material derived from occupation of the site, including charcoal-enriched soil, animal bones and Class II pottery. One pit had had four objects placed at its base, and its fill contained bones from six sets of pig's feet and the lower leg of a sheep. The objects were two lignite pendants (Fig. 5.1.11: 1–2), a bone bead (Fig. 5.1.11: 3) and a highly polished animal tooth fragment (Fig. 5.1.11: 4). The placement of these objects with the animal bones must have been some type of ritual act.

A blue glass bead was recovered from the 'living floor'. Blue glass beads were also found on other late Bronze Ages sites on Knockadoon (Ó Ríordáin 1954; Grogan and Eogan 1987) and elsewhere in Ireland, including the hillfort at Rathgall, Co. Wicklow (Waddell 2000, 273). Analysis of the chemical composition of the beads from Lough Gur confirmed that the glass was comparable to glass from late Bronze Age levels at Lake Neuchâtel, Switzerland; the beads may have been imported to Lough Gur from northern Italy or Switzerland, or manufactured at Lough Gur from glass imported from these areas (Henderson 1987).

Few metal artefacts were recovered from the excavation of the C-shaped enclosure and there was no evidence of on-site metal production. A fragment of a small copper bead, two small bronze

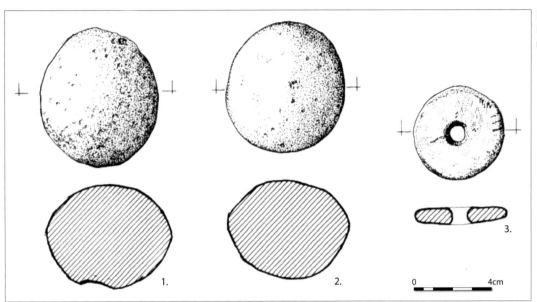

Fig. 5.1.13—Finds from Knockadoon: 1 hammer-stone; 2 rubbing stone; 3 perforated disc (spindle-whorl).

bars, which may have been ingots or parts of larger objects, and a hone used to sharpen metal were found within the enclosure. A small piece of sheet gold (Fig. 5.1.12: 2) was found on the occupation floor level and its thinness suggests that it was used as a decorative inlay such as on the spearhead recovered from Lough Gur (see below) or used to cover an object made from base metal or made into a bead (Cahill 2003). A 14.8mm-long gold bar fragment (Fig. 5.1.12: 1) found in a pit may have been from a bracelet or part of a necklace (*ibid.*). Hammer marks on the fragment also indicated that the gold might have been in the process of being reshaped into sheet gold.

Other artefacts from the enclosure included fifteen fragments of polished stone axeheads, some of which were from the 'living floor'. Three hammer-stones (Fig. 5.1.13: 1) may have been used to strike flint for tool-making. Five rubbing stones (Fig. 5.1.13: 2) from the site had very smooth surfaces and were possibly used to grind corn. A perforated stone disc (Fig. 5.1.13: 3) with a diameter of 47mm and a central perforation may have been a spindle-whorl used in the production of wool. There was some evidence of flint- and chert-working on the site, and finished tools of possible Bronze Age date consisted of scrapers and blades.

Animal bones from the enclosure indicated that equal numbers of cattle and pigs were kept. The cattle were primarily for meat, although some older animals supplied milk. The muddy shoreline of Lough Gur was suitable for the wallowing and rooting habits of pigs, and the enclosure around the houses probably prevented stock from entering the settlements. Butchered sheep remains were also found and sheep may have been kept for wool. Some salmon bones suggest fishing in the nearby rivers, but fish was not a major part of the diet of the Bronze Age inhabitants of Knockadoon. Horse bones and teeth from the site showed that horses were primarily kept as mounts, pack animals or for status but were also occasionally eaten. The cereal remains from the site indicated that barley was the commonest crop, with some wheat and infrequent amounts of oats. The rubbing stones suggested on-site crop-processing, although there were no quernstones recovered to confirm this. Hazelnuts were consumed as a seasonal food. Weeds contemporary with site occupation were nettles, which indicated broken cultivated ground near the site.

Fig. 5.1.14—Knockadoon: field fence west of C-shaped enclosed habitation site.

The enclosure wall continued downhill on the south-western side towards a field fence (Fig. 5.1.4). This was of similar construction to the enclosure and had large limestone kerbing on either side, with an infill of small stones and earth (Fig. 5.1.14). It was *c.* 2.4m wide and the excavated section was 0.5m high but it may have stood to a greater height in antiquity. Bronze Age Class II pottery was recovered from the wall fill and wall tumble on the northern side. Two human skull fragments, one of which was cremated, were found in the fence. While the possibility remains that these were accidentally included in the fence, the likelihood is that the fragments were deliberately placed within it as some type of amulet or charm to protect the settlement. Two radiocarbon determinations from charcoal in the wall and wall tumble provided a date range of 1392–1148 BC, showing that the fence and enclosure were in contemporaneous use.

Fences on Knockadoon were mapped by O'Kelly (1941) and were constructed in a variety of ways, including single rows of stones, stone and earthen banks, and double rows of stones retaining a stone and earth fill (Fig. 5.1.15). The fences were clustered in the ravine that extends from the peak at Back Hill on the south to Knockmore on the north. Sections of similar walls were recorded on Sites C and D and were described by Ó Ríordáin (1954, 323, 385–6) as an 'enclosure' (Site C) and 'terraces' (Site D). These walls were undated, although finds of Class II pottery and moulds for bronze axeheads indicated a Bronze Age date. Radiocarbon dating of the field fence excavated in 1991 to *c.* 1392–1148 BC suggests that similar walls on Knockadoon were constructed in the Bronze Age to protect crops from foraging animals, particularly pigs.

Dating of the C-shaped enclosure to the Bronze Age (*c.* 1600–1100 BC) allows a review of the dating of the enclosures of Circles J, K and L and Sites 10–12 excavated by Ó Ríordáin (Grogan and Eogan 1987). There is some confusion about the excavation of Sites 11 and 12, as no records of Site

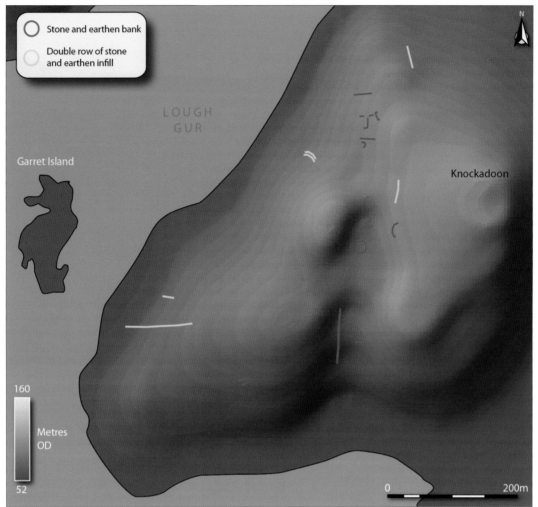

Fig. 5.1.15—Field walls on Knockadoon (after O'Kelly 1941).

11 and no excavation plans of Site 12 were located (*ibid.*, 462). The enclosures at Circles J, K and L were slightly bigger than the C-shaped enclosure, delimiting areas of *c.* 672m² (Circle J), 636m² (Circle K) and 552m² (Circle L). The enclosing walls around Circles J, K and L and Site 10 were 1.5–2.2m wide, built from continuously set limestone slabs and infilled with gravel, stones and earth, similar to that on the C-shaped enclosure. The absence of clear stratigraphy and details of the locations of finds from Circles J, K and L and Sites 10 and 12 makes precise dating difficult. The ceramic finds provide evidence that each site had Neolithic, Beaker period and Bronze Age phases of use. Sequential occupation resulted in material from earlier phases being incorporated into later features. As pottery identified as Class II which can now be ascribed to the Bronze Age was recovered from the infill of the enclosure walls, the date of enclosure construction can be placed in the Bronze Age.

Circle J
This site was on the east side of the Back Hill (Fig. 5.1.16). The enclosure was roughly circular, with maximum external dimensions of *c.* 26m (east/west) by 30m (north/south), and the surrounding

Fig. 5.1.16—Aerial photograph of enclosures at Circles J and K, Knockadoon (Photographic Unit, National Monuments Service).

wall comprised two concentric rows of kerbstones *c.* 1.8–2m apart (Fig. 5.1.17). Similar to the C-shaped enclosure, the kerbstones were set on limestone bedrock which was close to the surface. The wall fill was of earth and stones; where it overlay a pre-existing layer of Neolithic occupation on the south-east side, Neolithic finds were incorporated into the make-up of the wall. The remains of a Neolithic house survived under the enclosure wall (Chapter 3), as well as spreads of occupation material that extended inside and outside the enclosure and pits and post-holes within the enclosure (Grogan and Eogan 1987, 308–12). The post-holes within the enclosure were probably the vestiges of buildings but discernible building plans could not be deduced from the remains. The entrance to Circle J was not located during the excavation but may have been on the east side where the enclosure wall narrowed. A standing stone in the south-east quadrant and a second recumbent stone which may have been a fallen standing stone were tangible remains of Bronze Age activity within the enclosure (*ibid.*, 312). As the enclosure was also used as a burial ground in the late Iron Age/early medieval period much of the evidence for earlier activity was destroyed.

Bronze Age Class II pottery was found in pre-enclosure levels, was the main type of pottery within the enclosure and was also found incorporated into the enclosure wall. Some of the Class II pottery from Circle J has rows of dots below the rim which mimic perforations but are not bored through (Fig. 5.1.18: 1) and some is perforated (Fig. 5.1.18: 2). Elsewhere this type of pottery has been dated to the period *c.* 1150–1000 BC or the late Bronze Age. Apart from pottery, other finds of Bronze Age date from Circle J were two blue glass beads and a small piece of bronze. There was no evidence of Bronze Age houses within the enclosure but, given the disturbance caused by later burials and the difficulty of identifying structures where the archaeological stratigraphy was compressed into thin deposits, the absence of evidence of houses contemporary with the Bronze Age enclosure is not remarkable.

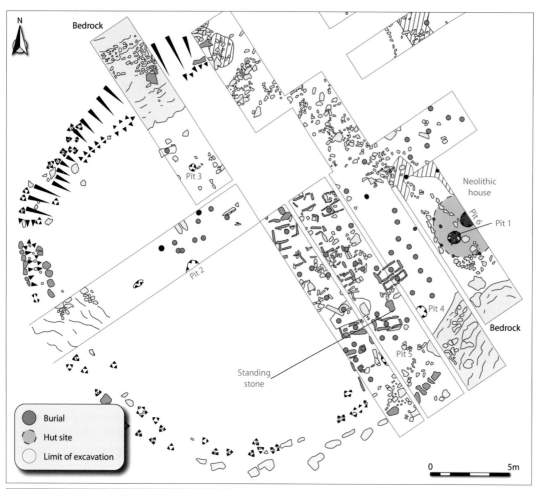

Fig. 5.1.17—Knockadoon: plan of Circle J.

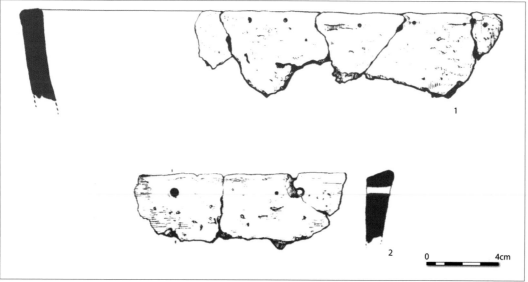

Fig. 5.1.18—Knockadoon: pottery from Circle J.

Circle K

Circle K was situated on a level plateau on the west side of the Back Hill (Figs 5.1.1, 5.1.16 and 5.1.19). A Neolithic house was recorded under the enclosure wall and there was another off-centre within the enclosure (Chapter 3). The enclosing wall was most likely fortuitously constructed on the early Neolithic house. Circle K was built in a saucer-shaped depression of weathered limestone, roughly circular in outline, with maximum external dimensions of *c.* 31m (east/west) by 27.7m (north/south). The surrounding wall comprised two concentric rows of kerbstones *c.* 1.5m apart (Fig. 5.1.20). The outer ring of stones was *c.* 0.9m high while those of the inner ring were lower; the kerbstones were set directly on bedrock, sometimes propped with packing stones. The wall infill between the kerbstones was a mixture of stones and earth. An entrance on the south-east side was *c.* 1.8m wide on the inner side and 2.4m externally. Paired post-holes at the entrance which probably held gateposts indicated that the entrance was closed by double wooden gates. A 3m-long row of stones extended externally from the southern side of the entrance.

The soil cover within the enclosure was only 0.1m deep over most of the area and the majority of the finds were recovered from crevices in the bedrock. The depth of soil in a natural hollow within the enclosure was *c.* 0.75m and Neolithic and Bronze Age pottery was recovered from this area. The bulk of the ceramic finds from the infill of the enclosure wall and, indeed, from within the enclosure consisted of Bronze Age Class II wares, suggesting that the enclosure was built in the Bronze Age.

Circle K produced a relatively large number of bronze objects (Grogan and Eogan 1987, 385), described as coming from the upper levels (*ibid.*, 364), although the excavation report suggested that as the stratigraphy was so thin it was not possible to separate out discrete phases. An awl (Fig. 5.1.21: 1), a thin decorated disc (Fig. 5.1.21: 2), a possible toggle (Fig. 5.1.21: 3), pin fragments (Fig. 5.1.21: 4), a button (Fig. 5.1.21: 5) and casting waste (Fig. 5.1.21: 6) were recovered. There was some evidence of on-site metal production, and six fragments of clay moulds were found on the north-east side outside

Fig. 5.1.19—Knockadoon: Circle K (Carleton Jones).

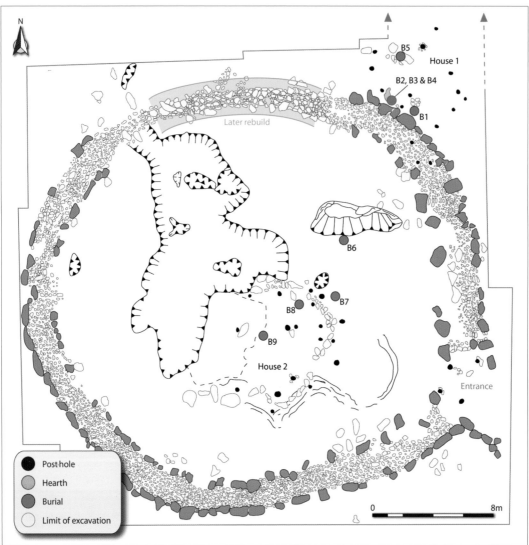

Fig. 5.1.20—Knockadoon: plan of Circle K.

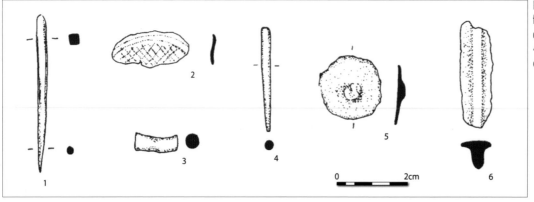

Fig. 5.1.21—Bronze artefacts from Circle K, Knockadoon: 1 awl; 2 decorated disc; 3 toggle; 4 pin fragment; 5 button; 6 casting waste.

the enclosure. The moulds were broken once the object was cast but the imprints suggested that they were used to manufacture late Bronze Age swords (*ibid.*, 383). What were described as a 'large number' of glass beads were also found at Circle K (*ibid.*, 385). There are no published details of the glass beads although they were likened to those from Site C, Knockadoon, which were blue-green, produced by winding a thin stick of heated glass around a wire (wire-wound) and then broken off to make the bead. Similar beads have been recovered from late Bronze Age levels at Rathgall hillfort, Co. Wicklow.

Circle L

This enclosure was on a level platform on the south-east side of Knockadoon Hill, overlooking the lake (Fig. 5.1.1). It was roughly circular, with a maximum external diameter of 25m, and the surrounding wall was *c.* 2m wide (Fig. 5.1.22). The western wall partly incorporated a cliff face. The enclosure wall was not as well built as those at Circles J and K; it was haphazard in places and had

Fig. 5.1.22—Knockadoon: overall plan of Circle L (Neolithic houses and Bronze Age enclosing wall).

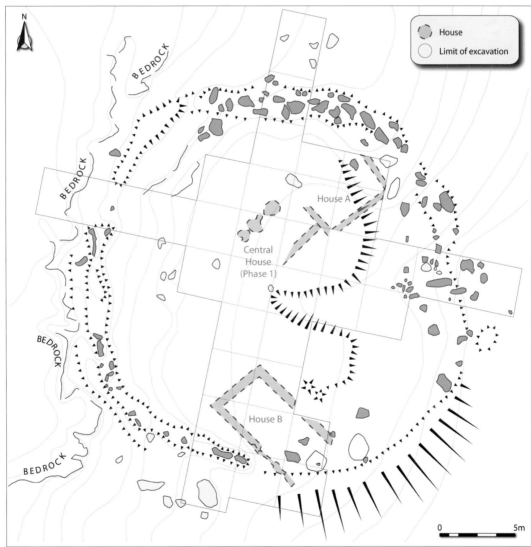

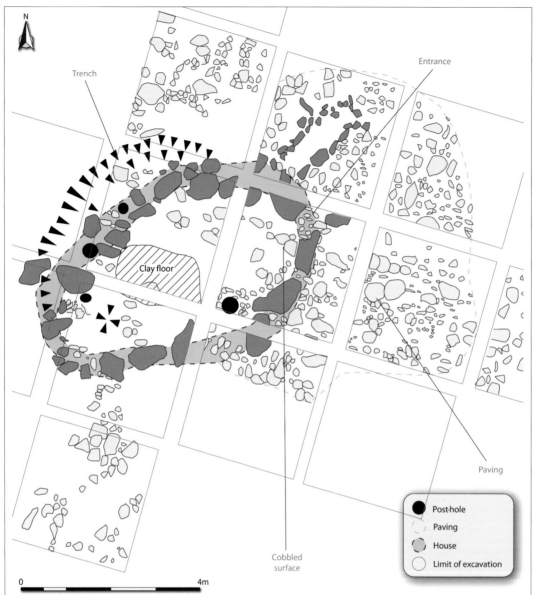

Fig. 5.1.23—Knockadoon: plan of Bronze Age house within Circle L.

Legend:
- Post-hole
- Paving
- House
- Limit of excavation

Labels on figure: N, Trench, Entrance, Clay floor, Paving, Cobbled surface

Scale: 0 ____ 4m

collapsed along the southern and western sides, where it had been constructed on loose habitation layers from earlier Neolithic occupation. Where best preserved it comprised an outer kerbing and an inner bank of smaller stones or a mix of small stones and clay. In some sections an inner and outer stone kerbing was recorded and the intermediary space was filled with stones, clay and incorporated habitation layers, including animal bones and charcoal from pre-enclosure occupation. The entrance was not located on the excavation. There are no published details of the finds recovered from the wall fill, as much of the contextual information of the finds from Circle L was lost at the time the site report was being prepared (Grogan and Eogan 1987), but the structural similarity to Circles J and K and the C-shaped enclosure suggests a Bronze Age date.

Fig. 5.1.24—Knockadoon:
pottery from Circle L.

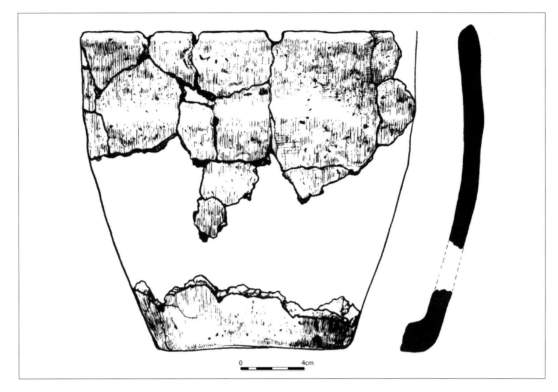

0   4cm

Three Neolithic houses were recorded within Circle L and one of these was a poorly preserved post-built house in the centre of the enclosure (Fig. 5.1.22; Chapter 3). A Bronze Age house was subsequently built over the central Neolithic house and was probably contemporary with the construction of the stone enclosure. This central Bronze Age house was oval in plan, 6.5m by 4m, and the foundations were a continuous line of large boulders up to 0.9m in length (Fig. 5.1.23). Three post-holes on the north-west line of boulders probably marked the vestiges of a post-built timber wall which may have had intermediary wicker walling. A trench abutting the north-west side was described as a footing trench for timber uprights (*ibid.*, 413) but may have functioned as a drip-gully for overhanging eaves. The floor was covered by a 0.1m-thick clay layer spread over the centre and the southern side, and the northern end was floored with rough cobbling which may originally have covered the entire floor. The house entrance was unrecorded, although a single post-hole on the eastern side suggested a door-jamb. A paved area measuring 6.8m by 5.2m extended from the eastern and northern sides of the house and was contemporary with the occupation of the house. A hearth was recorded 1m to the north-east of the house and may have been an outdoor cooking area for the household. A burial in an unlined or unprotected grave on the northern side of the paving was that of an adult male, aligned south-west/north-east with the head to the south-west. The date of the burial is unknown and it may have been unconnected to the occupation of the Bronze Age house.

As the location details of the pottery from the Bronze Age house are now lost it is not possible to be precise regarding its construction date. Over 50% of the pottery identified as coming from the enclosure phase of Circle L was Bronze Age Class II (Fig. 5.1.24), with some Neolithic Class I and minor quantities of Beaker pottery. Neolithic and Beaker pottery were probably churned up from

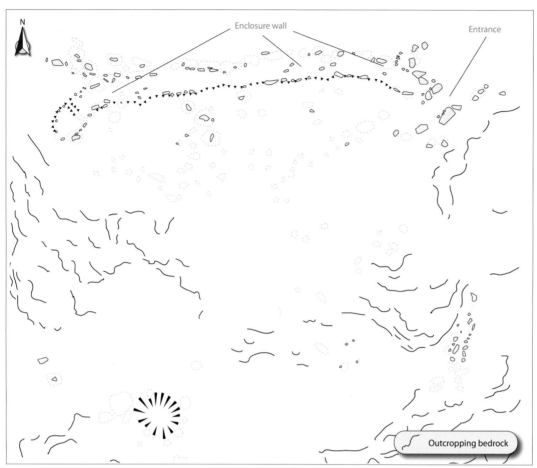

Fig. 5.1.25—Knockadoon: Site 10 enclosure.

earlier occupation when the central house and enclosure were constructed. Some of the Class II wares from Circle L were decorated with patterns of horizontal and vertical lines like the pottery from Chancellorsland, Co. Tipperary, which dated from 1600–1400 BC, and the enclosure and central house may have been constructed during this period.

Site 10

This was on a level platform on the south-west side of Knockadoon Hill (Fig. 5.1.1). It was C-shaped in plan, open to the south and similar to the C-shaped enclosure excavated in 1990–1 (Cleary 2003). The site was partially excavated and the results showed that a 34m-long enclosure wall was constructed along its northern end and joined outcropping limestone on the east and west sides, while the south side was unenclosed (Fig. 5.1.25). The enclosure wall was faced on the outside and inside with large boulders with an intermediary distance of 1.5m. The wall infill consisted of small stones and earth and included Neolithic and Beaker pottery from pre-enclosure levels. There was a well-defined 1.5m-wide entrance on the north-east side, where the enclosure wall abutted a rock outcrop (Fig. 5.1.26).

The excavation recorded eighteen post- and stake-holes on the south side of the excavated area and these may have been the vestiges of a lean-to building against a rock outcrop (Fig. 5.1.26). Six post-holes formed an arc and may have held posts for the external wall of a building with an estimated

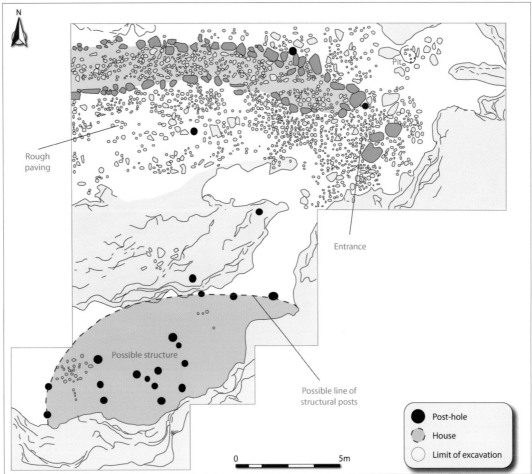

Fig. 5.1.26—Knockadoon: Site 10 enclosure and possible house.

diameter of *c.* 12.5m (east/west). A further twelve internal post-holes suggest roof-support posts or the remains of internal fittings. A roughly paved surface was laid down after the enclosure wall was constructed and occupation debris accumulated on it. The finds from the paved area consisted of pottery (mainly Bronze Age Class II, with a small quantity of Neolithic Class I), débitage from flint- and chert-working and finished tools, principally scrapers. A stone axehead and axehead chips were also recovered. Over 220 sherds of fragmented Beaker pottery and sherds of four Food Vessel Bowls were found around the paved surface and may have been churned up from earlier levels when the paving was laid, as some sherds were parts of vessels found at levels pre-dating the construction of the enclosure (Grogan and Eogan 1987, 460). The only bronze find was a pinhead, which came from the paved surface. It was conical and comparable to examples from Sites C and D that were dated to the late Bronze Age (Ó Ríordáin 1954, 361).

Site 12
This was partly excavated in 1954 but there is no surviving archive of site plans (Grogan and Eogan 1987, 462). The site was D-shaped and located on a level platform on the western side of Knockadoon (Fig. 5.1.1). A steep cliff extended north/south across the western side of the site and

Fig. 5.1.27—Knockadoon: excavation in progress at unenclosed Bronze Age houses.

bedrock was close to the surface. The enclosing wall was kerbed and had an infill of smaller stones. The pottery included Class II wares, which were probably contemporary with the construction of the enclosure in the Bronze Age.

Unenclosed settlement

Unenclosed Bronze Age houses on Knockadoon excavated by Ó Ríordáin (Ó Ríordáin 1954; Grogan and Eogan 1987) were dated by associated artefacts, particularly pottery. An excavation of three Bronze Age houses in 1985–8 provided a series of radiocarbon dates for the buildings and for Class II pottery that enabled a review of similar ceramics from older excavations (Cleary 1995). The 1985–8 excavation took place on a narrow plateau on the northern slope of Knockadoon Hill overlooking the lake (Figs 5.1.1 and 5.1.27). A cave which was a narrow crevice in a rock face to the south-west of the plateau was also excavated but did not produce any evidence that it had been used as a shelter in antiquity.

The sequence of construction of the houses was firstly a round house, followed by a rectangular house and finally by an oval-shaped house. The time interval between the successive houses may not have been great and it is possible that they represented occupation by a few generations of the same kin group. Architecturally the houses were simple structures, comprising vertically set posts of ash and oak with wattle walls, identified from charcoal from the vicinity of the houses as of willow and hazel.

The earliest house on the plateau was round in plan (Fig. 5.1.28) and was radiocarbon-dated to 1493–1091 BC. The diameter of the area enclosed by upright posts was 4.9m, although it is probable that these posts constituted an internal ring of roof supports and that a low-pitched roof

Fig. 5.1.28—Knockadoon: plan of Bronze Age round house.

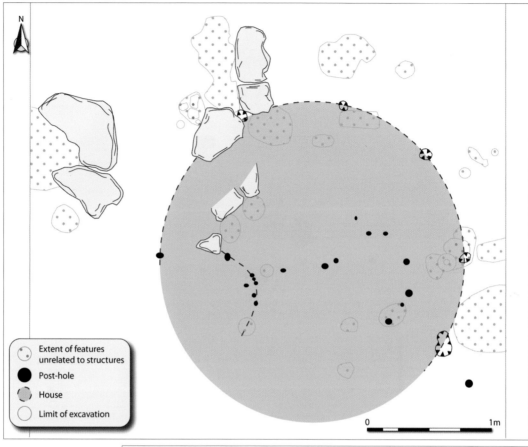

Fig. 5.1.29—Knockadoon: reconstruction of Bronze Age round house.

continued to external walls outside these uprights (Fig. 5.1.29). The external walls were probably low and built of wattle carried on light posts and plastered with mud, or they may have been made from piled-up turves. There was no trace of a hearth within the building; although the absence of a hearth had obvious disadvantages, such as the lack of heat within a building, leading to more rapid decay of timbers, a hearth within a timber house was a fire hazard. An arc of stake-holes was recorded on the south-west side of the house and may represent an internal stake-built screen or drying rack

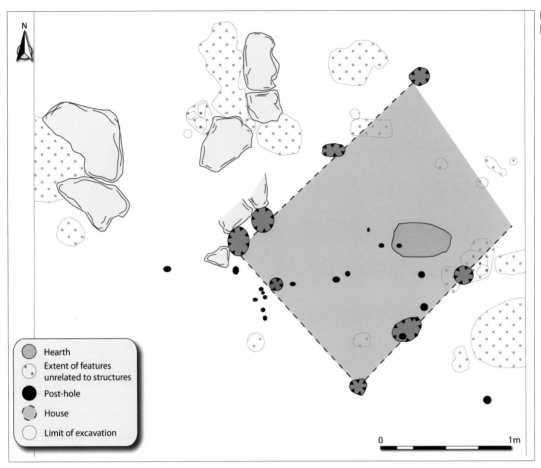

Fig. 5.1.30—Knockadoon: Bronze Age rectangular house.

Legend:
- Hearth
- Extent of features unrelated to structures
- Post-hole
- House
- Limit of excavation

0   1m

(Fig. 5.1.28). The round house was replaced by a rectangular house measuring 2.9m wide by at least 3m long and dated to 1154–811 BC (Fig. 5.1.30). Similar to the round house (above), the post-holes may have held internal roof supports, and the external walls were outside these and under a low-pitched roof. There was an off-centre hearth within the house.

After the houses were levelled, a trampled, compact layer of chert was laid along the southern edge of the area, and this was partly covered by layers of stony soil which formed an artificial platform overlying the foundations of the round and rectangular houses. A layer of burnt limestone and sandstone was then laid along the edge of the platform and this was dated to 1084–811 BC. The source of the burnt stone is unknown and may have derived from use in heating water, similar to activity at *fulachtaí fia* (ancient cooking sites), or perhaps from a house that was destroyed by fire. An oval house was constructed on the platform and the area enclosed by posts measured 4.8m (north/south) by 5.3m (east/west) (Fig. 5.1.31). Clusters of stake-holes within the house suggested internal screens, benches or drying racks. A stone hammer and a polished limestone pebble recovered from two of the post-holes may represent deliberate placement as some type of symbolic act related to house construction. Four large pits within the floor area were possibly used as rubbish pits, as animal bone fragments were recovered from the fills. One off-centre pit (Fig. 5.1.31: 1; see also Fig. 5.2.4) within the oval house was partly lined with limestone slabs and portions of an infant's skull

Fig. 5.1.31—Knockadoon: plan of Bronze Age oval house.

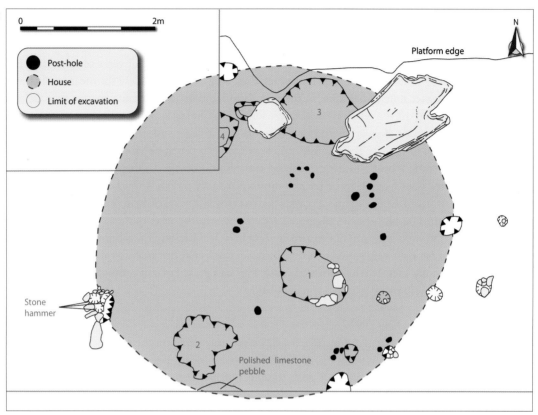

Fig. 5.1.32—Finds from Knockadoon: 1–4 scrapers; 5 blade; 6–7 arrowheads; 8 bronze earring.

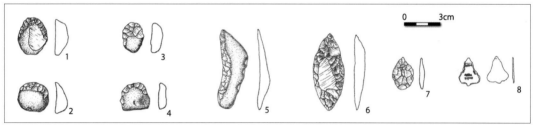

were found at its base. Three Bronze Age slab-lined graves and two unlined graves were recorded immediately north of the Bronze Age houses (see below).

Fourteen pits within the excavated area varied in size and depth. Most were filled with dark habitation refuse, including butchered animal bone. Some care had been taken to dig and line the paved base of one of the pits. Radiocarbon evidence showed that the pits ranged in date from 1609 to 792 BC, and one pre-dated house construction.

Finds from the Bronze Age houses mainly consisted of Class II pottery, which was in and around the houses but was mostly recovered from the layer of burnt limestone and sandstone. Other stone finds included a broken hone, rubbing stones, four flint scrapers (Fig. 5.1.32: 1–4), a blade (Fig. 5.1.32: 5) and two arrowheads (Fig. 5.1.32: 6–7). A pear-shaped bronze earring, which measured 5.5mm by 3.3mm (Fig. 5.1.32: 8), was decorated with a lightly incised zigzag pattern along the perimeter and two incised lines across its centre.

The animal bone assemblage from this excavation was the first from Knockadoon to be comprehensively studied using modern analytical techniques and produced some interesting results (Van Wijngaarden-Bakker 1995). The majority of the bones were from pigs; cattle were the next most frequent, with much smaller quantities of sheep/goat, horse and red deer. The pigs were moderately sized and of slender build and all were killed by three and a half years of age, while the cattle were generally killed by the age of four years. Pigs were bred exclusively for meat production, probably to counteract nutritional stress in the population and as an insurance against crop failure. Cattle were also killed off at a relatively young age rather than being kept for milk, and dairying was of secondary importance. Pigs are pernicious to crops and tillage, and crops were probably not a primary food source in the late Bronze Age at Lough Gur. No cereal remains were recovered from this site although some wheat and barley remains were found on the C-shaped enclosure (above). The presence of red deer suggests some limited hunting. A study by Van Wijngaarden-Bakker (1995) of the bird bones[3] from Ó Ríordáin's excavations enabled some reconstruction of the landscape around Lough Gur. The bird species suggested habitats where the environment near the lake was open wetland, with rough grassland in the surrounding hills. The lake itself was bordered by reedlands, and these types of habitats were suited to native birds such as geese, ducks, coots and marsh-harriers, and to seasonal visitors such as white-fronted geese. Pigs had plenty of soft ground in which to root and wallow. Cattle presumably grazed open grasslands.

Huts in the car-park excavations (1977–8)
The remains of four small circular huts (Fig. 5.1.33) were uncovered on the car-park excavation site (Cleary 1982a; 1982b; 1983). Huts 1, 3 and 4 had foundation or footing trenches, while Hut 2 was constructed using free-standing vertical posts for the wall perimeter. Where the evidence for the superstructure of Bronze Age huts survives, many are interpreted as having upright posts with intermediary woven wattle walls (Doody 2007, 91–3). There was no direct dating evidence for the structures excavated in the car park, although the size and ground-plans suggested that they were prehistoric. Hut 1 pre-dated the medieval House I and was also disturbed by the foundation of the

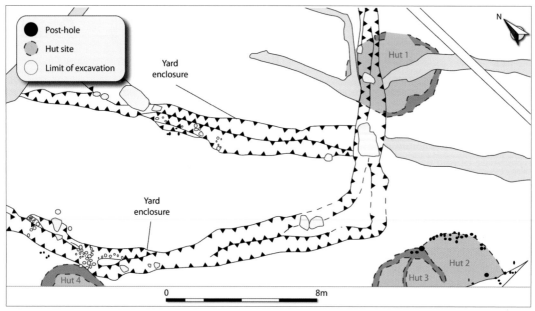

Fig. 5.1.33—Car-park excavations: hut sites.

medieval yard enclosure fence (Chapter 10). Hut 4 was also cut into by the yard enclosure fence. Huts 2 and 3 overlapped in floor plan and were probably built sequentially. The huts varied in diameter from 4m to 6m, a size common in the Irish Bronze Age (*ibid.*, 91).

Some flint artefacts of prehistoric date were recovered from the car-park area; they range in date from the late Neolithic to the Bronze Age and may indicate a prehistoric construction date for the huts, although there was no direct association between the structures and the flint. A flint Petit Tranchet Derivative (PTD), which was a type of arrowhead in use in the late Neolithic (3000–2500 BC), was found in the foundation of the medieval House II, three flint scrapers from the topsoil were of Neolithic or Bronze Age date, and some waste flakes show limited on-site flint-knapping. A stone axehead fragment of Neolithic date was reused as a hone in the medieval period. A piglet burial was found in the floor of Huts 2 and 3 and may represent some type of symbolic act or offering when the hut was built or abandoned.

House site (1977 excavations)
A house site was recorded when excavations were carried out in advance of construction of the interpretative centre (Cleary 1982a). An arc of post-holes that held vertical structural posts was recorded along the northern side of the building and defined part of the perimeter (Fig. 5.1.34). The estimated diameter was *c.* 8.5m. Posts in these positions may have been an inner circular setting of roof supports for a low-pitched roof which extended to a low wall; the vestiges of this wall were marked by a second arc of post-holes set at a distance of 3m from and concentric with the inner arc.

Fig. 5.1.34—Excavations 1977: plan of Bronze Age hut.

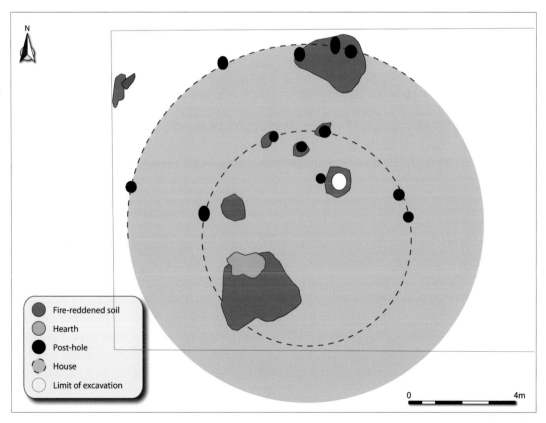

Legend:
- Fire-reddened soil
- Hearth
- Post-hole
- House
- Limit of excavation

0   4m

If the outer arc marked the external wall, the estimated overall diameter of the house was *c.* 13.5m. A similar type of building was suggested for a round house excavated on Knockadoon (see Fig. 5.1.29). The external walls may have been of wattle carried on light posts and plastered with mud. An internal hearth was also recorded. An area of burning visible on the external perimeter suggested that the building was damaged by fire. A 0.6m-deep pit with a diameter of *c.* 1m on the east side of the inner arc of post-holes had minute fragments of burnt bone in the fill. Pottery from the site[4] was similar to Class II ware and was decorated with linear motifs. The pottery is comparable to other Class II wares from Knockadoon and from Chancellorsland, Co. Tipperary, and a date range of *c.* 1600–1400 BC is suggested for the house.

Site C

Site C was excavated in 1940 and 1949 and produced evidence for three middle Neolithic (3600–3000 BC) houses and for occupation in the late Neolithic Grooved Ware phase (3000–2500 BC) and in the Beaker period (2500–2000 BC). The evidence of Bronze Age activity did not include a formal house. Ó Ríordáin (1954, 323) considered that a naturally occurring gravel/stone layer marked the abandonment of Site C in the Beaker period and that all finds below this layer were no later than the Beaker phase. Finds that included Class II pottery and bronze artefacts were recovered from below the gravel/stone layer, and it can be argued that these were intrusive from later levels owing to pit-digging in the Bronze Age. Much of the Class II pottery was in pits, which were frequent within the excavated area, particularly in the section excavated in 1949. Absolute dating by radiocarbon determinations of Class II pottery confirms a Bronze Age date, and the presence of Class II wares in the lower strata was undoubtedly due to later disturbance. Decorated sherds of Class II ware from Site C can be closely paralleled in more recently excavated sites such as Chancellorsland, Co. Tipperary (Cleary 2008), dated to 1600–1400 BC.

Other Bronze Age finds from Site C included whetstones, blue glass beads, bronze blades, pins, awls, knife blades, a socketed axehead and a tanged razor. Ó Ríordáin (1954, 382) described some of the bronze objects as coming from a low level in the area excavated in 1949 where most pits were recorded and indicated disturbance on the site by the Bronze Age phase of activity. Twenty sandstone whetstone fragments were found at Site C (1940 and 1949) and had surfaces smoothed from use in sharpening metal blades; one from Site C (1940) had pin-grooves from the sharpening of bronze pins. Two whetstones were found on the old ground surface at Site C (1940), indicating that the finds were intrusive in the earlier Neolithic strata. Nine complete and six fragments of blue glass beads found at Site C were like the glass beads from the C-shaped enclosure and Circles J and K and were probably late Bronze Age in date. Bronze objects including a blade fragment, a complete pin (Fig. 5.1.35: 1), a broken pin, an awl and six fragments of bronze were found below the gravel layer at Site C (1940). Ó Ríordáin (1954, 361) described the complete pin as 'nail-headed' and suggested a late Bronze Age date. A second complete pin (Fig. 5.1.35: 2) was found above the gravel layer. A broken double-edged blade (Fig. 5.1.35: 3) from a long, slender dagger or rapier had a perforated tang indicating a riveted handle and dated from the late Bronze Age (Ó Ríordáin 1954, 362). A razor (Fig. 5.1.35: 4) comprising a tang and a blade was made as one piece rather than riveted together and was also late Bronze Age in date. A small late Bronze Age socketed axehead found near the surface at Site C (1940) had a raised ridge fashioned into a rope-moulding motif at the socketed end and a loop for fastening a handle (Fig. 5.1.35: 5). A knife blade and two awls were found at Site C (1949).

Fig. 5.1.35—Bronze artefacts from Site C, Knockadoon: 1 'nail-headed' pin; 2 pin; 3 rapier blade; 4 razor; 5 socketed and looped axehead.

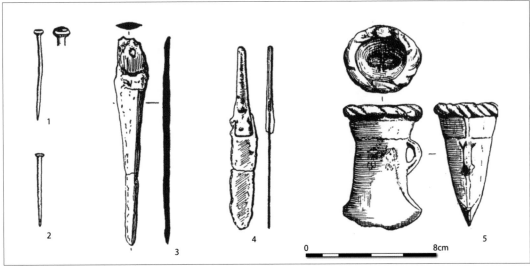

Site D

Walls visible on the surface prior to the excavation were interpreted by Ó Ríordáin (1954, 384–5) as stone foundations marking the basal levels of a house (House I[5]) that was roughly rectangular in plan, measuring 5.5m (north/south) by 3.5m (east/west) (Figs 5.1.36–7). The stones on the south-west side were set upright on a roughly cobbled surface or on exposed bedrock and were supported by smaller stones and sods wedged under the uprights. The foundation at the western end of the house was on a rock outcrop. The type of superstructure House I may have had is unknown, although Ó Ríordáin (1954, 385) suggested that the walls above the stone foundation may have been built of sods. There was a stone-lined post-hole, possibly for a roof support, near the centre of the house. House I partly overlay the floor area of a middle Neolithic round house (Chapter 3). There are no locational details of the finds from House I. Ó Ríordáin (1954, 392) noted that decoration on the Class II pottery was rare and this might indicate a date in the late Bronze Age. A number of sherds illustrated in the published record have perforations below the rims that also suggest a late Bronze Age date.

A line of large stones to the south of the house extended across a narrow valley to link with outcropping rock; a short section of a second wall at the eastern end of the line of stones was *c.* 1.2m to the north (Fig. 5.1.36). The intermediary space between the walls was used as a rubbish dump and a considerable amount of occupation debris, including Class II pottery and animal bones, was recovered from the area. Ó Ríordáin (1954, 385) suggested that the accumulation of rubbish inside the wall created a level surface that served as a yard for the house. Two other walls *c.* 15m to the north of the house also closed off the area around the house and were *c.* 3m apart. The northern wall was built of large stones, and occupation debris, including animal bones and Class II pottery, had accumulated against it. The southern wall was built of smaller stones set into a natural rock fissure. Ó Ríordáin (1954, 384–5) interpreted the walls to the north and south of the Bronze Age house as terraces to prevent soil and scree from washing down the hill. Alternatively, the walls could have formed an enclosure around House I similar to the enclosure at Site 10.

Fragments of a clay mould (Fig. 5.1.38: 1) were found to the north of House I at a depth of *c.*

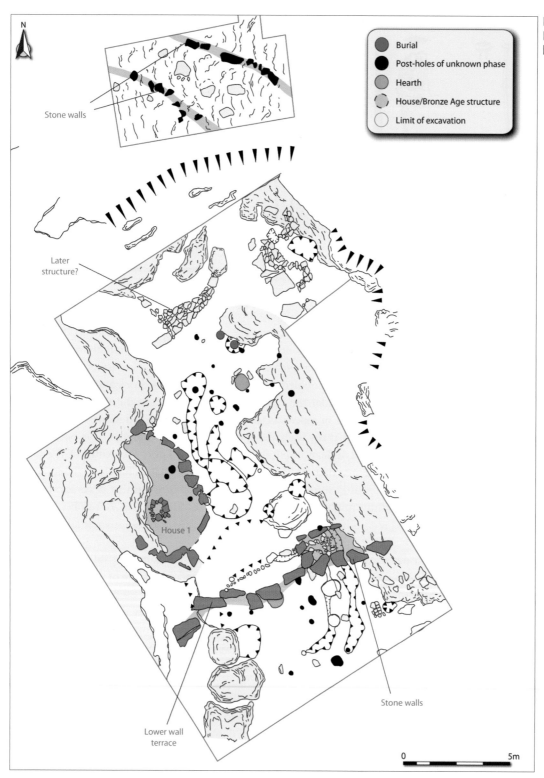

Fig. 5.1.36—Site D, Knockadoon: plan of Bronze Age house and enclosing walls.

Legend:
- Burial
- Post-holes of unknown phase
- Hearth
- House/Bronze Age structure
- Limit of excavation

Stone walls

Later structure?

House 1

Lower wall terrace

Stone walls

0   5m

Fig. 5.1.37—Site D, Knockadoon: Bronze Age house during excavation.

Fig. 5.1.38—Finds from Site D, Knockadoon: 1 fragment of clay mould for bronze spearhead; 2 fragment of stone mould for palstave axehead.

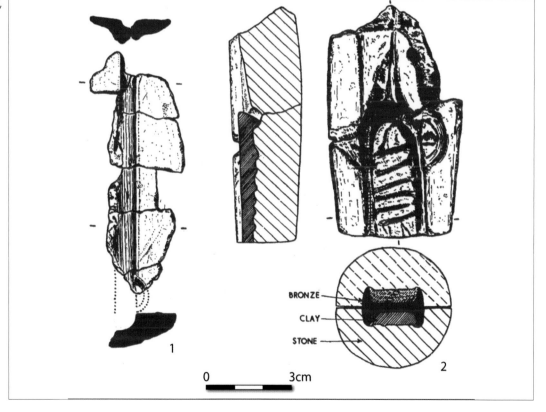

BRONZE

CLAY

STONE

0   3cm

1

2

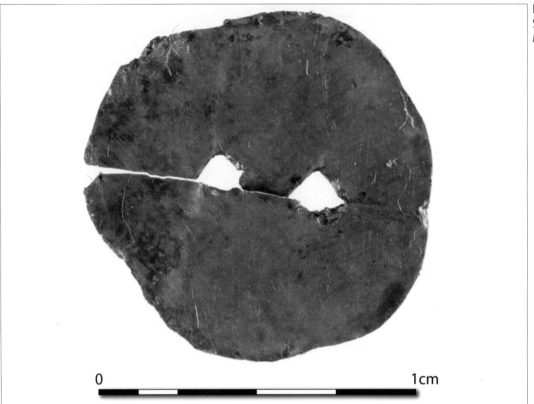

Fig. 5.1.39—Gold disc from Site D, Knockadoon (National Museum of Ireland).

0 1cm

0.18m below the sod. The mould had been broken to extract the artefact, but it was possible to fit some pieces together to show that it was for a looped spearhead of late Bronze Age date. Fragments of a sandstone mould (Fig. 5.1.38: 2) for a palstave axehead were recovered from inside House I and from north of the house. Part of the inner surface was covered with clay to allow the smith to cast flanges on the axehead. The provenances of six whetstones from Site D were not recorded, but these were used to sharpen metal blades and were probably from late Bronze Age horizons. A bronze nail-headed pin, like one from Site C, and two bronze awls were found in House I. A piece of the cutting edge of a bronze axehead and part of a bronze chisel were found near the south terrace/enclosure wall, and a bronze bracelet came from within the wall. The bracelet was oval, with an internal diameter of 62mm, and may have belonged to a child.

The locational details of an early Bronze Age small gold disc (Fig. 5.1.39) from Site D are unknown. It is made from very thin foil with an irregular edge and is almost circular, measuring 11.4mm by 11.5mm. Two perforations punched through the foil suggest that the disc was probably attached to a larger object as a decorative mount or cover (Cahill 2003, 175).

Sites E–I

Five hut sites were excavated on Knockadoon during Ó Ríordáin's campaign and were designated Sites E–I. Stone foundations of all the huts were visible on the surface prior to excavation. Except for Site F, which was probably early medieval in date, the recovery of Class II pottery from the huts suggests a Bronze Age date. Site F was the largest structure, measuring 8m by 6.3m, and was

Fig. 5.1.40—Site E,
Knockadoon: plan of hut.

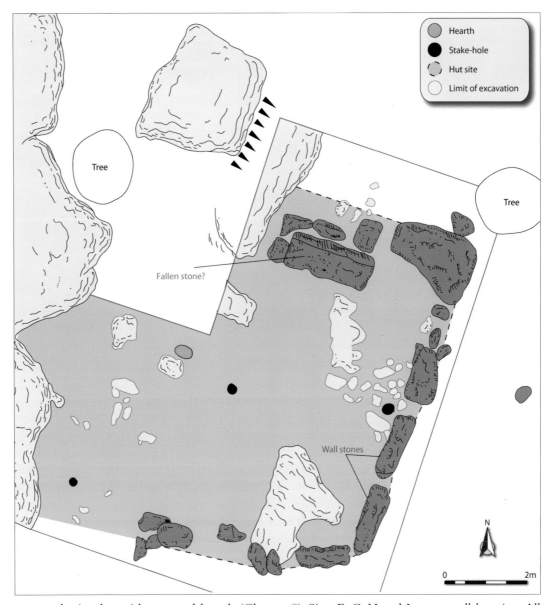

rectangular in plan with a central hearth (Chapter 8). Sites E, G, H and I were small hut sites. All were similar in construction methods and had haphazardly built stone foundations above which walls may have been built of sods or wood. Site E was on a narrow plateau on the west side of Knockadoon; Site I was in the narrow valley that runs north–south across Knockadoon Hill and Sites F, G and H were upslope from the lake on the south-west of Knockadoon (Fig. 5.1.1). Sites E, F and G incorporated cliff faces into the structures similar to the house excavated within the C-shaped enclosure (above; Figs 5.1.8–10). As the bedrock was close to the surface at each site, it was difficult to discern post-holes for structural upright posts where crevices in the bedrock had been opportunistically used to contain posts.

Fig. 5.1.41—Knockadoon: Site E during excavation (from north).

Site E

The hut measured 4.6m by 3.7m and its ground-plan was marked by large stones (Figs 5.1.40–41). These were placed on edge along the south and east sides and had fallen along the north side. The west end of the hut was formed by a rock face. The stones were set up on a gravel layer which may have been a floor level and some were propped up with smaller stones. The gravel layer was at a depth of 0.3m below the modern surface and may have been naturally occurring rather than deliberately laid. A small central post-hole suggested the location of a roof prop. A 0.5m spread of burnt soil on the floor was interpreted as a hearth and charcoal-enriched soil in and around the hut suggested that it burnt down, which may indicate that the walls were made of wood. There was no clear evidence of the date of construction as there were few finds, but the general morphology suggests parallels with the other Bronze Age huts excavated by Ó Ríordáin. Ó Ríordáin (1954, 415) also interpreted the hut as a temporary shelter owing to the lack of signs of prolonged occupation.

Site F

Ó Ríordáin (1954, 419) suggested a possible Bronze Age or early medieval date for stone house foundations of roughly rectangular plan at Site F. Early medieval finds, including an iron knife and pin from the western end of the north wall and a bone comb fragment inside the west wall, would seem to favour an early medieval date (Chapter 8). Pre-house activity on the site was indicated by a hearth and occupation soil under the north wall. An off-centre hearth within the house floor yielded mainly Class II pottery and a few sherds of Neolithic pottery. The site also produced evidence of Neolithic occupation from a layer near the house (Chapter 3). The Class II pottery was found in the main associated with clay moulds used to manufacture late Bronze Age weapons. A field wall also extended from the west side of the house and, although the excavation did not confirm a clear

Fig. 5.1.42—Site G,
Knockadoon: plan of hut.

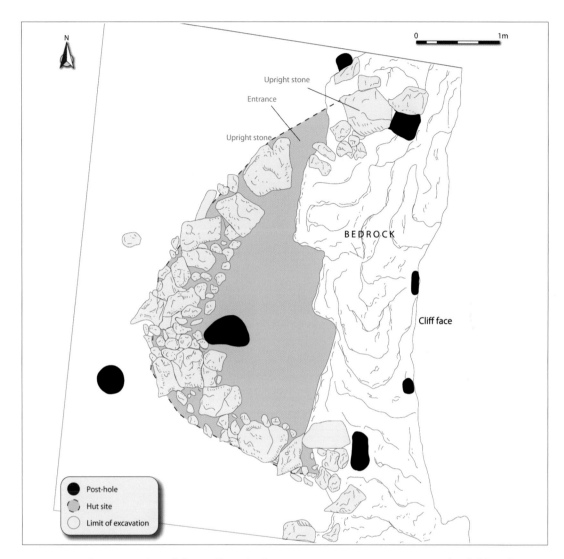

association, the proximity of the wall to the house suggests contemporaneity. The field walls were dated to the early medieval period by Ó Ríordáin (1954, 419).

Evidence of bronze-working, including clay mould fragments and bronze-working waste, was recovered from the hearth under the east end of the fence adjacent to the house. Fragments of clay moulds and some Class II pottery were also found under and within a fence to the south and in the fill of an adjacent ditch. Overall, fragments of about 100 clay moulds were recovered, and these were used in bivalve casting to produce late Bronze Age socketed looped spearheads and rapiers of middle Bronze Age date (1500–1000 BC). The number of clay mould fragments from Site F suggested that the site was a bronzesmith's workshop.

Site G

This small hut was built against a rock face to the north of Site F. It was defined by a semicircular stone setting and the straight face of a 2m-high cliff edge, which gave an overall D-shaped ground-

Fig. 5.1.43—Knockadoon: Site G during excavation.

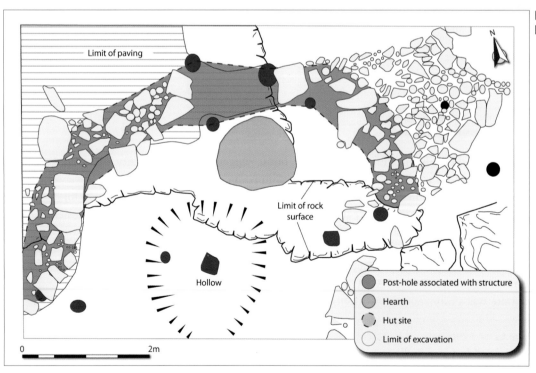

Fig. 5.1.44—Site H, Knockadoon: plan of hut.

Limit of paving

Limit of rock surface

Hollow

Post-hole associated with structure

Hearth

Hut site

Limit of excavation

0   2m

plan (Figs 5.1.42–3). The long axis was 3.4m (north/south) along the cliff face and the short axis was 2.4m (east/west). The stone foundation course was made by piling up variously sized stones to a height of 0.45–0.6m. Post-holes along the cliff edge, near the cliff face and at either side of the western wall foundation may have held wall posts or roof supports. A 1m-wide gap flanked by two upright stones on the north side of the hut marked the entrance. The floor of the east side was exposed bedrock and elsewhere a layer of clay and gravel that had been compressed from trampling. The only pottery found was Class II ware, which was found inside and outside the hut. The coarse fabric and perforations below the rims suggest that the pottery was late Bronze Age in date.

Animal bones from the site were identified as mainly cattle, with some sheep and pig. The upper portion of a human jaw of an individual aged 20–30 years was found in the stone foundation course. The teeth indicated chronic gum disease and were worn, presumably from the person's diet.

Site H

Only part of a more extensively occupied area was excavated at Site H. This created difficulties when drawing interpretative plans, as the site was multi-period and included Neolithic, Grooved Ware, Beaker and sherds of pygmy cups, which are more usually associated with early Bronze Age burials. Some post-holes under a section of a stone wall foundation and occupation layers that yielded animal bones and pottery pre-dated the Bronze Age hut. A paved area under the stone foundations on the north-west side pre-dated the building. Bedrock was also near the surface and there appears to have been little depth in the stratigraphy. The north side of the Bronze Age hut was the best-preserved section and had a randomly coursed stone foundation and evidence of a post-built wall, with paired post-holes recorded at either side of the stone foundation (Fig. 5.1.44). The hut appears to have been oval or circular in plan, with an estimated diameter of 6–7m. The floor level was formed by a natural rock surface and clay. Class II pottery was the main find from the floor, and its coarseness and perforations below the rims suggest a late Bronze Age date. Two bone points, a small bone bead, a clay bead and a blue glass bead were also found within the hut. A skull fragment from an adult was found on the floor level with the pottery.

Site I

This hut was within an area where there were some small field enclosures (Fig. 5.1.1). Ó Ríordáin (1954, 435) described these as 'terraces' marked by banks of stone and clay, small level areas delimited by large stones and a sunken trackway that extended from near the lake shore northwards through a narrow valley. The 'terraces' were small fields that enclosed naturally level areas. The enclosing banks were made of upright stones and in places combined with small stones and earth. These were of similar construction to the field fence excavated south-west of the C-shaped enclosure (above), which was dated by radiocarbon to 1392–1148 BC. Neolithic (Class I) and Bronze Age (Class II) pottery was found near but not within the walls.

The hut at Site I was built beside one of the field enclosures, c. 1m north of the enclosure wall but not bonded into it. The hut was roughly rectangular in plan and measured 3m by 2.5m[6] (Figs 5.1.45–46). Similar to Sites E–H, the stone foundations were a mix of large limestone blocks, smaller stones and earth. The stones were, however, set into a shallow foundation trench filled with small stones and earth, and the larger stones were set on top of this. The walls were built on top of the foundation, as at Sites E–H, and were probably made from sods. A c. 1m-wide break in the south-west side of the foundation suggested an entrance. Four post-holes within the floor area may have

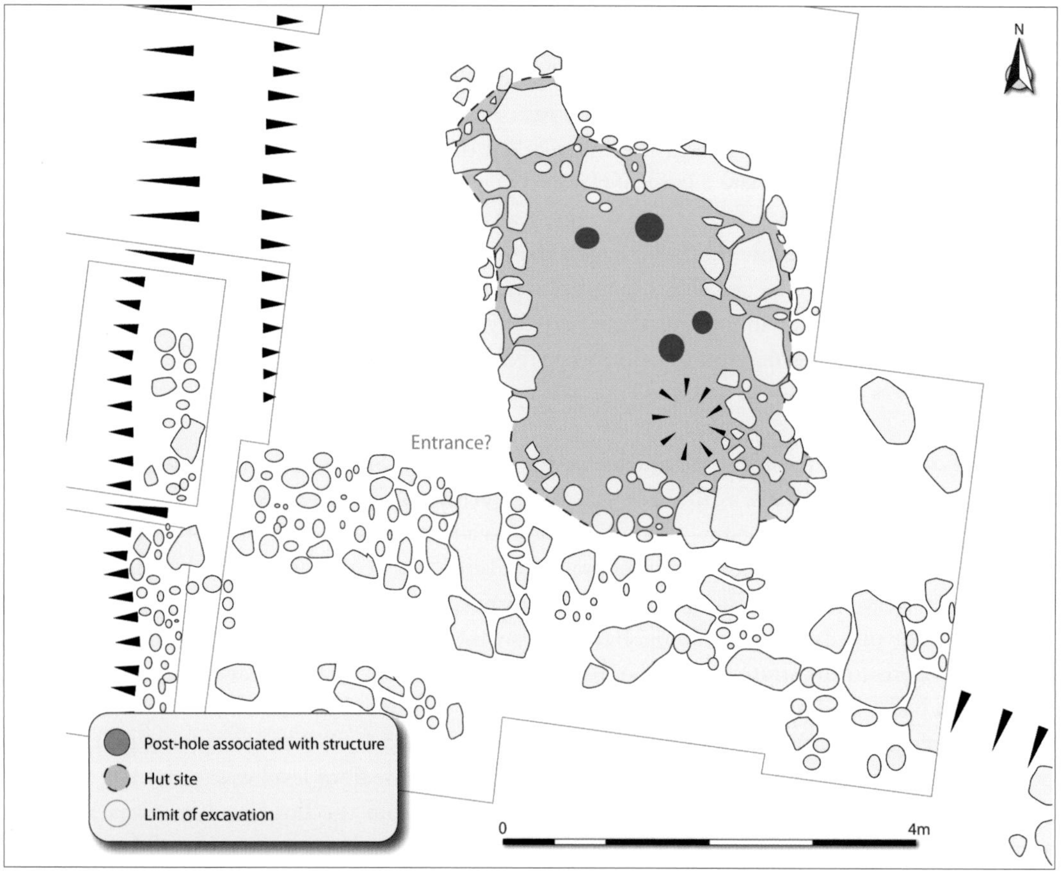

Fig. 5.1.45—Site I, Knockadoon: plan of hut.

Entrance?

Post-hole associated with structure

Hut site

Limit of excavation

0   4m

Fig. 5.1.46—Knockadoon: Site I during excavation.

held roof-support posts. A hearth site in a hollow adjacent to the south wall probably pre-dated the hut and included Neolithic pottery and animal bone fragments. The hut is difficult to date, as the pottery from the hearth and adjacent pit were Neolithic, although these may have pre-dated the construction of the hut. Neolithic pottery was also found in cuttings made across the field enclosure walls and probably represented earlier phases of site occupation. The similarity of construction and size of the hut at Site I to Site G may indicate a Bronze Age date.

5.2: BURIAL

Bronze Age burials at Lough Gur have been recorded on a variety of sites. The megalithic tomb excavated by Ó Ríordáin and Ó h-Iceadha (1955) was reused in the Bronze Age for burial, Bronze Age slab-lined graves were recorded on Knockadoon Hill and a burial in a pit was uncovered at Newchurch. There are also antiquarian accounts of finding burials that may date from the Bronze Age.

Megalithic tomb

A Bronze Age burial dated to 1731–1409 BC was inserted into the wedge tomb (Brindley and Lanting 1991–2, 24). The excavation also recorded that the western end or portico had been infilled with stones, and a small, slab-lined grave or cist was inserted c. 0.08m below the top of this infill (see Fig. 4.3.4). The cist grave was about 15in. (0.38m) square and contained fragments of cremated bone and pottery (Ó Ríordáin and Ó h-Iceadha 1955, 36). There was no dating evidence for the burial; details of the types of pottery within the cist grave are not provided in the published account, but the stratigraphic details suggest that the cist grave was later than tomb construction and the recovery of Class II pottery from around the megalithic tomb indicates that the site continued in use into the Bronze Age.

Knockadoon Hill

An excavation on the north side of Knockadoon Hill (Fig. 5.2.1) uncovered three slab-lined graves of Bronze Age date, evidence for casual deposition of human remains and the incorporation of parts of human remains in pits (Cleary 1995). All the burials were of infants. These slab-lined graves were immediately north of a Bronze Age settlement site, with which the burials were probably associated. A Neolithic burial dated to 3641–3372 BC (Chapter 3) and an Iron Age burial dated to 128 BC– AD 402 (Chapter 6) were also found.

Grave 1
This slab-lined grave was set into a bedrock crevice and was aligned east/west; it measured 0.86m (east/west) by 0.43m (north/south) by 0.16m deep, and was c. 0.15m below the modern surface (Figs 5.2.1–2). The floor was paved and two capstones partially covered the grave. The burial was of an infant aged 5–8 months and only the skull and some teeth remained; alternatively, the burial may have been a token interment, while the remainder of the body was buried elsewhere. The bones indicated that the child suffered from nutritional deficiency and illness prior to death (Ó Donnabháin 1995).

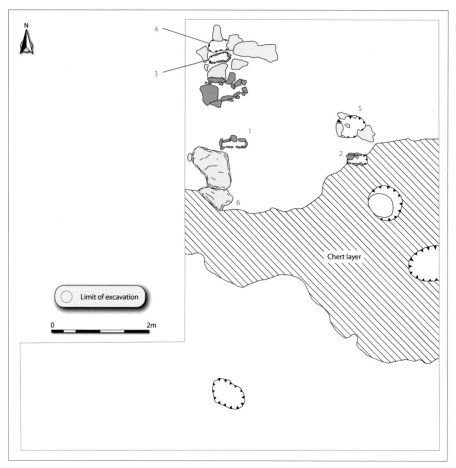

Fig. 5.2.1—Plan of burials on Knockadoon Hill.

Limit of excavation

0   2m

N

Chert layer

Grave 2

This slab-lined grave underlay a layer associated with the nearby settlement (Fig. 5.2.1). The layer was dated to 1607–1404 BC and the grave was in place before the layer accumulated. The grave cut into and post-dated a structural post of an oval house dated to 1493–1091 BC, and the grave itself may date from *c.* 1400 BC. It was aligned east/west and measured 0.65m (east/west) by 0.31m (north/south). There were no floor slabs or capstones. There were no human remains within the grave and it may be that it was never used.

Grave 3

The slab-lined grave was set into a crevice in the bedrock, and measured 0.7m (east/west) by 0.35m (north/south) by 0.22m high (Figs 5.2.1 and 5.2.3). The floor was paved and there were no capstones. The burial was of an infant aged 4–7 months.

Grave 4

This was a shallow oval pit measuring 0.66m (east/west) by 0.35m (north/south) by 0.15m deep (Fig. 5.2.1). One paving slab was recorded at the base. There were no human remains and the pit appeared to have been an unfinished grave. It was immediately north of Grave 3.

Fig. 5.2.2 (right)—Grave 1,
Knockadoon Hill.

Fig. 5.2.3 (far right)—Grave 3,
Knockadoon Hill.

Fig. 5.2.4—Knockadoon:
child's skull in pit within house
floor.

Grave 5

The remains of an infant aged 0–6 months were recovered from the base of a pit that measured 0.93m (east/west) by 0.63m (north/south) by 0.17m deep (Fig. 5.2.1). Only the skull and upper body parts were recovered; the remainder may have been buried elsewhere or may have disintegrated in the soil.

Grave 6

The remains of a skeleton were found lying directly on bedrock, and there was no apparent attempt to make a formal grave. The bones were those of an infant aged about three months and the head was to the west.

Partial burial

Body parts of other individuals were recovered from features associated with the settlement. The upper cranium of an infant was recovered from the base of a pit (Fig. 5.2.4) that was centrally located within an oval house (Fig. 5.1.31). The burial of a child's skull may have been some type of ritual act associated with the occupancy of the house. A single tooth of a juvenile aged about 12–14 years was also found in another pit associated with the settlement on the site. This may have been accidental loss rather than a deliberate burial.

Ballynagallagh

An excavation in 1978 at a destroyed megalithic tomb in Ballynagallagh townland uncovered two graves (Cleary and Jones 1980). The primary burial (Fig. 5.2.5) was a fragmentary cremated bone deposit and it was not possible to identify the age or sex of the individual. One of the side stones of a later cist grave was immediately south of the cremation pit but did not cut through it. The cist grave was 0.6m below the modern surface, polygonal in shape, with diameters of 1–1.2m and *c.* 0.45m in height. The side stones were set in an imbricated fashion and some were supported by packing stones. The floor was partially paved and there was no capstone *in situ*. The burial was a flexed inhumation with the head to the north. The bones were in poor condition but it was possible to age the individual on the basis of the teeth to 30–40 years. The teeth also showed some periodontal disease, and one of the long bones had evidence for an old fracture. While there are no absolute dates for either the primary cremation or the inhumation, the proximity of both graves suggest that the burials were possibly close in time, and the cist grave is similar to Bronze Age cist graves in Ireland. Animal bones were recovered from in and around the cist grave and, where identifiable, were mostly of cattle, from immature animals killed off between six and eighteen months of age; it may be speculated that these were from cattle slaughtered and eaten as part of the funeral rite.

Newchurch

A burial was unearthed during house construction in 1990. The burial was that of a juvenile aged 11–12 years and was placed in a simple pit; the bones were dated to 1387–1050 BC. The teeth showed that the child had suffered an illness prior to death.

Circle J

This was the location of the earliest excavation at Lough Gur, carried out by J. Harkness (Harkness 1869), who recorded the burial of a child aged 6–8 years in an unlined grave at a depth of *c.* 0.3m

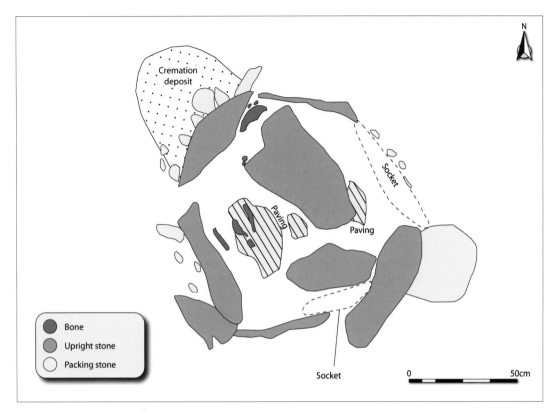

Fig. 5.2.5—Ballynagallagh: plan of graves.

Cremation deposit

Socket

Paving

Paving

Bone
Upright stone
Packing stone

Socket

0   50cm

below the surface and to the west of the standing stone (Fig. 2.17). A cist grave was also recorded in the south-west quadrant at a depth of 0.45m; this was partly covered by a flagstone and paved at the base (Harkness 1869, 391; Windle 1912, 299). It contained the remains of an adult, possibly female, and a child aged 6–8 years. Both bodies were aligned north/south, with the heads to the south. Pig bones and an antler fragment were placed in the grave with the burials (Harkness 1869, 392; Grogan and Eogan 1987, 333).

Circle J was partially excavated in 1946–7 by Seán P. Ó Ríordáin (Grogan and Eogan 1987). The site had been used as a burial ground possibly in the late Iron Age/early medieval period. Ó Ríordáin recorded nine slab-lined graves with associated burials, and a further nine slab-lined graves that were either empty or contained only fragmentary skeletal remains (ibid., 323). There was no unequivocal dating evidence for the slab-lined graves; they may have been late prehistoric or early medieval and are discussed in Chapter 8.

Ring-barrows and ring-ditches

Ring-barrows and ring-ditches have a surrounding ditch or fosse; the difference between them consists largely of a central mound within the barrow and sometimes an outer bank. These sites are often located in low-lying ground and are frequently observed in the landscape as circular features where the fosse is visible as a wetter area with lush grass growth or, indeed, with irises growing in the wet ground. Medium-altitude aerial photographic survey of east Limerick and parts of west Tipperary has documented 482 barrows and 128 ring-ditches (Doody 2008).

Dating can be problematic for sites excavated in the past, when radiocarbon dating was unavailable and sites were dated by associated finds, including ceramic vessels. Seán P. Ó Ríordáin excavated 21 ring-barrow sites at Lizzard near Galbally, Co. Limerick (Ó Ríordáin 1936). Most of these did not produce any finds that allowed him to date the monuments. One site at Lizzard had a burial associated with fragments of a cinerary urn similar to an urn type known as a 'cordoned urn' and datable to the period 1770–1550 BC (Brindley 2007). The excavation at Lizzard is also of interest in that the urn may have been covered by a large timber which Ó Ríordáin (1936, 175) suggested was a dugout canoe, noting that Lizzard 'is far from navigable water, but this may not have been the case in ancient times'. Much of the landscape around Lough Gur and further south was one of lakes, and dugout canoes would have been an ideal mode of transport in prehistoric times. Some ring-ditches excavated on the Limerick gas pipeline near Galbally were dated on the basis of ceramic finds to the late Bronze Age (1100–700 BC) (Gowen 1988). A ring-barrow with a diameter of 4m at Site C, Chancellorsland, near Emly, Co. Tipperary, was dated to 790–410 BC (Doody 2008, 341). The dating evidence from two other ring-barrows at Chancellorsland indicated that the tradition of using penannular enclosures surrounded by a ditch continued into the seventh–tenth centuries AD. O'Brien (2008, 662–3) suggested that these later penannular ditched enclosures were linked to Anglo-Saxon England, with a further connection evidenced by St Berihert of the Glen of Aherlow, whose name 'Berechtuine' derived from Old English.

Dating the ring-barrows and ring-ditches excavated at Lough Gur in the late 1940s is difficult, as the artefacts recovered ranged from Mesolithic microliths to Neolithic, Beaker, Food Vessel and Bronze Age pottery with a date range of over five millennia (8000–700 BC). The probability is that transient occupation took place where the ring-ditches and ring-barrows were subsequently constructed and that the earlier material was incorporated into later features. Where evidence is available, the floruit of ring-barrows and ring-ditches is in the Bronze Age (Cleary and Hawkes 2014).

A proposed function for ring-barrows and ring-ditches is that they were primarily part of a funeral rite (Corlett 2005; McGarry 2009). The excavated ring-barrows at Cahercorney, Ballingoola, Rathjordan and Grange Stone Circle B produced no evidence for burial. Ó Ríordáin (1947a; 1948) and MacDermott (1949a; 1949b) both argued that soil acidity had dissolved the bone or that the mound material of the barrows lightly covered inhumed burials which had 'completely disappeared' (Ó Ríordáin 1947a, 4). The most plausible explanation for the lack of burial evidence has, however, been suggested by Daly and Grogan (1993, 60), who hypothesised that ring-ditches and ring-barrows were part of a funeral rite rather than a final ossuary. Burnt animal bones have been recovered from many excavated sites and may represent the remains of ritual feasting. Other suggested purposes of ring-ditches include their being ritual places where the enclosed circle acted as an apotropaic cordon to turn aside evil (McGarry 2009, 420), places that represented ancestral powers and community history (Woodward 2000) or places of ceremony (Corlett 2005, 65). Some or all of these explanations may apply to ring-barrows and ring-ditches, although all suggest assembly.

Eight ring-barrows have been excavated around Lough Gur, at Rathjordan (1–4), Ballingoola (1–2 and possibly 5), Cahercorney and Knockfennell Hill. Three ring-ditches were also excavated within the Great Stone Circle (B) (Ó Ríordáin 1951), while a further three were detected by geophysical survey (O'Driscoll and Cleary 2016) and one was identified to the east outside the stone circle (Cleary and Hogan 2013).

Fig. 5.2.6—Rathjordan: location of barrows.

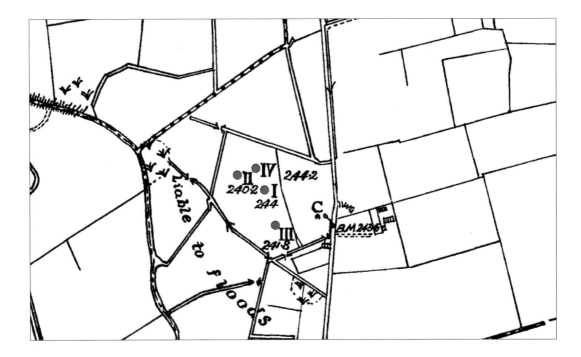

Rathjordan

Seán P. Ó Ríordáin excavated four ring-barrows in Rathjordan in 1946 (Barrow 1) and 1947 (Barrows 2–4), and these sites are about 3km north-east of Lough Gur (Ó Ríordáin 1947a; 1948). The sites were first drawn to his attention because 'an immense number of stone axes are said to have been found during tillage of a low-lying field there during World War I' (Ó Ríordáin 1947a, 1–2). A stone platform of possible Beaker period date (see Chapter 4) was also excavated in an adjacent field (Ó Ríordáin 1948). Barrows 1, 3 and 4 were on a ridge, while Barrow 2 was to the west and on the slope of the ridge (Fig. 5.2.6).

Ring-barrow 1

The site was visible as a low mound surrounded by a ditch and external bank with an overall diameter of 13m (Fig. 5.2.7). The partial excavation consisted of two 2m-wide cuttings north–south across the centre of the site. The low central mound, formed from ditch upcast, was *c.* 8m in diameter and no more than 0.2m at maximum height (Fig. 5.2.7: sectional profile). A layer of pebbles at the base of the mound was interpreted as part of the upcast from the ditch. The ditch was broad and V-shaped, *c.* 1.1–1.2m wide at the top and cut to depths of 0.3–0.5m below the original ground level, and had naturally silted up. A small area of burning with charcoal near the centre of the barrow produced a single minute fragment of unidentifiable cremated bone.

A pit 0.5m deep by *c.* 1.2m wide was slightly off-centre on the south-west side of the ring-barrow and was filled with burnt material, including burnt stone, oak charcoal and a small amount of cremated bone, identified as probably pig ribs and toe bones. A broken Neolithic pottery vessel from the base of the pit was dated to the period *c.* 3800–3500 BC. Ó Ríordáin (1947a, 3) argued that the pit was initially dug and immediately covered by the mound without any interval, as the top of the pit merged with the layer of pebbles at the base of the mound and with the pre-barrow

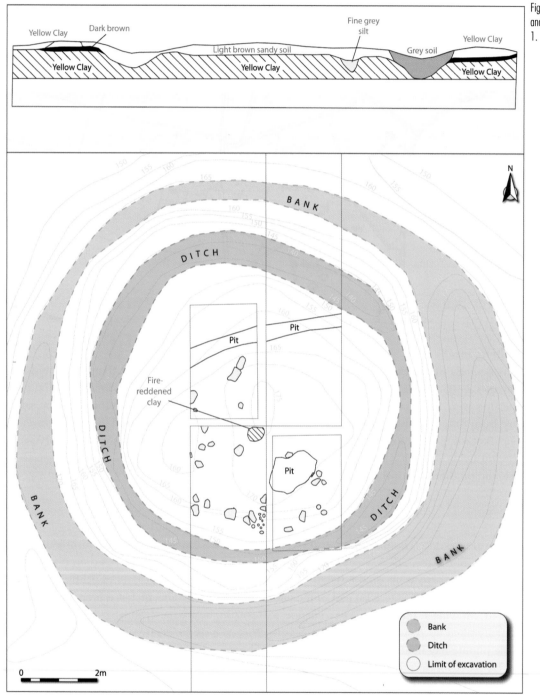

Fig. 5.2.7—Rathjordan: plan and sectional profile of Barrow 1.

old ground level, and therefore that the mound and the pit were contemporary. The pottery led Ó Ríordáin to date the construction of the barrow to the Neolithic. Two Mesolithic quartz microlithic points dating from *c.* 8000–6500 BC were also recovered from the pit, and a fragment of polished stone axehead was found in the mound. The recovery of Mesolithic artefacts and Neolithic pottery from the pit strongly suggests that these were accidental inclusions from earlier activity on the site and that they cannot be used to date the ring-barrow construction.

Ring-barrow 2
This site was to the north-west of Barrow 1, similar in size and slightly oval in plan, measuring 13m (north/south) by 12m (east/west). It was on a slope and was less well preserved than Barrows 1, 3 and 4. It had a low mound, surrounding ditch and external bank and was poorly preserved on the western side. The excavation took place mainly in the central area inside the ditch, and cuttings were made across on the north, south, east and west sides. Only a description and sectional profiles rather than site plans were published (Ó Ríordáin 1948, 20–2). The mound was formed by upcast from the digging of the ditch and was a mixture of topsoil mixed with yellow boulder clay. The sectional profiles suggest a mound height of *c.* 0.15–0.6m (Fig. 5.2.8). The thickest section of the mound was on the eastern side, where there was a natural hollow which was infilled with soil excavated from the ditch. Four sections excavated across the ditch showed that it was U-shaped in profile, cut to depths of *c.* 0.2–0.4m and 0.4–0.9m wide, being widest on the western side. Upcast from the ditch was also used to form the outer bank, which was best preserved on the northern side and 0.4m high. A central irregularly shaped pit under the mound was at maximum 1.5m in diameter and *c.* 0.5m deep, being deepest at the northern end and shallow (*c.* 0.15m deep) on the southern side. In some areas the

Fig. 5.2.8—Rathjordan: sectional profiles of Barrows 2 and 4.

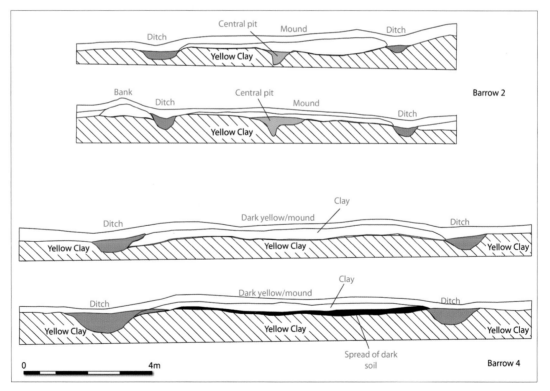

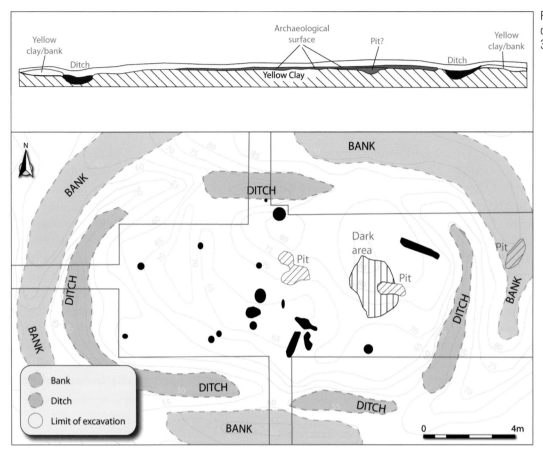

Fig. 5.2.9—Rathjordan: plan and sectional profile of Barrow 3.

surrounding bank had slipped back into the ditch, and this was particularly noticeable on the eastern side where the gradient was steeper. Ó Ríordáin interpreted dark layers at the base and side of the ditch fill as the remains of rushes that grew in the damp ditch and concluded that, as the rushes grew in the spring/summer, the barrow was constructed perhaps in late winter or spring (*ibid.*, 20–1).

The fill of the central pit consisted of charcoal-flecked clay with some burnt bone. Three early Mesolithic quartz microlithic points (*ibid.*, pl. III) dating from *c.* 8000–6500 BC, a leaf-shaped flint point identified as a Bann flake of later Mesolithic date (*c.* 6500–4000 BC), one sherd of undecorated Neolithic pottery (*c.* 3800–3500 BC) and a small chert blade were recovered from the pit (*ibid.*, 21–2). A second possible chert 'miniature Bann flake' was also recovered from the site but the report does not specify provenance (*ibid.*, 22). Like the material recovered from Barrow 1, the artefacts from the pit at Barrow 2 ranged widely in date, suggesting that they were accidentally incorporated into the pit when it was backfilled. Neolithic pottery, a chert scraper, fragments of greenstone axeheads and flint and chert débitage were also found at Barrow 2. The cremated bone from Barrow 2 was identified as being from non-specific animals, and the unburnt bones were fragments of ox teeth (*ibid.*, 22).

Ring-barrow 3
This lay to the south of Ring-barrows 1 and 2 and at the end of the ridge. It was oval, 22.5m

(north/south) by 12.5m (east/west), with an internal ditch and low external bank (Fig. 5.2.9). There was no evidence of a mound within the interior and the site was more like a ring-ditch than a ring-barrow. Most of the central area was excavated, as well as additional 1m-wide cuttings across the bank. The ditch was U-shaped in section, with an upper width of *c.* 1.5m and a depth of *c.* 0.5m. Ó Ríordáin interpreted the ditch fill as bank slippage that occurred soon after the external bank was thrown up.

The interior had randomly distributed post-holes, spreads of dark soil, short trenches and pits; one pit was under the eastern bank and pre-dated the construction of the ring-ditch. These types of features are more usually found on settlement sites. The pit fills included pottery fragments, flints and small fragments of unidentifiable burnt bone, possibly animal. The bulk of the pottery was recovered from the southern half of the interior, the enclosing ditch, internal pits and trenches, but mainly from the darker soil adjacent to these features (Ó Ríordáin 1948, 24). Overall, *c.* 250 pottery fragments were found and were from Neolithic and Bronze Age vessels (*ibid.*, fig. 5). Fifty Beaker pottery fragments from the site (Fig. 4.2.5: 1–6) dated from *c.* 2500–2300 BC. Fragments of at least three Bowl Food Vessels were also recovered (Fig. 4.2.5: 7–9) and date from 2160–1930/20 BC (Brindley 2007, 328).

Ó Ríordáin (1948, 23) argued for contemporaneity of the various pottery types, as the pottery was recovered from the same features. The range of pottery spans over 3,500 years, however, and the more likely scenario is that some features pre-dated the ring-ditch and that material residual from earlier phases of site occupation was incorporated into pits when these were dug and backfilled. Ó Ríordáin (1948, 23) interpreted the larger pits and charcoal-enriched soil spreads as originating from 'cooking', suggesting domestic activity, and prior to barrow construction the site may have been used as a seasonally occupied site from Mesolithic to early Bronze Age times.

Ring-barrow 4

This was to the east of Ring-barrow 2 (Fig. 5.2.6). A slight internal mound was surrounded by a ditch with an overall diameter of *c.* 12.5m (Fig. 5.2.8). Sectional profiles were published although there was no published plan. Ó Ríordáin (1948, 29) described the site as having a 6m-diameter central spread of dark soil at a depth of *c.* 0.4m below the modern surface. An unspecified number of pits were described as 0.3–0.4m deep with charcoal-flecked soil fill and some burnt bone. Fifty sherds of Neolithic pottery, a small leaf-shaped flint arrowhead, a tanged arrowhead (Beaker?), a chert arrowhead and six greenstone axehead fragments were found at Barrow 4, but there were no details of provenance and the relationship of the artefacts to the period of barrow construction is unknown. The only identifiable animal bone was a fragment of an ox tooth.

Ballingoola

Two ring-ditches were excavated in Ballingoola in 1948–9 by Máire MacDermott (MacDermott 1949a), and a possible ring-barrow was excavated by Seán P. Ó Ríordáin (1950). The ring-ditches at Ballingoola 1 and 2 were to the south of a former river course, which at the time of the excavation was visible as a dried-up stream bed (Fig. 5.2.10). There was evidence at Ballingoola 1 of activity that pre-dated the ring-ditch, including a hollow in the south-east quadrant which had been cut through by the enclosing ditch and charcoal spreads and burnt stone under the eastern bank (Fig. 5.2.11). A second hollow was also recorded within the ring-ditch but their stratigraphic relationship was unclear. The two hollows were *c.* 0.35m deep and filled with charcoal-enriched soil and burnt

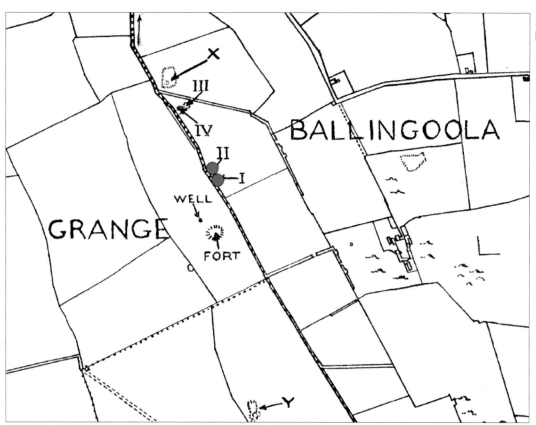

Fig. 5.2.10—Ballingoola: location of Barrows 1 and 2.

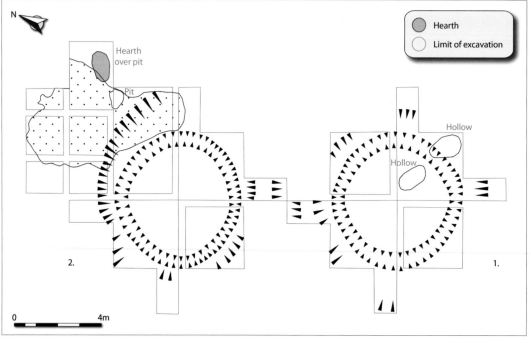

Fig. 5.2.11—Plan of Ballingoola 1 and 2.

Fig. 5.2.12—Sectional profiles of Ballingoola 2.

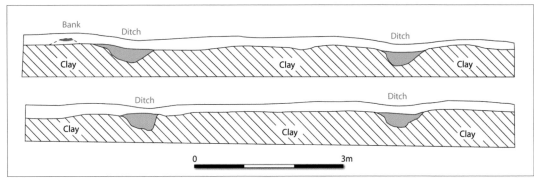

Fig. 5.2.12—Sectional profiles of Ballingoola 2.

stone. Pottery from the southern hollow was identified as 'some small fragments of coarse gritty pottery' (MacDermott 1949a, 142) which was not identified as to type, but the description suggests a Bronze Age date. Barrow 2 at Ballingoola was partly built on a stony layer where the dating evidence suggests use in the Beaker period (Chapter 4).

Ballingoola 1 and 2 had internal level areas surrounded by enclosing shallow ditches, and the absence of an internal mound suggested that these were ring-ditches rather than ring-barrows. The ring-ditches were *c.* 4m apart and were similar in size, with diameters of 6m. Before excavation, Ballingoola 1 (the southern site) had traces of an outer bank on the southern, south-eastern and northern sides. The ditch of Ballingoola 2 was visible on the south, north and west, and an outer bank was also visible on the western side (Fig. 5.2.12). The ditches were cut into this to a depth of *c.* 0.48m, and ditch upcast formed a slight bank or in some areas only a thin layer over the original ground level (MacDermott 1949a, 142). The ditches were subsequently rapidly infilled by bank slippage. The excavation did not recover any evidence of burial within either ring-ditch. Charcoal-enriched soil and burnt stone were recorded near the centre of Ballingoola 1. Apart from the pottery from the hollow in the south-east quadrant, the only other finds from Ballingoola 1 were a small flint flake and chert débitage.

Ballingoola 5 was west of Longford Bridge, south of the Camoge River; like the other excavated ring-ditches and barrows, it was situated on a slight rise in the low-lying marshy terrain. The site was interpreted as a house site (Ó Ríordáin 1950, 263) similar to Ballingoola III and IV (Ó Ríordáin 1949a; see Chapter 8) but, in the absence of any evidence of habitation and as the site had a central mound enclosed by a 0.48m-deep ditch, Ballingoola 5 was most likely a ring-barrow. The site was described[7] as *c.* 11m in diameter with an enclosing ditch and a possible causeway on the northern side, but this was not confirmed by excavation. The central area was a mound of redeposited boulder clay, and charcoal-flecked soil was recorded towards the centre of the site. The ditch was infilled by bank slippage.

Cahercorney

The ring-barrow was in marshy ground on the south side of the Camoge River (MacDermott 1949b), about half a mile to the south-west of the ring-barrows excavated at Rathjordan, which were to the north of the Camoge River. Before excavation the site was visible as a low circular mound surrounded by an enclosing ditch with a slight outer bank.[8] The overall diameter was *c.* 12m and the mound diameter was *c.* 4m. This mound and an external bank were formed by upcast from the ditch. The ditch was dug to a depth of about 0.5m and appeared to have been backfilled immediately, as there was no evidence of silting at the base. A spread of charcoal-flecked clay was recorded near the centre of the barrow at a depth of 0.13m and included some charred seeds, identified as possibly hawthorn. There were no traces of burial within the ring-barrow.

Finds included a polished greenstone axehead fragment, a Neolithic leaf-shaped chert arrowhead, which had broken during manufacture, and some waste fragments or débitage from the working of flint and chert. There are no details of exactly where these finds were recovered; they may have been from the pre-mound surface, the mound or ditch. One sherd of undecorated Neolithic pottery was found in the mound. As with the other excavated ring-barrows and ditches, there was no real evidence of the period of construction and the Neolithic pottery, arrowhead and stone axe fragment may have been residual from an earlier phase of site use.

Knockfennell Hill

Seán P. Ó Ríordáin excavated a small ring-cairn on the highest point of Knockfennell Hill in 1938. The site was interpreted as a ring-barrow with a central bowl-shaped depression which was defined by a bank formed by a rubble kerb and had a maximum diameter of 15.25m (O'Kelly 1941; 1944, 47). Pockets of unidentified cremated bone were found within the rubble kerb. Other finds were the butt of a stone axehead and animal bones. There was no evidence of date.

Grange Stone Circle B

Excavation by Ó Ríordáin (1951) and geophysical survey (O'Driscoll and Cleary 2016) identified six possible ring-ditches and one ring-barrow within the Great Stone Circle (B) (Fig. 5.2.13). The barrow (Fig. 5.2.13: G9) had a diameter of 5.2m and was the smallest enclosure. Three (Fig. 5.2.13: G4/5, G7/8, G13/14) of the ring-ditches had concentric ditches and were 7–9m in diameter. A possible ring-ditch with an overall diameter of *c.* 20m was also identified to the east of the stone circle (Cleary and Hogan 2013).

Other burials?

Antiquarian records suggest that other Bronze Age burials may exist around Lough Gur, although the exact locations of these are now unknown. An exception to this is the site of a possible Bronze Age burial ground uncovered when the reservoir at Caherguillamore was constructed in the early 1900s (Ó Ríordáin and Hunt 1942, 42). The work unearthed extended burials and urns; the urns suggest that some of the burials were Bronze Age. Nearer to Lough Gur, Lynch (1895, 290) recorded that 'In a field, now tilled, near Lough Gur Castle, are many graves lined with stone'. He also noted that, many years before he wrote of Lough Gur, 'several stone coffins of ordinary size were found, from eighteen [0.46m] to twenty-four inches [0.6m] below the surface' in a small garden 160 yards (146m) 'north of the Carriggally [Carraig Aille] group of stone circles' (Circles O and P). The same site may also have been referred to by Crofton Croker (1833, 110) when he mentioned 'Ardacolleagh, or Height of the Halter, for having been formerly used as a place of execution by the Earls of Desmond. Here, in making the road a few years since, some stone coffins, were found and several bones'. Crofton Croker also recorded that 'Near Mr John Hayne's house on Knockroe is a field containing numerous small stone graves a little under the surface, some of which, examined by Professor Harkness, contained human bones; and Mr Hynes told me he found iron implements in some others which he examined'. A field north-west of Circles O and P is recorded on the Ordnance Survey maps as 'Kistvaen Field'. A number of trial trenches were excavated in different parts of the field but nothing was found (O'Kelly 1944, 24).

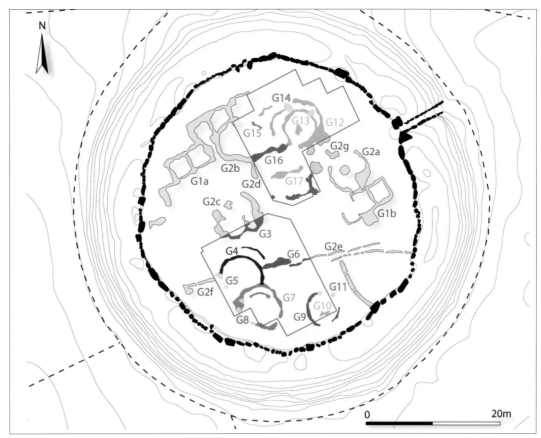

Fig. 5.2.13—Grange Stone Circle B: location of excavated ring-ditches and ring-ditches detected by geophysical survey.

Crofton Croker (1833, 108) also wrote that 'stone coffins had recently been dug up in the altar field', which was somewhere around the *Leaba na Muice* tomb in Ballynagallagh townland. These stone coffins were likely to have been Bronze Age slab-lined or cist graves. Lynch (1895, 257) also recorded that 'a stone coffin was found with a human skeleton close to Labanamuice [*Leaba na Muice*], and there is a tradition in the neighbourhood that two gold swords are buried near the grave'.

5.3: METALWORK

Bronze metalwork was recovered from Lough Gur after it was drained in the late 1840s. Metal and other finds were acquired by antiquarians who visited Lough Gur in the late nineteenth century. Day, the noted collector of portable antiquities, visited Lough Gur around 1885 and met John Fitzgerald of Holy Cross Cottage, of whom he wrote:

'He was in many ways a remarkable man, renting a dairy farm from Count de Salis … He could easily have formed a museum in his house, with good examples of all materials I have named, but was so generous that no visitor was permitted to go away empty from his home; and I am indebted to him for many objects that were found upon his farm and in the lake' (Day 1895, 303).

Day listed antiquities in his collection which he had acquired from a friend at Lough Gur, found himself or 'bought from rag and bone men in Bruff' (*ibid.*, 304): 23 stone axeheads, five bronze axeheads, two socketed bronze spearheads, three bronze pins/brooches and an unspecified number of bone pins. He recorded that Lough Gur was partially drained in the 'fifties' (1850s) and referred to the acquisition of portable antiquities by museums and private collectors in Britain (*ibid.*, 305). Indeed, Lynch (1895, 245) wrote that 'vast quantities of bones of various animals have been found near the crannogs … Relics from Lough Gur are scattered widely. They are to be seen in many museums of the learned societies, as well as in the numberless collections of private individuals.' Some antiquities were also found in ploughed fields or on destroyed sites, such as a cairn on Knockadoon where a bronze 'celt' or axehead was found (Lynch 1913, 8). Although antiquarians bought or were given artefacts, some were also melted down for the value of the metal.

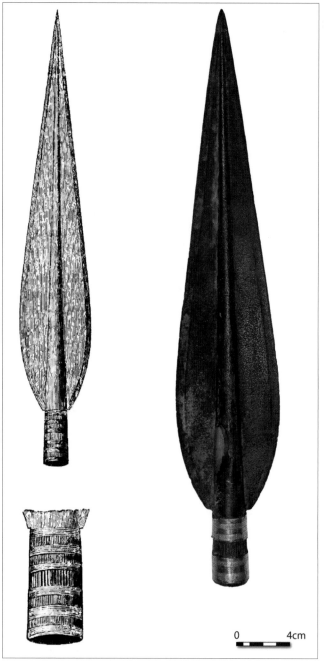

Fig. 5.3.1—Gold-mounted spearhead.

Among the finds from the immediate vicinity of the lake O'Kelly (1942–3, 97) listed 23 bronze axeheads of various types, twelve bronze spearheads and a stone mould for spearheads, two leaf-shaped swords, a rapier, three daggers and one halberd, and noted that this was by no means the full list. Many of the bronze axeheads and other artefacts catalogued by O'Kelly are in the Hunt Collection or the Limerick City Museum and remain local to Lough Gur. Other finds are part of the national collection in the National Museum of Ireland. Some bronze artefacts were given to the museum in University College Cork and are now in the Cork Public Museum, while some, such as the gold-mounted spearhead, were acquired by the Pitt-Rivers Museum in Oxford. Other bronze artefacts have been found over

the years in the neighbourhood of Lough Gur. The large number of precious objects that were in use around Lough Gur in the Bronze Age reflect the wealth and status of their owners. Few metal artefacts have been recovered from excavations of Bronze Age settlement sites except for a socketed axehead of late Bronze Age date from Site C.

Two of the most spectacular objects from Lough Gur are the gold-mounted spearhead (Fig. 5.3.1) and the bronze shield (Fig. 5.3.2), both of which can be dated to the late Bronze Age (1100–700 BC). Dowd (1896, 65) recorded that the shield and spearhead were recovered when the lake level was lowered. Lynch (1895, 245) noted that the spearhead was found near Bolin Island crannog and described it as follows:

'The head is seventeen inches [0.43m] long, and it is, I think, now fixed on a bog-oak handle about seven feet [2.13m] long. When discovered there were about eighteen inches [0.46m] of old handle left. Around the socket of the spear is a band of gold a little over two inches [51mm] in breadth, ornamented with a lineal pattern, alternating in perpendicular and horizontal order. This spear belonged to Lord Guillamore, was purchased at his sale by the Rev. Dr Neligan, of Cork, and is now the property of General Pitt Rivers. As if to match this spear, a small beautiful bronze circular shield was also found in the lake. It is in the museum of the Royal Irish Academy.'

This use of gold foil to decorate the spearhead socket is one of the few examples known in Ireland and Britain (Taylor 1980, 70). The decorative pattern on the spearhead socket consists of three bands of transverse grooves and two intermediary areas of longitudinal grooves (Fig. 5.3.1). Strips of thin (1mm thick or less) gold foil were hammer-welded into the 48 grooves and remain in place in four of them (Coles *et al.* 1964, 192). The Lough Gur spearhead is rare, and other examples of similar spearheads were found in Pyotdykes, Dundee, Scotland, and at Harrowgate in Yorkshire (*ibid.*). The

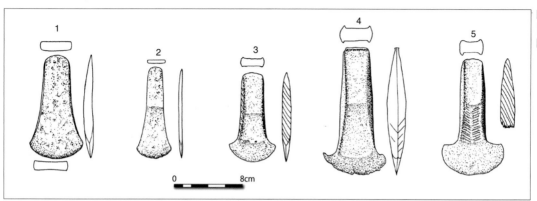

Fig. 5.3.3—Bronze axeheads: 1–2 Ballyvalley type; 3–5 Derryniggan type.

goldwork on the spearhead was the product of an Irish goldsmith and the spearhead is datable to the later part of the Bronze Age, possibly from 1400 BC (Taylor 1980, 70).

The Lough Gur shield is a superb example of sheet bronze-working; it is 0.71m in diameter and is decorated with six concentric repoussé ribs (ribs beaten out from the back), six intermediary rows of bosses and a central boss (Fig. 5.3.2). The handle to the back of the central boss is of sheet bronze bent in the form of a tube and riveted in place. There are a pair of perforated bronze tabs, which probably held a cord of some kind and allowed the owner to sling the shield over his shoulder. There appear to be residues of leather in the hollows at the back of the shield, suggesting an original leather backing. The shield itself was light and probably more for display than for practical self-defence, as the metal would not protect against a slashing blow from a sword. It probably dates from *c.* 1000–800/700 BC.

The spearhead and shield must have been prestigious items and the owners were probably high-ranking individuals, such as warriors or chiefs within a hierarchical society. O'Kelly (1942–43, 97) also referred to a 'gold crown or diadem' found in Kilpeacon townland near Fedamore. The object was sold to a Dublin goldsmith and was presumably melted down. It was described as having the form of a large oyster shell and may have been a late Bronze Age gorget. Gorgets were crescentic neck ornaments made of sheet gold with elaborate decoration and date from the period 1000–800/700 BC.

As Lough Gur includes four townlands—Grange, Knockfennell, Ballynagallagh and Lough Gur—it is not always possible to give accurate locations for portable antiquities and much of the information on find-spots is also lost. Harbison recorded five Beaker period bronze axeheads from Lough Gur (Chapter 4). Two axeheads (Fig. 5.3.3: 1–2) are classified by Harbison (1969a) as of Ballyvalley type and date from 2000–1600 BC. These bronze axeheads had wide cutting edges; some had slight flanges that show a technological improvement on hafting techniques from earlier bronze axeheads and were intended to fit into an angled wooden haft. Three other axeheads (Fig. 5.3.3: 3–5) of are Derryniggan type and date from 1600–1500 BC (Harbison 1969a). One axehead from Lough Gur (Fig. 5.3.3: 5) was decorated with a herringbone motif which was integrated into the casting process. Another decorated example of a Derryniggan-type axehead from Lough Gur is in the possession of the de Salis family, and a replica can be seen in the Cork Public Museum (Fig. 5.3.4). A palstave axehead (Fig. 5.3.5) in the National Museum of Ireland is recorded as having been found at Lough Gur and dates from *c.* 1500–1300 BC. A decorated looped socketed axehead from Site C (Fig. 5.1.35: 5) is one of the few complete bronze artefacts found on the excavations on

Fig. 5.3.4—Decorated axehead (Cork Public Museum).

Fig. 5.3.5 (right)—Palstave axehead (National Museum of Ireland).

Fig. 5.3.6 (far right)— Socketed axehead (National Museum of Ireland).

Knockadoon. An undecorated looped socketed axehead in the National Museum of Ireland (Fig. 5.3.6) also came from Lough Gur and both were probably made around 1000–900 BC.

Three bronze swords were recovered from Lough Gur, and clay mould fragments for casting swords from outside the enclosure at Circle K suggest on-site manufacture (Grogan and Eogan 1987, 383). The swords date from the late Bronze Age (1100–800/700 BC) and were the property of a warrior class. Swords needed to be made from good-quality metal with a high tin content in order to be serviceable weapons. The swords were cast in bivalve moulds and finished by hammering the blade to harden the thrusting and cutting edge. A wooden handle was then riveted onto the weapon. A sword (Fig. 5.3.7: 1) from Lough Gur that was acquired in 1888 by the National Museum of Ireland has an overall length of 0.56m and, although the terminal is missing, six rivet holes on the butt show how a wooden handle was hafted to the blade. A second sword (Fig. 5.3.7: 2) from Lough Gur, now in the Salisbury Museum, has an overall length of 0.43m, with rivet holes on the tang and butt. A sword (Fig. 5.3.7:3) from Holycross in the Limerick City Museum is 0.62m long and has two rivet holes in the tang and two in the butt.

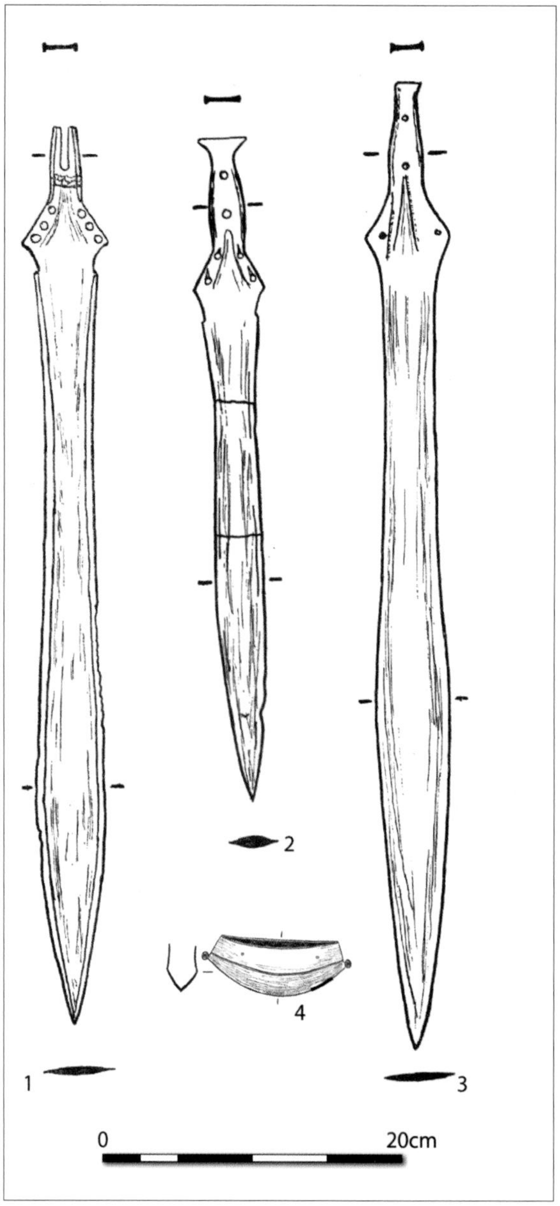

Swords were carried in scabbards made of leather or perhaps wood. The end of the scabbard, where the sword tip was housed, was covered by a metal chape of thin bronze, protecting both the weapon and the bearer from accidental damage. A scabbard chape (Fig. 5.3.7:4) found at Lough Gur was acquired by the National Museum of Ireland in 1886. It is purse-shaped, 82mm wide, with two knobs at the sides and two tiny holes on each side for attachment to the scabbard.

Some evidence for the production of Bronze Age weapons and tools was recovered from Ó Ríordáin's excavations on Knockadoon Hill (Ó Ríordáin 1954; Grogan and Eogan 1987). Apart from the clay moulds for casting swords from Circle K, moulds for casting spearheads, a stone mould for casting looped palstave axeheads (Fig. 5.1.38: 2) and a clay crucible were found associated with

Fig. 5.3.7—1–3 Swords; 4 scabbard chape.

House I at Site D (Ó Ríordáin 1954, 400–1). Clay moulds for looped spearheads and possibly rapiers and some casting waste were recovered from a hearth outside the house and under a bank at Site F (*ibid.*, 422). Ó Ríordáin considered that a bone point or gouge from Site F was used in the manufacture of the clay moulds, either in mixing the clay or in shaping the template for the spearheads in the clay prior to pouring the metal (*ibid.*, 425). The excavation at the megalithic tomb (Ó Ríordáin and Ó h-Iceadha 1955) recovered several fragments of clay crucibles from the western chamber and part of a stone bivalve mould for casting spearheads (Fig. 5.3.8). These items were deposited perhaps up to 1,200 years after the tomb was constructed and, although the megalithic tomb may have remained a special or a sacred place in the minds of late Bronze Age people in Lough

Fig. 5.3.8—Stone mould fragment from Lough Gur wedge tomb and suggested reconstruction of socketed spearhead from mould.

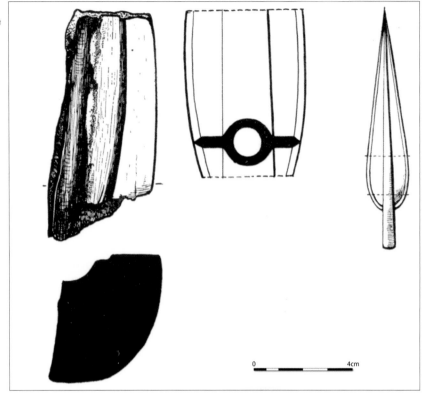

Fig. 5.3.9—Mould for kite-shaped spearheads found in Lough Gur and now in the British Museum.

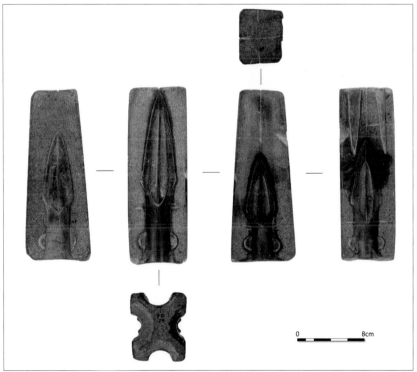

Gur, there is no direct link between metal-working and the tomb. A four-sided mould (Fig. 5.3.9) used around 1600–1500 BC to make four different kite-shaped, end-looped spearheads is now in the British Museum[9] and the find-spot is given as on the estate of J.F.W. de Salis Esq.

Hones or whetstones for sharpening metal tools were found on many prehistoric sites on Knockadoon Hill and represent the maintenance of the cutting edges of metal tools and weapons. Two sandstone hones were found at Site H, and one complete example and two fragments were recovered from Site I (Ó Ríordáin 1954, 435, 440). Twenty stones described as 'whetstones' were found at Site C and some bore grooves from the sharpening of pins (ibid., 349, 380). Six whetstones from Site D had worn surfaces from sharpening. Whetstones were also recovered from Sites G and F (ibid.) and from the C-shaped enclosure, an unenclosed site on Knockadoon and the car-park excavations in 1978 (Cleary 1982a; 1982b; 1995; 2003).

5.4: MONUMENTAL REMAINS

Stone circles and standing stones dot the landscape around Lough Gur. The bank around the Great Stone Circle (B) at Grange was built between 2950 and 2850 BC (Chapter 4), and the inner stone circle was probably constructed in the Beaker period (2500–2200 BC). Circle C at Grange survives intact, while only the north-western arc of stones remains at Circle D (Chapter 4). Geophysical survey has recorded the sites of possible stone circles near the Great Stone Circle (B) and near Circles O and P, but there are now no above-ground remains of these (Cleary and Hogan 2013). The Ordnance Survey recorded an arc of a possible stone circle on the western side of the foot of Knockfennell Hill but O'Kelly (1942–3, 85) considered this doubtful.

There are 45 standing stones in Small County barony and seventeen of these are around Lough Gur (O'Kelly 1942–3, 87). There is no precise dating of the stones; some may be ancient and some may have been erected in more modern times as scratching posts for cattle. Those of antiquity have elsewhere been associated with token burials within the socket dug to erect the stone. The function of the stones has been variously interpreted as that of territorial markers, prehistoric signposts and sites of ritual activity.

One of the most prominent standing stones in Lough Gur is that on the west-facing side of Ardaghlooda Hill, known locally as 'the Pillar Stone' (Fig. 5.4.1). Of volcanic breccia, it is *c.* 3m high, 2m wide and 0.6m thick. An ancient road known as *Cladh na Leac* extends from north of the Pillar Stone to the modern road from Holycross to Lough Gur and possibly further south. *Cladh na Leac* is a sunken track marked on either side by low banks and boulders placed along the banks at intervals. Apart from proximity, there may be no connection between the track and the Pillar Stone, although a linear group of standing stones east of Lough Gur (see below) appears to mark another ancient route. A standing stone to the south-east of the Great Stone Circle (B) is recorded as *Cloghavilla*, which Lynch (1895, 299) translated as 'the stone of the ancient tree', stating that 'an ancient line of Munster kings were inaugurated' under the tree. The stone is 3m long, 1.5m high and 1.4m thick (Fig. 5.4.2). An alternative translation of *Cloch-a-bhile* is 'the stone of the bill [tax?]', and this may have been a traditional location for the payment of dues or tribute in early historic times. The stone may also mark the traditional inauguration site for Gaelic kings (see Chapter 11).

A standing stone and a second (now recumbent) stone at Circle J may have been some type of grave-marker associated with the use of the site as a graveyard in the late Iron Age or early medieval

Fig. 5.4.1—The 'Pillar Stone' on Ardaghlooda Hill.

Fig. 5.4.2—Cloghavilla standing stone.

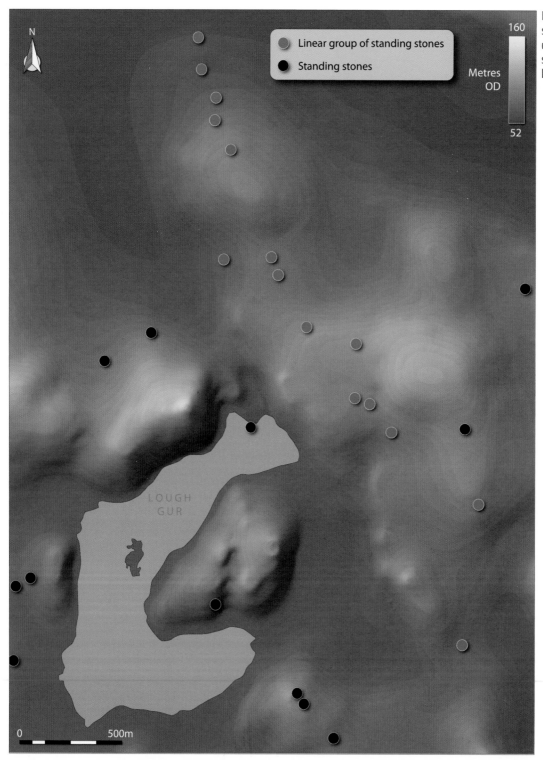

Fig. 5.4.3—Linear group of standing stones (red) to east and north-east of Lough Gur; standing stones (black) around Lough Gur.

Fig. 5.4.4—Standing stone incorporated into modern field boundary.

period (Grogan and Eogan 1987, 312). They may also have been erected in the Bronze Age when the site was enclosed. The standing stone is 0.85m high and the prostrate stone would have stood to a height of *c.* 1.5m.

A linear grouping of fifteen limestone standing stones extended from the Cross of Lough north to Ballingoola (Fig. 5.4.3). Some of these stones stood to *c.* 1m, while those on the southern side were taller and varied from 1.2m to 2.4m (O'Kelly 1942–3, 179–80; 1944, 29). One tall stone, almost 2.5m high, is now incorporated into a modern field boundary (Fig. 5.4.4). The standing stones were interpreted as marking an ancient routeway, and O'Kelly (1942–3, 180) recorded that part of a trackway was visible at the northern end in Ballingoola townland. When part of the trackway was ploughed in 1941, the surface was visible as limestone chippings.

NOTES

[1] Pottery of similar form to the bucket-shaped Lough Gur Class II ware was recovered from in and under the embankment at Grange Stone Circle B and was at the time likened to Scottish Grooved Ware (Ó Ríordáin 1951). Recent dating has confirmed the Grooved Ware identification of the Grange pottery and dated it to 3000–2500 BC (Chapter 4). Flat-based pottery (Grooved Ware) was also recovered from Site H at Knockadoon (Ó Ríordáin 1954) and from Geroid Island (Liversage 1958).

[2] Information from Katharina Becker, Archaeology Department, UCC.

[3] Few animal bones were retained from the early excavations on Knockadoon, although a selection of the bird bones was kept.

[4] Originally identified as Beaker (Cleary 1982a, 4) but the sherd thickness suggests decorated Class II ware.

[5] Houses II and III were Middle Neolithic round houses (Chapter 3).

[6] The scale bar on Ó Ríordáin's published plan (1949b, pl. LIII) indicated a building measuring 10.5m (north/south) by 8m (east/west). This is probably inaccurate and the measurements in the published text are taken as correct.

[7] There were no published plans in Ó Ríordáin's (1950) account of the site.

[8] There are no published plans and this description is taken from MacDermott's (1949b) published account.

[9] Museum No. 1862, 1206.1. Acquired by the British Museum around 1850.

6. The Iron Age

The Irish Iron Age probably began around 800/700 BC and lasted until about AD 400, when there was some contact with the Roman world (Chapter 7), and into the beginning of the early medieval period (Chapter 8). The introduction of iron-working technology overlapped with the late Bronze Age, and the new knowledge and skills may have been quickly adopted by smiths competent in bronze-working. The stimulus for these changes was contact with the Celtic world on the Continent and in Britain. This contact is visible in the archaeological record as new weapon types, ornaments and decorative art styles on artefacts. The bulk of Iron Age artefacts in Ireland are, however, of native manufacture and there are few pieces that can be considered imports. There has been much debate about the mechanisms by which changes in Ireland occurred, and Celtic invasions have been mooted as a possibility. There is little evidence to support this hypothesis, as there is an absence in Ireland of Continental and British Iron Age burial customs, house sites and domestic items such as pottery that would confirm a migration of a distinct group of people. The most likely influences may have come via contact between those on the island of Ireland and Celtic-speaking peoples in Britain and continental Europe. These 'Celts' perhaps spoke a common language but were also diverse in many aspects of their economic, social and political structures. Greek and Roman writers have provided insights into the world of the 'Celts'. In Ireland, an oral tradition of history was written down with the coming of literacy that accompanied Christianisation. The historical narrative is interspersed with myths, legends, ancient stories and folklore. The absence of archaeological evidence for the structure of society may, however, be counterbalanced by insights into earlier society provided by early Irish sagas, which confirm a highly structured society with royal personages, warriors and druids but offer little information about the rest of the population.

The Iron Age is divided into two periods based on characteristic artefacts found on an early Iron Age site at Halstatt in Austria and a late Iron Age site at La Tène in Switzerland. In Ireland the beginning of the Halstatt phase around 800/700 BC saw the introduction of iron-working; by *c.* 300 BC stylistic influences on metalwork produced in Ireland came from the Continental La Tène Iron Age and continued into the fourth/fifth centuries AD.

Iron ore deposits are relatively extensive in Ireland and the availability of raw material for the production of iron tools and weapons may have allowed for the widespread adoption of iron-working technology. The technology itself involved heating iron ore in a small bowl-shaped furnace; after smelting, metallic iron was produced which was then heated and hammered to anneal the metal, and the iron was made into useful tools or, when required, weapons. Bronze and gold continued to be produced and were used for more ornamental items, such as jewellery and decorative fittings. As iron does not survive well in the soil, bronze and gold objects are the best preserved. Carved stones also have distinctive Iron Age motifs but these are mostly found in Connaught and Ulster. The Iron

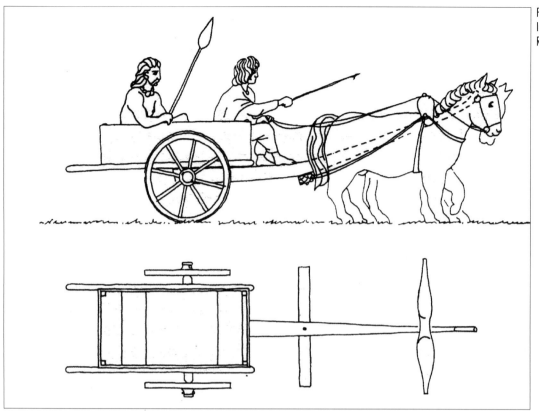

Fig. 6.1—Reconstruction of Irish Iron Age chariot (after Raftery 1997).

Age, particularly in Munster, has left little trace, and settlement sites are infrequent in the archaeological record.

Broad indicators of the vegetational landscape in east Limerick/west Tipperary in the period 390 BC–AD 300 show some woodland regeneration, with continued pastoral and arable farming; from around AD 300 pastoral farming became dominant (Molloy 2008, 29–30). An increase in population pressure during the late Bronze Age and early Iron Age is indicated by some use of land which was wetter and where heavier soils occurred, and 'a complete removal of woody vegetation' was recorded at Lough Gur (Almgren 1989). A major upsurge of agricultural activity centred on *c.* AD 300 is also suggested (Molloy 2008, 30).

The evidence for the Iron Age at Lough Gur includes a few finds of La Tène date and some burials. A pair of tubular, cast-bronze horn-like objects which may have been fittings for a chariot were found in 'a fort on an island in Lough Gur' (Raftery 1983, 80). The 'island' may refer to Knockadoon Hill, Geroid Island or perhaps Bolin Island. The chariot mounts are now in the British Museum. Two-wheeled chariots were used in Britain and, based on archaic descriptions, a reconstruction of the Irish chariot suggests a two-wheeled vehicle with spoked wheels drawn by two horses (Fig. 6.1). The horses were harnessed onto a central pole or yoke, and the bronze fittings from Lough Gur would have fitted onto the ends of the yoke as decorative mounts. The yoke mounts are of cast bronze and *c.* 16cm in length; small holes in the pieces suggest that they were nailed to the yoke (Fig. 6.2). They are decorated with three bands of hatching which were made when they were cast. The top of the mounts also has cast motifs, which are moulded bands encircling the heads

Fig. 6.2—Chariot-yoke mounts from Lough Gur (after Raftery 1983).

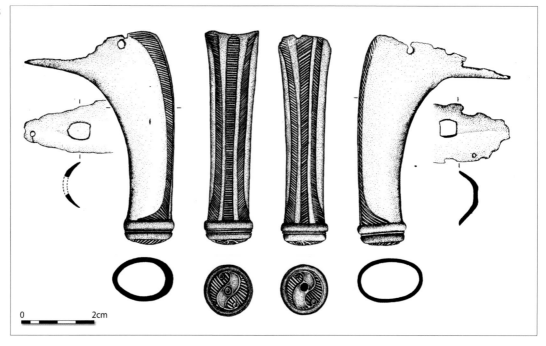

Fig. 6.3—Iron sword with bone handle from Lough Gur townland (left: National Museum of Ireland).

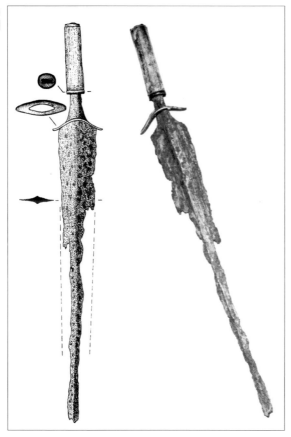

and an S-shaped motif surrounded by hatching.

An Iron Age sword which was acquired by the Royal Irish Academy in 1852 was found in the townland of Lough Gur and is now in the National Museum of Ireland. It is fragmentary, with a surviving length of *c.* 0.35m and a straight-sided blade that converged to the tip (Fig. 6.3). An arched mount or hilt-guard at the top of the blade is of bronze and the handle or grip is of polished bone. The sword probably dates from the second or third century BC.

A bronze safety-pin brooch or fibula (Fig. 6.4) was found at a depth of *c.* 0.3m in the middle of the excavated area of Site C (1940). The brooch is 91mm in length and the bow is straight-sided; the pin and spring are missing, and a surviving rivet at the end of the bow held the pin in place. The brooch may date from the last few centuries BC or the first century AD.

The Iron Age burial record at Lough Gur is provided by the excavations on

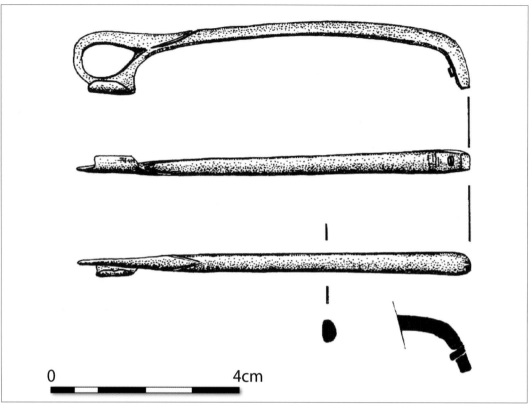

Fig. 6.4—Safety-pin brooch (fibula) from Site C, Knockadoon.

0   4cm

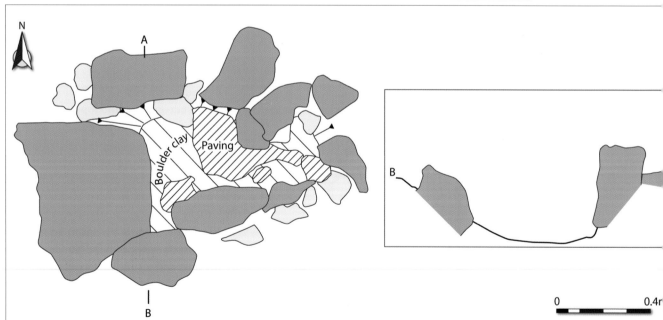

Fig. 6.5—Slab-lined grave on Knockadoon.

0   0.4r

Knockadoon Hill. A slab-lined grave excavated in 1986 was dated to 128 BC–AD 402 (Cleary 1995). The grave was wedge-shaped in plan, being higher and wider on the west side, with an overall length of 1.45m (Fig. 6.5). With the exception of one infant burial, the human remains were scattered throughout the grave and appeared to have been randomly placed in it, perhaps having been originally interred elsewhere and subsequently moved to a final burial place. The remains were of at least two infants aged 6–10 months, one possible newborn and one child aged 2–3 years. The grave also contained an adult right hand and some adult ribs. There was no surviving evidence that the adult hand was severed, as the wrist bones were not present. It may have been placed within the grave as some type of charm for the protection of the children.

Excavations at Circle J uncovered 48 burials, the majority of which were orientated east/west in the Christian manner (Grogan and Eogan 1987), but five were orientated north/south and may date from pre-Christian or Iron Age times. The bodies were also partly crouched and the majority appeared to have been buried in pits unprotected by stone lining. Later burials at Circle L were generally orientated east/west and many were in slab-lined graves. Some of the unexcavated ring-ditches around Lough Gur may date from the Iron Age, as similar excavated enclosures elsewhere have been dated to the third and second centuries BC and yielded cremated human remains.

There are other indications of Iron Age activity around Lough Gur in the Knockainy district, where the Déisi tribe had made their headquarters; by the fourth century the Déisi had been superseded by the Eóganacht. Knockainy can be considered one of the royal sites of Iron Age Munster.

7. The Roman period

Ireland was not part of the Roman Empire and, although its proximity to Roman Britain ensured contact, the numbers of Roman finds in Ireland are relatively few. Imports from the Roman provinces date from the first/second century AD—with a break in the third century, possibly owing to disruptions in the Romano-Gallic Empire and the incursions of barbarian tribes into Gaul (Bateson 1973, 28)—and from the fourth/early fifth century. The latter period overlapped with the early medieval phase of Irish archaeology and was contemporaneous with the advent of Christianity (particularly in the Munster region) and the construction of ringforts. The introduction of Christianity also resulted in increased contact with Europe and the importation of wine for religious rites.

Contact between the Roman world and the Lough Gur region may have been via the Waterford coast, as the area around Lough Gur was part of the Déisi territory that extended from Waterford to east Limerick. Lough Gur is in the centre of the barony of Small County, whose name (*In Déis Becc*) is a memento of Déisi lordship, while the name of the village of Bruff (*Brugh na Déisi*) is also derived from association with the Déisi (Ó Ríordáin 1947b, 45). The Déisi had colonised Wales and thus there was contact with and importation of Roman material in the south of Ireland. Other mechanisms for the importation of Roman goods included Irish raids on Britain from the end of the third century to the early fifth century, Irish mercenaries returning home after service with the Roman army, Irish traders, travellers or refugees who came to Ireland with Roman objects, or Palladian missionaries (Bateson 1973, 29–30).

A Roman coin, a toilet implement and a stylus were recovered from the excavations at Carraig Aille. The coin was found under a large stone collapsed from a wall on the site of houses to the north of and outside the enclosure at Carraig Aille II. Described as an imitation of a coin of Constantius II or Constans (Ó Ríordáin 1949b, 93), it is bronze, *c.* 13mm in diameter and its inscription is worn (Fig. 7.1). The obverse bears the letters DN CON, with a bust which is diademed, draped and cuirassed (wearing a defensive breastplate and back-plate). The reverse bears faint traces of two or three letters on the right. There are faint traces of a warrior standing to the left and driving a spear at a horseman fallen beside his horse (Ó Ríordáin 1947b, 76). The coin was described by Bateson (1973, 48) as 'an extremely barbarous imitation of the major issue of Constantius (324–361) and is firmly associated with the 350s'. Roman coins were minted in France (Roman Gaul) at Trier, and this mint was the main source of Roman coinage in Britain and Gaul up to AD 355, followed by mints in Lyons, Arles and Siscia (Bateson 1973, 29). The coin from Carraig Aille therefore originated in France.

The bronze toilet implement (Fig. 7.2: 1) was found 0.4m below the surface within the Carraig Aille II enclosure and may have been a native copy of types found in Roman Britain (*ibid.*, 26). It is 67mm long and may be a nail-cleaner; the handle has moulded decoration of nail-head type

Fig. 7.1—Roman coin from
Carraig Aille II.

Fig. 7.2—1 Bronze toilet
implement from Carraig Aille II
(Ó Ríordáin 1949b, fig. 8); 2
bronze stylus from Carraig Aille
II; 3 bronze ring from Ballinard
townland.

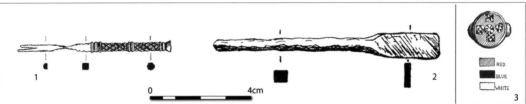

projections between intersecting diagonal lines, while the lower section is forked at the end and filed in the middle to a very thin width (Ó Ríordáin 1949b, 71–2). Cahill Wilson (2014, 38) described this as a cast tubular type and dated it to the fourth century AD.

A bronze stylus (a writing implement) (Fig. 7.2: 2) was found under paving within the rampart of Carraig Aille II and at the lowest stratigraphic levels. It had a square shaft with a tapering shank and a spatulate end, and measured 74mm in length (Ó Ríordáin 1949b, 73). The lower end is broken and may have had a point.

A bronze finger-ring from Ballinard townland, just east of Herbertstown, was found by William Corbett while he was digging in a field in 1941; he also found a stone axe and a blue glass bead (Ó Ríordáin 1947b, 57). The ring is 16mm in diameter and its small size suggests that it was worn by a woman (Fig. 7.2: 3). It has a circular recessed setting or bezel for red enamel, and there are five insets of millefiori or coloured glass. The central glass setting is circular with a white square and blue and white radiating lines, and the other four settings are square with an irregular diaper or diamond pattern of blue and white triangles (Ó Ríordáin 1947b, 57). The use of chequered millefiori glass and red enamel is reminiscent of Roman glass in Britain and the Ballinard ring is thought to be an Irish copy of a Roman type (Bateson 1973, 84). Finger-rings are frequent in the Roman world but almost unknown from early medieval Ireland (Ó Ríordáin 1947b, 59).

The Roman silver hoard from Balline, near Knocklong, was discovered in 1940 by Mr James Flynn in a gravel pit about 0.6m under the ground. The hoard consists of seven pieces of silver: two silver ingots and parts of two others, and three pieces of silver dishes (*ibid.*, 45). The ingots are narrower in the middle, with expanded ends (Fig. 7.3). The inscription on one ingot reads EXOFFI IS (reversed) ATIS and can be read *Ex Offi[cina] Istatis*, whereby the 'Ex offi' names the official (Istatis)

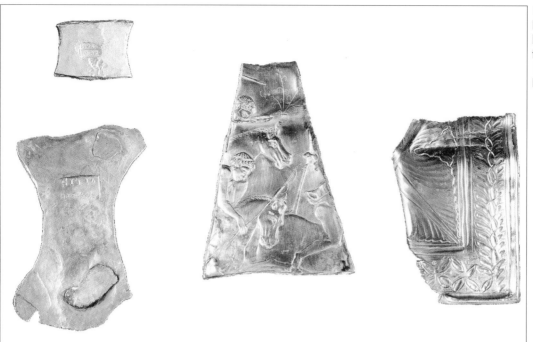

Fig. 7.3—The Balline silver hoard: ingots (left); dish with hunting scene (centre); dish with foliage and acanthus pattern (right) (National Museum of Ireland).

rather than the mint. The inscription is enclosed in a beaded frame; an intermediary beaded line between the upper and lower lines of the inscription marked the middle of the ingot and allowed it to be cut along into two halves (*ibid.*, 45–6). This ingot is the same as one found on a Roman fort at Richborough in east Kent, England. The second ingot bears the inscription EX Ж OFC VILIS (X with a vertical line is interpreted as a Christian monogram or Chi-Rho) and can be read as *of[fi]c[ina] Vilis*. The stamped Chi-Rho is the earliest Christian inscription from Ireland (Cahill Wilson 2014, 49). Both inscribed ingots weigh 10oz., 2dwt. and 12 grains. The fragmentary ingot (3oz., 11dwt.) has the inscription EX•O NON (*Ex o[fficina] Non[ni]* or *Non[ii]*). There were rim fragments from two dishes; one is flat with beading along it, while the other bears a foliage pattern or wreath and an acanthus pattern (Fig. 7.3). The third dish (Fig. 7.3) bears a hunting scene depicting three youths on horseback (Ó Ríordáin 1947b, 48–52). The silver dishes were of high quality and were originally used as tableware (Cahill Wilson 2014, 43). Bateson (1973, 73–4) identified the dish rim with foliage pattern as probably Romano-British and the dish with the hunting scene as possibly from the Mediterranean area; he dated the fragments to the late fourth century. The dating indicates a time when the Roman Empire was in decline and the find circumstances suggest that the material was buried for temporary safety and was meant to be retrieved (Ó Ríordáin 1947b, 44). The silver hoard may have been booty brought into Ireland via the Waterford coast by a Déisi raiding expedition (*ibid.*, 51–3) or payment made to a mercenary in the Roman army (Cahill Wilson 2014, 43).

Christian rites require wine, and this was transported in large ceramic vessels or amphora from Roman Gaul. Excavations by John Hunt at Ballingarry near Garryspillane, to the south of Lough Gur, uncovered a pottery sherd similar to a Roman amphora fragment. A sherd of Roman Samian ware was also recovered from Ballingarry (McCormack, forthcoming). Samian ware was produced in Roman Gaul in the first three centuries AD and is a common find on Roman sites.

Overall, while the amount of Roman material from the Lough Gur area is small, the finds suggest contact with Roman Britain and Gaul. The material probably came to the area through the Déisi connection with Roman Britain and via mechanisms such as raiding, gift exchange, commerce and perhaps payment to those who served in the Roman army. Cahill Wilson (2014, 24) also suggested that the acquisition of exotic items imparted status to the owner and may reflect a social élite. The Balline hoard was found near the Morningstar River, which was probably an ancient routeway or crossing place, and the hoard was possibly booty. The Roman coin from Carraig Aille may represent trade or a souvenir. The decoration on the finger-ring from Ballinard was an Irish copy of Roman motifs rather than an import. Amphora pottery from Ballingarry can be related to Christianity or, in the case of Samian ware, a souvenir brought back by an early traveller. Where it is possible to date the artefacts, most seem to be from the fourth century, when the Roman Empire was in decline.

8. The early medieval period

POLITICAL HISTORY

For County Limerick, as elsewhere in Ireland, historical details of the period on the cusp of and during the arrival of Christianity—and, with it, literacy and written records—are an amalgam of pseudo-historical accounts, myth and the narrative of historical record. The history of Munster lacks early annals and this adds to the obscurity of the period. Westropp (1906–7, 174) provided a historical account of the barony of Small County, where Lough Gur is situated, as follows:

> 'Tradition states that in the middle of the third century a branch of the Déisi settled in the district after their expulsion by Cormac mac Airt. From it was derived the name "Deisbéag" in contrast to the Decies in Waterford, hence the Norman "Desbeg" and the strange term "Small County", which dates at least from Tudor times. The barony contains the important centres of Aine and Lough Gur.'

The boundaries of the territory of 'Deisbéag' were defined by the river systems.

> 'It is probable that the river Commoge [Camoge] formed the ancient northern limit of Deisbeg, and the Saimer[1] or Morning Star River the southern limit … The portion between the Maigue and Commoge is probably the old tribal land. The great early "fair" of *Enach-clochair, -beag* or *cuilin*, was held on the Commoge near Monasteranenagh Abbey' (Westropp 1906–7, 174).

The Déisi colonisation of Wales contributed to the importation of Roman material to the south of Ireland and may explain the presence of Roman artefacts in the Lough Gur area (Chapter 7).

The Déisi were superseded by the Eóganacht, who by the fourth century AD had expanded their territories and had a *caput* or headquarters at Knockainy (O'Kelly 1942-3, 79). Tradition has it that the Eóganacht Áine of east Limerick 'claimed descent from Ailell, son of Natfróich, son of Corc, brother of Oengus' (*ibid.*). Oengus was the father of Eochaid and Feidlimid; Eochaid was the ancestor of the Eóganacht Glennamnach (Glanworth) and Eóganacht Airthir Cliath (also in east Limerick), and Feidlimid the ancestor of the Eóganacht Áine and Eóganacht Cashel (*ibid.*). The Eóganacht of Caisil, Áine, Glenomain and Airthir Cliach belonged to a single family styled Uí Maic Láire, who originated in the area around Knockainy (east Limerick/west Tipperary) but later expanded and fragmented into the main Eóganacht dynasties. Eóganacht Áine or Uí Énna Áine remained around Knockainy but after the eighth century lost out in the battle for access to the overkingship to their erstwhile kin who had settled around Cashel. As they gradually became less important, they appear to have taken offices at Emly, the principal ecclesiastical establishment of Munster, by way of recompense.[2] The Eóganacht Áine of Knockainy were minor kings who ruled their tribal area or *tuath* but were ancestrally connected and subordinate to the Eóganacht Cashel. They supplied a number of kings of Munster; the last certain king of their line was Eterscél mac Máel hUmai, who died in 721 (Ó Corráin 1972, 5), although Ólchobar, who died a century later and claimed the kingship of Munster, may also have been from the Eóganacht Áine. The last of their kings to be mentioned in the annals died in 999, and after that the Eóganacht Áine 'are recorded as mere lords of Inis Cúle, a small area in the barony of Small County' (*ibid.*).

The Eóganacht were defeated at the Battle of Belach Mugna in 908; their king, King Cormac of Munster, was slain and thus they were shattered as a political force for some time (*ibid.*, 113). The demise of the Eóghanacht was matched by the rise of the Dál Cais. This tribe were originally Déisi who conquered and settled in east Clare in the early eighth century (*ibid.*, 114). The Dál Cais had emerged as a dominant power in Munster by the late tenth century, and when Brian Boru succeeded his brother Mathgamain he ultimately achieved enough control of the country to be able to claim the high-kingship of Ireland in 1005 (*ibid.*, 125).

A reference to Dún Gair (Lough Gur) occurs in *Lebor na Cert* (the Book of Rights),[3] in which details of rents and taxes paid to the king of Cashel were recorded (Dillon 1962, xiii). Westropp (1906–7, 61) dates the forts listed in *Lebor na Cert* and claimed by the king of Cashel to the period 870–900. The Book of Rights records that in 902 the 'fort of Gair [Dún Gair] was claimed by the King of Cashel' (*ibid.*, 179). P.J. Lynch (1906–7, 128) also noted that the Dún Gair mentioned in the Book of Rights was one of the Munster seats of the kings of Cashel. The site of the fortification of Dún Gair was located on the first (1844) edition of the Ordnance Survey map on Knockmore, the eastern hill on Knockadoon. J.F. Lynch (1913, 11) also noted that 'the Knockadoon height above Bourchier's Castle is called Carraigmore, or great rock, on which height I have been informed was the site of Dún Gair'. In terms of defence, the location of Dún Gair on Knockadoon was more likely to have been at the natural entrance where Bourchier's Castle now stands, and the Ordnance Survey location is probably erroneous.

Another seat of the Eóganacht Cashel was recorded at a site named as *Cathair Chinn Chonn*, where Máelduin, king of Munster, was defeated in 637, and he also was at Aine (Knockainy) in 666 (Westropp 1906–7, 61). An entry in *Chronicon Scotorum*[4] recounts a battle at *Cathair Chinn Chonn* in 639 between Aengus Liathdána and Máelduin, son of the king of Cashel (Lynch 1906–7, 128). Westropp (1906–7) identified the location of *Cathair Chinn Chonn* as Rockbarton, and Lynch (1906–7, 128) noted that the site was 'about a mile to the south-west of the lake, at Rockbarton' in Caherguillamore. The Ordnance Survey (1844) shows the site of '*Cathair Chinn Chon*' on the hill where Grange Castle was subsequently constructed. Lynch (1895, 247, footnote 2) also cited an entry in *Chronicon Scotorum* referring to Loch Ceann, which he identified as a lake between Knockainy and Lough Gur. The king of Cashel (Eóganacht Cashel) had a seat or headquarters at Loch Ceann, and the death of Gorman, son of Lonan, royal heir of Cashel, in 856 is recorded there in the *Chronicon Scotorum*.

Richard Rolt Brash (B.R.R. 1865, 243) cited a reference in the Annals of the Four Masters to a raid on Lough Gur in 1088, when 'in that year Dowhnell, the son of MacLochlainn, King of Ireland, and Rodrick [Ruaidri] O'Connor, King of Connaught, made a raid into Munster, and plundered Emley, Lough Gair, and Bruree'. The political history of the Lough Gur area from the seventh to the eleventh century appears to be one of intermittent warfare interspersed with periods of relative peace.

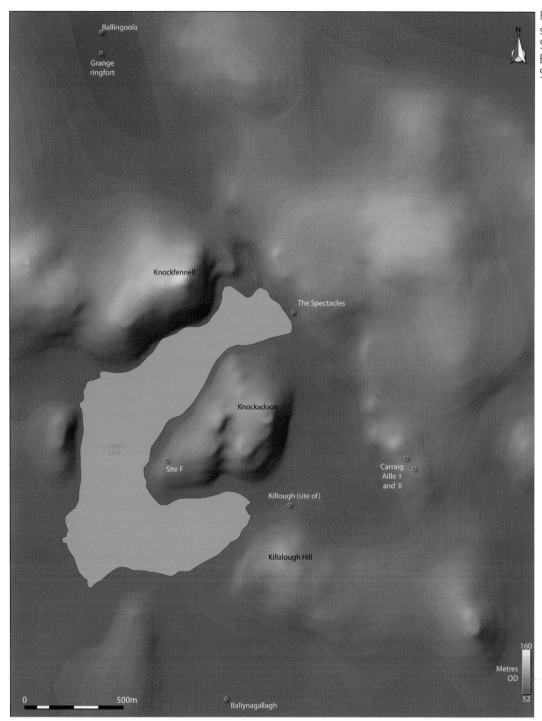

Fig. 8.1.1—Location map showing Carraig Aille I and II; the Spectacles; Grange ringfort; Ballynagallagh; Ballingoola; and Site F, Knockadoon.

8.1: SETTLEMENT

Settlement in the early medieval period was typically within ringforts. Ringforts are the most widespread archaeological field monument in Ireland. Usually known by the names *rath* or *lios*, they are circular or subcircular areas enclosed by a single or multiple earthen banks formed from material thrown up from an external concentric fosse (ditch). Variations on the enclosing element include stone-faced banks or stone walls (*caher*). Although comparatively few ringforts have been excavated, it is accepted that they have a long period of use with a floruit of about 500–900, and some may have been reoccupied in the medieval and post-medieval period. Ringforts can be considered as the enclosed farmsteads of strong farmers, affording the inhabitants some protection as well as status. Few historical details survive on these sites. Westropp (1906–7, 59) recorded at least 2,150 ringforts (earthen forts) in County Limerick. The early medieval period was also a time when there was an expansion of agriculture (Stout 1997, 46). Mitchell's (1954) pollen diagram from Lough Gur showed an increase in herbs and grasses, and species diversity suggests increased land use and a decline in forest cover. A pollen core taken in 2017 from Lough Gur also confirmed agricultural expansion beginning around 500 and continuing until about 800.[5] The pollen recorded in the core included cereal-type pollen and pollen associated with weeds found on cultivated ground.

Excavation at Lough Gur investigated four early medieval enclosures: the stone forts at Carraig Aille (Ó Ríordáin 1949b), a ringfort at Grange (Ó Ríordáin 1949a) and an enclosure at Ballynagallagh (Cleary 2006) (Fig. 8.1.1). An unenclosed site was also excavated at 'the Spectacles' (Ó Ríordáin 1949b). Two houses in Ballingoola (Ó Ríordáin 1949a) and Site F on Knockadoon (Ó Ríordáin 1954) may also be early medieval in date. A number of artefacts from later strata on prehistoric sites excavated on Knockadoon are also early medieval in date. A late Iron Age/early

Fig. 8.1.2—Carraig Aille forts, looking west (Photographic Unit, National Monuments Service).

medieval cemetery was excavated at Circle J on Knockadoon, where a pre-existing enclosure was used (Grogan and Eogan 1987).

Carraig Aille

The archaeological excavations at Carraig Aille and the Spectacles were undertaken in 1937–8[6] and published by Seán P. Ó Ríordáin in 1949 in the *Proceedings of the Royal Irish Academy*. The name 'Aille'[7] may refer to the precipitous cliff on the western side of the ridge on which the sites are located (Fig. 8.1.2). The ground also slopes steeply on the northern and eastern sides, while the gradient is gentler to the south. The local pronunciation of the name is '*Carraig Geal*', and *geal* may refer to the white limestone blocks that were used in the construction of the ramparts and are clearly visible on the ridge. Lynch (1895, 250) considered that the name might derive from 'the hill of the White Galls or Norse'. The site had not been excavated at the time of Lynch's writing and there was no obvious link with the Vikings. Excavation some 40 years later, however, recovered a Viking silver hoard from the inner side of the rampart of Carraig Aille II.

Crofton Croker (1833, 110) published a description of Carraig Aille:

'This eminence is called Carrig-galla, and upon it I found two circular works, marked M [on his plan; see Chapter 2, Fig. 2.4], constructed with regularly squared stones, resembling those used in building quays, placed and fitted one to the other, but without any appearance of mortar being used. The height of this circular wall may have been nearly ten feet [3m], and it seemed as if built about a mound of earth, as the grass-covered enclosed space was level with the highest part.'

Harkness (1869, 394) recorded Carraig Aille II as '142' [43.2m] in diameter. It consists of a wall in some portions about 4' [1.2m] in height and about 11' [3.3m] in thickness.' Carraig Aille I was described as having 'a diameter of 138' [42m] and is in a less perfect state'. Lynch (1895, 250) wrote that 'there are forts … connected by a wall on the east … very little of the fort on the south pinnacle is left. It had a diameter of one hundred and forty-two feet' (42.6m). The ramparts of the forts had apparently fallen into some disrepair in the period between Crofton Croker's (1833) description and those of Harkness (1869) and Lynch (1895). Oddly, only Carraig Aille I is mapped on the 1844 edition of the Ordnance Survey.

The archaeological remains at Carraig Aille consist of two stone forts identified as Carraig Aille I at the northern end of the ridge and Carraig Aille II to the south, a series of houses and enclosures to the north of Carraig Aille II and slight evidence of earlier use of the site in the Neolithic (Chapter 3). One house was also excavated outside the southern rampart of Carraig Aille II and there are surface indications of possible house sites further south; these are unexcavated but indicate a more extensive settlement on the ridge than that recorded on the excavation. Stone forts are themselves not common around Lough Gur, where most of the enclosed early medieval sites are ringforts with earthen ramparts.

The ridge on which the Carraig Aille stone forts are located is elevated above the surrounding terrain and about 400ft (122m) above OD (Fig. 8.1.1). The eastern side overlooks ground that was part of the lake at the time of occupation and became marshland when the lake was drained in the late 1840s (Fig. 8.1.2). The ridge slopes downward from the northern end, where Carraig Aille I is located, towards Carraig Aille II, and the ground between is relatively level (Fig. 8.1.3). The distance between the forts is about 130ft (40m).

Fig. 8.1.3—Carraig Aille forts, looking east (Photographic Unit, National Monuments Service).

Carraig Aille II

On excavation, Carraig Aille II was the best preserved, although much of the site had been covered by collapse and general accumulation of debris within the fort. Some parts of the stone ramparts were rebuilt when the excavation was completed, but restoration was minimal. The enclosing stone rampart was originally built following the contour of the ground and was subcircular in plan; the western end was wider and almost straight-sided, and the enclosure narrower and curved on the southern and eastern sides (Figs 8.1.3 and 8.1.6). Ó Ríordáin (1949b, 41) considered that the planning of the layout of the rampart was 'somewhat haphazard', as the curvature of the wall was changed about 3m north of the entrance to bring it into line with the southern side of the entrance. The stone facing tended to dip in places where the underlying bedrock dipped, and some straight joint lines were considered fortuitous rather than an indication that the wall was built in sections by separate gangs of workmen. The maximum diameter (south-west/north-east) was 156ft (47.5m). The rampart was 12–14ft (3.6–4.2m) thick and stood to heights of 1–3½ft (0.3–1m). It was faced externally and internally with large, well-shaped, rectangular limestone blocks laid in fairly regular horizontal courses, with small stones or spalls between the blocks to keep them in position. The limestone facing was of stones of varying sizes, averaging 1ft by 1½ft by 1ft (0.3m by 0.45m by 0.3m) although some were much larger, up to 6ft by 2ft by 15in. (1.8m by 0.6m by 0.4m). The rubble core was comprised of smaller blocks of stone and rubble. Steps (Fig. 8.1.4) along the inner face suggest that the rampart was originally higher than 1m; the steps were recorded at five locations, four of which were in the eastern side closest to the entrance and where the ground slope was gentler. The steps were about 2ft (0.6m) wide, with a tread that was 1ft (0.3m) deep and a rise of between 4in. and 1ft (0.1–0.3m). Based on the 45° angle of the steps on the southern side of the rampart, Ó Ríordáin (1949b, 42) postulated that the rampart was in the region of 6–8ft (1.8–2.4m) high, with

Fig. 8.1.4—Carraig Aille II: steps.

Fig. 8.1.5—Carraig Aille II: entrance.

Fig. 8.1.6—Carraig Aille II: plan of Phase I occupation.

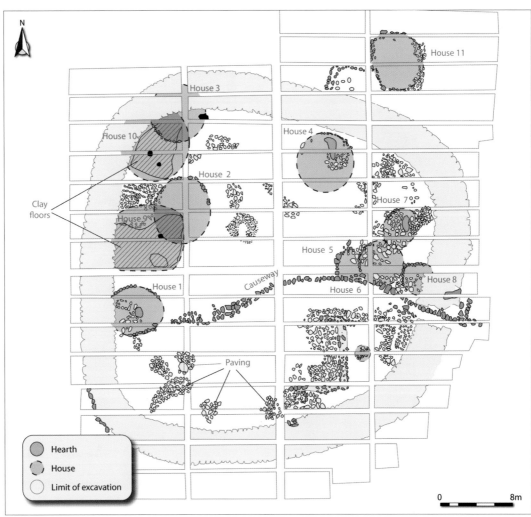

an inner wall-walk and outer bulwark. The quantity of collapsed stone from the rampart also confirmed that the ramparts were significantly higher than the extant remains at the time of the excavation. It is possible that the bulwark was at least partly constructed from a timber palisade.

The entrance (Fig. 8.1.5) to the fort, located on the eastern side, was on average 5ft (1.5m) wide, and the terminals of the rampart were wider than elsewhere at 14ft (4.2m). The entrance was paved on the northern side with large (0.3m) blocks of limestone, up to 0.3m thick. Cobbling on the southern side consisted of small, closely set rounded or flat stones, set lower and abutting the base of the paving. It was clear that both cobbling and paving were laid at the same time; Ó Ríordáin (1949b, 43) suggested that the paving was for use by humans while the cobbled surface was for animals and slip-proof for cloven feet or shod horses. The original surface of the entrance and the causeway were most likely laid down during the initial occupation (Phase I) of the fort. The paving extended from the entrance in a curved fashion into the fort for a distance of c. 25m (Fig. 8.1.6). The paving and cobbling were subsequently covered with gravel and some square stones were roughly set as steps; this surface became hard-packed from trampling. The gravel along the entrance

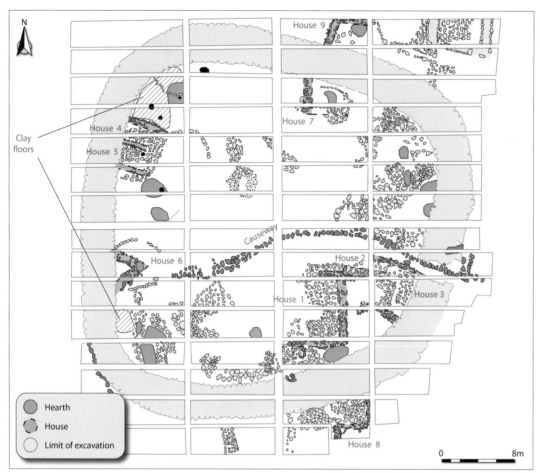

Fig. 8.1.7—Carraig Aille II: plan of Phase II occupation.

surface was mixed with dark habitation soil that may have derived from later activity (Phase II) within the fort. Over time the gravel surface was covered by general habitation refuse from occupation within the fort. There were recesses, 5ft (1.5m) long, in the rampart terminals at a distance of 3½ft (1m) from the outer face of the rampart; that on the northern side was set into the wall for a depth of 9in. (0.22m) and that on the south to a depth of 7in. (0.18m). These allowed a gate to be set back flush with the sides of the entrances; two recesses indicate a double gate. A niche on the eastern side of the northern recess may have held a gatepost.

The fort enclosed a number of houses, some of which were in contemporary use while others were sequential. The descriptions of the houses are not detailed in the report and it is at times difficult to make out the ground-plans from the published site drawings. The houses have been divided into two phases. Phase I comprises the earlier houses with curvilinear plans that were built directly on the rock and clay surfaces that formed the original ground level (Fig. 8.1.6). Up to ten houses can be deduced from the published site plans and descriptions. The causeway leading into the fort from the entrance was considered to be contemporary with the Phase I occupation, although one house (House 5, below) was under the causeway (Ó Ríordáin 1949b, 44). There were also some paved areas which were laid in Phase 1. Two clay and gravel floors in the north-west quadrant may also be the vestiges of houses. The later houses of Phase II were roughly rectangular in plan and the walls stone-faced on both sides with a rubble fill (Fig. 8.1.7). These houses were constructed within the fort, against the outer edge of the southern rampart, over the rampart on the northern side and along the ridge between Carraig Aille I and II. This phase of occupation represented a time when the rampart was redundant as an enclosure.

Phase I—round houses

These were stratigraphically the earliest structures on site. The evidence for the houses was arcs of stones, forming a circular plan, which survived to a height of one course and marked the perimeters of houses. Ó Ríordáin (1949b, 44) considered the structures to be of 'light construction'. As these arcs of stones consisted of a single course they did not form structural walls. Excavations at Deer Park Farms, Co. Antrim, where the level of preservation was exceptional, can throw some light on the interpretation of the Carraig Aille houses. At Deer Park Farms the seventh- and eighth-century houses were constructed from double wattle walls with intramural packing that functioned as insulation (Lynn and McDowell 2011). The inner house walls were sturdier than the external walls. The evidence from Deer Park Farms also confirmed that the roof was probably of woven wattle and a continuation of the internal wall woven to the apex of the roof. Arcs of stones similar to those at Carraig Aille II surrounded the round houses at Deer Park Farms and were interpreted as retaining features for clay platforms on which the houses were built. These arcs of stones were either adjacent to the structural walls or up to 0.2–0.5m outside them. The estimated house diameters at Carraig Aille II may therefore be less than the extant external kerbing or arcs of stones; the distance between the external kerb and the house wall is not possible to calculate now. The clay was also banked up against the lower section of woven wattle walls at Deer Park Farms in order to provide a damp course that diverted water seepage to the exterior of the houses (*ibid.*, 598–9). In dryland sites such as Carraig Aille I and II, where the preservation of organic material such as structural stakes was poor and where continuous occupation probably obliterated earlier phases, little remained of the upright stakes that were used to construct the walls. Excavation of a house at Ballingoola III (see below) in low-lying marshy ground confirmed the use of a clay platform which formed the house floor, a low clay bank on which the wattle walls were constructed and an arc of stones along the external perimeter that probably retained the clay platform (Ó Ríordáin 1949a).

As there are no detailed descriptions of the houses in the excavation report for Carraig Aille, for ease of reference the houses have been numbered 1–10 (Fig. 8.1.6). A further possible house (No. 11) may have existed external to and on the north side of the rampart. There were up to five houses (Nos 1–3 and 9–10) in the western area of the fort and five houses (Nos 4–8) in the north-east quadrant. Houses 1, 3 and 10 in the north-west quadrant may have pre-dated the rampart. There is no surviving evidence for doorways in the houses.

A 2.4m-long channel on the south-east side of the fort may have been part of the flue of a corn-drying kiln; it had upright stones on the sides and was covered with flat stones. Spreads of burnt earth to the east of the flue may have been rake-out from the kiln. The flue/corn-drying kiln was located away from the Phase I houses, presumably to prevent accidental fire. The burnt layer was under the paving of and pre-dated the Phase II House 3. Other burnt spreads within the fort were interpreted as evidence of the destruction of houses by fire (Ó Ríordáin 1949b, 47).

House 1. The house was D-shaped in plan and Ó Ríordáin (1949b, 44) considered that the stone wall of the rampart formed its western wall. It is also possible that the house wall continued under the unexcavated rampart and pre-dated the enclosure. The external arc of stones survived and, if it abutted the wall, the house dimensions can be estimated as 5m (north/south) by 6m (east/west), or perhaps slightly smaller if the arc marked the edge of a clay platform that extended beyond the confines of the house. This was one of the few houses that had a central hearth.

House 2. The house was oval in plan and the external arc of stones gives a maximum diameter of *c.* 7.5m north–south and *c.* 6m east–west.

House 3. Like House I, this appeared to abut—or, more likely, pre-date—the rampart wall and was D-shaped in plan, with a diameter of *c.* 6.5m east–west and *c.* 3.5m north–south. A possible further house (House 10) represented by a clay floor may have been earlier or later than House 3. A hearth site within and extending beyond the southern perimeter of House 3 was probably unrelated to the structure.

House 4. The northern external arc of stones survived. A line projected from this arc suggests a circular plan with a maximum diameter of *c.* 6.5m. A stone-kerbed hearth was recorded within the confines of the house.

House 5. This house pre-dated the causeway and the north-west section of the external kerbing survived. The plan was oval or circular with a maximum diameter of *c.* 6m.

House 6. The ground-plan of this overlapped with House 5. This house was considered by Ó Ríordáin (1949b, 44) to have been 'adapted to the position of the causeway' and was therefore constructed when the causeway was in place; consequently it post-dated House 5. The house may have been circular or oval in plan, with an estimated maximum diameter of *c.* 4.8m.

House 7. This was north-east of and adjacent to House 6 and, if in contemporary use, formed a figure-of-eight ground-plan with it. The estimated maximum diameter was *c.* 4.8m. A hearth within the house perimeter was visible as a large spread of oxidised soil up to 1.5m in length; this may have been overspill from a more confined hearth area.

House 8. This was immediately east of the entrance and also appeared to have abutted the rampart. The vestiges of the structure comprised an arc of stones along the north-east side with an estimated diameter of *c.* 3m. Its position and its small size may indicate that this was some type of sentry hut positioned to guard the entrance. Alternatively, the remains may also have been the north-west section of a larger building which continued under and pre-dated the rampart.

House 9. An irregularly shaped clay and gravel floor measuring *c.* 7.5m by 5.8m abutting the western rampart may have been the remains of a house. The projected line of the building reflecting the maximum spread of the floor suggests a house with an estimated maximum diameter of *c.* 7.5m. A post-hole on the eastern side within the projected house perimeter and a small off-centre hearth were also recorded. The floor plan of House 9 overlapped with that of House 2 and these buildings were likely to be sequential but the phasing is unknown.

House 10. The remains of this possible house consisted of a clay floor with maximum dimensions of *c.* 5.5m (north/south) and *c.* 4m (east/west). This house, like Houses 1 and 3, appeared to abut or pre-date the rampart, and the maximum estimated diameter was *c.* 8m. There were two post-holes within the area of the clay floor.

House 11. This was external to and north of the rampart. The remains consisted of an almost complete circle of stones possibly marking the perimeter of a house with a maximum diameter of *c.* 6m.

Phase II—rectangular houses

This stage of occupation of Carraig Aille II was marked by a lowering of the rampart along the north-west side, where the stones were removed in some places to one course or a height of *c.* 1ft (0.3m), leaving a gap *c.* 14ft (4.2m) wide in the wall. The reduction in wall height allowed expansion of settlement and access to the houses north of and outside the rampart (Ó Ríordáin 1949b, 41). A Viking silver hoard dated to 850–950 was inserted into a space between two stones in the inner face of the lowered rampart, suggesting that the rampart may have been lowered in the late ninth or tenth century. The rampart as an enclosing or defensive feature had become redundant at that stage.

Structural remains of houses from this phase of occupation survived better than those of Phase I and were in the main rectangular in plan (Fig. 8.1.7), marking a change in architectural style from the preceding round houses. Phase II houses were 'more substantial buildings than those at the lower levels' (*ibid.*, 45). Many of the house remains within the fort were fragmentary, however, and only the paved floors remained in the north-east quadrant adjacent to the rampart. Where best preserved, the stone walls of the houses were faced internally and externally with stone blocks and had rubble cores. These walls had collapsed over time and, as much of the area around the houses was paved, it was difficult for the excavators to distinguish the paving from the collapsed walls. As with Phase I, there are no detailed descriptions of the houses in the excavation report and for ease of reference they have been numbered Houses 1–7 within the rampart, House 8 to the south of the rampart and House 9 immediately north of the rampart (Fig. 8.1.7). The remains of a further eight houses were located outside the northern rampart of Carraig Aille II and along the ridge towards Carraig Aille I. The nomenclature for these used in the excavation report—Structures I–VII—is retained; two phases of house construction were recorded at Structures IV and VI. The floor area of some of the Phase II houses was paved. Paving that extended out from the rampart was also recorded in the north-east quadrant on the site plan (Fig. 8.1.7) and interpreted as the remains of house floors.

House 1. This was on the south side of the fort and the eastern wall and sections of the northern and southern walls survived. The house plan may have been either rectangular or square, with an internal width of *c.* 20ft (6m) (Fig. 8.1.7). The walls were *c.* 2½ft (0.75m) thick and the floor was paved with large flat slabs (Ó Ríordáin 1949b, pl.VI, 3). The external surface along the northern wall was paved. A poorly preserved small stone structure with internal dimensions of 4ft by 5ft (1.2m by 1.5m) abutted the south wall. Ó Ríordáin (1949b, 46, pl.VI, 3) interpreted this small annexe as either part of House 1 or a separate structure and noted a gap of *c.* 3ft (0.9m) and a step between the annexe and the southern wall of House 1, although this is not evident on the plan or photograph.

House 2. A fragment of an east/west-aligned wall extended east from House 1 and Ó Ríordáin considered that this was part of a discrete house, as the walls did not meet at a right angle.

House 3. Wall fragments and a paved area may represent a house located immediately inside and to the south of the original entrance to the fort. The walls were *c.* 5m apart and aligned roughly east–west, with an intermediary paved area. The estimated internal dimensions were *c.* 5m (north/south) by *c.* 6m (east/west).

House 4. This was on the north-west side of the fort and was in the footprint of House 9 in the earlier sequence of round houses. The remains of this house consisted of a northern wall built at right angles to the rampart and paving to the south.[8] The extant wall was *c.* 5m (east/west) in length and appeared to be in poor condition. The rampart wall on the western side may have been incorporated into the structure; the eastern and southern walls did not survive. Paving extended southwards from the northern wall for at least 6m and the plan of House 4 was probably rectangular.

House 5. This was immediately south of House 4 and was of later construction, as the northern wall of House 5 was built on the paved floor of House 4. The remains of House 5 consisted of a northern wall with a surviving (east/west) length of *c.* 5m. This wall extended into the rampart and linked to a wall built along the top of the rampart, which was also interpreted as a structural wall of House 5. The wall along the rampart was at least 9m in length (north/south) and the probability is that House 5 was a large rectangular structure. A poorly preserved wall within House 5, *c.* 2m south of the northern wall and *c.* 4m in length, may have been an internal division, indicating that House 5 was at least two-roomed or part of a discrete structure.

House 6. Fragmentary walls on the western side of the fort suggested a house at that location. House 6 was within the footprint of the Phase I House 1. There is no description of House 6 in the published account but it is shown on the site plan (Fig. 8.1.7). The wall fragments were at right angles; the eastern wall survived to a length of *c.* 3.5m and the extant length of the northern wall was *c.* 2m. It is unlikely that the walls formed part of a house that incorporated the rampart, as was the case with House 5, as the enclosed space was too small. The walls were possibly fragments of a house or houses that extended to the east into the enclosure rather than the north-east corner of a house that continued into the rampart.

House 7. This was on the northern side of the fort and within the footprint of the Phase I House 4. The western wall survived for a length of *c.* 3.8m and Ó Ríordáin (1949b, 46) recorded it as extending from the rampart; this section of the rampart was lowered to allow access to the houses to the north of and outside the fort, and it is unclear whether House 7 pre-dated the lowering of the rampart. It may have incorporated the rampart as part of the structure. The floor of House 7 was trampled clay with rock spalls and was paved on the eastern side. Paving was also laid outside the western wall. A stone-kerbed hearth within House 7 was up to 2.3m in length (north/south) and *c.* 1m wide (east/west). A quernstone was used at the northern end of the hearth as part of the kerbed surround.

Houses (?) in the north-east quadrant. The north-east quadrant of the fort had extensive paving, which was interpreted by Ó Ríordáin (1949b, 46) as the remains of house floors but 'too discontinuous to give any knowledge of the shapes or sizes of the houses'. The paving appears to have been on different levels and this probably indicates that sequential houses were built at this location. There were also

Fig. 8.1.8—Carraig Aille II:
House 8, Phase II. Plan of
rectangular stone-built house
south of rampart.

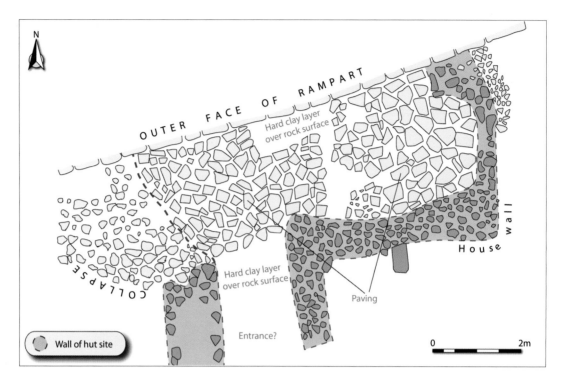

four hearths within the paved areas, possibly related to houses there.

House 8. This was to the south and outside the rampart (Figs 8.1.7–8) and was one of the few houses of which a detailed plan was published. The remains consisted of a southern wall *c.* 5m in length and a western return of *c.* 4.8m, with an enclosed paved area of, at maximum, 3m by 7.2m. The western wall was in a collapsed condition. The northern wall was formed by the rampart. Ó Ríordáin (1949b, 47) considered that a field wall to the south that terminated at the house was in contemporary use. A projecting wall *c.* 1.5m to the west and parallel to the field wall was interpreted as an entrance feature. The entrance had a hard clay surface, and the projecting wall and field wall may have formed some type of porch.

House 9. This was immediately outside and to the north of the rampart; it is shown on the published plan (Fig. 8.1.7) but not described in the report. The house was located in the area where the rampart was lowered and it is unknown whether it was built at that stage or before the lowering of the rampart. It appears to have been rectangular in plan and the western wall extended northwards from the rampart for *c.* 3.5m; a return wall, also *c.* 3.5m in length, formed part of the northern wall. A hearth on the site plan (Fig. 8.1.7) may have been associated with the house and was off-centre towards the northern wall, which was abutted by external paving.

Extramural houses to the north of the fort
Before excavation, these houses were visible as mounds and banks along the ridge between Carraig Aille I and II, enclosing roughly rectangular spaces (Fig. 8.1.9). They were of similar construction to the Phase II houses within the fort and some also had enclosed yards. A number of them may have

237

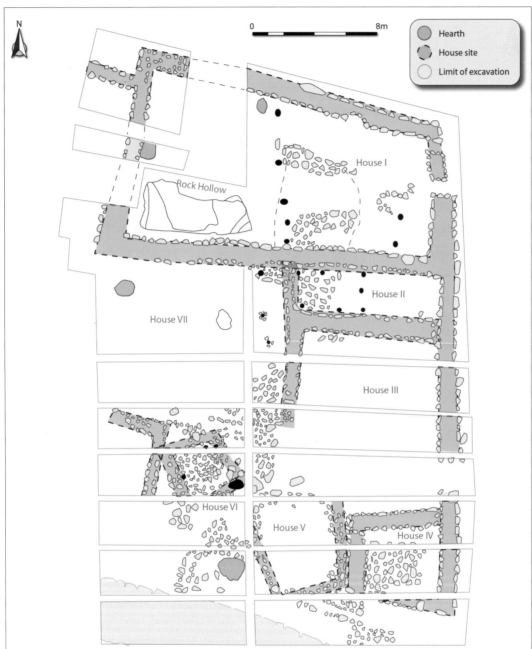

Fig. 8.1.9—Carraig Aille II: extramural houses north of rampart.

been in contemporary use with the houses within the fort. There was also evidence that at least two houses were constructed close to or within the footprint of earlier houses. The sequence of construction was interpreted from north to south, beginning with a large house c. 21m north of the northern rampart of Carraig Aille II. The enumeration of Ó Ríordáin's (1949b, 47–52) published account is retained here.

House I. This was the northernmost of the extramural houses and Ó Ríordáin (1949b, 52) considered it to have been the first house built outside the rampart. The structure was interpreted as a house on the eastern side and an enclosed yard at the western end. The house measured 7.5m (north/south) by 10m (east/west) internally. The stone walls were on average 4ft (1.2m) thick and survived to a height of 2ft (0.6m). They were well constructed on the eastern side within the footprint of the house, faced externally and internally with limestone blocks, and had a rubble and earth core. Apart from the south-western side, the wall angles were off-square. Ó Ríordáin (1949b, 49) suggested that the western wall of the house was constructed from posts which were set in holes cut into the rock and at a distance of 10m from the eastern wall. The intermediary wall between the posts may have been of woven wattle plastered with mud but no evidence of this survived. Stone foundations parallel to the northern wall extended from the western (post-built?) wall for a distance of *c.* 3.6m and may have been a footing for an internal division within the house. This partition wall was built with large stones, was 4ft (1.2m) wide and survived to a height of 1ft (0.3m). The space between it and the southern wall was labelled a 'clay and gravel bank' (Ó Ríordáin 1949b, pl. 1). As habitation material accumulated over the clay bank, it may have been a levelled-out, pre-construction feature. The entrance to the house was off-centre in the eastern wall and 2ft 8in. (0.8m) wide. A second break in the eastern wall near the north-east corner was wall collapse. A hearth, set in a natural hollow and kerbed, was *c.* 1.2m west of the entrance but almost directly in front of it. A niche in the northern wall may have been a press or some type of storage area.

The unroofed yard on the west of the house was enclosed by walls; that on the south was of similar construction to those in the house, but the eastern and northern walls were built of small stones and clay. Entry to the yard was likely to have been from the house, although there was probably also access on the western side. A large rock hollow on the southern side of the yard was entered via three rock-cut steps on the eastern side that led downwards from the yard. The hollow was 24ft (7.2m) long, 8ft (2.4m) wide and 4ft (1.2m) deep. Its base was deliberately infilled with large stones, and an area on the south-west was hard-packed with yellow clay to create a level floor. The hollow is probably best interpreted as equivalent to a souterrain or underground chamber used to store perishable food and as a hideaway in times of danger. The chamber may have been a natural fissure in the bedrock that was advantageously used as a cellar and may have been roofed over with timber. Ultimately the hollow was filled in with stones and occupation refuse, including animal bones, either deliberately or gradually over time. No dating evidence was recovered from the fill of the rock hollow but souterrains in the Irish archaeological record were in the main built between *c.* AD 750 and 1250 (Clinton 2001).

House II. This was immediately south of House I. Ó Ríordáin (1949b, 50) considered it to be a separate structure, although it is possible that it was a room in House I, as the only entrance appears to have been a step in the north wall which led up into House I. The eastern wall was a continuation of the eastern wall of House I, and the northern wall was a party wall between Houses I and II. The western wall of House II was not keyed into the structural wall of House I, indicating that it was a later addition. House II was narrow and rectangular in plan, with internal dimensions of *c.* 9.3m (east/west) by *c.* 2.8m (north/south) and an extant wall height of *c.* 0.45m. The floor was exposed bedrock with some paving at the western end. Seven paired post-holes measuring *c.* 0.2m in diameter and *c.* 0.25m deep were recorded against the internal walls of House II, and there was a further post-hole in the centre of the building. Ó Ríordáin (1949b, 50) interpreted posts in these positions as holding the roof down rather than as load-bearing to support a roof.

House III. This was a large structure with an enclosed area of *c.* 11m (north/south) by *c.* 8.5m (east/west). Ó Ríordáin (1949b, 50) interpreted it as being part house, part yard, similar to House I. In this instance, however, the yard was on the east and the habitable section was on the west. The interpretation of the western section as the domestic area was based on dark soil or residue from occupation. There were no indications of posts dividing the domestic section from the yard. The eastern wall was a continuation of the long wall that extended southwards from Houses I and II, the northern wall was a party wall between Houses II and III and the western wall was poorly preserved. The entrance on the eastern side was marked by a 5ft 6in. (1.55m) gap in the wall. Ó Ríordáin (1949b, 51) suggested that House III pre-dated Houses IV and V to the south.

House IV. Ó Ríordáin (1949b, 52) considered that two houses were built at this location and that the earlier house remained as wall fragments and a habitation layer underlying the paved floor of House IV. House IV was due south of House III and its eastern wall was a continuation of the long wall of Houses I–III. The northern wall of House IV was not bonded into the long wall and it was unclear whether it was a party wall between Houses III and IV. Remains of the western wall of House IV appear to have continued as far as the rampart, implying that the house was larger than shown on the plan. The northern area of House IV was an almost square room measuring 15ft 6in. (4.7m) by 13ft 6in. (4.1m), and the paved floor overlay a 0.3m-thick layer of habitation refuse. A *c.* 2m section of wall extending eastwards from the western wall of House IV may have been an internal partition or, indeed, part of an earlier structure.

House V. This was in the footprint of House 11 in the earlier round house sequence. It lay to the west of House IV and the walls were poorly preserved, although some paving remained to mark the floor area of the eastern end. The northern wall may have been a party wall with House III and the eastern wall was shared with House IV. Estimated internal measurements suggested a room *c.* 6m square.

House VI. Two houses and possibly a third were recorded at this location (Figs 8.1.9–10). House VI (a) was the earliest in the sequence and part of the northern and western walls remained extant (Fig. 8.1.10). The northern wall was *c.* 1.2m thick and 7m long and may have continued further east. The western wall was fragmentary but was of a similar thickness and survived for a length of *c.* 3.5m. Paving was recorded in the floor area and externally along the north-eastern side. House VI (b) was built within the footprint of House VI (a) and was rectangular in plan, with an internal width of 3.6m and a minimum length (east/west) of *c.* 6m. Only part of the north-eastern wall and possibly a small section of the south-eastern side survived *in situ* and the plan is otherwise conjectural. The walls were *c.* 1m thick. The floor may have been paved. A wall on the north-western side may represent a third house (House VI (c)) which was built across the western wall of House VI (a).

House VII. Ó Ríordáin (1949b, 52) described this as a house but there was no evidence of western or southern walls and the area may be best interpreted as a yard or space bounded by House I on the north and Houses II and II on the east. A hearth was recorded on the north-western side.

Fig. 8.1.10—Carraig Aille II: House VI (a).

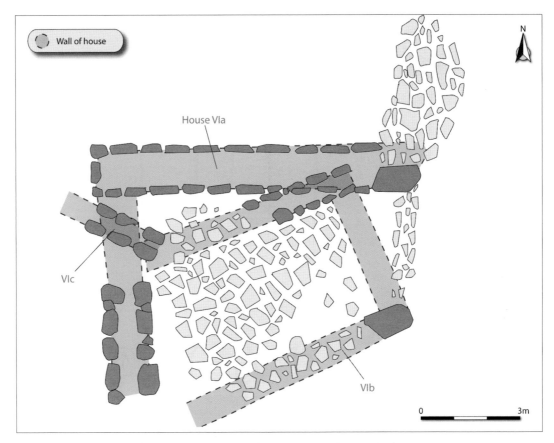

Finds

The finds from Carraig Aille II and the extramural house sites included bronze, iron, bone, stone, jet, glass beads and clay crucibles. Industrial activity such as iron-working was probably a home industry or in some instances the product of travelling smiths. A Viking silver hoard and bronze drinking-horn terminal are discussed in Chapter 9. An imitation Roman coin, a bronze toilet implement and a bronze stylus from Carraig Aille II originated in provincial Roman Britain or Gaul and probably date from the fourth century AD (Chapter 7). One sherd of prehistoric pottery, flint tools and stone axeheads from Carraig Aille II were residual from earlier site use (Chapter 3).

Twenty bronze ringed pins and fragments of ringed pins and sixteen iron ringed pins were recovered from Carraig Aille II and one bronze ringed pin from House VII. Ringed pins, comprising a pin and a swivel head, were used to secure clothing and were also decorative (Fanning 1994, 124–8). The bronze ringed pins were either cast or wrought into shape by a craftsman and manufacture did not require any great skill (*ibid.*). The iron ringed pins were made by bending over the pin heads to hold the rings, although some examples were perforated to hold the ring. Where find details are recorded at Carraig Aille II, all the bronze ringed pins came from the lower strata. A bronze ringed pin from under a stone in a collapsed wall of the extramural House VII may not have been contemporary with occupation. The bronze ringed pins are baluster-headed with spiral rings (Fig. 8.1.11: 1–2, 4, 6–8), while the iron examples (Fig. 8.1.11: 10–15) have, in the main, plain rings. Where measurements are given, the pins range in length from 60mm to 132mm with ring diameters of 15–

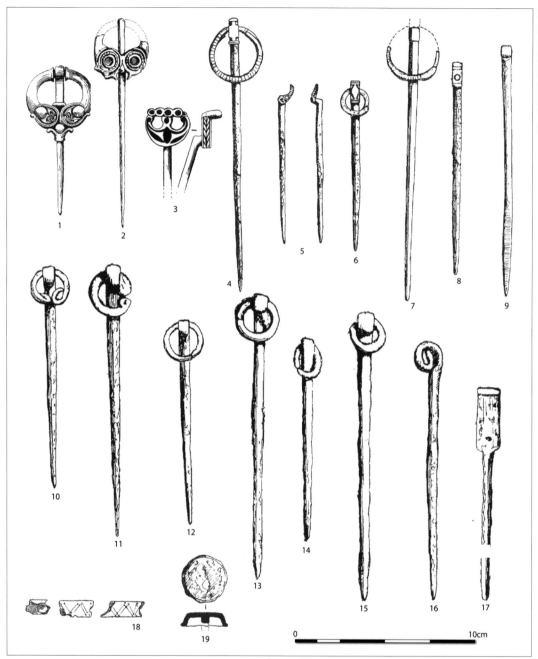

Fig. 8.1.11—Finds from Carraig Aille II: 1 bronze ring-pin/brooch; 2 bronze ring-pin; 3 bronze enamelled hand-pin; 4–9 bronze ring-pins; 10–15 iron ring-pins; 16 iron pin with spiral head; 17 flat-headed iron pin; 18 decorated bronze strip; 19 bronze button.

27mm. These ringed pins may date from as early as the fifth/sixth century AD (*ibid.*, 16). Similar ringed pins were found at Garryduff ringfort, Co. Cork, and were dated by the excavator to the seventh century (O'Kelly 1962). The short pin (66mm) of one ringed pin (Fig. 8.1.11: 1) suggests that it was a brooch, as the head does not move freely on the hoop. The terminals have bosses at the end of the hoop and each has a raised edging which forms a frame for an interlaced design. Ó Ríordáin (1949b, 69) proposed an eighth-century date for it. A second ringed pin (Fig. 8.1.11: 2) with an ornamental head has joined terminals which have a circular space surrounded by three concentric circles; two circles are raised and the middle circle is of dots. Ó Ríordáin (1949b, 68) proposed an eighth- or early ninth-century date for this example. A bronze enamelled hand-pin (Fig. 8.1.11: 3) was found at a depth of 0.45m and close to the toilet implement (Fig. 7.2.1). It may be a derivative of a Romano-British pelta brooch (Caulfield 1981, 209) and has red enamel insets on the brooch head. The pin has five 'fingers' and two openings under the fingers that form a 'palm', and the curvilinear metal surrounds have red enamel insets. Ó Ríordáin (1949b, 68) suggested a seventh- or early eighth-century date, but a review of the dating of hand-pins indicates a slightly earlier date in the late sixth/early seventh century (Youngs 1989).

The ring of one ringed pin (Fig. 8.1.11: 4) has lightly incised parallel lines and may date from the early sixth century (Ó Ríordáin 1949b, 68). A pin with a broken head (Fig. 8.1.11: 5) was different from the others in that the head appeared to have been fixed rather than to swivel on the top of the shaft and Ó Ríordáin (1949b, 69) compared it to ibex-headed pins dating from the first to third centuries AD. The ring of another ringed pin (Fig. 8.1.11: 6) has overlapping ends with a lozenge-shaped panel on each terminal, and the ringed pin from the extramural House VII is similar in design to this. One ringed pin (Fig. 8.1.11: 7) has a broken head that had decorated panels of light ribbing. Ringed-pin shafts that survived without the ring were mostly baluster-headed (Fig. 8.1.11: 8). One example (Fig. 8.1.11: 9) has the top of the shaft rolled over to house the ring. The iron ringed pins are similar to the bronze examples except that the ring was held by bending over the iron to form a loop (Fig. 8.1.11: 10–15). The ends of one ring (Fig. 8.1.11: 10) form loops, while another (Fig. 8.1.11: 11) has expanded terminals. An iron pin (Fig. 8.1.11: 16) from the extramural House III has a spiral head. An iron shaft with a flat head (Fig. 8.1.11: 17) came from under a stone wall of the house outside the southern rampart. The object may be a decorative pin but it does not fit in with the usual types from the early medieval period.

A fragment of very thin bronze plate (Ó Ríordáin 1949b, fig. 8:90), which was in poor condition, was compared with cauldrons and hanging bowls found in Norse graves (ibid., 73), but it was too thin to have functioned practically as a cauldron. Other bronze artefacts included a fragment of three strands of wire, twisted with a loop at one end, which have may have been a handle for a small pot, and thin strips of bronze which were possibly bronze mounts. A decorated bronze strip (Fig. 8.1.11: 18) with incised line and dot decoration was found under the paving in Phase 2 House 7 within the fort. A bronze button with a flat circular top and a central shank (Fig. 8.1.11: 19) may have been attached to clothing. An iron rivet with a bronze cap was also recovered from outside the rampart. A ring of bronze wire and fragments of a bronze ring were recovered from the extramural House VII.

Apart from ringed pins, most of the iron artefacts from Carraig Aille II were tools for household use or related to farming. Fifty-four iron knives were recovered from all levels on the excavation; no specifics of location are given in the published report (ibid., 74–7). A further eight knives were found in the extramural houses. Most knives have curved backs, straight cutting edges and triangular tangs (Fig. 8.1.12: 1–4), and some tangs (Fig. 8.1.12: 5) are flush with the blade. A few knives are also shorter (Fig. 8.1.12: 4) or longer (Fig. 8.1.12: 6) than the norm. The knife handles were probably of wood or bone, although no bone examples survive. A stone with a central deep boring (Fig. 8.1.15: 4) may have been a knife handle but would have made the knife heavy and cumbersome. An antler handle was found at Carraig Aille I (see Fig. 8.1.20: 6).

Other iron objects from Carraig Aille II included shears (Fig. 8.1.12: 7) for cutting cloth or

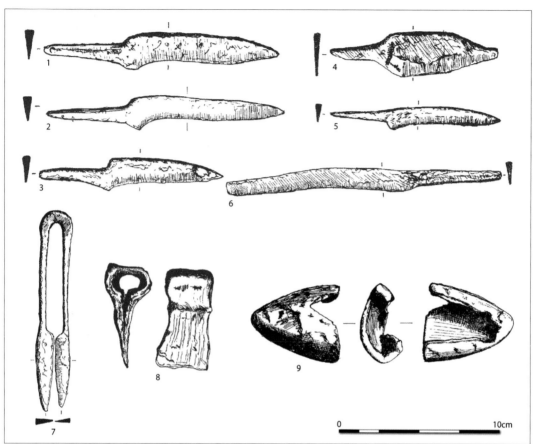

Fig. 8.1.12—Finds from Carraig Aille II: 1–6 iron knives; 7 iron shears; 8 axehead; 9 plough-sock.

shearing sheep, possible weaving combs, fragments of three saws, chisels, awls, nails, wall-brads, fragments of two small spearheads and harness fittings. Part of a corroded iron vessel found on a hearth in the north-east quadrant of the enclosure may have been in use during Phase 2 occupation, as this area had sequences of paving which were probably house floors. A poorly preserved tanged arrowhead was recovered from under the paving of Phase 2 House 1. A corroded iron axehead (Fig. 8.1.12: 8) was found below paving in the south-west quadrant of the fort. It has an oval socket and the overall length of socket and blade is 97mm. The socket was formed by bending the metal and welding the two sides together to make the blade. An iron plough-sock (Fig. 8.1.12: 9) was found over a hearth in the south-west quadrant of the fort. The plough-sock (or share) fitted over the cutting edge of the coulter or on the mould-board. The coulter cut the sod and the mould-board turned it. This type of plough may have been introduced into Ireland in the early seventh century or earlier and was known in Britain from the mid-fifth century (Mitchell 1976, 172). Excavations elsewhere in Ireland indicate a mid-seventh-century date for the coulter plough in Ireland (O'Sullivan *et al.* 2013, 195).

The worked bone from Carraig Aille II comprised 22 portions of bone combs, 34 bone pins, a needle, points, spindle-whorls, beads, gaming pieces and some bone that was worked but not finished into artefacts. The combs were manufactured from fresh bone or perhaps antler when the raw material was still malleable. The combs, similar to modern combs, were used to comb head and

Fig. 8.1.13—Finds from Carraig Aille II: 1–9 bone combs; 10–13 bone pins; 14 bone needle; 15–17 bone spindle-whorls; 18–19 bone scoops or gouges; 20–22 bone gaming pieces (?) or beads (?).

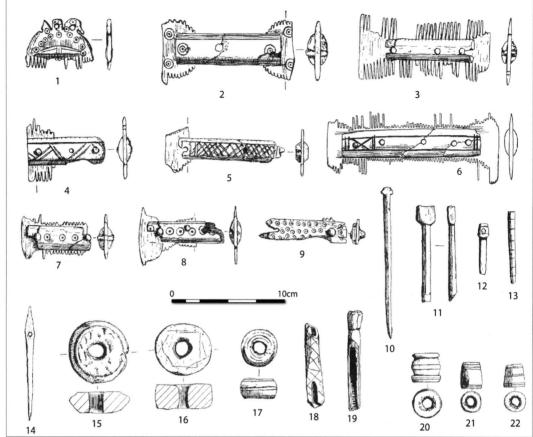

facial hair and indicate concern with personal appearance and hygiene. With the exception of one example (Fig. 8.1.13: 1), all the combs from Carraig Aille II are double-sided and were made by placing a thin bone plate between two side pieces and securing the three parts together with rivets or pegs. The teeth were then cut and the side plates were frequently ornamented with dot-and-circle or cross-hatched designs. The combs from Carraig Aille II were found at all levels. Dunlevy's (1988) classification of early Irish combs allows some dating of the combs from Carraig Aille II. One comb (Fig. 8.1.13: 1) from the extramural houses is single-sided with a high back and a suspension-hole in the centre top, and is decorated on one side with an ornithomantic crest and dot-and-circle motifs. This type of comb belongs to Dunlevy's Class A2 and has a broad date range from the fifth to the tenth century, albeit many examples are considered to be fifth- or sixth-century in date (Dunlevy 1988, 352–3). Wear patterns on the comb indicate that it was worn as a clothing ornament rather than being a functional comb. One comb (Fig. 8.1.13: 7) identified by Dunlevy as a Class B has a broad date range between the third and the ninth/early tenth century. More closely dated Class B combs from Deer Park Farms were recovered from seventh/eighth-century levels (Hurl *et al.* 2011, 258). The majority of the combs (Fig. 8.1.13: 2–6) from Carraig Aille II belong to Dunlevy's Class D1, are decorated with dot-and-circle and criss-cross motifs and date from between the fifth and tenth centuries. Examples of this type of comb from the ringfort excavation at Raheennamadra, close to Garryspillane, have been radiocarbon-dated to AD 520–690 (Stenberger 1966, 49, 52, fig.

3). Some combs (Fig. 8.1.13: 8–9) are identified as of Dunlevy Class D2 (1988, 390) and may be eighth- to tenth-century in date. These are also decorated with dot-and-circle motifs.

Thirty-four bone pins were found within the enclosure of Carraig Aille II and a further five from the area around the extramural houses. They vary in size and were probably used to fasten clothing such as a cloak, or to keep hair in place. Some pins have carved heads (Fig. 8.1.13: 10–12) or incised shafts (Fig. 8.1.13: 13) and may have been decorative as well as practical clothes-fasteners. One pin (Fig. 8.1.13: 11) is similar to an example from Garryduff, Co. Cork (O'Kelly 1962, fig. 12: 105), dated to the seventh century. Bone pins may also have been pin beaters used in weaving cloth or in basketry work. Pins with perforations or 'eyes' (Fig. 8.1.13: 14) were probably used as needles for stitching leather or cloth.

Spindle-whorls were used to maintain the momentum of a spindle when wool was spun to make thread, which was then knitted or woven into garments (Hurley and McCutcheon 1997, 588–9). Twelve spindle-whorls from within the enclosure at Carraig Aille II are of bone, except for one (Fig. 8.1.13: 15) made of deer horn. A further three, which were dome-shaped, were found in the extramural houses. Some of the spindle-whorls (Fig. 8.1.13: 15–17) are decorated with incised concentric circles around the central hole. One (Fig. 8.1.13: 16) has scratched lines on one surface that are geometric in style but may have been no more than doodles.

Some of the bone objects described by Ó Ríordáin (1949b, 83) as 'scoops' or 'gouges' (Fig. 8.1.13: 18–19) have been reinterpreted as spearheads (Mullins 2007, 52). These were made from sheep tibia and most were perforated to secure a haft that would render the spearhead a viable projectile. Bone spearheads may have been used in hunting or fishing rather than in warfare. Some of the bone spearheads are decorated with incised lines (Fig. 8.1.13: 18). One example with a carved head (Fig. 8.1.13: 19) was probably a gouge. Small, barrel-shaped bone objects (Fig. 8.1.13: 20–2) were lathe-turned and may have been beads or gaming pieces.

Thirty-five fragments of rotary quernstones were recovered from Carraig Aille II. Two fragments were reused as paving stones in the extramural houses and a further fragment was used as building stone in a house wall. The quernstones vary in thickness from 60mm to 80mm and taper towards the edges (Fig. 8.1.14: 1–2). About 75% of them are made from sandstone and the remainder from conglomerates. A few of the upper stones have raised collars around the central hole. Thirty-three whetstones used to sharpen metal objects were found at Carraig Aille II and eleven were recovered from the extramural houses. Some have perforations that allowed the owner to suspend the whetstone around the neck. Although common on many secular and ecclesiastical sites, some whetstones were valued possessions, as indicated by two examples from Carraig Aille II which were perforated: when they broke along the perforation, a second hole was drilled (Fig. 8.1.14: 3) to allow the owner to continue using the same stone (O'Connor 1991, 46). Round-ended whetstones were also used (Fig. 8.1.14: 4) and some bore pin grooves. Some whetstones showed extensive use and one example (Fig. 8.1.14: 5) was worn to a point by rubbing on both sides. Two stone axeheads had also been reused as whetstones and had pin grooves. One rotary grindstone (Fig. 8.1.14: 6) was found within the fort; it has an external diameter of 99mm and is 19mm thick. The central hole is circular, with a diameter of 50mm. Rotary grindstones were used to sharpen iron tools and weapons and were operated by a crank handle inserted through the central hole. They are not precisely datable, being recovered from early medieval (Stevens 2007) and Viking sites in Ireland (Carey 2014, 299). A single-cresset stone lamp (Fig. 8.1.14: 7) of sandstone was recovered. A second stone may also have been a lamp, although the bowl for the wick and tallow is shallow, and part of a stone lamp was recovered from the extramural houses.

Fig. 8.1.14—Finds from Carraig Aille II: 1–2 quernstones; 3–5 whetstones; 6 rotary grindstone; 7 single-cresset stone lamp.

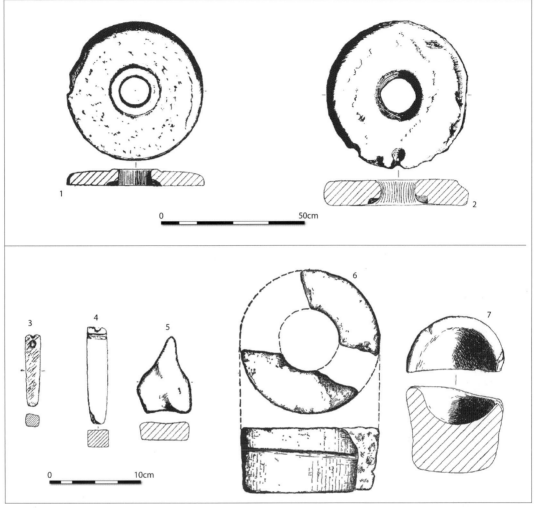

The stone spindle-whorls from Carraig Aille II are centrally perforated (Fig. 8.1.15: 1–2) and one (Fig. 8.1.15: 2) has lines scratched on the surface as simple decoration. Ó Ríordáin (1949b, 86) interpreted five small, flat stone discs (Fig. 8.1.15: 3) as unfinished spindle-whorls, but these may have been gaming pieces similar to modern draughts counters. Ó Ríordáin (1949b, 87) described two objects as 'stone handles', and one of these (Fig. 8.1.15: 4) has a deep central perforation which may have held the tang of an implement such as an awl.

Items of personal dress from Carraig Aille II included two portions of stone bracelets (Fig. 8.1.15: 5) and 33 fragments of jet bracelets. Three jet bracelet fragments and a polished jet bead were also found on the extramural house sites. The cross-sections of the jet bracelets are oval (Figs 8.1.15: 6, 8) or D-shaped (Fig. 8.1.15: 7). One jet bracelet (Fig. 8.1.15: 8) was perforated, possibly for suspension, and may have been worn as part of a necklace or as an earring. The internal diameters of the bracelets are *c*. 50mm or smaller, which may suggest that they were worn by women or children. A stone bead (Fig. 8.1.15: 9) recovered from Carraig Aille II was also an item of personal adornment.

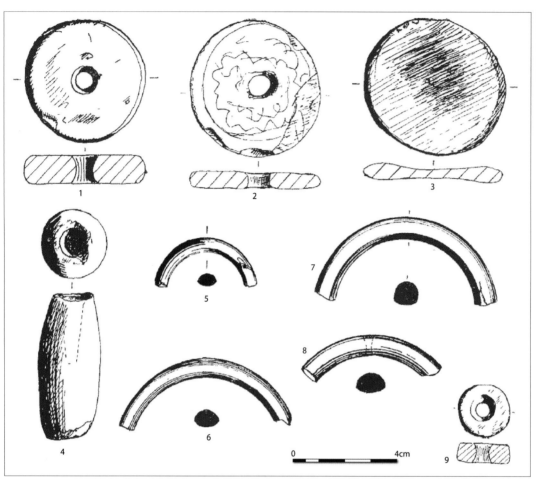

Fig. 8.1.15—Finds from Carraig Aille II: 1–2 stone spindle-whorls; 3 stone disc; 4 stone handle; 5 stone bracelet; 6–8 jet bracelets; 9 stone bead.

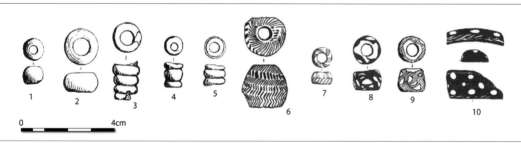

Fig. 8.1.16—Finds from Carraig Aille II: 1–9 glass beads; 10 glass bracelet fragment.

Glass beads from Carraig Aille II, which were presumably from necklaces or bracelets, comprised twelve blue glass beads and eight of more complex manufacture. The blue glass beads are 12–16mm in external diameter and generally barrel-shaped (Fig. 8.1.16: 1) or flat (Fig. 8.1.16: 2). Three blue glass beads are segmented (Fig. 8.1.16: 3–5), with three to five segments. The other beads include an example with yellow and yellowish brown zigzag ornament (Fig. 8.1.16: 6) over a core of yellow glass; one bead has a blue and white zigzag pattern (Fig. 8.1.16: 7), and another has wavy blue and white lines (Fig. 8.1.16: 8). Three blue glass beads, one translucent green glass bead and one bead with wavy blue and light blue lines (Fig. 8.1.16: 9) were found on the extramural house sites. A blue

Fig. 8.1.17—Clay crucibles
from Carraig Aille II.

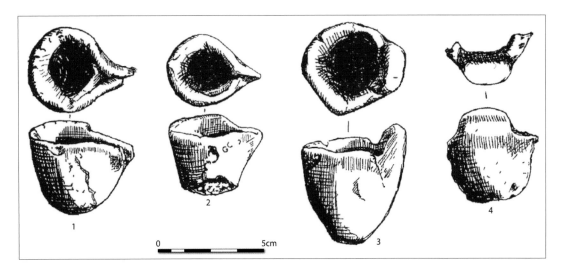

glass bracelet fragment (Fig. 8.1.16: 10) with white spots and light white lines was also found within
the enclosure.

Clay crucibles from Carraig Aille II provide evidence for the manufacture of bronze at the site.
Some (Fig. 8.1.17: 1–4) are small, with capacities of 4–9cc. Copper residues were visible in the
crucible bowls and some inner surfaces were vitrified from the intense heat of melting bronze. The
smaller crucibles are cup-shaped with flat bases and a triangular projection at the rim (Fig. 8.1.17:
1–2); this projection was used as a handle whereby the crucible could be held over the heat with
tongs. Other crucibles (Fig. 8.1.17: 3–4) have handles extending from the top of the rim, and one
has a slight pouring spout (Fig. 8.1.17: 3). Fragments of larger clay crucibles were also found on site;
these had wall thicknesses of up to 24mm and internally vitrified surfaces from contact with heat.

Carraig Aille I
This was to the north of Carraig Aille II at a distance of *c*. 130ft (40m) and on the highest part of
the ridge (Fig. 8.1.3). The rampart encircled the crest of the ridge and the central enclosed area was
higher than some of the surrounding ground. Part of the northern rampart was removed by
quarrying. The rampart was similar to that of Carraig Aille II and was 11–14ft (3.3–4.2m) thick,
standing to a height of *c*. 3ft (1m). The enclosure was oval in plan (Fig. 8.1.18), being widest along
the east–west axis, with an overall diameter of *c*. 140ft (42m). Ó Ríordáin (1949b, 53) considered
the stonework of the rampart of Carraig Aille I to be inferior to that of Carraig Aille II; the stones
used were larger and not as well placed, perhaps giving the masonry a rougher appearance. Two sets
of steps, 0.9m wide and 0.2m deep, were recorded, one *c*. 2m north of the entrance and one almost
directly opposite on the western side of the rampart. Similar to Carraig Aille II, these steps gave
access to the rampart, indicating that it was originally higher and that a palisade may have existed
along the top. A stone in the south-west quadrant which was set back in the rampart face may also
have given access to the rampart. The entrance was on the east and had recesses on either side to
house double gates which were set back flush with the wall when open; the recesses were *c*. 0.2m
deep, *c*. 1.5m long on the southern side and *c*. 1.7m long on the northern side. The entrance was *c*.
2.3m wide and the surface at the exit was paved with flagstones. A trench marked the limit of the
paving and Ó Ríordáin (1949b, 53) interpreted this as holding a wooden beam that acted as a

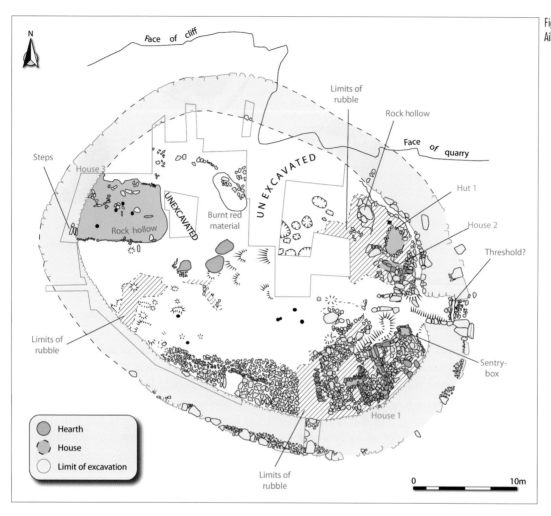

Fig. 8.1.18—Plan of Carraig Aille I.

threshold. A post-hole just outside and to the north of the entrance may have held a gatepost for an external gate. The paving at the entrance was laid over an accumulation of habitation refuse up to 0.3m thick, perhaps suggesting occupation of the site before the rampart was built.

The fort enclosed at least three houses and possibly more, and these appear to have been in the main stone-built and rectangular in plan. One possible oval-shaped hut can be deduced from the published plan and this was located north of the entrance. The remains of this hut were represented by an arc of stones which, similar to the Phase I round houses in Carraig Aille II, marked a retaining feature around a clay platform on which the hut was built. This hut had an estimated diameter of *c.* 3m but, based on its proximity to the rampart, it is possible that its eastern side continued under and pre-dated the rampart; the hut may therefore have been larger. There are no detailed descriptions of the rectangular stone buildings within the fort and the nature of the structures must be inferred from the published plans. At least one house (House 1) was immediately south of the entrance. The area around House 1 was paved and may indicate that there was a sequence of houses. House 1 was marked by an extant southern wall, *c.* 5m long (north-west/south-east), which abutted the rampart and a second wall that extended (east/west) at a right angle for *c.* 2m and was probably the vestiges of a northern wall. The walls were faced externally with stone blocks and probably had rubble cores, similar to the Phase II houses at Carraig Aille II. The enclosed area was paved. Three hearths within the house were all close to the rampart. These were thick (up to 0.45m) accumulations of burnt material and may have been dumps of burnt material rather than formal hearths. Vestiges of walls to the south-west enclosed an area *c.* 1.5m long, possibly an annexe to House 1 or part of an earlier or later house. The enclosed area was also paved. A north/south-aligned wall *c.* 5.7m west of House 1 was probably also part of a house. A stone structure *c.* 4ft (1.2m) square adjacent to the northern wall of House 1 and about 7ft (2.1m) south-west of the entrance was interpreted as a sentry-box (Ó Ríordáin 1949b, 54). There are no details of the structure although it is unlikely that a building with a single course of stones stood to any great height. It may have had a wooden superstructure or the foundations may have had some other function, perhaps as an annexe to House 1 or a small animal pen.

A stone setting immediately north of the entrance was of similar construction to House 1 and may represent the vestiges of a stone house (House 2). The western side was *c.* 2m long (east/west) and the eastern wall was *c.* 1m long; a *c.* 0.7m-wide space between these may have been the doorway. Paving led south from this towards the entrance.

House 3, on the western side of the enclosure, was built to take advantage of shelter provided by a natural rise in the rock on the east and by the rampart on the west. The house was 8m (east/west) by 6m (north/south), semi-underground and built within a natural rock fissure or hollow that was probably deepened to accommodate it. The illustrated cross-section (*ibid.*, pl. IX, A–B) indicates a depth of *c.* 0.7m within the rock hollow. The rock sides were straight, suggesting that they were hewn from the rock face and the walls were then stone-lined. The stone lining was described as poorly constructed although poor survival may also be a factor and, as the stone lining was built on an existing layer of black habitation material, there may have been some pre-construction use of the natural hollow. Three rock-cut post-holes clustered in the centre of the house suggest load-bearing posts for roof supports. The house floor was subsequently covered by an initial layer of clay and gravel that included some animal bones and a final layer of black habitation material; these layers indicate deliberate infill after the house was abandoned.

Three hearths and a spread of burnt material within the rampart were unlined and were possibly outdoor fires. The spread of burnt material may have been no more than casual dumping. A rock hollow in the north-east quadrant was filled with habitation debris and large rocks and may initially have functioned as a souterrain-like structure which was later infilled. Ó Ríordáin (1949b, 55) described the occupation of the fort as one 'of slovenly living', an impression garnered from the amount of accumulated habitation refuse within the site.

The artefacts from Carraig Aille I were fewer than from Carraig Aille II and were of bronze, iron, bone, stone, jet, glass and amber. Similar to the published details for Carraig Aille II, there is very little information on the locations of the finds. Pre-enclosure activity at Carraig Aille I was indicated by occupation layers under the rampart (Ó Ríordáin 1949b, 54), and some finds may have been recovered from these layers as well as from features associated with occupation within the rampart.

There were nine bronze artefacts from Carraig Aille I, comprising five ringed-pin fragments and four scraps of bronze. An iron hand-pin (Fig. 8.1.19: 1) from Carraig Aille I is unusual, as this type of decorative artefact was more commonly manufactured in silver or bronze. The hand-pin has three 'fingers' and a palm at the top of the shaft and may date from as early as the fifth century (*ibid.*,

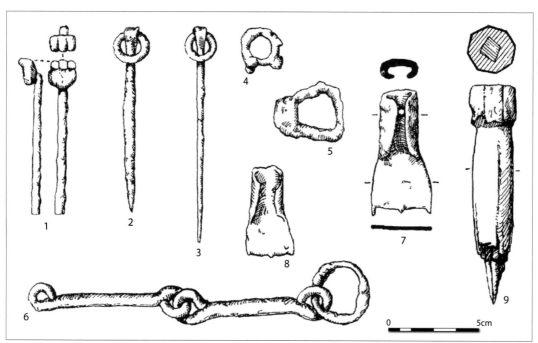

Fig. 8.1.19—Iron artefacts from Carraig Aille I: 1 hand-pin; 2–3 ringed pins; 4 ring; 5 strap end; 6 horse-bit; 7–8 scribing tools (?); 9 punch.

97) or from the late sixth/early seventh century (Youngs 1989). Two iron ringed pins (Fig. 8.1.19: 2–3) and fragments of others from Carraig Aille I were similar to those from Carraig Aille II. Nine iron rings of various sizes were recovered and may be parts of horse trappings. An S-hook from Carraig Aille I may also have come from a harness. One ring (Fig. 8.1.19: 4) with protruding knobs and a second D-shaped object (Fig. 8.1.19: 5) may have been strap ends. One complete horse-bit (Fig. 8.1.19: 6) and two fragments of horse-bits were recovered, and their size suggests that they were for small horses or ponies. Two iron artefacts (Fig. 8.1.19: 7–8) described as 'pronged implements' (Ó Ríordáin 1949b, 98) had three short prongs projecting from one end; where best preserved, the prongs were *c.* 4mm in length. One (Fig. 8.1.19: 7) had a hole at the shaft end that may have served as a nail hole to secure a wooden handle or as a suspension hole. Two similar objects were recovered from Carraig Aille II (*ibid.*, fig. 10). The function of these implements is unknown, but the prongs suggest some type of scribing tool for circles with a diameter in the region of 20–30mm—too large for the dot-and-circle motifs on bone combs but fitting those of some of the bone spindle-whorls. A similar object from the ringfort excavation at Raheennamadra was described as a 'leather-scorer' (Stenberger 1966, 46), which may indicate use to produce decorative motifs on or enabling the cutting of leather. Six iron punches and two awls were also found; one punch (Fig. 8.1.19: 9) had a pointed spike and an octagonal head. Other iron objects from Carraig Aille I consisted of a small wedge, saw fragments, shears fragments and nails.

Twenty-five bone combs from Carraig Aille I included fragments and complete combs. All were double-sided (Fig. 8.1.20: 1) and ornamented with incised dot-and-circle motifs or criss-cross lines. The combs were not available to Dunlevy (1988) for study but, like those from Carraig Aille II, have a broad date range between the fifth and tenth centuries. One comb plate (Fig. 8.1.20: 2) has double criss-cross lines with intermediary circles, while another (Fig. 8.1.20: 3) has double criss-cross lines with circles at the terminals. Three bone pins were also recovered from Carraig Aille I. A decorated

Fig. 8.1.20—Finds from
Carraig Aille I: 1–3 bone combs;
4 decorated bone strip; 5 bone
gaming piece or bead; 6 antler
handle; 7–8 bone spindle-
whorls; 9 bone scoop or gouge.

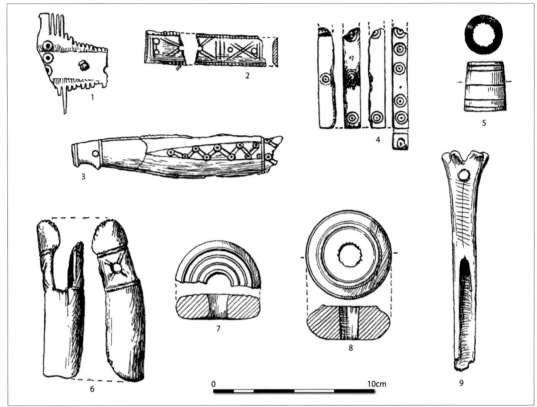

bone strip with irregularly spaced dot-and-circle motifs (Fig. 8.1.20: 4) was described as a 'dice' but
cannot be thrown (Ó Ríordáin 1949b, 100). It may have been used in a game similar to dominos. A
small, barrel-shaped bone object (Fig. 8.1.20: 5) may also have been a gaming piece. An antler tine
(Fig. 8.1.20: 6) has a slot at one end to receive a tang and a rivet hole to fasten the handle in place.
The handle has parallel decorative lines extending from the rivet hole and two bands of circular lines
around the handle. Twelve bone spindle-whorls from Carraig Aille I were better-finished than those
from Carraig Aille II (*ibid.*, 99). Three were decorated with concentric lines (Fig. 8.1.20: 7) and one
(Fig. 8.1.20: 8) was decorated on both sides. Of the sixteen bone scoops from Carraig Aille I, ten
were perforated and one example (Fig. 8.1.20: 9) was decorated with a scratched central line with
short crossing lines. Raw material for antler-working, including tines, a burr and a hollow cylinder,
was also recovered from Carraig Aille I.

The twelve quernstone fragments from Carraig Aille I were undecorated and similar to those
from Carraig Aille II. A rotary grindstone was also recovered. The number of whetstones from Carraig
Aille I totalled 55, which was 40% more than from Carraig Aille II. Other stone artefacts from Carraig
Aille I included ten spindle-whorls, five flat discs that were up to 120mm in diameter and may have
served as pot lids, and a possible stone handle similar to one from Carraig Aille II. Two fragments of
a jet bracelet were also recovered.

Of the three glass beads found at Carraig Aille I, one (Fig. 8.1.21: 1) is a small pink bead with
bands of lighter pink. The remaining two are blue glass and more complex in design. One bead (Fig.
8.1.21: 2) has applied pale blue glass that resembles a rope motif and a collar of twisted blue and

Fig. 8.1.21—Glass beads from Carraig Aille I.

white glass. The other (Fig. 8.1.21: 3) is five-sided with applied threads of blue and white glass and a collar of blue and white glass. This type of bead is described by Laing (1975, 337) as a 'horned eye bead'; it was a common find in the Iron Age, rare in the early medieval period in western Europe but known from the Viking period.

Two tons of animal bones were recovered from Carraig Aille I and almost four tons from Carraig Aille II. Ninety per cent were from cattle and the remainder mostly of sheep and pig, with some horse. The only evidence for red deer consisted of antler tines, which were used to make implements. Other animal bones were from medium-sized to large dogs, cat, badger, hare, ferret and fox. A few fish vertebrae unidentifiable to species were also found. Bird bones were from domestic fowl, marsh harrier, black-headed gull, wild duck, tufted duck, greylag and barnacle goose, Berwick's swan, whooper swan, cormorant, moorhen and coot. The swans and geese are winter visitors to Ireland and were probably opportunistically hunted.

To the north-west of Carraig Aille I was a level plateau below the fort and bounded on the western side by the vertical cliff face; Carraig Aille I stood at the edge of this cliff. The plateau was *c.* 36m long and 11m wide and was accessed via a formal entrance on the south-east side which was marked by two large upright stones with an intermediary distance of *c.* 1m (Fig. 8.1.22). A large post-hole over 1.2m in diameter and 0.6m deep adjacent to the north-east of the entrance suggests a substantial gate-post here. It was latterly covered by a large flat stone, indicating that the gate had become redundant. Ó Ríordáin (1949b, 56) considered that the plateau was a cattle corral associated with the occupation of the forts on Carraig Aille.

Fig. 8.1.22—Enclosed cattle corral west of Carraig Aille I.

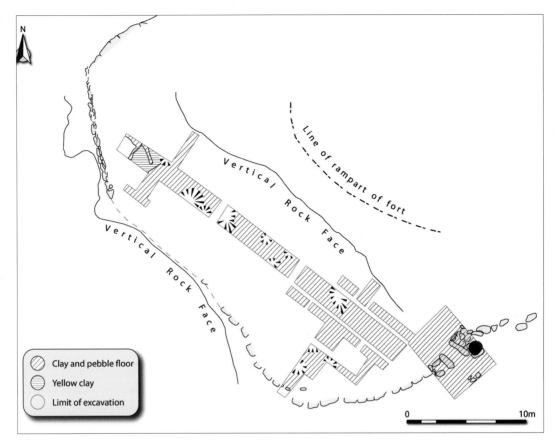

Structures north-west of Carraig Aille I

Three structures on the hill slope north-west of Carraig Aille I were visible on the ground prior to excavation as large stones almost 1m high (Fig. 8.1.23). They were interpreted as 'unroofed pens' (Ó Ríordáin 1949b, 56) and, given their small size, may have been sheepfolds. The structures were undated and the only finds recovered were animal bones.

Structure A. This was the most southerly of the structures, rectangular in plan and measuring 4.2m (east/west) by 3.6m (north/south) (Fig. 8.1.23). There was no apparent entrance. The external area on the north-eastern side between Structure A and Structure B was paved.

Structure B. This was circular in plan, just under 4m in diameter and possibly open-ended on the northern side (Fig. 8.1.23). A double setting of stones along the southern side may indicate a more substantial wall or part of another building further south that continued into an unexcavated area.

Structure C. This was the largest of the structures and the ground-plan had the appearance of two conjoined buildings which were roughly rectangular in plan (Fig. 8.1.23). The overall internal measurements were *c.* 7.8m (north/south) by 5.4m (east/west) and the eastern side incorporated the adjacent rock face. The upright stones of Structure C were kept in place by the piling of stones around their bases.

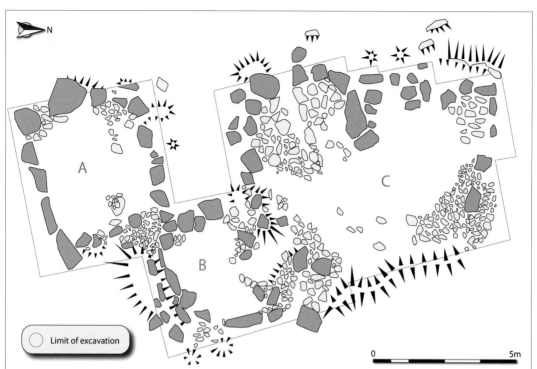

Fig. 8.1.23—Plan of Structures A–C north-west of Carraig Aille I.

Fig. 8.1.24—The Spectacles.

A small plateau *c.* 33m further north of Structures A–C was enclosed in antiquity, and a small enclosed area *c.* 25m across was recorded to the south-west of the structures; both enclosures may have been stock corrals similar to that on the plateau west of Carraig Aille I.

The Spectacles

These house sites were on the lower slope of Drumlaegh Hill and north-west of the present interpretative centre (Fig. 8.1.1). The Spectacles were excavated at the same time as the Carraig Aille complex (Ó Ríordáin 1949b). Ordnance Survey mappers during the 1920–4 revision used the name 'spectacles' because of the resemblance of the surface remains to eyeglasses. The site is on a narrow plateau, *c.* 100m (north/south) by 35m (east/west), which slopes slightly downwards towards the lake on the southern side, the rock face being almost vertical thereafter; the northern side is a steep rock face which rises to the top of Drumlaegh Hill. The site can be considered to be naturally enclosed by the physical terrain. The excavation uncovered three houses and one narrow building interpreted as a byre (Fig. 8.1.24). Three stone-faced field fences and an earthen fence run north/south across the plateau. A more substantial stone field fence extends east/west across the plateau and continues towards the summit of Drumlaegh Hill. Each house was within a separate field that can be described as a 'kitchen garden' or 'haggard', as they are known in an Irish context, with an enclosed area of *c.* one-seventh of an acre (0.06ha).

House A

This was the most northerly of the houses, *c.* 4m north of the east/west stone fence. It was circular in plan externally, while a slight flattening of the internal walls resulted in a roughly square internal plan with rounded corners (Fig. 8.1.25) and a diameter of 15ft (4.5m). The walls had a facing of large stone blocks and a rubble core and were over 3ft (0.9m) thick. There were twelve post-holes with an average diameter of 7in. (0.18m) and a depth of 7–9in. (0.18–0.23m) within the house; eight of these were adjacent to the wall and four were within the floor area. Posts at these locations possibly held ancillary roof supports, although the walls were thick enough to be load-bearing. A further four post-holes adjacent to the external wall may have held roof-support posts. Two larger post-holes, 9in. (0.23m) in diameter and 1ft (0.3m) deep, on either side of the entrance were interpreted as supports for a porch or for projecting eaves over the door. The entrance was on the southern side and was marked by two large in-turned stones, 4ft (1.2m) apart. A paved pathway edged with stones led into the entrance and a step at the door gave access to the house. The pathway continued southwards for *c.* 12m to the east/west stone field fence. The internal floor was uneven, with outcropping bedrock. Two hearths within the house were kerbed by two stones that projected from the walls. A pit, 2ft (0.6m) long, 1ft (0.3m) wide and 7in. (0.18m) deep, partly underlay the hearthstone of the hearth opposite the entrance. The second hearth, against the northern wall, was 2ft (0.6m) wide and 9in. (0.23m) deep; it was burnt red, and the wall behind it was also affected by heat. Ó Ríordáin (1949b, 58) suggested that the positioning of two hearths within the house might have been dictated by wind direction.

House B

This was built against the east/west stone field fence and about 6.5m south of House A. The ground-plan was oval, with internal dimensions of *c.* 4.8m (north/south) by 2.5m (east/west). The western stone wall was extant for *c.* 3.5m, faced on either side with large stones, and had a rubble core (Fig.

Fig. 8.1.25—The Spectacles: Houses A and B.

8.1.25). It curved northwards and was against the east/west stone field wall, which must have been in place before the house was built and may have been used as part of the northern wall of House B. Ó Ríordáin (1949b, 59) considered that the western stone wall was built as a revetment to counteract the steep drop in ground level on the western side of House B. The line of the house on the southern and eastern sides was visible as paired post-holes with intermediary distances of *c.* 0.8–1.3m. Ó Ríordáin (1949b, 59) suggested that this section of the house wall was built from wood or partly from turves, or possibly constructed of mud. Placement of posts along the internal and external perimeter of the wall was similar to House A, and posts in these positions probably helped to support the roof. An internal paved hearth with burnt layers was recorded on the southern side of the house. There was no apparent entrance in the surviving remains but this was probably on the eastern or southern side.

House C

This narrow building, no more than 1m wide (north/south) internally and with an overall length (east/west) of *c.* 4.2m, was interpreted as an animal shelter rather than a domestic building. The walls were built by placing large stone blocks between rock outcrops, and it is unlikely that the structure stood to any significant height. The space between the stone blocks and the rock outcrops was filled in to provide a good surface and to counteract the natural slope from east to west. The internal space was cobbled. Post-holes to the north and north-east of House C may have been part of another building or a fence.

House D

This was on the southern side of the plateau and was rectangular in plan (Fig. 8.1.26), with internal dimensions of 14ft (4.2m) (north/south) by 12ft (3.6m) (east/west). The walls were stone-faced with a clay core, in contrast to the rubble cores of walls at Houses A and B at the Spectacles and the rectangular buildings at Carraig Aille. At the southern end of House D there were three post-holes that may have held posts forming part of a timber wall; this feature was recorded on the extramural houses at Carraig Aille II. Two extramural post-holes outside the eastern and western walls were in a line with those forming the southern wall. A further three post-holes within the house, *c.* 1.5m from the back (northern) wall, may have held roof-support posts. Also within the house were a hearth

Fig. 8.1.26—The Spectacles: House D.

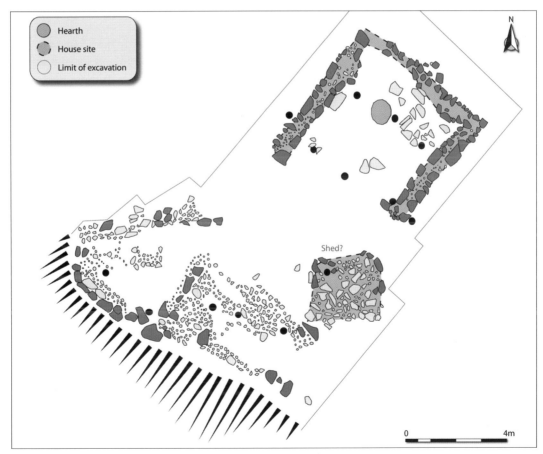

and traces of a paved floor. A small, stone-built structure of roughly rectangular plan, measuring *c.* 3m (east/west) by 2.5m, with a paved floor to the south of House D was interpreted as an outbuilding. The remains comprised a single line of stones and the structure is unlikely to have stood to any significant height.

A paved surface between House D and the cliff edge had been initially laid and was subsequently repaved. This paving was partially excavated along the cliff edge (Fig. 8.1.26) and led to Houses A and B. There were steps leading to the lake shore adjacent to the paved path south of Houses A and B. Examination of the pre-drainage lake levels during test-trenching in 1977 confirmed that the lake had extended up to 10m to the north and under the present access road to the farm by Lough Gur, and that the modern ground level was formed by introduced sand, gravel and occasionally waste from the limekiln (Cleary 1982a). The steps leading from the Spectacles may, however, have led to a narrow pathway between the base of the southern cliff edge at the Spectacles and the former lake edge.

Three of the north/south field fences at the Spectacles were stone-faced with rubble cores (Fig. 8.1.25), and the most easterly was an earthen bank. The east/west fence was also stone-faced with a rubble core and part of a more extensive enclosure system. The section of this fence between Houses A and B was initially *c.* 1.2m wide; an extra section was added on the southern side, making the fence 6ft (1.8m) wide. A 0.9m-wide entrance through the primary fence was blocked up when the fence was widened.

Finds

The number of finds from the Spectacles was relatively small and came mostly from House A. The metal artefacts included two pin fragments of bronze ringed pins, an iron pin and six iron knives. Bone objects from Houses A and D consisted of pins, spearheads, points and comb fragments. All the stone objects were from House A and comprised a quernstone from over the paving outside the entrance, three spindle-whorls and eight whetstones. Four fragments of jet bracelets were found: two in House A, one fragment from outside the house and one fragment in the hearth of House D. One blue glass bead with yellow glass trails was found just outside House A and a blue glass bead came from the hearth on the north side of House A. About half a ton of animal bones were recovered from the Spectacles and were similar to those from Carraig Aille I and II in terms of species, being primarily from cattle, with some pig and sheep. Bones from a terrier-sized dog and a cat, the skull of a large fish and one bone each from a teal and a rook were also recovered.

The fields at the Spectacles represent rare instances in which the small enclosures surrounding early medieval houses survive in the archaeological record. These small fields may be equated with the vegetable garden referred to in the seventh-century law text *Bechbretha* as being often situated outside the *lios* or fort (Kelly 1997, 368). Alternatively, the *Crith Gablach* defined the area outside the settlement as the *airlise*, which extended for the length of a spear cast outside the *lios* and included enclosed fields for cultivation and grazing (*ibid.*, 369). The stone walls forming the enclosures at the Spectacles fit within the class defined in the *Bretha Comaithchesa*, which specified that the walls should be 3ft thick and twelve fists (4ft) high (*ibid.*, 374).

Grange ringfort and hut sites in Ballingoola

A small ringfort known locally as 'the Mote' was excavated in Grange townland in 1948 (Ó Ríordáin 1949a) in a marshy valley north of Lough Gur (Fig. 8.1.1). The ringfort enclosure was a bank and ditch, and traces of an outer bank were uncovered by excavation (Figs 8.1.27–28). The ringfort was

Fig. 8.1.27—Grange ringfort before excavation.

Fig. 8.1.28—Grange ringfort: plan of excavation.

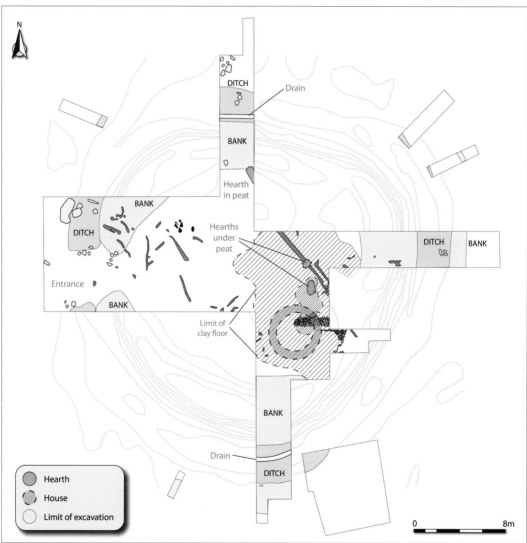

roughly circular in plan, although the northern and south-eastern circuit of the bank was almost straight in places. The average diameter, including the ditch, was *c.* 32m, and the surviving bank height was 0.5–0.8m. The ringfort was built on a peat layer formed on top of alluvial clay and the ditch was dug through the peat to a depth of 0.5m into the underlying clay. Material for the bank was sourced from the excavated ditch, and the basal level was peat on which was piled-up clay. Ó Ríordáin (1949a, 128) suggested that some of the peat from the excavated ditch was thrown into the interior of the site. Timber logs and tree stumps within the interior may have been small trees cut down when the site was initially cleared of alder, willow and poplar. Ash and oak logs were also uncovered but Ó Ríordáin (1949a, 128) considered that these had been brought onto the site.

The entrance was on the western side, where the ground was drier. There was no evidence for

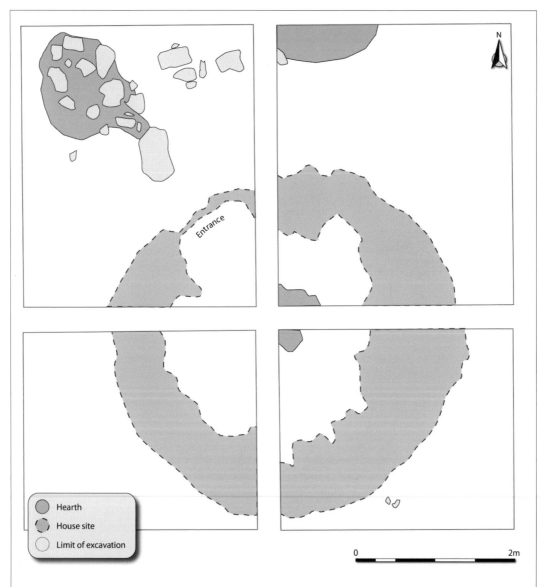

Fig. 8.1.29—Grange ringfort: plan of house.

- Hearth
- House site
- Limit of excavation

0   2m

Fig. 8.1.30—Grange ringfort: house site during excavation.

a formal gate, although one post-hole midway across the entrance may represent the vestiges of a central gatepost for a double gate. There was an extensive charcoal and brushwood layer mixed with clay around the entrance and under the peat on which the ringfort was built. This may have been laid down to keep the entrance dry, or it may pre-date ringfort construction. The vestiges of stone settings that defined the entrance remained at the ditch terminals.

Prior to excavation, the foundations of a house site were visible as a low mound with a central hollow in the south-east quadrant. An extensive, 0.2m-thick spread of clay was introduced into the south-east quadrant and the house, which was 5m in diameter, was built on this (Figs 8.1.28–29). The clay continued under the bank to the south-east and was contemporary with ringfort construction. The house had burnt down and the imprint of the structure remained as a circular band of oxidised clay (Fig. 8.1.30). Ó Ríordáin (1949a, 131) envisaged the house as a conical structure whose walls and roof were constructed as a single unit. A 1m-wide entrance on the north-west was marked by a gap in the oxidised clay, and charred wood probably represented the remains of a timber threshold. Charcoal fragments within the confines of the house were likely to have been from burnt wattle walls, which were probably plastered with daub to retain heat. A central hearth was also recorded in the house. Two other hearths within the ringfort probably indicate cooking areas outside the house. Finds from the ringfort included fragments of iron slag from various places in the peat and the clay floor around the house, five whetstone fragments, a stone spindle-whorl and two rounded stones which may have been hammer-stones. Cattle and sheep bones were also recovered and give some indication of diet.

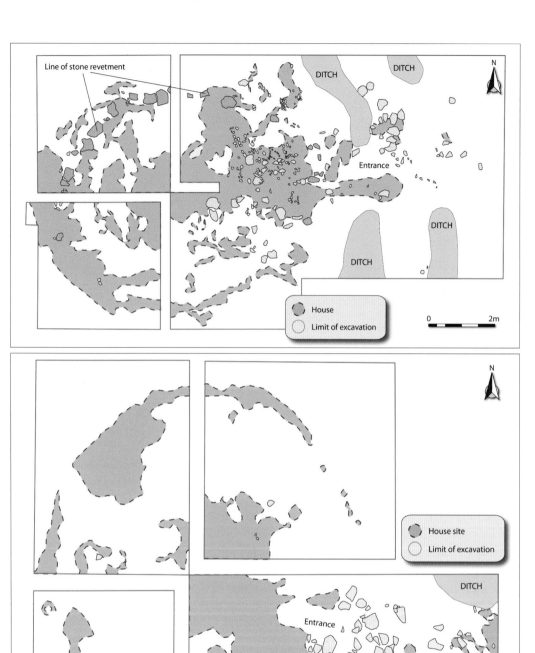

Fig. 8.1.31—Ballingoola III: plan of house site.

Fig. 8.1.32—Ballingoola IV: plan of house site.

Fig. 8.1.33—Ballynagallagh:
site location.

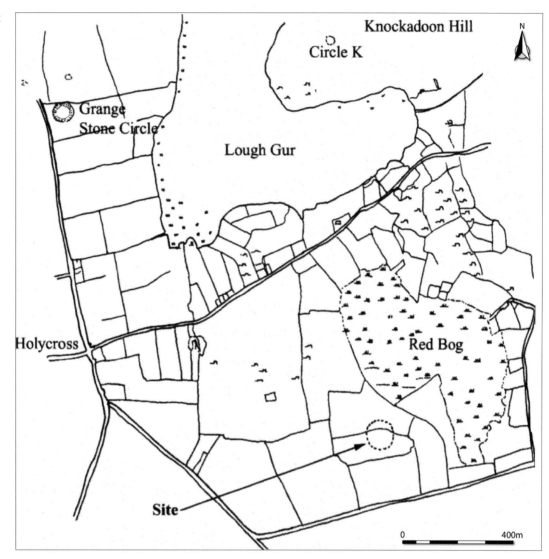

There were two house sites, designated Ballingoola III and IV, to the north of the ringfort at Grange and separated by a narrow stream. The remains of the Ballingoola III house consisted of oxidised clay layers on a clay floor, indicating that the house had burnt down. An arc of stones skirting the perimeter of the house was similar to stone arcs around the circular houses at Carraig Aille II and is best interpreted as a retaining feature for a clay platform on which the house was built. The house was slightly oval in plan, with an average diameter of *c.* 6m (Fig. 8.1.31). Walls of wattle may have been set into a low clay bank. The entrance was on the eastern side and was in part paved with flat slabs. A central hearth was recorded within the house. Two ditches skirting the perimeter of the house may have been dug to provide the clay for the low bank on which wattle walls would have been constructed and clay for the house floor, besides keeping water away from the floor area, as the house was built on low-lying marshy ground. The only finds from Ballingoola III were two butt ends of stone axeheads and a piece of chipped flint from the ditch, which may have been residual finds from earlier site use.

The Ballingoola IV house had a clay floor, and the position of the wattle walls was indicated by a circular band of charcoal *c*. 6m in diameter, the charred wood indicating that the house had burnt down (Fig. 8.1.32). The entrance was on the eastern side and was paved. A central hearth was also recorded. A ditch on the east side, like Ballingoola III, probably provided the clay for the floor and served to draw water away from the house.

There were no datable finds from the Ballingoola houses and the sites were dated on their architectural similarities to the house within the ringfort at Grange. The absence of datable finds from the Grange ringfort and the Ballingoola houses led Ó Ríordáin (1949a, 138) to speculate that these sites were linked to the use of the adjacent lands for summer grazing and transhumance. Cattle bones were found at Ballingoola III and cattle, pig, horse and dog bones at Ballingoola IV.

Ballynagallagh

The site was on the western edge of the 'Red Bog' (Fig. 8.1.33), which is to the south of Lough Gur and separated from it by a limestone ridge. The 'Red Bog', a former lake that has degenerated into bog possibly through silting, excessive weed growth and other environmental factors, was obviously an attractive settlement location and, although smaller than the nearby Lough Gur, would have provided the same resources, such as water and supplementary food sources from wildlife, particularly wild birds. The excavated site at Ballynagallagh was a large oval enclosure (140m by 100m) that was first detected by medium-altitude aerial photography (Fig. 8.1.34) undertaken as part of the Bruff aerial survey (Doody 1993; 2000) and visible as a circular crop mark with differential grass growth, although a very low bank was barely perceptible. Geophysical prospection techniques indicated evidence of archaeological remains inside and outside the enclosure. The excavated area was small

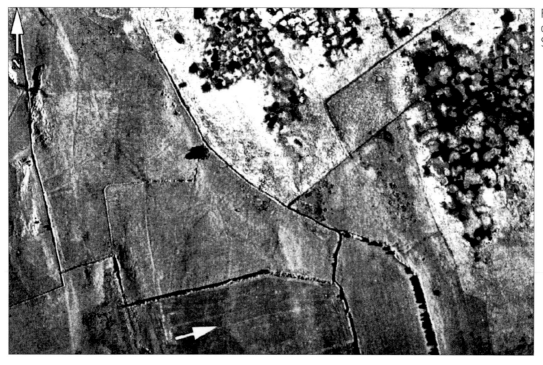

Fig. 8.1.34—Aerial photograph of Ballynagallagh (Bruff Aerial Survey).

Fig. 8.1.35—Plan of circular house at Ballynagallagh.

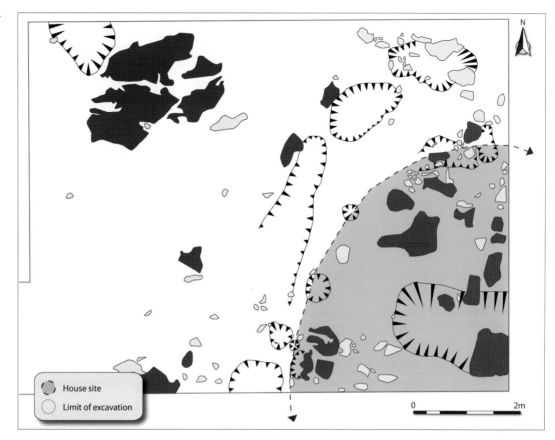

House site

Limit of excavation

0   2m

relative to the size of the site and radiocarbon dates from animal bones from the site place its use in the period AD 460–1150.

The earliest dated feature on the site was a section of a round or oval house constructed with substantial earthfast posts that formed the perimeter walls (Fig. 8.1.35). A radiocarbon date for one post-hole places the structure in the period AD 460–630. The estimated diameter of the house was in the region of 8m and a possible entrance was represented by a cluster of post-holes on the western side. The perimeter posts were likely to have supported the roof but other internal roof-support posts may have been necessary to support the span of roof trusses. Part of a second post-built structure was also recorded on the excavation; this was smaller, with an estimated diameter of 4.5–5m. The footing for a fence line on the site remained as a linear trench where charred ash and Scots pine fragments probably represent the remains of a timber fence. The fence was dated to the period AD 560–730 and may have been erected around the larger house. A considerable number of cattle bones were recovered from the trench fill; as these were mainly from butchering waste, it is likely that butchering took place near the fence and that the waste was thrown into the trench as part of the infill.

The excavation established that the enclosure detected by aerial photography and topographic and geophysical survey was a double palisade, constructed in the period 760–900, consisting of two lines of large posts with an intermediary distance of 1.4m (Fig. 8.1.36) and an estimated circumference of *c.* 380m. Drawing on the seventh-century *Bretha Comaithchesa*, Ó Corráin (1983, 249) described post-and-wattle farm fences as having posts *c.* 0.2m apart, 1.8m high and 0.6m wide at the base, bound together by three courses of wickerwork and built to withstand both small and large animals. If those stipulations were followed for the enclosure fence at Ballynagallagh, it would have required vast quantities of wooden posts and wattle, and these resources must have been harvested from a wide area. No evidence for houses in contemporary use with the palisade was uncovered on the excavation, but this may have been due to the limited extent of the area investigated. Seven large pits were found on the excavation and they yielded animal bone waste and some charred cereals that confirm rubbish disposal within the palisade enclosure. Radiocarbon dates of AD 620–870 and AD 950–1130 from pits indicate that the site was in use over a lengthy period. Two pits were stone-lined (Fig. 8.1.37) and show care in construction. Lewis (1837, 108) and Dowd (1896, 79) provided an initial foundation date of 941 for the nearby nunnery of Ballynagallagh, which may have used the enclosure as a convenient rubbish disposal site.

Fig. 8.1.36—Palisade trench, Ballynagallagh.

Fig. 8.1.37—Stone-lined pit within the enclosure at Ballynagallagh.

There was a stone trackway *c.* 1.4m west of and outside the palisade enclosure. It was 2m wide and its metalled surface comprised stones of various sizes. A date of AD 660–780 was obtained from animal bone in the stone surface, confirming that the trackway was in place before the enclosing palisade was erected. The stone surface was also partly covered by upcast from the digging of the palisade post-holes, but the trackway may have still been in use. Part of a second stone trackway, 2.6–3.3m wide, lay 50m to the south of the trackway beside the palisade; it was adjacent to and west of a 1.4–2m-wide ditch. Radiocarbon dating places the use of this trackway and probably the adjacent ditch in the period 910–1080.

The settlement at Ballynagallagh included fifth/seventh-century circular houses that may have been unenclosed, and a double palisade fence around the site that was constructed in the eighth/ninth century. Pits within the enclosure had similar dates to the palisade, while others date from the early twelfth century. A trackway on the western side of the enclosure was in use from the seventh century. The site had a long period of use and this may have been relatively continuous. Evidence for the economy was provided by the animal bones, which indicated a reliance on cattle; there was also some barley cultivation. The relatively few finds from the site consisted of one whetstone and one hone, a clay bead, a small clay mould, part of a lignite bracelet and a lignite pendant, a bronze tube and some corroded iron objects of unknown function. Some iron slag and fired clay indicated iron-working on the site.

Knockadoon

The excavations undertaken on Knockadoon in 1939–40 and 1949 also uncovered evidence of early medieval activity (Ó Ríordáin 1954). Site F was a house or hut of roughly rectangular plan that may date from the early medieval period (Figs 8.1.38–40). Its remains consisted of roughly coursed stone footings that measured 27ft (8m) north/south by 21ft (6.3m), and the eastern side incorporated a rock shelf (Fig. 8.1.39). Ó Ríordáin (1954, 416) suggested that the walls may have been of mud built on stone footings, as the surviving stone walls were poorly constructed. An opening 8ft (2.4m) wide in the north-west corner was interpreted as an entrance, and a post-hole on the southern side possibly held a door-jamb. A central hearth and an off-centre hearth within the structure were probably contemporary with the house. A hearth also extended under the north wall. Layers of occupation debris that extended under the stone footings were likely to be from earlier occupation. The finds from Site F included evidence of the casting of socketed looped spearheads and rapiers of middle Bronze Age date (1500–1000 BC; see Chapter 5) and represent an earlier phase of activity. Finds that were possibly contemporary with the stone house were an iron knife with a curved blade and a corroded iron fragment from the western end of the north wall and an iron pin from stones displaced from the north wall. A fragment of a double-sided bone comb was also recovered from rubble inside the west wall.

A field fence extended from the western end of the north wall of the house and there was a second field fence *c.* 60m to the north (Fig. 8.1.38). Both were aligned east/west. The northern fence extended to the pre-drainage lake edge. It was stone-faced on both sides, 4ft (1.2m) wide and stood to a height of 2ft (0.6m). There was a ditch, 3ft (0.9m) wide and 2ft (0.6m) deep, immediately north of the fence. The second fence, with a parallel ditch, 2ft (0.6m) deep, to the south, extended from the west side of the house, was about 30m long and was not as well constructed as the northern fence. The ditches were interpreted by Ó Ríordáin (1954, 418) as source material for bank construction. Contemporaneity between the house and the adjacent fence could not be established, and Ó Ríordáin (1954, 418) suggested that the house walls were robbed to provide stone for the fence. This, however, contradicts his interpretation of the house walls as being constructed from mud. The probability is that the house and fences were contemporary and similar to the field walls that enclosed the houses at the Spectacles. A hearth site under the eastern end of the fence adjacent to the house yielded evidence of Bronze Age metal-working, including clay mould fragments and bronze-working waste. Fragments of clay moulds and some late Bronze Age pottery were also found under and within the fence and in the ditch fill to the south. Construction of the field fence had clearly disturbed earlier levels.

Two late ninth/early tenth-century silver coins (Fig. 8.1.40:1–2) were found at Site C (1940). One was a silver penny struck by Plegmund, archbishop of Canterbury (890–914). The obverse bears the inscription *Plegmund Archiep* between two concentric circles, and there is a small cross with expanded ends (pattée) in the centre; the inscription on the reverse reads *Wilrc Mo*, the name

Fig. 8.1.38—Site F, Knockadoon: general plan.

Fig. 8.1.39—Site F, Knockadoon: plan of stone house.

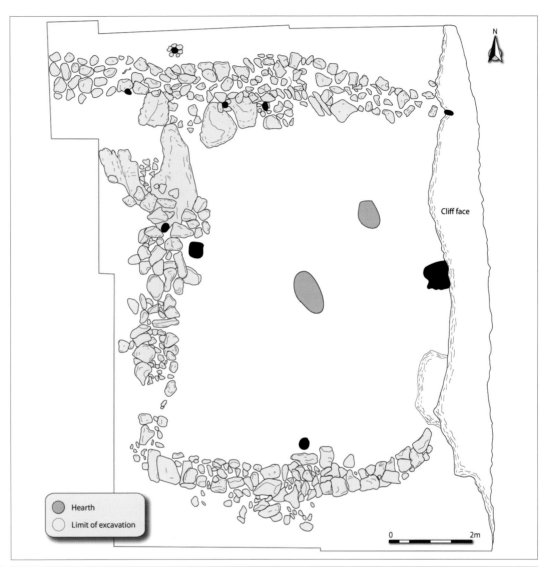

Cliff face

N

Hearth

Limit of excavation

0   2m

Fig. 8.1.40—1 Silver penny of Plegmund, archbishop of Canterbury; 2 silver penny of Edward the Elder.

(probably a corruption of Wulfric) and title of the moneyer. The ornament consists of a group of three pellets above the inscription while below it are three small pattée crosses across the centre. The second coin is half a silver penny of Edward the Elder (900/901–25). The full inscription would read *(Eadv)veard Re(x)*, of which the letters VEARD and RE are left, and is between two circles with three pellets above. The inscription on the reverse, the name of the moneyer, appears to be *Erihp*, a rendering of Erinw(ald) (sometimes spelled Ernwald), a known moneyer of Edward the Elder. Above the name are three pellets and below there are traces of three small crosses. The dates of the coins are sufficiently close to indicate that both were lost at the same time. The Canterbury penny was found on the stones of the enclosing wall at the south-west corner of Site C (1940); the other penny was from a stony surface. A scrap of silver, irregular in outline and about 20mm across, was found on the gravel layer on the western side of Site C.

Other early medieval finds from Site C were bone spearheads (Ó Ríordáin 1954, fig. 26: 16–20) similar to those from Carraig Aille, a bone bead with zigzag incised lines (*ibid.*, fig. 26: 39) and fragments of a bone comb with diamond-shaped motifs filled with parallel incised lines (*ibid.*, fig. 26: 33). A yellow glass bead, a blue glass bead with inlaid white glass and a glass stud (*ibid.*, 358) date from the early medieval period, while beads of greenish-blue glass may be earlier. The ring of a bronze ringed pin (*ibid.*, fig. 28: 21), two iron loops (*ibid.*, fig. 29: 10–11) from ringed pins and eleven iron knives (*ibid.*, fig. 29: 4–6) were also found. A dark blue glass bead and a pale blue glass bead with white cable decoration and an iron knife were found on Site C (1949) and date from the early medieval period (*ibid.*, 382, 383–4).

A clay crucible from Site D had a thick base and was similar to crucibles from early medieval sites (*ibid.*, 401). An iron knife from the upper stratum at Site G, Knockadoon, may also be early medieval in date (*ibid.*, 443).

Overview

The excavations at Carraig Aille I and II, the Spectacles, Grange, Ballingoola III and IV, Site F at Knockadoon and Ballynagallagh have provided considerable evidence for life in Lough Gur during the period 400–1100. Prehistoric artefacts, including flint and pottery from Carraig Aille and the Spectacles, indicate previous site use in the Neolithic. There is some evidence that flint may have been regarded as having magical properties and was kept as a charm in the early medieval period (O'Sullivan *et al.* 2013, 100). Some of the flint from Carraig Aille and the Spectacles may have been collected from elsewhere and brought to the site. Fourteen stone axeheads, some of which were fragmentary, were recovered from the Carraig Aille sites and two fragments from the Spectacles. Two stone axeheads had been reused as whetstones, and some may have been found and retained as curiosities. A Roman coin dated to the 350s AD and a bronze toilet implement and bronze stylus, both of Romano-British style, were found within the rampart of Carraig Aille II. These finds may indicate settlement pre-dating the stone forts or, as the items are so few, were perhaps heirlooms belonging to the earlier inhabitants.

Carraig Aille I and II were enclosed by strong stone ramparts; such sites are known as 'cashels' or *cathracha* and are stone enclosures equivalent to the ringfort. The use of stone for the ramparts at Carraig Aille was likely due to the predominance of good-quality limestone along the ridge where the sites are located. Indeed, part of the northern rampart of Carraig Aille I was quarried away for limestone in modern times. Carraig Aille I and II both had ramparts over 4m thick with steps leading to their tops, which were likely augmented by wooden palisades to increase protection as well as perhaps to create visual prominence and status. Both cashels were guarded by sturdy gateways with double gates. Access to the enclosures was therefore controlled and, according to the *Críth Gablach*, fines could be imposed for uninvited entry (Kelly 1997, 431).

In contrast to the Carraig Aille stone forts, the site at Ballynagallagh was a large palisaded enclosure with two sturdy fences set 1.4m apart and an estimated perimeter of 380m. This enclosure must have appeared a formidable feature on the landscape. Radiocarbon dating indicated that it was constructed sometime between 760 and 900. It may have been a gathering site rather than a place of permanent settlement, a place similar to an *aonach*, where people assembled to conduct business and trade and to participate in various sports, including horse-racing. There were several major festivals in Ireland in early medieval times and presumably these were mirrored by more local gatherings. Freemen were expected to gather for the *airecht*, where legal business was transacted (Kelly 1997, 458). A 2m-wide gravel trackway, dated to 660–780, beside the enclosing fence at Ballynagallagh was probably in use when the palisaded enclosure was constructed. A road, even a byroad, gave land added value and local farmers were responsible for maintenance (*ibid.*, 390–2).

The Spectacles was an unenclosed site where defence was unnecessary. Initial unenclosed settlement may be inferred at Carraig Aille II, where there is some evidence to suggest that Houses 1 and 3 of Phase 1 pre-dated the rampart, as their outlines appear to have continued under it. Ó Ríordáin (1949b, 44) argued that they abutted the rampart but this may be incorrect, as the plans indicated round houses. A small circular hut was also recorded outside the northern rampart at Carraig Aille II. In the latter phase of occupation at Carraig Aille II the rampart became redundant; settlement spread out from the enclosure and the rampart was deliberately lowered to accommodate this.

Carraig Aille II provided the best evidence for house types. The earliest architectural style was the round house; up to eleven were evident in the surviving archaeological record, although others may have existed of which traces did not survive. Not all the houses were in contemporary use and some were clearly sequential, replacing earlier houses. On the published evidence, the houses were largely along the western perimeter of the rampart, with a concentration just north of the entrance. A house of circular/oval plan with an estimated diameter of 8m and a smaller house 4.5–5m in diameter were found at Ballynagallagh. Houses A and B at the Spectacles were also circular/oval in plan and of similar dimensions to those at Carraig Aille II, albeit with sturdy stone foundations.

At Carraig Aille II, houses of rectangular plan replaced the round form and were in the main located in the footprint of the earlier buildings within the rampart. Houses of rectangular plan were also built outside the rampart—House 8 on the southern side and House 9 on the northern side. These were built against the rampart and would have compromised any defensive function. Houses of rectangular plan and more elaborate houses with attached enclosed yards were built on the ridge between Carraig Aille I and II. House 3 at Carraig Aille I was a large semi-underground building enclosing an area of 48m² (8m long by 6m wide). This type of structure has parallels with souterrains or underground chambers found elsewhere in ringforts such as at Cush, near Glenbrohane (Ó Ríordáin 1940), and Raheennamadra, near Knocklong (Stenberger 1966). The souterrains at Cush and Raheennamadra had stone-lined walls but were much narrower and unsuitable for permanent occupation. That at Raheennamadra was 9m long but only 2m wide at the base (*ibid.*, 41). House 3 at Carraig Aille I is not easy to parallel, although semi-underground sunken structures of early medieval date and circular plan are known along the western seaboard, while semi-underground buildings are recorded in urban contexts but of late eleventh- to twelfth-century date (Walsh 1997, 52). House D at the Spectacles was rectangular in plan, similar to the later houses at Carraig Aille II.

The nature of the superstructure of the Phase 1 round houses at Carraig Aille II, Ballynagallagh and the Spectacles was indicated by the surviving foundations. Wattle and daub probably formed the upper walls of the circular houses at Carraig Aille II and Ballynagallagh. The arcs of stones interpreted by Ó Ríordáin as walls of the round houses at Carraig Aille II were more likely to have been stones delimiting clay floors, as they were too flimsy to be structural. Excavations of the ringfort at Grange and two houses at Ballingoola confirmed wattle walls, and the house at Ballingoola III had an arc of stones delimiting the clay floor of the building. Sods or mud may also have been used as wall material, and the excavations at Raheennamadra uncovered evidence for sod walls (Stenberger 1966, 39–40). The published account of the rectangular stone-built houses at Carraig Aille and the Spectacles suggests that the basal thicknesses of the stone walls—up to 1m—were sufficient to support stone walls perhaps up to 2–2.5m high. The walls were possibly load-bearing for the roofs, which were probably thatched with reeds from the ample supply around the lake and in nearby marshland. There is little recorded detail on the internal layout of the circular houses at Carraig Aille II. These ranged in diameter from 3m to 7.5m, and where the houses were adjacent to the rampart the doorways presumably faced out towards the centre. Some houses had surviving internal hearths and some had clay floors. Houses 6 and 7 may have been conjoined. The larger circular house at Ballynagallagh was 8m in diameter. The stone rectangular houses along the western rampart within Carraig Aille II presumably had entrances facing eastwards towards the centre of the enclosure. Of the extramural houses on the northern side of Carraig Aille II, Houses I and III had east-facing entrances. Paved floors were also noted within the stone houses, although in some cases this appeared to have been no more than exposed fissured bedrock.

There are parallels in the archaeological literature of east Limerick for the architectural styles recorded on the excavations at Lough Gur. A large circular house (House J) excavated at Knockea (O'Kelly 1967), about 10km north of Lough Gur, had an estimated diameter of *c.* 7m and was similar to the round houses at Carraig Aille II. It was earlier than the ringfort enclosure, as it was cut through by the ringfort ditch. A round house at Raheennamadra, *c.* 10km to the south-east of Lough Gur, was 6–7m in diameter; the entrance at that site was on the north-west side and was marked by a cluster of post-holes similar to the circular house at Ballynagallagh (Stenberger 1966). The smaller round houses at Carraig Aille II and Ballynagallagh, with diameters of 3–5m, were similar to a small hut at Knockea (O'Kelly 1967).

In the absence of radiocarbon determinations, the dating of the construction of the forts at Carraig Aille and houses at the Spectacles, Grange and Ballingoola was largely based on the artefacts recovered. There is a circularity in this method of dating, as artefacts from sites used as comparanda do not allow definite dating but only provide a floating chronology within a broad time-frame of centuries. The difficulty of using artefacts from Carraig Aille is compounded by the lack of published detail on the contexts for many finds, and the material may belong to the round house or the later rectangular stone house phase. The forts at Carraig Aille may have been in use for several generations and it is possible that some of the round houses were constructed prior to the massive stone ramparts. The Romano-British and some undiagnostic finds from Carraig Aille may belong to an unenclosed phase of site use. The Viking silver hoard recovered from the rampart of Carraig Aille II (Chapter 9) is broadly dated to the tenth century and confirms use of the site at that time. Based on the artefacts and art historical dating, Ó Ríordáin (1949b, 108) concluded that the main phase of occupation was probably from the eighth to the eleventh century. This dating has largely been followed by other writers (O'Sullivan *et al.* 2103, 66). Bronze and iron artefacts similar to those from Carraig Aille and the Spectacles have been found on other excavated ringforts, including Raheennamadra (Stenberger 1966), Garryduff,[9] Co. Cork (O'Kelly 1962), and Deer Park Farms, Co. Antrim (Lynn and McDowell 2011), where site occupation extended from the sixth century into the eighth/ninth century. The iron knife types from Carraig Aille were in use at Deer Park Farms from the seventh century and continued in use to the tenth century. The glass beads from Carraig Aille can be paralleled by similar finds from Garryduff, Co. Cork, and by beads dated to between the seventh and tenth centuries at Deer Park Farms.

Radiocarbon dates are available only for the large circular house at Ballynagallagh, which was dated to AD 460–630. Based on architectural style, the round houses at Carraig Aille II may be just as early. At Raheennamadra, a round house 6–7m in diameter and probably constructed from wattle walls set into a footing trench was similar to the round houses at Carraig Aille II. Four charcoal samples from Raheennamadra returned radiocarbon dates of AD 520–670 (Stenberger 1966, 52–3). A series of radiocarbon dates from Deer Park Farms, Co. Antrim, which had similar circular houses to Carraig Aille II, confirmed construction in the period 545–780 (Warner 2011, table 12.5) and may indicate a slightly earlier date for the round house phase at Carraig Aille II than that proposed by Ó Ríordáin. A review of the dating evidence for Carraig Aille by Caulfield (1981) and Laing and Laing (1990) suggests that the sites may have been occupied as early as the fourth century AD. This putative early dating may be part of a pre-enclosure occupation at Carraig Aille indicated by pre-rampart round houses as well as early artefacts.

The evidence for the lives of the people who inhabited Lough Gur in the early medieval period can in some ways be reconstructed from the archaeological remains, including structures and artefacts. These remains are fragmentary, however, and it is never possible to provide anything like a complete picture of what daily life was like, how people subsisted, how they produced the items necessary for the home and farm and how they spent their leisure time. The production of items from stone, bone, antler, iron and bronze may have been by local people skilled in these crafts but who were part of the household, or some items may have been bought from specialised craftworkers.

Quernstones from Carraig Aille and the Spectacles confirm that cereals were processed on site. An iron plough-sock from Carraig Aille II shows cultivation in the locale. Animal bones from these sites, while not the subject of a specific archaeozoological study, show that cattle predominated in the economy. Harness fittings and horse-bits indicate horse-riding and the use of horses for farming. Ó Ríordáin considered that the cobbled surface at the gate in Carraig Aille II was intended to prevent horses from slipping. Horses were associated with men of high rank (Kelly 1997, 89), suggesting that the occupants of Carraig Aille were at least of the status of strong farmers. The size of some horse-bits from Carraig Aille was suitable for small horses or ponies. Horse bones were also recovered from the house at Ballingoola III. Household items such as knives were probably used within the house and outside on the farm. Shears used for cutting cloth or shearing wool, spindle-whorls, possible weaving combs and bone pin beaters indicate cloth production, probably mainly from wool although flax seeds from Carraig Aille II may indicate that linen was also produced. Bone points with eyes were probably used for sewing. Leather for garments, belts, saddles, bags and other items was likely processed from hides. Carpentry is attested at Carraig Aille by the recovery of iron saw fragments, an axehead, chisels, awls, nails and wall-brads. Ash and oak logs at Ballingoola III were drawn into the site and presumably used for house construction and other woodwork. The large timber palisade at Ballynagallagh also showed large-scale building in timber. Iron slag and crucible fragments from Carraig Aille and iron slag and baked clay from Ballynagallagh indicate iron- and bronze-working. Whetstones, used to sharpen iron implements, were also frequent finds.

In terms of the individual, bone combs from Carraig Aille, the Spectacles and the upper levels of Site C, Knockadoon, attest to some concern with personal appearance. Glass beads were common at Carraig Aille and were also recovered at the Spectacles. These may have been strung to form necklaces or bracelets. Two amber beads were also found at Carraig Aille I. Jet bracelets from Carraig Aille were frequent and their small diameter suggests that they were worn by children or women. Bracelets were included as tribute paid to the king of Cashel; they are referred to in *Lebor na Cert* on ten occasions and are frequently mentioned with chess sets, which were also items used to pay tax (Dillon 1962). The jet bracelets recovered on the excavations at Lough Gur may have been prized possessions, as indicated by the value of bracelets as tribute. Ringed pins made of bronze or iron were frequent finds from Carraig Aille; these were not only functional clothes-fasteners but also decorative, like brooches.

The picture of society in Ireland in the period 400–1000 is somewhat elucidated by early Irish law tracts. Early medieval society has been described as 'tribal, rural, hierarchical and familiar' (Binchy 1969, 54). The political structure was one whereby an area or *túath* was ruled by the local king or *rí*, who governed his own territory (which was similar in size to a modern barony) and who in turn may have been subordinate to a higher king or may himself have been an over-king to other local kings. Kingship was hereditary and dynastic. In the early medieval period the local king in the Lough Gur area was a scion of the Eóganacht who paid tribute to the Eóganacht king of Cashel, and by the late tenth century this Eóganacht hegemony had been replaced by the Dál Cais.

Society was essentially hierarchical. Difference in status was the cornerstone of Irish law; although most men were free, slavery was also part of the social structure (*ibid.*, 56). Below the king was the aristocracy or warrior class and then the 'men of art' or *aes dána*; when Christianity was accepted, the clergy came under this rank (*ibid.*, 57). Of the commoner classes, the *bóaire* was the strong farmer who owned 21 *cumals* of land; a *cumal* is equated to three or more cows, and a *bóaire* had land capable of supporting at least 63 milch cows (Kelly 1997, 33, 574). The less wealthy farmer or *ócaire* had farmland worth seven *cumals*, or land for 21 milch cows. The stone forts at Carraig Aille were probably the home of a *bóaire*, whereas the ringfort at Grange and the unenclosed sites at the Spectacles and at Ballingoola III and IV may have been those of an *ócaire*. It has been proposed that these unenclosed sites and the extramural houses at Carraig Aille were the homes of labourers or slaves (O'Sullivan *et al.* 2013, 112). The stone houses within Carraig Aille I and II and the extramural stone houses were of similar construction, however; if anything, those outside were larger and cannot be used to indicate a lesser social ranking than a *bóaire*. Houses A, B and D at the Spectacles were also of sturdy construction and similar to the stone houses at Carraig Aille. The absence of enclosure may reflect the absence of a need for defence rather than social status.

The basic unit in early Irish society was the family rather than the individual and hence the term 'familiar' is used (Binchy 1967, 54). Extended families occupied ringforts and stone enclosures. The number of houses within Carraig Aille II, and less so in Carraig Aille I, probably reflects people who were kin and lived in separate houses within the enclosures. Not all of these houses may have been contemporary and some were probably repaired, replaced or rebuilt over time. There is no evidence of ranking in the layout and dimensions of the circular houses at Carraig Aille II; in the stone houses of Phase 2, House 1 appears to have been slightly larger than the other buildings but was smaller than the extramural Houses I and III.

The Spectacles is one of the few early medieval sites in Ireland where the settlement was unenclosed, as most excavated domestic sites of this period are within ringforts. The natural topography of steep cliffs to the north and south of the Spectacles and the lake shore at the base of the southern cliff face must have provided some modicum of security, if not defence. The small fields attached to the houses represent an almost unique survival of early medieval gardens.

The excavations of early medieval settlements at Lough Gur have provided an insight into life, home and hearth, society, economy, crafts and pastimes. Although some sites at Lough Gur were excavated almost 80 years ago and before scientific dating methods, it has been possible to review the archaeological evidence in the light of more recently excavated sites.

8.2: CRANNOGS

The term 'crannog' is used to describe an artificially constructed island with an enclosing timber palisade. A ring of closely set timber piles was set into a lake, and layers of peat, brushwood, timbers, stones and soil were mounded up within the piles to create an island. Most dating evidence suggests that crannogs were built in the sixth/seventh century AD but occupation may have continued into later times (O'Sullivan 1998, 131). There are other types of artificially constructed stone platforms at Lough Gur; these were excavated at Rathjordan (Ó Ríordáin and Lucas 1946–7), Rockbarton (Mitchell and Ó Ríordáin 1942) and Geroid Island (Liversage 1958) but yielded no evidence of having been enclosed by palisades, while occupation layers indicated a late Neolithic/Beaker period date (Chapter 4).

Crannogs are mostly found on lakes in the midlands, north-west, west and north of Ireland. There are four recorded crannogs on Lough Gur and these were encircled by the lake prior to drainage in the late 1840s (Fig. 8.2.1). Dowd (1896, 67) wrote of these that 'There are four diminutive islets to be observed, evidently of an artificial character, two of them rising but a foot above the surface'. He included the crannogs at Bolin Island and Crock Island as well as the natural Garret Island and Church Island. Church Island was marked on the 1844 Ordnance Survey maps as close to the southern shore of Lough Gur but was not recorded in subsequent editions; a crannog[10] on the lake shore in Ballynagallagh townland may be the site of Church Island, now on dry land after the lake drainage in the late 1840s. Dowd (1896, 68–9) described two other crannogs as 'two slight elevations perceptible above the level surface of the drained ground east of Knockadoon, and named Balic Islands, which also appear to be crannogs'. These were immediately east of Knockadoon Hill (Fig. 8.2.1) in an area that is now bog but was part of the lake prior to the post-Famine drainage. They are no longer visible and may have been removed when turf was cut from the bog (Glennon 1847). The name 'Balic' was ascribed to the islands on the 1844 Ordnance Survey map and may have been a misnomer. O'Kelly (1944, 28) recorded the crannog sites as the 'Bailey Islands', and this name was connected to Mr John Baylee, whose family occupied Bourchier's Castle as agents of the Fane family from the late seventeenth century.

Bolin Island, on the north-east side of Lough Gur, has an overall diameter of 27m (Figs 8.2.2–3). It was constructed by laying a boulder foundation in a ring and then infilling the central area with layers of brushwood and soil. Ó Ríordáin cut a trial trench at Bolin Island in 1938, confirming how the crannog was built, but there were no finds to indicate the date of construction (O'Kelly and O'Kelly 1978). Crock Island was originally in a narrow inlet of water between the south-western end of Knockfennell Hill and the northern end of Ardaghlooda Hill. Similar to Bolin Island, large stones were placed in a circle within the lake and the central area was filled with earth and brushwood to form a platform. Crock Island was also 27m in diameter and now stands to a height of almost 2m above the surrounding ground level. Lewis (1837, 27) proposed that the name 'Crock Island' was due to the discovery of a large pot or crock on the crannog prior to the lowering of the lake after the Famine.

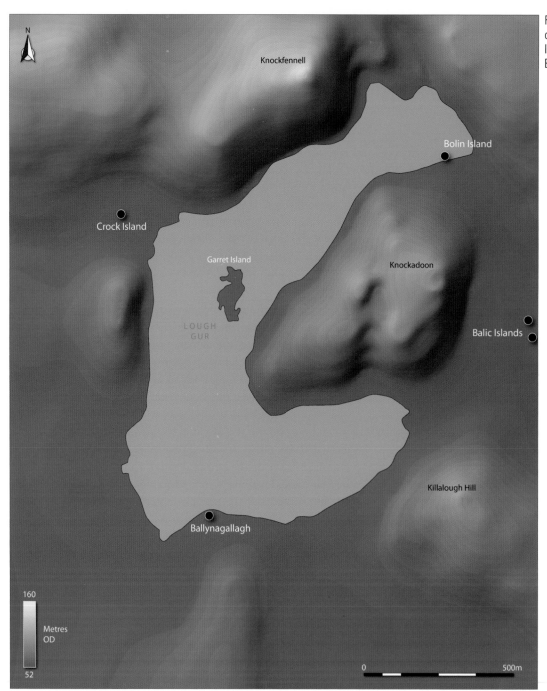

Fig. 8.2.1—Location of crannogs (Bolin Island, Crock Island, Balic Islands and Ballynagallagh).

Fig. 8.2.2—Bolin Island.

Fig. 8.2.3—Bolin Island.

Once the lake was drained, many artefacts and animal bones were recovered from the vicinity of both Bolin Island and Crock Island. Lynch (1895, 245), drawing on Harkness's 1869 account, noted that 'On or near these crannogs have been found many of the simple instruments which were used by the lake dwellers … Bone implements in the form of large pins and pincers, and many stone weapons, have been found.' Harkness's account (1869, 395–6) referred to Geroid Island rather than the crannog of Crock Island, and he noted that many stone axeheads as well as large quantities of butchered animal bone were exposed on and around Geroid Island when the lake level was lowered. Lynch also documented the recovery of the gold-mounted spearhead (Fig. 5.3.1) near Bolin Island crannog and noted that vast quantities of bones of various animals were found near the crannogs. Richard Rolt Brash (B.R.R. 1865) wrote of Crock Island that 'On the last lowering of the lake, a *crounogue* [crannog], or artificial island was discovered, in which were, as usual, found a large quantity of the bones of domestic animals, with several ornaments of bone; and ornaments and weapons of bronze'. The crannogs at Lough Gur are relatively small and were originally close to the lake shore. The Ordnance Survey (1844) pre-drainage map of lake levels indicated that they were surrounded by water but may have been fairly accessible. It is possible that the positioning of the crannogs was not entirely guided by a need for defence and exclusion and that they were built for some other purpose, such as specialist workshops, although there is no archaeological evidence to support this hypothesis.

8.3: THE CHURCH

Early church sites are usually recognised in the landscape by circular enclosures, some physical remains of a church, cross-inscribed slabs, proximity to a holy well and bullaun stones,[11] or by the evidence of place-names or townland names. There is some indication that churches were located on the edge of ringfort clusters on *túath* (tribal) boundaries (Stout 1997). Early churches were probably built in the main of timber and later replaced by mortared stone buildings (Leask 1960). The Irish word *dairthech* ('oak house') was used to describe timber churches and, as these do not survive above ground, the foundations can only be discovered and dated through archaeological excavation. Similarly, churches constructed from other perishable materials such as wattle or turves (sods) leave few, if any, above-ground traces. The transition to mortared stone churches occurred in the early tenth century (from 900 onwards). The organisation of the early church in Ireland was based on a federation of monasteries under the control of an abbot/bishop who claimed lineage from a founder. Apart from early monastic sites, some churches probably fulfilled a pastoral role, and private churches were also built for the use of individual families.

A church site at Lough Gur, recorded on the second-edition (1924) Ordnance Survey map as 'Killalough', was located just south-east of Black Castle (Fig. 8.1.1). The first-edition (1844) OS map shows the lake to the west and a large tract of water (now bogland) to the east, and the church site may have been on a narrow isthmus of land between these two water bodies. Little now remains above ground and the site is marked by a slight mound. The place-name 'Killalough' can be translated as 'the church of the lake'. The church may have been built of timber. A bullaun stone[12] located to the north, near Bourchier's Castle and some distance from the church site, may be unconnected to the early church. It is a naturally occurring rock outcrop which has a bowl-shaped depression hewn out of the top of the rock. Water from the hole is said to cure warts. O'Kelly (1941) recorded a rectangular building on the eastern slope of Knockadoon Hill, to the north-east of Black Castle, which he suggested may have been an early church site. It consists of a stone foundation of rectangular plan, measuring 7.3m (north/south) by 12m (east/west), with a projection on the south-west corner which extended for a further 2.4m. The walls were stone-faced with a rubble and earth core. The building is undated but its size and orientation may indicate a church site. It is known locally as 'the Money Hole', as tradition has it that treasure was buried there. This tradition also states that the treasure must be dug for at midnight and that a white bull comes down the hill and scatters those digging at the spot.

There is a reference to an ancient road at Lough Gur that may date from the advent of Christianity, perhaps part of a routeway by which missionaries traversed Munster. In his essay on the ancient roads of Ireland, Ó Lochlainn (1940, 468) cited 'The Tripartite Life of St Patrick' and noted an ancient road that traversed the southern part of Ireland from Kilkenny to Ballyhoura. The road went from Kilkenny to Cashel, Co. Tipperary, via Kilteely, Pallas Grean and Ballineety to Lough Gur, and from there to Holy Cross, Bruff, Kilmallock, Ardpatrick and Ballyhoura. He was confident of the veracity of the life of St Patrick as a source and stated that roads listed in this 'may be taken as established from early times' (1940, 471).

8.4: BURIALS

The enclosure at Circle J was constructed in the Bronze Age (Chapter 5). The site was subsequently used as a cemetery in the late Iron Age/early medieval period. Burials were mainly within the enclosure, although the cemetery spread outside and there were eight burials outside the north-eastern section of the wall. The pre-existing enclosed site was most likely opportunistically used as a burial ground in the early medieval period. Of the 58 excavated graves, five were orientated north/south, partly crouched, and the majority appeared to have been buried in unprotected pits and may date from pre-Christian or Iron Age times. The remaining burials were mainly orientated east/west in the Christian manner, and many were in slab-lined graves. Where the bones were identifiable as regards sex or age, those interred at the site comprised at least ten males, nine females, sixteen children and six infants, ranging in age from two to 50 years; the majority of the adults were aged 25–30 years and the children were aged 2–10 years. There was also evidence that some burials, particularly those in slab-lined graves, were in groups, perhaps indicating close familial groups. Circle J was possibly a cemetery where the dead of one kin group from a nearby settlement were buried. It may have been in use from the period when conversion to Christianity was beginning to have an impact on early medieval society.

NOTES

[1] Westropp (1906–7, 174) cites footnote 1 in the Civil Survey (Simington 1938), where 'even in 1655, the rivers Camoge and "Cavoyer" were meares [pools; wet land]'. The Saimer is named in the charter of Magio (Monasternenagh) in 1186. 'The name is equated with the ancient river-names Samara and Shamar. "Cavoyer" shows that the later "Camhair" has at least an antiquity of several centuries.'

[2] Information from Dr Paddy Gleeson, School of Natural and Built Environment, Queen's University, Belfast.

[3] The text of *Lebor na Cert* (the Book of Rights) is in verse and is a tenth-century recension of earlier texts (Dillon 1962, ix). The Book of Rights is preserved in later manuscripts, including the Book of Ballymote (late thirteenth century), the Book of Lecan (early fifteenth century) and the Book of Lismore (late fifteenth century) (*ibid.*, xxi) .

[4] *Chronicon Scotorum* is a collection of annals which chronicle events from prehistoric times to AD 1150 (Hennessy 1866). The battle at *Cathair Chinn Chonn* is also recorded in the Annals of Ulster (U640.1).

[5] Information from Kevin Kearney, Department of Archaeology, UCC.

[6] The published report does not specify the excavation year but it is recorded in the O'Kelly files on his barony survey of Small County (1941), housed in the Department of Archaeology, UCC.

[7] *Aill* can be translated as cliff or precipice.

[8] Ó Ríordáin (1949b, 46) referred to a wall at a right angle to the south in Cutting 18, but this is not shown on plan and may be unrelated to House 4.

[9] A single radiocarbon determination from a hearth site at Garryduff returned a date of AD 593–679 (GrN-12614). Art historical dating of Period II at Garryduff I suggests an eighth-century AD date (O'Kelly 1962, 118–19).

[10] Listed in the Record of Monuments and Places for County Limerick as a crannog (RMP LI 032-015) in Ballynagallagh townland.

[11] These are stones that have a depression in the centre and are frequently found near ancient churches or monasteries. They are usually filled with rainwater and are regarded as either curing or cursing stones.

[12] Recorded as RMP LI 032-038.

9. The Vikings

The earliest Viking (Norse) fortification on the River Shannon may have been established in the 840s at Athlunkard, Co. Clare, *c.* 2km north of the historic core of Limerick City. Earthworks at Athlunkard have been identified as the likely location of an early Viking settlement of the type known as a *longphort* (Kelly and O'Donovan 1998). Based on annalistic evidence, Ferrar (1767, 4) gives the date of 853 for the fortification of Limerick City by the Vikings. Hall (2007, 88) suggested a date before 887 for the foundation of the Viking settlement at Limerick, although the precise location of the settlement within the modern city has not yet been identified by archaeological investigation. Indeed, there is very little archaeological evidence for occupation in Limerick City before the twelfth century (O'Rahilly 1995).

The ethnic mix within Viking port towns is unknown, although a cultural mix is evident in the artefactual remains from cities such as Dublin, Waterford and Cork where there have been extensive archaeological investigations and where the cultural phases are known as 'Hiberno-Norse' or 'Hiberno-Scandinavian'. Although Viking communities were essentially sea-traders, control of the towns became linked over time to regional dominance and the Vikings were drawn into wider power struggles, and thus conflict arose between the various port towns. Rivalry between Limerick and Waterford Vikings led to the Vikings from Waterford going overland into Limerick in 926 and launching their ships on Lough Gur (Ó Corráin 1972, 103). The *Chronicon Scotorum* suggests that the Waterford Vikings established a *longphort* at Lough Gur, but this is likely to have been a temporary raiding base rather than a permanent settlement (Valante 2008, 104, 116). The Annals of Inisfallen record that a coalition of Limerick Vikings and Irish inflicted 'a slaughter of the foreigners of Waterford at Cillmahallock [Kilmallock]' in 927 (*ibid.*, 104; Ó Corráin 1972, 103). How the Vikings managed to traverse the countryside from Waterford to Lough Gur may be understood in terms of the terrain that existed in the hinterland of Lough Gur in the tenth century. Viking ships could navigate the River Suir and its tributary the River Aherlow. Low-lying tracts of land to the south of Lough Gur may have been lakes in the early historic period (Synge 1966, 19), facilitating access to Lough Gur by Viking ships.

The political history of Limerick in the tenth-century records is one of internecine strife within the Irish kingdoms and warfare between the Irish and the Vikings, and between the Irish and coalitions of Vikings and their Irish allies. The Vikings were defeated by Mathgamain, king of the Dál Cais, at the Battle of Sulchóid (near Limerick Junction) in 960 (Ó Corráin 1972, 116). Mathgamain also burned the Viking settlement in Limerick and on the following day devastated the land of Eóganacht Áine, whose territories included Lough Gur and Knockainy (*ibid.*, 116–17). Indeed, Lenihan (1866, 43) remarked that the 'interminable feuds of the Eóganacht and Dalgais desolated the whole province of Munster'. An alliance was forged between Donnubán, king of Uí

Fidgente (a tribe in Limerick), Máel Muad mac Briain of the Eóganacht Raithlind and the Vikings of Limerick (Ó Corráin 1972, 116). Mathgamain was captured by Donnubán, handed over to Máel Muad and executed in 976. He was succeeded by his brother, Brian Boru, who set about avenging his brother's death, killing Ivar, king of the Limerick Vikings, defeating the Uí Fidgente and killing Máel Muad in the battle of Belach Lechta in 978.

Brian Boru consolidated his position in Munster and expanded his power over much of Ireland; by 1005 he was king of Ireland (*ibid.*, 125). An entry in the *Cogadh Gaedhel re Gallaibh* ('The War of the Irish with the Foreigners'[1]) for 1002[2] recorded that 'King Brian fortified Dún Gair and the Island in Loch Gair' (Westropp 1906–7, 179). Other sites fortified by Brian Boru between 1002 and 1012 were Áine (Knockainy) and Loch Ceann (also recorded as Inis Loch Cend; MacCotter 2006, 68), located between Lough Gur and Knockainy (O'Kelly 1942-3, 81). The Annals of the Four Masters recorded that in 1056 the Norse and Irish 'destroyed the Lough Gur fort reconditioned by Brian' (*ibid.*, 81), suggesting that the fortification at Lough Gur was not built by Brian Boru but that he strengthened ('reconditioned') an existing defensive earthwork. The death of Cormac Mac Carthy is recorded in 1143 at Lough Gur, where he was being held in captivity by Turlough O'Brien (Dolley 1972, 32). This suggests that there was still a fortification at Lough Gur in the mid-twelfth century. Dún Gair was plundered by O'Collins of Cleanglas in 1178 (Westropp 1906–7, 179), reaffirming the continued survival of a *dún* at Lough Gur.

The archaeological evidence of a Viking presence at Lough Gur consists of a sword retrieved from the lake and a silver hoard from Carraig Aille II fort. The Viking sword from Lough Gur was donated to the British Museum by J.F.W. de Salis and the find-spot is recorded as the lake bed, although there is a possibility that it came from a crannog (Peirce and Oakeshott 2005, 95). These types of locations are watery places, and the sword may have been deliberately thrown into the lake as an offering to the gods or perhaps for safe-keeping until the owner returned; alternatively, it may have been lost in battle. The ritual of depositing precious items in wet areas, including lakes and bogs, is well attested in Ireland from prehistoric times. Hoards recovered from the Bog of Cullen, Co. Tipperary, *c.* 18km to the east of Lough Gur, included Bronze Age gold as well as two Viking hoards, one of which was silver (Wallace 1938; Graham-Campbell and Sheehan 2009).

The sword from Lough Gur is short, suggesting that it belonged to a child or a youth (Davidson 1994, 40). It is well preserved and has a double-edged blade with inlaid decoration on both sides near the hilt (Fig. 9.1). The decorative patterns are symmetrical; on one side they comprise three vertical bars, a cross, a central circle, a cross and three vertical bars, while on the reverse the pattern is three vertical bars, an omega-like symbol (Ω), a cross, an omega-like symbol and three vertical lines. The decoration is similar to that on swords found in Norwegian Viking graves and the markings may identify the owner or maker. The blade is surmounted by a cross-guard, above which is the grip and a pommel. The blade is pattern-welded, which was a method of forging whereby the smith beat the iron into narrow bars, carburised the iron and welded the bars together, resulting in patterning on the blade (*ibid.*, 25–30). Finally, the sword was quenched and tempered to produce a strong, sharp blade. This type of sword blade was produced by Viking smiths from the mid-eighth century, and the example from Lough Gur is dated to the tenth century (Peirce and Oakeshott 2005, 95). The Lough Gur Viking sword blade also has a strongly marked groove or *fuller* down the blade known as a 'blood-channel' (Davidson 1994, 39–40). The blade is 0.68m long, with a grip of only *c.* 60mm between the rings; the hilt has gold ornament, and it may have been made for a high-born boy who began his training in swordplay before he grew to manhood (*ibid.*, 40, 212).

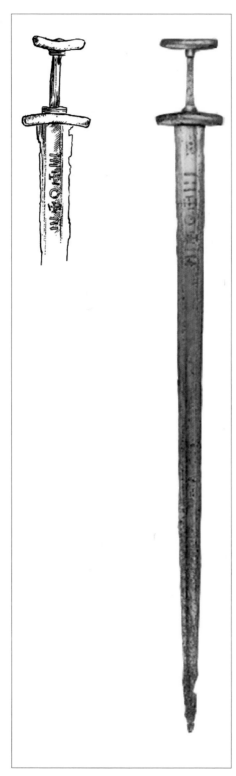

Fig. 9.1—Viking period child's sword from Lough Gur.

A small hoard of Viking silver, a single silver ingot and a silver ring were found in Carraig Aille II fort (Ó Ríordáin 1949b, 62–4, pl. XVII). The hoard was found in a space between two stones in the inner face of the rampart on the northern side of the fort, and the ingot was 0.15m away in the rubble fill of the rampart. The hoard comprises a ring, a bracelet fragment, two decorated pieces cut from arm-rings and three ingots. This is known as 'hack silver'—silver items that were deliberately cut either for ease of carrying before melting down for reuse or cut into units for their bullion value (currency by weight). The ring (Fig. 9.2: 1) is plain, oval-shaped and 4mm thick, with a maximum external diameter of 29mm and tapering ends which are not quite closed. Ó Ríordáin (1949b, 63) identified this as a finger-ring, but these objects are now known as 'bullion rings' and are interpreted as currency rather than jewellery; they are datable to 850–950 (Graham-Campbell 1995, 30; 2011, 87). A silver object described as a 'bracelet' (Ó Ríordáin 1949b, 63) has an extant length of 60mm and a lozenge-shaped cross-section (4mm by 3.5mm); the ends are roughly cut (Fig. 9.2: 2). The fragment is probably derived from an arm-ring and is comparable in size to arm-ring fragments from Woodstown, Co. Waterford (Sheehan 2014, 204). It has punched decoration along one edge and the motif is indented in a row on either side on the angle. Two fragments of silver were cut from thin (1.5–2mm), flat, broad-band arm-rings, and both are ornamented with punched decoration (Fig. 9.2: 3–4). The patterns consist of rows of pendant triangles on one fragment (Fig. 9.2: 3) and rows of ellipses with a central raised ridge on the other (Fig. 9.2: 4). The style of these broad-band arm-rings is Hiberno-Scandinavian, of a type dated to 850–950 (Sheehan 2011). The three silver ingots appear to be rods and range in length from 20mm to 48mm (Fig. 9.3: 1–3). Ingots were a means of storing bullion and are a significant component of around half of the 80 known Viking hoards from Ireland, particularly hoards dated to the tenth century (Sheehan 2014, 196). Two of the ingots from Carraig Aille have impressions on the metal from contact with fabric when molten (Fig. 9.3: 1–2). These fabric impressions, which are probably from linen, are paralleled in a hoard from Cuerdale, near

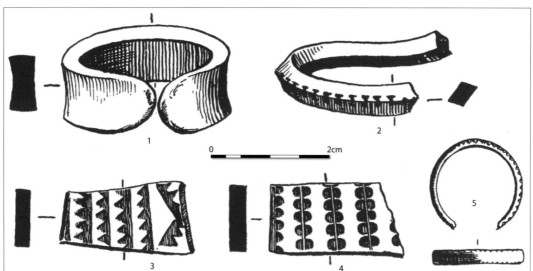

Fig. 9.2—Carraig Aille Viking hoard: 1 ring; 2 bracelet; 3–4 arm-rings; 5 ring.

Preston in Lancashire, which is the largest hoard of Hiberno-Scandinavian silver from western Europe; it was buried between 905 and 910 (Kruse and Graham-Campbell 2011). A broken silver ring from the rampart of Carraig Aille II and not directly associated with the hoard was found at a depth of *c.* 0.15m under the pavement on the southern side of the fort. It has a diameter of 16mm and was perhaps from a chain (Fig. 9.2: 5). It has triangular nicks on the outer edges; nicking silver was a characteristic Scandinavian method of assessing its quality (Sheehan 2014, 198).

The Viking silver hoard from Carraig Aille II is broadly dated to the tenth century. This is indicated by its composition, the decorative motifs on the bracelet fragments and the rod shape of the silver ingots. Viking hoards were most frequently deposited in the tenth century, as this period was marked by the return of the Vikings after the initial raiding and plundering phase in the ninth

Fig. 9.3—Silver ingots from Carraig Aille.

286

Fig. 9.4a—Drinking-horn (National Museum of Ireland).

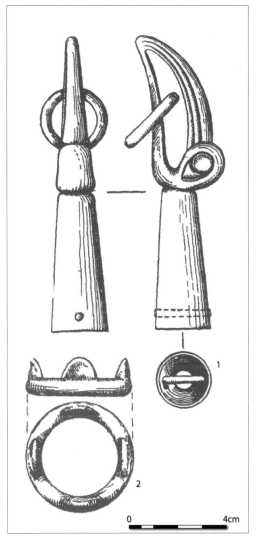

Fig. 9.4b—Finds from Carraig Aille: 1 drinking-horn; 2 chain link (National Museum of Ireland).

century. The tenth century saw an upsurge in violence between Gaelic kingdoms and the Vikings (Edwards 1996, 178, fig. 88b). The Carraig Aille II hoard was recovered from a settlement site and one can only speculate about how it came to be deposited there. It may have been hidden away during a raid on the fort, intended for trade with the Vikings in Limerick, or paid as a ransom or tribute to the inhabitants at Carraig Aille (*ibid.*, 176). An Irish raid on the Viking settlement at Limerick in the late tenth century claimed booty of gold and silver as well as jewels, decorated saddles and exotic cloth (de Paor 1977, 145). It is tempting to ascribe the source of the hoard at Carraig Aille II to an Irish raid or payment for the release of a Viking captive. Ó Ríordáin (1949b, 63) suggested that the hoard was deliberately hidden among the stones in the rampart face. Turbulent political times, including internecine warfare between the Dál Cais and Eóganacht and between the Dál Cais and Vikings, resulted in the devastation of the lands of Eóganacht Áine in which Carraig Aille was located (Ó Corráin 1972, 116–17). The hoard from Carraig Aille II may have been placed in the rampart for safe-keeping until the return of more peaceful times.

Other artefacts from Carraig Aille that may have been linked to the Vikings include a bronze terminal mount for a drinking-horn and a chain link (Fig. 9.4b: 1–2) found together within the Carraig Aille II enclosure (Ó Ríordáin 1949b, 64–6). The terminal mount once fitted on the pointed end of an ox horn; the attached link was part of a chain that joined the bronze terminal to the rim of the drinking-horn and was used to hang up the item when not in use. The drinking-horn terminal measures 65mm in length and has one socketed end with a 10mm internal diameter. The mount has the shape of a conventionalised bird's head (*ibid.*, 64). These types of drinking-horn mounts are Irish in origin but terminal mounts with animal and bird forms have been found in ninth- and tenth-century Viking graves in Norway, although production of these may have been as early as the eighth century (*ibid.*, 65–6). The chain link (Fig. 9.4: 2) may also be part of a drinking-horn mount. The ring is circular in cross-section with an internal diameter of 18mm, having four projections on one side which may have fitted into a groove on a drinking-horn. Raw materials used by Viking craftsmen included jet and amber (Russell and Hurley 2014). Three fragments of jet bracelets and a jet domed bead and two small fragments of amber were also found in Carraig Aille II (Ó Ríordáin 1949b, 95, 102).

The evidence for a Viking presence in Lough Gur is slight and comprises historical references as well as a few artefacts. To date, there is no archaeological evidence to confirm that a Viking *longphort* or earthwork fortification was established at Lough Gur, although it may have been more of a temporary raiding base than a semi-permanent occupation site. Indeed, the Annals of Ulster suggest that the Vikings were firmly beaten and that 'the Eóganacht of Cashel inflicted a rout on the heathens at "Dún Maíle Tuile", in which five hundred fell' (Valante 2008, 44). The location of the battle site, 'Dún Maíle Tuile', is unknown but it may have been in east Limerick, and the battle ended the Viking incursions (*ibid.*, 44, footnote 41). The Viking child's sword, a silver hoard and a terminal mount for a bronze drinking-horn could have come to Lough Gur through a variety of mechanisms, including trade, exchange, looting, gifts or tribute. The date range for contact with the Vikings is the ninth and tenth centuries, and the artefacts may have been the result of either a Viking presence in the Lough Gur area or more sporadic contact through trade.

NOTES

[1] The *Cogadh Gaedhel re Gallaibh* was compiled sometime between 1086 and 1114 (MacCotter 2006, 69).

[2] Based on annalistic accounts, MacCotter (2006, 69) suggested a date of AD 995 for the fortification of Lough Gur.

10. The Anglo-Normans, 1170–1300

POLITICAL HISTORY

The Anglo-Norman invasion of Ireland in 1169 began a process which was to change the political and social fabric of Ireland. The invading army made piecemeal progress across the country, forging alliances with some Gaelic chiefs and defeating others. The goal was land and, with it, wealth. For the first ten years there was a period of consolidation of territorial gains. The lands in the vicinity of Lough Gur were the subject of grants to the Anglo-Norman families of de Braose, de Marisco and de Clare. There is, however, sparse information on the land grants in Limerick, as little survives in the way of charters or documentation (Empey 1981, 5). King Henry II granted the kingdom of Limerick (Thomond) to the Anglo-Norman adventurer Philip de Braose in 1177, although the lands remained in the hands of Donal Mór Ó Brien (Dolley 1972, 86). The pattern of subinfeudation was complex and was also compounded by the fact that King John 'was in the habit of making successive grants of the same place to different people' (Empey 1981, 4–5). By 1201 most of what is now County Limerick had been transferred by Prince John, then lord of Ireland, to William de Braose. In the environs of Lough Gur, Geoffrey de Marisco held the cantred of Any (Knockainy). The Fitzgeralds (who ultimately became the Desmond Geraldines) were assigned as tenants to holdings including Shanid, Croom and Kilteely (Dolley 1972, 100). Although they began as relatively modest landowners, they remained a constant in landholding and ultimately emerged as the powerful earls of Desmond in 1329. Maurice Fitz Gerald acquired land in Munster from the late 1170s, and this was expanded by his son Thomas from 1199 and subsequently by Thomas's son, John of Shanid, who 'transformed his family's position from relatively minor landowners in Co. Limerick into a substantial regional power' (McCormack 2005, 29). This expansion and consolidation may have been achieved in part by judicious marriages. Lynch (1895, 247) recorded that 'Thomas Fitz Maurice married Eleanor [Ellinor] daughter of Jordan de Marisco and thus the Desmond Geraldines probably obtained in this way some of the estates of Marisco'. Ellinor brought extensive property in County Kerry to the marriage (Graves 1869). Sir Geoffrey de Marisco was appointed justiciar or chief governor of Ireland in 1212 and obtained a grant of a yearly fair lasting for six days in his manor of Awny (Knockainy). By 1276 the lands around the Lough Gur region had passed to Thomas de Clare and the Fitzgeralds continued as landholders. De Clare also held lands at Caherconlish and the Grean (Pallasgrean) and rented the castles at Kilcullane and Ballinard to tenants (Westropp 1906–7, 185–7). The Desmond Geraldines emerged as the dominant power in Limerick and had been confirmed in these lands by the late thirteenth century, in the reign of Edward I. The fourteenth century saw English power in Ireland dissipated by the emergence of strong Anglo-Norman and Gaelic families and continual internecine strife (Lydon 1973). The de Clares and their colony of Thomond were wiped out by Gaelic chiefs at the Battle of Dysert in 1318 (Westropp 1906–7, 67).

The Desmond Geraldines, however, appeared to grow in strength and, despite treason, rebellion and crime, Maurice (fitz Thomas), the first earl of Desmond, was appointed justiciar (chief justice) of Ireland in 1355 (Lydon 1973, 56).

After the invasion in 1169, the Anglo-Normans had built castles to secure their Irish properties once the more active Gaelic resistance was crushed (Westropp 1907, 29). Early Anglo-Norman castle-building in Munster was a 'deliberate and slow process' (Westropp 1906–7, 64). Westropp (1907, 33) noted that Anglo-Norman fortresses 'spread in a network over all its districts guarding passes, routes, rivers and fords'. These early castles were earth and timber fortresses rather than stone and are known as 'motte-and-baileys' (O'Conor 1998, 17; O'Keeffe 2000, 15). In his survey of the barony of Small County, in which Lough Gur is situated, O'Kelly (1941, 50) recorded thirteen mottes, although none are close to Lough Gur. A large motte-and-bailey still stands in Kilfinnane, 18km south of Lough Gur. A possible motte at Garryheakin, shown on Ordnance Survey mapping as 'Rahard', is to the east of Lough Gur near Old Pallasgrean (O'Dwyer 1964). Other Anglo-Norman defensive sites were ringworks, where the mound was lower than in mottes and surrounded by outer earthen ramparts. A number of ringworks were recorded by O'Kelly (1942–3) in the barony of Small County but none in the vicinity of Lough Gur. There are, however, a number of sites around Lough Gur that are classified as platform-type ringforts, and some of these may be Anglo-Norman defensive earthworks (O'Keeffe 2000, 29–30). Platform ringforts are generally in low-lying terrain and have a single surrounding fosse; some have visible house foundations within the enclosures (O'Kelly 1941, 41). Excavations by John Hunt of an earthwork at Ballingarry, near Galbally, confirmed that the site had various periods of occupation, and in the final phase the top of a pre-existing mound was used by Anglo-Norman settlers as the site of three houses of rectangular plan (McCormack, forthcoming). These early Anglo-Norman fortifications, including the motte-and-bailey and ringworks, appear to have continued in use for 100–150 years after they were first built (O'Conor 1998, 35).

Pre-Anglo-Norman fortifications, such as those erected by Brian Boru in 1002 when he 'fortified Dún Gair' (Lough Gur), were used and perhaps improved by the Anglo-Normans. 'Dún Gair' was plundered by O'Collins of Cleanglas in 1178, and at his death in 1287 Thomas de Clare held '"Le Dun" at Loych Gir' (Westropp 1906–7, 179). The precise location of 'Dún Gair' is unknown and O'Kelly (1941, 25–6) suggested that the Ordnance Survey's positioning of 'Dún Gair' on Knockmore Hill, Knockadoon, is incorrect. A defensive earthwork was more likely to guard the natural entrance to Knockadoon, where Bourchier's Castle now stands.

Westropp (1907, 66) recorded that some 'manors on which no castles are mentioned include Any (with Lough Gur)'.[1] The Fitzgerald (Desmond) family held de Clare's manor at Lough Gur and there is no tangible evidence that it included a castle. The existing castles at Lough Gur, including the Black Castle and Bourchier's Castle, are later and were built in the late fourteenth/fifteenth century (*ibid.*, 37).

SETTLEMENT

Archaeological evidence for Anglo-Norman settlement at Lough Gur (Fig. 10.1) was uncovered at Caherguillamore (Ó Ríordáin and Hunt 1942) and during excavations in advance of car-park development on the north-east shore of Lough Gur in 1977–8 (Cleary 1982b; 1983). These excavations uncovered medieval houses of rectangular plan dated to the thirteenth and fourteenth centuries. The houses were probably those of tenants of the Fitzgeralds. The inhabitants may have been a mix of Gaelic

Fig. 10.1—Location map.

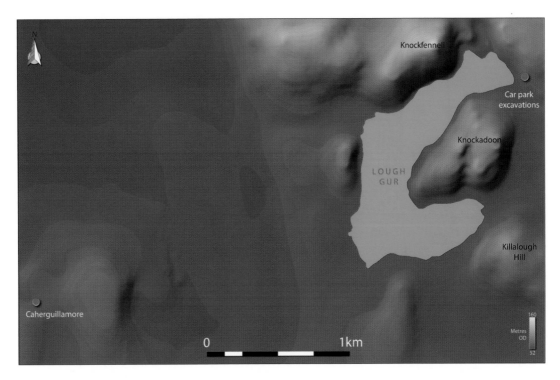

and Anglo-Norman. Culturally, the material remains show Anglo-Norman influence, and parallels for the artefactual remains can be found in Anglo-Norman Britain and from excavations of medieval levels in Anglo-Norman-dominated Irish cities. The Lough Gur excavations were limited in extent and the excavated remains may be part of a more extensive nucleus of houses.

Caherguillamore

Earthworks were recorded at Caherguillamore by the antiquarians Lynch (1895) and Dowd (1896) at the end of the nineteenth century. Of the name 'Guillamore', Lynch (1895, 251) noted that 'The Right Hon. Standish O'Grady, Chief Baron of the Exchequer in Ireland, who was raised to the peerage in 1831 took his title of Viscount Guillamore'. He described the earthworks at Caherguillamore as the

> 'remains of an ancient city … the sites of streets, gates, and fortifications are still to be traced, extending in some places into the adjoining parishes. The two chief streets of the city cut each other at right angles, and there are several side streets. Stones were taken from the city to build the houses of Rockbarton and Caher, and also to carry out various improvements in the two demesnes.'

Dowd (1896, 80) dismissed Lynch's interpretation of the site as 'the remains of an ancient city of great extent', remarking that 'history knows nothing of the "city"'. He noted that 'part of the garden wall adjacent to the residence of Viscounts Guillamore is evidently a portion of some fortified enclosure of considerable extent, probably the Caher which gives its name to the place'.

Westropp (1906–7, 178–9) published the historical details of Caherguillamore in his survey of the ancient castles of County Limerick; he noted that the castle at Caherguillamore was unmarked on the

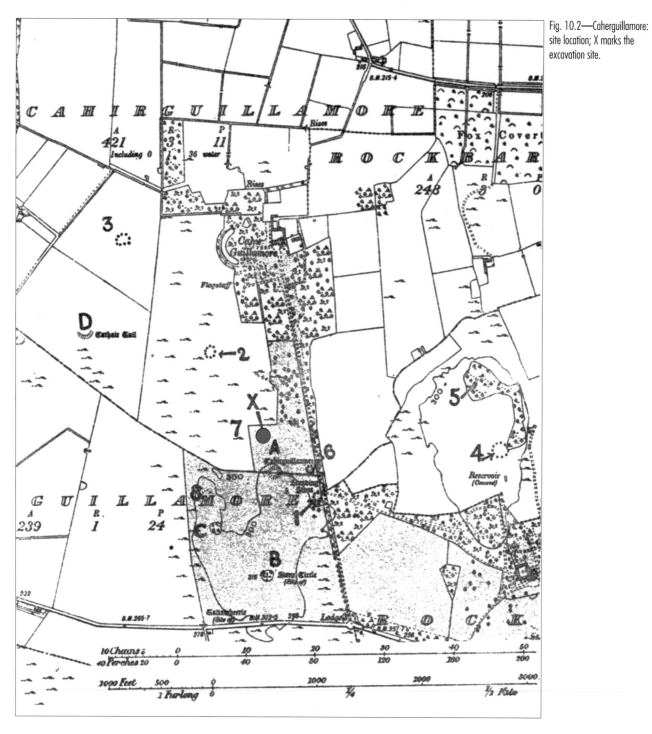

Fig. 10.2—Caherguillamore: site location; X marks the excavation site.

Ordnance Survey map but was recorded as 'Rockbarton Castle' in the Ordnance Survey Name Book. The plea rolls calendar[2] of 1289 recorded 'Cathyrgilmora' (Westropp 1906–7, 178). There are references in both the Desmond rolls[3] and the Peyton survey (1584–6) to a castle and village (*vill*) in Caherguillamore, listed as *Cahir a Gillimo* in the Desmond rolls and as 'Kaheragyllymoore in Any' (Knockainy) in the Peyton survey. These surveys confirm the survival of a nucleated settlement at Caherguillamore in the mid-sixteenth century. The term 'vill' can refer to a village, manor or territorial unit.

A local tradition in the early twentieth century referred to the earthworks at Caherguillamore as an 'ancient city' and this drew the attention of Seán P. Ó Ríordáin and John Hunt to the site (Ó Ríordáin and Hunt 1942). The site is *c.* two miles (3km) west of Lough Gur. The Irish Air Force flew over the site and provided the excavators with aerial photographs which enabled them to trace and map extensive earthworks over an area of *c.* 200ha (500 acres) (*ibid.*, fig. 2). The Ordnance Survey mapped two stone forts marked 'Caherguillamore' and 'Caher Gail' (*Cathair Gheal*) in the deer-park adjacent to Caherguillamore House, as well as the site of a stone circle (Fig. 10.2). The aerial photographs taken by the Irish Air Force in 1940 showed many other sites, including stone forts, a D-shaped structure, a ruined megalithic tomb, possible sites of prehistoric date, remains of ancient field systems and extensive earthworks that were probably part of a deserted medieval village. Ó Ríordáin and Hunt (1942, 42) also recorded that work on a reservoir at Caherguillamore in the early 1900s unearthed extended burials and urns. The Caherguillamore area was included in the medium-altitude Bruff Aerial Survey and was flown over in 1986 (Fig. 10.3). These photographs also show an extensive complex of

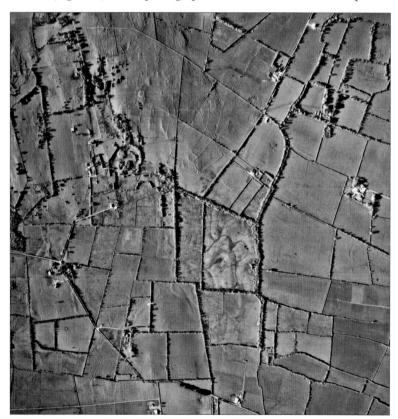

Fig. 10.3—Field systems at Caherguillamore (Bruff Aerial Survey).

archaeological sites, including a network of ancient field systems. Ó Ríordáin and Hunt (1942, 44) listed the number of houses in their survey of Caherguillamore at about twelve, each within a small square or rectangular enclosure, either a yard or a garden, and possibly one larger house or yard. Other houses may have existed in the general vicinity of the excavated site and Ó Ríordáin and Hunt (1942, 44) suggested that the stone from these could have been removed to build the nineteenth-century wall of the deer-park. At the time of the excavation little remained of the wall stones of the houses. There was also a strong local tradition that the settlement was once much larger.

This settlement at Caherguillamore may have initially developed from the migration of Anglo-Norman peasantry to Ireland in the wake of the invasion of 1169. Peasant immigration into Ireland occurred in the first two generations after 1169 and peaked around 1200–20 (Otway-Ruthven 1968, 113–14). The peasants probably came from western England and Wales (Graham 1993, 73). The reasons for migration from the peaceful lands of rural England and Wales to what was a hostile, politically unstable and troubled countryside included the opportunity to better themselves and rise up the social ladder to the status of free tenant with hereditary rights and personal freedom (Otway-Ruthven 1968, 116–18; O'Conor 1998, 42). O'Conor (1998, 42) also suggested that a further inducement may have been that labour services were lighter on Irish manors than on British manors and that work on Anglo-Norman Irish demesnes was carried out by cottiers or labourers rather than by free tenants. There may also have been some coercion on the part of Anglo-Norman lords, compelling their British tenantry to locate to their Irish manors (O'Conor 1998). The settlement at Caherguillamore can best be interpreted as a rural borough or village, populated initially by tenants of Thomas Fitz Maurice. There is some evidence that there was a decline in village life after *c.* 1300, when tenants moved from manorial centres to lands around the nucleated settlements, prompted by an economic change towards pastoral farming (*ibid.*, 46). Historical and archaeological evidence appears to confirm that many of these villages were deserted by *c.* 1400, and possibly considerably earlier, owing to the combined effects of Gaelic resurgence, the Bruce Wars (1315–18) and plagues, including the Black Death in 1348–50, which was rampant in areas where there was a clustered population and where the disease spread easily (*ibid.*, 47).

Archaeological excavations at Caherguillamore in 1940 were described as 'trial excavations' and were limited to two house sites (Ó Ríordáin and Hunt 1942, 39). Full excavation of even part of the whole complex of monuments was not possible given the resources available at the time.

The excavation

House I was two-roomed, measuring a maximum of 13m (east/west) by 5.7–6.3m (north/south) externally, and was sub-square and narrower at the western end (Figs 10.4–5). The walls were straight, 0.7–0.8m thick, well built and rounded at the external corners. The wall stones were dressed or had natural flat surfaces; they were bonded with a mixture of yellow boulder clay and small stones and were laid directly on bedrock, which was only *c.* 80mm below the modern surface. A 25–40mm-thick layer of burnt wattle was recorded as skirting the foot of the internal walls and extending out from the wall for a distance of 0.45m. The wattle remains were small—twigs 13–25mm thick over a clay layer 50–80mm thick—and were in turn covered by a similar clay layer. Ó Ríordáin and Hunt's (1942, 45) interpretation of the wattle and clay was that the internal stone house walls were initially plastered with clay to create a smooth surface; wattle lining was then pressed into the wet clay and plastered over with more clay. This lining would have insulated the walls and created a warm house.

The eastern room measured *c.* 9m (east/west) by 4.8m (north/south) internally, and the western

Fig. 10.4—Plan of medieval houses at Caherguillamore.

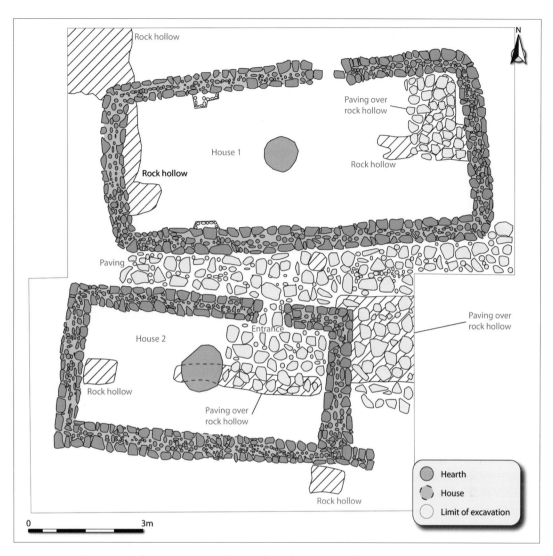

room 2.4m (east/west) by *c.* 4.5m (north/south). The division between the rooms was marked by two opposing post-holes, set against the north and south walls, which held posts that supported the internal partition; this may have been a wattle wall. The post-holes, 0.6m (east/west) by 0.3m (north/south) in diameter, were cut into the bedrock to a depth of *c.* 0.22m, and their size indicated relatively large posts. The house floor was flat bedrock that had the appearance of a cobbled surface, and any fissures were infilled with fine dark soil and small stones, which levelled the floor. A natural hollow in the bedrock in the north-east corner was infilled with black soil and some animal bone and was paved over to even up the floor. A hollow in the bedrock at the western end of the house continued under the wall and extended beyond the external face of the west wall; it was filled with yellow soil but was not paved over. The fireplace, marked by a layer of turf ash, was in the centre of the floor of the eastern room, just west of the door. The smoke presumably exited through a smoke-hole in the roof.

The door was in the north wall, off-centre in the external façade, *c.* 4.5m from the north-east

Fig. 10.5—Caherguillamore: the houses during excavation.

corner and midway along the wall of the larger eastern room. The external walls were slightly thicker at the doorway to accommodate the door-jambs. The doorway was 0.9m wide externally and splayed inwards, with an internal width of just over 1m. A stone threshold of three flags, 0.1m thick by 0.2m wide, lay midway across the door opening. This was laid down at the same time as the walls were being built, as the eastern threshold stone was built into the base of the wall. A second external doorway, which was blocked up, in the south-west corner of the house led into the smaller western room. The original door-jamb stones were larger than those of the adjoining wall and the doorway was not splayed like that in the north wall. The blocking material in the doorway comprised large stones that were not bonded into the main walls. The inner blocked-up wall was plastered over with clay and wattle, similar to elsewhere along the internal walls, and this covered over the original opening.

There was no surviving evidence for the roof but examples of vernacular architecture suggest that the walls were probably load-bearing, with roof trusses springing from the wall-heads and supporting purloins and rafters (Gailey 1984, fig. 69). There was no evidence at Caherguillamore that the roof trusses sprang from ground level or that there was any internal support for the roof, as no post-holes were detected within the building other than the two marking the division between the eastern and western rooms. The roofing material may have been layers of fitted sods (scraws) which served as an underthatch, with a thatch of straw or possibly reeds, given the proximity of marshy ground in Rockbarton.

House II was immediately south of House I, with an intermediary distance of 1.2m on the

Fig. 10.6—Caherguillamore: quernstone *in situ* in yard between Houses I and II.

western side and 2m at the eastern end (Fig. 10.4). A 0.2m-thick layer of habitation refuse from House I accumulated around the south wall of House I and extended southwards. The western end of House II was built on top of this refuse accumulation, confirming that House II was slightly later than House I. Once House II was built, the space between the two houses was paved, forming a passage that continued eastwards around the north-east corner of House II and along the south wall of House I, forming a small yard. A complete quernstone (Fig. 10.6) was used as part of the paving and covered a small pit or hollow close to the south wall of House I. House II was slightly smaller than House I, being at maximum 9.8m (east/west) by 5.5–5.7m (north/south) externally. The House II walls were straight, 0.8–1m thick, with squared external corners. The east wall, however, was wider at the south-east end. Ó Ríordáin and Hunt (1942, 48) described House II as being less well built than House I, with smaller wall stones and on the eastern side 'a mass of small stones, and this faulty construction had caused it to slip and disintegrate'. As House II was built over the soft ground of refuse accumulation, the foundations were poor and this may have caused settling. A 0.6m-wide buttress projected 0.8m from the south-east corner of the house to counteract settlement.

The floor plan indicated a single room with internal dimensions of 8.4m (east/west) by *c.* 4m (north/south). The floor was formed by the exposed limestone bedrock, which sloped gently downwards from the south-west to the north-east. A dip in floor level in the north-east corner was levelled up with habitation debris and paved over, and the paving included several broken quernstones. A linear fault or fissure in the bedrock, 0.4–0.6m wide, ran east/west across the floor of the house; this was also filled in with occupation deposits mixed with pebbles and paved over. The central hearth was in this fissure, giving the appearance of a sunken hearth, filled with reddish ash. Similar to House I, the smoke probably exited directly through a smoke-hole in the roof. The door of House II was in the north wall, off-centre and *c.* 2.4m from the north-east corner. It was *c.* 0.7m wide and splayed inwards. An almost complete though broken quernstone was laid as a threshold in the doorway.

An external hollow in the bedrock at the north-east corner of House II was a continuation of the dip or hollow within the house. This was up to 0.9m deep, measured 2.8m (north/south) by 3m (east/west) and extended beyond the excavation limits to the east. It was filled with soil containing a large quantity of animal bone, and the fill was paved over to form the yard between the two houses.

The shallowness of the stratigraphy does not allow for close association with specific periods of occupation. The infill below the paving in the houses produced only animal bone and no closely datable artefacts. The artefacts from both houses were of bronze, iron, lead, stone, bone and pottery and provide some dating evidence for the occupation of the houses. A worn silver penny identified as a late issue of Edward I (1272–1307) was recovered from the floor of House I. Two bronze strap

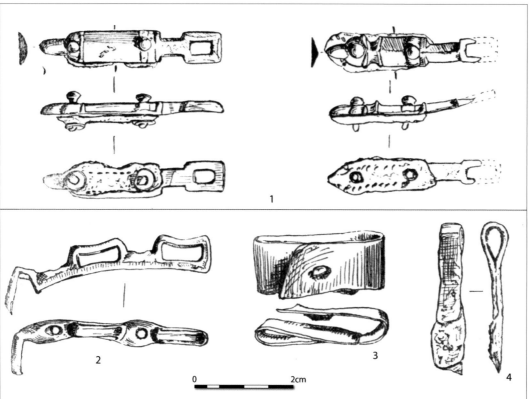

Fig. 10.7—Bronze strap ends or cheek-pieces from Caherguillamore.

ends from a belt or perhaps cheek-pieces and part of a horse harness (Fig. 10.7: 1–2) were found 0.45m apart at the bottom of a habitation layer outside the west wall of House I. These objects were described as 'gilt'[4] and much of this remained on the surfaces (Ó Ríordáin and Hunt 1942, 51). The strap ends/cheek-pieces are dated to the thirteenth/fourteenth century (Clarke *et al.* 2004). A strip of bronze secured at the end by a rivet (Fig. 10.7: 3) from within House II was interpreted as a mount from a dagger sheath. A piece of bronze bent to form a loop (Fig. 10.7: 4) may be tweezers and was found under the paving inside House II.

The iron artefacts comprised six knives, a door key, a small key, a latch-lifter, a hasp, a buckle, a spur rowel, shears, a chisel, nails, wall-brads, a staple, a ring, a hook and some unidentifiable fragments. Knives of the form found at Caherguillamore have a long currency of use and were found on the stone forts at Carraig Aille, which possibly date from 500–800, and at 'the Spectacles' (Ó Ríordáin 1949b); they are frequently found on urban medieval excavations, where they date from the eleventh to the fourteenth century (Scully 1997a; 1997c). A broad-bladed knife (Fig. 10.8: 1) is interpreted as a carving knife while the others were multi-purpose. A whittle-tanged knife (Fig. 10.8: 2) found inside House II, just above the bedrock floor, is of a form typically of thirteenth-century date (Scully 1997c). A knife with a 'pommel-shaped' bone handle (Fig. 10.8: 3) recovered at a depth of 0.2m was dated by the excavators to the fourteenth/fifteenth century but may be later. One knife with a bone handle (Fig. 10.8: 4), found at a depth of 0.1m inside House II, was dated to the sixteenth century. The blade curvature may, however, suggest an earlier date, and similar blades from Irish urban excavations are dated to between the late eleventh and mid-thirteenth centuries (Okasha 1997; Scully 1997c).

Fig. 10.8—Finds from Caherguillamore: 1–4 iron knives; 5–6 door keys; 7 latch-lifter; 8 hasp; 9 spur rowel; 10 buckle; 11 shears; 12 chisel.

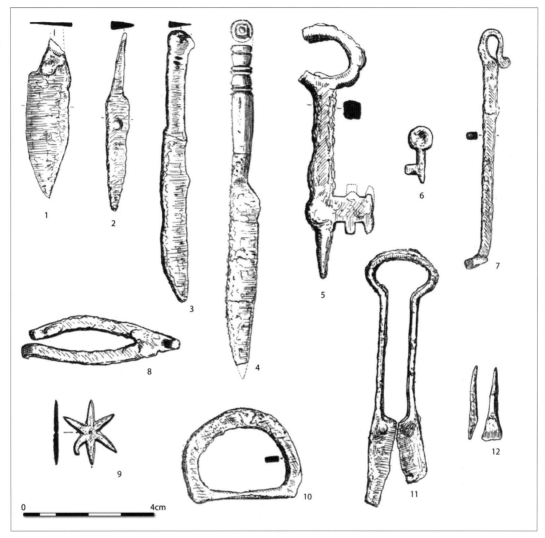

The large door key (Fig. 10.8: 5) came from inside the door of House I, and similar keys from Waterford date from the early/mid-twelfth century (Scully 1997c, 460). A second key (Fig. 10.8: 6) from outside the house is a casket key of thirteenth/fourteenth-century date (*LMMC* 1940, 144). An object described as a 'latch-lifter' (Fig. 10.8: 7) does not have a pivot point, and the right angle at the bottom suggests that it may instead be identified as a barrel padlock key. Barrel padlock keys were used to open casket locks and date from early medieval times to the twelfth/thirteenth centuries (Scully 1997c, 459). A hasp (Fig. 10.8: 8) that was part of a padlock for a door or chest was found at a depth of *c.* 0.35m outside House II and was dated to the medieval period. A spur rowel (Fig. 10.8: 9) from the south-west corner outside House I is a six-pointed star of a type dated to the fourteenth century (*LMMC* 1940, 107–8). A large buckle (Fig. 10.8: 10) found outside House II is for a broad belt, which Ó Ríordáin and Hunt (1942, 55) identified as being used with armour and possibly belonging to a soldier rather than a civilian. Alternatively, the buckle may be from a horse harness and similar to some of the larger buckles recovered from thirteenth-century levels in Waterford

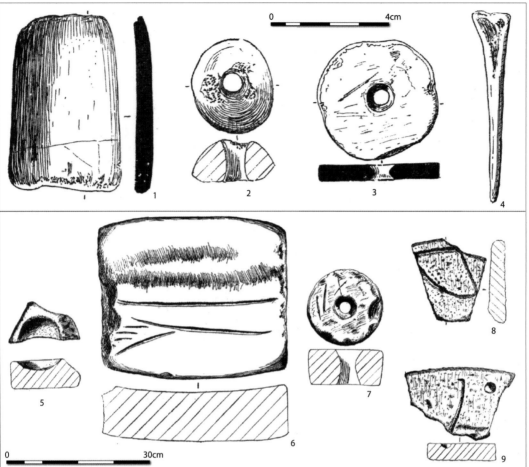

Fig. 10.9—Finds from Caherguillamore: 1 bone box; 2–4 spindle-whorls; 5 stone lamp; 6 whetstone; 7 rotary grinding stone; 8–9 quernstones.

(Scully 1997c). The remaining iron finds, such as the shears (Fig. 10.8: 11), a small spatula–like object identified as a chisel (Fig. 10.8: 12) and nails, were usual household items. A small piece of iron slag found in the pit between Houses I and II suggests a blacksmith or farrier working near the houses.

A lidded bone box (Fig. 10.9: 1) was found at a depth of 0.33m outside the south-east wall of House II. Three spindle-whorls, one of bone (Fig. 10.9: 2) from outside House I and two of stone (Fig. 10.9: 3) from inside House I, were found at depths of 0.15–0.2m below the surface and indicate wool-spinning within the households. Wisps of woollen fleece were wrapped around a distaff or stick, fed to a spindle, spun and dropped as thread; the momentum of the spinning was maintained by a weight or whorl (Hurley and McCutcheon 1997, 588–9). The thread was then knitted or woven into garments for the household. A bone with a central perforation, identified as a bobbin used in weaving (Ó Ríordáin and Hunt 1942, 56), was also found in House I. A 75mm-long bone point (Fig. 10.9: 4) came from outside the house on the south-west.

The basal section of a single-cresset stone lamp (Fig. 10.9: 5) was found outside House I. Eighteen sandstone whetstones were recovered from the houses and a number of these bore pin grooves from sharpening (Fig. 10.9: 6). A small rotary grinding stone (Fig. 10.9: 7) found at a depth of 0.15m in House I measured 17.5cm in diameter and 80mm thick; it is larger than examples from twelfth- and thirteenth-century levels in Waterford, although the shape is similar (McCutcheon 1997, 422). Pin grooves on one surface indicate that it was also used as a sharpening stone or hone. Thirty-two sandstone quernstones, including fragments, were recovered on the excavation, and some of these were reused as paving slabs in the threshold and floor of House II and in the yard between the houses (Fig. 10.6). The quernstones indicate cereal-processing and consumption. They appear to have been disc querns (Fig. 10.9: 8–9)—rotary handmills used to grind grain, which was poured into a central hole between an upper and lower stone. Some of the quernstones from Caherguillamore were decorated with grooved lines, and pin grooves show that some were used as hones after breaking. These types of quernstones are not closely datable but are generally found on medieval sites (Caulfield 1969). Their secondary use suggests that they were redundant at the time of house construction and were used as building stones.

About 70 pottery sherds found inside and outside Houses I and II were the fragments of a number of vessels (Ó Ríordáin and Hunt 1942, fig. 2). At the time of the excavation (1940) little was known about medieval pottery in Ireland, and this field of archaeological study has progressed significantly owing to many excavations in urban centres. The pottery from Caherguillamore has been reassessed;[5] the majority of the vessels date from the thirteenth century and were manufactured in the Limerick area. A small quantity of Saintonge green-glazed pottery, possibly from Cognac in the Bordeaux region of south-west France, was recovered; this also dates from the thirteenth century. About fourteen potsherds from the site were of modern earthenware; these date from the later seventeenth to the nineteenth century and are unrelated to house construction.

While there is no detailed analysis of the Caherguillamore animal bones, a brief account states that the assemblage was predominantly made up of cattle and pig, with lesser quantities of sheep or goat (Ó Ríordáin and Hunt 1942, 60). The types of animals enable an assessment of the meat diet of the inhabitants. Bones from three dogs and two cats were also recovered. Wildlife was represented by rabbits, geese and a rat. The number of horse bones from the site was unusually high; these were identified as being from a pony and a larger horse, possibly a farm horse.

Dating of the houses at Caherguillamore can be revised in the light of several excavations in Ireland over the last four decades, and the artefactual range indicates a thirteenth/early fourteenth-century period of occupation. A worn silver penny (1272–1307) from House I corroborates the date. Both excavated houses were rectangular in plan and stone-built. Ó Ríordáin and Hunt (1942, 61) suggested that House I was built before House II but may have been in contemporary use, House II being built slightly later than House I. There is nothing in the artefactual material associated with the structures that indicates a significant time difference in occupation, and the paving between the houses was interpreted as a passageway between the houses, again indicating that at some stage both were occupied at the same time. House II was considered by the excavators to be less well built than House I (Ó Ríordáin and Hunt 1942, 48).

The excavations were of the basal remnants of stone walls, 0.7–0.1m thick, of sufficient size to support an upper storey or at least some type of loft. A central hearth may indicate that the smoke exited directly through a hole in the roof and that an upper level was more likely to have been a loft on one side of the building rather than a complete floor across the entire room. Two posts set against the north and south walls at the western end of House I were interpreted as support posts for a wooden partition of wattle or wooden planks dividing the ground floor into two rooms; it may also have been a support structure for a loft. House I initially had two doors, one in the north wall and one in the south-west corner which was blocked up. An internal wattle and clay lining, interpreted as a layer of insulation, was plastered onto the walls and also covered the blocked-up door, indicating that this insulation layer was added to the house sometime after it was remodelled by the blocking of the south-west door. A clay layer at the base of the external walls was also interpreted as an external render. The use of wattle insulation on the walls is not closely paralleled in the archaeological record in the stone houses on urban excavations. Where the evidence survives, rendered internal walls are a feature of some castles. As the wattle was identified as carbonised, this may suggest that the house burnt down and that the clay and wattle ultimately slipped from the walls when the house was abandoned. An alternative explanation is that the carbonised wattle and clay were part of a collapsed roof rather than wall insulation. Evidence for the structure of the roof did not survive, but the rafters were probably set into the tops of the walls and covered by thatch. House II was smaller and less well built than House I; poor foundations over soft ground, particularly in the south-east corner, caused settlement and the wall was buttressed. Both houses had central hearths and this hearth location is paralleled in thirteenth- and fourteenth-century houses from urban excavations in Waterford and Cork (Hurley 2001).

The range of artefacts from both houses included some high-quality items indicative of wealth: pottery imported from France, possibly gilded strap ends/cheek-pieces from a horse harness, a silver penny from House I and a bronze mount from a dagger sheath from House II. A small casket key and a barrel padlock key suggest that the occupants had goods that they wished to keep locked and secure in caskets. Horse bones, a spur rowel and a buckle from a broad belt perhaps used in horse trappings indicate horse-riding. Other artefacts show a range of household crafts, including cloth production, evidenced by spindle-whorls and iron shears, perhaps used to cut cloth. A small fragment of iron slag indicates some iron-working, and whetstones were used to sharpen tools.

North-east shore of Lough Gur

Excavations undertaken in 1977–8 in advance of developments along the north-east shore of Lough Gur (Fig. 10.10) uncovered two medieval houses (Houses I and II) in the area designated 'Car-Park Area 2', 130m north of Bourchier's Castle (Cleary 1982a; 1982b; 1983). Prior to the Famine drainage scheme of the late 1840s, this area was the natural access point to Knockadoon Hill, the other being the artificial causeway at Black Castle. There were no indications of houses in the car park prior to the excavation.

The excavation
House I was subrectangular in plan, with an external length (east/west) of 14.5m and width (north/south) of 7.6m (Fig. 10.11). There was no surviving evidence for internal partitions and the floor plan appears to have been a single room. The south-west corner was square

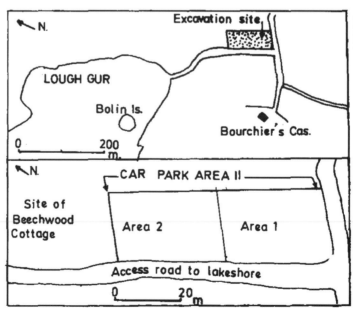

Fig. 10.10—Car park: site location (after Cleary 1982b).

Fig. 10.11a—Car park: plan (Colin Rynne).

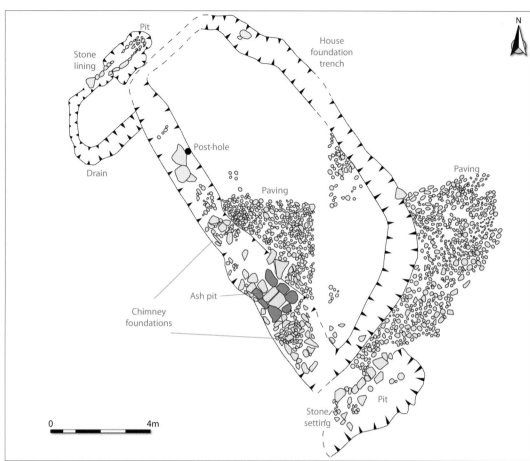

Fig. 10.11b—Reconstruction of House 1 (Colin Rynne).

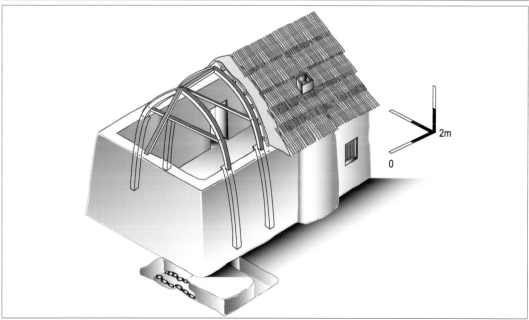

while the north-east and south-east corners were rounded. The northern end of the house was cut through and disturbed by a trench for a yard fence associated with House II. The foundation trench of House I was U-shaped, 0.5–0.75m deep and 0.8–1.4m wide, being best preserved on the southern and eastern sides. Little stone was recovered from the foundation trench and the walls were probably constructed either entirely of mud or of post and wattle liberally coated with mud. There was no evidence of post-holes in the foundation trenches to indicate that timber uprights were used as a frame, although the nature of the soil in Lough Gur does not easily allow for the recognition of post-holes unless the posts were driven into the underlying boulder clay. Over 500 large fragments of unweathered animal bone were recovered from the foundation trenches and their condition suggested that they were used as temper in the mud walls, which would have reduced excessive shrinkage as the mud dried (J. Monk 1984, 39). Mud walls may have been up to 1.5m thick. There was no surviving evidence for the roof; it may have been supported by a cruck-frame (Fig. 10.11) or, similar to the houses at Caherguillamore, the walls may have been load-bearing. As the corners were rounded on the north-east and south-east ends of the house, it is possible that the roof was hipped. Charred plant remains from the house confirmed that barley was grown and this may have provided straw for thatch; alternatively, reeds from the lake shore may have been used.

The southern wall trench was wider, and a stone-built hearth and ash pit were recorded there. A basal layer of stone marked the hearth but its floor did not survive. An ash pit immediately to the south was a stone-lined, box-like structure measuring 1.5m (north/south) by 0.8m (east/west) and set into the wall foundation below the floor level. Closely set paving in front of the hearth extended across the floor towards the east wall, and elsewhere the floor was clay. There was no trace of a break in the foundation trench to indicate an entrance. The threshold in House II (below) was laid over part of the foundation trench which was infilled, and it appears that in House II the builders dug the foundations without planning the door location. External paving along the east and south walls of House I may suggest that an entrance existed there.

A stone-lined drainage channel in the north-west corner of the house led out under the wall to a rectangular pit, 2m by 1m wide. The pit fill included charred weeds of creeping buttercup (*Ranunculus* sp.), rushes (*Juncus* sp.) and sedges (*Carex* sp.), which are commonly found in damp areas; the weeds may have been brought in with rushes used as bedding in the house. A second pit, 0.7m south of the house, was also stone-lined and rectangular in plan, 4.5m long by 2m wide. The paving on the eastern side of the house continued to the edge of the pit. The pit contained some animal bone that was discoloured owing to contact with human bodily waste, indicating that at some stage the pit was used as a latrine adjacent to the house.

Dating of this house is based on the pottery finds, which consisted of fragments of thirteenth/early fourteenth-century green-glazed jugs, including some decorated examples made in the Limerick area. Ten sherds were recovered from the house foundation trench, two from the internal paving and two from the pit on the north-west corner. Other finds were iron nails, an iron hook (Fig. 10.12: 1) and part of a horseshoe (Fig. 10.12: 2) from within the house and an iron buckle (Fig. 10.12: 3) from the pit on the south-west side. Some iron-working residues were found in the house foundation trench. A bone die with well-polished surfaces (Fig. 10.12: 4) was recovered from the north-west pit and the values were indicated by dot-and-circle impressions. The die is not a perfect cube and the sides measure 8.3–9.2mm.

House II, to the north-west of House I, was larger, rectangular in plan and divided into two sections (Figs 10.13–14). The structure was originally interpreted as having two rooms (Cleary

Fig. 10.12—Finds from House I: 1 iron hook; 2 horseshoe fragment; 3 iron buckle; 4 bone die.

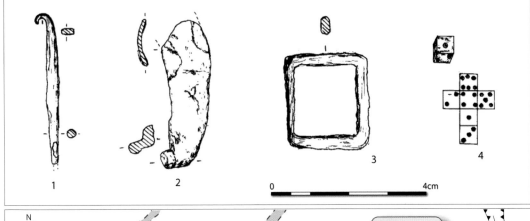

Fig. 10.13—Car park: plan of House II and yard enclosure foundation trenches.

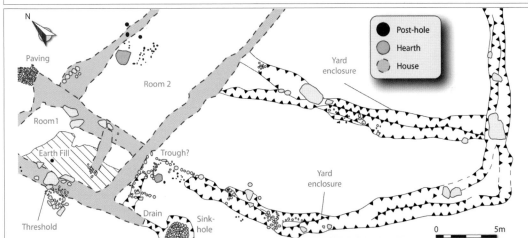

Fig. 10.14—Car park: foundations of House II.

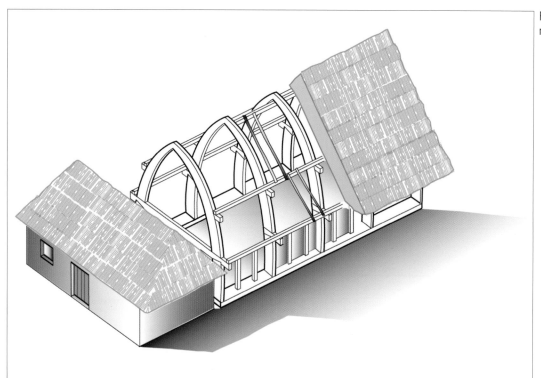

Fig. 10.15—Car park: reconstruction of House II.

Fig. 10.16—Car park: foundation of east wall of House II.

Fig. 10.17—Car park: threshold of House II.

1982b), although it is more likely that the western side was a house and that the larger 'room' on the eastern side was some type of barn (Figs 10.14–15). The southern wall foundation continued eastwards to form the wall foundation of the barn, and both the house and barn were probably built as a single structure. The western wall foundation extended for 3m beyond the end wall and formed part of a stone-built annexe for House II. The house was rectangular in plan, with maximum external dimensions of 11.2m (north/south) by 8m (east/west). Internally, the floor plan measured 8.6m by 5m. The foundation trenches were 1.2–2m wide and 0.5–0.7m deep and, similar to House I, it is suggested that the house was mud-built with thick walls set into foundation trenches. Stones were more frequent in the basal levels of the House II foundations than in House I (Fig. 10.16). Four large boulders that were natural glacial erratics were left in the eastern trench, as presumably they were too awkward to move, and they remained as part of the foundation. The foundation trenches also contained unweathered animal bone and, as at House I, this was interpreted as 'temper' included in the wall to reduce the amount of shrinkage when the mud dried and solidified. Over 3,000 animal bone fragments were recovered from in and around the house, including the wall foundation trenches, a spread of earth inside the door and a midden outside the door. As at House I, there was no evidence for the roof but it may have been cruck-framed or supported on wall-plates laid along the top of the walls. The roof was most likely thatched with straw or reeds.

The door was on the west side and was marked by a stone threshold (Fig. 10.17). The foundation trench was continuous here and the threshold was set into a section of the trench that was infilled with stones. The door location was apparently undecided until the foundations were dug. The threshold was slightly off-centre in the wall and comprised one large stone, *c.* 1m long on the inside, and a roughly paved area extended outwards from the door. The threshold/paved area was at maximum 1.2m wide and the door was probably slightly narrower. A post-hole on the northern side probably marked the door-jamb. As the house was built on a slope, the builders introduced a layer of earth to level up the floor. This earth fill was thickest (0.25m) at the threshold and petered out towards the east within the house. The purpose of a post-hole within the earth layer is unknown. A foundation trench on the south-east corner may have marked an internal division. If this was the case, the enclosed space was irregular in plan and was 3.4m long (east/west) by 1.5–2m wide, being widest at the eastern end. There was no evidence of a hearth within the house. An external well-laid

Fig. 10.18—Car park: House II stone annexe.

paved area was set in a shallow foundation against the north wall of the house. Much of the paving was, however, disturbed by a modern horse burial.

Two parallel trenches, set 6.5m apart internally, extended from the eastern side of the house, and this section of the structure is interpreted as a barn or byre attached to the house (Figs 10.13 and 10.15). The archaeological evidence for the type of building suggests that it was of similar construction to the house, being a thick-walled mud-built structure with some stones at the basal levels of the foundation trench. The foundation trench on the southern side was clearly a continuation of the house wall trench. The northern foundation trench was dug separately from the house foundation. Only the basal sections of both trenches survived on the eastern side and were truncated by modern ploughing. The southern trench was 1–1.2m wide; that on the north was more irregular and up to 2m wide at the junction with the east wall of the house, where a 2m-long section of stone revetting was recorded along its outer edge. The revetting may have provided some type of buttress against the wall or may be residual from a more substantial outer stone course along a mud-built wall. The quantity of animal bone in the barn foundation trenches was considerably smaller than in the house, comprising about 360 fragments or 12% of the number of bones in the house, and it was a mixture of weathered and fresh bone. It is possible that the walls of the barn, although mud-built and tempered with animal bone, were not as thick and sturdy as those of the house.

Two large post-holes (0.35–0.5m in diameter) on either side of the northern foundation trench may mark the position of a wide or double door on the north side of the barn; a wide door would have facilitated the passage of stock or carts into the barn. The vestiges of 27 post-holes immediately south of the possible entrance may mark some internal fitting such as a manger, a hayrack or perhaps a sty. A hearth that was simply a spread of oxidised soil and charcoal almost abutted the north wall of the barn.

A part-stone and part-mud-walled structure on the southern side of the house appears to have been an annexe or shed (Fig. 10.18). It was an open-ended, lean-to building constructed against the south wall of House II. The west wall was a continuation of the house wall; the east wall was drystone-built, and a stone wall was also partially built against the south wall of the house (Fig. 10.13). The eastern stone wall was a *c.* 5m-long single row of stones that survived to a height of two courses or 0.5m. The remains do not indicate a free-standing wall; it may originally have contained more stones at foundation level or may be the remains of a stone-faced earthen wall whose earthen component did not survive in the archaeological record. The west wall may have supported a lean-to roof that was also carried on a lower east wall. A 2.7m-long stone wall within the shed consisted of a double row of stones and was either an internal division or a rebuilding of the shed wall in stone. A small, stone-built, trough-like feature in the north-east corner measured 1m (north/south) by 1.5m (east/west) and part of it used the stone revetting against the south wall of the house. A drain cut to a depth of 0.25m below its base led from the trough, under the west wall of the shed and into a large, stone-filled sink-hole. There was a marked concentration of animal bones from around the stone annexe, the sink-hole and the yard fence foundations adjacent to the annexe. These were tinged green and were probably in contact with human or animal waste, and it is possible that a dunghill existed just outside the stone annexe and adjacent to the yard fence.

There were foundation trenches for fencing around a large enclosure or yard to the south of the house (Fig. 10.13). The fences, constructed after House I had been levelled, were erected over part of the foundation trench of its north wall. They were 0.5–1.5m wide and 0.2–0.3m deep below the boulder clay level but were probably deeper when dug from the contemporary ground surface; they were interpreted as the footings or bedding trench for timber or wattle fences. The yard was at maximum 25m wide (north/south) and the excavated length was 18m (east/west) but it continued outside the excavation limits. The fence trench extended from the east wall of the stone annexe of House II and the fence was likely to have been in use when House II was occupied. The yard fence to the south of House II was probably repaired or replaced over time and this is evidenced by the recutting and realignment of foundation trenches. Wooden fences usually decay at ground level within ten to fifteen years and need regular replacement.

There was a large oval pit to the east side and about 1.5m south of the yard fence. Its dimensions (2.75m east/west by 1.3m north/south) and alignment, the displaced large stone blocks which may have lined its sides and the charred remains of bread wheat, barley and oats suggested that it was used to dry corn. The kiln was poorly preserved but may have been keyhole in plan, similar to medieval kilns (M. Monk 1984; 2013). It was necessary to dry corn prior to threshing, particularly after a damp harvest, and also to parch the grain prior to grinding in either a handmill (quernstones) or in a larger, commercially run mill. The excavations on the car-park site also produced a number of quernstone fragments, showing that cereals were ground on site for domestic consumption. The fill of the corn-drying kiln included a sherd of locally made late thirteenth/early fourteenth-century pottery and an iron key (Fig. 10.19: 2) of twelfth/thirteenth-century date, and the kiln may have been contemporary with House I or II. A stone-built hearth, 1m south of the barn wall, had two rows of stones with an intermediary stone. Stake-holes around the hearth indicated a spit over the fire, which either allowed for roasting meat or perhaps held pots to cook cereals or bake outside the house. A sherd of early fourteenth-century pottery from the hearth suggested that it was in use at the same time as House II. Also within the yard was a 4m-long stone-covered drain leading to a stone-covered pit on the east side.

Finds from the foundation trenches and floor area of House II included sixteen sherds of late

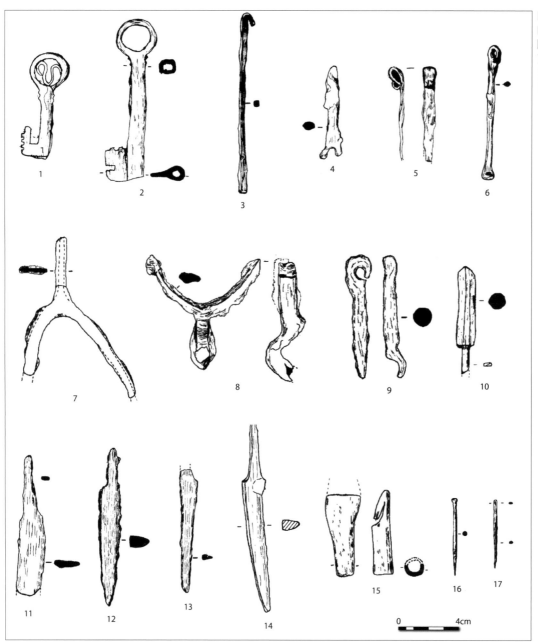

Fig. 10.19—Iron artefacts from House II, car park: 1–2 door keys; 3–6 barrel padlock keys; 7–8 stirrups; 9–10 horse-bits; 11–14 knives; 15 arrowhead; 16 stick-pin; 17 needle.

thirteenth/early fourteenth-century pottery jugs, probably made in the Limerick area. One sherd of green-glazed pottery was from an imported vessel from the Saintonge region of south-west France. Eighteen sherds of locally made late thirteenth/early fourteenth-century pottery and one sherd of green-glazed Saintonge ware were also found in the foundation trenches of the yard enclosure. Ten iron nails were found in the house foundations and a further seven in the yard enclosure trenches. A door key (Fig. 10.19: 1) of twelfth/thirteenth-century style (*LMMC* 1940, 136–7) and three barrel padlock keys (Fig. 10.19: 3–4, 6) for a chest came from the house, while a third barrel padlock key

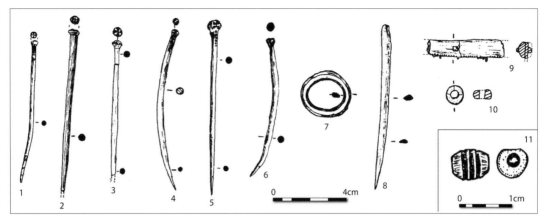

(Fig. 10.1.19: 5) of thirteenth-century date (*ibid.*, 148) was recovered from the fence trench around the yard. Part of an iron prick-spur (Fig. 10.19: 7) was found in House II, and a second prick-spur (Fig. 10.19: 8) of thirteenth-century style (*ibid.*, 95–9) came from the yard fence trench. A two-link horse-bit (Fig. 10.19: 9), common in Britain from the beginning of the eleventh century (*ibid.*, 81), and part of a second horse-bit were found in the house, and a horseshoe fragment came from the yard fence trench. A tanged object with a pointed head (Fig. 10.19: 10) from the yard enclosure trench may have been a reamer. Four whittle-tanged iron knives (Fig. 10.19: 11–14) were found in the house; the blades were triangular in section with the tangs extending from the blade back. Similar knives from urban excavations date from the eleventh to the thirteenth century in Cork and Waterford (Scully 1997a, 165; 1997c, 454). A socketed triangular-bladed arrowhead (Fig. 10.19: 15) with the head bent back towards the socket was found in the fill of the yard enclosure trenches. This type of arrowhead is dated to the twelfth and thirteenth centuries (Halpin 1997, 540). An iron stick-pin (Fig. 10.19: 16) with a domed head was found in the house and similar pins from Waterford are dated to the thirteenth century (Scully 1997c, 439). Other iron objects included an iron strip and rod from the house and an iron needle (Fig. 10.19: 17) from the yard fence foundation.

Four bronze stick-pins (Fig. 10.20: 1–2, 4–6) were found in the house and one (Fig. 10.20: 3) came from the yard trench. These had club-shaped heads and were decorated with rows of dots on the shafts and a cross pattern on one head. These types of pins were used to fasten clothing or may have been used to keep women's hair in place. They were in use from the twelfth to the fourteenth century (Scully 1997c, 439). An oval-shaped bronze ring (Fig. 10.20: 7) was found inside the house and may be from a horse harness. A bone pin (Fig. 10.20: 8) was also found in the house and, like the stick-pins, may have secured clothing or hair. A single-sided fine-toothed bone comb (Fig. 10.20: 9) and a fragment of a second bone comb were found in the house and are thirteenth-century in form (Dunlevy 1988). An amber bead (Fig. 10.20: 10) from the house may be part of a paternoster (rosary beads) or necklace. A bone bead (Fig. 10.20: 11) was found in the yard fence trench; it is decorated with grooving while one side is flat, suggesting that it might have been sewn against fabric or leather as a decoration.

Stone artefacts from House II included three hones or whetstones (Fig. 10.21: 1–3) and a small fragment of a fourth. A Neolithic polished stone axehead (Fig. 10.21: 4) was reused as a hone and has pin grooves on the surfaces. Hones were small, hand-held stones used to edge knives and to sharpen pins and other metal items used in the household. Fragments of quernstones were found in

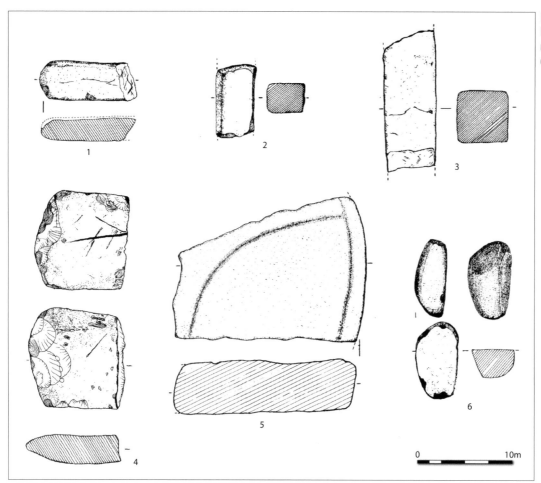

Fig. 10.21—Finds from House II, car park: 1–3 whetstones; 4 reused stone axehead; 5 quernstone; 6 plough pebble.

the yard fence foundation trench. One fragment of an upper stone has a picked-out decorative line (Fig. 10.21: 5) which was probably a cross motif. The quernstones confirm on-site corn-grinding associated with the corn-drying kiln (see above), indicating that the inhabitants were self-sufficient in flour production. A large shale pebble with a worn surface from House II (Fig. 10.21: 6) may be a plough pebble (discussed below).

Pottery and other artefacts give a broad date in the thirteenth and early fourteenth centuries for the houses in the car park. House I was earlier than House II, as the yard fence foundation trench associated with House II cut into the western wall foundation of House I, and it seems that House I was at that stage demolished. House I was single-roomed, and a drain leading from the north-west side may indicate that the northern end of the building was used as a byre for small animals, such as nursing sows, kept within the house. This partial use of houses as byres is well recorded in the nineteenth century, and the byre-dwellings included a drainage channel to drain animal waste outside the house (Gailey 1984, 142–8). House II had an internal partition and an attached barn or byre. The lean-to shed adjacent to House II was also probably a sty or byre. The condition of some of the animal bones from around the sty showed that there was probably an adjacent dunghill.

Both houses were probably mud-built, and many unweathered bones in the foundation trenches suggested that animal bones were incorporated into the mud during construction to reduce shrinkage as the mud dried. The stone footings in House II were similar to a foundation for a mud-walled building in a thirteenth-century house at Jerpoint, Co. Kilkenny (O'Conor 1998, 50). The use of mud-built walls is well attested in vernacular architecture of the sixteenth to twentieth centuries (Gailey 1984, 30–2, 42–3). Foundation trenches 1–2m wide in Houses I and II indicated fairly thick walls which must have provided good insulation. The construction of mud-walled houses in the Anglo-Norman period is supported by documentary evidence: in 1298 the Fitz Maurice Anglo-Norman manor of Insula, Co. Kerry, had buildings with earthen walls (*ibid.*, 265). Timber posts were used as a frame in conjunction with mud walls up to recent times (Danaher 1978, 65–8). The deep foundation trenches of the houses may indicate that posts were erected in these to form a frame and that the intermediary space was then infilled with wattle and plastered over with clay. Similar techniques are known from the archaeological remains of twelfth-century houses on urban sites in Ireland (Hurley 2003; Scully 1997b) and from vernacular houses in Wales (Peate 1940, 172–82). Mud-walled houses survived in the Lough Gur area up to the recent past and building took up to a year (Ó Ríordáin and O'Kelly 1940, 235).

The floor plan of House I showed that the building had rounded corners on the east side and probably square corners on the west side. The hearth of House I was built into the south wall, with an adjacent ash pit also within the foundation trench. The hearth was the only area within the foundation trenches where there was any marked quantity of stone, and the foundation trench on the south wall was also wider, presumably to accommodate the hearth. Hearths incorporated into walls are unusual in Ireland in the medieval period, as almost all the excavated houses in urban and rural contexts have hearths in the middle of the floors, such as at Caherguillamore and in thirteenth- and fourteenth-century houses in Cork and Waterford (Hurley 2003; 2014). An exception, however, was a late thirteenth/early fourteenth-century stone house excavated in one of the backyard plots off North Main Street, Cork (Hurley 1995, 53), where the archaeological evidence showed that a paved hearth and stone chimney-breast were constructed against a wall. Evans (1957, 62–3) suggested that the adoption of a hearth or fireplace against a wall dates from the sixteenth century onwards. Artefactual and stratigraphic evidence dates House I at Lough Gur to the thirteenth century, pre-dating Evans's proposition by two to three centuries. It is possible that, rather than a stone-built chimney, the structure over the fire was a canopy and that the smoke exited via a smoke-hole above. Canopies over chimneys are known in vernacular architecture and channelled the smoke out through the roof (Gailey 1984, 115–22). Evidence from the construction of vernacular houses in the Lough Gur area shows that canopies over hearths were constructed using a timber frame whereby the front of the canopy was carried by a wooden beam and the back rested on the house wall. The canopy itself was made of grass ropes known as *putóga*, which were soaked in and covered with mud, wound around the timber frame and subsequently plastered over (Ó Ríordáin and O'Kelly 1940, 230–1). This type of structure would not leave any trace in the soil at Lough Gur. In Ireland, the time-frame for the evolution from a free-standing central hearth to a wall hearth is unknown, but the evidence from House I of the car-park houses suggests that this occurred as early as the thirteenth century. The stone-lined ash pit adjacent to the hearth in House I stored ashes, perhaps for use as fertiliser or charcoal for use in iron production. Ash pits in old vernacular houses were either a hole in front of the fire or in the wall beside the fire (Evans 1957, 62).

House II was originally interpreted as a two-roomed building (Cleary 1982b), but more likely the eastern 'room' was a barn or byre attached to the house. An entrance is suggested by post-holes

Fig. 10.22—Plough as illustrated in the Luttrell Psalter.

on the northern foundation trench, and access from the barn/byre into the enclosed yard was probably via a doorway in the south wall. The attachment of a barn/byre or outhouses to a dwelling house to form a continuous line is known in east Limerick and examples exist in the modern landscape around Lough Gur. Another typical farm-building layout in east Limerick is of outhouses being built around a rectangular yard, as in the case of 'the Farm by Lough Gur', beside Knockfennell Hill.

Residues of what people ate in the medieval period sometimes survive as charred plant remains. These are extracted from the soil in modern excavations and allow for an assessment of the cereal and vegetable diet of the inhabitants. Cereals recovered from the medieval occupation of the car-park area included barley, wheat, oats and cultivated peas (M. Monk 1982; 1984). Some of these cereals were likely processed on site for home consumption, as evidenced by the quernstone fragments and the corn-drying kiln. Legumes such as peas were grown as part of a land management system whereby field rotation involved pasture and tillage and legumes were set as soil-improvers to fix nitrogen in the soil in tilled ground (Postan 1975, 55–7). The area surrounding the medieval houses at Caherguillamore included field systems, visible on aerial photographs, which may have been in contemporary use with the medieval occupation (Ó Ríordáin and Hunt 1942, 43). The arrival of the Anglo-Normans saw level, good ground brought into tillage and the plough horse was extensively used (Brady 1988). The plough had an iron share, a coulter knife fixed in front of the share to cut the furrow and a mould-board parallel with the share to turn the cut and lay it on its side (Postan 1975, 49–50). This type of plough is illustrated in the Luttrell Psalter[6] (1335–40), where various agricultural activities, including tillage, are shown (Fig. 10.22). Small, hard pebbles known as 'plough pebbles' were inserted into the wooden parts of ploughs to prevent the wood from wearing when the soil was turned (Brady 1988). Five plough pebbles were found in the 1977–8 excavations at Lough Gur (Fig. 10.21: 6). These date from the Anglo-Norman period, and this type of mechanised ploughing may have been introduced in the mid-twelfth century (Cleary 1982a, 11).

A study of the animal bones from the 1977–8 car-park excavations at Lough Gur showed that the majority of the bones derived from cattle, sheep and pig, with some domestic fowl, horse, dog, cat and hare bones (J. Monk 1982; 1984). The cattle were generally from a small variety similar to the modern Kerry cow; some were killed off mainly between 2½ and 3½ years, which is the prime slaughtering age for beef, while older cows were likely to have provided milk and its by-products butter and cheese. Butchering took place on site, presumably for home consumption. Wear on some cattle bones also showed that cattle were used for traction, perhaps for ploughing. Sheep were also eaten, while spindle-whorls provided evidence of wool production. Pigs were kept and killed off between the ages of one and three years. These pigs were long-legged and not similar to the modern pig. Horses were also eaten, although most of the horse bones were from older animals that showed signs of arthritis in the legs, presumably from use as farm animals. Horse-bits, harness buckles and rowel- and prick-spur fragments from both Caherguillamore and the car-park excavations also confirm horse-riding. The dogs were of both large and small varieties and may have been hunting dogs, farm dogs or pets. Bird bones from the site included domestic fowl (ducks and hens). A concentration of hawk, raven and crow bones were found in the yard enclosure foundation and these may have been hung up to deter predatory birds. Other bird bones included wild geese and duck, which were presumably opportunistically hunted and eaten. The remains of a swan, a buzzard and perhaps a golden eagle were also found.

Iron-working residues of mainly iron slag and one tuyère fragment were uncovered on the excavations at the car park. The tuyère was a clay nozzle at the junction of the bellows pipes and the furnace. Much of the iron slag was found within the yard of House II and some came from various other locations. Almost 12kg of iron slag was recovered, suggesting small-scale, on-site smithing for the manufacture of household items such as knives and farm equipment such as shears, sickles and ploughs. Hones from the site and evidence of the reuse of quernstones as sharpening stones indicate iron-working and the maintenance of tools. The raw iron may have been sourced from bog ores.

THE CHURCH

The church in Ireland, as elsewhere in Europe, underwent reformation and structural changes prior to the Anglo-Norman invasion. The Irish church had fallen out of line with Roman rule; lax practices in canon law and church rites were widespread, and church organisation was dominated by the monasteries rather than a diocesan structure. Much of the impulse for reform came from Munster, beginning with the Council of Cashel in 1101. Reformation in Ireland was led by St Malachy of Armagh, who also spent time in the south of Ireland at Lismore and who had Cormac McCarthy of Cashel as his patron. Prior to reform, the chief centre for the church in north Munster was the monastery at Ardpatrick, which, along with the monastery at Mungret, owed allegiance to the archbishop of Cashel rather than to the bishop of Limerick. In Limerick the change from a monastic to a diocesan system was led by Gille (or Gilbert), bishop of Limerick City (Fleming 2009). Gille was probably of Norse origin, from the cantred of the Ostmen in Limerick. As papal legate he presided over the Synod of Rathbreasil (1111), whereby fourteen dioceses were established in Ireland and in County Limerick the Church of St Mary in Limerick became the cathedral church (*ibid.*, 3). The Synod of Rathbreasil began the displacement of monastic rule in favour of diocesan organisation whereby bishops ruled and were free of the authority of lay rulers. It established the territorial boundaries of the dioceses; the diocese of Limerick, as outlined in the Book of Clonenagh, included the following territories:

'The see of Luimneach, the Maoilchern eastwards, Ath ar Choinne, Lodan and Loch Gair [Lough Gur], and the Laitheach Mhor from Aine westwards, and Ard Padraig to the south and Bealach Feabhradh and Tulach Leis, the Fell westwards and Tairbeart and Cuinche in Thomond and Cossa in Sliabh Uidhe in Riogh and the Dubhabhann' (*ibid.*, 6).

Church reform also included the introduction of Cistercian monks, a contemplative order following the Rule of St Benedict. The first Cistercian foundation in Ireland was at Mellifont, Co. Louth, in 1142; this was followed by the foundation of eight daughter houses, including one at Monasteranenagh in 1148. Turlough O'Brien, king of Limerick, built the monastery at Monasteranenagh beside an ancient *aenagh* or fair site, from which the name 'Monasteranenagh' was derived. The monastery was dedicated to St Maria de Magio, 'de Magio' referring to the flat lands or plain surrounding the foundation. The monastic lands of Monasteranenagh extended as far east as Lough Gur and included Grange, Camas and Cahercorney. The name 'grange' originates from monastic estate land. In 1186 a charter bestowed Loc Geir (Lough Gur), with the island and Grange, to Magio Abbey (Monasternenagh) (Westropp 1906–7, 179).

Although church reform in Ireland began before the Anglo-Norman invasion in 1169, the arrival of Henry II in 1171 cemented the process. The Irish church was brought into conformity with the English church, and the powerful Anglo-Norman lords became significant church benefactors—an example that was in turn followed by the great Gaelic lords. Anglo-Norman and Gaelic patronage enabled the introduction of other monastic orders, and in County Limerick these included monasteries established in the late thirteenth century by the Dominicans at Kilmallock (1291) and by the Franciscans at Buttevant (1276–9). Religious life for women was a feature of the reforming church. A nunnery dedicated to St Catherine was founded by the Fitzgibbon[7] family at Ballynagallagh in 1283 for the canonesses of St Augustine[8] (Seymour 1913, 136). It was recorded as being on the site of an earlier convent, founded in 941, which was destroyed by Viking raids (Dowd 1896, 79). Lewis (1837, 15) recorded that the convent was of the Order of St Augustine and was called *Monaster-ni-Cailliagh Juxta Arny*.[9] He noted that a preceptory or estate/buildings was founded at Ballynagallagh in 1226 which subsequently became the property of the Knights of St John of Jerusalem (the Knights Hospitallers), who built a church in nearby Hospital in 1215. He also recorded that a friary for Eremites[10] of the Order of St Augustine was founded by John Fitzgerald[11] at Ballynagallagh in 1349. Dowd (1896, 79) noted that in 1360 the Augustinian priory at Llanthony, Gloucestershire, owned the land at *Calliaghtown juxta le Loghir et le Loghgir*.[12] The Augustinian canons of Llanthony also established a monastery at Duleek, Co. Meath, and Ballynagallagh was probably a daughter house.

The nuns at Ballynagallagh followed the Rule of St Augustine (Arroasian Rule), which was introduced into Ireland by St Malachy of Armagh in the mid-twelfth century (Watt 1972, 22). The nunnery survived until the dissolution of the monasteries, and the house of 'Ballenegallaghe by

Fig. 10.23—Ballynagallagh nunnery.

Loghguyre' was granted to Edmund Sexton in *c.* 1548 (Seymour 1913, 136).[13] Graves were reputedly uncovered in the field where the church is located (O'Kelly 1941, 5). Crofton Croker (1833, 108) noted of Ballynagallagh that there had 'formerly been a nunnery here, and that stone coffins had recently been dug up in the altar field'; old walls and trenches were still to be seen near a farmhouse at that time.

The remains of the nunnery at Ballynagallagh are now partly incorporated into the western wall of the graveyard (Fig. 10.23). It is possible that the graveyard wall itself was constructed from former stone buildings on the site. The upstanding remains consist of a gable end of a building constructed of undressed limestone stones bonded with lime mortar. The gable wall is *c.* 1m thick, stands to a height of 4.5m and is 3m long. The remains of a slightly splayed window-jamb are visible. The wall enclosing the graveyard is modern, probably built in the late nineteenth century. It measures 35m (east/west) by 32m (north/south) and has dressed limestone quoins at the corners. Entrance to the graveyard is via a stile in the north-west corner, of similar construction to the entrance at Newchurch.

Lynch (1895, 289), citing local tradition, stated that there was another nunnery at Grange, where Grange Roman Catholic church now stands, and that the nuns from this convent 'were accustomed to meet the nuns from Ballynagallagh convent at the site of Holy Cross, which is somewhat to the east of the present Holy Cross'. This meeting place was supposedly on the line of an ancient trackway known as *Cliadh na Leac*, which extends from Grange to Ballynagallagh. Lynch (1895, 290) also referred to a Franciscan friary founded at Lough Gur (in Ballynebrahir) in the thirteenth century by the family of Clan Gibbon. This was recorded by the Ordnance Survey as an 'abbey', and Lynch (1895, 290) noted that 'only a mere crumb of the building is left. It is situated on the bank of the river Camogue … the friary was called Ballynebrahirbeg, or Little Friarstown, to distinguish it from Friarstown, in the parish of Fedamore'.

NOTES

[1] Westropp (1906–7, 66; 1907, 31) made reference to a castle at Aqi or Agni (Knockainy), which he recorded as 'Castle Dany stood in Knockainy in 1199' and as 'standing in 1287'. This may initially have been an earthwork, later replaced with a stone castle; the extant castle at Knockainy is a tower-house of fifteenth-century date.

[2] Plea rolls were a record of the court system used from the late thirteenth century in which the outcomes of civil and criminal cases were noted. Caherguillamore is in the Plea Rolls Calendar vol. ii, p. 77.

[3] The Peyton survey (1584–6) and the Desmond rolls (1585–6) recorded lands forfeited as a result of the Desmond rebellion in preparation for the plantation of Munster.

[4] In the absence of a metallurgical analysis it is not possible to confirm Ó Ríordáin and Hunt's identification of gilding on the strap ends. Bronze develops a patina when buried and this may have been mistaken for gilding.

[5] Clare McCutcheon, Archaeology Department, UCC.

[6] Similar ploughs are also shown in the manuscript of the poem 'Piers Ploughman', written sometime between 1370 and 1390.

[7] The head of the family then was Gilbert, son of John Fitzgerald (Lynch 1895, 252).

[8] Crofton Croker (1833, 108) referred to Archdale's *Monasticon Hibernicum*, in which the nunnery of Negillagh or *Monaster ni calligh*, dedicated to St Catherine, near Lough Gur was mentioned. Westropp (1904–5, 395) noted that the site of Ballynagallagh, Lough Gur, has been confused with St Catherine's Abbey or Manisternagalliagh, Shanid, founded around 1240.

[9] *Monaster* = monastery; *ni-Cailliagh* = of the nuns [literally witches]; *juxta* = beside; *Arny* = Knockainy.

[10] Hermits.

[11] He was also known as Fitz-Robert.

[12] *Calliaghtown* = Ballynagallagh; *juxta* = beside; *Loghir* = Lough Gur.

[13] Lynch (1895, 289) recorded that after the dissolution of the monasteries (from 1530 onwards) the lands were granted to Sir Henry Wallop, while Lewis (1837, 15) recorded a grant by Queen Elizabeth to Edward, John and Mary Absely; these land grants may have been sequential.

11. Tower-houses and settlement, 1400–1700

THE EMERGENCE OF THE FITZGERALD DYNASTY AND THE EARLS OF DESMOND

From the fourteenth century the political history of east Limerick was dominated by the Fitzgeralds or Geraldines, who were ennobled as the earls of Desmond in 1329. By 1282 Thomas fitz Maurice had begun an expansion and consolidation of holdings, and his son Maurice, the first earl of Desmond, 'added substantially to the Desmond estates' (McCormack 2005, 31–2). The Desmonds were essentially magnates who were powerful 'at the periphery [London] of central politics' (*ibid.*, 18). Gerald (Gearóid Iarla), the fourth earl, began a policy of making their possessions more contiguous when he acquired the manor of Askeaton in 1375 and connected up parcels of land. This was continued by his sons John and James (*ibid.*, 32–3). The Desmonds became 'virtually Irish chieftains' and by 1400 Earl Thomas held de Clare's manors at Lough Gur (Westropp 1907, 34, 37).

The fortified stone residences built by Anglo-Norman lords and Gaelic chiefs from about 1380 to 1600 are known as 'tower-houses', or sometimes 'peel towers', which to all intents and purposes were castles that combined defensive and administrative functions and were also family homes. Tower-houses are particularly common in areas where the land is of good agricultural quality, such as County Limerick. A survey of County Limerick by Westropp (1906; 1906–7) listed over 400 castles and sites of castles, and most of these are tower-houses. The building of tower-houses increased from the fifteenth century onwards and was linked to the division of land between free tenants who paid rent or gave services to the earl of Desmond (Donnelly 2009, 71). It is also suggested that during the lordship of James (1411–62), sixth earl of Desmond, which was a particularly stable period, sufficient wealth was generated to support tower-house construction (*ibid.*, 72).

The structure of local government under Anglo-Norman rule was based on cantreds, and for administrative purposes these were subdivided into 'chapters' (or parish groups) and coroners' districts (Westropp 1906–7, 57). The main locus of financial administration was the manor, where feudal dues and rents were paid. Income was derived from levies charged on fairs, tolls in towns and fines imposed in courts (McCormack 2005, 48–9). Coyne and livery (a tax used by Gaelic chiefs) was also imposed and was used to support the household and troops (*ibid.*, 51). These administrative and financial transactions took place in tower-houses and consequently space was allocated for such functions, usually in the main hall at first- or second-floor level. In time the Anglo-Normans became Hiberno-Normans, taking on the customs and manners of Gaelic Ireland. Like Gaelic chiefs, Hiberno-Norman lords became patrons of bards, poets and historians, who also resided in the tower-house. McCormack (2005, 46) estimated that the household within a tower-house might number between 80 and 100, and noted that in 1533–4 Henry Bourchier employed 50 servants at Bourchier's Castle. Bourchier also administered a judicial system and based the legal administration on the Gaelic customs of the *aonach* and the *oireachtas*, which were gatherings that included legal, social and sporting activities (*ibid.*, 48).

Some of the tower-houses in County Limerick may have been built from as early as the 1380s–90s. Leask (1973, 76–7) proposed that one stimulus for the construction of tower-houses was a statute of Henry VI in 1429 which paid a £10 subsidy to every liegeman within the English Pale (Dublin, parts of Kildare, Louth and Meath) who built a castle to the specified size of 6m by 5m by 12m high. Some of the County Limerick tower-houses, however, pre-date the £10 castle grant by up to 50 years. The origin of the architectural style of the tower-house is unknown; Westropp (1907, 26) suggested that the late introduction of styles of building and ornament to Ireland and the conservativeness of building traditions make it difficult to assess foreign parallels and building evolution. The Irish tower-house may be an Irish response to the need for a defendable house in times of periodic political unrest and internecine strife between various powerful Anglo-Norman families and between the Anglo-Norman and Gaelic clans. Apart from their defensive and administrative functions, tower-houses were also status symbols and territorial markers (Donnelly 2009, 72). Their significance in the latter regard meant that they were located along routeways in order to control trade and access and egress from a region.

There were seven tower-houses in the vicinity of Lough Gur: five built by the Geraldines (Desmonds) and two by the Bourkes of Caherelly. Two Geraldine tower-houses, Bourchier's Castle and Black Castle (also known as Killalough), are located on Knockadoon Hill, one is on Geroid Island, one at Grange (Fig. 11.1) and one at Caherguillamore. The castles survive in varying states of preservation, and P.J. Lynch (1906–7, 128), writing in the early twentieth century, noted that 'vandalism in its worst form appears to have run riot at Lough Gur, castles have been removed to build modern mansions'. The tower-houses around Lough Gur are generally at defendable locations. The Black Castle and Bourchier's Castle were located at the only access points to Knockadoon Hill, which was virtually an island before the lake was drained in the late 1840s. The tower-house on Geroid Island was surrounded by the lake. Grange Castle was located on a rock outcrop and the surrounding lower ground, now bog, was probably a lake.

The castles were simple oblong buildings, with four walls rising from a base batter to crenellated parapets (Leask 1973, 79). The internal layout of the buildings was relatively uniform in being divided into two main sections, one side containing the winding stairs and a number of small chambers and the other side containing the larger rooms (*ibid.*, 79). This division is clearly visible in some Limerick tower-houses, and an external joint line is evident between the two sections, suggesting that the part containing the stairwell and smaller chambers was built first (*ibid.*, 79). The stairwell section of a tower-house provided the only access to the upper chambers and battlements, and it could be easily defended and offered a last retreat for a garrison if the main building was taken by assault. This section was also a refuge in the event of fire, as it was independent of the rest of the structure and likely to escape if the larger rooms were burnt.

Precise dating of tower-house construction at Lough Gur is difficult, given the poor survival of most of the structures, with the exception of Bourchier's Castle and Caherelly West. The architectural style and available historical information suggest that the Lough Gur tower-houses were built by the earls of Desmond (Fitzgeralds) in the late fourteenth to fifteenth century (Grene Barry 1903a; Westropp 1906–7; 1907). There is limited historical documentation for County Limerick for the period *c.* 1390–1540, although the *Castle Founders List* for neighbouring County Clare indicates

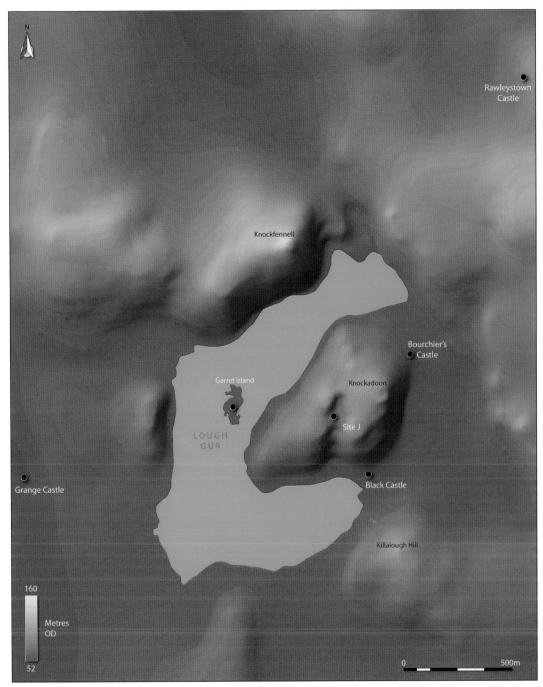

Fig. 11.1—Location map.

that 'the building of peel towers began about 1390, was feverishly active from 1440 to 1490, and then fell off' (Westropp 1907, 38).

Westropp (1907, 37) described the fifteenth century as 'probably the most active in castle-building', when

> 'there sprung up in every direction a crop of peel towers … along with these, the larger and older castles were repaired and enlarged … a time of … no inconsiderable wealth and peace … the Crown hardly interfered; the Earls of Desmond ruled as independent chiefs from the Maigue westwards; the towns paid peace-money to the Irish chiefs, and were immersed in successful trade'.

FORTIFICATIONS ON KNOCKADOON

The name 'Knockadoon' ('the hill of the fort [*Dún Gair*]') suggests a fortification which historical accounts[1] link to Brian Boru, who may have strengthened existing defences. Strategically this fortification would be best placed on or near the natural access point where Bourchier's Castle now stands. The Ordnance Survey (1840) located the site of 'Dún Gair' on Knockmore, the north peak on Knockadoon Hill, and high above the natural entrance to Knockadoon at Bourchier's Castle, but this is more likely just a rock outcrop (O'Kelly 1941, 25–6). Westropp (1906–7, 180) described Bourchier's Castle as being built within an earlier fort. Bourchier's Castle is also identified as 'Castledoon' (*ibid.*, 180; Grene Barry 1903a, 196–7) and this name is presumably derived from its location within or near a *dún* or fort. 'Bourchier Castle, properly Castledoon, was erected on the site of an older fortification, which guarded the natural and only passage into the island of Knockadoon. That this was the only access to the island is certain before the building of a great causeway across the lake' (Grene Barry 1903a, 196).

BOURCHIER'S CASTLE

Westropp (1906–7, 180) described Bourchier's Castle as a 'peel tower 49 feet [14.9m] by 33½ feet [10.2m] outside, 75 feet [22.8m] high, and well preserved'. The tower-house is rectangular in plan, with the long axis east/west (Figs 11.2–4). It was built in two sections on the same foundations with a wide base batter of about 1.5m, and the joint line is clearly visible externally (Fig. 11.5). The stairwell and smaller compartments occupy the north-east corner. The portion of the castle that contains the doorway and staircase comprises about one-quarter of the whole structure, with quoin stones at the external angles that are bonded at intervals into the rest of the building.

The main door of Bourchier's Castle is on the east side (Fig. 11.6) and has a pointed carved limestone decorative moulding (Fig. 11.7). A hinge bracket on the north side and a chain hole on the south side of the door suggest an iron gate or yett, which would have provided extra defence for the doorway. The existing wooden door at Bourchier's Castle, which may not be original, has a shot hole in the centre. Revd J.F. Lynch (1895, 248) wrote of Bourchier's Castle: 'Lough Gur Castle is very strongly built, and is likely to last for centuries yet to come … The heavy oak door, thickly studded with bolts, still bars the entrance to the castle.' Internally the door leads into a narrow porch

Fig. 11.2—Bourchier's
Castle (Photographic Unit,
National Monuments
Service).

Fig. 11.3 (above right)—
Bourchier's Castle
(Photographic Unit, National
Monuments Service).

Fig. 11.4—Bourchier's
Castle (Photographic Unit,
National Monuments
Service).

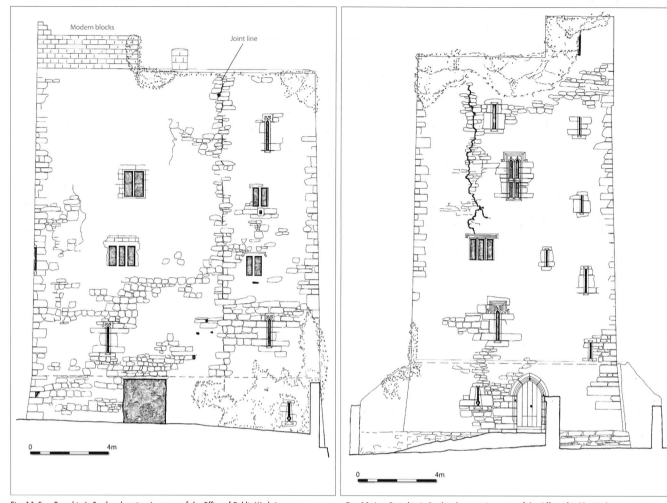

Fig. 11.5—Bourchier's Castle: elevation (courtesy of the Office of Public Works).

Fig. 11.6—Bourchier's Castle: elevation (courtesy of the Office of Public Works).

(Fig. 11.8), a view of which was provided by a 'murder-hole' in the ceiling (Fig. 11.9). The 'murder-hole' was a defensive feature that allowed defenders to protect the entrance lobby. Lynch (1895, 248–9) described the roof of the porch at Bourchier's Castle: 'there is the usual *poul na morrough*, "murdering hole", through which boiling oil, pitch, darts, and other missiles could be thrown at the enemy who succeeded in entering the porch'.

Bourchier's Castle is now a five-storey building but was probably originally higher (see below). Unusually, there is a basement under the ground floor to the left of the doorway and partly under the porch (Figs 11.9–10). There are two stone vaults, one above the first floor and one at fourth-floor level (Fig. 11.10), the undersides of which still bear visible impressions of the woven wicker used to support the stone during construction. As is typical of all tower-houses, the timber floors in Bourchier's Castle were carried on beams resting on projecting stone corbels, and these beams supported the timber joists on which the floors were laid. The projecting stone corbels are visible above the ground-, second- and third-floor levels (Fig. 11.10). Bourchier's Castle was renovated by

Fig. 11.8—Bourchier's Castle: door (Joseph Lennon).

Fig. 11.7—Bourchier's Castle: door (Joseph Lennon).

Count de Salis in the early twentieth century and the floors may have been replaced at that stage, although it is possible that some of the existing wall-plates, joists and floor timbers are original. The castle was used as a site office and as accommodation for archaeologists during the excavations in the late 1930s to the early 1950s, and by Michael J. O'Kelly (later professor of Archaeology at UCC) as accommodation during his survey of the monuments of the barony of Small County in 1940.

Craig (1982, 97) has described tower-houses as being essentially vertical, in that the main rooms were laid out in various storeys rather than side by side. The larger rooms had a variety of uses. The cellar below the entrance lobby at Bourchier's Castle is accessed via a trapdoor. Alcoves in the walls suggest that it was used for storage; cool conditions would have made it suitable for a larder, although there is no stair to allow access. The basement may have been a cell for prisoners. The ground floor has an entrance lobby, two rooms and a spiral staircase that leads to the upper floors (Fig. 11.11). The smaller room is to the left of the door and the main room is entered via the entrance lobby. The small room directly above the cellar has a timber floor and two single-light windows, one on the east wall and one on the south wall, both of which have gun ports near their bases. There is a wall press or alcove on the west wall and a fireplace on the east side. The larger room is *c.* 8.5m by 6.5m and has three embrasures or splayed openings that housed windows in the north, south and west walls (Fig. 11.11). The large door now on the south side is a later insertion and was formerly the location of a window (Fig. 11.5). There are wall presses or alcoves on the western ends of the north and south walls and a fireplace on the east wall.

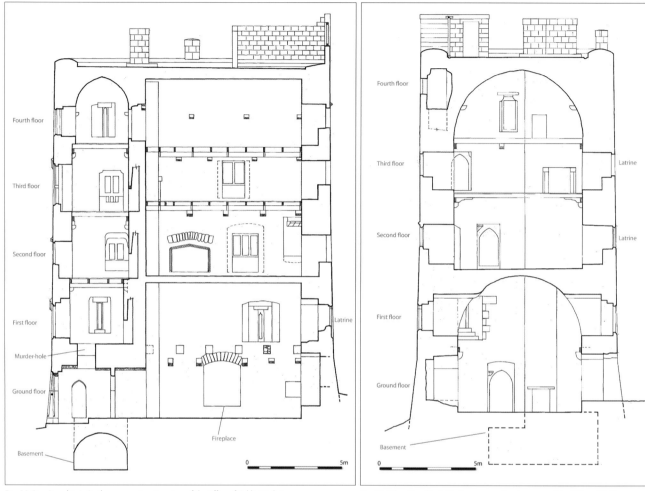

Fig. 11.9—Bourchier's Castle: cross-section (courtesy of the Office of Public Works).

Fig. 11.10—Bourchier's Castle: cross-section (courtesy of the Office of Public Works).

The first floor (Fig. 11.12) has a small room above the entrance lobby that is accessed from the stairwell; it may have housed watchmen or guards, as it is directly above the 'murder-hole'. This room has two windows, one each in the south and east walls, and four wall presses. The larger first-floor room is of similar size to the large room on the ground floor, has three windows and may have served as accommodation for retainers. The second to fourth floors have small rooms entered from the stone stairwell and which were probably used as bedchambers or private rooms, and there is also a latrine or toilet (Figs 11.13–15). The latrine emptied into a chute, visible on the north side of the castle, which carried the waste to the ground at the base of the castle. The larger rooms on the second and third floors have fireplaces; the room on the second floor may have been the great hall where business was transacted, while that on the third floor was probably a living room for family use. The fireplace on the second floor has a carved limestone surround (Fig. 11.16) and that on the third floor has decorative limestone half-columns carved with spiral motifs and surmounted by capitals (Fig. 11.17). The stones of the overmantle are now gone, presumably removed in the past. Lynch (1895,

Fig. 11.11—Bourchier's Castle: ground-floor plan (courtesy of the Office of Public Works).

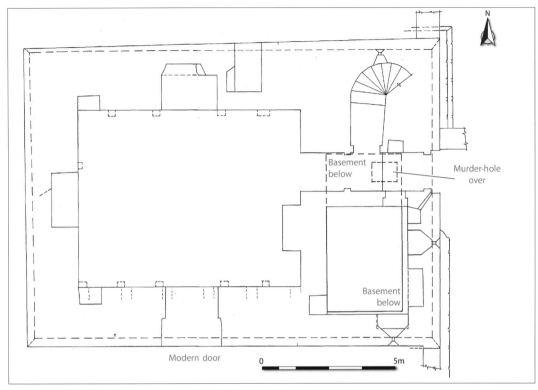

Fig. 11.12—Bourchier's Castle: first-floor plan (courtesy of the Office of Public Works).

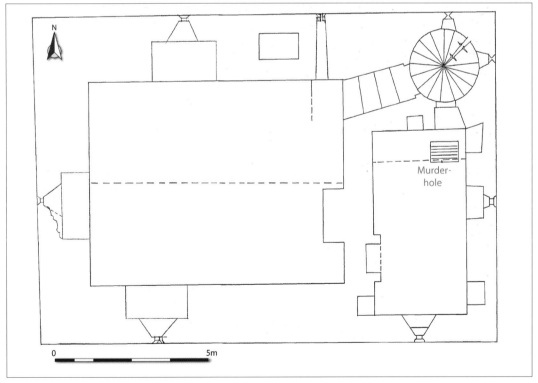

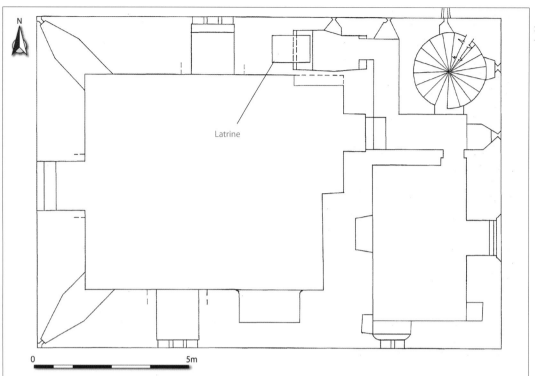

Fig. 11.13—Bourchier's Castle: second-floor plan (courtesy of the Office of Public Works).

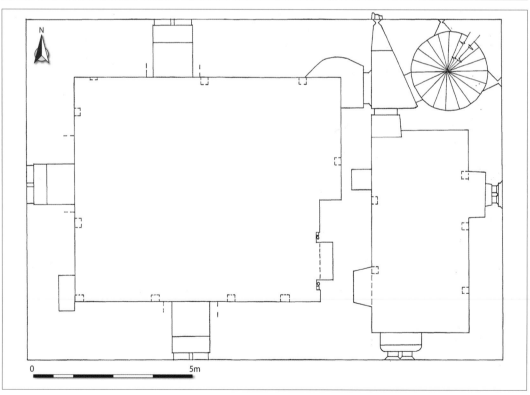

Fig. 11.14—Bourchier's Castle: third-floor plan (courtesy of the Office of Public Works).

Fig. 11.15—Bourchier's Castle: fourth-floor plan (courtesy of the Office of Public Works).

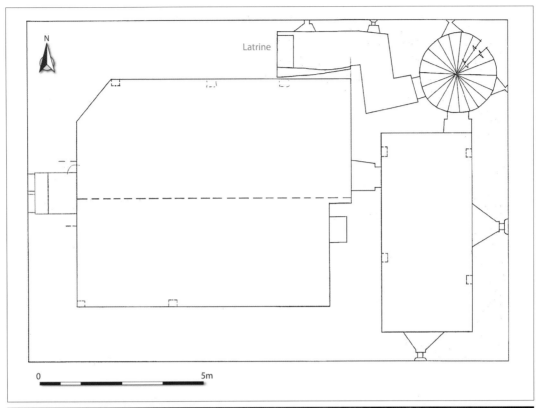

Fig. 11.16—Bourchier's Castle: second-floor fireplace (Joseph Lennon).

Fig. 11.17—Bourchier's Castle: third-floor fireplace (Joseph Lennon).

249) noted of Bourchier's Castle that 'many of the beautiful well-cut stones have been torn from their places'. The second- and third-floor windows at Bourchier's Castle are large (Figs 11.5–6), suggesting that these floors were spaces used for daily life and business. The fourth floor had a small bedchamber on the east end, a latrine on the north and a large room or main chamber which was poorly lit by a single window. Some of the larger windows at Bourchier's Castle have square hood-mouldings as well as ornamental stonework above narrow slit windows (Fig. 11.6).

The journal of Thomas Dineley gives an account of his visit to Ireland in 1681 (Shirley 1856). Although Westropp (1907, 27) did not consider Dineley a 'sound historian', the usefulness of Dineley's journal lies in his sketches. His sketch of Bourchier's Castle in 1681 shows six floors and crenellations or stepped battlements (Fig. 11.18). It is possible that the castle was originally two floors higher than it is today, and the absence of any evidence for a roof above the fourth floor suggests that there was at least another floor above. Lynch (1895, 249), describing Bourchier's Castle, wrote that since Dineley's visit in 1681, 'when it was inhabited by the Bayley family, the battlements, the roof and the bower chamber [lady's private room] have fallen away'. The original roof was presumably gabled, with the gables rising from slightly inside the faces of the walls and a narrow wall-walk inside the parapet. The roof was probably of slates or thin flagstones and there may have been attic space under it. The upper wall now has modern concrete blocks, added during the restoration works carried out by Count de Salis (Figs 11.9–10).

The defensive features in tower-houses include narrow loops, corner loops and shot holes positioned at different locations within the building, which were designed to keep attackers at bay, as well as a crenellated parapet (Donnelly 2009, 73). The winding stone staircase on the north-east corner at Bourchier's Castle hindered attackers from reaching the upper levels. Grene Barry (1903a, 197) remarked that the stair at Bourchier's Castle, 'as is usual, winds from right to left, to allow the

Fig. 11.18—Dineley's sketch of Bourchier's Castle.

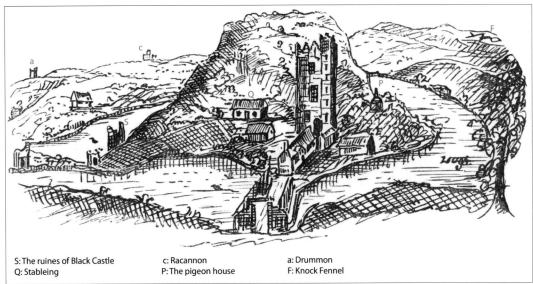

| S: The ruines of Black Castle | c: Racannon | a: Drummon |
| Q: Stableing | P: The pigeon house | F: Knock Fennel |

defender the free use of his sword-arm', while the thickness of the interior wall and the grouted floors hampered a breach from the ground floor of the tower-house. Lynch (1895, 249) also recorded that the interior of Bourchier's Castle had 'a splendid spiral staircase [that] leads to the upper apartments'. The stairwell was lit by narrow single- or two-light windows (Figs 11.5–6).

Dineley's sketch of Bourchier's Castle in 1681 shows the lake completely surrounding Knockadoon Hill, a building immediately east of the castle, a gatehouse and a bridge across the lake (Fig. 11.18). Dineley described Lough Gur as 'an island and castle of strength environ'd with a deep large Mote or Logh … upon the edge thereof neer the present bridge is seen the castle' (Shirley 1867, 287). His sketch shows a moat which was cut to allow the water to extend to either side of the isthmus that linked Bourchier's Castle to the mainland, or the moat may have been cut through the isthmus and crossed by a drawbridge to provide an outer defence for the castle (Grene Barry 1903a, 197). The moat was probably drained when the lake was lowered in the late 1840s, and it was filled in sometime in the early twentieth century. The gatehouse and an addition on the east side of the tower-house shown in Dineley's sketch were built in the mid-seventeenth century by the countess of Bath (*ibid.*, 197). Other buildings shown in Dineley's sketch are the columbarium or pigeon-house to the north of Bourchier's Castle, barns and a stable block to the south, and the ruins of Black Castle and its outer gatehouse in the distance to the south (Fig. 11.18).

The positioning of Bourchier's Castle and Black Castle on Knockadoon Hill suggests that it was necessary to defend two access points—the natural access at Bourchier's Castle and the artificial causeway at Black Castle. A wall on the lower eastern slope of Knockadoon Hill which extended from Bourchier's Castle into the bawn wall of Black Castle also confirms that both castles were connected and in contemporary use. Hayman (1868–9, 415) described it as 'a strong wall … drawn all along the edge of the lake till it met the Black Castle'. Lynch (1895, 247) wrote that it was 'nearly fifteen feet [4.5m] high and eight feet [2.4m] thick, made up of immense blocks of stone. They were the largest that can be seen in any building of this kind in the country.' Brash (B.R.R. 1865, 243) described 'the remains of a massive wall of regular masonry in large blocks … finished the same on both sides'.

The construction date of Bourchier's Castle is addressed in various accounts. Westropp (1907, 40) suggested that it was probably built sometime after 1450, when Lough Gur became one of the chief seats of the Desmonds. Land forfeitures after the Desmond rebellion (1579–83) resulted in the granting of the tower-house to George Bourchier. A petition in 1587 by Eleanor, the widowed countess of Desmond, confirmed that the tower-house was not built by Bourchier but was previously her home and she sought its return (Langrishe 1905, 22). Crofton Croker (1833, 105) wrote of Knockadoon: 'It is now connected with the mainland by two causeways, which approaches were respectively defended by a massive tower or castle, probably constructed in the fifteenth century by the Geraldines. The tower [Bourchier's Castle] which protects the northern causeway is the larger and more perfect of the two.' Lynch (1895, 302) also affirmed that 'Lough Gur was very closely connected with the fortunes of the Geraldines. It witnessed the rise and fall of that great family … and Lough Gur saw the "Great Earl", once the owner of five hundred thousand acres and castles innumerable, fleeing a landless and homeless man from the bloody battle at Manister, fought not far from it in 1579.' Bourchier's Castle and other tower-houses in the environs of Lough Gur were most likely erected by the earls of Desmond, who had numerous castles within their huge estates (McCormack 2005, 41).

Some of the historians who provided general accounts of the history of County Limerick gave a date for the construction of Bourchier's Castle in the reign of Elizabeth I, who acceded to the throne in 1558 (Fitzgerald and McGregor 1826; Lewis 1837; Dowd 1896). The antiquarian Richard Rolt Brash (B.R.R. 1865, 243), who wrote specifically about Lough Gur in the *Dublin Builder*, suggested that Bourchier's Castle was built by George Bourchier, who was granted Desmond lands in the reign of Elizabeth I. Hayman (1868–9, 415) referred to Dineley's drawing (1681) and noted that the 'castle and bridge in the foreground were built by the Bourchiers after Desmond's fall'. Both Brash and Hayman were probably incorrect in assigning the construction of the castle to Bourchier.

Historical references to Bourchier's Castle

Bourchier's Castle is the best-preserved castle in Lough Gur and a number of surviving historical references are recorded by Westropp (1906–7; 1907) and other authors, including Dineley in 1681 (Shirley 1856). As there is some confusion between Bourchier's Castle and Black Castle, some of the references may be to either castle. Attacks on Bourchier's Castle are detailed in various accounts of its history. These attacks included cattle-raiding, which in later medieval Ireland provided the attackers with income, as cattle were the principal commodity of wealth, while harrying was designed to terrorise the local population into submission (Donnelly 2009, 78–9). Cattle-raiding is documented between the earls of Desmond and the O'Briens of Thomond in the late fourteenth century (*ibid.*, 80).

Maurice (fitz Thomas) succeeded as the tenth earl of Desmond in 1487; he held the title for 34 years, making him the longest-serving earl, and his territories remained relatively quiet and stable (McCormack 2005, 64). During the 1510s the peace of the earldom was broken. The Annals of Ulster recorded that in 1515 James, son of the earl of Desmond, captured Knockainy Castle from his uncle John and then attacked Lough Gur Castle (Donnelly 2009, 81; McCormack 2005, 63). James besieged Lough Gur again in 1516 with the assistance of MacCarthy and other allies. The attack is recorded by Brash (B.R.R. 1865, 243), whereby 'in AD 1516 James Fitz Maurice, with a large army, laid siege to it [Lough Gur], but the O'Briens of Thomond raised the siege, and compelled the Geraldines to retreat'.

After a succession dispute on Maurice's death, his son James became the eleventh earl in 1520 and thereafter there was ongoing conflict with the Butlers of Ormond. Lynch (1896, 140) refers to accounts of Lough Gur in the *Calendar of State Papers*[2] which detail that on 9 August 1536 the Lord Treasurer Butler laid claim to the Desmond lands in right of his wife Joan, daughter to the earl of Desmond, and took Desmond's castle at Lough Gur. A letter from James Butler to Thomas Cromwell in the *Calendar of the Carew Manuscripts*[3] (1515–74, 101–7) noted that 'As Sir John of Desmond's sons would incline to no good conformity we foraged and committed semblable destruction'; as the Desmonds left no ward (guard) at the castle, it was easily taken, and Butler wrote that he 'set up doors and made it defensible, and warded it with my own men' (Donnelly 2009, 81). When James Fitzgerald, the son of Sir John, declared himself the earl of Desmond, the lord deputy, Lord Leonard Grey, and his council of Ireland decided to suppress this claim by force in 1536. They moved into Desmond territory and marched on James's manor at Lough Gur (*ibid.*, 81). On arrival, Lord Deputy Grey found 'Lokkere, a strong castle of James (fitz John) of Desmond, and found it deserted and open; the roof, doors and windows burned or removed' (Westropp 1906–7, 179). Over the following year James achieved a *rapprochement* with the Crown. Brash (B.R.R. 1865, 243) recorded that on 17 December 1537 James, earl of Desmond, from Lough Gur was 'received into great favour by the King'. James went again to England in 1542 with letters of recommendation from Lord Deputy St Leger.

The Great Earl

Queen Elizabeth I succeeded to the English throne in 1558 and Gerald (fitz James) Fitzgerald became the fourteenth earl of Desmond. Gerald was seized by Crown forces in Dublin and, with his wife Eleanor and brother John, was imprisoned for five years in the Tower of London. During this detention he wrote several letters protesting his loyalty (Hayman 1868–9, 416). After his release in 1563, Gerald made a 'Feoffment [grant of possession of a property in land] of his baronies and manors in Co. Limerick to Lords Dunboyne and Curraghmore to be held in trust for himself and his wife, and the survivor' (Grene Barry 1897–1900, 3). The manors in County Limerick were Portdrinarde near Abbeyfeale, Lough Gur, Glenogra, Rathmore and Aney (Hospital) (*ibid.*).

An ongoing feud between Gerald and Thomas Butler, earl of Ormond (Kilkenny and south Tipperary), with political intrigue and sporadic violence, dominated the period 1558–67. Lough Gur is referred to in the 'Unpublished Geraldine documents' in relation to the Desmond–Butler conflict (Hayman 1868–9). Lysaghe McMorishe Moyle O'Connor, an ally of Gerald's, swore in a deposition taken in Kilkenny that on 1 April 1565 he and 'Lysaghe McMoroughe with others of his retinue [were] in the said Earl of Desmonds company at his house of Loughgirre' (*ibid.*, 401–2). Ormond attacked Gerald at the Battle of Affane in 1565 because of the latter's proposed incursion into Decies (Waterford and some parts of south Tipperary). Ormond was victorious and Gerald was captured (McCormack 2005, 99–100). Hayman (1868–9, 415) described Lough Gur as 'the place where some of the followers of Desmond lay, till cured of the wounds received at Affane'. On 1 July 1566 Sir Warham St Leger met with Gerald at Lough Gur (Lynch 1896, 140; McCormack 2005, 104) to resolve the dispute between the earl of Desmond and Sir Maurice of Decies, whose lands were under threat. Gerald was again detained in London in 1567, and his cousin James fitz Maurice took his place as ruler of Desmond.

The first Desmond rebellion (1569–73) was motivated in part by religion but also by Sir Peter Carew's attempts to renew land titles and by a general sense of grievance and dislocation in Munster

(McCormack 2005, 116–19). Humphrey Gilbert became colonel and governor of Munster in 1569 and waged a brutal war against all rebels (*ibid.*, 119). Westropp (1907, 153) described the period as one of 'wholesale surrender of Desmond's castles to the English in 1569', whereby English settlers were given possession of the castles, and during the rebellion many castles were almost ruined, including Aney (Knockainy) Castle.

In 1573 Gerald fitz James Fitzgerald was released from his imprisonment and returned to Ireland. The Crown and the privy council in Whitehall tried to control the earl and to limit his power, issuing him with a series of articles intended to ensure his obedience (McCormack 2005, 127). Gerald was under curfew when he arrived back in Dublin, but under the ruse of going hunting at Grangegorman he simply walked out of Dublin and headed south-west to his lands in Limerick (Edwards 2016, 341). His allies, Rory Oge O'More and Piers Grace, met him with horses and escorted him to the south. On his return to Munster, Gerald received widespread support. 'His wife met him at Bealadrohid[4] and they continued to Lough Gur' (McCormack 2005, 132). Edwards (2016, 342) records that when the earl arrived at Lough Gur 'he was greeted by an assembly of local landowners who gathered at the ancient Gaelic inauguration site that stood close by', and that 'with great ceremony he removed the clothes he had worn since leaving Dublin, his "English apparel", and "put on his Irish raiment"'. The inauguration site may have been located at Grange,[5] where Lynch (1895, 299) noted that 'an ancient line of Munster kings were inaugurated' under the tree near the standing stone at *Cloghavilla*. Changing into Irish dress was an ostentatious affirmation that Gerald wished to continue in his former ways as an independent lord, and he quickly re-established his authority. Wearing Irish dress also contravened an ordinance introduced in 1570 by Sir John Perrot, president of Munster, whereby it was forbidden 'to wear mantels or Irish coats, but to wear some "civil garment", and no maid or single woman shall wear or put on any great roll or kerchief of linen cloth upon their heads, neither any great smock with great sleeves, but to put on hats, caps, French hoods, tippets or some other civil attire upon their heads' (Grene Barry 1897–1900, 5–6). On his return to Lough Gur, Gerald also refused to deliver his castles to Captain Bourchier. Bourchier had been captured by Gerald's cousin, James fitz Maurice, in 1574 and the earl was asked to secure his release (McCormack 2005, 133).

The second Desmond rebellion (1579–83) broke out when James fitz Maurice returned from France and gathered supporters (*ibid.*, 145). Initially it consisted of small-scale skirmishes, and James fitz Maurice was killed by the Clanwilliam Bourkes in August 1579 (*ibid.*, 146). It developed into a Munster-wide military conflict from October 1579 to June 1581 (*ibid.*, 146) and a few pitched battles took place, including one at Monasteranenagh in 1579 in which the earl of Desmond was defeated. In 1579 the lord deputy placed troops in the castles of Rathmore, Lough Gur, Adare and Kilmallock (B.R.R. 1865, 243). Increased English military activity under Lord Arthur Grey in alliance with the Butlers of Ormond saw the imposition of a scorched earth policy and the capture of all the castles in rebel hands (McCormack 2005, 155). Gerald was finally tracked down and killed near Tralee in 1583. According to Hayman (1868–9, 415–16), Gerald

'By his unhappy rebellion, worked the ruin of his house [and] is in popular tradition, the guardian spirit of Loughgur. He is held beneath its waters by enchantment, which will cease, and he shall return to life, when the silver shoes of his grey charger, which he rides over the surface of the lake once in seven years, are worn out.'

Westropp (1907, 154) details the catastrophic effect of the rebellion:

'During the rebellion, ruin seized on numbers of the castles. We know few more terrible records—far more terrible than the most rhetorical history—than that ghastly list of doom in the margins of the Desmond Roll.[6] There we read hundreds of dry, methodical, quiet entries, as unemotional as an account-book, recording the doom of Desmond and his adherents, "slain in rebellion," "by execution," "died attainted," "died in battle," written within and without with death—"sword and fire, red ruin, and the breaking up of laws".'

Elizabethan plantation

Overall, 800,000 acres were confiscated from the earl of Desmond, and in 1586 planters were allocated 'seignories' (manors) of 12,000 acres, 6,000 acres and 4,000 acres (Grene Barry 1897–1900, 8–10). The land grantees (called undertakers) were given specific instructions. Those with 12,000 acres had to enclose a demesne of 2,100 acres and settle six farmers, each holding 400 acres; six freeholders, holding 300 acres each; 42 copyholders, holding 100 acres each; and the rest in 'mean tenure' in 50-, 25- and ten-acre holdings among at least 36 families. Undertakers with 8,000, 6,000 and 4,000 acres had *pro rata* requirements for demesne enclosures and tenants. Every undertaker had to build a castle enclosed by a strong courtyard, and those who got 1,500 acres were required to finish a house and bawn within two years (*ibid.*, 9; Lynch 1895, 248).

Sir George Bourchier was granted 12,880 acres in Lough Gur, Glenogra and Crean in the barony of Small County at the rent of £137 13s. 4d. 'There were eight Englishmen settled on this seignory, the rest was occupied by Irishmen "most in controversy" [whereby the land boundaries were not fixed]' (Grene Barry 1897–1900, 11; Langrishe 1905, 23). Bourchier was required to build 94 houses for tenants and a residence for himself. As the lands had been devastated during the Desmond rebellion, it was some time before the estates became profitable, and Bourchier appears not to have had sufficient funds to build a new house as required in his land grant. It is likely that he occupied the existing tower-house on the north-east of Knockadoon Hill rather than constructing a new house, and from then on it became known by his name. The Bourchier family held tenure at Lough Gur from 1583 to 1641 (Westropp 1906–7, 180).

In 1583 the Desmond roll recorded:

'The Manor of Lough Gur, a large and excellent castle, in a good state of repair; a chief house of the late Earl of Desmond, with an iron door at the entrance, strongly situated at the foot of a round, rocky hill to the east. A fishery is included, called a "Logh", replete with river fish. The castle in itself includes nine separate rooms … and a barbican, built of stone, at an angle of which is a little round turret for defence. There are two entrances [to Knockadoon], that at the east by a narrow "causea" and two doors; the other to the south-west where is another small castle [Black Castle] or peel. An island, an orchard, a garden, and divers other edifices or cottages, with gardens adjoining (where dwell divers tenants)' (*ibid.*, 180).

Bourchier's ownership of the castle is confirmed in 1587, when a petition from Eleanor, the widowed countess of Desmond, stated that the castle was 'one of the strongest that my lord my husband had; and a parcel of my jointure,[7] being the best furnished house I had, my straight charge and commandment to the keepers always was, that none should come within the said castle except it were the Queen's officers, whom I willed should be received at any time. Whereupon the Sheriff of Limerick ... was willingly received ... [and] took possession thereof, and it was in the hands of a keeper for George Bourchier' (Langrishe 1905, 22).

Eleanor was successful in her petition, as Bourchier wrote in 1588 that 'some parts of the manors of Any [Knockainy], Clonegor and Loughe [Lough Gur] [were] taken from him and given to the Countess of Desmond' (*ibid.*, 22). In 1589 Bourchier complained that his lands were in controversy and that the boundaries had not been fixed (*ibid.*, 23). The Calendar of State Papers for 1611 recorded 'The castle and lands of Loughgur, granted to Sir George Bourchier, now Sir John Bourchier. In demesne 14 acres, in fee farm 1,000 acres, leasehold 3,700 acres, small tenants 23. Evicted and delivered land, 2,588 acres. The abated [lowered] rent is £111 14s. He has 9 horse and 15 foot' (Grene Barry 1897–1900, 18).

Overall, the Elizabethan plantation was not entirely a success, as the undertakers lived within a hostile environment and the dispossessed began to regain their lands.

'These English planters suffered "war to the knife" ... the old proprietors or their descendants hastened to repossess themselves of their old estates, and with fire and sword drove out the intruders. The misery of the English ... the wealthier sort leaving their castles ... [and went] into walled towns. The meaner sort were slain—man, woman and child, and such as escaped came all naked into the town' (*ibid.*, 16).

The Bourchier family survived, however, and retained their estates, including the lands of Lough Gur. Westropp (1906–7, 180) noted that the Bourchiers continued to reside there in 1641.

Documents relating to the Elizabethan plantation of Munster in 1622 record the seignory (manor) of Logher as

'Alias Bourchier's Hall, containing 12,880 English acres to Sir George Bourchier, rent 145 pounds 19s and 9d, of which there hath been no abatement though there be much wanting of the number of acres at first granted, as is alleged. And your Majesty's letters for a new survey and abatement of rent and other conditions proportionate hath been procured. The castle of Logher is covered and there hath been little cost bestowed upon it; but it is intended that it shortly be well repaired and a strong bawn built to it' (Dunlop 1924, 130).

George Bourchier

The Bourchier family's original base was in south-east England and they ultimately settled in Essex, where the family rose in prestige and to the title of baron in the fourteenth century (Langrishe 1904, 367). George Bourchier was probably born between 1535 and 1540. He was sent to Ireland as a military captain in 1567, and in 1571 commanded the garrison of Kilmallock, comprising 200 English soldiers, who were to hold the Geraldines in check (*ibid.*, 374). While at Kilmallock, Captain Bourchier and Sir Thomas of Desmond tried to contain the rebellious activities of James fitz Maurice.

Fitz Maurice captured Bourchier in 1574 and held him prisoner for two months. On his release, the queen granted Bourchier lands in Dublin, Kildare, Tipperary, Westmeath and Wexford, and he was knighted in 1579 in Aherlow. At the onset of the Desmond rebellion, Bourchier was asked to defend Kilmallock. He wrote to the earl of Ormond, saying that he had not received four months' pay for the soldiers, was short of provisions and had 'not fifty pounds of [gun] powder' (*ibid.*, 378). Part of Desmond's forces were in south Cork (Youghal and Imokilly) and the rest were in the woods in the Glen of Aherlow, where Bourchier made a sortie against them in April 1580, killing 60 (*ibid.*, 378). He was promoted to colonel of the army of Munster and was asked to ravage the Desmond lands in Kerry. In September 1580 he sent 1,400 cows and stud horses to Askeaton Castle. He returned to Kilmallock in February 1581 and again complained to the privy council that he had insufficient provisions for his 400 soldiers.

After the suppression of the Desmond rebellion the military companies, including that of Sir George Bourchier, were disbanded in 1581 and 1582. Bourchier left for England in 1581 to look after his estate there. He was then in his forties and he married Martha Howard. The union is described as a 'love match, for there was no great fortune to be obtained on either side' (Langrishe 1905, 21). The Bourchiers had seven sons; those commemorated on a memorial slab erected by George and Martha in St Canice's Cathedral, Kilkenny, were the infants Charles and Fredrick Philip Bourchier, who died in 1584 and 1587 (Langrishe 1904). Lady Bourchier died in October 1589 and was buried in Christ Church Cathedral in Dublin. In September 1605 George Bourchier wrote to request the earl of Salisbury's favour for his sons, as his fortunes were not good and he 'leaves poor children, the most miserable sons of an unhappy father' (Langrishe 1905, 25). He died two days later, leaving three sons.

The Sugán Earl rebellion

A period of relative peace ensued after the second Desmond rebellion (1579–83) until the last few years of the 1590s. A rebellion in Ulster led by Hugh O'Neill and Hugh O'Donnell was mirrored in Munster by the Geraldine revolt (1598–1601) led by the Sugán Earl of Desmond, James (fitz Thomas) Fitzgerald, and his clansmen with the aim of restoring the earldom of Desmond. Westropp (1907, 155) described the time: 'All seemed fairly settled, when, as the century drew to a close, the rebellion of the Sugán Earl, James of Desmond, broke out [in 1598]. Had the English done their duty at the outset, it might have been nipped in the bud, or greatly restricted.' George Bourchier had sublet his manor house at Lough Gur to Robert Rowley, who gave it in charge to Ulick Browne, and in 1598 Browne gave it to the followers of the Sugán Earl (Langrishe 1905, 24). Bourchier's Castle was of strategic importance, as it 'commanded the communications between Kilmallock and Limerick, so that for two years previous the road was impassable for anyone in the English interest' (Dowd 1896, 72). The castle 'was held against Queen Elizabeth by the rebel John Fitz Thomas' (Shirley 1867, 288). In 1600 Captain Francis Slingsby was commander of the lord president of Munster's foot company and garrison at Kilmallock, where a strong force of troops was stationed in order to control and harass the Geraldines (*ibid.*, 288). A surprise attack on Bourchier's Castle on 29 April 1600 aimed to carry off the cattle on which the maintenance of the garrison at Lough Gur depended. Dowd (1896, 72) gives an account of the raid, which was narrated in the *Pacata Hibernia* (Stafford 1633, 80–4):

'The party, consisting of one hundred and twenty foot and twenty horse under the command of Captain Slingsby, set out from Kilmallock in the night and concealed themselves in the neighbourhood, waiting till the herds would be led out across the causeway in the morning to graze in the adjacent meadows. The cattle were brought out as usual, and the escort suspected no danger. Suddenly the English, watching their opportunity, overpowered the guards by a sudden and unexpected rush, captured the cattle, and hurried off with them towards Kilmallock. The garrison sallied forth, a sharp skirmish ensued, but the Irish were unable to obtain possession of their cattle, and their supplies must have been seriously diminished till some successful foray on their part restored the commissariat.'

Surrender of Bourchier's Castle, 1600

The Sugán Earl's rebellion in Munster was quashed by Sir George Carew, who landed in Waterford in April 1600 and became the lord president of Munster. Carew's arrival saw the tide turn against the earl of Desmond. An account of the surrender of Bourchier's Castle in the text of *Pacata Hibernia* included a description of the 'rendering of Loughguyree in May 1600' (Stafford 1633, 80–4; see Appendix 1). Bourchier's Castle was held by John fitz Thomas, younger brother of the Sugán Earl, who left the castle in the charge of Owen Grome (or Groome) when he went to join his men in Aherlow. Grome was described as 'a stranger from the North' (*ibid.*, 80), suggesting that he was a mercenary soldier. John fitz Thomas had ridden out with two men, one named John Coppinger and the other named Nugent. Nugent had been in the employment of Sir Thomas Norris, a previous president of Munster, but had deserted the English service and attached himself to the Sugán Earl, rising high in fitz Thomas's favour. Despite being one of his most trusted followers, Nugent attempted to kill fitz Thomas but was prevented from doing so by Coppinger (Dowd 1896, 73–4).

The following extract from the *Pacata Hibernia* (in Elizabethan English) narrates Carew's first reconnoitre of Bourchier's Castle:

'He found it to bee a place of exceeding strength, by reason that it was an Island, encompassed by a deepe lough, the breadth thereof being in the narrowest place a Calievers shot over, upon one side thereof standieth a verie strong castle, which at the time was manned with a good garrison, for there was within the Island, John fitz Thomas, with two hundred men at least, which shewed themselves prepared to defend the place. The President being approached within shot, to discover the ground, they discharged some twentie muskets at him and his company but without hurt done: and having effected as much he intended at that time, they casting foorth some reviling speeches, he left the place' (Stafford 1633, 80).

Owen Groome betrayed the castle for a pardon and a sum of 60 pounds, and so Carew took it 'without striking a blow' (Dowd 1896, 75). The surrender at least ensured that the castle survived, whereas after this 'Carew went on to waste castles in Clanwilliam' (Westropp 1907, 155–6). George Carew[8] wrote of the castle that 'It standeth very pleasantly upon the foot of an Iland [island], containing 80 acres, environed with great water and mountains, and rocks without same; munited and warded more by nature than by man's hand'.

After the defeat of the Sugán Earl, English settlement resulted in almost 40 years of peace in which 'The English interest had rather fallen away than increased, and some of the stern Elizabethan settlers were represented by men holding the faith and political opinions of their grandfathers' opponents' (*ibid.*, 158). Thus it would seem that these English settlers acquiesced in the relative autonomy from English governance. Under the new dynasty, 'the exhausted land had rest for nearly forty years, though a broken and irritated rest' (*ibid.*, 158).

The 1641 rebellion and the siege of Bourchier's Castle

The 1641 rebellion began as an attempt by the dispossessed landowners to recover their lands and evolved into an alliance or confederation of Catholics, including Gaelic and 'Old English', who determined to defend their religion, their rights and their property. The revolt cost thousands of lives and was finally suppressed by the arrival of Oliver Cromwell. Violent acts in County Limerick were relatively few; according to Westropp (1907, 159), 'most of the outrages named in the depositions were ordinary acts of war, "commandeering" horses, cattle, and supplies, cutting off scouts and messengers, and laying ambushes'. Dineley remarked that Bourchier's Castle in 'the time of the Irish rebellion was always a garrison for one side or other; beside, being an island of above a mile in circumference encompassed with a large and deep Lough or Poole, it was a receptacle not only for man but beast to defend from the enemy' (Shirley 1867, 195).

The 1641 siege of Bourchier's Castle during the Confederate Wars (1641–52) was recorded in depositions[9] given by Constables William Weekes and Richard Harte in 1653 in Kilkenny (Welply 1919). The castle was besieged for 24 weeks from early February 1641. A besieging force of 1,500 from the baronies of Small County, Clanwilliam and Connagh and other places, under the command of Dr Higgins, gathered near Bourchier's Castle (see Appendix 2). An account in the 1641 Depositions noted:

> 'Lough Gur still held out under William Weekes, but the garrison was "watched and waited on" by a Dr Higgins and the Irish. The blockade was varied by occasional sallies of the garrison, in one of which they burned the village of Ballynegalliagh [Ballynagallagh]. The Irish, fearing a like attack on Bruff, went in force to the hill near it. The English fell back, but some of Lacy's force went to Gransha [Grange], on the shore of the lake, and took two men, servants to Weekes. John Lacy gave strict orders on the safety of the prisoners; but during his absence, and despite his orders, and frantic protests of his wife, they were taken and hanged on the gallows of Bruff' (Westropp 1907, 161).

Dame Barbery Browne was one of those blockaded in Lough Gur Castle from March 1641, until 'Eddie Lacy seized her horses and household stuff when she fled to Castletown' (*ibid.*, 161). The Depositions recorded that the castle was surrendered to Lord Castleconnell.

Cromwellian plantation

The arrival of Cromwellian forces in 1649—the 'New Model Army' of 12,000 soldiers complete with siege train—saw the establishment of a network of fortified positions (Donnelly 2009, 86–7). A number of castles in County Limerick, including Bourchier's Castle, were reused as fortifications; 'the new role was not as a fortified residence but as a defended garrison' (*ibid.*, 88). In 1652, after the Cromwellian Wars, the population in Ireland was only slightly over half of what it was in 1641, and the country is described as 'depleted of men and money, stricken with fire and sword, without cattle or growing crops, and with a plague-stricken and starving population' (Grene Barry 1900, 24). Land forfeited by the Catholic population was given to English Protestants, many of whom had invested in the Cromwellian campaigns. Most of the soldiers who were granted land sold it to their officers (*ibid.*, 29). 'About two-thirds of the county of Limerick changed hands in the … Desmond and the Cromwellian settlements' (*ibid.*, 32). There was no change in landownership at Lough Gur, where Henry Bourchier, son of George, remained in possession (Grene Barry 1903b, 211). The castle was garrisoned by English troops and in 1653 Capt. Jas. Synnocke got 100s.[10] 'for the garrison at Logighur', and as much 'for corne taken from Edmond Rawley by the garrison' (Account Rolls, Limerick District,[11] 1650–8, 8).

Bourchier's Castle 1655–1800

In 1655 'Loghguir castle and six houses were in the possession of Henry Earl of Bath', the son of George Bourchier (Simington 1938, 10). On Henry's death Bourchier's Castle was inherited by his widow, Elizabeth (Lynch 1895, 301). In 1681 Dineley noted Bourchier's Castle as a 'castle of great strength … belonging to Countess of Bath … with ye late buildings erected by the conveniency of the present inhabitant, Mr John Bayly [Baylee]' (Shirley 1867, 195). Baylee had come to Ireland 'as a confidential agent to the Fane family', and his descendants were still at Lough Gur in 1833 (Crofton Croker 1833, 105).

As Henry and Elizabeth had no children, the Bourchier estates ultimately came to Sir Henry Vane or Fane. In 1718 Charles Fane Esq. of Bassilden was created baron of Lough Gur (Lynch 1895, 301). His only son, Charles, died without issue in 1782 and his estates in County Limerick devolved on his sisters' descendants, of whom Mary had married Jerome, Count de Salis, in Switzerland, and Dorothy had married John, earl of Sandwich. The Irish property was divided after some years between Count de Salis and the earl of Sandwich (*ibid.*).

According to Crofton Croker's (1833, 106) description of Bourchier's Castle, which was no longer inhabited, 'about the year 1700 Mr John Baylee built the present dwelling-house, in the fashion of the period, adjacent to the castle'. Croker also recorded in a footnote that 'on a pier of the stable gateway is sculptured the initials of Henry, son of John and probably Susanna Baylee'. The residence of Count de Salis was Grange House (Lynch 1895, 301). Lynch (1913, 11) also noted that 'about the year 1700 Thomas O'Connellan, Minstrel-Bard, died at Bourchier's Castle, when he was the guest of Mr Baily'. The Sligo-born O'Connellan was buried at New Church (*Teampall Nua*) in an unlettered tomb, at the north-eastern gable of the church.

BLACK CASTLE (KILLALOUGH CASTLE)

The poorly preserved remains of Black Castle consist of a tower on the western side, a bawn wall with an entrance gateway and an artificial causeway extending from the gateway across a tract of ground that either was under lake water or was bogland prior to the draining of Lough Gur in the late 1840s (Fig. 11.19). Grene Barry (1903a, 196) wrote that the lake here was 'at its narrowest, and was fordable, to judge from that portion between the two castles, which was drained many years ago, and is now a cutaway bog, and over the level of the present lake'. A strong wall that extended from Black Castle along the southern edge of Knockadoon Hill to Bourchier's Castle suggests that both were in contemporary use.

Fig. 11.19—Black Castle:
Ordnance Survey map showing
castle and causeway.

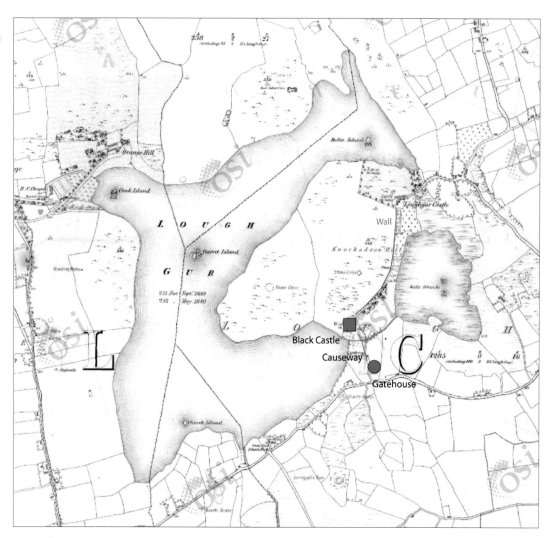

The tower within the bawn wall is in poor condition and the west side has fallen. Both Dowd (1896, 70) and Westropp (1906–7, 181) gave similar measurements of '25 feet [7.6m] by 13½ feet [4.1m] inside. The lower story is vaulted; the sides 35 feet [10.6m] high to the south, 12 feet [3.6m] high elsewhere, and 7½ feet [2.2m] thick.' The tower stood to a height of three storeys when it was sketched by Du Noyer in the 1860s (Fig. 11.20). A watercolour possibly by Mrs Croker and dated to *c.* 1870 also shows it as more intact than it is today (Fig. 11.21). The tower was rectangular in plan and contained the reception hall where business was transacted and family rooms, as well as the kitchen and stores. A stone vault remains over the ground floor, and the imprint of wickerwork used to support the vaulting during construction is visible in the undersurface of the arch. Dowd (1896, 70) noted that 'the arched roof of the lower storey is still remaining'. Part of the stone stair at Black Castle also remains. The tower does not survive to roof level but Dineley's sketch (Fig. 11.18) suggests stepped battlements. Hayman (1868–9, 415), referring to Dineley's drawing (1681), noted that the 'old Desmond fortress, called the Black Castle, and which was ruinous even in Dineley's time, is shown in his sketch'. Dowd (1896, 70) also referred to the foundations of an extensive series of

Fig. 11.20—Black Castle: Du Noyer's sketch (1860s).

Fig. 11.21—Black Castle c. 1870.

Fig. 11.22—Black Castle: bawn wall and entrance (Joseph Lennon).

buildings adjacent to the gateway within the bawn wall enclosure at Black Castle.

Entrance was via a stone causeway guarded by a gateway (Fig. 11.22) with surrounds of dressed limestone; rebates in the walls indicate the locations of internal bolts. The imprint of wickerwork is also visible in the gateway arch. Brash (B.R.R. 1865, 243) recorded that 'the entrance gateway [is] still perfect, showing in the jambs the massive stone rings and sockets in which the pivots of the gates swung'. Lynch (1895, 247) wrote that a 'very strong arched gateway in this wall was the entrance into the hill. Over the arch, which is about fifteen feet [4.5m] in depth, was another strong building, and on each side were two lodgements with loopholes.' These loopholes or embrasures are narrow on the external (southern) side and widen internally. The openings are too confined for the use of a longbow and the crossbow was probably the weapon of choice at these locations. The wide inner embrasure allowed the archer scope to shoot sideways as well as directly ahead. This type of defence remained in use after the advent of firearms. The bawn wall of Black Castle formed an outer defence for the main tower and was constructed from large limestone blocks (Fig. 11.22). It continued eastwards and joined a wall on the eastern lower slope of Knockadoon Hill which extended to Bourchier's Castle (Fig. 11.19).

The stone causeway zigzags southward and was probably just above or under the water level before the lake was drained; any visitor to the castle would need to have known the route or else chance losing the track and ending up in the water. There is a break or fosse across the causeway at a distance of about 70m from the bawn wall which must also have proved a hidden danger. Dowd (1896, 70) says that 'at the island extremity the approach was intersected by a moat crossed by a drawbridge, and the island was entered through a strongly fortified gateway'. He also described the causeway construction as being 'between two walls of stone, and is higher on the western side than on the eastern'. Hayman (1868–9, 415) wrote of Knockadoon as being 'connected with the land by a causeway, solidly built of stone 432 feet [131.6m] long, by 22 feet [6.7m] wide. It is 7½ feet [2.3m] high on the eastern and about 10 feet [3m] on the western side.'

A gatehouse on the southern (landward) side of the causeway is shown on Dineley's 1681 sketch (Fig. 11.18) but is marked 'site of' on the first-edition Ordnance Survey (*c.* 1840) maps of Lough Gur, and so the standing building had probably been removed by that stage. The foundations of the gatehouse and part of the causeway were removed in the 1970s. Hayman (1868–9, 415) described the external gatehouse and causeway as 'the only approach to the island, was defended by a castle (long since levelled to the ground, but shown on Dineley's sketch) placed 77 feet [23.5m] from the causeway. The foundations of this castellated gateway are quite visible, and are 23½ feet [7m] square. 162 feet [49.3m].' Black Castle may have fallen out of use in the sixteenth century, as in 1536 Lord Grey noted that the castle of James of Desmond was deserted and open (Westropp 1906–7, 179).

Black Castle was frequently confused with Bourchier's Castle in early descriptions. Brash (B.R.R. 1865, 243) wrote of the Desmond fortress on Knockadoon, 'which before the lowering of the lake and the invention of artillery, must indeed have been a formidable stronghold in the hands of a native chief. The only entrance to this island was by a causeway at the south side, built of large blocks of regular masonry; at the end of this causeway, on the island, are the remains of a tower.' Dowd (1896, 70) wrote of Black Castle: 'Geraldines constructed here one of their most formidable military works … the castle [the gatehouse on the landward side of the causeway] on the south end has disappeared. Black Castle on the island is still standing, though greatly injured.'

GEROID ISLAND

There are now no surface traces of the former castle on Geroid Island (Fig. 11.23). Westropp (1906–7, 181) considered it to be a 'doubtful site', although he recorded (1907, 153) on 'Garrod's Island, in the lake, traces of a building, said to be a castle of Earl Garrod, whose ghost is doomed to ride over the lake once in seven years, till the silver horseshoes are worn away'. Crofton Croker (1833, 105) described Geroid Island as 'the site of a small castle, of which the base is still visible. The castle must have been a picturesque object, has been pulled down by Mr Croker of Grange for building material … and with the stones he erected a lime-kiln on the opposite shore.' Lynch (1895, 245–6) noted that 'On Garrode Crannog are the remains of an old stone fortification … amongst the rest, the Desmond fortifications on Knockadoon have suffered dreadfully—one of the castles having been actually taken away piecemeal to build a mansion in the neighbourhood'. The castle was described by Brash (B.R.R. 1865, 243) as 'the remains of an octagon building, the ruined wall enclosing it is 8 feet [2.4m] thick, and built of heavy masonry; when the lake was lowered a small stone circle and a cistvaen were found on the shore, which had been under water previously'. Access to Geroid Island may have been by boat. O'Kelly (1941, 56) noted that a causeway built on wooden piles once connected the island with Knockadoon, and it is possible that these piles were exposed when the lake was lowered in the late 1840s, although none are now visible. A letter to Seán P. Ó Ríordáin from Count John de Salis in December 1938[12] confirmed that there was no surviving trace of wooden piles in the lake; de Salis wrote that 'I have never seen a trace of anything of the kind [wooden causeway], and I have searched and waded all over it when I was a boy, looking for signs of crannogs or a causeway'.

Fig. 11.23—Geroid Island in the centre of the lake, with Knockfennell (right) and Knockadoon (left).

Excavations on the west side of Garret Island (Geroid Island) undertaken in 1956 by David Liversage confirmed the existence of the castle on the island and exposed what was identified as 'a large circular pile of stones resembling a crannog … [which] preceded the building of Desmond's Castle' (Liversage 1958, 80). The excavation established that this stone platform was over 2m in depth and 40m in diameter. A high wall built on the platform was described as 'built with mortar, but has now almost fallen, follows the circumference of the stone platform in a series of straight legs, and so encloses a polygon. Within the enclosure are traces of sunken rooms, and the wall contains a suggestion of an entrance and a few surviving quoin stones' (*ibid.*, 67). The description is imprecise as regards the plan of the castle foundations, although the term 'polygon' suggests a multi-sided structure. Such a polygonal plan is unusual for an Irish castle of any period, although Westropp (1906–7, 178) noted an octagonal tower-house at Glenogra to the west of Lough Gur which was built between 1400 and 1420 by Thomas, earl of Desmond (O'Kelly 1941, 12). A castle at Shanid which may have been built by John of Shanid is polygonal in plan, and the earliest historical record of Shanid dates from 1230 (Leask 1973, 42).

Gearóid Iarla

Brash (B.R.R. 1865, 243) ascribed the name of the castle on Garret Island to 'the unfortunate Earl of Desmond' or Gerald fitz James Fitzgerald (fourteenth earl of Desmond). Local tradition, however, suggests that the castle was built by Gerald (Gearóid Iarla), fourth[13] earl of Desmond. Gearóid Iarla is associated with the myths and legends of Lough Gur and is credited with the composition of

345

sophisticated bardic poetry (McCormack 2005, 46). Little is known of his life, although it is documented that he was captured at the Battle of Monasteranenagh in 1370, when Brian O'Brien of Thomond defeated the Desmonds (*ibid.*, 39). In Graves's (1869) pedigree of the Desmonds, Gerald is listed as the Poet Fourth Earl of Desmond, son of Ellinor or Aveline third wife of Maurice Fitz Thomas. Ellinor was the daughter of Nicholas Fitzmaurice, third lord of Kerry and Lixnaw. Gerald had two sons, John and James.

Gearóid Iarla was lord justice of Ireland in 1370. He disappeared in 1398 and Graves (1869, 463) states that he 'is believed by the peasantry to live beneath the waters of Lough Gur. Carew and the Cotton Manuscript say he was slain by O'Brien in Thomond, 1398.' Gearóid Iarla ruled for 40 years (Curtis 1938, 280–1) and the castle on Garrett Island is reputed to have been built in his time (1358–98).

Gilbert (1865, 227–8) wrote of Gerald as follows:

'On the retirement of Duke Lionel, in 1367, the Viceroyalty was committed to Gerald, fourth Earl of Desmond, styled "the poet", who, from his learning and acquirements, was generally regarded as a magician. Some fragments of Anglo-Norman verse, entitled "Proverbs of the Earl of Desmond", still survive. Becoming closely allied with the natives, the Earl obtained royal license to send his son James to be fostered and brought up among the O'Briens, in Thomond, notwithstanding the prohibition under the "Statute of Kilkenny". The native writers describe Earl Gearoitt, or Gerald, as a lord of marvelous bounty and mirth, cheerful in conversation, charitable in his deeds, easy of access, a witty and ingenious composer of Gaelic poetry, a learned and profound chronicler, and one of the foreign nobles that held the learning of Erin and its professors in greatest reverence.[14] The Earl lived long in Irish legends, according to which, he once in seven years revisited his castle in Lough Air, or Gur, near Limerick. The Four Masters thus mention him:— "A.D. 1398. Gerald, Earl of Desmond, a man of gaiety and affability, the most distinguished of the English of Ireland, and also of many of the Irish, for his attainments and knowledge of the Irish language, of poetry, history, and of other branches of literature which he had acquired, died after he had gained the victory of repentance".'

GRANGE CASTLE

Grange Castle is to the west of Lough Gur and stands on the summit of a rock overlooking surrounding marshy ground. The Ordnance Survey (1840) recorded '*Cathair Chinn Chon*' and 'Grange Castle (in ruins)' on the same rock. Lynch (1906–7, 128), writing on Lough Gur, described the location of *Cathair Chin Chon* as being 'about a mile [1.6km] to the south-west of the lake, at Rockbarton' in Caherguillamore, contradicting the Ordnance Survey map location.

Westropp (1906–7, 179) noted Grange Castle as being on Carriganilea Rock and as having foundations of '40 feet [12.1m] by 30 feet [9.1m] and fragments 10 feet [3m] overall and 6½ feet [2m] thick'. Dowd (1896, 76–7) described Grange Castle as follows: 'The crag and walls are covered with lichen, moss and ivy, and it is barely possible to distinguish the one from the other. No window or doorway can be found in the little that is left of the castle, and the outer casing of walls appears to have been removed.' Lynch (1895, 251) also noted of Grange Rock Castle that 'most of the stones were taken from this castle to build Raheen House, which is now in ruins'.

Westropp (1906–7, 179) recorded that the lands around Grange were one of the 'granges' or farms of Magio (Monasteranenagh). The pipe rolls[15] for 1348–9 confirmed that the abbot of Magio accounts for issues of lands in Grangehawe (Gransha) in the king's hands by attainder (conviction) of Maurice, earl of Desmond. In 1583 the Peyton survey[16] detailed the Graunsha de Lough (Gur), or Castleanedroyde. The Civil Survey in 1655 identified Grangew (Grange) as being in the tenure of Lord Bath (Henry Bourchier) (*ibid.*).

CAHERGUILLAMORE

There are now no visible traces of this castle and there is also some confusion about its location. Westropp (1906–7, 178–9) noted that 'The castle is not marked on the Ordnance Survey but called "Rockbarton Castle" in the Ordnance Survey Name Books' and described the remains as a 'rectangular foundation, 150 feet [45.7m] to east of a stone ring, which the Ordnance Survey Letters record as having been built with the ruins in 1835'. The castle may have been in the demesne of Caherguillamore House and it is possible that the stone circle erected in 1835 was a folly within the demesne landscape. Excavations at Caherguillamore in 1940 (Chapter 10) uncovered a nucleated settlement of thirteenth- and fourteenth-century date (Ó Ríordáin and Hunt 1942) and these houses may have been in the environs of a castle. It is possible that Westropp (1906–7, 179) misidentified the footings of medieval houses for those of the castle.

The castle was recorded in 1289 as 'Cathyrgilmore' in the plea rolls.[17] In 1298 it was held by Thomas fitz Maurice (*ibid.*, 178). Westropp recorded that in 1564 Dominic White of Limerick held 'Cahiringuillimore, redeemed from the late Earl of Desmond, and purchased from its rightful owner' (*ibid.*, 178–9). This castle was probably a tower-house built sometime in the late fourteenth or early fifteenth century. In 1583 the Desmond rolls record the castle and vill of 'Cahir a Gillimo', and 'Kaheragyllymoore in Any' is recorded in the Peyton Survey. According to the inquisitions chancery[18] James Stritch held the castle in 1639, as did his grandfather, J. Stritch, and in 1665 the Down Survey[19] confirmed the castle as being held by W. and E. Stritch. The Settlement Act[20] recorded that in 1667 the castle was granted to Capt. Robert Morgan and to A. Reymon.

RAWLEYSTOWN CASTLE

This castle, described on the Ordnance Survey map as 'Rawleystown Court', is in low-lying ground to the south of the Camoge River (Fig. 11.1). The castle at Rawleystown no longer stands but the bawn wall remains. The Down Survey (1655–7) shows a square tower within a bawn wall with turrets at the angles (Fig. 11.24). Westropp (1906–7, 186) recorded that 'The two Down Survey maps show it as a battlemented peel tower in a square court, with turrets at each angle'. The bawn wall is best preserved along the northern side, and sections of the flanking towers remain (Figs 11.25–26). Rawleystown tower-house was described by Fitzgerald and McGregor (1826, 304) as 'an ancient building consisting of a bawn 180 feet [55m] long and 120 feet [36.5m] wide, the wall of which is twelve feet [3.65m] high and four feet [1.2m] thick', with the tower-house itself being 'a strong house of lime and stone, three stories high, and eighty feet [24.4m] long by thirty feet [9.1m] in breadth'. A photograph[21] taken around 1940 (Fig. 11.27) shows the extant gable wall of a three-storey building with large windows, a central fireplace and chimney.

From architectural details (windows and flankers) Fitzgerald and McGregor (1826, 305) suggested that Rawleystown Castle was 'built in the reign of James I,[22] possibly granted to Mr Carew Raleigh son of Sir Walter Raleigh or to Captain George Raleigh, his nephew'. Lynch (1895, 248) cites 'Raleighstown' as an example of the Elizabethan land grants of 1,500 acres, and the estate is supposed to have been granted to Carew Raleigh, son of Sir Walter Raleigh, 'as a sort of expiation [compensation] for Sir Walter's

Fig. 11.24—Down Survey sketch of Rawleystown Castle.

Fig. 11.25—Rawleystown Castle: bawn wall.

Fig. 11.26—Rawleystown
Castle: bawn wall.

death'. This attribution to the family of Sir Walter Raleigh is disputed by Westropp (1906–7, 186), who recorded: 'The Rawleys or de Releics are one of the oldest Anglo-Norman families in Co. Limerick, having settled there before 1222. In later days they have been confused with the supposed descendants of Sir Walter Raleigh.' Westropp attributes this error to Fitzgerald and McGregor.

Westropp noted significant dates in the history of the castle as follows. In 1587 the fiants[23] record that Sir E. Fytton was granted the head-rent of James Rowley of Ballinrowley. In 1600 the fiants record the pardon of Richard Rowlie, or Raleigh, of Raleighstown after the Sugán Earl's rising. The patent rolls[24] record that in 1607 the head-rent of James Rawley of Ballinrowley was granted to Nicolas Haward. Inquisition chancery records show that in 1609 the castle was held by D. O'Grady of Kilballyowen, and the patent rolls record that O'Grady and James Rawley were granted the castle in 1610. In 1655 'Rawlighstown' castle was ruinous and owned by Redmond Rawley. Lenihan (1866, 746) gives the epitaph (in the Church of the Recollects, Paris) of 'Messire Michel Raleigh de la famille de Raleighstown', Knight of the Order of St Louis, who died in 1732, aged 76. The Settlement Act confirmed Lord Kingstown as owner in 1667. The castle was held in 1709 by E. Croker.

CAHERELLY CASTLES

Westropp (1906–7) recorded 56 castles in Clanwilliam Barony and practically all belonged to the Bourkes. 'Both Hynes and Clanchy [Clancy] got their estates through intermarriage with the Bourkes' (Grene Barry 1905–8). There were two tower-houses in Caherelly, known as the 'East Castle' and the 'West Castle'. The East Castle, also known as the 'Black Castle', was the O'Heynes'

349

Fig. 11.27—Rawleystown Castle: three-storey building within bawn wall *c.* 1940.

Fig. 11.28—Caherelly Castle (Joseph Lennon).

residence; it was repaired by a Mr Hannan before 1826 but was levelled before 1840 (*ibid.*, 138). Westropp (1906–7, 91) recorded the East Castle as a tower-house '60 feet [18.2m] high and 20 feet [6m] wide' (Fig. 11.28). The West Castle was 'built near a former lake, 300 yards [183m] west of the church … [and was] repaired and roofed by Michael Furnell some sixty years ago [1845–8] and was in a good state of preservation' (Grene Barry 1905–8, 138). One of the castles is depicted on the Down Survey (1655–7) as a tower-house with battlements and at least four storeys high (Fig. 11.29).

The history of the Caherelly castles is recorded sporadically. The plea rolls document a suit of J. de Norragh concerning Caherelly in 1283 and a dispute in 1323 between Almeric de Bellofago and T. Fitz Rhys about Milltown watermill (Westropp 1906–7, 91). The Desmond rolls recorded 'Carelii duo castell' (two castles of Caherelly) in the ownership of William Bourke in 1583. Westropp noted that Bourke's successor, Tadeus O'Heyne, died there in 1599 (*ibid.*). The inquisition chancery documented that in 1622 O'Heyne's son Conor died and his son 'Donat entailed [settled on his heirs] the castle, hall, bawn, and vill of Le Caherelly and in 1629 Donat was pardoned for alienation of Caherelly West'. Dan Hayne held Caherelly in 1655 (Simington 1938, 28). Tadeus O'Heyne's sons or grandsons, Teige and Donal, had possession of Caherelly East and West, and their castles and lands of about 1,200 Irish acres were granted to Sir W. King as part of the Cromwellian plantation in 1667. Caherelly West was occupied by Surgeon Owen Connory in 1677; he sold it to Patrick Furnell,

Fig. 11.29—Down Survey sketch of Caherelly Castle.

who died in 1750 and whose table tomb is in Caherelly graveyard (Grene Barry 1905–8). The connection of the O'Heynes with Caherelly remained at least until 1748, when Hynes of Cahirelly and Clanchy of Ballyvorneen were the only gentry between Ballinaguard and O'Brien's Bridge who were not Bourkes (Fitzgerald and McGregor 1826, 284).

Grene Barry (1905–8) recounted a romance of Caherelly Castle in the *Journal of the Limerick Field Club*. The background was a cattle raid at Caherelly. There was some enmity between the Bourkes of Caherelly and the Fitzgeralds (Desmonds), as the Bourkes took sides against the Desmonds. The Camoge River divided the Desmond lands from those of the Bourkes, and Caherelly Castle was the nearest stronghold to the Fitzgeralds at Lough Gur, being only two and a half miles (4km) away across the ford of *Ath-fhada*, or Longford Bridge. The Fitzgeralds of Lough Gur Castle raided Bourke's cattle while William Bourke was away with his kinsman of Castleconnell fighting the O'Briens of Thomond. 'The Fitzgeralds were noted robbers, and used to drive cattle of their neighbours whenever they got a chance.' Only an old man, William's daughter's tutor Teige O'Heyne and a boy remained at Caherelly Castle. Teige O'Heyne, the old man and the boy set out to rescue the cattle. They waited until the Fitzgeralds had to cross a ford in the Camoge at Longford Bridge. When they saw the raiders in the middle of the ford, they attacked, turning the cattle back; three of the robbers were killed and the cattle were saved. The daughter fell in love with the tutor and eventually married him in St Aille's Church, so O'Heyne succeeded to the Bourke estate at Caherelly.

ARCHAEOLOGICAL EXCAVATIONS

It is unknown whether the main excavation campaigns of Seán P. Ó Ríordáin included any investigation of the tower-houses on Knockadoon. M.J. O'Kelly referred to some trial excavation at the base of the garderobe chute at Bourchier's Castle but no record of this survives.

Car-park excavations

Archaeological excavations (1977–8) in advance of the car-park development at Lough Gur uncovered two complete skeletons and parts of a third (Cleary 1983, 72; Fraher 1984). The graves were located to the north-east of Bourchier's Castle, outside the surrounding moat and gatehouse depicted in Dineley's sketch of 1681 (Fig. 11.18). The graves were shallow and aligned north–south with the heads to the north. This alignment is not usual in the Christian rite and the bodies were also interred without coffins, suggesting that the graves were hastily dug and the bodies thrown into holes in the ground. The complete skeletons were of young males aged in their mid-twenties and relatively tall. It is possible that both lost their lives in some attack on Bourchier's Castle, perhaps during the 1641 siege or during an earlier violent incident. Both skeletons showed abnormalities in their bones that would have given them a 'freakish' appearance. One had considerable outward bulging at the back of his head and a low, prominent forehead. The other man had a number of abnormalities, including some scoliosis or curvature of the spine; his skull bones were distorted and asymmetrical, giving the impression that his face was being squashed over to the left side, and he had an old fracture in his left hand which left it twisted and bent forward. He also had crowding in his teeth, and an extra tooth had grown between his front teeth. Little survived of the third skeleton, which was buried close to the surface and may have been disturbed by ploughing.

Paving that extended (north/south) across the eastern edge of the excavated area continued beyond the limits of the excavation under the modern road that leads into Lough Gur (Cleary 1982b, fig. 2). The paving was due east of Bourchier's Castle and may have been laid as a trackway out of the gatehouse on the east side of the tower-house; this gateway was probably built by the countess of Bath in the mid-seventeenth century. Finds from the surface of the paved area included one complete and two fragmentary horseshoes of twelfth/thirteenth-century date, two broken iron knives, an iron pin fragment, a hone fragment and a broken bone spindle-whorl. The pottery from the pavement surface included seven sherds of mid-fourteenth-century locally made wares, which may have been incorporated into the paving during the construction of the trackway. Four sherds of seventeenth-century English pottery were probably contemporary with the use of the paved surface (*ibid.*, 87). A shelter of rectangular plan recorded in the car-park excavations may have been some type of byre or animal pen (*ibid.*, 86). Its foundation trenches measured *c.* 6m (north/south) by 5m (east/west) and were open-ended on the northern side. Seventeenth-century pottery from north Devon was recovered from over the foundation trenches and probably dates the construction. The foundation of a 3.3m-wide stone wall which traversed the car-park excavation area in an east/west direction lay over the paved area and may also have been related to activity at Bourchier's Castle. German stoneware from the basal levels of the wall suggests a seventeenth-century construction date. Other finds recovered from the topsoil in the car-park site included seventeenth-century pottery

from north Devon and German stoneware, which were likely to relate to the later occupation at Bourchier's Castle. English clay pipes dating from 1610–40 may have been lost by Bourchier's troops stationed at the castle, while English and Irish clay pipes dating from 1650–90 possibly originated during or after the Cromwellian campaigns. A copper halfpenny (Fig. 11.30) countermarked with five castles arranged in a circle and minted for the Confederate Catholics in 1642–3 was also recovered.

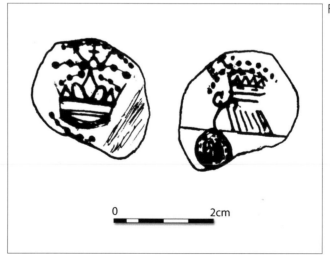

Fig. 11.30—Confederate coin.

0   2cm

Fig. 11.31—Plan of Site J.

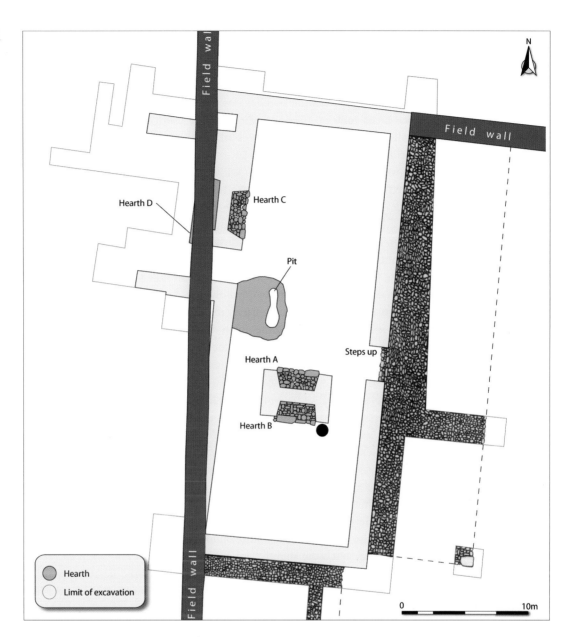

Site J, Knockadoon

An excavation on Knockadoon Hill carried out by Seán P. Ó Ríordáin and Caoimhín Ó Danachair in 1945 exposed the basal levels of a seventeenth-century house at Site J (Ó Ríordáin and Ó Danachair 1947). This was in the valley between the two peaks on Knockadoon Hill. Owing to the lack of resources, the site was not fully excavated and the complete plan of the house was not exposed. The house was partially under a modern drystone field fence. It was L-shaped in plan (Fig. 11.31), probably a single-storey building, with a main rectangular block, aligned north/south, and a projection on the northern section of the west side. The overall external length was 17.3m (north/south) with a width of 6.8m (east/west) across the main north/south block, while the projection had external

353

dimensions of 7m in width (north/south) and 4.05m (east/west) in maximum length. The stone foundations of the main block were laid directly on boulder clay. The walls of the projecting section on the west side used existing clay banks, which were stone-faced. The western ends of the walls of the projecting room were evenly built; the excavators suggested that the basal levels of the north wall were built against a vertical face in a natural boulder clay bank and that the wall was not free-standing. The north wall was faced only on the southern side. The south wall was faced on both sides and it is unclear whether its western end was also built against a boulder clay bank, as the western ends of both walls consisted of loose stone and clay.

The house foundation walls were on average 0.75m wide, neatly built of limestone mortared with yellow clay; they survived best on the northern end to a height of 0.6–0.7m, and to 0.15–0.2m in height on the southern side. The west wall was under the base of a modern field wall, which was not removed during the excavation owing to limited funding for the project. Window glass was recovered from the excavation, indicating a number of windows within the house. Some slate from the site may indicate a slate roof.

The entrance to the house was a 1.25m-wide doorway on the east side. The internal floor level was 0.2–0.25m below the level of the threshold and two shallow steps led down from the door into the house. The clay floor was worn into a hollow immediately inside the doorsteps. A second 1.25m-wide doorway in the west wall led into the room on the north-west side of the house. There was no evidence of internal partitions within the main rectangular block and the excavators suggested that the house was of open plan. There were two double fireplaces: one was c. 1.2m from the main door and in the middle of the room, while the second was built into the northern end of the west wall. The stone-built fireplaces were placed back to back with a dividing wall between. The fireplace of Hearths A and B (Fig. 11.31) was free-standing and rectangular in plan, measuring 2.5m (east/west) by 1.8m (north/south), and the extant wall height was 0.75m. The hearths within the fireplace narrowed from the front to the back; Hearths A and B were c. 1.5m wide, narrowing to c. 1.2m, and both were 0.6m deep. They were paved and this surface was slightly higher than the clay floor of the room. A post-hole adjacent to the eastern side of Hearth B was 0.3m wide and 0.25m deep and probably held the crane from which cooking-pots hung over the fire. Hearths C and D were incorporated into the west wall; Hearth C faced into the large rectangular room, while Hearth D faced into the projecting room on the north-west side of the building. Like Hearths A and B, Hearths C and D narrowed towards the back but were slightly larger. Hearth C was 0.9m wide and 0.8m deep. Hearth D was not fully exposed during the excavation but the back of the hearth appears to have been almost 2m in length. All the hearths had the residues of fires and contained soot and ashes.

The areas outside the south and east walls of the house were paved with well-set cobbles. Exploratory trenches confirmed that the paving extended for a distance of 4.2m from the east wall and the edge was marked by carefully set larger cobbles. The paving on the southern side extended for at least 7.8m and the edge was not uncovered on the excavation. The excavators also referred to a large stone immediately south of the main door (Ó Ríordáin and Ó Danachair 1947, 43, pl. XII: 3), which they interpreted as a 'mounting block' for riders.

Later activity on the site included the construction of field walls and a sheep pen in the centre of the site; this probably resulted in the reuse of stone from the house, leading to variable preservation. Part of the site was also used as a potato garden, and stones may have been removed to facilitate cultivation.

The pottery from the excavation mainly consisted of internally glazed red earthenwares dating

Fig. 11.32—Finds from Site J:
1 spoon; 2 ornamental piece; 3
jew's harp; 4 bone handle; 5–7
whetstones.

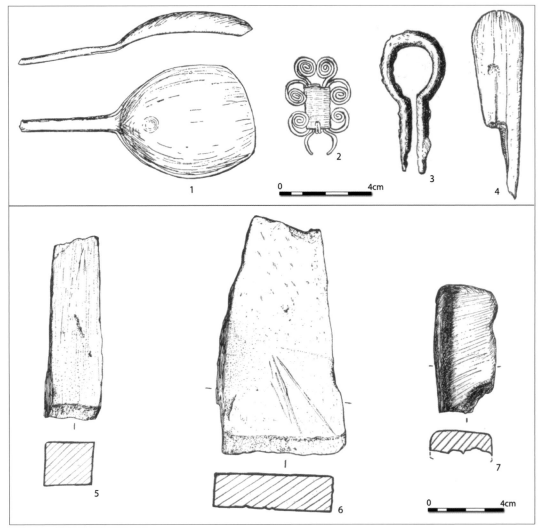

from the seventeenth century. These earthenwares were used both in the kitchen and as dairy pans. Imported pottery was identified as the basal section of a Rhenish or Cologne stoneware pot known as 'Gris de Flandres', imported into England from Flanders. Pottery similar to Dutch delftware but made in England and a fragment of English sgraffito ware were also found on the site.

A money weight from the site dated from c. 1615. The obverse bore a bust of James I and the letters 'I.R. MA. BRIT.', while the reverse had a crown and the letters 'XXII.S.' within a beaded circle. A latten[25] spoon (Fig. 11.32: 1) with a wide bowl was stamped with a ring or maker's mark. A dress-fastener (Fig. 11.32: 2) of coiled bronze wire, an iron jew's harp (Fig. 11.32: 3), a bone knife handle (Fig. 11.32: 4), iron nails, wall-brads and door- or chest-fasteners were also found. Three sandstone whetstones (Fig. 11.32: 5–7) and a Neolithic greenstone axehead reused as a whetstone were recovered. These were used for sharpening kitchen knives and other implements, including farmyard tools. Some sherds of a glass vessel were also recovered. Twelve clay pipe fragments with small-sized bowls are similar to seventeenth-century clay pipes. The record of the animal bones from the site is meagre but ox bones are mentioned, suggesting cattle-based farming. Carbonised barley grain was recovered from Hearth C, indicating the consumption of cereals.

Few houses of the type at Site J, Knockadoon, are known in the Irish archaeological record. A direct parallel can, however, be cited at Drumlummin, Co. Tipperary (Cleary 1987). The house at Drumlummin was T-shaped in plan but of similar dimensions and construction to Site J, Knockadoon, with an overall length of 18m, a room width of *c.* 5–6m and double fireplaces between the rooms. It was dated to the mid-seventeenth century on the basis of artefactual material, a money token of 1650–60 and historical information; it was probably similar in date to Site J.

A silver coin was recovered from the topsoil between Site J and a stone terrace *c.* 43m to the south (Ó Ríordáin 1954, 440). It is an Irish halfpenny of Edward IV (1470–8), sixth issue. The obverse bears the inscription 'EDV' with a crown bust, while the reverse bears a long cross with three pellets in each angle and the inscription '. . . ITAS DVB'. Two pottery sherds from Site J were yellow-glazed and appear to be seventeenth-century North Devon sgraffito ware. An iron ploughshare (*ibid.*, fig. 53) from the site may also be seventeenth-century or later.

The period 1400–1650 at Lough Gur is represented in the main by upstanding remains of tower-houses. These were constructed in the fifteenth and sixteenth centuries and are testament to the wealth and prestige of the earls of Desmond, but also to the continuous need for defence of the eastern borders of the Desmond territories against powerful adversaries, including the earls of Thomond and the Butlers of Ormond and their allies. The tower-houses were built with defence in mind but also served as homes and as the administrative centres of large territories. Their date of construction and use cannot be firmly established, and they may have been in contemporary or sequential use. The tower-houses at Lough Gur, and in particular Bourchier's Castle, are unusual in that some historical information survives on the buildings.

The archaeological excavations at Lough Gur have documented some of the material from the fifteenth to seventeenth centuries. The excavation at Site J revealed one of the few seventeenth-century houses to be excavated in Ireland. The excavations in the car-park area recovered some artefacts, three burials and evidence of a road linked to the activity at Bourchier's Castle.

NEWCHURCH

Newchurch or *Teampall Nua* is located on the south-eastern shore of Lough Gur. It may originally have been a parish church endowed by the Fitzgeralds (Desmonds). Parish churches and chapels of ease[26] provided pastoral care and the sacraments for the general population and were financed by the levy of tithes from the parishioners; the tithe supported the priest and maintained the upkeep of the church building. While pastoral care preceded the Anglo-Norman invasion, parish churches proliferated under the patronage of Anglo-Norman lords and many were constructed in the fourteenth and fifteenth centuries.

Grene Barry (1903a, 195) wrote of Newchurch that 'The church, or chapel-of-ease, is, if not of earlier date, at least coeval with the Desmond stronghold on the island opposite … it was, without doubt, Desmond's "Chapel-of-ease".' Architectural features at Newchurch such as the ogee-headed windows are characteristic of the fifteenth century (Leask 1971, 124) and corroborate Grene Barry's dating. There were many examples of chapels of ease attached to and located near castles in east Limerick when the parish church was some distance away. These sites were also the burial places of

Fig. 11.33—Newchurch.

the old families of the district, and in the case of Lough Gur that family was the Fitzgeralds.
Newchurch was in a ruinous state after 1642 and was restored in 1679 by Rachel, countess of Bath,
who added the belfry on the west gable. The name 'Newchurch' came from its use for Protestant or
Reformed worship rather than the construction of a new church. Fitzgerald and McGregor (1826,
311) recorded that Countess Rachel endowed the church with £20 sterling per annum. Gifts of a
chalice and paten were also made, the chalice bearing the following inscription: 'The gift of the
Right Hon. Rachel, Countess Dowager of Bath, to her Chapel in the Kingdom of Ireland, Ann.
Dom. 1679'. Dineley (Shirley 1867, 194) wrote during his 1681 journey around Limerick that the
Countess of Bath, who owned the castle, also 'built the said new church for the use of Protestants,[27]
and bestow'd a Rich Pulpitt Cloth, Silver Chalice, Plate, Bible and Service Book'. Dowd (1896, 80)
recorded that 'the chalice and paten bestowed by the Countess were, on the decay of the edifice
[Newchurch], presented to Knockainey Church'. Lewis (1837, 16) noted that, the property at
Newchurch 'having descended to the Count de Salis, and the church not being registered in diocesan
records, the nobleman discontinued the appointment of a chaplain, and the church has fallen into
ruins'.

The church is rectangular in plan, gable-ended (Figs 11.33–34) and measuring 17m (east/west)
by 6.4m (north/south). The entrance on the south side has an external rounded arch with dressed
limestone surrounds (Fig. 11.35); the arch is flat on the inside. The east window is round-headed
and has a wide internal splay. It originally had two lights; the window mullion is now gone, but
traces of the pointed decorative trefoil at the top of the window remain. There are single-light

Fig. 11.34—Newchurch.

windows in the west gable and the south wall; that in the south wall has a square hood-moulding (Fig. 11.36) similar to hood-mouldings on the larger windows at Bourchier's Castle. Traces of an annexe that projected from the north side of the church are visible in the stonework and there is also a blocked-up door; the annexe may have been a sacristy. O'Kelly (1944, 30) recorded that Count de Salis conserved the church sometime after 1900 and that the edges of the gables were stabilised and repointed. A coloured glazed plaque of the Madonna and Child was inserted high up on the south wall (Fig. 11.35). The graveyard surrounding the church is still in use. Owen Bresnan (1847–1912), a local poet and historian, is buried in Newchurch. The minstrel-bard Thomas O'Connellan, who died at Bourchier's Castle, is also said to have been buried in Newchurch graveyard. An ode to O'Connellan was printed in the *Dublin Penny Journal*:[28]

> 'By Lough Gur's waters, lone and low the minstrel's laid—
> Where mouldering cloisters dimly throw sepulchral shade.
> Where clustering ivy darkly weeps upon his bed,
> To blot the legend where he sleeps—the tuneful dead!
> And fallen are the towers of time, in dust in lone,
> Where the ringing of his fairy chime so well was known!
> Where song was sweet and mirth was high and beauty smiled,
> Thro' roofless halls the night winds sigh, the owl shrieks wild.'

CAHERELLY CHURCH

Caherelly parish church, *c.* 3km to the north-east of Lough Gur, was founded in 1296 (Westropp 1904–5, 442). It is similar in layout to Newchurch, albeit smaller, with a length of *c.* 10m, and more ornate. The two south windows had large pointed lights divided by mullions (Figs 11.37–38). Caherelly is in the diocese of Emly and tradition has it that the church was founded by St Ailbe, who may have had a connection to Caherelly; the parish church was built almost 800 years after the death of St Ailbe, however, and the link possibly arose from a misunderstanding of the name (*ibid.*, 443).

Fig. 11.35—Newchurch: door with modern coloured glazed plaque of the Madonna and Child (top left).

Fig. 11.36—Newchurch: window in south wall.

Fig. 11.37—Caherelly church.

Fig. 11.38—Caherelly church: window in south wall.

NOTES

[1] *Cogadh Gaedhel re Gallaibh* ('The War of the Irish with the Foreigners') recorded for AD 1002 that 'King Brian fortified Dún Gair and the Island in Loch Gair' (Westropp 1906–7, 179). *Cogadh Gaedhel re Gallaibh* was compiled sometime between 1086 and 1114, and MacCotter (2006, 69) suggests a date of 995 for the fortification of Lough Gur. The fortification of Dún Gair is also recorded in *Lebor na Cert* ('Book of Rights'), a tenth-century account of tribute paid to the king of Cashel (Dillon 1962, xiii).

[2] Ellis and Murray 2017.

[3] Brewer and Bullen 1867–73.

[4] Bealadrohid, Co. Tipperary, was one of the earl's landholdings, where he owned 1,000 acres

(Edwards 2016, 341).

5 Knockainy was also the traditional inauguration site of Gaelic chiefs.

6 The Desmond rolls are a survey (1585–6) of lands forfeited as a result of the Desmond rebellion in preparation for the Munster plantation.

7 A jointure is property settled on a woman after her marriage to be enjoyed after her husband's death.

8 George Carew compiled a series of manuscripts on Munster during his period as president of Munster. This extract is from Carew i, p. 103.

9 The 1641 Depositions provided testimonies on the 1641 rebellion.

10 This equals £5. This can be calculated in terms of today's monetary value (value of income and wealth) at about £27,000 (about €36,600).

11 These were Cromwellian account books and included entries such as 'hay for horses' at the garrisons, including Lough Gur (Westropp 1906, 202).

12 File in the Department of Archaeology, UCC.

13 McCormack (2005, 39) lists Gearóid Iarla as third earl of Desmond; Graves's (1869) pedigree of the earls of Desmond recorded him as the fourth earl.

14 This description is recorded in the Annals of Clonmacnoise (Curtis 1938, 280).

15 These were financial records of the exchequer and were annual accounts.

16 The Peyton survey (1584–6) was of County Limerick and, like the Desmond rolls, recorded lands forfeited by the earl of Desmond, the lands of 'attainted' persons (persons convicted of treason) and the lands of religious houses. One of the surveyors, Sir Henry Wallop, expressed an interest in acquiring an estate in the Knockainy–Lough Gur district. Another surveyor, Valentine Browne, acquired lands in Hospital during this process.

17 Plea rolls were a record of the court system, used from the late thirteenth century, in which the outcomes of civil and criminal cases were noted. Caherguillamore is in the Plea Rolls Calender vol. ii, p. 77.

18 This was again a survey of forfeited lands.

19 The Down Survey (1656–8) was a detailed survey of lands forfeited by the Catholic Irish for settlement by merchant adventurers and English soldiers.

20 This act (1662 and 1665) partly reversed the Cromwellian Settlement Act (1652), whereby lands forfeited and taken by Cromwellian settlers were returned to 'Old English' (Royalists) and 'innocent Catholics' (Catholics who had not taken part in civil wars or massacres of English Protestants).

21 Department of Archaeology, UCC archive.

22 James VI of Scotland, king of England, Ireland and Scotland from 1603 until 1625.

23 Fiants were warrants directed to the Irish chancery and included land grants and leases. The fiants here refer to those of the reign of Elizabeth I.

24 These were the administrative records of the English chancery. They include grants.

25 The term 'latten' refers to the metal, which was tin plate or brass.

26 A chapel of ease was a church other than the parish church which was within the parish boundary and was attended by those who could not conveniently go to the parish church.

27 This statement is clearly incorrect, as the architectural details indicate a fifteenth-century date, and it is likely that the countess renovated an existing church.

28 *Dublin Penny Journal*, 20 October 1832.

APPENDIX 1

The following account of the capture of Bourchier's Castle in May 1600 is from *Pacata Hibernia*, compiled in 1633 by Thomas Stafford (1633, 80–4). The original spelling is largely retained.

The five and twentieth, the armie encamped at Brough [Bruff] *where the President* [Lord Carew, president of Munster and earl of Totnes] *left a ward, partly to offend the rebels of Loughguirre (Guire) which was as yet held by the rebels, the President attended with a troope of horse, rode to take a particular view of the strength and situation thereof, as also by what way he might most conveniently bring canon to annoy the same. He found it to be a place of exceeding strength, by reason that it was an Island, encompassed by a deepe lough, the breadth thereof being in the narrowest place a Calievers shot over, upon one side thereof standieth a verie strong castle, which at the time was manned with a good garrison, for there was within the Island, John fits Thomas, with two hundred men at least, which shewed themselves prepared to defend the place. The President being approached within shot, to discover the ground, they discharged some twentie muskets at him and his company but without hurt done: and having effected as much he intended at that time, they casting foorth some reviling speeches, he left the place. That night the President came to Limerick, the armie incamped with a little more than a mile thereof … [The President] directed the smiths and carpenters to get canon mobilised according to the proportions he gave, they wrought, and in the end a demie-canon was mounted and drawn towards the gate of the Cittie, that leadeth to the Island of Loghguire before named. The rebels within the castle receiving intelligence thereof one Owen Grome, a stranger from the North (to whose charge John fits Thomas had committed the custodie of the castle) sent word that for his pardon, and a competent summe of money, he would deliver it up unto her Majesties use. The President considering that many impediments would arise, if he should attempt the taking of it by force, and that it must needs bee chargeable to the Queen, cost the lives of many of his men, and a great delay for the prosecution of other services, which he intended, accordingly to his demands, and received the castle, the monie (which was threescore pounds) being paid by the Presidents order, by one Rowlye, who lost the same to the rebels: whilst these things were in handling, Nugent intending no longer to deferre the enterprise, attempted the execution of this sort. The President being past Loghguire, John fits Thomas riding forth of the Island towards the fastness of Arloghe* [Aherlow], *where most of his men remained, with one called John Coppinger. Nugent rode behind John fits Thomas, intended to shoot him in the back. Coppinger at the instant snatched the pistol from him, crying treason: whereby John fits Thomas turning himself about perceived his intent. Nugent spurred his horse, the horse stumbled and Nugent was taken. The next day after examination and confession of his intent* [Nugent was] *hanged. For now was John fits Thomas possessed with such a jealous suspicion of everyone, that he durst not remain long at Loghguire, for feare of some other attempt that might be wrought against him; and therefore leaving the castle in the custodie of said Owen (who as before, kept it very short time after) departed suddenly into his brother's camp. Loghguirre being now possessed for the Queene and the armie well refreshed marched into Clan-William a countree of the Burkes.*

APPENDIX 2

During the Confederate Wars (1641–52), Bourchier's Castle was besieged for 24 weeks from early February 1641. A besieging force numbering 1,500, drawn from, *inter alia*, the baronies of Small County, Clanwilliam and Connagh, gathered near Lough Gur Castle (Bourchier's Castle).

A verbatim copy of the account of the siege by William Weekes and Richard Harte, constables of the castle, is preserved in the Sloane Collection in the British Museum (Welply 1919). No attempt has been made to alter the spelling or the punctuation, or to expand any of the contracted words (*ibid.*, 79). Note that the word 'or' is a contraction of 'our', 'wch' is a contraction of 'which', and 'yt' is a contraction of 'that'.

A declaratione of William Weekes steuard to the Right honerabele the lord of Baeth & Richard Harte of Dunkipp both appointed to be Constabeles of the Castele of Loegar by Sr William Saintleger lord president of Munster, of Cariadge before & after begininge of the seidge.

Imprimis about Candelmas [2 February] *last there gathered together of the barronie Clanwilliam & the barronie of the small Countie & the barronie of Connagh & other places the number of 1500 neire* [near] *the Castele of Loegarr* [Lough Gur], *the Chiefe Conmanders, Castele Cormell, Perce Walsh, of the abbie of onie, Mr. William Burck, the second sonne of the lord of Brettis mortoe Brian of Doeharroue. One Ó Kenidie of the silvermines, Knohar Ó Clansie of Clenwilliam john Clansie of Limbrick, merchant his brother, Tibbott Burck of Ballingard & two of his brothers, Doctor Daniell Higgins; after this they sent to the Constabele of the said Castele to yeld upp the said Castele wch was denied vpponn yt there was 2 letters sent to the said Constabele one by the lord of Brettis desiringe him to deliver to him otherwise it* [the castle] *should be battered doune the other Ire* [letter] *from Portewalch to the same effect wch two letters were sent by the Constabele to the lord of president about a fortnight after Richard Harte was desired by the lord of Castele Connell to come out: to them vpponn a parly to one Morriss Raulies of Raulies toune* [Rawleystown], *there Castele Connell Perce walch John Lacie of the Bruse, Doctor Higgins Tibbott Burck of Ballingard Conor Ó Clansie & diverse others pswaded* [persuaded] *him to goe unto mase & yt he should have his goods restored againe wch he denied to doe, nevertheless yt if he would lieu at his Castele of Dunkipp he should the verie next morninge his said Castele of Dunkipp was betrayed & takene by one Edie lacie of Brurie & others, & at yt same time the lord of Castele Connell & the rest pretenid* [pretended] *great love to the lord of Baeth pmissed* [promised] *yt none of the Castell should be stir'd nor none molested vppon the lands after all this they laid three several Ambusses to cutt the said ward of Contrarie to there oath & pmise* [promise] *by gods divine hand they were prevented. The day after St. Patrick day or Iland* [Knockadoon] *was besieged & the Castele in 3 quarters Castele Connell & Doctor Higgins of one quarter, Perce Walch & Morriss Baggott of Baggotts toune* [Baggotstown] *of another quarter the other quarter by the gentlemen of Clenwilliam Called themselves volunteers & they were to maintaine 60 menn. There* [their] *Captain they appointed was one Patrick Breett of Clennogarr, about a weeck afte we were besieged Doctor Higgins brought a great boat from Limbrick & toock or Iland* [Knockadoon] *wth great force of menn & wole Packs to defend them from shott afterward they toock the brew-house stable a pigeon house & one of or watch houses all wch was wth in halfe muskeett shott of the Casteles about a sennight* [a week] *after they assaulted the kitchen adioininge to the Castele & made a great breach yt two menn might enter, we beate them yt & kild* [killed] *some of thear menn. They continued their seidge against us wth as great extremitie as could be vsed* [used] *we having to the number of menn wemenn & children two hundred and fortie or there about, & not sufferinge vs* [us] *to have one dropp of milck or springe watter wch we desired for wemenn yt laid sick nor suffer us to burie those yt died, without butt was inforced to burie the dead in the kitchen, vntill yt we toock the watch house from them & thenn we had the command of the garden after this they brought a peace of or ordinance from Limbrick & planted it in the Iland, sent a menacinge letter if we would not deliuer* [deliver] *the Castele they would not spare a mothers childe. They made 3 shotts at the Castele & carried there peace awaie againe about the same time we were relieved by Captaine Bridges wth* [with] *pouder we told him yt wee were not abell to houlde out a fortnight for want of victuals he tould vs* [us] *yt wee should be releaved wth in tenne days at the fardest we continued in the castele 7 weecks yt we were druine* [driven] *into greate extremitie after this one Richard Harte one of the Constabbells of the ward haueing nothinge to releue him his wife & children desired a quarter to go to Limbrick, to git wha monnie was owinge him, two of the besegers* [besiegers] *went a longe wth him the agrement what munnies the said Richard Harte should pcure* [procure] *they should haue* [have] *half of it they were for yt to convaie* [bring] *him & his familie to the English armie articeles* [agreements] *were made & oaths past nottinge performed they receauinge* [receiving] *of the said Richard Harte the some of 48£, he pcured* [procured] *a convaie from S'Chareles Bavisser, to receive him, they most falslie not pforming* [performing] *articells nor oaethe kept ther until Loegarr was yelded after this the besiegers of the Castele desired to parle* [talk] *with the steuard the Steuard beinge drivne to yt extremitie for want of victuals did yeald the said Castele vppon articells one articele was the convaieinge safe in boddie & goods to or arme he & the warde* [keeper], *the time wth or goods went out was in the Eveninge beinge pswaded* [persuaded] *to goe one 3 miles forward in or waie to one Morrish Baggetts one of the besiegers yt verie night all the besegers* [besiegers] *beinge with us we were rob'd of 7 load of or goods & as we conceiud the besegers were accersarie* [accessories] *for there was no stir made when the said loads were takene awaie, many were takene and affirmed by them to be authors of the robberrie butt let goe againe after that, this wee Continued fooure dayes before we could goe yt the poore people were infarct to sell most of there goods for littell or nothing after we were to goe unto Mitchells toune* [Mitchelstown] *we staid at Mr. Mc Gibbons Castele called Ballinhinch & there they beinge Conscious of there breach of quarter, desired the said Constabells to wrieght under there hands of the faithfull pformance of there quarter pmised* [promised], *wch they were enforced wreight under there hands for the safe gard of there liues* [lives] *and goods & there Companie wth them, or liues & goods were in great danger after all this if we should relate the Cruelties duringe the time we were besieged wch was 24 weecks during yt time we had not any fresh meate butt 3 sheep and one beife all wch we toock from them, their Crueltie in Killinge wemenn and Childrene gatheringe of earbs & sorrel we buried duringe the time of the seidge about foure scoare* [80] *psonns* [persons], *the goods at the time there armie approach the Castele wch was about Candelmas last past they toock of the lord of Baeth sheepes the number of 5000 sheepe, 360 horses mares & Coultes beside they burnt the reecks of Corne of his all wch was divided amonge them. The lord of Castle Connell the lord of Brettis Perce Walch Mortoe Briann & the reste divided the stude & the sheepe, a list of the names of the voluntears Tibbett Burck of Ballingard of Clenwilliam Thomas Burck of Ballilehann of the foure baronies Walter Burck of Killonam, Tibbott Burckes sonn of Carginlish* [Caherconlish] *viz., Richard Burck his Eldest sonne Pattrick Burck Tibbott Burck oge* [óg] *Knohar Clansie of Ballibricken Daniell Ó Hine of Carrellie & his Eldest sonne Doniell hine of Carellie Daniell Ó*

Clansie of Ballievear John Fitch Edmund Burck of the skirt, Edmund Raulie of Ballingoelie Tibbott Burck unkle to Tibbott Burck of Ballingard Captaine Foxe of Bulduegine of the small Countie Walter Burck of Luddunbegg in Clenwilliam Garrett Marshall & his eldest Sonne Miles Burck Ralph Jourdenn John Bourck the brother of the said Miles & his Eldest sonne Walter Roe Burck of Rothes toune Tibbott Burck Fitch John his brother of Ballinwilliam Pattrick brett of Clemogarr there Captaine wth many others of Clanwilliam wch we cannot well remember at this time.

Witnesse or hands at Youghall the 7th of Septe 1641 Willm Weekes Richard Harte [Endorsed:] A declaration of the seidge of Loeggar

12. Summary

The imprint of human activity at Lough Gur began as far back as 8000 BC, when the first hunter-gatherer or Mesolithic communities traversed the countryside around the lake. The landscape then differed from that of today, with more of the region covered by lakes. Lough Gur remains the only surviving large lake, and some bogs in its hinterland are the locations of former lakes. Indeed, the expanse of Lough Gur itself was reduced in the post-Famine period, when it was partly drained around 1847–8. The drainage exposed many artefacts, which were collected by local people. Many of these finds are now in museums, some were sold to visiting antiquarians and some were inevitably lost or destroyed.

The advent of farming just after 4000 BC was the result of the arrival of new populations of Neolithic people, probably from Britain, who managed the landscape to provide food and the basic requirements of human existence through crop and animal husbandry. Farming communities were sedentary and they constructed houses of rectangular plan; the footings of these survive on Knockadoon Hill. Around 3500 BC that architectural house style was replaced by houses of circular plan. Pottery in which to cook food and stone tools characteristic of the Neolithic period were made at Lough Gur. Contact with Britain persisted throughout the Neolithic, as evidenced by the importation of stone axeheads from Cumbria in north-west England. Stone axeheads were also procured from as far away as County Antrim. Connections with other parts of Ireland are confirmed by artefacts such as serpentine beads, for which at least the raw material was sourced in the Connemara area of County Galway. A type of pottery, known as Carrowkeel Ware, from Caherguillamore is usually found in passage tombs in the megalithic cemeteries in the northern half of Ireland, particularly in counties Sligo and Meath, and the Caherguillamore pottery therefore shows contact with these areas.

Lough Gur is not an area where megalithic tombs dominate the landscape, although portions of two surviving examples may date from the early Neolithic. There are, however, some unprotected burials on Knockadoon Hill, demonstrating a belief in the afterlife. The artefacts left behind, the remains of houses and farming practices provide some insight into the lives of these early communities in Lough Gur, including how people lived, how their society was structured and what they believed.

The advent of new beliefs around 3000 BC was marked in the Lough Gur landscape by the construction of the embankment at the Great Stone Circle at Grange and probably of a timber circle at the nearby Circle D. These sites were a focus for rites and religious practices which are now obscure, but the monumental remains suggest places of community assembly. Grooved Ware pottery from the Great Stone Circle, Geroid Island and Knockadoon Hill and stone maceheads from Lough Gur show connections with the Orkney Islands off the north-east Scottish coast, beginning at around

3000 BC and continuing until 2500 BC. Evidence for the advent of new cultures in what is known as the Beaker period is widespread around Lough Gur. These new cultures show a broadening of contact with Britain, France and the Iberian regions and the introduction of metal-working. Radiocarbon evidence from elsewhere in Ireland and the styles of Beaker pottery found at Lough Gur confirm that Beaker cultures were established at Lough Gur around 2500 BC. The physical remains of this time include the stone circle at the Great Stone Circle in Grange and possibly Stone Circle C and the now-destroyed Stone Circle D. Concentrations of Beaker pottery at occupation sites on Knockadoon (particularly Site D) and at seasonally used sites at Ballingoola, Rathjordan and Cahercorney are testament to extensive settlement in Lough Gur at the end of the third millennium BC. Beaker pottery and possibly a burial inserted into an older burial site in Cahergullamore show continued use of what was then an ancient site. Bronze axeheads, bronze ingots, copper awls and bracelets found at Lough Gur attest to the acquisition of metal artefacts reflecting wealth and status. A Beaker period type of dagger known as a halberd and similar to a ceremonial staff was probably recovered from the lake when it was drained in the mid-nineteenth century. Other Beaker period objects from Lough Gur include stone wrist-bracers and barbed and tanged arrowheads, which suggest archery as a sport or perhaps for hunting. Structural evidence for Beaker period houses at Lough Gur is, as elsewhere in Ireland, not easily recognised in the archaeological record and the evidence of occupation is only clear in the artefactual material. The apparent absence of Beaker period houses may be connected to the types of shelters used, which left few physical, easily recognisable remains. Megalithic tombs known as wedge tombs were constructed towards the end of the Beaker period and there may have been up to eight of these in the immediate hinterland of Lough Gur. Modern dating of the human bones from the Giant's Grave, close to the lake shore, indicated that interments took place around 2202–2162 BC. The site continued in use over several hundred years into the Bronze Age, and a later burial was inserted into the tomb around 1700 BC. The Giant's Grave must have continued as a focus for the community over several generations.

The Bronze Age in Lough Gur began around 2000 BC, when changes in society were reflected in new burial practices and monument types. The era also saw widespread use of metal tools and weapons indicating wealth and status. Of these, the late Bronze Age Lough Gur shield and gold-mounted spearhead are the epitome of high-quality craftsmanship and symbolic of power and wealth. A consciousness of a need for security and perhaps status is reflected in stone enclosures built around settlements; six of these were excavated on Knockadoon Hill and have been dated to the later Bronze Age either by radiocarbon dating or on the basis of the artefact types, particularly pottery. Unenclosed settlements are also recorded on Knockadoon Hill. Some field enclosures on Knockadoon Hill and in the hinterland of Lough Gur are Bronze Age and provide proof of managed farmland. Burials were in simple graves that were either stone-lined or unprotected. Ring-barrows and ring-ditches are frequent around Lough Gur and are interpreted as playing a part in funeral rites rather than being final ossuaries. Standing stones were also erected around Lough Gur; some indicate ancient routeways while others may demarcate territory.

The Iron Age in Munster is an obscure period in Irish prehistory and no less so at Lough Gur. Iron Age burial sites were uncovered during excavations on Knockadoon Hill and some artefacts from Lough Gur are dated to about AD 300 or the late Iron Age. Historical records confirm that the Déisi were the ruling tribe around Lough Gur at this time, and the name of the barony of Small County (*In Déis Becc*) is a memento of Déisi lordship. The Déisi had contact with Roman Britain, and finds such as a silver hoard from Balline, near Knocklong, as well as some artefacts from the

Fig. 12.1—The Lough Gur
shield.

excavations at Carraig Aille show connections with the Roman world.

Excavations of the sites of historic date at Carraig Aille, the Spectacles, a ringfort at Grange, house sites at Ballingoola, an enclosure and house sites at Ballynagallagh and some of the Knockadoon sites provided information on early medieval settlement and society, helping to reconstruct the lives of these past communities in Lough Gur. This time saw the arrival of Christianity, the beginning of literacy and historical records which are an adjunct to understanding the physical remains either still visible in the landscape or uncovered through archaeological excavation. Early medieval sites investigated in the late 1930s–40s at Lough Gur were dated from the artefacts found on sites, based on similar styles found elsewhere in Ireland. Radiocarbon dating of material from modern excavations can establish a broad dating for these settlements at Lough Gur, beginning in the fifth or sixth century AD and continuing to the eighth or ninth century. These excavations produced a wealth of information on the development of house types and the varied artefacts that were in use—some of which were mundane, while others were rare and expensive. The crannogs on Lough Gur were most likely constructed at this time. A church site at Killalough and Christian burials on Knockadoon are testament to the introduction of Christianity.

There is also some historical evidence that Vikings came to Lough Gur; indeed, a Viking sword was recovered from the lake. Brian Boru consolidated his position as king of Munster and among the sites that he fortified was Lough Gur, around 995. The next great change in Ireland was the Anglo-Norman invasion of 1169, which altered the political and social structure of the country. Anglo-Norman land grantees in east Limerick included the Fitzgeralds or Geraldines, who in time emerged as the dominant landowners and ultimately became the earls of Desmond, wealthy magnates and independent of government in London. The Geraldine dynasty reigned supreme over much of County Limerick from the fourteenth to the sixteenth century. Although Lough Gur was manorial land, there is no evidence of an early castle there. Peasant settlements were uncovered on excavations at Caherguillamore and in the car park at Lough Gur. Castles built by the Geraldines at Lough Gur included Bourchier's Castle and the Black Castle. George Bourchier was granted the castle at the entrance to Knockadoon Hill in 1583—hence the name. The historical information on this castle is relatively plentiful and various sieges are recorded.

Lough Gur has a wide range of monumental remains from prehistoric and historic times. The care of these monuments is not entirely the preserve of State agencies but rests also with the local communities. The preservation of sites reflects traditional respect for the fragments left behind by our ancestors. A reluctance to disturb or destroy old resting places helps to protect archaeological sites. Some destruction of monuments happened in prehistoric times, where an ancient structure was found to overlie an earlier one (Ó Ríordáin 1955, 8). When Ó Ríordáin (1955) wrote a paper entitled 'Preserve, examine, illustrate: a commentary on the position of Irish archaeology' over 60 years ago, it was at a time of large-scale schemes of land improvement, drainage and other works, as well as the introduction of power machinery, which resulted in the destruction of field antiquities on a scale unprecedented in the history of the country. This pattern has continued elsewhere in Ireland. In some respects, the monuments at Lough Gur have been saved thanks to the absence of tillage and to an appreciation in the locality of the unique landscape. There was some monument destruction in the nineteenth century, including the removal of megalithic tombs by the time of the first Ordnance Survey in the early 1840s, and Lynch (1895, 246) decried the demolition of castles to obtain stone for building mansions. Although there has been some modern levelling of archaeological sites, this has remained minor, albeit regrettable. At Lough Gur there will always be a continuity of community, and this local community are the primary guardians of the archaeological heritage of the area. There will also be a continuity of archaeological research and presentation of its results, encouraging public awareness of the unique landscape that is Lough Gur.

Bibliography

Ahlberg, K., Almgren, E., Wright, H.E. and Ito, E. 2001 Holocene stable-isotope stratigraphy at Lough Gur, County Limerick, Western Ireland. *The Holocene* **11** (3), 367–72.

Almgren, E. 1989 Woodland establishment, expansion, and regression in association with prehistoric and later human settlements around Lough Gur, Co. Limerick, Ireland. Unpublished Ph.D thesis, University of Minnesota, Minneapolis.

Almgren, E. 2001 The sedimentary record of woodland reduction in association with prehistoric and later settlements around Lough Gur, Co. Limerick, with special emphasis on the Neolithic and Bronze Age periods. *Proceedings of the Royal Irish Academy* **101**B, 161–2.

Armit, I., Murphy, E., Nelis, E. and Simpson, D. 2003 Irish Neolithic houses. In I. Armit, E. Murphy, E. Nelis and D. Simpson (eds), *Neolithic settlement in Ireland and western Britain*, 146–8. Oxbow Books, Oxford.

Ashe-Fitzgerald, M. 2000 *Thomas Johnson Westropp 1860–1922: an Irish antiquary*. Seandálaíocht Monograph Series, Department of Archaeology, UCD, Dublin.

Baillie, M.G.L. 1995a Dendrochronology and the chronology of the Irish Bronze Age. In J. Waddell and E. Shee Twohig (eds), *Ireland in the Bronze Age*, 30–7. Stationery Office, Dublin.

Baillie, M.G.L. 1995b *A slice through time*. Batsford, London.

Baillie, M.G.L. 1999 *Exodus to Arthur*. Batsford, London.

Bateson, J.D. 1973 Roman material from Ireland: a re-consideration. *Proceedings of the Royal Irish Academy* **73**C, 21–97.

Beaufort, L.C. 1828 An essay upon the state of architecture and antiquities, previous to the landing of the Anglo-Normans in Ireland. *Transactions of the Royal Irish Academy* **15**, 101–241.

Binchy, D.A. 1969 Secular institutions. In M. Dillon (ed.), *Early Irish society*, 52–65. Mercier Press, Dublin.

Borlase, W.C. 1897 *The dolmens of Ireland*. Chapman and Hall, London.

Bradley, R. 2007 *The prehistory of Britain and Ireland*. Cambridge University Press, Cambridge.

Brady, N.D.K. 1988 The plough pebbles of Ireland. In G. Lerche, A. Fenton and A. Steensberg (eds), *Tools and Tillage* **6** (1), 47–60. National Museum of Denmark, Herning.

Brewer, J.S. and Bullen, W. (eds) 1867–73 *Calendar of the Carew Manuscripts*. Longman, Green, Reader and Dyer, London.

Brindley, A. 1980 The Cinerary Urn tradition in Ireland—an alternative interpretation. *Proceedings of the Royal Irish Academy* **80**C, 197–203.

Brindley, A. 1999a Irish Grooved Ware. In R. Cleal and A. McSween (eds), *Grooved Ware in Britain and Ireland*, 23–35. Oxbow Books, Oxford.

Brindley, A. 1999b Sequence and dating in the Grooved Ware tradition. In R. Cleal and A.

McSween (eds), *Grooved Ware in Britain and Ireland*, 133–44. Oxbow Books, Oxford.

Brindley, A. 2007 *The dating of Food Vessels and Urns in Ireland*. Department of Archaeology, National University of Ireland, Galway.

Brindley, A.L. and Lanting, J.N. 1989–90 Radiocarbon dates for Neolithic single burials. *Journal of Irish Archaeology* **5**, 1–7.

Brindley, A.L. and Lanting, J.N. 1991–2 Radiocarbon dates from wedge tombs. *Journal of Irish Archaeology* **6**, 19–26.

B.R.R. 1865 An antiquarian ramble. *Dublin Builder* **7**, 242–4.

Burgess, C. 1979 The background of early metallurgy in Ireland and Britain. In M. Ryan (ed.), *The origins of metallurgy in Atlantic Europe*, 207–47. Stationery Office, Dublin.

Burl, A. 1976 *The stone circles of the British Isles*. Yale University Press, New Haven.

Butler, D.J. 2004 The churches and plate of the Church of Ireland in the dioceses of Cashel, Emly, Waterford and Lismore. *Journal of the Royal Society of Antiquaries of Ireland* **134**, 91–165.

Cahill, M. 2003 Two fragments of scrap gold. Appendix V in R.M. Cleary, 'An enclosed Later Bronze Age site on Knockadoon, Lough Gur, Co. Limerick'. *Proceedings of the Royal Irish Academy* **103**C, 173–4.

Cahill Wilson, J. 2014 Romans and Roman material in Ireland: a wider social perspective. In J. Cahill Wilson and G. Dowling (eds), *Late Iron Age and 'Roman' Ireland*, 11–58. Wordwell, Dublin.

Camden, W. 1607 *Britannia: A chorographical description of the flourishing kingdoms of England, Scotland, and Ireland, and the islands adjacent; from the earliest antiquity. Translated and enlarged by R. Gough (1789)*. J. Nichols, London.

Carbery, M. 1973 *The farm by Lough Gur* [reprint]. Mercier Press, Cork.

Carey, A. 2014 Stone. In I. Russell and M. Hurley (eds), *Woodstown: a Viking-age settlement in Co. Waterford*, 299–320. Four Courts Press, Dublin.

Carte, M.D. 1866 Of some indented bones of the *Cervus Megaceros*, found near Lough Gur, County of Limerick. *Journal of the Royal Geological Society of Ireland* **1**, 151–4.

Case, H.J. 1966 Were Beaker-people the first metallurgists in Ireland? *Palaeohistoria* **12**, 141–77.

Caulfield, S. 1969 Some quernstones in private possession in Co. Kerry. *Journal of the Kerry Archaeological and Historical Society* **2**, 59–73.

Caulfield, S. 1981 Some Celtic problems in the Irish Iron Age. In D. Ó Corráin (ed.), *Irish antiquity: essays and studies presented to Professor M.J. O'Kelly*, 205–15. Tower Books, Cork.

Chambers, A. 2011 *Eleanor, Countess of Desmond*. Gill and Macmillan, Dublin.

Cherry, J. 2009 Landlords, estates, demesnes and mansion houses in County Limerick *c.* 1870–1920. In L. Irwin, G. Ó Tuathaigh and M. Potter (eds), *Limerick history and society*, 533–56. Geography Publications, Dublin.

Clarke, J. (ed.) 2004 *The medieval horse and its equipment*. Museum of London, London.

Clarke, J., Egan, G. and Griffith, N. 2004 Harness fittings. In J. Clarke (ed.), *The medieval horse and its equipment*, 43–74. Museum of London, London.

Cleary, K. 2011 Stone bead and pendant. In R.M. Cleary and H. Kelleher, *Archaeological excavations at Tullahedy, County Tipperary: Neolithic settlement in north Munster*, 402–5. Collins Press, Cork.

Cleary, R.M. 1982a Excavations at Lough Gur, Co. Limerick, 1977–78, Pt I. *Journal of the Cork Historical and Archaeological Society* **87** (245), 2–20.

Cleary, R.M. 1982b Excavations at Lough Gur, Co. Limerick, 1977–78, Pt II. *Journal of the Cork Historical and Archaeological Society* **87** (246), 77–106.

Cleary, R.M. 1983 Excavations at Lough Gur, Co. Limerick, 1977–78, Pt III. *Journal of the Cork Historical and Archaeological Society* **88** (247), 51–80.

Cleary, R.M. 1984 Bone-tempered Beaker potsherd. *Journal of Irish Archaeology* **2**, 73–5.

Cleary, R.M. 1987 Drumlummin, Co. Tipperary. In R.M. Cleary, M.F. Hurley and E.A. Twohig (eds), *Archaeological excavations on the Cork–Dublin gas pipeline*, 116–41. Cork Archaeological Studies No. 1. Department of Archaeology, University College Cork.

Cleary, R.M. 1993 The Later Bronze Age at Lough Gur: filling in the blanks. In E. Shee Twohig and M. Ronayne (eds), *Past perceptions: the prehistoric archaeology of south-west Ireland*, 114–20. Cork University Press, Cork.

Cleary, R.M. 1995 Later Bronze Age houses and prehistoric burials from Lough Gur, Co. Limerick. *Proceedings of the Royal Irish Academy* **95**C, 1–92.

Cleary, R.M. 2000 The potter's craft in prehistoric Ireland, with specific reference to Lough Gur, Co. Limerick. In A. Desmond, G. Johnson, M. McCarthy, J. Sheehan and E. Shee Twohig (eds), *New agendas in Irish prehistory*, 119–34. Wordwell, Bray.

Cleary, R.M. 2003 An enclosed Later Bronze Age site on Knockadoon, Lough Gur, Co. Limerick. *Proceedings of the Royal Irish Academy* **103**C, 97–189.

Cleary, R.M. 2006 Excavations of an early-medieval period enclosure at Ballynagallagh, Lough Gur, Co. Limerick. *Proceedings of the Royal Irish Academy* **106**C, 1–66.

Cleary, R.M. 2008 The pottery from Site A. In M. Doody, *The Ballyhoura Hills Project*, 259–303. Discovery Programme Monograph No. 7. Wordwell, Bray.

Cleary, R.M. 2010 Appendix II (A). In R. Gillespie and A. Kavanagh, *Of troughs and tuyères: the archaeology of the N5 Charlestown Bypass*, 1–55. NRA Scheme Monograph 6. National Roads Authority, Dublin.

Cleary, R.M. 2011 The pottery. In R.M. Cleary and H. Kelleher, *Archaeological excavations at Tullahedy, County Tipperary: Neolithic settlement in north Munster*, 322–83. Collins Press, Cork.

Cleary, R.M. 2015 Excavation at Grange Stone Circle (B), Lough Gur, Co. Limerick, and a review of dating. *Journal of Irish Archaeology* **24**, 51–77.

Cleary, R.M. and Hawkes, A. 2014 Munster ring-ditches, *fulachtaí fia* and the excavations at Carrigtohill, Co. Cork. *Journal of Irish Archaeology* **23**, 97–121.

Cleary, R.M. and Hogan, N. 2013 Recent survey work at Lough Gur. *North Munster Antiquarian Journal* **53**, 79–98.

Cleary, R.M. and Jones, C. 1980 A cist burial at Ballynagallagh, near Lough Gur, Co. Limerick. *North Munster Antiquarian Journal* **10–12**, 3–7.

Cleary, R.M. and Kelleher, H. 2011 *Archaeological excavations at Tullahedy, County Tipperary: Neolithic settlement in north Munster*. Collins Press, Cork.

Cleary, R.M. and O'Driscoll, J. 2014 Archaeological remains and geophysical surveys at Lough Gur and Grange Stone Circle. *Irish Quaternary Association Field Guide No. 32*, 31–44.

Clinton, M. 2001 *The souterrains of Ireland*. Wordwell, Bray.

Coles, J.M., Coutts, H. and Ryder, M.L. 1964 A late Bronze Age find from Pyotdykes, Angus, Scotland, with associated gold, cloth, leather and wood remains. *Proceedings of the Prehistoric Society* **30** (11), 186–98.

Collins, T. and Coyne, F. 2006 As old as we felt. *Archaeology Ireland* **20** (4), 21.

Condit, T. and Simpson, D. 1998 Irish hengiform enclosures and related monuments: a review. In A. Gibson and D. Simpson (eds), *Prehistoric ritual and religion: essays in honour of Aubrey Burl*, 45–61. Sutton, Stroud.

Cooney, G. 2000 *Landscapes of Neolithic Ireland*. Routledge, Abingdon.

Cooney, G. 2007 In retrospect: Neolithic activity at Knockadoon, Lough Gur, Co. Limerick. *Proceedings of the Royal Irish Academy* **107**C, 215–25.

Cooney, G. and Grogan, E. 1994 *Irish prehistory: a social perspective*. Wordwell, Dublin.

Corlett, C. 2005 Ring-barrows: a circular argument with a ring of truth? In T. Condit and C. Corlett (eds), *Above and beyond: essays in memory of Leo Swan*, 63–71. Wordwell, Bray.

Craig, M. 1982 *The architecture of Ireland from the earliest times to 1880*. Eason and Son, Dublin.

Crawford, O.G.S. 1920 Account of excavations at Hengwm, Merionethshire, August–September 1919. *Archaeologia Cambrensis* **20**, 99–128.

Crofton Croker, T. 1833 Druidical remains near Lough Gur, Co. Limerick. *Gentleman's Magazine* (February 1833), 105–12.

Cropper, C. 2014 Glass. In I. Russell and M.F. Hurley (eds), *Woodstown: a Viking-age settlement in Co. Waterford*, 282–5. Four Courts Press, Dublin.

Cummins, V. and Fowler, C. 2004 *The Neolithic of the Irish Sea: materiality and traditions of practice*. Oxbow Books, Oxford.

Curtis, E. 1938 *A history of medieval Ireland from 1086 to 1513*. Methuen, London.

Daly, A. and Grogan, E. 1993 Excavation of four barrows in Mitchelstown West, Co. Tipperary: final report. *Discovery Programme Reports* **1**, 44–60.

Danagher, P. 1973 Longstone. In T.G. Delaney (ed.), *Excavations 1973: summary accounts of archaeological work in Ireland*, 24–5. Association of Young Irish Archaeologists, Belfast.

Danaher, K. 1978 *Ireland's vernacular architecture*. Mercier Press, Cork.

Daniel, G. 1960 Professor Seán Ó Ríordáin: an appreciation. *University Review* **2** (1), 59–61.

Davidson, H.E. 1994 *The sword in Anglo-Saxon England*. Boydell Press, Woodbridge.

Davies, O. 1939 Stone circles in Northern Ireland. *Ulster Journal of Archaeology* **2**, 2–14.

Day, R. 1895 Supplemental notes on some of the antiquities discovered in Lough Gur. *Journal of the Cork Historical and Archaeological Society* (ser. 2) **1**, 303–5.

Dempsey, C. 2013 An analysis of stone axe petrography and production at Lough Gur, Co. Limerick. *Journal of Irish Archaeology* **22**, 23–50.

de Paor, M. 1977 The Viking impact. In P. Cone (ed.), *Treasures of early Irish art 1500 BC to 1500 AD*, 144–52. Metropolitan Museum of Art, New York.

de Valera, R. and Ó Nualláin, S. 1982 *Survey of the megalithic tombs of Ireland. Volume 4. Counties Cork–Kerry–Limerick–Tipperary*. Stationery Office, Dublin.

Dillon, M. 1962 *Lebor na Cert: the Book of Rights*. Educational Company, Dublin.

Dineley, T. 1870 [1681] *A voyage through the kingdom of Ireland in the year 1681*. Dublin.

Dolley, M. 1972 *Anglo-Norman Ireland*. Gill and Macmillan, Dublin.

Donnelly, C.J. 2009 Architecture and conflict: Limerick's tower houses, *c.* 1400 to 1650. In L. Irwin, G. Ó Tuathaigh and M. Potter (eds), *Limerick history and society*, 71–89. Geography Publications, Dublin.

Doody, M. 1993 The Bruff Aerial Photographic Survey. *Tipperary Historical Journal* (1993), 173–80.

Doody, M. 2000 Bronze Age houses in Ireland. In A. Desmond, G. Johnson, M. McCarthy, J.

Sheehan and E. Shee Twohig (eds), *New agendas in Irish prehistory*, 135–60. Wordwell, Bray.

Doody, M. 2007 *Excavations at Curraghatoor, Co. Tipperary*. University College Cork, Cork.

Doody, M. 2008 *The Ballyhoura Hills Project*. Discovery Programme Monograph No. 7. Wordwell, Bray.

Dowd, Revd J. 1896 *Round about the county of Limerick*. G. McKern and Sons, Limerick.

Dunlevy, M. 1988 A classification of early Irish combs. *Proceedings of the Royal Irish Academy* **88**C, 341–422.

Dunlop, R. 1924 An unpublished survey of the Plantation of Munster in 1622. *Journal of the Royal Society of Antiquaries of Ireland* **24**, 128–46.

Edwards, D. 2016 Geraldine endgame: reassessing the origins of the Geraldine rebellion, 1573–9. In P. Crooks and S. Duffy (eds), *The Geraldines and medieval Ireland*, 341–78. Four Courts Press, Dublin.

Edwards, N. 1996 *The archaeology of early medieval Ireland*. Routledge, London.

Egan, G. 1998 *The medieval household: medieval finds from excavations in London*. HMSO and Museum of London, London.

Egan, G. 2004 Buckles, hasps and strap hooks. In J. Clarke (ed.), *The medieval horse and its equipment*, 55–60. Museum of London, London.

Ellis, S.G. and Murray, J. (eds) 2017 *Calendar of State Papers 1509–1547*. Irish Manuscripts Commission, Dublin.

Empey, C.A. 1981 The settlement of the kingdom of Limerick. In J. Lydon (ed.), *England and Ireland in the later Middle Ages*, 1–25. Irish Academic Press, Dublin.

Eogan, G. 1965 *Catalogue of Irish bronze swords*. Stationery Office, Dublin.

Evans, E.E. 1957 *Irish folk ways*. Routledge and Kegan Paul, London.

Evans, J. 1881 *The ancient bronze implements, weapons, and ornaments of Great Britain and Ireland*. Longmans, Green and Co., London.

Fanning, T. 1994 *Viking Age ringed pins from Dublin*. Royal Irish Academy, Dublin.

Ferrar, J. 1767 *A history of the City of Limerick*. A. Welsh, Limerick.

Finch, O. 1997 Bottles and window glass. In R.M. Cleary, M.F. Hurley and E. Shee-Twohig (eds), *Skiddy's Castle and Christ Church, Cork: excavations 1974–77 by D.C. Twohig*, 193–205. Cork Corporation, Cork.

Finch, T.F. and Ryan, P. 1966 *Soils of Co. Limerick*. National Soil Survey of Ireland Bulletin No. 16. An Foras Talúntais, Dublin.

Finnegan, R. (ed.) 2008 *A tour in Ireland in 1775, by Richard Twiss*. University College Dublin, Dublin.

Fitzgerald, P. and McGregor, J.J. 1826 *The history and topography of the county and city of Limerick with a preliminary view of the history and antiquities of Ireland*. G. McKern, Limerick.

Fleming, J. 2009 The formation of the medieval church in Limerick. In L. Irwin, G. Ó Tuathaigh and M. Potter (eds), *Limerick history and society*, 1–15. Geography Publications, Dublin.

Fraher, J.P. 1984 Report on the skeletal material from Lough Gur: excavations at Lough Gur, Co. Limerick, 1977–78, Pt IV. *Journal of the Cork Historical and Archaeological Society* **89** (248), 35–7.

Frazer, J.G. 1911–15 *The golden bough*. Macmillan, London.

Gailey, A. 1984 *Rural houses of the north of Ireland*. John Donald, Edinburgh.

Gilbert, J.T. 1865 *History of the viceroys of Ireland with notice of the Castle of Dublin and its chief occupants in former times*. J. Duffy, Dublin.

Glennon, R. 1847 On the discovery of bones of the Extinct Deer, etc. at Lough Gur in Co. Limerick. *Zoologist* **5**, 1589.

Gowen, M. 1988 *Three Irish gas pipelines: new archaeological evidence in Munster.* Wordwell, Dublin.

Graham, B.J. 1993 The High Middle Ages: *c.* 1100–*c.* 1350. In B.J. Graham and L.J. Proudfoot (eds), *A historical geography of Ireland*, 58–98. Academic Press, London.

Graham-Campbell, J. 1995 *The Viking-age gold and silver of Scotland.* National Museum of Scotland, Edinburgh.

Graham-Campbell, J. 2011 *The Cuerdale hoard and related Viking-age silver and gold from Britain and Ireland.* Research Publication 185. British Museum, London.

Graham-Campbell, J. and Sheehan, J. 2009 Viking Age gold and silver from Irish crannogs and other watery places. *Journal of Irish Archaeology* **18**, 77–93.

Graves, J. 1869 The Earls of Desmond. *Journal of the Royal Society of Antiquaries of Ireland* **1**, 459–98.

Grene Barry, J. 1897–1900 Limerick during the reign of Queen Elizabeth. *Journal of the Limerick Field Club* **1** (1), 1–19, 47; **1** (2), 45–6.

Grene Barry, J. 1900 The Cromwellian settlement of the county of Limerick. *Journal of the Limerick Field Club* **1** (4), 16–33.

Grene Barry, J. 1901 The Cromwellian settlement of the county of Limerick. *Journal of the Limerick Field Club* **2** (5), 43–9.

Grene Barry, J. 1903a Notes on Bourchier Castle and New Church, Loughgur. *Journal of the Royal Society of Antiquaries of Ireland* **13**, 194–7.

Grene Barry, J. 1903b The Cromwellian settlement of the county of Limerick. *Journal of the Limerick Field Club* **2** (7), 211–16.

Grene Barry, J. 1905–8 The romance of Caherelly Castle. *Journal of the Limerick Field Club* **3** (11), 134–8.

Griffiths, N. 2004 Harness pendants and associated fittings. In J. Clarke (ed.), *The medieval horse and its equipment*, 61–71. Museum of London, London.

Grimes, W.F. 1963 The stone circles and related monuments of Wales. In I. Ll. Foster and L. Alcock (eds), *Culture and environment: essays in honour of Sir Cyril Fox*, 93–152. Routledge and Kegan Paul, London.

Grogan, E. 1996 Neolithic houses in Ireland. In T. Darvill and J. Thomas (eds), *Neolithic houses in northwest Europe and beyond*, 41–60. Oxbow Books, Oxford.

Grogan, E. 2002 Neolithic houses in Ireland: a broader perspective. *Antiquity* **76**, 517–25.

Grogan, E. and Eogan, G. 1987 Lough Gur excavations by Seán P. Ó Ríordáin: five enclosed habitation sites of the Neolithic and Beaker period on the Knockadoon Peninsula. *Proceedings of the Royal Irish Academy* **87**C, 299–506.

Grogan, E. and Roche, H. 2010 Clay and fire: the development and distribution of pottery traditions in prehistoric Ireland. In M. Stanley, E. Danaher and J. Eogan (eds), *Creative minds: production, manufacturing and invention in ancient Ireland*, 27–45. National Roads Authority, Dublin.

Hall, R. 2007 *Exploring the world of the Vikings.* Thames and Hudson, London.

Halpin, A. 1997 Archery material. In M.F. Hurley, O.M.B. Scully and S.W.J. McCutcheon, *Late Viking Age and medieval Waterford: excavations 1986–1992*, 538–52. Waterford Corporation, Waterford.

Hammer, C.U., Clausen, H.B. and Dansgaard, W. 1980 Greenland ice sheet evidence of post-glacial volcanism and its climatic impact. *Nature* **288**, 230–5.

Harbison, P. 1969a *The axes of the Early Bronze Age in Ireland*. Prähistorische Bronzefunde 9:1. C.H. Beck'sche Verlagsbuchhandlung, Munich.

Harbison, P. 1969b *The daggers and halberds of the Early Bronze Age in Ireland*. Prähistorische Bronzefunde 6:1. C.H. Beck'sche Verlagsbuchhandlung, Munich.

Harbison, P. 1976 *Bracers and V-perforated buttons in the Beaker and Food Vessel cultures in Ireland*. Archaeologia Atlantica Research Report No. 1. Moreland and Co., Bad Bramstedt.

Harkness, J. 1869 The pre-historic antiquities of and around Lough Gur. *Quarterly Journal of Science* **6**, 388–96.

Hayman, S. (ed.) 1868–9 Unpublished Geraldine documents. *Journal of the Royal Society of Antiquaries of Ireland* **1**, 356–416.

Henderson, J. 1987 The chemical analysis of glass from Lough Gur and its archaeological interpretation. In E. Grogan and G. Eogan, 'Lough Gur excavations by Seán P. Ó Ríordáin: five enclosed habitation sites of the Neolithic and Beaker period on the Knockadoon Peninsula'. *Proceedings of the Royal Irish Academy* **87**C, 502–6.

Hennessy, W.M. 1866 *Chronicon Scotorum: A chronicle of Irish affairs from the earliest times to AD 1135*. Longmans, Green, Reader and Dyer, London.

Herity, M. and Eogan, G. 1977 *Ireland in prehistory*. Routledge and Kegan Paul, London.

Hunt, J. 1967 Prehistoric burials at Cahirguillamore, Co. Limerick. In E. Rynne (ed.), *North Munster studies: essays in commemoration of Monsignor Michael Moloney*, 20–42. Thomond Archaeological Society, Limerick.

Hurl, D., McDowell, J.A., Bourke, C. and Okasha, E. 2011 Objects of bone, copper alloy, lignite and decorated pieces. In C.J. Lynn and J.A. McDowell, *Deer Park Farms: the excavation of a raised rath in the Glenarm Valley, Co. Antrim*, 258–70. Stationery Office, Norwich.

Hurley, M.F. 1995 Excavations in Cork City: Kyrl's Quay/North Main Street and at Grand Parade (Part 1). *Journal of the Cork Historical and Archaeological Society* **100**, 47–90.

Hurley, M.F. 2001 Domestic architecture in medieval Cork and Waterford (11th–17th century). In M. Gläser (ed.), *Lübecker Kolloquium zur Stadtarchäologie im Harseraum III: Der Hausbau*, 15–34. Verlag Schmidt-Römhild, Lübeck.

Hurley, M.F. 2003 A review of domestic architecture in Cork. In R.M. Cleary and M.F. Hurley (eds), *Excavations in Cork City 1984–2000*, 151–70. Cork City Council, Cork.

Hurley, M.F. 2004 Bone artefacts In E. Fitzpatrick, M. O'Brien and P. Walsh (eds), *Archaeological investigations in Galway City, 1987–1998*, 463–76. Wordwell, Bray.

Hurley, M.F. 2014 Appraisal of the evidence. In M.F. Hurley and C. Brett (eds), *Archaeological excavations at South Main Street 2003–2005*, 470–94. Cork City Council, Cork.

Hurley, M. and McCutcheon, S.W.J. 1997 Wooden artefacts. In M.F. Hurley, O.M.B. Scully and S.W.J. McCutcheon, *Late Viking Age and medieval Waterford: excavations 1986–1992*, 553–634. Waterford Corporation, Waterford.

Irwin, L. 2009 Thomas Johnson Westropp. In L. Irwin, G. Ó Tuathaigh and M. Potter (eds), *Limerick history and society*, 483–97. Geography Publications, Dublin.

Jones, C. 2007 *Temples of stone*. Collins Press, Cork.

Kelleher, J.V. 1967 The rise of the Dál Cais. In E. Rynne (ed.), *North Munster studies: essays in commemoration of Monsignor Michael Moloney*, 230–41. Thomond Archaeological Society,

Limerick.

Kelly, C. 2004 *The Grand Tour of Limerick*. Cailleach Books, Allihies.

Kelly, E.P. and O'Donovan, E. 1998 A Viking *longphort* near Athlunkard, Co. Clare. *Archaeology Ireland* **46**, 13–16.

Kelly, F. 1997 *Early Irish farming*. Dublin Institute for Advanced Studies, Dublin.

Kemmy, J. 1996 The Fitzgerald and McGregor history. *Old Limerick Journal* (1996), 11–12.

Knight, J., Coxon, P., Marshall McCabe, A. and McCarron, S.G. 2011 Pleistocene glaciations. In E. Ehlers, P.L. Gibbard and P.L. Hughes (eds), *Quaternary glaciations—extent and chronology: a closer look*, 183–91. Elsevier, Amsterdam.

Kruse, S. and Graham-Campbell, J. 2011 Classification and discussion of the Cuerdale objects. In J. Graham-Campbell (ed.), *The Cuerdale hoard and related Viking-age silver and gold from Britain and Ireland*, 73–84. Research Publication 185. British Museum, London.

Laing, L. 1975 *The archaeology of late Celtic Britain and Ireland c. 400–1200 AD*. Methuen and Co., London.

Laing, L. and Laing, J. 1990 *Celtic Britain and Ireland, AD 200–800: the myth of the Dark Ages*. Irish Academic Press, Dublin.

Lane Fox, A. 1869 Notes on a marble armlet and a bronze spear. *Journal of the Ethnological Society of London* (1869–70), 35–8.

Langrishe, R. 1904 The Bourchier tablet in the Cathedral Church of St Canice, Kilkenny, with some account of that family. *Journal of the Royal Society of Antiquaries of Ireland* **34**, 365–79.

Langrishe, R. 1905 The Bourchier tablet in the Cathedral Church of St Canice, Kilkenny, with some account of that family. *Journal of the Royal Society of Antiquaries of Ireland* **35**, 21–33.

Leask, H.G. 1960 *Irish churches and monastic buildings*, vol. 1. Dundalgan Press, Dundalk.

Leask, H.G. 1971 *Irish churches and monastic buildings*, vol. 2 [reprint]. Dungalgan Press, Dundalk.

Leask, H.G. 1973 *Irish castles and castellated houses*. Dundalgan Press, Dundalk.

Lenihan, M. 1866 *Limerick; its history and antiquities, ecclesiastical, civil and military from the earliest ages*. Mercier Press, Cork.

Lennon, A.M. 2003 Grattan Street. In R.M. Cleary and M.F. Hurley (eds), *Excavations in Cork City 1984–2000*, 61–77. Cork City Council, Cork.

Lewis, S. 1837 *A topographical dictionary of Ireland*. Reprinted (1980) as *A history and topography of Limerick City and County*. Mercier Press, Cork.

Liversage, D. 1958 An island site at Lough Gur. *Journal of the Royal Society of Antiquaries of Ireland* **88**, 67–81.

LMMC 1940 *London Museum Medieval Catalogue*. London.

Lydon, J. 1973 *Ireland in the later Middle Ages*. Gill and Macmillan, Dublin.

Lynch, J.F. 1895 Lough Gur. *Journal of the Cork Historical and Archaeological Society* (ser. 2) **1**, 241–58, 289–302.

Lynch, J.F. 1896 Fragments. *Journal of the Cork Historical and Archaeological Society* (ser. 2) **2**, 140–3.

Lynch, J.F. 1897 The myths and monuments of Loch Gair. *Journal of the Cork Historical and Archaeological Society* (ser. 2) **3**, 332–60.

Lynch, J.F. 1913 Antiquarian remains at Lough Gur. *Journal of the Cork Historical and Archaeological Society* **19**, 8–22.

Lynch, J.F. 1920a Laiche Hi Fiaich. *Journal of the Cork Historical and Archaeological Society* **26**, 29–31.

Lynch, J.F. 1920b Ruaidhri Ruadh. *Journal of the Cork Historical and Archaeological Society* **26**, 84.

Lynch, P.J. 1906–7 Cromleacs in Co. Limerick. No. III. Lough Gur. *Journal of the Limerick Field Club* **3** (11), 127–33.

Lynn, C.J. and McDowell, J.A. 2011 *Deer Park Farms: the excavation of a raised rath in the Glenarm Valley, Co. Antrim.* Stationery Office, Norwich.

McCarthy, M. 2008 Faunal remains, Site C. In M. Doody, *The Ballyhoura Hills Project*, 393–6. Discovery Programme Monograph No. 7. Wordwell, Bray.

McClatchie, M., Bogaard, A., Colledge, S., Whitehouse, N., Schulting, R., Barratt, P. and McLaughlin, R. 2015 Farming and foraging in Neolithic Ireland: an archaeobotanical perspective. *Antiquity* **90**, 302–18.

McCormack, A.M. 2005 *The earldom of Desmond 1463–1583: the decline and crisis of a feudal lordship.* Four Courts Press, Dublin.

McCormack, G. (forthcoming) John Hunt's excavations at Ballingarry ringfort, 1949–51: a medieval settlement in Co. Limerick.

McCormick, F. 1985–6 Faunal remains from prehistoric Irish burials. *Journal of Irish Archaeology* **3**, 37–48.

McCorry, M. 1997 Coarse Ware pottery from Phase 3. In D.M. Waterman, *Excavations at Navan Fort 1961–71* (ed. C.J. Lynn), 72–9. Stationery Office, Belfast.

MacCotter, P. 2006 The rise of Meic Carthaig and the political geography of Desmumu. *Journal of the Cork Historical and Archaeological Society* **111**, 59–76.

MacCotter, P. 2008 *Medieval Ireland: territorial, political and economic divisions.* Four Courts Press, Dublin.

McCutcheon, S.W.J. 1997 The stone artefacts. In M.F. Hurley, O.M.B. Scully and S.W.J. McCutcheon, *Late Viking Age and medieval Waterford: excavations 1986–1992*, 404–32. Waterford Corporation, Waterford.

MacDermott, M. 1949a Two barrows at Ballingoola. *Journal of the Royal Society of Antiquaries of Ireland* **79**, 139–45.

MacDermott, M. 1949b Lough Gur excavations: excavation of a barrow in Cahercorney, Co. Limerick. *Journal of the Cork Historical and Archaeological Society* **54**, 101–2.

McGarry, T. 2009 Irish late prehistoric ring-ditches. In G. Cooney, K. Becker, J. Coles, M. Ryan and S. Sievers (eds), *Relics of old decency: archaeological studies in later prehistory*, 413–23. Wordwell. Dublin.

McSparron, C. 2008 Have you no homes to go to? *Archaeology Ireland* **22** (3), 18-21.

Manning, C. 1985 A Neolithic burial mound at Ashleypark, Co. Tipperary. *Proceedings of the Royal Irish Academy* **85**C, 61–100.

Mitchell, G.F. 1951 Studies in Irish Quaternary Deposits: No. 7. *Proceedings of the Royal Irish Academy* **53**C, 111–206.

Mitchell, G.F. 1954 A pollen diagram from Lough Gur, County Limerick (Studies in Irish Quaternary Deposits: No. 9). *Proceedings of the Royal Irish Academy* **56**C, 481–8.

Mitchell, [G.]F. 1976 *The Irish landscape.* Collins, London.

Mitchell, G.F. and Ó Ríordáin, S.P. 1942 Early Bronze Age pottery from Rockbarton Bog, Co. Limerick. *Proceedings of the Royal Irish Academy* **48**C, 255–72.

Molloy, K. 2008 Palaeoenvironment. In M. Doody, *The Ballyhoura Hills Project*, 23–30. Discovery Programme Monograph No. 7. Wordwell, Bray.

Monk, J. 1982 The animal bones. Excavations at Lough Gur, Co. Limerick, 1977–78. Pt II. *Journal of the Cork Historical and Archaeological Society* **87** (246), 101–6.

Monk, J. 1984 The animal bones. Excavations at Lough Gur, Co. Limerick, 1977–78. Pt IV. *Journal of the Cork Historical and Archaeological Society* **89** (248), 37–54.

Monk, M. 1982 The charred seeds and cereal remains. Excavations at Lough Gur, Co. Limerick, 1977–78. Pt II. *Journal of the Cork Historical and Archaeological Society* **87** (246), 100–1.

Monk, M. 1984 The charred seeds and cereal remains. Excavations at Lough Gur, Co. Limerick, 1977–78. Pt IV. *Journal of the Cork Historical and Archaeological Society* **89** (248), 33–7.

Monk, M. 2013 Overview of sites from the early medieval period. In K. Hanley and M.F. Hurley, *Generations: the archaeology of five national road schemes in County Cork*, 240–9. National Roads Authority, Dublin.

Motherwell, E. 2012 LiDAR and its potential contribution to archaeological survey in Ireland. Unpublished MPhil. thesis, Department of Archaeology, University College Cork.

Mullins, C. 2007 Socketed longbone points: a study of the Irish material with reference to British and Continental examples. *Journal of Irish Archaeology* **16**, 35–59.

Newman, C. 1997 *Tara: an archaeological survey*. Discovery Programme Monograph No. 2. Royal Irish Academy, Dublin.

Noel Hume, I. 1991 *A guide to artefacts of Colonial America*. Vintage Books, New York.

O'Brien, E. 2008 The extended use of Site C for burial. In M. Doody, *The Ballyhoura Hills Project*, 658–63. Discovery Programme Monograph No. 7. Wordwell, Bray.

O'Brien, W. 1993 Aspects of wedge tomb chronology. In E. Shee Twohig and M. Ronayne (eds), *Past perceptions: the prehistoric archaeology of south-west Ireland*, 63–74. Cork University Press, Cork.

O'Brien, W. 2004a *Ross Island: mining, metal and society in early Ireland*. Department of Archaeology, National University of Ireland, Galway.

O'Brien, W. 2004b (Con)Fusion of tradition? The circle henge in Ireland. In A. Gibson and A. Sheridan (eds), *From sickles to circles: Britain and Ireland at the time of Stonehenge*, 323–38. Tempus, Stroud.

O'Brien, W. and O'Driscoll, J. 2018 *Hillforts, warfare and society in Bronze Age Ireland*. Archaeopress, Oxford.

O'Connor, L. 1991 Irish Iron Age and Early Christian whetstones. *Journal of the Royal Society of Antiquaries of Ireland* **121**, 45–76.

O'Connor, P.J. 1988 The maturation of town and village life in County Limerick 1700–1900. In W.J. Smyth and K. Whelan, *Common ground: essays on the historical geography of Ireland*, 149–72. Cork University Press, Cork.

O'Conor, K.D. 1998 *The archaeology of medieval rural settlement in Ireland*. Discovery Programme Monograph No. 3. Royal Irish Academy, Dublin.

Ó Corráin, D. 1972 *Ireland before the Normans*. Gill and Macmillan, Dublin.

Ó Corráin, D. 1983 Some legal references to fences and fencing in early historic Ireland. In T. Reeves-Smyth and F. Hamond (eds), *Landscape archaeology in Ireland*, 247–52. British Archaeological Reports, British Series 116. Oxford.

Ó Donnabháin, B. 1995 The human remains. In R.M. Cleary, 'Later Bronze Age houses and prehistoric burials from Lough Gur, Co. Limerick'. *Proceedings of the Royal Irish Academy* **95**C, 59–63.

O'Donovan, J. 1840 *Letters containing information relative to the antiquities of the county of Limerick collected during the progress of the Ordnance Survey in 1840.* [Reproduced under the direction of Revd M. O'Flanagan, Bray, 1929.]

O'Driscoll, J. and Cleary, R.M. 2016 Grange Stone Circles, Lough Gur, Co. Limerick: geophysical survey at Stone Circles B, C and D, and review of dating and phases of monument use of Circle B. *North Munster Antiquarian Journal* **56**, 27–46.

O'Dwyer, M. 1964 A survey of the earthworks in the district of Old Pallasgrean. *North Munster Antiquarian Journal* (1964), 111–15.

Okasha, E. 1997 The inscribed knife. In M.F. Hurley, O.M.B. Scully and S.W.J. McCutcheon, *Late Viking Age and medieval Waterford: excavations 1986–1992*, 524–8. Waterford Corporation, Waterford.

O'Keeffe, T. 2000 *Medieval Ireland: an archaeology.* Tempus, Stroud.

O'Kelly, M.J. 1941 A survey of the antiquities in the barony of Small County, Co. Limerick. Unpublished MA thesis, Department of Archaeology, University College Cork.

O'Kelly, M.J. 1942–3 A survey of the antiquities in the barony of Small County, Co. Limerick. *North Munster Antiquarian Journal* **3** (2), 75–97, 169–84, 222–41.

O'Kelly, M.J. 1944 A survey of the antiquities in the barony of Small County, Co. Limerick, part 4. *North Munster Antiquarian Journal* **5**, 16–53.

O'Kelly, M.J. 1951 An Early Bronze Age ring-fort at Carrigillihy, Co. Cork. *Journal of the Cork Historical and Archaeological Society* **56**, 69–86.

O'Kelly, M.J. 1962 Two ring-forts at Garryduff, Co. Cork. *Proceedings of the Royal Irish Academy* **63**C, 17–125.

O'Kelly, M.J. 1967 Knockea, Co. Limerick. In E. Rynne (ed.), *North Munster studies: essays in commemoration of Monsignor Michael Moloney*, 72–101. Thomond Archaeological Society, Limerick.

O'Kelly, M.J. and O'Kelly, C. 1978 *Illustrated guide to Lough Gur.* Claire O'Kelly, Cork.

Ó Lochlainn, C. 1940 Roadways in ancient Ireland. In J. Ryan (ed.), *Féilsgríbhinn Eóin Mhic Néill. Essays and studies presented to Professor Eoin MacNeill*, 465–74. Three Candles, Dublin.

Ó Nualláin, S. and Cody, E. 1996 A re-examination of four sites in Grange townland, Lough Gur, Co. Limerick. *North Munster Antiquarian Journal* **37**, 3–14.

O'Rahilly, C. 1995 Medieval Limerick: the growth of two towns. In H.B. Clarke (ed.), *Irish cities*, 163–76. Mercier Press, Cork.

Ordnance Survey of Ireland 1991 *Ordnance Survey of Ireland: an illustrated record.* Ordnance Survey of Ireland, Dublin.

Ó Ríordáin, S.P. 1936 Excavations at Lissard, Co. Limerick, and other sites in the locality. *Journal of the Royal Society of Antiquaries of Ireland* **66**, 173–85.

Ó Ríordáin, S.P. 1940 Excavations at Cush, Co. Limerick. *Proceedings of the Royal Irish Academy* **45**C, 83–181.

Ó Ríordáin, S.P. 1946 Prehistory in Ireland, 1937–46. Paper No. 6. *Proceedings of the Prehistoric Society* **12**, 142–71.

Ó Ríordáin, S.P. 1947a Excavation of a barrow at Rathjordan, Co. Limerick. *Journal of the Cork Historical and Archaeological Society* **52**, 1–4.

Ó Ríordáin, S.P. 1947b Roman material in Ireland. *Proceedings of the Royal Irish Academy* **51**C, 35–83.

Ó Ríordáin, S.P. 1948 Further barrows at Rathjordan, Co. Limerick, and other sites in the locality. *Journal of the Cork Historical and Archaeological Society* **53**, 19–31.

Ó Ríordáin, S.P. 1949a Lough Gur excavations: three marshland habitation sites. *Journal of the Royal Society of Antiquaries of Ireland* **79**, 126–39.

Ó Ríordáin, S.P. 1949b Lough Gur excavations: Carraig Aille and the 'Spectacles'. *Proceedings of the Royal Irish Academy* **52**C, 39–111.

Ó Ríordáin, S.P. 1950 Lough Gur excavations: Ballingoola V. *Journal of the Royal Society of Antiquaries of Ireland* **80**, 262–3.

Ó Ríordáin, S.P. 1951 Lough Gur excavations: the Great Stone Circle (B) in Grange townland. *Proceedings of the Royal Irish Academy* **54**C, 37–74.

Ó Ríordáin, S.P. 1954 Lough Gur excavations: Neolithic and Bronze Age houses on Knockadoon. *Proceedings of the Royal Irish Academy* **56**C, 297–459.

Ó Ríordáin, S.P. 1955 Preserve, examine, illustrate. A commentary on the position of Irish archaeology. *Journal of the Royal Society of Antiquaries of Ireland* **85**, (1), 1–21.

Ó Ríordáin, S.P. and Hunt, J. 1942 Medieval dwellings at Caherguillamore, Co. Limerick. *Journal of the Royal Society of Antiquaries of Ireland* **72**, 37–63.

Ó Ríordáin, S.P. and Lucas, A.T. 1946–7 Excavation of a small crannog at Rathjordan, Co. Limerick. *North Munster Antiquarian Journal* (1946–7), 68–77.

Ó Ríordáin, S.P. and Mitchell, G.F. 1942 Early Bronze Age pottery from Rockbarton Bog, Co. Limerick. *Proceedings of the Royal Irish Academy* **48**C, 255–72.

Ó Ríordáin, S.P. and Ó Danachair, C. 1947 Lough Gur excavations: Site J, Knockadoon. *Journal of the Royal Society of Antiquaries of Ireland* **85**, 34–50.

Ó Ríordáin, S.P. and Ó h-Iceadha, G. 1955 Lough Gur excavations: the megalithic tomb. *Journal of the Royal Society of Antiquaries of Ireland* **77**, 39–52.

Ó Ríordáin, S.P. and O'Kelly, M.J. 1940 Old house types near Lough Gur, Co. Limerick. In J. Ryan (ed.), *Féilsgríbhinn Eóin Mhic Néill. Essays and studies presented to Professor Eoin MacNeill*, 227–36. Three Candles, Dublin.

O'Sullivan, A. 1998 *The archaeology of lake settlement in Ireland.* Discovery Programme Monograph No. 4. Royal Irish Academy, Dublin.

O'Sullivan, A., McCormick, F., Kerr, T.R. and Harney, L. 2013 *Early medieval Ireland, AD 400–1100: the evidence from archaeological excavations.* Royal Irish Academy, Dublin.

O'Sullivan, W. 1997 A finding list of Sir James Ware's manuscripts. *Proceedings of the Royal Irish Academy* **97**C, 69–99.

Otway-Ruthven, A.J. 1968 *A history of medieval Ireland.* Benn, London.

Peate, I.C. 1940 *The Welsh house: a study of folk culture.* The Honourable Society of Cymmrodorion, London.

Peirce, I. and Oakeshott, E. 2005 *Swords of the Viking Age.* Boydell Press, Woodbridge.

Postan, M.M. 1975 *The medieval economy and society.* Penguin, Harmondsworth.

Raftery, B. 1983 *A catalogue of Irish Iron Age antiquities.* Marburg.

Raftery, B. 1984 *La Tène in Ireland.* Marburg.

Raftery, B. 1997 *Pagan Celtic Ireland: the enigma of the Irish Iron Age.* Thames and Hudson, London.

Raftery, J. 1936–9 Excavation of two stone circles at Lough Gur (1936). Excavation of stone circle and two stone forts at Lough Gur (1937). Excavations at Lough Gur (1938). *North Munster Antiquarian Journal.* 1, 82–83, 124–5.

Raftery, J. 1939 An early Iron Age sword from Lough Gur, Co. Limerick. *Journal of the Royal*

Society of Antiquaries of Ireland **9**, 170–1.

Roche, H. 2004 The dating of the embanked stone circle at Grange, Co. Limerick. In H. Roche, E. Grogan, J. Bradley, J. Coles and B. Raftery (eds), *From megaliths to metals: essays in honour of George Eogan*, 109–16. Oxbow Books, Oxford.

Russell, I. and Hurley, M.F. (eds) 2014 *Woodstown: a Viking-age settlement in Co. Waterford*. Four Courts Press, Dublin.

Scarre, C., Arias, P., Burenhult, G., Fano, M., Oosterbeek, L., Schulting, R., Sheridan, A. and Whittle, A. 2003 Megalithic chronologies. In G. Burenhult and S. Westergaard (eds), *Stones and bones: formal disposal of the dead in Atlantic Europe during the Mesolithic–Neolithic interface, 6000–3000 BC*, 65–111. Archaeopress, Oxford.

Schulting, R.J., Murphy, E., Jones, C. and Warren, G. 2011 New dates from the north and a proposed chronology for Irish court tombs. *Proceedings of the Royal Irish Academy* **112**C, 1–60.

Scully, O.M.B. 1997a Ferrous and non-ferrous metal artefacts. In R.M. Cleary, M.F. Hurley and E. Shee-Twohig (eds), *Skiddy's Castle and Christ Church, Cork: excavations 1974–77 by D.C. Twohig*, 165–90. Cork Corporation, Cork.

Scully, O.M.B. 1997b Domestic architecture: houses in Waterford from the eleventh century to post-medieval times. In M.F. Hurley, O.M.B. Scully and S.W.J. McCutcheon, *Late Viking Age and medieval Waterford: excavations 1986–1992*, 34–44. Waterford Corporation, Waterford.

Scully, O.M.B. 1997c Metal artefacts. In M.F. Hurley, O.M.B. Scully and S.W.J. McCutcheon, *Late Viking Age and medieval Waterford: excavations 1986–1992*, 438–89. Waterford Corporation, Waterford.

Seymour, S.J.D. 1913 *The diocese of Emly*. Church of Ireland Printing and Publishing, Dublin.

Shee Twohig, E. 1990 *Irish megalithic tombs*. Shire Publications, Princes Risborough.

Sheehan, J. 2011 Hiberno-Scandinavian broad arm rings. In J. Graham-Campbell (ed.), *The Cuerdale hoard and related Viking-age silver and gold from Britain and Ireland*, 94–109. Research Publication 185. British Museum, London.

Sheehan, J. 2014 Silver. In I. Russell and M.F. Hurley (eds), *Woodstown: a Viking-age settlement in Co. Waterford*, 194–222. Four Courts Press, Dublin.

Sheridan, A. 2010 The Neolithization of Britain and Ireland: the 'big picture'. In B. Finlayson and G. Warren (eds), *Landscapes in transition*, 89–105. Oxbow Books, Oxford.

Sheridan, A. 2013 Early Neolithic habitation structures in Britain and Ireland: a matter of circumstance and context. The house through the Irish Neolithic. In D. Hofmann and J. Smyth (eds), *Tracking the Neolithic house in Europe: sedentism, architecture, and practice*, 283–300. Springer, London.

Shirley, E.P. 1856 Extracts from the journal of Thomas Dineley, Esquire, giving some account of his visit to Ireland in the reign of Charles II. Notes by J.P. Prendergast. *Journal of the Kilkenny and South-East of Ireland Archaeological Society* (ser. 2) **1**, 143–6, 170–88.

Shirley, E.P. 1867 Extracts from the journal of Thomas Dineley, Esquire, giving some account of his visit to Ireland in the reign of Charles II. Notes by R. O'Brien and J. Graves. *Journal of the Kilkenny and South-East of Ireland Archaeological Society* (ser. 2) **6**, 73–91, 176–204, 268–90.

Simington, R.C. (ed.) 1938 *The Civil Survey, AD 1655–1656. Vol. 4: Limerick*. Irish Manuscripts Commission, Dublin.

Simpson, D.D.A. 1988 The stone maceheads of Ireland. *Journal of the Royal Society of Antiquaries of Ireland* **118**, 27–52.

Simpson, D.D.A. 1996 Irish perforated stone implements in context. *Journal of Irish Archaeology* **7**, 65–76.

Simpson, D.D.A. and Gibson, A. 1989 Lyles Hill. *Current Archaeology* **10** (7), No. 114, 214–15.

Smyth, J. 2006 The role of the house in Early Neolithic Ireland. *European Journal of Archaeology* **9**, 229–57.

Smyth, J. 2007 Neolithic settlement in Ireland: new theories and approaches. Unpublished Ph.D thesis, University College Dublin.

Smyth, J. 2010 The house and group identity in the Irish Neolithic. *Proceedings of the Royal Irish Academy* **111**C, 1–31.

Smyth, J. 2013 Tides of change? The house through the Irish Neolithic. In D. Hofmann and J. Smyth (eds), *Tracking the Neolithic in Europe: sedentism, architecture, and practice*, 301–27. Springer, New York.

Smyth, J. 2014 *Settlement in the Irish Neolithic: new discoveries at the edge of Europe*. Oxbow Books, Oxford.

Stafford, T. 1633 *Pacata Hibernia—or A history of the wars in Ireland, during the reign of Queen Elizabeth. Taken from the original Chronicles* [reprinted 1810]. Hibernia Press, Dublin.

Stenberger, M. 1966 A ring-fort at Raheennamadra, Knocklong, Co. Limerick. *Proceedings of the Royal Irish Academy* **65**C, 37–54.

Sternke, F. 2011 The stone tools. In R.M. Cleary and H. Kelleher, *Archaeological excavations at Tullahedy, County Tipperary: Neolithic settlement in north Munster*, 216–71. Collins Press, Cork.

Stevens, P. 2007 Clonfad 3: a unique glimpse into early monastic life in Co. Westmeath. *Seanda* **2**, 42–3.

Stout, G. 1991 Embanked enclosures of the Boyne region. *Proceedings of the Royal Irish Academy* **91**C, 245–84.

Stout, M. 1997 *The Irish ringfort*. Four Courts Press, Dublin.

Synge, F.M. 1966 Glacial geology. In T.F. Finch and P. Ryan, *Soils of Co. Limerick*, 12–20. National Soil Survey of Ireland Bulletin No. 16. An Foras Talúntais, Dublin.

Taylor, J. 1980 *Bronze Age goldwork of the British Isles*. Cambridge University Press, Cambridge.

Todd, J.H. 1867 *Cogadh Gaedhel re Gallaibh*. Longman, Green, Reader and Dyer, London.

Trotter, J.B. 1819 *Walks through Ireland in the years 1812, 1814 and 1817 described in a series of letters to an English gentleman*. Sir Richard Phillips and Co., London.

Valante, M.A. 2008 *The Vikings in Ireland: settlement, trade and urbanization*. Four Courts Press, Dublin.

Van Wijngaarden-Bakker, L.H. 1995 Subsistence in the Late Bronze Age at Lough Gur. In R.M. Cleary, 'Later Bronze Age houses and prehistoric burials from Lough Gur, Co. Limerick'. *Proceedings of the Royal Irish Academy* **95**C, 79–92.

Waddell, J. 2000 *The prehistoric archaeology of Ireland*. Wordwell, Bray.

Wakeman, W.F. 1891 *Archaeologia Hibernica: a hand-book of Irish antiquities, pagan and Christian: especially of such as are easy of access from the Irish metropolis* (2nd edn). Hodges Figgis, Dublin.

Wallace, J.N.A. 1938 The Golden Bog of Cullen. *North Munster Antiquarian Journal* **3**, 89–101.

Wallace, P.F. 2004 Adolf Mahr and the making of Seán P. Ó Ríordáin. In H. Roche, E. Grogan, J. Bradley, J. Coles and B. Raftery (eds), *From megaliths to metals: essays in honour of George Eogan*, 254–63. Oxbow Books, Oxford.

Walsh, C. 1997 Sunken buildings. In M.F. Hurley, O.M.B. Scully and S.W.J. McCutcheon, *Late*

Viking Age and medieval Waterford: excavations 1986–1992, 45–53. Waterford Corporation, Waterford.

Ware, J. 1705 *The antiquities and history of Ireland*. A. Crook, Dublin.

Warner, R. 2008 Appendix 1. Radiocarbon dates from Chancellorsland site A. In M. Doody, *The Ballyhoura Hills Project*, 665–8. Discovery Programme Monograph No. 7. Wordwell, Bray.

Warner, R.B. 2011 An analysis of the radiocarbon dates from Deer Park Farms. In C.J. Lynn and J.A. McDowell, *Deer Park Farms: the excavation of a raised rath in the Glenarm Valley, Co. Antrim*, 228–34. Stationery Office, Norwich.

Watt, J. 1972 *The Church in medieval Ireland*. Gill and Macmillan, Dublin.

Watts, W.A. 1960 C14 dating and the Neolithic in Ireland. *Antiquity* **34**, 111–16.

Welply, W.H. 1919 The siege of Lough Gur castle, Co. Limerick, 1641. *Journal of the Cork Historical and Archaeological Society* **25**, 79–81.

Wesley, J. 1785 *The journal of John Wesley*. Published 1906, J.M. Dent and Sons, London.

Westropp, T.J. 1889 History of the abbey and battles of Monasteranenagh, Croom, County Limerick, 1148–1603. *Journal of the Royal Society of Antiquaries of Ireland* **9**, 232–8.

Westropp, T.J. 1904–5 A survey of the ancient churches in the county of Limerick. *Proceedings of the Royal Irish Academy* **25**C, 327–480.

Westropp, T.J. 1906 Cromwellian account books, Limerick. *Journal of the Royal Society of Antiquaries of Ireland* **16**, 202–4.

Westropp, T.J. 1906–7 The castles of the County Limerick (north-eastern baronies; central and south-eastern baronies). *Proceedings of the Royal Irish Academy* **26**C, 55–108, 143–208.

Westropp, T.J. 1907 The principal ancient castles of County Limerick. *Journal of the Royal Society of Antiquaries of Ireland* **17**, 24–40, 153–64.

Westropp, T.J., Macalister, R.A.S. and MacNamara, G.U. 1916 *The antiquities of Limerick and its neighbourhood*. Hodges, Figgis and Co., Dublin.

Windle, B. 1912 Megalithic remains surrounding Lough Gur, Co. Limerick. *Proceedings of the Royal Irish Academy* **30**C, 283–306.

Woodman, P. 2015 *Ireland's first settlers: time and the Mesolithic*. Oxbow Books, Oxford.

Woodman, P.C. and Scannell, M. 1993 A context for the Lough Gur lithics. In E. Shee Twohig and M. Ronayne (eds), *Past perceptions: the prehistoric archaeology of south-west Ireland*, 53–62. Cork University Press, Cork.

Woodman, P.C., Anderson, E. and Finlay, N. 2006 *The archaeology of a collection: the Keiller-Knowles Collection of the National Museum of Ireland*. National Museum of Ireland Monograph 2. Wordwell, Bray.

Woodward, A. 2000 *British barrows: a matter of life and death*. Tempus, Stroud.

Young, T. 2014 Ceramics: crucibles and cupels. In I. Russell and M.F. Hurley (eds), *Woodstown: a Viking-age settlement in Co. Waterford*, 267–82. Four Courts Press, Dublin.

Youngs, S. 1989 Fine metalwork to *c*. AD 650. In S. Youngs (ed.), *'The work of angels': masterpieces of Celtic metalwork, 6th–9th centuries AD*, 20–9. British Museum Publications, London.

Index

A

Abbeyfeale, 333
Account Rolls, 340
Adare, 334
aerial photography, 40, 267, 293
Aherlow, 194, 337–8, 363
Aherlow, River, 283
Aine, goddess, 141
Aney (Hospital), 333, 334
Anglo-Norman Lough Gur, 15, 289–318 *passim*, 319
  Anglo-Norman families, 289, 320
  Anglo-Norman invasion, 289, 316, 356, 369
  Anglo-Norman land grantees, 369
  Anglo-Norman lords, 294, 316, 319, 356
Anglo-Saxon England, 194
antiquarian accounts, 17–18, 189
antler handle, 243, 253
antler tines, 74, 253–4
antlers, 7–8, 91–2, 244, 275
Antrim, 56, 91, 233, 274–5, 367
Antrim coast, north, 4
archaeological research, 1, 17, 19, 21, 23, 25, 27, 29, 31, 33, 35, 37, 39, 41, 48
archaeological time, 13–15
Arctic fox, 6
Arctic lemming, 6
Ardaghlooda, 4
Ardaghlooda Hill, 29, 107, 145, 147, 210–11, 277
Ardanreagh townland, 145
Ardpatrick, 281, 315
Armagh, 151, 315–16
arm-rings, 285–6
Arroasian Rule, 316
arrowheads, 86, 113, 126, 175, 177, 202, 310–11
  barbed and tanged, 55, 114, 123–4, 125, 126, 130, 199, 368
  laurel-shaped, 66
  leaf-shaped, 14, 55, 60, 62–3, 66, 68, 72–3, 76, 77–8, 85, 91, 92, 156
  lozenge-shaped, 55, 66, 68, 72–3, 75–6, 91, 113–14
  Petit Tranchet Derivative (lopsided), 102, 113, 114, 118, 177

ash pits, 304
Askeaton, 319
Askeaton Castle, 337
Ath-fhada (Longford Bridge), 351
Athlunkard, 283
Augustinian canons, 316
Augustinian nunnery, 15
Augustinian priory, 316
Austria, 215
awls, 113–14, 133, 165–6, 178, 244, 247, 252, 275
Awny (Knockainy), 289
axe factories, 56, 91
axeheads, bronze, 131–2, 178, 182, 204, 206–7, 208
axeheads, copper, 123
axeheads, iron, 244, 275
axeheads, stone, 14, 44, 55, 56–7, 60, 63, 68, 72–3, 75, 78, 85, 91, 92, 93, 127, 129, 202, 204, 241, 246, 265, 272, 280, 367
  granite, 66, 69
  greenstone, 56, 60, 66, 68, 75, 91, 93, 198–9, 202
  porcellanite, 56–7, 91
  socketed, 14, 178, 205, 207

B

Baggotstown, 6, 364
Balic/Bailey Islands, 277
Ballinaguard, 351
Ballinard, 221, 223, 289
Ballinard finger-ring, 15
Balline, 221, 368
Balline hoard, 15, 222, 223
Ballineety, 281
Ballingarry, 222–3, 290
Ballingoola, 9, 14–15, 29, 40, 93, 102, 130, 194, 199–201, 213, 226–7, 260, 274, 368–9
Ballingoola III, 201, 233, 265–6, 272, 274, 275, 276
Ballingoola IV, 201, 264, 266, 272, 276
Ballinrowley, 349
Ballyhoura, 281
Ballylanders area, 6
Ballynagallagh, 15, 25, 35, 41, 132, 136, 145, 192–3, 203, 206, 226–7, 265–9, 272–5, 277, 278, 282,

316–18, 339, 369
Ballynagallagh convent/nunnery, 25, 268, 317
Ballynebrahir, 317
Ballynebrahirbeg, 318
Ballyvorneen, 351
Bann flakes, 14, 44, 46, 47, 198
    miniature, 46, 198
    possible, 44, 46
barrel padlock keys, 299, 302, 310
barrows, 32, 45–6, 93, 129–30, 147, 150, 193–5, 197–9,
    201–2
    excavation of, 45, 129
    location of, 195, 200
Bassilden, 340
Bath, 18, 331, 340, 352, 357
Bath, Lord, 347
Battle of Affane, 333
Battle of Belach Lechta, 284
Battle of Belach Mugna, 225
Battle of Dysert, 289
Battle of Monasteranenagh, 346
Battle of Sulchóid, 283
Battle of Waterloo, 19
Baylee, John, 277, 340
Baylee, Stackpoole, 12
Baylee, Susanna, 340
Bayley family, 330
Bayly, Henry, 19
beads
    amber, 311
    bone, 66, 69, 73–4, 75, 86, 91, 96, 99, 159, 244,
      246, 272, 311
    clay, 114, 187, 269
    copper, 159
    glass, 153, 159, 163, 167, 178, 187, 221, 241,
      248–9, 253–4, 260, 272, 275
    jet, 247
    shell, 99
    stone, 63, 66, 73–4, 75, 79, 91, 99, 131, 247,
      367
Beaker culture, 102, 112–13, 123, 125–6, 128–30, 140,
    145, 156, 187, 194, 199, 214, 368
Beaker pottery, 14, 72, 90, 100, 112–13, 124–5, 129–
    30, 138, 140, 169–70, 368
Bealadrohid, Co. Tipperary, 334, 361
Beechwood Cottage, 39
Black Castle, 12, 15, 20–1, 24–5, 280–1, 302, 320, 331–
    2, 335, 340–4, 349, 370
Black Death, 294
blades, flint, 47, 60, 130, 140
Bog of Cullen, 47–8, 124, 284
Bolin Island, 205, 216, 277–80
bone artefacts
    beads, 66, 69, 73–4, 75, 86, 91, 96, 99, 159, 244,
      246, 272, 311

box, 300
    combs, 184, 244–5, 252–3, 272, 275, 311
    cylinders, 75
    gaming pieces, 245, 253
    handle, 217, 298, 355
    needle, 245
    pin beaters, 275
    pins, 68–9, 100, 244–6, 252, 311
    points, 66, 72–4, 76, 78–9, 85–6, 91, 114, 187,
      275
    scoops, 245, 253
    spearheads, 85–6, 101, 246, 272
    spindle-whorls, 245, 252–3
    strip, decorated, 253
bones
    bird, 10, 63, 86, 141, 176, 214, 254, 315
    cattle and sheep, 263
    elk, 6
    Giant Irish Deer, 13
    notched, 86, 91–2
Book of Clonenagh, 316
Book of Lecan, 282
Book of Lismore, 282
Book of Rights, 225
Bordeaux region, 301
Boru, Brian, 15, 29, 225, 284, 290, 322, 369
Bourchier, Charles, 337
Bourchier, Elizabeth, 340
Bourchier, Fredrick Philip, 337
Bourchier, George, 332, 334, 335–7, 340, 370
Bourchier, Henry, 319, 340, 347
Bouchier, Sir John, 336
Bourchier, Martha, 337
Bourchier family, 18, 336
Bourchier's Castle, 15, 18, 20, 23–5, 29, 225, 290, 319–
    20, 322–32, 337–40, 343, 344, 351–2, 356, 358,
    363–4
    siege of, 339
    surrender of, 338
Bourke, William, 350
Bourkes, 320, 349, 351
Bowl Food Vessels, 140, 147, 199
bowls, round-bottomed, 53, 98–9
Boyne Valley, 103
bracelets, 113–14, 133, 149, 160, 182, 247–8, 276, 285–
    6, 368
Bretha Comaithchesa, 260
Britain, 6, 12, 39, 43–4, 56, 85, 123–4, 131, 133, 204–5,
    215–16, 220–1, 244, 367–8
British Grooved Ware, 112
British Museum, 119, 209, 214, 216, 284, 364
bronze, 11–12, 15, 178, 182, 215, 217, 220–1, 241–3,
    249, 251, 272, 275–6, 280, 287–8, 297–8
    sheet, 114, 206
    strip, 242–3, 298

Bronze Age, 1, 44–6, 125–6, 149–51, 153, 159–63, 165,
169, 171–9, 183–5, 187, 189, 191–5, 199, 201–3,
205–11
    buildings, 125, 158
    Class II pottery, 55, 68, 72, 85, 156–7, 161,
        163, 165
    early, 102–3, 105, 107, 109, 111–13, 115, 117,
        119, 121, 123, 125, 127, 129, 147
    gorget, 206
    in Lough Gur, 368
    middle, 14, 48, 140
    sites, 48
bronze artefacts, 149, 166, 178–9, 204–5, 243, 251
    awls, 133, 182
    axeheads, 11, 14, 131–2, 149, 161, 182, 204,
        206, 368
    bracelets, 113, 133, 182
    button, 242–3
    chisel, 182
    earring, 175
    ingots, 368
    pins, 165, 178
    pins/brooches, 204
    plaque, 17
    ring-pin/brooch, 242
    spearheads, 11, 181, 204, 208
    stick-pins, 311
    stylus, 221, 241, 272
    swords, 208
    toilet implement, 220–1, 241, 272
bronze-casting, 15, 165–6, 208, 270
bronzesmith's workshop, 185
brooches, 217, 242, 276
    safety-pin, 15, 218
Browne, Dame Barbery, 339
Browne, Ulick, 337
Browne, Valentine, 362
Bruce Wars, the, 294
Bruff, 11, 20–1, 23–4, 32, 204, 220, 281, 339, 363
Bruff Aerial Survey, 32, 36, 41, 104, 266, 293
Bruree, 225
buckle, 298–9, 302
bullaun stones, 280
burials, 14–15, 66, 95–8, 101, 123–4, 138, 140–1, 145,
169, 189–90, 192–4, 202, 219, 281, 368
    Beaker, 124
    child, 68, 80, 95
    cremated Mesolithic, 44
    crouched, 98–9, 101
Butler, James, 333
Butler, Thomas, 333
Butler conflict, 333
Butlers of Ormond, 333–4, 356
Buttevant, 316
byre-dwellings, 312

C
Caher Gail, 293
Cahercorney, 7, 14, 21, 40, 93, 102, 194, 201, 316, 368
Caherelly Castles, 4, 349–50, 351
Caherelly church, 359
Caherelly East, 349–50
Caherelly West, 320, 349–50
Caherguillamore, 14, 15, 19, 25, 40–1, 93, 98–100, 102,
125, 130, 131, 290–301, 304, 313–15, 318, 346,
347, 362, 367–8
Calliaghtown, 316, 318
Camas, 316
Camoge River, 4, 7–10, 43, 45–6, 127–8, 201, 224,
347, 351
canon law, 315
Canterbury, 270–1
Canterbury penny, 272
Cappamore, 44
Carew, Sir George, 18, 338
Carew, Lord, 363
Carew, Sir Peter, 333
Carew Manuscripts, 333, 346
Carraig Aille, 10, 15, 92–3, 220, 223, 226–9, 233, 235,
237, 243, 249–57, 259–60, 272–6, 285–7, 369
Carraig Aille II, 15, 93, 220–1, 228–33, 235, 237–8,
241–54, 259, 265, 273–6, 284–5, 286–8
    hoard, 287
Carriganilea Rock, 346
Carrowkeel Ware, 99, 367
Cashel, 42, 225, 272, 276, 281, 288, 315
    king of, 225, 276, 361
casket key, 299
Castleconnell, Lord, 339
Castledoon, 322
Castlepook, Co. Cork, 6
castles, 18–19, 24, 26, 117, 289–91, 318–20, 322, 326,
330–41, 343–7, 349–50, 352, 356–7, 363–4, 370
    early, 290, 369
    extant, 318
Cathair Chinn Chon, 225, 346
Catholics, 339, 340, 352, 362
cauldrons, 149, 243
Celtic invasions, 215
Celtic world, 215
Celticism, 18
Chalcolithic and early Bronze Age, 102
chalice, 357
Chancellorsland, 55, 126, 150, 170, 178, 194
    pottery, 150
chapel-of-ease, 356
chariot-yoke mounts, 217
cheek-pieces, 298
chert, 75
    arrowheads, 75
    artefacts, 73, 75

blade, 62
débitage, 93, 198, 201
knives, 68
scraper, 93, 124, 198
Chi-Rho, 222
chisels, 244, 275, 298–300
Christ Church Cathedral, Dublin, 337
Christianity, introduction of, 215, 220, 224, 369
Christian rites, 222, 315, 351
Chronicon Scotorum, 26, 225, 282
church(es), 280–1, 315–17, 356
early, 280–1, 282
mortared stone, 280
parish, 356
timber, 280
Church Island, 277
Cistercian monks, 316
Civil Survey, 9, 281, 347
Cladh na Leac, 210
Clanchy family, 349, 351
Clan Gibbon, 318
Clanwilliam barony, 338–9, 349, 364
Clanwilliam Bourkes, 334
Class II pottery, 14, 53, 55, 59, 64, 86, 112, 118, 140,
150–1, 152, 153, 156, 158–9, 162, 163, 172, 175,
178–9, 184–5, 187, 214
climatic deterioration, 149
Cloghavilla standing stone, 144, 210, 334
Clonegor, 336
Clonenagh, 316
Clonmacnoise, 362
cloth production, 246, 275, 302
Cogadh Gaedhel re Gallaibh, 284, 288, 361
coin, Roman, 15, 220, 272
Colby, Col. Thomas, 27
columbarium, 331
Confederate coin, 352
Confederate Wars, 339, 352, 364
Connagh barony, 339, 364
Connemara area, 63, 85, 367
Connory, Owen, 350
Constans, Emperor, 220
Constantius, Emperor, 220
Constantius II, Emperor, 220
Cooper, Austin, 20
copper, 11, 114, 123, 149
awls, 133, 368
halfpenny, 352
metallurgy, 14, 123
residues, 249
Coppinger, John, 363
Cork Examiner, 13, 24
Cork Public Museum, 204, 206–7
Cormac, king of Munster, 225
Cormac mac Airt, 224

Cornwall, 4, 56
Council of Cashel, 315
crannogs, 15, 117, 129, 204, 277–8, 280, 282, 284, 344–
5
Crean, 335
Críth Gablach, 260, 272
Crock Island, 277–8, 280
Crom Dubh, 147
Cromwell, Oliver, 15, 333, 339
Cromwellian account books, 362
Cromwellian forces, 339
Cromwellian plantation, 339, 350
Cromwellian settlement, 340
Croom, 289
crucibles, 14, 141, 208, 241, 249, 272, 275
cruck-frame, 304
Cuerdale, Lancashire, 285
Cumbria, 4, 56, 91, 367
Curraghmore, Lord, 333
Cush, 273

D
daggers, 114, 123–4, 149, 204, 368
slender, 178
dagger sheath, 113–14, 298, 302
Dál Cais, 225, 276, 283, 287
darts, 47, 324
Day, Robert, 37
de Bellofago, Almeric, 350
de Braose, Philip, 289
de Braose, William, 289
de Clare, Thomas, 289
de Marisco, Geoffrey, 289
de Marisco, Jordan, 289
de Norragh, J., 350
de Salis, Count, 13, 24, 39, 108, 203, 325, 330, 357, 358
de Salis, Count Jerome, 340
de Salis, Count John, 344
de Salis, J.F.W., 210, 284,
de Salis family, 206
Decies, 224, 333
deer, red, 176, 254
Deer Park Farms, 233, 245, 274–5
Deisbéag/Deisbeg/Desbeg, 224
Déisi, 15, 219–20, 223, 224–5, 368
Desmond, earls of, 13, 15, 289–90, 319–20, 322, 332–
8, 340, 344–7, 351, 356, 362, 369
castles, 117, 333–4, 345
estates, 319
fortifications, 344
lands, 333, 337, 351
lordship, 15
rebellion, 318, 332, 335, 337, 362
rolls, 293, 318, 335, 347, 350, 362
territories, 333, 356

diocesan system, 315
dogs, domestic, 86
dolmens, 134, 136, 144
Dominicans, 316
Doneraile, Co. Cork, 6
Donnubán, king of Uí Fidgente, 283–4
Down Survey, 18, 19, 347, 350, 362
drainage, 9–13, 23, 25, 277, 367, 370
    arterial, 10
drinking-horn, 15, 287–8
Drumlaegh Hill, 257
Drumlummin, 356
Du Noyer, George, 20
Dublin, 21, 283, 320, 333–4, 337
Dublin Builder, 332
Dublin Penny Journal, 358, 362
dues, feudal, 319
dugout canoes, 194
Duleek, Co. Meath, 316
Dunboyne, Lord, 333
Dundee, Scotland, 205
Dún Gair, 225, 284, 290, 322
    fortification of, 225, 361
Dún Maíle Tuile, 288
Duntryleague, 93, 107
Dutch delftware, 355

E
Edward I, 297
Edward IV, 356
Edward the Elder, 271–2
eels, 9, 44
Elizabeth I, 318, 332, 333, 337, 362
Elizabethan land grants, 348
Elizabethan plantation, 335–6
Elizabethan wars, 18
Eóganacht, 219, 224–5, 276, 283, 287
Eóganacht Áine, 15, 224–5, 283, 287
Eóganacht Airthir Cliath, 224
Eóganacht Cashel, 224–5, 288
Eóganacht Glennamnach, 224
Eóganacht hegemony, 276
Eóganacht king of Cashel, 276
Eterscél mac Máel hUmai, 225

F
Famine Relief, 10
Fane, Charles, 340
Fane, Sir Henry, 340
Fane family, 19, 277, 340
farm, fee, 336
farming practices, 367
Fedamore, 6, 206, 318
fiants, 349, 362
fibula, 15, 217–18

field boundary, modern, 213
field fence, 1, 14, 48, 144, 153, 161, 187, 269–70
field rotation, 314
field systems, 37, 150, 293
field walls on Knockadoon, 162
financial administration, 319
finger-rings, 221
Fionn Mac Cumhal, 134
fish stocks, 44
Fitzgerald, Edward, 108, 144
Fitzgerald, Garrett, 13
Fitzgerald, Gerald (Gearóid Iarla), 4th earl of Desmond, 319, 345–6, 362
Fitzgerald, Gerald fitz James, 14th earl of Desmond, 13, 332, 333–4, 345
Fitzgerald, James fitz Maurice, 333
Fitzgerald, John, 25, 109, 145, 203, 316, 318
Fitzgerald, John fitz Thomas, 338, 363
Fitzgerald, Maurice fitz Thomas, 1st earl of Desmond, 290
Fitzgerald, Maurice fitz Thomas, 10th earl of Desmond, 332
Fitzgerald, Thomas fitz Maurice, 319, 347
Fitzgerald dynasty, 15, 319, 351
Fitzgibbon family, 316
Fitzmaurice, Nicholas, 346
Fitz Maurice, Thomas, 289
Fitz Rhys, T., 350
Flanders, 355
flax seeds, 275
flint flakes, 46, 96, 117, 129
flint knife, 66, 68
Flynn, James, 221
food sources, 9–10, 44
Food Vessel(s), 80, 112, 117, 130, 140, 145, 146–7, 150, 156
Food Vessel Bowls, 147, 171
Food Vessel burials, 14, 124
foraged foods, 10, 44, 48
fortifications, 29, 283–4, 291, 322, 339
fortified stone residences, 319
fowling, 128–9
France, 220, 302, 334, 368
Franciscan friary, 317
Franciscans, 316
Freestone Hill, Co. Wicklow, 151
French Revolution, 19
Friarstown, 318
fulachtaí fia, 126, 174, 373
furnace, small bowl-shaped, 215
Furnell, Michael, 350
Furnell, Patrick, 350
Fytton, Sir E., 349

G

Galway, County, 63, 367
gaming pieces, 244, 246–7, 253
Garret (Geroid) Island, 10, 102, 103, 117–18, 129, 214, 216, 277, 280, 320, 344–5, 346
Garrode Crannog, 344
Garryduff, 246, 274–5, 282
Garryheakin, 290
Garryspillane, 222, 245
Gaul, 15, 220, 241
geology, 4
geophysical prospection techniques, 35, 266
geophysical survey, 33–7, 104–5, 122–3, 194, 202–3, 210, 267
Geraldine revolt, 337
Geraldine tower-houses, 320
Geraldines, 319–20, 332, 336–7, 344, 369–70
Geraldines, Desmond, 289–90
Geroid Island, *see* Garret (Geroid) Island
Geroid Island Castle, 15
Giant Irish Deer, 7–8, 13
Giant's Grave, 25–6, 29, 31, 93, 102–3, 124, 134, 136–8, 144–5, 368
Gilbert, Humphrey, 334
Gille (Gilbert), bishop of Limerick, 315
glacial erratics, 9
glaciation, 4, 6
Glanworth, 224
glass bracelet fragment, 248–9
Glenbrohane, 273
Glenogra, 333, 335, 345
Gloucestershire, 316
gold, 11, 160, 205, 215, 287
        sheet, 123, 160, 206
gold bar, 159
gold collars, 149
gold crown or diadem, 206
gold disc, 14, 182
gold foil, 159, 205
gold inlay, 12
gold jewellery, 149
gold swords, 141, 203
Golden Vale, 8
gorgets, 149, 206
gouges, 208, 245–6, 253
government, local, 319
Grace, Piers, 334
Grange, 10, 14, 23–4, 29–31, 33–7, 104, 106–7, 112–13, 117, 150, 210, 274, 316–17, 347, 367–9
        Great Stone Circle (B), 9, 18–20, 24–5, 27–9, 31, 35–7, 53, 55, 102, 104, 107, 144–5, 148, 150, 210, 367, 368
Grange Castle, 15, 25, 225, 320, 346
Grange church, 37
Grange Hill, 4

Grange House, 340
Grange monument complex, 104
Grange ringfort, 14, 15, 46, 93, 226, 260, 261–3, 266
Grange Rock Castle, 346
Grange Roman Catholic church, 317
Grange Stone Circles, 18–21, 25–6, 28–9, 35–6, 41, 93, 103–4, 106–15, 117–18, 133, 144, 146–7, 202–3
Grange townland, 9–10, 27, 260
Grangegorman, 334
Grangehawe, 347
Gransha, 339, 347
graves, 95–8, 136, 141, 143, 147, 150, 189–93, 202–3, 219, 346, 351–2, 362, 368
graveyard wall, 317
Grean, 289
Great Famine, 16
Great Langdale, 56, 91
Grey, Lord Arthur, 334
Grey, Lord Leonard, 333, 344
Grome, Owen, 338, 363
Grooved Ware, 14, 80, 102–3, 107, 112, 115, 118, 148, 156, 187, 214, 367
        timber circle, 104
Guillamore, Lord, 12, 205

H

hafting techniques, 206
haggard, 257
halberds, 123, 133–4, 204, 368
Halstatt, 215
hammer-stones, 85, 156, 160, 263
handle
        riveted, 178
        wooden, 207–8, 252
hand-pins, 243, 252
        enamelled, 242–3
hare, 6, 254
harness fittings and horse-bits, 275
Harrowgate, Yorkshire, 205
Harte, Constable Richard, 339, 364–6
Haward, Nicolas, 349
Hayes, Gabrielle, 40
Hekla, 149
henges, 103–4
Henry II, 289, 316
Henry VI, 320
Herbertstown, 221
Higgins, Dr, 339
history, political, 224–5, 283, 289, 319
Holocene, 8, 371
        early, 44, 100
Holy Cross, 281, 317
Holy Cross Cottage, 18, 37, 203
hood-mouldings, 330, 358

Hooker, J.D., 12
horse-bits, 252, 275, 310, 315
horse-racing, 273
horse trappings, 252, 302
horses, plough, 314
horseshoe fragment, 305, 311
Hospital, 316, 333, 362
Hunt Collection, Limerick, 131, 132, 204
hunter-gatherer communities, 14, 43–4
hut sites, 14–15, 41, 176, 260

I
Iberian Peninsula, 131
Iberian regions, 123, 368
ibex-headed pins, 243
Iceland, 149
ice sheets, 6
inauguration site, ancient Gaelic, 334
ingots, 160, 221–2, 285
instruments, musical, 149
interpretative centre, 14, 41, 147, 151, 177, 257
Irish Air Force, 293
Iron Age, 15, 78, 189, 210, 215–17, 219, 254, 368
iron buckle, 304–5
iron hand-pin, 251
iron key, 309
iron knives, 243–4, 260, 272, 299
iron needle, 311
iron pin, 242–3, 260, 269
        flat-headed, 242
iron ploughshare, 356
iron prick-spur, 311
iron punches, 252
iron shears, 244, 302
iron slag and crucible fragments, 275
iron sword, 217
iron-working technology, 15, 215
Ivar, king of the Limerick Vikings, 284

J
Jackson, Thomas, 18
James I, 348, 355, 362
Jerpoint, Co. Kilkenny, 313
jet bracelets, 247–8, 253, 260, 276, 288
jew's harp, 355
John, King, 289

K
Kerry, County, 289
keys, 298–9, 310
Kilballyowen, 349
Kilcullane House, 8
Kildare, 320, 337
Kilkenny, 281, 313, 333, 337, 339
        Statute of, 346

Killalough, 14–15, 24–5, 31, 40, 103, 124, 280, 320
Killalough Castle, 340
Killalough Hill, 136–8, 145
Killuragh Cave, 44
Kilmallock, 13, 20, 281, 283, 316, 334, 336–8
Kilteely, 281, 289
Knights Hospitallers, 316
knives, 66, 68, 72–3, 75, 243, 275, 298, 310–11, 315
Knockadoon, 14–15, 29, 37–41, 45–53, 55, 57–8, 60–
        4, 92, 150–75, 178–86, 225–8, 269–72, 322, 344–5
Knockadoon Hill, 15, 74, 77, 92–3, 95, 100, 102, 125,
        153, 189–91, 208, 210, 320, 331, 367–8
        unprotected burials on, 95, 367
Knockainy, 4, 141, 219, 224–5, 283–4, 289, 293, 318,
        334, 336, 362
Knockderc, 6–7
Knockea, 274
Knockfennell, 4, 10, 21, 206, 345
Knockfennell Hill, 6, 10, 14, 29, 40, 47, 194, 202, 210,
        277, 314
Knockmore, 48, 161, 225, 322
Knockmore Hill, 144, 290
Knockroe, 6, 202
Knowth passage tomb, 102

L
La Tène period, 215, 216
Lacy, Eddie, 339
Lacy, John, 339
lake drainage, 10, 13–14, 23, 47, 277
Lake Neuchâtel, 159
Landnam, 47
Lane Fox, Colonel, 12
Larcom, Lt. Thomas, 27
latch-lifter, 298–9
Late Neolithic Grooved Ware, 103, 105, 107, 109, 111,
        113, 115, 117, 119, 121, 123, 125, 127, 129, 131
law tracts, early, 276
Leaba na Muice, 23, 24, 25, 26, 29, 31, 42, 134, 136,
        141–3, 203
Leahy, James, 144
Leo, James, 145
LiDAR, 36, 37
lignite pendants, 159
Limerick, 8, 13, 19–21, 23–6, 283–4, 287, 289, 315–16,
        333–4, 336–7, 346–7, 349, 357, 363
Limerick, County, 18–19, 24, 26, 224, 227, 289, 291,
        316, 319–20, 332–3, 339–40, 369
Limerick Basin, 4
Limerick City Museum, 132, 204, 208
Limerick Field Club, 26
Limerick gas pipeline, 194
Limerick Junction, 283
Limerick tower-houses, 320
Limerick Vikings, 283

Limerick Volcanics, 6
Linkardstown-type pottery, 73, 99
Lismore, 282, 315
Little Friarstown, 318
Llanthony, 316
Loch Ceann, 225, 284
Longford Bridge, 201, 351
Longstone, Co. Tipperary, 107
Lough Gur, 4, 8–26, 34–44, 46–58, 130–4, 140–6,
    148–52, 202–10, 216–20, 224–8, 280–6, 288–90,
    312–20, 330–40, 366–70
        besieged, 332
        fortification of, 288, 361
Lough Gur area, 4, 6, 15, 18, 27, 31–2, 37, 41, 44, 51,
    147, 150, 222, 224–5, 313
Lough Gur Castle, attacked, 332
Lough Gur Class II pottery, 126, 148, 150, 152, 153
Lough Gur Shield, 11, 14, 149, 205–6, 368
Luttrell Psalter, 314

M
Mac Carthy, Cormac, 284, 315
MacDermott, Máire, 1, 40, 199
maceheads, 102, 103, 118–19, 367
Máelduin, king of Munster, 225
Máel Muad mac Briain, 284
Magio Abbey (Monasteranenagh), 281, 316, 347
Mahr, Adolf, 38
Maigue Drainage Scheme, 7
Maigue River, 4
Manisternagalliagh, 318
medieval period, 332
        early, 92–3, 224–5, 227, 229, 231, 233, 235,
        237, 239, 243, 253–5, 269, 271–3, 275–7,
        281
Mediterranean area, 222
megalithic cemeteries, 367
megalithic tombs, 14, 23–6, 29, 31–2, 95, 102–4, 134–
    41, 144–5, 147, 150, 189, 208, 367–8, 370
        destroyed, 24, 41, 136, 144, 192
        excavated, 136
        extant, 93, 137
        possible, 28, 30, 107, 136
megaliths, 24, 137–8, 140–1, 143, 144, 145
Mellifont, Co. Louth, 316
Mesolithic, 9, 14, 43–5, 46, 47, 56, 194, 198, 199
Midlandian phase, 7
migratory birds, 10
Milltown watermill, 350
Monaster, 318
Monasteranenagh, 26, 281, 316, 334, 346–7
Monasteranenagh Abbey, 224
monasteries, 280, 315–16, 318
monastic orders, 316
money token, 356

money weight, 355
Morgan, Captain Robert, 347
Morningstar River, 4, 224
mottes, 290
moulds, 132, 141, 149, 161, 167, 182, 208–9
        bivalve, 207, 208
        clay, 14, 165, 179, 181, 184–5, 208, 270
        four-sided, 208
        stone, 14, 140, 181, 204, 208, 209
mounts, 113–14, 160, 216, 298
mud-walled houses, traditional, 40
Mulkear River, 4, 43–4
Munster, lord president of, 337, 338, 364

N
Napoleonic Wars, 19
National Monuments Service, 106–7, 119, 137–8, 163,
    227, 229, 323
National Museum of Ireland, 38–9, 54, 132, 133, 152,
    182, 204, 206–8, 217, 222, 287
Navan Fort, Co. Armagh, 151
necklaces, 73, 75, 79, 95–6, 160, 247–8, 276, 311
needle, 244, 246, 310
Neligan, Revd W.C., 12, 205
Neolithic, 1, 44, 47–8, 55–6, 62, 64, 80, 91–3, 150, 153,
    156, 162–3, 165, 167, 187, 189, 199
        early, 14, 49, 57, 98
        middle, 14, 53, 79–80, 178–9, 214
Neolithic burial, 87, 93, 95, 189
Neolithic house foundations, 63
Neolithic houses in Lough Gur, 48
Neolithic pottery, 45, 47, 53–5, 59, 72, 92–3, 97, 112,
    130, 153, 184, 189, 197–9, 202
        round-based, 80
Neolithic settlement, 47–8, 86
Neolithic stone axeheads, 4, 9
Newchurch, 21, 25, 29, 31, 40, 189, 192, 317, 356–60
Newgrange, Co. Meath, 113
New Model Army, 339
Norris, Sir Thomas, 338
Norse, 228, 283–4
Norse graves, 243
Norway, 288
Norwegian Viking graves, 284

O
O'Brien, Brian, 346
O'Brien, Turlough, 316
O'Brien's Bridge, 351
O'Collins of Cleanglas, 284, 290
O'Connellan, Thomas, 340, 358
O'Connor, Lysaghe McMorishe Moyle, 333
O'Connor, Rodrick (Ruaidri), 225
O'Donnell, Hugh, 337
O'Grady, Standish, 291